Georgina Campbell's

Tipperary Water Guide

IRELAND'S FINEST PLACES TO
EAT DRINK & STAY

Ireland

2000

Georgina Campbell's Guides

Editorial Director Georgina Compbell
Production Editor Graham Smith

Georgina Campbells Guides Ltd.,
PO Box 6173
Dublin 13
Ireland

website: www.ireland-guide.com
email: info@ireland-guide.com
Guide rcommendations for the Greater Dublin area can be found
on the Dublin Live section of the Irish Times On Line: www.ireland.com

Front Cover/Jacket Design: Rai Uhlemann
Front Cover: Jacobs Ladder, New Quay, Dublin
          Linnane's Lobster Bar, Co. Clare
          Glin Castle, Glin, Co. Limerick

Designed and typeset in Ireland by Brian Darling, The Design Station
Image Scanning by The Design Station
Printed in Ireland by Colour Books Ltd.

First published 1999 by Georgina Campbell Guides Ltd.

ISBN: 1 903164 00 1

Foreword

by Dr. James McDaid T.D.,
Minister for Tourism, Sport and Recreation

I was delighted to be asked again to provide a short greeting to the readers of *Georgina Campbell's Tipperary Water Guide to Ireland*. This is an objective, quality reference guide that will prove invaluable to many throughout the millennium year.

When a leading food writer like Georgina Campbell produces a guide to Ireland, people sit up and take note. Her passion for perfection, her commitment to excellence and her vision for the future of Irish food, an integral part of our tourism industry in which dining and hospitality play major parts, all make the Georgina Campbell Tipperary Water Guide to Ireland an important publication.

This guide makes it crystal clear that there's never been a better time to eat out in Ireland. Quality, diversity and value are the hallmarks of the Irish dining and hospitality experience, from pubs to family-run restaurants, from hotels to our award-winning, gourmet establishments.

The finest, purest Irish ingredients are to be found in the vast array of ethnic food now available here. Indeed, today Ireland hosts Thai, African, Mediterranean, Malaysian, Middle-Eastern and Oriental restaurants of the first order. And they're priced to suit every budget, from early-bird specials, to table d'hôte, to extensive à la carte offerings. The choice is endless for the prospective diner and visitor.

Moreover, the number of four and five-star hotels increases apace, attracting a sophisticated, discerning, high-spending clientèle. The benefits of such a clientele transfer throughout the industry from transport, to shopping, to entertainment.

For the establishments recommended by this guide, inclusion is an accolade in itself. I congratulate all who have made it into these influential pages, and pay particular compliment to those chosen for special awards.

With this publication, Georgina Campbell and Tipperary Water make a crucial contribution to Ireland's tourism and hospitality industry. I am confident that Irish people and overseas visitors alike will find it to be a useful, highly-credible companion.

Dr. James McDaid, TD

How to Use the Guide

Location/Establishment name
- Cities, towns and villages arranged in alphabetical order within countries, ith the exception of Dublin, Cork and Belfast, which come first within their categories
- Establishments arranged alphabetically within location.

Category(ies) of Establishment

Address/contact details
(please phone/fax/email ahead for additional directions if required)
- includes an email address if available

Rating - for outstanding cooking and accommodation

☆	- Demi-Star: restaurant approaching full star status
★	- For cooking and service well aboe average
★★	- Consistent excellence, one of the best restaurants in the land
★★★	- The highest restaurant grading achievable
🏛	- Outstanding Accommodation of its type
🏛🏛	- De Luxe Hotel
[PUB★]	- Outstanding Pub - good food and atmosphere
✗	- Establishment data not supplied
✗	- Establishment data not complete

PRICES & OPENING HOURS

PLEASE NOTE THAT PRICES AND OPENING HOURS MAY HAVE CHANGED SINCE THE GUIDE WENT TO PRESS. TIMES & PRICES ARE GIVEN AS A GUIDELINE ONLY AND SHOULD BE CHECKED BEFORE TRAVELLING OR WHEN MAKING A RESERVATION.

Prices in the Republic of Ireland are given in Irish punts and those in Northern Ireland in pounds sterling.

Thanks and Acknowledgements

The publication of this guide would not have been possible without the support and encouragement of a large number of organisations, companies and individuals. Particular thanks must go to all the sponsors, of course, for having faith in this second edition which is an all-Irish project and the first of its kind. Those who have given invaluable assistance are too numerous to mention individually but, on behalf the Guide, I would like to thank you all.

Georgina Campbell,
Editorial Director.

Contents

*Patrick and
Marie Cooney*

Where else in the world would you find the simple natural
pleasures that make Ireland so special? The natural warmth
of the welcome. The natural abundance of fresh produce.
The natural beauty of the unspoilt Irish landscape.

As a wholly Irish-owned company we are delighted to sponsor
this new, wholly Irish guide, which highlights and rewards
Ireland's finest hotels, restaurants and other establishments.
As award-winners in our own right (we have three international
gold medals to our name) we are also proud to sponsor the
awards for Ireland's hotel, restaurant and chef of the year.

We are proud too that Tipperary Bottled Waters grace the
very best tables in Ireland and abroad. You will find that our
delicious Sparkling, Still and Naturally Flavoured waters are
the perfect complement to the finest Irish cuisine.

And, because every precious drop is drawn from our source at
Borrisoleigh, in the unspoilt countryside of County Tipperary,
you will find that our natural mineral water is remarkably pure.
Like the natural hospitality, we are confident you will find it
delightfully refreshing.

Marie T. Cooney
Marketing Director

Patrick J. Cooney
Managing Director

Introduction

by Georgina Campbell
Editorial Director

Welcome to the second edition of Georgina Campbell's Tipperary Water Guide to Ireland. The guide provides comprehensive independent recommendations on the best food, accommodation and hospitality throughout Ireland, both North and South. While no guide can ever be exhaustive, we aim to provide everyone travelling in Ireland with a selection of the best places for their purpose in every part of the country.

We use a unique combination of local knowledge and professional assessment to achieve this aim - and this is the only guide to take into consideration the needs of both leisure and business travellers. From the warm reception given to the first edition, it is clear that a comprehensive guide, based solely on merit, is very much in demand - and the number of changes necessary in this year's entries is an indication of the importance for travellers to have up-to-date information to hand.

As well as giving the best recommendations to readers, for virtually any occasion and over a wide range of prices, the guide aims to raise standards by highlighting the best that Ireland has to offer. We do this through each recommendation given, but more specifically through the stars awarded to restaurants, ratings for deluxe hotels and other outstanding accommodation - and, especially, through our annual Awards which are presented to exceptional establishments in a variety of categories. These include major awards for the leading establishments and individuals, but also others carefully tailored to highlight excellence in specialist areas: the creative use of the best Irish produce whatever it may be - seafood, farmhouse cheeses, beef, lamb or pork - the provision of outstanding facilities for business and pleasure, and recognition for those special people and places that ensure a memorable visit: the exceptional hosts, the keenest sommeliers and even hotels where not only the guests but also their pets are made welcome.

Already, just a short year after our first edition was published, the changes we are recording are immense. The huge surge of international interest in Ireland as a destination for discerning travellers who appreciate quality in all areas of hospitality - and, of course, the growing numbers of Irish people who take regular short breaks in their own country through the year - has triggered a great deal of development; consequently many new hotels, guesthouses, restaurants and pubs have opened during the last few months, or are due to open shortly. The prospect of new five-star hotels opening in Dublin has caused a flurry of activity amongst the competitors, sharpening up standards all round. This has to be good news for consumers.

In the middle market, some good budget accommodation has come on stream with the emphasis on facilities rather than service; the long term results for visitors remain to be seen, but this development is bound to put pressure on the best guesthouses and small hotels, particularly in the major cities, where prices charged are similar but personal service, rather than spacious new facilities, is the main characteristic. In recognition of the importance of professional service and genuine hospitalilty, the Guide is pleased to announce its first Skills Development Award, given to an outstanding figure in the industry, who not only trains the many young people who pass through his establishment, but inspires them with a sense of real hospitality and its worth.

Perhaps it is the imminent arrival of a new millennium that is causing the enormous stir we are currently feeling throughout the hospitality industry. Or perhaps it is connected with that mythical creature the Celtic Tiger. Chefs and hoteliers hardly retire but a number of major figures in the hospitality industry have chosen this year to change direction - Declan Ryan, of Arbutus Lodge, Cork;Gerry Galvin, of Drimcong House, Galway (recipient of our major Irish Food Award last year) and Brian Cronin, of the Blue Haven in Kinsale are among those who have handed on the baton and will be much missed.But the energy of an upcoming generation of chefs and hoteliers and greater public awareness of many of the issues that concern professionals, especially in the catering sector, is inspiring a new attitude of commitment to high standards in a changing world. Debate about the safety and provenenace of food, animal safety and massive issues like genetic engineering has a sense of great urgency. Euro-Toques, the European association of chefs committed to defending regional and traditional foods, is committed to developing specific food supply networks which allow ensure traceability of origins. Diners in Ireland will be pleased to know that many of the chefs featured in this guide are members of Euro-Toques - and the Guide has established a new Natural Food Award to highlight the best practices in this area.

While the trend for highly decorative, multi-cultural and perilously stacked food has not yet run its course, there are signs that there is a general move towards more natural foods. Mould-breaking vegetarian restaurants are now out there making a fashion statement, juice bars are popping up all over and a growing number of restaurants are claiming to use as much organic produce as possible. Indeed, where high style is coming into play it is from a new direction, and very pure in its philosphy and application - the place to look for it is in the new wave of Japanese food. Regional foods are attracting growing attention and our major New Irish Cuisine Award is a reflection reflection of the developing interest in that area.

And wherever changing fashions may lead, the small, family run restaurant with a proprietor chef in charge, is still the backbone of Ireland's best eating out experiences.Many of these are out around the country, clustered in small rural or coastal towns - Kenmare, Dingle, Clifden, Carlingford are all examples, also midland towns such as Athlone. Some of these great little places are pubs as well as restaurants, often providing a uniquely relaxed atmosphere as well as good food, and there's no doubt that they generally provide a great experience for the dining public.

What we always seek on your behalf is professionalism, genuine hospitality, high standards and value for money. However, there can be disappointment as well as delight. We hope that you will enjoy visiting the establishments recommended here or, if problems arise, that they can be satisfactorily and quickly settled. But, if you have any outstanding experiences - good or bad - at recommended establishments, please tell us how you fare. Similarly, if you know of places you feel deserve assessment for the next edition, we would like to hear from you.

Alupui Campbell

It's All Great Sport

Sport and recreation are so totally entwined through life in Ireland that their metaphors and attitudes define everything else. The Irish way of life and the manner in which the countryside readily lends itself to outdoor pursuits of all kinds makes this state of affairs seem nothing other than completely natural, so much so that one of the highest forms of praise you'll find for almost any activity whatever is that "it's all great sport".

This is very much to the benefit of the visitor seeking recreation and relaxation, because people in Ireland really do subscribe to the notion that it's much more important to take part than to win. Their attitude is that if you're having fun, then you're succeeding regardless of what the final score may be.

Mount Juliet Golf Course

That said, like everyone else the Irish enjoy seeing their teams win. But the warm welcome which the country's soccer fans receive when they travel overseas in support of the national squad shows that this understandable desire to win is kept in a healthy perspective, with joy in victory being balanced by good-humoured acceptance of defeat.

And at home, when Ireland is hosting an international rugby match, the atmosphere is so totally convivial that even those from overseas who have been unable to get a ticket for the match will happily travel to Dublin in order to watch it on the big screen in one of the city's many pubs. As for those seeking a uniquely Irish occasion, the massive extension of the GAA headquarters at Croke Park in Dublin, coming on stream in 2000, will provide the perfect setting for epic hurling and Gaelic football finals.

An enthusiasm for sport and its central role in the national psyche have been recorded in Irish history from the earliest mists of time. Today's busy all-Ireland Gaelic Games programme reflects this tradition, with inter-county rivalries being kept cheerfully active on a year round basis. But people's sporting and recreational interests are much wider than the high media profile given to stadium sports might at first suggest. That passionate supporter of the county's hurlers or the national rugby team is equally likely to be someone who gets as much pleasure from a day's gentle fishing from a boat on the neighbourhood lake, or a quiet game of golf with friends. And as for knowledge of horses, well, if you don't know about horses, or at least wish to know about horses, then you're not really Irish at all.

THE EQUESTRIAN WORLD

Down in the County Kildare and other well-pastured places, they'll tell you it isn't true that the horse has Godlike status in Ireland - it's actually much more important than that... Certainly the horse might have been invented with the Irish countryside in mind. Whether racing or hunting or taking part in the sacred festival of the annual Kerrygold Dublin Horse Show in early August or simply enjoying a beautiful meadow or revelling in a gallop along a flawless beach, the horse is one of Ireland's most wondrous ornaments.

Ballycormac House, Co. Tipperary

Yet despite his divine status, the world of the Irish horse has an accessibility which often seems lacking in other countries. For locals and visitors alike, Ireland's easily reached race-courses, hospitable hunting packs, and thoroughly professional equestrian centres make this a world to be shared and enjoyed. And if you happen to spread your enthusiasm to all manner of four-legged sporting creatures, then the good news is that Ireland also has no less than sixteen greyhound tracks, some of them located in decidedly comfortable stadia to offer a grand night out in the heart of town.

GOLF

As the Irish countryside was also specifically invented for the playing of golf, it's a good thing there's so much of it in order to provide space for golfers and horse folk alike. The hold which golf has taken in contemporary Ireland is nothing less than a phenomenom. Even in areas which in times past might have been thought somewhat impoverished, the local golf course is now expected as a normal part of the environment. And in the regions which lend themselves especially well to the ancient game, the courses and links are heaven on earth, a matter of pilgrimage for golfers worldwide, while the style and friendliness of the clubs makes such visitors more than welcome.

FISHING

The announcement that "the mayfly is up" is an item of national news in Ireland. The hatching in late May of this brief-lived insect, its effect on the trout population, and its interest not just for the nation's many anglers but also for folk in general, is indicative of the way that fishing in all its forms permeates the way of life.

The variety of fishing available on lake, river, canal and sea is almost beyond comprehension, and throughout the country and along the coasts of sea and lake alike, you'll find friendly and experienced establishments which will help you to catch your fish in areas of breathtaking beauty, and then help you to celebrate afterwards.

BOATING, SAILING AND SURFING

In such a watery land of rivers, lakes and canals, with 3,000 miles of seacoast, boats are at home. The fleets of motor-cruisers which are available for hire along the inland waterways and the lordly Shannon may seem large on paper, but the reality is that so much space is available that you can easily find somewhere to yourself should you so wish, while convivial ports of call are always within easy reach.

Sailing particularly appeals to the Irish sporting instinct, and it has a long history going back even beyond the foundation of the world's oldest club, the Royal Cork Yacht Club, in 1720. Hospitable clubs continue to be the organisational backbone of the sport, but while sailors respect their history, they also look

Photo W.M. Nixon

enthusiastically to the future, and those same Royal Cork people host one of the world's most successful modern regattas, the biennial Ford Cork Week, which in July 2000 is going to be one of Ireland's major millennial events.

The ready availability of open water also means that windsurfing thrives, while the fact that three of our four coastlines face oceanwards into clear seas makes Ireland a surfing venue of international standard.

CLIMBING, WALKING, CYCLING

One of the most remarkable and attractive aspects of the Irish landscape is that each and every range of hills and mountains seems to have its own special and individual character. Thus although it is only natural to have a favourite region, you could happily spend many years finding somewhere different each time out.

But you don't need to take on the challenge of rock-climbing or full-scale mountaineering to savour the Irish landscape in all its continuing variety. Hill-walking and rambling provide a very satisfying holiday and a special insight into the life of the countryside. And the wide availability of routes away from the main roads means that cycling is increasingly popular, particularly using the convenient group system whereby everyone's baggage is conveyed by van to the evening's comfortable destination.

And that, of course, is the dream which all visitors to Ireland can fulfill. A good day out, a day of great sport whichever way you prefer it. And a hospitable and convivial place beckoning a welcome as evening approaches. It's all great sport.

W. M. Nixon

The Best of the Best

Bord Bía
Irish Food Board

BORD BIA STARRED RESTAURANTS

★★ / ★ / ☆ Republic of Ireland:

2 Star: ★★
Dublin, Thornton's

1 Star: ★
Dublin, Le Coq Hardi
Dublin, Peacock Alley
Dublin, Restaurant Patrick Guilbaud
Co Clare, Dromoland Castle, Newmarket-on-Fergus
Co Cork, Ballymaloe House, Shanagarry
Co Cork, Longueville House, Mallow
Co Galway, Erriseask House, Ballyconneely
Co Kerry, Park Hotel, Kenmare
Co Kerry, Sheen Falls Lodge, Kenmare
Co Kildare, Kildare Hotel, Straffan
Co Sligo, Cromleach Lodge, Castlebaldwin

Demi-Star: ☆
Dublin, Chapter One
Dublin, Clarence Hotel, Tea Room

Demi-Star *(continued):* ☆
Dublin, L'Ecrivain
Dublin, Mange Tout
Dublin, O'Connell's
Dublin, One Pico
Cork, Isaacs
Co Dublin, Morels, Sandycove
Co Cavan, MacNean Bistro, Blacklion
Co Kerry, D'Arcy's, Kenmare,
Co Limerick, Mustard Seed at Echo Lodge, Ballingarry
Co Mayo, Ashford Castle, Cong
Co Westmeath, Crookedwood House

Northern Ireland
1 Star: ★
Belfast, Deane's

Demi-Star: ☆
Co Down, Shanks, Bangor

DELUXE HOTELS

Dublin, The Berkeley Court, Ballsbridge
Dublin, The Clarence, Temple Bar
Dublin, The Four Seasons, Ballsbridge
Dublin, The Merrion, Merrion Street
Dublin, The Shelbourne, Stephen's Green
Dublin, The Westbury, Grafton Street
Cork, Hayfield Manor Hotel
Co Clare, Dromoland Castle, Newmarket-on Fergus
Co Kerry, Park Hotel, Kenmare
Co Kerry, Sheen Falls Lodge Hotel, Kenmare
Co Kildare, Kildare Hotel, Straffan
Co Kilkenny, Mount Juliet, Thomastown
Co Limerick, Adare Manor, Adare
Co Mayo, Ashford Castle, Cong,
Co Wexford, Marlfield House, Gorey

Northern Ireland
Belfast, Culloden Hotel

OUTSTANDING ACCOMMODATION

Dublin, The Towers at Jurys Hotel, Ballsbridge
Dublin, The Conrad, Earslfort Terrace
Co Dublin, Portmarnock Hotel & Golf Links
Cork, Maryborough Hotel
Co Cork, Aherne's, Youghal
Co Cork, Ballymaloe House, Shanagarry
Co Cork, Ballyvolane House, Castlelyons,
Co Cork, Longueville House, Mallow
Co Cork, Perryville House, Kinsale
Galway city, Killeen House, Bushypark
Co Clare, Carnelly House, Clarecastle,
Co Clare, Gregans Castle Hotel, Ballyvaughan
Co Galway, Cashel House Hotel, Connemara
Co Galway, Fermoyle Lodge, Costello
Co Galway, St Cleran's, Craughwell
Co Galway, The Quay House, Clifden
Co Kerry, Caragh Lodge, Caragh Lake
Co Kerry, Killarney Park Hotel, Killarney
Co Kerry, Shelburne, Kenmare
Co Kildare, Barberstown Castle, Straffan
Co Kildare, Moyglare Manor, Maynooth
Co Limerick, Dunraven Arms Hotel, Adare
Co Limerick, Echo Lodge, Ballingarry
Co Limerick, Glin Castle, Glin
Co Mayo, Newport House, Newport
Co Monaghan, Hilton Park, Clones
Co Offaly, Kinnity Castle, Kinnity
Co Sligo, Coopershill House, Riverstown
Co Sligo, Cromleach Lodge, Castlebaldwin
Co Wicklow, Humewood Castle, Kiltegan
Co Wicklow, Rathsallagh House
Co Wicklow, Tinakilly House

Northern Ireland
Belfast, Hilton Hotel
Co Antrim, Galgorm Manor, Ballymena
Co Londonderry, Ardtara House, Upperlands
Co Londonderry, Beech Hill House Hotel, Londonderry
Co Tyrone, Grange Lodge, Dungannon

OUTSTANDING PUBS (for good food & atmosphere)

[PUB★]
Dublin, The Porterhouse
Dublin, Nancy Hands
Co Dublin, Johnnie Fox's Pub, Glencullen
Co Cork, Bushe's, Baltimore
Co Cork, Mary Ann's, Castletownshend
Co Cork, Hayes Bar, Glandore
Co Clare, Monk's Bar, Ballyvaughan
Co Galway, Moran's Oyster Cottage, Kilcolgan
Co Kerry, The Point Bar, Caherciveen
Co Kildare, The Ballymore Inn, Ballymore Eustace
Co Offaly, The Thatch, Crinkle
Co Tipperary, Sean Tierney's, Clonmel
Co Waterford, Buggy's Glencairn Inn
Co. Waterford, Maddens Bar, Lismore
Co Wexford, Kehoe's, Kilmore Quay
Co Wicklow, Roundwood Inn, Roundwood
Northern Ireland:
Belfast, Crown Liquor Salon

Bord Bia Awards of Excellence

Irish Food Board

Annual awards for the best establishment and staff in a variety of categories, sponsored by leading Irish companies and organisations

Hotel of the Year

When Longueville House opened its doors to guests in 1967, it was one of the first Irish country houses to do so. The present house, a particularly elegant Georgian mansion of pleasingly human proportions, dates from 1720, and overlooks the ruins of the O'Callaghan family's original home, Dromineen Castle. Many things make Longueville special, most importantly the warm, informal hospitality and charm of the O'Callaghans themselves – Michael and Jane, now joined by their son (and talented chef) William and his wife Aisling. The location, overlooking the River Blackwater, is lovely. The river, farm and garden respectively supply fresh salmon in season, the famous Longueville lamb and all the fruit and vegetables. In years when the weather is kind, the estate's crowning glory is its own house wine, a light refreshing white fittingly named "Coisreal Longueville". Graciously proportioned reception rooms include a bar and drawing room both elegantly furnished in country house style - yet they are next in line in the endless rota of refurbishment which keeps this lovely old house in tiptop condition. Accommodation is equally sumptuous and bedrooms – which include a suite, six mini-suites and six rooms designated non-smoking – are spacious, superbly comfortable and stylishly decorated to the highest. As well as being one of the finest leisure destinations in the country, this all adds up to a good venue for small conferences and business meetings.

2000

1999 Winner:
Sheen Falls Lodge, Kenmare

Natural
Mineral Water

THE NATURAL CHOICE

Longueville House Hotel, Mallow, Co. Cork

Tipperary Water
congratulates

Longueville House Hotel

winner of
Hotel of the Year

TO THE

connoisseur

IT'S THE

purist

WATER

IT'S NOT WHAT IS IN A MINERAL WATER

THAT DETERMINES ITS QUALITY,

IT'S WHAT IS ABSENT. IN THAT RESPECT,

TIPPERARY NATURAL MINERAL WATER

IS OF THE HIGHEST QUALITY.

IT HAS THE LOWEST MINERALISATION

OF ANY IRISH MINERAL WATER

AND A PERFECT PH BALANCE.

—

FROM THE PUREST ENVIRONMENT,

THE PURIST'S WATER.

Tipperary
Natural
Mineral Water

THE NATURAL CHOICE

Natural Mineral Water

THE NATURAL CHOICE

Restaurant of the Year

Since opening in 1977, John and Catherine Howard's elegant Ballsbridge restaurant has been, in its quiet way, a leading light in Ireland's food revolution. Famous for his refusal to be a slave to food fashions, John's steadfast sureness of purpose has served the restaurant well in guiding an excellent kitchen team - working, since 1982, under head chef James O'Sullivan - through a culinary minefield of fast-changing tastes. John's background of classical French cooking has blended happily with traditional Irish themes to produce dishes that show New Irish Cuisine at its best. Alongside old favourites which have earned a permanent place on the menu, such as the Scottish-inspired "Coq Hardi" Smokies (a hot starter of smoked haddock, baked with tomato, cream and cheese), upbeat modern Irish classics appear in dishes like Clonakilty black pudding served with a traditional potato cake and apple sauce, baked white fish served with bacon and cabbage with a whiskey cream sauce and a wonderful roast loin of kassler with green cabbage, fresh herb mash and Calvados jus (selected for the Guide's Irish Pork Award last year). But a restaurant is about more than its food. Service, under Catherine Howard's discreet direction, is superb and indicates the underlying strengths of Le Coq Hardi: training and teamwork. And, then of course, there's the small matter of how best to accompany fine food - and the answer lies in an outstanding wine list which is particularly strong in John's favourite areas: Bordeaux, Burgundy, Loire, and Champagne.

2000

1999 Winner:
Deane's, Belfast

Le Coq Hardi
Dublin

Tipperary Water
congratulates

Le Coq Hardi

winner of
Restaurant of the Year

TO THE

connoisseur

IT'S THE

purist

WATER

IT'S NOT WHAT IS IN A MINERAL WATER

THAT DETERMINES ITS QUALITY,

IT'S WHAT IS ABSENT. IN THAT RESPECT,

TIPPERARY NATURAL MINERAL WATER

IS OF THE HIGHEST QUALITY.

IT HAS THE LOWEST MINERALISATION

OF ANY IRISH MINERAL WATER

AND A PERFECT PH BALANCE.

—

FROM THE PUREST ENVIRONMENT,

THE PURIST'S WATER.

Tipperary
Natural Mineral Water

THE NATURAL CHOICE

Chef of the Year

Set in the hills just above Lough Arrow, Cromleach Lodge enjoys one of the finest views in Ireland. The building, which is uncompromisingly modern in style, takes full advantage of its location and Moira Tighe's growing reputation for outstanding cooking is an even more powerful magnet. The restaurant (which is totally non-smoking) is beautifully simple - crisp linen, modern silver and crystal, fine, understated Rosenthal china with fresh flowers a single focal point of colour - which all combine with immaculate maintenance to provide a fit setting for dinner, the high point of every visit to Cromleach. Moira - who, amazingly, is a self-taught cook - and her personally trained all-female kitchen team work superbly well together.They have a growing number of established specialities that are in constant demand, so menus must juggle these with the essential creativity of new dishes. An 8-course Gourmet Tasting Menu offered to residents allows full appreciation of the talent at work.Throughout, carefully sourced local ingredients are evident and details are superb, from the appetisers served with aperitifs in the bar to the irresistible plate of petits fours that round off the evening.

2000

1999 Winner: Kevin Thornton, Thornton's Restaurant, Dublin

MERRYS

Moira Tighe
Cromleach Lodge, Co. Sligo

Bord Bia Irish Awards of Excellence

TO CREATE THEIR OWN

Gold Medal

WINNING

Irish Cream

LIQUEUR

TAKE ESSENTIAL NATURAL INGREDIENTS

- MERRYS IRISH WHISKEY

- THE FRESHEST IRISH CREAM

- THE FINEST IRISH SUGAR

- AND SPECIAL INDIVIDUAL FLAVOURINGS

—

TO BLEND THE DISTINCTIVELY UNIQUE

MERRY'S IRISH CREAM LIQUEUR

NOW IN FIVE SMOOTH TASTING FLAVOURS

*Butterscotch, White Chocolate,
Peaches & Cream, Strawberry Ripple
and Cappuccino.*

*Merrys Irish Cream Liqueurs
- Simplicity with Excellence*

Bord Bia

Irish Food Board

New Irish Cuisine Award

In 1996, recognising that the Irishness of our food was in danger of being lost in the current tidal wave of international influences, the Restaurants Association of Ireland and Bord Bia got together to encourage Irish chefs to consider the regionality of their menus. Visitors were crying out for food with a genuinely Irish flavour, talented young Irish chefs aplenty were returning from experience abroad and the quality of Irish raw materials was recognised - to bring these elements together, New Irish Cuisine was born. The term describes updated traditional Irish food, seen in dishes that have their roots in the past and their heads in the present - dishes that utilise traditional and native ingredients in a colourful, contemporary style. It would be hard to think of a better example than Michael Ryan to demonstrate the potential vitality of the concept: a Cork man, who rightly takes great pride in the produce and specialities of his native city and county, Michael has a knack of including both the produce and the dishes in an international repertoire that brings Irish food bang up to date - and downright irresistible to the dining public.At Isaacs, the atmospheric restaurant that brought the contemporary cafe-brasserie concept to Cork in 1992 with a flourish, Michael and Catherine Ryan together with partner and head chef Canice Sharkey, make a magnificent team - tempting, colourful dishes cleverly combine sunny Mediterranean influences and comforting Irish traditions thus, for example, potato and leek soup sits easily on the menu alongside tempura of prawns with soya and ginger. A perfect environment for the development of New Irish Cuisine and Michael's energetic and inspiring pursuit of excellence and respect for Irish culinary traditions within the framework of international trends.

2000

Bord Bía
Irish Food Board

Michael Ryan,
Isaac's Restaurant, Cork

Bord Bía
congratulates

Michael Ryan

winner of
New Irish Cuisine Award

Ireland
the

Welcome to Ireland, the Food Island.

In Bord Bia, Irish Food Board, we work to increase the consumption of Irish food and drink at home and overseas. We have found that the very best way to promote Irish food is simply for people to taste it - personal experience of the flavour, quality and variety of Irish products leaves a lasting, positive impression.

Ireland is often referred to as the Emerald Isle because of the lush green grass, on which our important dairy and beef cattle and sheep are reared. They are as much a part of the Irish landscape as mountains or rivers.

Bord Bia operates a number of Quality Assurance schemes, over and above those of the regulatory bodies.

Bord Bia
Irish Food Board

Clanwilliam Court, Lower Mount St.
Dublin 2, Ireland
Tel+353-1- 668 5155   Tel+353-1- 668 7521

nd
Food Island

These assure chefs and consumers alike that best practice
has been followed and a wholesome product results.

I encourage visitors to Ireland to explore our culinary heritage,
which blends the modern and the traditional. Returning home,
what better way to relive your memories of visiting Ireland than
to revisit the taste of Irish food, by seeking it out in your own
countries. Irish food is now available in 80 countries around
the world.

I am certain that you will find much to please you in this guide,
not least the winners of the Bord Bia Irish Awards for Excellence.
I wish you a pleasant and flavoursome stay.

Michael Duffy, Chief Executive.

Bord Bia

Irish Food Board

Irish Beef Award

*Fillet of Beef served with Clonakilty Pudding Mash,
Crispy Bacon and Wholegrain Mustard Cream*

Eugene and Breda McSweeney's period house on the edge of Kilkenny city has been the leading restaurant in the area for over 15 years. Eugene is a well-known Euro-Toques chef, who has respresented Ireland many times in culinary competition, while Breda was the Guide's 1999 Sommelier of the Year. In line with the Euro-Toques principles of using the best local ingredients, supporting local producers and thus, in the words of Paul Bocuse "defending the ingredients that are the building blocks of good cooking", Eugene is an enthusiastic supporter of local produce. A particular speciality is beef, which is raised by a local famer known personally to Eugene and always on the menu in a current speciality dish. On a recent visit, Eugene's Fillet of Beef served with Clonakilty Pudding Mash, Crispy Bacon and Wholegrain Mustard Cream turned out to be a dream of a dish. The Clonakilty pudding - enough to add interest without weight - is worked into a creamy, well-flavoured mash, topped with the steak then a single rasher set jauntily alongside, and a slightly crunchy mustard cream around it: admirably simple, with excellent flavour and texture. An example of how successful New Irish Cuisine can be, when traditional elements are developed in a contemporary style.

2000

*1999 Winner: Stefan Matz,
Erriseask House Hotel, Co. Galway*

Bord Bía
Irish Food Board

Lacken House Restaurant, Kilkenny

Bord Bía
congratulates

Lacken House Restaurant

winner of
Irish Beef Award

why choose Quality Assured egg

Ireland is one of only four countries which have an EU approved salmonella plan. Under the plan all farms are tested and monitored by the Department of Agriculture and Food. This places Ireland in the world premier league in terms of salmonella control.

The Quality Assured Scheme is designed to build on the general high health status of the country's laying flock.

Special features of the scheme include:

- All incoming stock for egg laying must be certified free of salmonella

- Ongoing production must be regularly monitored for salmonella on a monthly basis

- Only heat-treated feed can be used

- Management systems must ensure full traceability of eggs

- Each egg carries the logo, best before date and house code

- Producer suppliers must be inspected and approved

- All systems must be independently audited before the Quality Assurance Mark is awarded

Irish Food Board

Irish Lamb Award

Roast Loin of Kerry Mountain Lamb with Filo Wrapped Lambs Kidney, Duxelles and Roasted Shallot

Local seafood naturally features strongly on the menu at Pat and John Moore's elegant restaurant, which is named after one of the nearby Blasket Islands. But Kerry mountain lamb is an equally attractive option and very much a speciality of the house in cooking that is never too clever or pretentious, but always an experience to relish due to the sheer quality of ingredients and an imaginative but disciplined approach. Rack of lamb is as far as most restaurants get with this versatile ingredient which is a pity - so three cheers for restaurants like Beginish, where the dish may vary, but you can be sure it will be a little different -and their Roast Loin of Kerry Mountain Lamb with Filo Wrapped Lambs Kidney, Duxelles and Roasted Shallot is a current favourite. Mountain lamb, which comes into season in mid summer and is available through the autumn, is smaller and leaner than the earlier lowland lamb but, having been raised on mountain herbs and grasses, it makes up in flavour anything it may lack in size. At Beginish it is always an experience to relish.

2000

1999 Winner: Phil McAfee, Restaurant St. Johns, Co. Donegal

Bord Bia
Irish Food Board

Beginish Restaurant
Dingle, Co. Kerry

Bord Bia
congratulates

Beginish Restaurant

winner of
Irish Lamb Award

bac

It takes the individual skill
of a chef to transform
raw ingredients into superb
meals. But as any chef
will tell you, the quality
of a meal depends on
the quality of the
ingredients.

Locating the very best foodstuffs can be difficult. But in conjunction with Bord Bia, bacon suppliers have developed a strict code of practice which ensures that the quality of their product is never less than excellent.

• **Traceability:** Quality Assured bacon can be easily tracked from the original farm through the entire factory process.

**QUALITY
ASSURED BACON**
BORD BIA – IRISH FOOD BOARD

• **Consistency:** Once the Quality Assured mark is issued, standards are maintained by fully auditing every member on a regular basis.

• **Peace of mind:** Knowing that such rigorous standards are applied in such a consistent fashion means real peace of mind for anyone involved in the purchasing of bacon products.

• **Product Standards:** By insisting on limits to the amount of water, salt and fat, shrinkage is minimised.

Quality Assured Bacon gives you an added guarantee of consistent excellence.

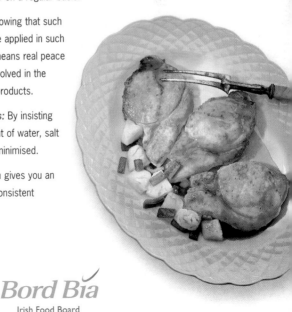

Bord Bia
Irish Food Board

Bord Bía

Irish Food Board

Irish Bacon Award

Roast Loin of Bacon with a Clove & Irish Mist Glaze, served on a Bed of Braised Cabbage & a Potato Cake

The restaurant is a growing attraction at Catherine and Kevin Dundon's impressive country house hotel just across the river from Waterford. Beyond the pleasure garden, a distant organic vegetable and fruit garden bodes well for the, as total self-sufficiency is the eventual aim. Meanwhile, chef/proprietor Kevin succeeds unusually well in combining classical and international influences with local produce and Irish themes. Specialities of the house are marked on the menu with a rosette - these special temptations include starters such as seared magret de canard foie gras and main courses such as local salmon baked on an oak plank and scented with smoked hickory chips - and the dish that specially caught the guide's admiring attention on a recent visit, Roast Loin of Bacon with a Clove & Irish Mist Glaze, served on a Bed of Braised Cabbage & a Potato Cake. Despite the importance of the pig in our culinary history - and indeed the present - too few chefs are currently making the best use of pork and, especially, bacon so this dish came as a breath of fresh air. In it, Kevin works with the best local produce to combine familiar traditional themes with contemporary elements - this is an excellent example of New Irish Cuisine and we applaud it.

2000

1999 Winner: John Howard, Le Coq Hardi, Dublin

Bord Bia
Irish Food Board

Dunbrody House Hotel, Arthurstown, Co. Wexford

Bord Bia
congratulates

Dunbrody House Hotel

winner of
Irish Bacon Award

enjoy
nature's best

chee

Irish farm cheeses
capture the pure,
true flavours of the
Irish countryside,
using only the freshest,
purest milk from
small herds.

se

From the tangy, wave-blown pastures of West Cork's dramatic jagged coast, to the mild, undulating meadows of the east, cheesemakers are reviving a lost art - using traditional skills to make cheese with character.

Some have farmed their land for generations; others have sought new lives in remote rural havens. All are dedicated artisans, committed to creating cheese with life and flavour. Using only the freshest, purest milk, from small herds grazing on Irish grass and herbs, these cheesemakers allow intricate tastes and aromas to flower. Their cheese might be fluffy and creamy-mild, or delicately, tenderly goaty, or long matured and magnificently hard and rich.

The exciting range of varieties means there's an Irish farm cheese to suit every palate.

Bord Bia
Irish Food Board

Bord Bia Irish Awards of Excellence

Seafood Restaurant of the Year

Although not exclusively devoted to seafood, this dashing new contemporary Japanese restaurant is especially deserving of the Guide's Seafood Restaurant of the Year Award. The owners are the Hoashi family, who established Dublin's first Japanase restaurant, Ayumi-Ya, in Blackrock 16 years ago and, since then, have been delighting an increasingly knowledgeable clientele with their authentic traditional Japanese cuisine. The Japanese appreciation of seafood is of course well-known and, as sushi has recently become popular in mainstream restaurants, Dubliners heard with delight that Yoichi Hoashi was planning to introduce the city to a totally new concept - a conveyor sushi bar, restaurant and Japanese food hall.The dining highlight is a full on-line menu offering a wide range of sushi, all authentically Japanese - although, of course, most of the fresh fish used is locally caught in Irish waters. Aya also offers takeaway sushi, fresh and frozen meals and a small selection of Japanese ingredients. The main menu covers all the bases and is impressively wide-ranging, serving everything from well-priced bento boxes at lunchtime to more exotic fare in the evening. This restaurant also has great style - deep-red velvet, beech laminated tables - the service is excellent and, to add to the fun, the staff wear very distinctive grey and red uniforms inspired by 'Dr. No', of James Bond fame. This innovative restaurant is run by true professionals and provides an experience not to be forgotten.

2000

1999 Winner:
Lawrence Cove House, Bere Island

BIM Ireland

Aya@Brown Thomas, Dublin

BIM
congratulates

Aya@Brown Thomas, Dublin

winner of
Seafood Restaurant of the Year

BIM *Ireland*

Seafood is versatile, easy to prepare, quick to cook and the perfect choice for every dining occasion.
Go on, get hooked on Seafood!

RAY WITH BLACK BUTTER

Ray wings have sweet pleasant flesh which slides easily off the soft ribs of the fish. This is the classic recipe for ray and the butter is served not black but a deep nut brown. Final cooking must be done quickly in order to serve the dish   piping hot!

INGREDIENTS

700g/1¹/₂lbs ray wings, cut into 4 pieces
600mls/1pt warm water seasoned with onion,
bayleaf, parsley stalk and lemon slice
75g/3ozs butter
3 tablespoons white wine vinegar
chopped parsley and capers
Nasturtium flowers to garnish (optional)

METHOD

1. Add the wings to the warm seasoned liquid in a wide pan.
2. Simmer gently until cooked, and transfer to a warm serving dish.
3. Meanwhile, heat the butter in a small saucepan till golden brown. Pour all over the fish.
4. Quickly return saucepan to the heat and de-glaze with the wine vinegar, stir well until it reduces and pour over the fish.
5. Scatter on capers and chopped parsley. Serve piping hot immediately.

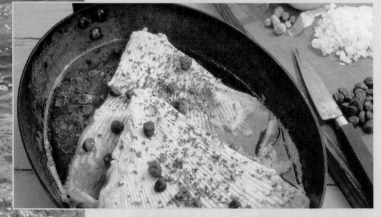

IRISH SEA FISHERIES BOARD/BIM, P.O. BOX 12, CROFTON RD, DUN LAOGHAIRE

SALMON SOUP

Salmon is called The King of Fish and few people can resist that appetising colour, together with a flavour that is both rich and delicate.

INGREDIENTS

FISH STOCK:
1 kg/2 lbs fish bones and trimmings
85g/3 ozs in total of roughly chopped white of leek, carrot, celery
30g/1 oz mushroom trimmings
150 mls/ 1/4 pt dry white wine
1 litre/2 pts water
Salt and peppercorns, egg white and crushed eggshell
SOUP:
100g/4 ozs salmon, cut in diamond shape
100g/4 ozs brill, cut in diamond shape
30g/1 oz green part of leek, cut in very fine strips
30g/1 oz carrot, cut in very fine strips
30g/1 oz celery, cut in very fine strips
Sprigs of dill, pink peppercorns

METHOD FOR STOCK

1. Reduce wine to half in large saucepan.
2. Add vegetables, fish bones, trimmings and water. Simmer gently for 20 minutes. Season and simmer for a further 5 minutes. Skim occasionally. Strain through muslin, reserving 1 tablespoon of solids.

TO CLARIFY

3. Return stock to a clean pan. Add reserved solids, egg white and shell. Bring to the boil gently, whisking continuously. Carefully strain through double thickness of muslin.

TO COMPLETE SOUP

4. Add prepared leek, carrot and celery to clarified stock. Cook for 3 minutes. Add salmon and brill. Simmer for 2 minutes. Scatter pink peppercorns and sprigs of dill over before serving in warmed soup bowls.

CO. DUBLIN, IRELAND   TEL: + 353 1 2841544   FAX: + 353 1 2841123

JAMESON®

IRISH WHISKEY

Pub of the Year

Everyone, especially visiting and local sailors, feels at home in this famous old bar – which is choc-a-bloc with genuine maritime artefacts such as charts, tide tables, ships' clocks, compasses, lanterns, pennants et al – but it's the Bushe family's hospitality that makes it really special. Since Richard and Eileen took on the bar in 1973 it's been "home from home" for regular visitors to Baltimore, for whom a late morning call is de rigeur (in order to collect the ordered newspapers that are rolled up and stacked in the bar window each day). Now there's a new generation of Bushes involved with the business, so all is humming nicely. Simple, homely bar food starts early in the day with tea and coffee from 9.30, moving on to home-made soups and a range of sandwiches including home-cooked meats (ham, roast beef, corned beef), salmon, smoked mackerel or – the most popular by far – open crab sandwiches, served with home-baked brown bread. And all at around a fiver or less. This is a terrific pub, at any time of year, and a very worthy recipient of our Jameson Pub of the Year Award.

2000

1999 Winner:
The Porterhouse, Dublin

JAMESON®

IRISH WHISKEY

Bushe's Bar, Baltimore, Co. Cork

Jameson congratulates

Bushe's Bar, Baltimore.

winner of
Pub of the Year

Bord Bia Irish Awards of Excellence

rush
hour
nyc

JAMESON
WHAT'S THE RUSH?

Irish Distillers Limited Wines and Spirits

Skills Development Award

Since 1985, when Francis Brennan became proprietor and general manager of this renowned hotel, Park Hotel Kenmare has earned international acclaim for exceptional standards of service, comfort and cuisine. Once inside the granite Victorian building, a warm welcome and the ever-burning fire in the hall begin weaving the Park's special magic: any tendency to formality in the antique furnishings is offset by amusing quirks of taste and despite the constant quest for perfection, the atmosphere is relaxed. Public rooms are grand but not overpowering and several open onto a verandah overlooking river and gardens; luxurious bedrooms are spacious, with excellent bathrooms and are furnished to exceptional standards of comfort. However, the most remarkable aspect of the Park Hotel - and one for which it is rightly renowned throughout the length and breadth of Ireland and far beyond - is its staff. The exceptional standard of training overseen by Francis Brennan through the years has had a very significant effect on standards not only in the hotel, but as a ripple effect throughout the country (and, possibly, the world) as those trained under his management have moved on to other positions. In recognition of his unique contribution in this area, the Guide is proud to award Francis Brennan its new Skills Development Award, which will allow him to nominate a promising trainee for a bursary sponsored by Irish Distillers Wines & Spirits.

2000

Irish Distillers Limited
Wines and Spirits

Francis Brennan,
Park Hotel Kenmare, Co Kerry.

Irish Distillers Wines & Spirits
congratulates
Francis Brennan,
Park Hotel Kenmare
winner of
Skills Development Award

Cork Dry Gin

Host of the Year

Since 1980, to growing acclaim, Reggie Ryan and Phil McAfee have run Restaurant St John's in their substantial period house overlooking Lough Swilly and it is one of the most hospitable houses in Ireland. Reggie has a way with guests which must be pretty well unrivalled, making each one feel especially welcome and - oh joy of joys - making the whole occasion relaxed and fun, a time when it is no crime to let your hair down a little after dinner. Restaurant St John's has hosted many an international figure and we are in no doubt that he has had the same effect on them all, welcoming them with warmth and leaving each with memories that will always be treasured. The conservatory extension has allowed for Lough views in addition to the original cosy inside rooms, all a fit setting for Phil's cooking, which combines a respect for tradition and understanding of the value of simplicity with a willingness to experiment, ensuring that the many guests who regularly return always have a meal that is both stimulating and relaxing. Given the location, seafood is very popular but Phil uses a wide range of local ingredients, including game in winter and Donegal mountain lamb, which is an established favourite. (Her "Rack of Donegal Mountain Lamb with Rosemary and Mascarpone Risotto" earned Restaurant St John's the Guide's Irish Lamb Award in 1999). A fairly priced wine list includes nine house wines, a special seasonal selection and a good choice of half bottles adds to the hospitable atmosphere.

2000

1999 Winner: Ray Byrne & Jane English, Wineport Restaurant, Athlone

Bord Bia Irish Awards of Excellence

Cork Dry Gin

Reggie Ryan, St John's Country House,
Fahan, Co. Donegal.

Cork Dry Gin
congratulates
Reggie Ryan,
St John's Country House
winner of
Host of the Year

C·D·C

FINEST

Cork Dry Gin

TRIPLE DISTILLED FROM THE FINEST
GRAIN FOR THE UTMOST PURITY

"Where Good Taste Prevails"

Cork Dry Gin ~ One Of The Fine

When It Comes To Perfecting A U n i q u e Tasting Gin, Mr Coldwell Wrote The Book.

In 1799, a distiller at Old Watercourse, William Coldwell, began recording the development of a recipe for a fine gin. His recipe book, which has been handed down through eight generations of Cork distillers, was the inspiration for one of the finest tasting gins in the world - Cork Dry Gin.

Today, that book is jealously guarded at the offices of the Cork Distilleries Company. However, if you want to know how the story ends - simply taste a Cork Dry Gin. We think you'll agree, it's a rather thrilling climax.

asting Gins In The World

Irish Distillers Limited
Wines and Spirits

Wine List of the Year

Sarah and John McDonnell's craft shop and restaurant is beautifully located and the restaurant, which offers excellent home-made self-service fare throughout the day, has magnificent sea view. On Fridays and Saturdays in July and August, evening brings a more formal dining arrangement, offering the same good cooking and excellent value in imaginative dinner menus based on local produce.Tempting vegetarian dishes, nice homely desserts – and, of course, an especially interesting wine list. John's passion for wine led him to operate The Australian Wine Bureau in Ireland, but the restaurant wine list travels much further afield and the pleasure with which he has sourced Whitethorn's liquid offerings is tangible in the reading. What's more, he makes out individual wine suggestions to match specific dishes on the dinner menus - and even sits down with guests while they're considering the menu, to help with making the best choices to suit the food, individual taste and the mood of the moment. All this is done with the lightest possible touch, without a hint of the dread wine snobbery that can be so intimidating - and John's sheer enthusiasm is infectious.

2000

1999 Winner:
Moyglare Manor, Maynooth

Irish Distillers Limited
Wines and Spirits

Whitethorn Restaurant,
Ballyvaughan, Co. Clare

Irish Distillers Wines & Spirits
congratulates

Whitethorn Restaurant

winner of
Wine List of the Year

Irish Distillers Limited Wines and Spirits

Sommelier of the Year

Dromoland is one of Ireland's grandest hotels, and also one of the best-loved. Today, the grandeur of the surroundings gives a sense of occasion, without overpowering.The most beautiful room, the Earl of Thomond Dining Room, is magnificent, with crystal, gilding and rich fabrics – and also suprisingly relaxed. Guests ease into the dining experience with an aperitif in the Library Bar while reading the menu and wine list before moving through to beautifully presented tables and the gentle background music of a traditional Irish harpist - a fit setting for Head Chef David McCann's excellent cuisine. Service, under restaurant manager Tony Frisby, is excellent and the wine list – about 250 wines, predominantly French – is under the constant review of sommelier Pascal Playon, who is not only knowledgable, but an exceptionally thoughtful and helpful wine host. Unusually Pascal, who is from Brittany, is self-taught - which may partly explain his encouragingly enthusiastic and approachable attitude when guiding guests' wine choices. Having worked with Alain Bras shortly after he gained the title of Best Sommelier in Ireland in 1996, Pascal was inspired to read, attend wine tastings and travel to wine regions to increase his knowledge. In September 1998 he was selected to represent Ireland at the finals of the Waterford Crystal "Wine Service Award", inspiring him to still greater efforts. As he says himself "Still the best is the next one to come, with wine a lifetime is not enough..."

2000

1999 Winner: Breda McSweeney, Lacken House Restaurant, Kilkenny

Irish Distillers Limited Wines and Spirits

Pascal Playon, Dromoland Castle Hotel, Newmarket-on-Fergus, Co. Clare.

Irish Distillers Wines & Spirits congratulates

Pascal Playon, Dromoland Castle Hotel winner of
Sommelier of the Year

Ireland on the Web

Looking for info on...

Theatre

Music

Cinema

Comedy

Restaurants

Pubs

Shopping

Sights

Accommodation

IRISH
HEART
FOUNDATION

Happy Heart Eat Out Award

Head chef Johanna Hill has been supervising the production of the famously wholesome home-cooked food at Avoca Handweavers Restaurant since 1995 and people come here from miles around to tuck into fare which is as healthy as it is delicious, much of which meets the Irish Heart Foundation's definition of a Healthy Choice, i.e. dishes with lots of fruit and vegetables that are high in fibre and low in fat. Healthy dishes bursting with vitamins and many of them low-fat,include a wide range of salads. Although traditional home cooking is the overall theme, many dishes, such as Mediterranean vegetable & chevre tart, roasted vegetable & chicken pancake stack and green bean and coconut soup, have a welcome a contemporary twist. Hot food includes traditional dishes such as beef and Guinness casserole and vegetarians are especially well catered for, both in special dishes – nut loaf, vegetable-based soups – and the many that just happen to be meatless. Johanna Hill and her team have proved that healthy, natural foods are very much in demand - and to underline the point, Avoca is shortly publishing a cookery book based on their restaurant dishes. Baking is another strong point; typical breads made daily include traditional brown soda, cheese bread and a popular multigrain loaf.

2000

1999 Winner:
101 Talbot, Dublin

IRISH
HEART
FOUNDATION

Avoca Handweavers, Kilmacanogue, Co. Wicklow

*Irish Heart Foundation
congratulates*

Avoca Handweavers

winner of
Happy Heart Eat Out Award

Eat Out

For a Happy Heart ...
Go For Low Fat Healthy Eating

Just Ask

More and more people are interested in healthy eating when eating out, and yet still want to enjoy delicious food. A recent customer survey conducted by the Irish Heart Foundation indicated that over three-quarters of people ask for the healthier choice.

Many chefs and restaurants are responding to this demand for lighter cuisine. To help you offer your customers a wider and more creative range of healthy choices, the Irish Heart Foundation and the Health Promotion Unit in the Department of Health and Children organise **HAPPY HEART EAT OUT** for the month of June each year.

The theme is 'Go For Low Fat Healthy Eating' and customers are encouraged to *Just Ask* for the low fat healthy choice. Our evaluations show that many establishments continue to provide low fat choices all year round.

For information and suggestions on healthy choices and recipes contact the Irish Heart Foundation, Telephone: 01 668 5001.

NATIONAL HEALTHY EATING CAMPAIGN

IRISH
HEART
FOUNDATION

HEALTH
PROMOTION
UNIT

Farmhouse Cheese Award

An old leather tannery has been imaginatively converted to make Paul and Maire Flynn's stylish contemporary restaurant. The kitchen is open to view as guests go upstairs to the first-floor dining area and the tannery theme is echoed throughout the light, clean-lined interior, creating a sense of history that, along with dramatic paintings and fresh flowers, adds greatly to the atmosphere. Paul's colourful, modish dishes are equally contemporary, presented on elegant white plates set against unadorned lightwood tables. Wide-ranging menus inspired by global trends are based mainly on local ingredients: local seafood features in a successful modern rendition of traditional fish chowder, made with smoked haddock and spring onions and main courses such as a fillet of John Dory served with wild rice, and a morel and parma ham cream. Dashing desserts are tempting but don't miss the cheese. A selection of four farmhouse cheeses is presented in perfect condition and, although they are sourced from the celebrated Dublin cheesemongers Sheridans of Anne Street (who ensure that everything supplied is in perfect condition), the selection tends to be fairly local. A ripe Cashel Blue will often be included and west Cork will usually be represented - by Durrus or Milleens, perhaps, or if you are lucky the West Cork Cheese Company's wonderful nutty-flavoured mature Gabriel, Desmond or Mizen. Mine Gabhar fresh goats cheese may be offered in season (April-October) and they sometimes offer a continental cheese such as Pont l'Eveque alongside the Irish ones. Whatever the day's quartet may be, it is very attractively served on a board with a selection of biscuits, celery, walnuts and fruit.

2000

1999 Winner:
Casino House, Kilbrittain, Co. Cork

Tannery Restaurant, Dungarvan, Co. Waterford

Jacob's Biscuits
congratulates

Tannery Restaurant

winner of
Farmhouse Cheese Award

Jacob's ~ ORIGINAL & BEST ~ Cream Crackers ~ SINCE 1885 ~

TUNA CRUNCH

Mix a tin of tuna with some sweetcorn. Add in a tablespoon of mayonnaise and a teaspoon of tomato ketchup. Spread thickly on to a Jacob's Cream Cracker topped with a couple of slices of cucumber. Season with black pepper before eating.

SPICY PRAWN

Mix some cottage cheese with finely chopped spring onion. Spread on to a Jacob's Cream Cracker. Place three or four fresh peeled prawns on to the mix and season with paprika.

FRUIT PATE

A thick spread of your favourite pate topped off with a slice of succulent kiwi. A savoury and sweet Jacob's Cream Cracker suitable for any time.

MINI PIZZA

Ideal for entertaining or a tasty lunch. Spread some tomato puree onto a Jacob's Cream Cracker. Add a little mozzarella and then top with your favourite pizza toppings. For example, we chose salami and ham. Place under a moderately heated grill until the cheese is melted. Serve hot.

TOP THEM WITH YOUR IMAGINATION

Jacob's
~ ORIGINAL & BEST ~
# Cream Crackers
~ SINCE 1885 ~

CREAM OF THE SEA

Thickly spread cream cheese on to a Jacob's Cream Cracker. Then place a generous slice of smoked salmon neatly on top. Finish off with a squeeze of fresh lemon juice and serve.

MEXICAN MIX

An exciting way to spice up a party! Peel and slice half an avocado on to a buttered Jacob's Cream Cracker. Chop some spring onion and a green pepper and sprinkle on top of the avocado. Add a small pinch of chilli powder and a squeeze of lemon juice to taste.

BLUE ORCHARD

Slices of green apple arranged alternatively with some slices of blue cheese on a Jacob's Cream Cracker. A tasteful way to finish a pleasant meal.

MOZZARELLA MUNCHIE

Top a Jacob's Cream Cracker with a large slice of juicy tomato. Grate some mozzarella cheese and sprinkle it on top. Add some slices of green and red pepper and pop into the microwave for 15-20 seconds (per cracker). Eat hot served with coleslaw.

TOP THEM WITH YOUR IMAGINATION

Atmospheric Restaurant of the Year

The O'Donnell family have run Danny Minnie's since 1962 and, far from tiring of the challenge, they continue to welcome back old friends and delight new ones each year. For, hidden behind a frontage of overgrown creepers, this cool, sophisticated gem of a place amazes first time guests. It's like finding a little palace at an oasis: antiques, elegantly appointed candle-lit tables, Terri O'Donnell's warm welcome and helpful service from kind waitresses. They do the menu in both Irish and English (but not the wine list, which is probably just as well) and Michael O'Donnell's cooking is a good match for the surroundings - fine, with imaginative saucing. On a wide-ranging à la carte menu, seafood stars in the main courses – lobster and other shellfish, availability permitting, and baked fillet of turbot with prawn sauce and pesto, perhaps, or monkfish and courgette with a ginger & herb cream. There is also a strong selection of meats including Donegal mountain lamb, typically served with caramelized onions, blackcurrant & mint jus and and Donegal beef, served various ways including classic Beef Wellington. Vegetables are a strength and gorgeous desserts such as crepes suzette with orange and Grand Marnier can be relied on to create an appropriately dramatic finale. Great food, warm hospitality and a lovely room seen in the warm glow of candlelight always make for a memorable evening.

2000

1999 Winner:
Restaurant Le Chateau, Athlone

RATHBORNES
ESTABLISHED 1488

Danny Minnie's Restaurant,
Annagry, The Roses, Co. Donegal

Rathborne Candles
congratulates

Danny Minnie's Restaurant

winner of
Atmospheric Restaurant of the Year

Several of us have now worked under you ...

...od you have evinced much zeal for our int...

...ich deserves praise ; for this we tender ...

...ed that when each ... from our labo...

...and blandness ... the produc...

...d that wh ... rning the...

...and bian ... our labo...

...ks with ... he produ...

...loyer and ... urting the...

...and pros ... a healthy t...

...r hail ... ortant Esta...

...appines ... Mo...

...al urba...

...lways

Pet-Friendly Establishment of the Year

This historic country house is close to many places of interest, including medieval Kilkenny, New Ross (where river cruises are available) - and Kildare's National Stud. Animals are important to Lorum Old Rectory, both on and off the premises - close by is Gowran Park racecourse and there's also a riding school (offering both outdoor and indoor tuition) and many interesting animals around the property, which are always a source of great entertainment to visiting children. Elegant, spacious and very comfortable accommodation includes a lovely drawing room for guests and a bedroom with a four-poster- but it is Don and Bobbie Smith's hospitality that really keeps bringing guests back.Bobbie, who is a member of Euro-Toques, prepares good home cooked dinners for residents, based mainly on organic ingredients and served at a long mahogany table. This is a family-friendly place where children enjoy swings in the orchard as well as the relaxed attitude to animals - and it should come as no surprise that guests are welcome to bring their dogs (who tend to become part of the family) by arrangement.

2000

1999 Winner:
Kylenoe, Co. Tipperary

Lorum Old Rectory,
Bagnelstown, Co. Carlow

Master Foods
congratulates

Lorum Old Rectory

winner of
Pet-Friendly Establishment
of the Year

Supporting Pet Friendly Accommodation

Don't leave home without your pet!

⊡ **Electrolux**

ELECTROLUX GROUP (IRELAND) LTD.

Natural Food Award

Home to the Bourke family for generations, this gracious 17th century manor house was first opened to guests in 1965 by Hugh and the late Eleanor Bourke, and it's now run by their son Joe, with his wife Hazel, who is the personification of Euro-Toques principles which aim to preserve the quality of natural and traditional foods. Wonderful food, much of it from their own organic walled kitchen garden, is one of the main reasons people keep going back to Assolas. Hazel is renowned for imaginative and skilled use of local produce, used in seasonal cooking that is refreshingly natural in both style and content and genuinely reflects the region. Seafood features regularly, in starters like Rosscarbery oysters grilled with garden herbs or warm salad of new potatoes with Kenmare mussels, a dish that recently won acclaim for its "audacious simplicity, superb flavour and natural ingredients". The garden also inspires wonderful soups – sorrel, perhaps, or potato and leek. Main courses are also admirably simple - Kanturk lamb from the local butcher served with homemade mint jelly, perhaps, or tender local roast free-range duckling which is a speciality of the area. Desserts tend to be classic and very seasonal as they grow a lot of fruit – raspberries and cream or blackcurrant fool with vanilla shortbread – and local farmhouse cheeses are superb.

2000

⊠ Electrolux

ELECTROLUX GROUP (IRELAND) LTD.

Hazel Bourke, Assolas Country House, Kanturk, Co. Cork

Electrolux/Euro-Toques
congratulates

Hazel Bourke, Assolas Country House

winner of
Natural Food Award

Euro-Toques

Guardians of European Food

Euro-Toques is a 2,500 strong association of chefs throughout Europe who have banded together in order to preserve the quality of natural and traditional foods. They are committed to supporting producers of the best foods in Europe, so that the fine quality and flavour of ingredients can be maintained. By the same token, they also wish to maintain the traditional dishes and the traditional ways of preparing and cooking the regional foods of Europe.

Euro-Toques sees itself as guardian of European cultures of good food and of a good quality of life. It is not an elitist organisation but open to members who wish to follow a code of honour which includes a commitment to promote the use of fine quality and traditional artisan foods and to avoid convenience products.

Each country operates a Chapter through a group of commissioners led by a Commissioner-General – Ireland's is currently Derry Clarke of L'Ecrivain, Dublin – supported by a Founder Member and regional Commissioners. For a small country the Irish Chapter is very strong, with over a hundred members. This is largely due to the inspired leadership and energy of the Irish Commissioners, notably Mrs Myrtle Allen of Ballymaloe House, Cork. She was the Founder Member for Ireland when Euro-Toques was established in 1986 by its first

Myrtle Allen and Lars Pluto Johannison

President M Pierre Romeyer, chef-patron of the Brussels restaurant Maison de Bouche. In 1994, Mrs Allen succeeded the famous French chef Paul Bocuse as President. The current President is Lars Pluto Johannison of Sweden

Euro-Toques' foundation was supported by the then President of the EC, M Jacques Delor, who welcomed this "European Community of Cooks". The Brussels connection is extremely important to Euro-Toques, as it is the only organisation of chefs recognised by the EU as a lobbying group on European Food Legislation, and it is in this area that much of the group's most urgent work is done. They have lobbied successfully on topics such as defending the sale of unpasteurised milk cheese and ensuring that the quality aspect of food be a factor in food legislation, rather than simply safety. Current lobbying areas include genetic engineering of food, additives and labelling.

Euro-Toques is responsible for selecting an Irish representative to the world's most prestigious cooking competition, the Bocuse d'Or, which is held in Lyons, France, every two years. Within Ireland they have also nurtured young talent through the Baileys Young Chef Competition which, since 1990, has given some of Ireland's most promising young chefs the opportunity to gain experience under leading chefs in some of Europe's finest kitchens.

There is also a lighter side to the organisation, as each branch organises activities such as mushroom hunts, visits to food producers and a European Day of Taste, when members visit schools to teach young children about taste. In true chef style, Euro-Toques outings involve much bonhomie and, through enjoyment, commitment to their common goal is strengthened.

European Partners

Electrolux and Euro-Toques

Electrolux, the world's largest manufacturer of household appliances, is currently committed to a three year European sponsorship of Euro-Toques. Citing Euro-Toques as "a partner for the new millenium", Electrolux is building on its traditional areas of strength with added concentration on all aspects of Food Care, from safe refrigeration to sophisticated cookery. Euro-Toques and Electrolux share many values and the two organisations are highly compatible: both are concerned to serve their customers good, healthy and exciting food. Restaurateurs need the

Derry Clarke, Irish Commissioner-General of Euro-Toques

best equipment and Electrolux, with advice from Euro-Toques chefs, will also be well placed to provide home cooks with the best products for preparing top quality meals.

Electrolux aims to position the brand as the authority and leader in food preservation and cooking in Europe. According to Matsola Palm, Head of Global Marketing: "We will be having fun doing what we do best: bringing a stream of innovative and great new products onto the market at competitive prices to help us all to be Europe's favourite chefs."

For a free copy of the booklet listing
Euro-Toques Chefs and Restaurants
of Ireland contact:

Euro-Toques Irish Branch
11 Bridge Court
City Gate
Dublin 8
Tel: + 353 1 677 9999

Electrolux

ELECTROLUX GROUP (IRELAND) LTD.

An Bord Glas
THE HORTICULTURAL DEVELOPMENT BOARD

Vegetarian Dish of the Year

*Goats' cheese, pinenut and oven-roasted
tomato charlotte, served with
wilted greens and puy lentils in basil oil*

Denis Cotter and Bridget Healy's mould-breaking vegetarian restaurant has been a great success since it opened six years ago - and 1999 saw the philosophy reach a far wider public with the publication of the lovely Cafe Paradiso Cookbook. Here you will find (amongst many other culinary gems) the recipe for our Vegetarian Dish of the Year: goats' cheese, pinenut and oven-roasted tomato charlotte, served with wilted greens and puy lentils in basil oil. This dish is a good example of the reason why vegetarian food never seems the same after eating at Café Paradiso: it's exciting mainstream cooking and even the most committed carnivores love every mouthful. Any chef with a goat cheese starter on the menu should take a look at Denis Cotter's goats' cheese charlotte and see how it lightens up an ingredient which can easily be too heavy and is often a disappointment. The little restaurant where all this vegetarian creativity takes place is lively with a buzzy atmosphere and the staff, under the direction of Bridget Healy, are not only friendly and helpful but obviously enthusiastic about their work.

2000

*1999 Winner: Ballymore Inn,
Ballymore Eustace, Co. Kildare*

An Bord Glas
THE HORTICULTURAL DEVELOPMENT BOARD

Café Paradiso,
Cork

Jörg Köster

An Bord Glas
congratulates

Café Paradiso, Cork

winner of
Vegetarian Dish of the Year

An Bord Glas
THE HORTICULTURAL DEVELOPMENT BOARD

Make more of Nature's Treats . . .

with Fruit & Vegetables

For further information or recipe leaflets, please contact the
Fresh Fruit & Vegetable Information Centre at T: 01 6614105

Irish Distillers Limited
Wines and Spirits

Business Hotel Award

Conference and meeting facilities, video-conferencing, business centres and secretarial back-up, bedrooms with personal photocopiers and ISDN lines - all these and off-duty amenities like golf courses and leisure centres are seen in a growing number of hotels - but some have been practising longer than others. Lynch Hotels have been meeting the needs of business guests with exemplary efficiency since the 1960s. The West County, in Ennis, has long been a leading example of the genre, offering a good mix of leisure and business facilities with that all important ingredient - hard won experience in looking after business guests and successfully managing business events. Its nearby sister hotel The Clare Inn is perhaps more leisure-orientated, but they also do an excellent job for conferences. The more recent flagship Limerick establishment, South Court Hotel, is conveniently located for both local and visiting business guests and has been designed with the requirements of the business traveller particularly in mind, offering outstanding facilities, spacious and well-equipped bedrooms - and the same high standard of service. Although all of their hotels are also of interest for leisure, it is greatly to their credit that Lynch Hotels have been serving the business community so consistently for over 30 years and this award is well deserved.

2000

1999 Winner:
Jurys Hotel and Towers, Dublin

Irish Distillers Limited
Wines and Spirits

Lynch Hotels

Irish Distillers Wines & Spirits
congratulates

Lynch Hotels

winner of
Business Hotel Award

BUSHMILLS

International Hospitality Award

The origins of Straffan House go back a long way – the history is known as far back as 550 AD – but it was the arrival of the Barton wine family in 1831 that established the tone of today's magnificent building, by giving it a distinctively French elegance. It was bought by the Smurfit Group in 1988 and, after extensive renovations, opened as an hotel in 1991. Set in lush countryside, and overlooking its own golf course, the hotel boasts unrivalled opulence. Under the guidance of Ray Carroll, who has been with the hotel from the outset and was general manager for two years before taking over responsibility for the Golf and becoming Chief Executive of the Resort, it is run with apparently effortless perfection. Ray's illustrious career in the hotel business has taken him from Park Lane in London's West End, to Barbados and Cashel, Co Tipperary - a variety indicative of the range of experience required when it comes to offering international hospitality at the the very top of the market. The Kildare Hotel & Country Club has deservedly received many accolades and, like the golf course which is host to the Smurfit European Open, has continued to develop and improve. At the time of going to press, Ray's international hospitality skills are due to be energetically exercised, as both the hotel and golf course are on the point of embarking on major developments in preparation for the Ryder Cup, which the K Club will host in 2005.

2000

1999 Winner: Johnny & Lucy Madden,
Hilton Park, Co. Monaghan

BUSHMILLS

Ray Carroll,
Kildare Hotel & Country Club

Bushmills
congratulates
Ray Carroll,
Kildare Hotel & Country Club
winner of
International Hospitality Award

Our Days Are often Soft, Our Malt Is always Mellow.

Close by the stunning Antrim coast, nestles the time-touched village of Bushmills.

There, in a distillery licenced since 1608, we first ferment and then triple-distil Irish malted barley. Ten maturing years follows in American oak bourbon barrels and European oak sherry casks creating the unique mellowness that characterises Bushmills Single Malt Irish Whiskey.

In just one smooth sip, you'll discover why Bushmills Malt was a Gold Medal Winner at the World Spirits Championships and noted as having:

"A silky mouthfeel; a soft, elegant finish with expanding warmth."

Above all, you'll savour a rare softness and mellowness that reflects a quiet land and a warm people.

Come softly to Bushmills Malt.

Come softly.

Bushmills Malt.
The Single Malt Whiskey from Ireland.

Bord Bía
Irish Food Board

Bord Bía congratulates

Maddybenny Farmhouse,
Portrush, Co. Antrim

Farmhouse of the Year

Rathsallagh House,
Dunlavin, Co. Wicklow

Country House of the Year

Barrowville Townhouse,
Carlow, Co. Carlow

Guesthouse of the Year

2000

Winners 2000

Maddybenny Farmhouse

Rathsallagh House

Barrowville Townhouse

Bord Bia Irish Awards of Excellence

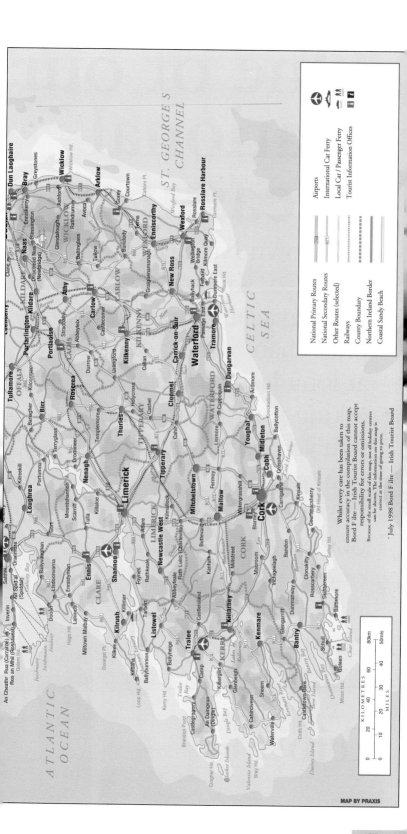

MAP BY PRAXIS

95

One of our National Treasures

"Our own No. 1 Brew from Co. Kildare appears to be available in more pubs than ever before and at long last people are asking for it by name. If you've never tasted it, you're missing out on one of our national treasures."

Tom Doorley

Tribune The Sunday

6 June 1999

DUBLIN City
A Town for our Times

This year of 2000 is Dublin's year, but the place is so busy they'll scarcely have time for any special celebrations. Yet Dublin is a city whose time has come. It's an old town whose many meandering stories have interacted and combined to create today's busy riverside and coastal metropolis. Through a wide variety of circumstances, it has become an entertaining place ideally suited for the civilised enjoyment of life as the 21st Century gets into its stride.

Dubliners tend to wear their city's history lightly despite having in their environment so much of the past in the way of ancient monuments, historic buildings, gracious squares and fine old urban architecture that still manages to be gloriously alive. They may not quite take it for granted, but nevertheless they have to get on with everyday life. Indeed, these days they've a vigorous appetite for it. So they'll quickly deflate any visitor's excessive enthusiasm about their city's significance with some throwaway line of Dublin wit, or sweep aside highfalutin notions of some figure of established cultural importance by recalling how their grandfathers had the measure of that same character when he was still no more than a pup making a nuisance of himself in the neighbourhood pub.

The origins of the city's name are in keeping with this downbeat approach. From the ancient Irish there came something which derived from a makeshift solution to local inconvenience. Baile Atha Cliath - the official name today - means nothing more exciting than "the townland of the hurdle ford". Ancient Ireland being an open plan sort of place without towns, the future city was no more than a river crossing.

But where the Irish saw inconvenience, the Vikings saw an opportunity. When they brought their longships up the River Liffey, they found a sheltered berth in a place which the locals of the hurdle ford called Dubh Linn - "the black pool". Although the name was to go through many mutations as the Vikings were succeeded by the Normans while they in turn were in the business of becoming English, today's name of Dublin is remarkably similar to the one which the Vikings came upon, although the old Irish would have pronounced it as something more like "doo-lin".

The name makes sense, for it was thanks to the existence of the black pool that Dublin became the port and trading base which evolved as the country's natural administrative centre. Thus your Dubliner may well think that the persistent official use of Baile Atha Cliath is an absurdity. But it most empatically isn't the business of any visitor to say so, for although Dublin came into existence almost by accident, it has now been around for a long time, and Dubliners have developed their own attitudes and their own way of doing things.

Located by a wide bay with some extraordinarily handsome hills and mountains near at hand, the city has long had as an important part of its makeup the dictates of stylish living, and the need to cater efficiently for individual tastes and requirements. Quite often the facade has been maintained through periods of impoverishment, but even in earliest mediaeval times this was already a major centre of craftmanship and innovative shop-keeping. Today, the Dublin craftsmen and shop-keepers and their assistants are characterful subjects worthy of respectful academic study. And in an age when "going shopping" has become the world's favourite leisure activity, this old city has reinvented herself in the forefront of international trends.

For Dublin virtually shunned the Industrial Revolution, or at least took some care to ensure that it happened elsewhere. The city's few large enterprises tended to be aimed at personal needs and the consumer market, rather than some aspiration towards heavy industry. Outstanding of them all was of course Guinness's Brewery, founded in 1759. Today, its work-force may be much slimmed in every sense, but it still creates the black nectar, and if a new mash is under way up at the brewery and the wind is coming damply across Ireland from the west, the aroma of Guinness in the making will be wafted right into the city centre, the moist evocative essence of Anna Livia herself.

When Dublin was expanding to its present size during the mid-20th Century with people flocking in from all over Ireland to work in the city, it was said that the only "real Dub" was someone who didn't go home to the country for the weekend. Today, with Dublin so popular with visitors, the more cynical citizens might well comment that the surest test of a real Dub is someone who avoids Temple Bar. But it is rather unfair of any Dubliner to dismiss that bustling riverside hotbed of musical pubs, ethnic restaurants, cultural happenings and nightclubs as being no more than a tourist ghetto. For at the very least, it is Temple Bar which maintains the Dubliner's international reputation as a round-the-clock party animal. And now that the area has settled down and achieved a certain mellowness in its new role, you will occasionally meet "real Dubs" there.

Nevertheless, come nightfall and your discerning Dubliner is more likely to be found in a pleasant pub or restaurant in one of the city's many urban villages, delightfully-named places such as Ranelagh or Rathmines or Templeogue or Stoneybatter or Phibsborough or Donnybrook or Glasnevin or Ringsend or Dundrum or Clontarf or Drumcondra or Chapelizod, to name only a few. And then there are places like Stepaside or Howth or Glasthule or Foxrock or Dalkey which are at sufficient distance as scarcely to think of themselves as being part of Dublin at all. Yet that's where you'll find today's real Dubs enjoying their fair city every bit as much as city centre folk. Happy is the visitor who is able to savour it all, in and around this town for our times.

Local Attractions and Information

Abbey and Peacock Theatres	Lower Abbey Street 01 878 7222
Andrew's Lane Theatre	off Exchequer Street 01 679 5720
Bank of Ireland (historic)	College Green 01 661 5933
Christchurch Cathedral	Christchurch Place D8 01 677 8099
Drimnagh Castle (moat, formal 17th century gardens)	Longmile Road 01 450 2530
Dublin Airport	01 814 4222
Dublin Castle	Dame Street 01 677 7129
Dublin Film Festival (April)	01 679 2937
Dublin Garden Festival, RDS (June)	01 490 0600
Dublin International Organ & Choral Festival (June)	01 677 3066
Dublin Theatre Festival (October)	01 677 8439
Dublin Tourism Centre (restored church)	Suffolk Street 1850 230 330
Dublin Writer's Museum	Parnell Square 01 872 2077
Dublinia	Christchurch 01 475 8137
Gaiety Theatre	South King Street 01 677 1717
Gate Theatre	Cavendish Row 01 874 4045
Guinness Brewery	St. James's Gate 01 453 6700 ext 5155
Hugh Lane Municipal Gallery	Parnell Square 01 874 1903
Icon at the Baileys Centre	Leopardstown Rd Foxrock 01 289 1000
Irish Antique Dealers Fair, RDS (October)	01 285 9294
Irish Film Centre	Eustace Street 01 679 3477
Irish Museum of Modern Art/Royal Hospital	Kilmainham 01 671 8666
Irish Tourist Board/Bord Failte	Baggot Street Bridge 01 602 4000
Iveagh Gardens	Earlsfort Terrace 01 475 7816
Kilmainham Gaol	Kilmainham 01 453 5984
Landsdowne Road Rugby Ground	Ballsbridge 01 668 4601
Mother Redcaps Market	(nr St Patricks/Christchurch) Fri-Sun 10am-5.30 pm
National Botanic Gardens	Glasnevin 01 837 7596
National Concert Hall	Earlsfort Terrace 01 671 1888
National Gallery of Ireland	Merrion Square West 01 661 5133
National Museum of Ireland	Kildare Street 01 677 7444
National Museum of Ireland	Collins Barracks 01 677 7444
Natural History Museum	Merrion Street 01 661 8811
Newman House	St Stephen's Green 01 475 7255
Northern Ireland Tourist Board	Nassau Street D2 01 679 1977
Number Twenty Nine (18c house)	Lower Fitzwilliam Street 01 702 6165
Olympia Theatre	Dame Street 01 677 7744
Point Depot (Concerts & Exhibitions)	North Wall Quay 01 836 6000
Powerscourt Townhouse	South William Street 01 679 4144
Pro Cathedral	Marlborough Street 01 287 4292
Royal Hospital	Kilmainham 01 671 8666
St Michans Church	Dublin 7 (mummified corpses) 01 872 4154
St Patrick's Cathedral	Patrick's Close 01 475 4817
Temple Bar Food Market	Saturdays 11am – 4 pm (all year)

The Dillon Garden	45 Sandford Rd Ranelagh D6 01 497 1308
The Old Jameson Distillery	Smithfield D7 01 807 2355
Tivoli Theatre	Francis Street 01 454 4472
Trinity College Book of Kells and Dublin Experience	01 677 2941
War Memorial Gardens (Sir Edwin Lutyens)	Islandbridge D8 01 677 0236

Dublin 4   *66 Townhouse*

66 Northumberland Road Ballsbridge Dublin
GUESTHOUSE   Tel: 01 660 0471 Fax: 01 660 1051

Conveniently located close to the RDS exhibition centre and with a limited amount of off-street parking, this comfortable guesthouse is well sited for out-of-town guests attending shows or anyone wanting a relaxed, family home feel in a city setting. Breakfast is excellent. Parking. No pets. **Rooms 9** (8 suites, 1 en-suite, 4 no-smoking) B&B £40pps. MasterCard, Visa.

Dublin 1   *101 Talbot Restaurant*

101 Talbot Street Dublin
RESTAURANT   Tel/Fax: 01 874 5011

Ever since opening 101 Talbot in 1991, Margaret Duffy and Pascal Bradley have created a real buzz around this groundbreaking northside restaurant. Its proximity to the Abbey and Gate theatres and the constantly changing art exhibitions in the restaurant have been partly responsible for drawing an interesting artistic/theatrical crowd, but its popularity with this discerning clientele is also due to the joyfully creative and healthy food that has earned the 101 such a fine reputation from the start. Always interested in experimentation, and exceptionally willing to help with any particular dietary requirements, the Mediterranean and Middle Eastern influences at work in the kitchen here explain the uniquely enjoyable wholesomeness across the complete range of dishes, always including strong vegetarian options. 101 Talbot was our 1999 Happy Heart Eat Out Award Winner. No private parking. Children welcome. **Seats 80.** Open 5-11, Mon to 10. A la carte. No-smoking area. Closed Xmas, New Year, Bank Hols. Amex, Diners, MasterCard, Visa.

Dublin 4 ✻   *Aberdeen Lodge*

53-55 Park Avenue Ailesbury Road Ballsbridge Dublin
Tel: 01 283 8155 Fax: 01 283 7877
ACCOMMODATION   email: aberdeen@iol.ie

Centrally located (close to the Sydney Parade DART station) yet away from the heavy traffic of nearby Merrion Road, this handsome period house offers all the advantages of an hotel at guesthouse prices. Small conference (50). Garden. Parking. Children welcome. No pets. **Rooms 17** (all en-suite, 2 suites, 15 mini-suites, 5 no-smoking). B&B £40pps, ss £25. Residents' meals available, £24 + all-day menu. Licensed. 24-hr room service. Open all year. Amex, Diners, MasterCard, Visa.

Dublin 2   *Adams Trinity Hotel*

28 Dame Street Dublin
HOTEL   Tel: 01 670 7100 Fax: 01 670 7101 email: adamshtl@indigo.ie

Plumb in the centre of the city, within a stone's throw of Trinity College, this compact hotel offers a high standard of accommodation at a reasonable rate. Rooms, which include two suitable for disabled guests and 14 executive rooms (including four designated lady executive), are individually decorated and very well-appointed with well-planned en-suite bathrooms and double glazing to cut out noise from the busy street below. The foyer is actually at the back entrance, from Dame Court, which is much handier for dealing with luggage. The Mercantile Bar & Grill, next door, is part of the same premises; it can get very busy but developments in progress at the time of going to press include a Residents' Bar. Own parking. Children welcome (under 10s free in parents' room, cots available.) **Rooms 102** (4 suites, 40 no-smoking rooms, 2 for disabled). B&B from £75 pps, ss from £75; sc 12.5%. Wheelchair access. Lift. Closed 24-26 Dec. Amex, Diners, MasterCard, Visa.

Dublin 2   *Alexander Hotel*

Merrion Square Dublin

HOTEL   Tel: 01 607 3700   Fax: 01 661 5663   email: alexanderhotel@eircom.net

This hotel opened in 1997 and is very well situated at the lower end of Merrion Square. Although large and new it is remarkable for classic design that blends into the surrounding Georgian area quite inconspicuously. In contrast to its subdued public face, the interior is strikingly modern and colourful, both in public areas and bedrooms, which are all to executive standard, spacious and unusual. Conference/banqueting (400/350). Business centre. Secretarial services. Video conferencing. Gym. Parking.Wheelchair access. Children welcome (Under 2s free in parents' room; cots available). No pets. **Rooms 102** (all en-suite, 4 suite, 40 no-smoking, 2 for disabled). Lift. B&B from £75pps, ss from £75. Open all year. Amex, Diners, MasterCard, Visa.

Dublin 4   *Anglesea Townhouse*

63 Angelsea Road Ballsbridge Dublin 4

GUESTHOUSE   Tel: 01 668 3877   Fax: 01 668 3461

Helen Kirrane's Anglesea Town House brings all the best "country" guesthouse qualities to urban Dublin – a delightful building and pleasant location near Herbert Park, Ballsbridge; comfortable, attractive bedrooms; good housekeeping; a warm, welcoming drawing room with a real period flavour and wonderful breakfasts that prepare guests for the rigours of the most arduous of days. Thoroughly recommended for its creativity and perfectionism in re-defining what a guesthouse can be, Anglesea Townhouse was a very worthy winner of our 1999 Irish Breakfast Award. Garden. Parking. Children welcome (Under 3s free in parents' room; cots available). No pets. **Rooms 7** (all en-suite, 5 shower only, all no-smoking). B&B £45pps, ss £5. Closed Xmas and New Year. Amex, MasterCard, Visa.

Dublin 2 ❋ ✗   *Ar Vicoletto Osteria Romano*

5 Crow Street Temple Bar Dublin 2
Tel: 01 670 8662

Genuine little Italian restaurant, doing authentic, restorative food in a relaxing atmosphere and at very moderate prices. Very friendly helpful staff too - one of the pleasantest spots in Temple Bar. MasterCard, Visa.

Dublin 4 ❋   *Ariel House*

52 Lansdowne Road Ballsbridge Dublin

GUESTHOUSE   Tel: 01 668 5512   Fax: 01 668 5845

Conveniently located near Lansdowne Road DART station, this Victorian mansion - which has been in the same ownership since the 1950s - has been carefully restored over the years to create a luxurious guesthouse with period furniture, original paintings and good service. Morning coffee and afternoon tea are served in the Drawing Room and there's cosy Wine Bar. Own parking. Children over 8 welcome (Under 12s free in parents' room). No pets. **Rooms 40** (36 en-suite, 4 shower only, 4 mini-suite, 25 executive rooms, all no-smoking, 1 for disabled). B&B £48pps, ss £15.50. Lift. Closed Mid Dec-Mid Jan. MasterCard, Visa.

Dublin 6 ✗   *Ashtons*

Clonskeagh Dublin
Tel: 01 283 0045

PUB

This famous pub fronts onto a busy road and is built on a steep slope reaching down to the River Dodder. It has an interesting interior and an unexpectedly tranquil atmosphere at the back, where the river view is always full of interest. The range and quality of their lunchtime buffet – a roast, hot dishes including a wide selection of seafood, cold buffet and salads – that has earned this pub its enviable reputation. Meals£

Dublin 2 ❋   *Aya @ Brown Thomas*

Clarendon Street, Dublin

RESTAURANT   Tel: 01 677 1544   Fax: 01 677 1546   email: mail@aya.ie

Seafood Restaurant of the Year

Deep-red velvet, beech laminated tables and just wall-to-wall style. This is Dublin's first conveyor sushi bar, restaurant and food hall, offering takeaway sushi, fresh and frozen meals and a small selection of Japanese ingredients. Although not exclusively devoted to seafood, this dashing new contemporary Japanese restaurant is especially deserving of the Guide's Seafood Restaurant of the Year Award. The owners are the Hoashi family, who established Dublin's first Japanese restaurant, Ayumi-Ya, in Blackrock 16 years ago and, since then, have been delighting an increasingly knowledgeable clientele with their authentic traditional Japanese cuisine. Nobody knows more about fresh seafood than the Japanese and, as sushi has recently become popular in mainstream restaurants, Dubliners heard with delight that Yoichi Hoashi was planning to introduce the city to this totally new concept. The dining highlight is a full on-line menu offering a wide range of sushi, all authentically Japanese - although, of course, most of the fresh fish used is locally caught in Irish waters. Aya also offers takeaway sushi, fresh and frozen meals and a small selection of Japanese ingredients. The main menu covers all the bases and is impressively wide-ranging, serving everything from well-priced bento boxes at lunchtime to more exotic fare in the evening. The service is excellent and, to add to the fun, the staff wear very distinctive grey and red uniforms inspired by 'Dr. No', of James Bond fame. This innovative restaurant is run by true professionals and provides an experience not be forgotten. Wheelchair access. Children welcome before 8pm. **Seats 60.** No-smoking area. Air conditioning.Open daily. Breakfast 7.30-11. L 12-3, Mon-Sat, Sun brunch 11-4. D 5.30-11, Mon-Sat, Sun D to 10. All à la carte. House wine from £12. SC discretionary. Toilets wheelchair accessible. Closed 25-26 Dec, 1 Jan, Good Fri. Amex, Diners, MasterCard, Visa.

Dublin 2   *The Bad Ass Café*

9-11 Crown Alley Temple Bar Dublin
CAFE   Tel/Fax: 01 671 2596

Original and still the best – the Bad Ass Café has been charming youngsters (and a good few oldsters) with its particular brand of wackiness and good, lively food since 1986, when most people running Temple Bar restaurants were still at school. Kids love the food (the Bad Ass burger is still one of the favourites, and very good too), the warehouse atmosphere, the loopy menu and the cash shuttles (from an old shop) that whizz around the ceiling. Fourteen years after opening, young people still find it cool.Wheelchair access. Children welcome. **Seats 85.** Open daily. 11:30am-12 midnight. Set L £4.75. Tourist menu £11.95 all day. A la carte available. House wine £11.95. No-smoking area. Air conditioning. SC discretionary. Xmas & Good Fri. Amex, MasterCard, Visa.

Dublin 4   *Batts Bistro*

10 Baggot Lane Dublin
RESTAURANT   Tel: 01 660 0363 Fax: 01 298 5653 email: aguy@indigo.ie

In a laneway just across the road from the Hibernian Hotel, owner-chef Leonie Guy has built up a well-deserved reputation for good cooking, based on the best of ingredients. During the last year she has completely renovated the bistro, creating separate dining rooms for 6-8 and 46-50 guests. The upstairs area is especially bright and spacious and, with a balcony and outdoor service, just the place for sunny days. Her food has an indefinable character, best described as home cooking at its best. Children welcome. **Seats 78** (private rooms, 8 + 50) L 12-3 Mon-Fri. D 6-10 Mon-Sat. Closed Sat lunch, Sun all day. Set L £9.50. Set D £20, early bird menu £10.95 6-7:30 pm. A la carte available. House wine £11. Toilets wheelchair accessible. No-smoking area. Air conditioning. SC discretionary. Closed Xmas week & Bank Hols. Amex, Diners, MasterCard, Visa.

Dublin 2 ✳   *Belgo Dublin*

17-19 Sycamore Street Dublin
RESTAURANT   Tel: 01 672 7555 Fax: 01 672 7550

A recent Dublin off-shoot of the Belgo restaurants in London and elsewhere, this large, trendy restaurant in Temple Bar offers Belgian specialities, including a huge range of beers and other drinks you're unlikely to come across elsewhere in Ireland. The food goes a lot further than moules & chips -wild boar sausages, for example, and a lot of other seafood. They do a couple of trademark Belgo Bargains - a Fiver Lunch (12-3 Mon-Fri, to 4 at weekends) and Beat the Clock (Mon-Fri 5.30-7.30) - you pay the price of the time you order, eg order at 6.40, pay £6.40. It's just another early-bird really, but it's fun and suits the place. Otherwise, prices are quite steep for the informality of the food and service. Children welcome. **Seats 220** (private room, 90) No-smoking area. Air conditioning.Open daily. L 12-3. D 5-11. Set L £5. Set D £20, early evening menu £10 6-7 pm only. A la carte L&D available. House wine £10.95. SC 12.5%. Toilets wheelchair accessible. Closed 25 + 31 Dec. MasterCard, Visa.

Dublin 4   *Bella Cuba*

11 Ballsbridge Terrace Dublin

RESTAURANT   Tel/Fax: 01 660 5539

Authentic Cuban cuisine is presented at its very best in this small, intimate restaurant, which demonstrates so well the Spanish, Caribbean and South American influences on this unique country's cooking. Pork dishes are prepared particularly well, and the atmosphere, style of cooking and presentation indicate perhaps a greater degree of culinary formality than is normally associated with the region; the Cajun cooking of Louisiana across the Bay of Mexico, for example. Well worth a visit to experience something genuinely different. Parking by arrangement with nearby carpark. Children welcome before 7:30. **Seats 26** L 12:30-2:30 Tue-Fri. D 6-11 daily. Set L £10.50. A la carte available. House wine £10.50. SC discretionary (10% parties & 6+). Closed 25-26 Dec. Amex, MasterCard, Visa.

Dublin 4 🏨🏨   *Berkeley Court Hotel*

Lansdowne Road Ballsbridge Dublin

HOTEL   Tel: 01 660 1711   Fax: 01 661 7238   email: berkeleycourt@doylehotels.com

Set in its own grounds, and within easy distance of the city centre, this luxurious hotel is well-known as a haunt of the rich and famous when in Dublin. It is particularly spacious, with groups of seating areas arranged around an impressive chandeliered foyer, with bars, restaurants and private conference rooms leading off it. The hotel is famous for its high standards of service and accommodation, which includes two rooms especially suitable for disabled guests, six suites and 24 executive rooms; 20 of the bedrooms are designated non-smoking. Bedroom amenities include computer modem, mini-bars and luxurious extras such as robes and slippers. On-site facilities, including a hair salon and boutique, are augmented by an arrangement with the exclusive Riverview Club, for tennis, squash and swimming. Conference/banqueting (450/290) Business centre. Secretarial services. ISDN lines. Video conferencing. Safe. Leisure centre. Wheelchair access. Own parking. Children welcome (under 12s free in parents' room; cots available). **Rooms 188** (all en-suite, 6 suites, 24 executive rooms, 25 no-smoking, 2 for disabled). Lift. Room rate £195, max. 2 guests. SC15%. Open all year. Amex, Diners, MasterCard, Visa. **Berkeley Room:** A fine restaurant with very professional staff and some reliable specialities - seafood dishes are especially good and they are renowned for their roast beef. **Seats 60.** Air conditioning. Open Daily. L 12:30-2:15. D 6:30-9:15. Set L £22.50. Set D £29.50. A la carte available. Toilets wheelchair accessible. SC 15%.

Dublin 4✳   *Bewley's Hotel, Ballsbridge & O'Connell's Restaurant*

Merrion Road Ballsbridge Dublin
Tel: 01 668 1111   Fax: 668 1999

HOTEL + RESTAURANT   email: res@bewleyshotels.com

This new hotel has been cleverly built to incorporate a landmark period building next to the RDS (entrance by car is on Simmonscourt Road, via Merrion Road or Anglesea Road). Like its sister hotel at Newlands Cross (see entry), you get a lot of comfort and style here at a very reasonable cost. Small conferences (30). ISDN lines. Garden. Wheelchair access. Parking. Children welcome. No pets. **Rooms 210** (all en-suite, 84 suites, 108 no-smoking). Room rate £69, max 3 guests. Lift. Closed 6pm 24 Dec - 6pm 26 Dec. Amex, Diners, MasterCard, Visa.

O'Connells Restaurant ☆ (Tel: 647 3400) The restaurant has no connection with the cafe chain of the same name and is in the very safe hands of Tom O'Connell who was, until recently the general manager of the Berkeley Court Hotel. He is also the brother of Darina Allen (of Ballymaloe Cookery School fame) and it is clear that this restaurant has embraced many elements of the Ballymaloe philosophy: modern Irish cooking, quality ingredient driven - simple food, with natural flavours. The basement room is surprisingly large with dark wood panelled walls, floor to ceiling windows and crisp white table linen. But the food is the star here and it's allowed to speak for itself with all the ingredients being carefully sourced - the fish comes from Ballycotton every day, and is as fresh as it could be. For starters, a very light fish mousse with crab, tomato & ginger beurre blanc and leek & roast pepper tart with chive hollandaise - a creamy and moist filling encased in crisp buttery pastry - are typical examples of excellence. Fresh catch of the day might be perfectly judged spiced goujons of brill with aioli & chilli relish or the grilled hake with tomato & basil sauce served with roast potatoes, seasonal vegetables and a nicely dressed green salad. To finish choose between the weekly selection of Irish farmhouse cheese or a classic dessert like Crepes Suzette with vanilla ice cream. Superb food and good service make this a restaurant with a great future. **Seats 160.** No-smoking area. Air conditioning.L 12:30-2:15 Mon-Sat, Sun L 1-4. D 6-10:30 Mon-Sat, Sun D 7-9:30. Set Sun L £15. A la carte available. House wine £13.50. SC discretionary (10% on parties & 6+).Toilets wheelchair accessible. Closed 25-26 Dec. Amex, Diners, MasteCard, Visa.

Dublin 22   *Bewley's Hotel at Newlands Cross*

Newlands Cross Naas Road Dublin
HOTEL   Tel: 01 464 0140 Fax: 01 464 0900 email: res@bewleyshotels.com

The lobby gives a good first impression at this stylish budget hotel just off the N7. Bedrooms will confirm this feeling, especially at the price – a very reasonable room rate offers a large room with double, single and sofa-bed, a decent bathroom with bath and shower (except four rooms for disabled guests, which are shower only) and excellent amenities including a trouser press, iron and ironing board and fax/modem lines. Many more expensive hotels might take note of these standards. Good business facilities too (boardrooms for meetings from only £49 per day). The adjacent Bewley's Café provides very acceptable food and there is free parking for 200 cars. Small conference (20). Wheelchair access. Parking. Children welcome. (under 18s free in parents' room; cots available). No pets. **Rooms 260** (all en-suite, 5 shower only, 150 no-smoking, 6 for disabled). Room rate £49, max 3 adults. Lift. Closed 24-26 Dec. Amex, Diners, MasterCard, Visa.

Dublin 2 ❁   *Bewley's Principal Hotel*

19/20 Fleet Street Temple Bar Dublin
HOTEL   Tel: 670 8122 Fax: 6708103 email: bewleyshotel@eircom.net

This hotel is conveniently located in the heart of Temple Bar, within easy walking distance of all the city's main attractions, and is not connected to the other Bewleys hotels. It's fairly small, allowing an intimate atmosphere and a welcome emphasis on service.Parking by arrangement with nearby carpark. Children welcome (under 10s free in parents' room; cots available). No pets. **Rooms 70** (all en-suite, 40 shower only, 35 no-smoking). B&B £47pps, ss £17. Lift. Closed 24-26 Dec. Amex, Diners, MasterCard, Visa.

Dublin 2 ✗   *The Bistro*

4 & 5 Castle Market Dublin
RESTAURANT   Tel: 01 671 5430 Fax: 01 677 6016

Well located in the pedestrianised walkway between the Powerscourt Centre and George's Street Market, this relaxed, family-run restaurant has attractive warm-toned decor, a friendly atmosphere and good food cooked by co-owner Maire Block. Martin and Robert Block manage and look after front-of-house and it's a formula that brings people back. Expect tasty new-wave international cooking, with a few classics – Tarte Tatin, for example. Daily specials offer especially good value. L£ & D££ daily

Dublin 18   *Bistro One*

3 Brighton Road Foxrock Village Dublin
RESTAURANT   Tel: 01 289 7711 Fax: 01 289 9858

This interesting first floor restaurant is popular in the neighbourhood and can get very busy (which slows the service down) but there is a little bar on the way in, where guests are greeted and set up in comfort, and the attitude throughout is laid back but not without care. Tempting menus might include 6 or 8 choices per course, with starters such as seared marinated salmon on a chive potato cake or Bistro One's salad with crispy bacon and croutons. The pasta selection can be starter or main course as preferred – fettucine with smoked chicken and wild mushroom perhaps. Main courses include classics such as veal alla milanaise and updated club fare like lamb's liver with streaky bacon and red onion. There are generous side vegetables and a choice of farmhouse cheese; home made ice creams or classic puddings to finish. Children welcome. **Seats 45** D 7-11 Tue-Sat. Menu à la carte. House wine £13. SC 10%.No-smoking area. Closed Sun & Mon, and 24-26 Dec. MasterCard, Visa.

Dublin 8 ˣ   *Brazen Head*

20 Lower Bridge Street Dublin

PUB   Tel: 01 679 5186 Fax: 01 677 9549 email: info@brazenhead.com

Dublin's (possibly Ireland's) oldest pub was built on the site of a tavern dating back to the 12th century – and it's still going strong. Strong on genuine character, this friendly, well-run pub has lots of different levels and dark corners. Food is wholesome and middle-of-the-road at reasonable prices. Live music every night in the Music Lounge. L£ & D£ daily.

Dublin 2   *Brooks Hotel*

59-62 Drury Street Dublin
Tel: 01 670 4000 Fax: 01 670 4455
HOTEL/RESTAURANT   email: reservations@brookshotel.ie

A city sister for the Sinnott family's hotels in Galway – the Connemara Gateway and the Connemara Coast – Brooks is very well located, close to the Drury Street multi-storey car park and just a couple of minutes walk from Grafton Street. Described as a "designer/boutique" hotel, it's high on style in a comfortable country house-cum-club fashion and has been furnished and decorated with great attention to detail. All rooms have exceptionally good amenities, including well-designed bathrooms with power showers as well as full baths, air conditioning, ISDN lines, teletext TV and many other features. Small conference/private dining (70/30); back-up business services available on request. Children welcome (under 2s free in parents' room; cots available). No pets. **Rooms 75** (all en-suite, some no-smoking, some for disabled). B&B £92.50pps, ss £32.50. Lift. Open all year. Amex, Diners, MasterCard, Visa. **Francesca's:** Although it's on the lower ground floor, this restaurant is far from gloomy, with wooden floors, plaid-covered seating and beautiful book tapestries adorning the walls. Head chef Patrick McLarnon - who established his reputation at Ardtara Country House, County Derry - presents appealing à la carte and set menus, including signature dishes such as wild boar sausage with braised red cabbage & cornmeal pancake brought with him from the North. Cooking is very good, introducing both strong and subtle flavours to well thought out dishes. A classic such as seared foie gras comes with Asian spiced apple and quince chutney with toasted brioche, sitting happily alongside hot-smoked wild salmon on a bed of warm potato, olive, tomato and bean salad or smoked chilli dusted monkfish on a cream cheese risotto. [*Bar food is served from 10 am daily in the Butter Lane Bar.] **Seats 70** (private room, 30) No-smoking area. Air conditioning.D 7-10 daily. Set D £15.95 & £21.95, early bird menu £12.99 6-7:30. A la carte available. House wine £12.95. SC discretionary. Toilets wheelchair accessible. Closed Xmas.

Dublin 2 ✳   *Brownes Townhouse and Brasserie*

22 St Stephen's Green Dublin
TOWNHOUSE/RESTAURANT   Tel: 01 638 3939 Fax: 01 638 3900

A fine period house, on the stretch of St Stephen's Green between Grafton Street and the Shelbourne Hotel, has been stylishly converted to provide accommodation that has something of the atmosphere of a private home about it and includes a front first floor junior suite which can be converted for meetings and private parties, as the bed swings up into the wall. Small conference/banqueting (24/85). ISDN lines. Wheelchair access. Children welcome (Under 4s free in parents' room; cots available). No pets. **Rooms 12** (all en-suite, 2 suites, 10 executive rooms, 6 no-smoking, 1 for disabled). B&B £82.50. Lift. Open all year. Amex, MasterCard, Visa. **Brownes Brasserie:** Up a short flight of granite steps, the restaurant has a reception area furnished with antiques but curiously lacking in atmosphere (like a waiting room) and, on a recent visit, nobody present to receive. Once through into the restaurant, however, things improve - a long room, with big mirrors, it is well-appointed and has plenty of decorative interest to occupy guests between courses. The menu - a large, rather cheap'n'cheerful affair - seems at odds with the surroundings, but offers a wide choice of dishes suited to the brasserie style. It appears that kitchen and service have yet to settle into a consistent routine. Good breads accompanied a deep brown prawn bisque and 'sauteed baby squid' was actually deep-fried. Likewise a seafood pasta dish was not as described on the menu and (typical of over-long menus) a number of dishes were unavailable. However, a char-grilled striploin of beef, with burgundy jus, potatoes and ginger was an excellent dish and perfectly cooked. This is a pleasant, conveniently located, restaurant and, given some care, could be an asset to the area's dining options. **Seats 70** (private room, 26). No-smoking area. Air conditioning. L 12-3 daily, closed Sat. D 6:30-11 daily. Set Sun L £17.95. À la carte available. House wine £13.95. SC discretionary.Toilets wheelchair accessible.

Dublin 2 — *Bruno's*

RESTAURANT

30 East Essex Street Temple Bar Dublin
Tel: 01 670 6767 Fax: 01 677 5155

Open since 1997, Bruno's is poised to make quite an impact on the Dublin dining scene. The present restaurant is stylish, with clean lined lightwood and plain white walls providing a pleasingly simple background for owner-chef Bruno Berta's contemporary cooking. Children over 12 welcome until 8pm. *At the time of going to press Bruno is planning a second restaurant in Kildare Street (previously Mitchell's). It will be open for lunch 6 days and dinner daily; the emphasis will be on comfort. **Seats 60** L 12:30-4 daily. D 5-10:30 daily. Set L £11.95. Set D £13.95. House wine £13. Toilets wheelchair accessible. No-smoking area. Air conditioning. SC discretionary (10% on parties 4+). Closed Sat & Sun lunch, Sun dinner. Amex, Diners, MasterCard.

Dublin 2 — *Burlington Hotel*

HOTEL

Upper Leeson Street Dublin
Tel: 01 660 5222 Fax: 01 660 8496

Ireland's largest hotel, the Burlington has more experience of dealing with very large numbers efficiently and enjoyably than any other in the country. All bedrooms have been recently refurbished and banquets for huge numbers are not only catered for but can have a minimum choice of three main courses on all menus. The Burlington also offers good facilities for business guests; 250 of the 520 bedrooms are designated executive, with ISDN lines, fax machines and air conditioning. On-site entertainment is provided at Annabel's night club and their bar, Buck Mulligan's, has won numerous awards. Conference/banqueting (1500/1200). Business centre. Secretarial services. Video conferencing. Wheelchair access. Parking. Not suitable for children. No pets. **Rooms 504** (all en-suite, 4 suites, 2 mini-suite, 145 executive rooms. 60 no-smoking, 3 for disabled). Room rate £175 (max 2 guests). Lift. Amex, Diners, MasterCard, Visa.

Dublin 2 ❋ — *Buswells Hotel*

HOTEL/RESTAURANT

25 Molesworth Street Dublin
Tel: 01 6146500/6529 Fax: 01 676 2090

Home from home to Ireland's politicians, this old hotel close to the Dail (parliament) is held in great affection by Dubliners. What the original owners of this 18th century townhouse would make of it now is anyone's guess, but it's been an hotel since 1921 and, after major refurbishment in 1996/7, now offers a particularly good range of services for conferences, meetings and private dining. Accommodation is comfortable in the traditional style with good amenities and, as it's just a few yards from the city's prime shopping and cultural area, it also makes an ideal base for private visits. The lobby and bar (the latter is quite characterful) are very handy meeting places. Conference/banqueting (85/50). Secretarial services. Video conferencing. Wheelchair access. Children welcome (Under 4s free in parents' room; cots available). Pets by arrangement. **Rooms 69** (all en-suite, 2 suites, 8 no-smoking, 1 for disabled). Lift. B&B £80pps, no ss. Closed 24-26 Dec. Amex, Diners, MasterCard, Visa. **Trumans Restaurant:** This elegant well-appointed restaurant has a separate entrance from Kildare Street as well as access through the hotel and staff changes during 1999 seem to have brought a noticeable improvement in standards. Set 2/3 lunch menus and an à la carte option the evening all feature lively modern dishes and have the little touches that endear guests to an establishment, such as a tasty little amuse-gueule presented before the meal "compliments of the chef". Wisely, given the likely clientele, simpler dishes are always an option - notably roast beef or steaks presented various ways - and vegetarian dishes are particularly creative. Desserts are also interesting (eg, date-stuffed pear in a phyllo crown) or you can finish with Irish cheeses, which attract a small supplement on set menus. No children under 12 after 9pm. **Seats 45** (private room, 12). L 12:30-2 daily. D 6-10 daily. Set L £16. Set D £26. D also à la carte. House wine from £12. SC discretionary. Toilets wheelchair accessible. Closed Sun, Bank Hols.

Dublin 4 — *Butlers Town House*

GUESTHOUSE

44 Lansdowne Road Ballsbridge Dublin
Tel: 01 667 4022 Fax: 01 667 3960
email: info@butlershotel.com

On a corner site in the "embassy belt" and close to the Lansdowne Road stadium, this large townhouse/guesthouse has been extensively refurbished and luxuriously decorated in a Victorian country house style. Public rooms include a comfortable drawing room and an attractive conservatory-style dining room where breakfast is served. Rooms are individually decorated and furnished to a high standard, some with four-poster beds. Since a recent change of management there has been some refurbishment and more emphasis on service. Wheelchair access. Parking. Children welcome (Under 4s free in parents' room; cots available). No pets. **Rooms 19** (all en-suite, 1 shower only, 4 executive rooms, 1 for disabled). B&B £74pps, ss £25. Xmas week. Amex, Diners, MasterCard, Visa.

Dublin 2 *Café en Seine*

40 Dawson Street Dublin
CAFÉ + PUB   Tel: 01 677 4369 Fax: 01 671 7938

The first of the continental style café-bars to open in Dublin, in 1993, the large and lively Café en Seine is still just as fashionable now. It's a most attractive place, too, and offers sustenance as well as drinks at lunchtime (quiches, pasta dishes, smoked salmon salad and roast meats), snacks from late afternoon and coffee and pastries all day. Live jazz on Sundays, 1-4 pm, when a brunch menu is served. Wheelchair access. No children after 7pm. Bar open 10am-2am daily. Carvery lunch 12-3. Snack menu 4-10. Closed Xmas & Good Fri. Amex, MasterCard, Visa.

Dublin 2 *Camden Court Hotel*

Camden Street Dublin
HOTEL   Tel: 01 475 9666 Fax: 01 475 9677

A stylish new hotel (opened 1998) with two entrances – one next to the Bleeding Horse pub, the other via an arched passageway through a courtyard. The spacious reception area, with a partly tiled floor and lots of natural wood, leads to a smart restaurant, where an enticing breakfast buffet is laid out. But perhaps the hotel's finest asset is the atmospheric and rustic Piseogs pub, themed around Irish myths with differently decorated areas, the most intriguing being a fairytale forest! All of the bedrooms (some no-smoking) decorated with co-ordinating fabrics and practical fitted furniture and the usual facilities (plus satellite TV which can show your room bill, speeding check-out). Some 45 rooms have their own fax machines. Bathrooms are neat, but quite small.Staff are very friendly and the hotel seems to have 'lifted' this thriving locality, a mixture of big business and old shops. Conference (120). Leisure centre (indoor swimming pool, gym, sauna, steam). Wheelchair access. Parking. Children (Under 3s free in parents' room; cots available). No pets. **Rooms 246** (all en-suite, 3 mini-suite, 46 no-smoking, some for disabled). B&B £55pps, ss £15; no sc. Lift. Closed Xmas period. Amex, MasterCard, Visa.

Dublin 4 *Canaletto's*

71 Mespil Road Ballsbridge Dublin
RESTAURANT   Tel: 01 667 0699 Fax: 01 628 1120

Since 1992 Deborah Delaney's staff have been delighting diners at this unpretentious canalside restaurant with lively, wholesome cooking. In addition to good food – including a phone-in take-out service (no deliveries) – specialities of the house include Sunday brunch, from 10.30, which they also run on bank holiday Mondays. Most unusual however, is the in-house fortune teller every Monday night; advance bookings essential, fee £10! Children welcome. **Seats 65** No-smoking area. Air conditioning.Food service Mon-Sat: breakfast from 8am, self-service L 11-3, D 6-11. Sun from 10:30am. SC discretionary. Closed 3 days at Xmas and New Year. Amex, Diners, MasterCard, Visa.

Dublin 2 *La Cave Wine Bar & Restaurant*

28 South Anne Street Dublin
RESTAURANT   Tel: 01 679 4409 Fax: 01 670 5255 email: lacave@iol.ie

Margaret and Akim Beskri have run this well-known wine bar just off Grafton Street since 1989. With its classic French cooking and a wide range of wines by the glass (22), it makes a handy place to take a break from shopping. A first floor function room was recently opened, with seating for up to 32 - ideal for parties and small functions. Own parking. No children after 7pm. **Seats 48** (private room, 30) Air conditioning. L 12:30-4:30 daily, closed Sun. D 4:30-11 daily, Sun 6-11. L12-2 Sun only. Set menus £12.50-£18.50, early bird menu £6.95 4:30-7:30 pm only. A la carte available. House wine £10. SC discretionary. Closed 25-26 Dec, Good Fri, Bank Holiday lunches. Amex, Diners, MasterCard, Visa.

Dublin 4   *Cedar Lodge*

98 Merrion Road Ballsbridge Dublin
GUESTHOUSE   Tel: 01 668 4410   Fax: 01 668 4533

Conveniently located near the RDS show grounds and conference centre, this recently refurbished guesthouse has spacious rooms, with a full range of amenities. Public rooms are comfortably furnished and there is one room suitable for disabled guests. Parking. No children under 2 (Under 3s free in parents' room; cots available). No pets. **Rooms 16** (4 shower only, all no-smoking, 1 for disabled). B&B £60pps. Closed 24-27 Dec. Amex, MasterCard, Visa.

Dublin 2   *Central Hotel*

1-5 Exchequer Street Dublin
HOTEL   Tel: 01 679 7302   Fax: 01 679 7303   email: reservations@centralhotel.ie

Very conveniently located, as its name implies, this hotel is over a hundred years old and currently in the midst of a major refurbishment programme. The reception and central staircase areas have been completed and there is a very congenial library bar which serves light snacks. A very handy place to stay and not unreasonably priced; it's worth asking about special offers, including weekends. Conference/banqueting (150/100). Parking by arrangement with nearby carpark. Children welcome (Under 10s free in parents' room; cots available). No pets. **Rooms 70** (all en-suite, 20 shower only, 3 mini-suites). B&B £75pps, ss £20. Lift. Closed 24-27 Dec. Amex, Diners, MasterCard, Visa.

Dublin 1 ☆   *Chapter One*

18/19 Parnell Square Dublin
RESTAURANT   Tel: 01 873 2266/2281   Fax: 01 873 2330

Since 1993 chef-proprietor Ross Lewis and his partner, restaurant manager Martin Corbett, have been operating this successful restaurant in the basement beneath the Dublin Writers' Museum (where they also run a coffee shop, 10-5 pm daily). The restaurant has facilities for small conferences and secure parking – and they are most obliging about fitting in with the times of the nearby Gate Theatre: a most relaxing outing is to start with the early menu here, go along to the theatre after the main course and return later for dessert and coffee. Ross has built up a well-deserved following for confident, creative cooking which is classic French (chicken veloute with chives & rocket) overlaid with contemporary influences (grilled swordfish with beetroot risotto, fennel puree & chive vinaigrette); menus are always based on first class seasonal ingredients and have a pleasing leaning towards New Irish Cuisine (crepinette of pork with potato confit, glazed apples, cabbage & sage.) Lovely desserts - nougatglace with mixed berries, perhaos - or an unusual irish and continental cheese menu to finish. Interesting, informative wine list and excellent service complete a very fine package. Parking by arrangement with nearby carpark. Children welcome. **Seats 100** (private room, 20). Air conditioning. L 12:30-2:30 Tue-Sat. D 6-11 Tue-Sat. Set L £15.50. Early bird menu £15.50, 6-7:15. D à la carte. House wine £13.50. SC 10%. Toilets wheelchair accessible. Closed 25 Dec- 3/4 Jan. Amex, Diners, MasterCard, Visa.

Dublin 6 ✽   *Charleville Hotel*

Lr Rathmines Road Dublin 6
HOTEL/RESTAURANT   Tel: 4066100   Fax: 4066200

Well-equipped new hotel, mostly with suites (including sitting room kitchenette). Fax machines, CD players, ISDN lines, modem sockets, cable TV, hairdryer, trouser press with ironing board and tea/coffee-making facilities all included as standard. Own parking. Children welcome (under 4s free in parents' room; cots available). No pets. **Rooms 53** (Suites 43, executive rooms 10, no-smoking rooms 20). B&B £50 pps, ss £20. Lift. Annual closures TBC. Amex, Diners, MasterCard, Visa. **Carmines Restaurant:** Although the choice is much wider, pizzas and pastas are the backbone here, perhaps reflecting demands of the student population in the neighbourhood. However, the restaurant does have many plus points - interesting decor and food that, while not exactly inspired, is above average in the middle range - and, if there is disappointment, it may arise if comparisons are made with proprietor Alan O'Reilly's previous creation, Morels of Glasthule, which is outstanding. Prices are pitched pretty high for what is offered (perhaps because of the connection), but there is little competition in the neighbourhood.

Dublin 7 ❋   *Chief O'Neill's Hotel*

Smithfield Village Dublin

HOTEL   Tel: 01 817 3838   Fax: 01 817 3839   email: reservations@chiefoneills.com

This unusual new hotel is central to a new complex near the Old Jameson Distillery - and part of a major upgrading of the areas along Dublin's north quays. Accommodation has been designed in a striking modern style which guests will either love or loathe - the bathroom arrangements, for example, are sculptural rather than practical and have attracted some interesting comments. Lines are simple, colours strong and there's a distinctly youthful air about the place. Chief O'Neills' Cafe Bar features live traditional music and a combination of traditional and contemporary Irish food. Banqueting (110). Business centre. Leisure centre. Wheelchair access. Parking. Children welcome (Under 2s free in parents' room; cots available). No pets. **Rooms 73** (all en-suite, 63 shower only, 3 suites, 70 executive rooms, 19 no-smoking, 4 for disabled). Room rate £125. Lift. Amex, Diners, MasterCard, Visa.

Dublin 2   *The Chili Club*

1 Anne's Lane South Annes Street Dublin

RESTAURANT   Tel: 01 677 3721   Fax: 01 493 8284/677 3721

This cosy restaurant, in a laneway just off Grafton Street, was Dublin's first authentic Thai restaurant and is still as popular as ever a decade later. It is currently owned and managed by Patricia Kenna, who supervises a friendly and efficient staff. The head chef, Supot Boonchouy, prepares a fine range of genuine Thai dishes which are not "tamed" too much to suit Irish tastes. Children welcome. **Seats 42** (private room, 18) L 12:30-2:30 daily, closed Sun L. D 6-11:30 daily, Sun to 11. Set L £9.95. Early bird menu £13.50 6-7 pm. A la carte available. SC discretionary (10% on parties & 6+). Closed 25-27 Dec & 1 Jan. Amex, Diners, MasterCard, Visa.

Dublin 3   *Clontarf Castle Hotel*

Castle Avenue Clontarf Dublin

HOTEL   Tel: 01 833 2321   Fax: 01 833 2542   email: info@clontarfcastle.ie

This historic 17th century castle is convenient to both the airport and city centre. It has been family-owned and operated for 25 years (by the Houlihan family), who have recently completed a major refurbishment and extension programme. This has included banqueting, conference and business facilities (business centre and secretarial services, same day laundry and dry cleaning and exercise room for guests) as well as major changes to public areas and the addition of 100 rooms. Bedrooms, which include two executive suites and two junior suites, are furnished to a high standard and well-equipped for business guests with ISDN lines, voicemail and US electrical sockets in addition to the usual amenities; all south-facing rooms have air conditioning and bathrooms are well-designed and finished. The new building has been imaginatively incorporated into the old castle structure, retaining the historic atmosphere – some rooms, such as the restaurant and the original bar, have been left untouched and bedrooms have old-world details to remind guests of their castle surroundings. The "new" castle is very welcome in an area where extra facilities and accommodation were badly needed. Conference/banqueting (600/450). Business centre. Secretarial services. Leisure centre. Wheelchair access. Parking. Children welcome (Under 12s free in parents' room; cots available). No pets. **Rooms 111** (all en-suite, 3 suites, 1 mini-suite, 6 executive rooms, 42 no-smoking, 4 for disabled). B&B £55pps, ss £45. Lift. Closed 24-25 Dec. Amex, Diners, MasterCard, Visa.

Dublin 2 🏨   *The Clarence Hotel*

6-8 Wellington Quay Dublin
Tel: 01 670 9000   Fax: 01 670 7800

HOTEL/RESTAURANT   email: clarence@indigo.ie

The Clarence Hotel dates back to 1852 and – largely because of its convenience to Heuston Station – has long had a special place in the hearts of Irish people, especially the clergy and the many who regarded it as a home from home when "up from the country" for business or shopping in Dublin. Since the early '90s, however, it has achieved a different kind of fame through its owners, Bono and The Edge of U2 and Harry Crosbie, who have completely refurbished the hotel, creating the coolest of jewels in the crown of Temple Bar. No expense has been spared to get the details right, reflecting the hotel's original arts and crafts style whenever possible and complementing it with specially commissioned furniture and artefacts in contemporary style. Luxurious accommodation includes The Penthouse, which has wonderful river views (and an outdoor hot tub as well as a terrace from which to enjoy them to the full). All of the individually designed, double glazed bedrooms have king size beds, white-tiled bathrooms reminiscent of an earlier era and excellent amenities including mini-bar, private safe, PC/fax connections, remote control satellite television and video and temperature control panels. Public areas include the oak panelled, clublike Octagon Bar, which is a popular Temple Bar meeting place, and The Study, which has an open fire and makes a quieter spot for reading and writing. Conference/banqueting (50/60). Secretarial services. Wheelchair access. Children welcome (Under 12s free in parents' room; cots available). No pets. **Rooms 49** (all en-suite, 3 for disabled). Room rate £195. Lift. Open all year. Amex, Diners, MasterCard, Visa.

The Tea Room ☆ **:** Approached from its own entrance on Essex Street this high-ceilinged room is furnished in the light oak which is a feature throughout the hotel. Pristine white linen, designer cutlery and glasses, high windows softened only by the filtered damson tones of pavement awnings, all combine to create an impressive dining room. Under the direction of restaurant manager Kevin Watson, discreet staff move quietly, quickly offering aperitifs, menus and excellent breads which come with a dip. Head chef Michael Martin presents fashionably international seasonal menus which offer plenty of choice, including vegetarian options, but which are not overlong or overpriced. Seasonal à la carte dinner menus offer around nine starters – carpaccio of wild salmon with a salad of warm potatoes and fried quail egg, perhaps, or salad of aubergine crisps, mesclun leaves, roast garlic and red onion oil. The style is modern, bright and sassy, with strong but not overworked presentation. Desserts range from updated nursery classics like vanilla and coconut cream pot with rum raisin ice cream to an artistic assiette gourmandise, or there is farmhouse cheese, a nicely presented selection with tossed salad, grapes and toasted "brioche" and a choice of coffees or tea. Lunch menus offer a more restricted but well-balanced choice and are good value. **Seats 90.** No-smoking area. Air conditioning. L 12:30-2 daily. D 6:30-10 daily. Set L £17. Set D from £20. Gourmet menu £36. A la carte available. House wine from £14.50. SC discretionary.Toilets wheelchair accessible. Closed Sat & Sun lunch. Amex, Diners, MasterCard, Visa.

Dublin 2 ˣ   *Clarion Stephen's Hall Hotel*

The Earlsfort Centre Lower Leeson Street Dublin
Tel: 01 638 1111/661 0585 Fax: 01 638 1122
HOTEL/RESTAURANT   email: stephens@premgroup.com

Conveniently located just off St Stephen's Green, Dublin's only "all-suite" hotel has recently been refurbished and upgraded. Most suites now have wooden floors, all have ISDN lines, voice mail, modem access, fax machines and CD players – and computers are to be introduced to all rooms shortly. **Rooms 57** (all suites, 10 no-smoking). Wheelchair access.Lift. B&B £85 pps, ss £7.50.Annual closures TBC. Amex, Diners, MasterCard, Visa. **Restaurant:** Morels Bistro is in a semi-basement adjacent to the hotel and accessible directly from it or from offices at the back. Sister restaurant to the well-known southside restaurant Morels of Sandycove (proprietor Alan O'Reilly), the head chef is Adrian Spelman. Sunny decor and a bright and colourful style of cooking both echo the parent restaurant's Mediterranean theme. L£ Mon-Fri, D££+ daily.

Dublin 2   *The Commons Restaurant*

Newman House 85-86 St Stephen's Green Dublin
RESTAURANT   Tel: 01 478 0530/475 2597 Fax: 01 478 0551

Sited in the basement of Newman House, considered one of Dublin's finest examples of Georgian splendour, the restaurant (formerly the college dining room of University College Dublin) still evokes literary memories, with several works of modern art dedicated to James Joyce, a scholar at the turn of the last century. Other luminaries associated with the Palladian building are Cardinal John Henry Newman, former rector, and Gerald Manley Hopkins, professor. The spacious restaurant has French doors opening on to a secluded south-facing terrace (perfect for pre-meal drinks on a warm summer's day), elegantly presented tables and an array of unfailingly polite and professional staff. Little canapés on arrival, an amuse-bouche compliments of the chef and several freshly-baked breads demonstrate admirable attention to detail. Menus change weekly, but head chef Sebastien Masi has a liking for slightly unusual ingredients - specialities to look out for include loin of rabbit with Dublin Bay prawns & savoy cabbage and roast quail and foie gras, with baby spinach, rocket & tomato salsa. An imaginative main course that makes the most of a prime Irish ingredient is cannon of lamb baked in thyme & black pepper pastry, served with a potato torte & garlic jus. Service, under the supervision of restaurant manager Michael Andrews, is unfailingly excellent. **Seats 60** (private room, 60). No-smoking area. L 12-2:15 daily. D 7-10:15 daily. Set L £35. Gourmet menu £55. SC discretionary. Closed Sat & Sun lunch, and Bank Hols, 25 Dec-2 Jan & Good Fri. Amex, Diners, MasterCard, Visa.

Dublin 2 🏨   *Conrad International*

Earlsfort Terrace Dublin

HOTEL   Tel: 01 676 5555   Fax: 01 676 5424   email: sales@conrad-international.ie

Just a stroll away from St Stephen's Green and right opposite the National Concert Hall, the hotel celebrated its tenth anniversary in 1999. Continual refurbishment is a central characteristic of this fine hotel and facilities are constantly upgraded; air-conditioned bedrooms now have individual fax machines as well as three telephones, confirming the hotel's attraction to business/corporate guests, who also appreciate the fully-equipped and staffed business centre, complemented by an exceptional conference room (370 theatre-style), executive boardroom (12) and banqueting facilities (260). Many of the generously-sized bedrooms enjoy views of the piazza below and across the city, and offer plenty of workspace, at least one double bed, mini-bar, remote-control satellite TV with free in-house movie channel, clock/radio and safe. The well-equipped bathrooms have bathrobes and environmentally-friendly toiletries. A nightly turn-down service (hand-made Irish chocolates and bottles of mineral water are left beside the pillow) is provided, an example of the outstanding and professional service by committed staff, under the direction of long-serving general manager Michael Governey. Public areas include a raised lounge, two restaurants, the Alexandra and Plurabelle Brasserie (breakfast, lunch and dinner served here), and Alfie Byrne's Pub (serving splendid pub lunches) that opens on to an external terrace.Conference/banqueting (300/250). Business centre. Secretarial services. ISDN lines. Video conferencing. Air conditioning. Hairdresser. Fitness centre. Wheelchair access. Parking. Children welcome (Under 12s free in parents' room; cots available). No pets. **Rooms 191** (all en-suite, 9 suites, 60 no-smoking, 1 for disabled). B&B £133.50pps, ss £104.50, SC 15%. Lift.Open all year. Amex, Diners, MasterCard, Visa.

Dublin 2   *Cooke's Café*

14 South William Street Dublin

RESTAURANT   Tel: 01 679 0536   Fax: 01 679 0546   email: cookes1@iol.ie

John Cooke has always been ahead of fashions in the Dublin restaurant scene and his stylish café, Cooke's, was among the first of the current wave of trendy café-bistro style places doing Mediterranean and Cal-Ital food. The formula is still working well at Cooke's, where you can be sure of stylish, well cooked food based on the best of ingredients, either in the restaurant or on a heated pavement area with an awning, which is perfect for people-watching. The Rhino Room, a first floor restaurant over the café, has its own entrance on South William Street. The food is similar – pastas, salads, char-grilled meats and vegetables, all very competently prepared – but it is quieter and suits people who prefer a slightly more formal atmosphere and well-spaced tables. Nearby carpark. No children after 6pm. **Seats 60** (private room, 60).No-smoking area. Air conditioning. SC discretionary. L 12:30-3:30 daily. D 6-11 daily. Set L £16.50. Set D £16.50/18.50. A la carte available. House wine £14.50.Closed Bank Hols. Amex, Diners, MasterCard, Visa.

Dublin 4   *Coopers Restaurant*

Sweepstake Centre Ballsbridge Dublin

RESTAURANT   Tel: 01 660 1525   Fax: 01 660 1537

The flagship of the Coopers chain of restaurants, Coopers Café Ballsbridge is in dashing premises opposite the RDS. Well-situated for the Ballsbridge hotels and exhibition crowds, the Café serves global cuisine – salsa, szechuan, rocket and chilli are the kinds of words that leap off the menu – but it is reassuring to know that, on request, they will also cook a plain steak perfectly and serve it with a simple green salad.Children welcome. **Seats 185.** No-smoking area. Air conditioning. L 12:30-3 daily. D 5-11:30 daily (sun to 10). Set L £10.95. Set Sun L £13.95. L&D à la carte available. House wine £11.50. SC discretionary (10% on parties of 8+).Toilets wheelchair accessible.Closed 25-26 Dec & Good Fri. Amex, Diners, MasterCard, Visa.

*Other Coopers Restaurants are situated at: Lower Leeson Street (01-6768615), Greystones (01-2873914) and Kilternan (01-2959349)

Dublin 4 ★   *Le Coq Hardi*

35 Pembroke Road Ballsbridge Dublin
RESTAURANT   Tel: 01 668 9070 Fax: 01 668 9887
Restaurant of the Year Award

Since opening in 1977, John and Catherine Howard's elegant Ballsbridge restaurant has been, in its quiet way, a leading light in Ireland's food revolution. Famous for his refusal to be a slave to food fashions, John's steadfast sureness of purpose has served the restaurant well in guiding an excellent kitchen team - working, since 1982, under head chef James O'Sullivan - through a culinary minefield of fast-changing tastes. John's background of classical French cooking has blended happily with traditional Irish themes to produce dishes that show New Irish Cuisine at its best. Alongside old favourites which have earned a permanent place on the menu, such as the Scottish-inspired "Coq Hardi Smokies" (a hot starter of smoked haddock, baked with tomato, cream and cheese), upbeat modern Irish classics appear in dishes like Clonakilty black pudding served with a traditional potato cake and apple sauce, baked white fish served with bacon and cabbage with a whiskey cream sauce and a wonderful roast loin of kassler with green cabbage, fresh herb mash and Calvados jus (selected for the Guide's Irish Pork Award last year). But a restaurant is about more than its food. Service, under Catherine Howard's discreet direction, is superb and indicates the underlying strengths of Le Coq Hardi: training and teamwork. And, then of course, there's the small matter of how best to accompany fine food - and the answer lies in an outstanding wine list which is particularly strong in John's favourite areas: Bordeaux, Burgundy, Loire, and Champagne. All these factors add up to an exceptional establishment - and we are proud to award Le Coa Hardi with the title Restaurant of the Year. Own parking. Children welcome. **Seats 50** (private room, 35). No-smoking area. Air conditioning. L 12:30-2:30 daily. D 7-10:30 daily. Set L £25. L&D à la carte available. House wine £18. SC 12.5%. Closed Sundays, and 2 weeks in August, Xmas and Bank Hols. Amex, Diners, MasterCard, Visa.

Dublin 2   *Da Pino*

38-40 Parliament Street Dublin
RESTAURANT   Tel: 01 671 9308 Fax: 01 677 3409 email: m.jimenez@tinet.ie

Just across the road from Dublin Castle, this busy youthful Italian/Spanish restaurant is always full – and no wonder, as they serve cheerful, informal, well cooked food that does not make too many concessions to trendiness and is sold at very reasonable prices. The pizzas are especially good and are prepared in full view of customers. Children welcome. **Seats 80.** Open all day 12-11:30 daily. No-smoking area. Closed Xmas & Good Fri. Amex, Diners, MasterCard, Visa.

Dublin 2   *The Davenport Hotel*

Merrion Square Dublin
Tel: 01 607 3500 Fax: 01 661 5663
HOTEL   email: davenportres@ocallaghanhotels.ie

On Merrion Square, close to the National Gallery, this striking hotel is fronted by the impressive 1863 facade of Merrion Hall, which was restored as part of the hotel building project in the early '90s. Inside, the hotel has been imaginatively designed to be both interesting and comfortable, with a pleasing mixture of old and new influences and bold, confident colours used in both public areas and bedrooms. Conference/banqueting (300/400). Business centre. Secretarial services. ISDN lines. Video conferencing. Leisure centre. Wheelchair access. Parking. Children welcome (Under 2s free in parents' room; cots available). No pets. **Rooms 115** (all en-suite, 2 suites, 10 mini-suite, 45 no-smoking, 1 for disabled). B&B from £75pps, ss from £75. Lift. Open all year. Amex, Diners, MasterCard, Visa.

Dublin 2   *Davy Byrnes*

21 Duke Street Dublin
PUB   Tel: 01 677 5217 Fax: 01 671 7619

Just off Grafton Street, Davy Byrnes is one of Dublin's most famous pubs – having been mentioned in Joyce's Ulysses means it is very much on the tourist circuit. Despite all this fame it remains a genuine, well-run place and equally popular with Dubliners, who find it a handy meeting place and also enjoy the bar food. This is a particular point of pride and always includes a list of daily specials as well as the regular menu. Children over 7 welcome. Bar food served daily from 12-9. Closed 24-26 Dec & Good Fri. MasterCard, Visa.

Dublin 2 ✳   *Diep Le Shaker*

RESTAURANT

55 Pembroke Lane off Pembroke Street Dublin 2
Tel: 01 661 1829 Fax: 01 662 1004

Matthew Farrell opened this dashing if oddly-named two-storey restaurant to some acclaim in 1999. It's elegantly appointed, with comfortable high-back chairs, good linen and fine glasses, and bright - with sunny yellow walls and a long skylight along one side of the upper floor giving ample daylight at lunchtime and on summer evenings. Menus are considerately organised with Chinese dishes in blue and Thai ones in red and, in the Guide's experience, both cooking and service are excellent. An unusual dish singled out for special praise is steamed scallop with ginger and garlic: this is cooked in the shell, retaining its natural juices; to this is added finely chopped and blanched garlic and ginger, a sprinkling of very hot sesame oil and a little soy sauce. Sounds simple, but there's the skill. Diep Le Shaker is not inexpensive - expect to pay £80-£90 for dinner for two - but an unusual experience, enhanced by well-trained staff who know the menu and the principles of hospitable service. No children after 8 pm. **Seats 100** (private room, 12). No smoking area, air conditioning. L 12.30-2.30, D 6.30-11.Set L £15. House wine £14.50. SC 10%. Jazz 9 pm. Closed Sun. Amex, Diners, MasterCard, Visa.

Dublin 2   *Dish*

RESTAURANT

2 Crow Street Dublin
Tel: 01 671 1248 Fax: 01 671 1249 email: dish@indigo.ie

Trevor Browne and Gerard Foote have made quite an impact with their stylishly spartan restaurant in the Temple Bar area. Again we find the global cuisine which seems to have engulfed kitchens everywhere recently, but it is in Gerard Foote's capable hands here so you can be sure of substance as well as style. The best ingredients - organic beef and lamb, free-range chicken and a wide variety of fresh fish daily - provide the wholesome basis for menus that change regularly to make the most of seasonal produce. Smoked salmon tartare with ginger & horseradish; chicken and shrimp stir-fry; organic fillet steak; monkfish with lemon caper butter sauce are all typical of the repertoire. Children welcome. **Seats 50.** No-smoking area. Air conditioning. L 12-5 daily. D 5-11:30 daily. Menu à la carte. House wine £12. SC 10% on parties of 6+. Closed 25-26 Dec & Good Fri. Amex, Diners, MasterCard, Visa.

Dublin 2   *Dobbins Wine Bistro*

RESTAURANT

15 Stephens Lane Dublin
Tel: 01 676 4670/9, 01 661 3321 Fax: 01 661 3331

Now something of an institution, this restaurant has operated in a "Nissen hut" near Merrion Square since 1978 under the close supervision of owner John O'Byrne and manager Patrick Walsh. It has a conservatory area at the far end, which is very popular in summer, and a dark intimate atmosphere in the main restaurant. Gary Flynn, head chef since 1985, has attracted a loyal following for consistently good cooking in a style which has not abandoned tradition but incorporates new ideas too. Good details include generous, plain wine glasses and lovely home-baked brown bread. Valet parking. Children welcome. **Seats 120** (private room, 40). No-smoking area. Air conditioning. L 12:30-3 daily. D 7:30-11 daily. Set L £16.50. Gourmet menu £35. L&D à la carte available. House wine from £13. SC discretionary. Closed Sundays and Bank Hols. Amex, Diners, MasterCard, Visa.

Dublin 2   *The Dome*

St. Stephen's Green Shopping Centre Dublin
Tel: 01 478 1287

At the top of the shoppping centre is this bright and airy daytime restaurant with some excellent views of the top of Grafton Street. There are usually three to four hot meals to choose from, although the quality seems be hit and miss - salmon en croute (heated in the microwave) is destined to be disappointing, for example, although the accompanying vegetables should be better.The large salad bar is a much wiser option with a wide ranging and colourful selection. The mini quiches can be very good (if also a little compromised by a heating in the microwave - perhaps it's best to opt for one at room temperature). There is also a wide choice of desserts and confectionary which are oustanding and would be very hard to beat. Service polite and prompt, with table service for teas and coffees - overall the Dome is worth remembering as a lunch option. Children welcome. **Seats 150** No-smoking area. Air conditioning. Open Mon-Sat. 9:30-5:30. Menu à la carte. Wines from £2.95. SC discretionary. Toilets wheelchair accessible. Closed Sun, Bank Hols, 4 days at Xmas.

Dublin 22 ✗   *Doyle Green Isle Hotel*

Naas Road Dublin
HOTEL   Tel: 01 459 3406 Fax: 01 459 2178

Situated on the Naas Road, close to the major industrial estates, this is a popular hotel for conferences and business. Over half of the bedrooms are executive rooms and there are conference facilities for up to 250 delegates, four meeting rooms for a maximum of 50 each and some business back-up service if required. Acc££ Open all year. Amex, Diners, MasterCard, Visa.

Dublin 4 ✗   *Doyle Montrose Hotel*

Stillorgan Road Dublin
HOTEL   Tel: 01 269 3311 Fax: 01 269 1164

This south-city hotel near the University College campus has undergone extensive refurbishment. Removing balconies and rebuilding the whole front has updated the exterior, while interior improvements include the addition of more suites and rooms for the disabled. **Rooms 180.** Acc£££ Open all year. MasterCard, Amex, Diners, Visa.

Dublin 9 ✗   *Doyle Skylon Hotel*

Upper Drumcondra Road Dublin
HOTEL   Tel: 01 837 9121 Fax: 01 837 2778

Three miles north of the city centre, this 1960s hotel is conveniently situated for the airport, which is just four miles further out. Acc£££ Open all year.

Dublin 6 ✗   *Dunville Place*

25 Dunville Place Ranelagh Dublin
RESTAURANT   Tel: 01 496 8181 Fax: 01 491 0604

Michael Duignan and Sophie Ridley are operating a very stylish neighbourhood restaurant at Dunville Place, particularly in summer when the little courtyard at the back can also be used for drinks, or eating out in fine weather. The restaurant is informally well-appointed and Michael Duignan presents imaginative, contemporary seasonal menus which are carried through with style and include strong vegetarian choices. Asian influences come through quite strongly in the spicing, but Europe is represented too – in a vegetarian Greek plate with stuffed vine leaves, hummus, tabbouleh and various other little dishes, all served with warm pitta bread. Good desserts might include a classic crème brûlée. L£ daily, D££ Tues-Sat. Closed Bank Hols.

Dublin 2 ☆   *L'Ecrivain*

109a Lower Baggot Street Dublin
RESTAURANT   Tel: 01 661 1919 Fax: 01 661 0617

Owner-chef Derry Clarke, who is currently Ireland's Commissioner General for Euro-Toques, and his wife Sallyanne were in the process of a major extension and renovation programme at their highly regarded city centre restaurant. The new restaurant, which should open before Christmas 1999, will be more spacious but Derry's cooking style - classic French with contemporary flair and a strong leaning towards New Irish Cuisine - should not change. **Seats 90+** (private room, 30) No-smoking area. Air conditioning. L 12:30-2 daily. D 7-11 daily. Toilets wheelchair accessible. SC discretionary. Closed Sundays & Bank Hols. Amex, Diners, MasterCard, Visa

Dublin 2   *Eden*

Meeting House Square Temple Bar Dublin
RESTAURANT   Tel: 01 670 5373/2 Fax: 01 670 3330

In the heart of Temple Bar on Sycamore Street, next to the Irish Film Theatre and opposite Diceman's Corner (The Diceman, Thom McGinty, was a popular and well-known

Dublin street performer, particularly famous for his costumes), lies this spacious and modern restaurant, with its own outdoor terrace on the square. It is on two floors, with lots of greenery and hanging baskets and an open kitchen that ground floor customers can observe. Head chef Eleanor Walshe has established a house style which suits the restaurant and has become very popular, The lunch menu changes weekly, perhaps salmon tartare with crème fraîche and paprika, spicy lamb meat balls with lemon rice and tomato sauce, sticky toffee pudding with caramel sauce, while the dinner menu is seasonal, with many of the dishes employing organic produce. Classic desserts could include a caramelised lemon tart served with a scoop of blackcurrant sorbet. A well-balanced and not-too-expensive wine list offers several wines by the glass. Friendly staff are efficient and observant Children welcome. **Seats 110** (private room, 12).No-smoking area. Air conditioning. L 12:30-3 daily. D 6-10:30 daily. Set L £13. À la carte available. SC discretionary. Closed Bank Hols, 24-30 Dec. Amex, Diners, MasterCard, Visa.

Dublin 9   *Egan's Guesthouse*

7-9 Iona Park Glasnevin Dublin
Tel: 01 830 3611 Fax: 01 830 3312
GUESTHOUSE   email: eganshouse@eircom.net

Within walking distance of the Botanic Gardens, this long-established, family-run guesthouse offers comfortable, well-maintained en-suite accommodation and warm hospitality at a reasonable price. Wheelchair access. Parking. Children (Under 3s free in parents' room; cots available). Pets by arrangement. **Rooms 23** (all en-suite). B&B £25pps. Closed 24-27 Dec. MasterCard, Visa.

Dublin 4 ✼   *Eighty Eight*

88 Pembroke Road Ballsbridge Dublin
GUESTHOUSE   Tel: 01 660 0277 Fax: 01 660 0291

Conveniently located close to the RDS and Lansdowne Road, this luxurious guesthouse has all the amenities usually expected of an hotel. Small conference (10). Video conferencing. Leisure centre (indoor swimming pool). Tennis. golf. Wheelchair access. Parking. Children welcome (Under 8s free in parents' room; cots available). No pets. **Rooms 40** (all en-suite, 28 no-smoking, 2 for disabled). B&B £49.50pps, ss £30. Lift. Closed 22 Dec-4 Jan. Diners, MasterCard, Visa.

Dublin 2   *Elephant & Castle*

18 Temple Bar Dublin
RESTAURANT   Tel: 01 679 3121 Fax: 01 679 1399

John Hayes and Elizabeth Mee do a consistently good job at this buzzy Temple Bar restaurant – it was one of the first new-wave restaurants in the area and is still one of the best. Ingredients are carefully sourced and served in a range of big, generous and wholesome salads (their special Caesar salad is legendary), pasta dishes, home made burgers and great big baskets of chicken wings. Service can sometimes be a problem – waiting staff are usually foreign students and, although willing and friendly, it can take longer than anticipated to finish a meal here. Children welcome. **Seats 85.** No-smoking area. Air conditioning. Open daily from 8am-11:30pm, Sun from 12. Toilets wheelchair accessible. Closed 24-26 Dec & Good Fri. Amex, Diners, MasterCard, Visa.

Dublin 4   *Ernie's*

Mulberry Gardens Donnybrook Dublin
RESTAURANT   Tel: 01 269 3300 Fax: 01 269 3260

Not the easiest place for visitors to find (it's in a laneway opposite Ulster Bank; from city, take first left turn after Victoria Avenue), named after the late Ernie Evans and still owned by the family. The dining-room looks out on to a pretty courtyard garden, floodlit at night, though its main feature is the fantastic art collection, mostly Irish paintings, many of Kerry, that cover the walls entirely. Both the cooking and service are straightforward, with real old-fashioned classic sauces - a welcome respite in this new era of global cuisine and minimalist restaurants. However, there is a hint of modernism and a nod to foreign influences in some of the dishes: grilled bratwurst with wild mushrooms and onion jus, oven-baked parcel of brie served with fruit chutney and red pepper relish, home-made fish cakes on a bed of leaves with a pink peppercorn vinaigrette, and baked cod with fresh basil pesto and black olives. Alternatively, regular patrons can still enjoy dishes they have become accustomed to, such as roast rack of Wicklow lamb with a Madeira glaze, escalope of veal with a mushroom and Calvados cream sauce and pan-fried lambs liver with sage, avocado and red wine jus. For dessert, a gingered crème brûlée or poached pears and plums with Mascarpone cheese fit the bill perfectly. Good wine list, strong on clarets. Not suitable for children under 12. **Seats 60.** No-smoking area. Air conditioning. L 12:30-2 daily. D 7:30-10:30 daily. Set L £14.95. Set D £25. A la carte available. House wine £16.50. SC 12.5%. Closed Sun & Mon, and 2 weeks at Xmas. Amex, Diners, MasterCard, Visa.

Dublin 4   *Expresso Bar Café*

47 Shelbourne Rd Ballsbridge Dublin
CAFÉ BAR   Tel/Fax: 01 660 8632/280 9089

This cool, informal eating places is notable for clean-lined minimalism, and colourful Cal-Ital food, well-prepared and carefully presented with good coffee. Saturday and Sunday brunch are a must. A sister restaurant has opened at St Mary's Road, Ballsbridge (Tel: 01 660 0585). Children over 3 welcome. **Seats 50.** No-smoking area. Air conditioning.Open 7:30am-5:30pm Mon, 7:30am-9:30pm Tue-Fri, Sat brunch 9-5:30, Sun brunch 10-5:30. Closed 25-26 Dec, 31 Dec-1Jan & Good Fri. MasterCard, Visa.

Dublin 4 ✗   *Fitzers Ballsbridge Café*

Royal Dublin Society Merrion Road Dublin
RESTAURANT   Tel: 01 667 1301/2   Fax: 01 667 1303

Flagship of the Fitzers Café group, this dashing neo-classical restaurant is in the members' annexe of the Regency style Royal Dublin Society building – sculptures and old paintings from the RDS archives look stunning against deep orange walls. New and old meet well, providing a high level of comfort with great style – a dramatic setting for Cal-Ital influenced cooking. Private function rooms are also available and there is ample secure parking available exclusively to the restaurant. L£ Mon-Fri & Sun, D£££ Mon-Sat Closed Bank Hols. Other Fitzers Cafés are in Dublin at: Temple Bar Square (01-679 0440), Dawson Street (01-677 1155), National Gallery, Merrion Square (01-661 4496).

Dublin 2 ★   *Fitzwilliam Hotel*

St Stephen's Green Dublin
HOTEL   Tel: 01 478 7000   Fax: 01 478 7878   email: eng@fitzwilliamh.com

This stylish contemporary hotel enjoys a superb location overlooking St Stephen's Green and close to Dublin's most prestigious shopping area. Behind its deceptively low-key frontage lies an impressively sleek interior created by Sir Terence Conran's design group CD Partnership. Public areas combine elegant minimalism with luxury fabrics and finishes, notably leather upholstery and an unusual pewter bar counter – and, although only open a short time before we went to press, the bar was already becoming established as the chic place to meet in the Grafton Street area. Bedrooms, while quite compact for a luxury hotel, are finished to a high standard with fax/modem points, stereo CD players and minibars, and care has been lavished on the bathrooms too, down to details such as the choice of toiletries. The Fitzwilliam was the our Newcomer of the Year in 1999. Conference/banqueting (80/60). Secretarial services. Wheelchair access. Parking. Children welcome; (under12s free in parents' room; cots available). **Rooms 130** (all en-suite, all shower only, 2 suites, 29 no-smoking, 4 for disabled). B&B £118.50pps, ss £50. Lift. Open all year. Amex, Diners, MasterCard, Visa.

Peacock Alley ★: The culinary hierachy is changing so fast in Dublin that the coming year is hard to predict but, at the time of writing, Conrad Gallagher is Ireland's most talked about chef and Peacock Alley the most controversial restaurant. With a separate entrance from the Green, it's right at the top of the hotel, handy to the roof garden, with a small bar/reception - although it seems usual to show people straight to their tables, some of which overlook Stephen's Green and/or Conrad and his team at work in the open kitchen. As one would expect, it is impeccably appointed, with acres of crisp white linen, fine modern crystal and designer flowers (an unnervingly tall single specimen on each table). Although large, the room is lightly partitioned into three areas, creating a more intimate atmosphere. The ceiling is quite low and there have been problems with ventilation from the outset (unresolved at the time of going to press); the open kitchen probably accentuates this difficulty, which seriously affects an otherwise comfortable environment. The house style is theatrical and renowned for complicated dishes; from the time Conrad Gallagher opened his first restaurant (this is the third Peacock Alley and he now operates numerous other restaurants as well) critical opinion has been sharply divided: is it magnificent culinary entertainment, providing a total contrast to home cooking and all the better for that? Or is it all totally over the top, an expensive waste of good food? Nobody denies that the man can cook, however. Some examples from a recent Prix Fixe dinner to illustrate: the range of breads offered now requires two waiters bearing baskets to offer the selection. Likewise, amuse-bouches are offered from a huge tray (quite difficult to handle neatly with the fingers). A very pretty 'cappuccino' soup - pea emulsion with shiitake mushroom and langoustine - included a perfect whole Dublin Bay prawn (langoustine) but the fluffy, heavily garnished top posed a problem: how to get into it? A very green risotto of fresh peas local wild mushrooms and rillette of rabbit (served as a quenelle) was a well-textured, interesting dish. Roasted monkfish (with saffron and mussel emulsion, herb, gnocchi, eggplant and tomato followed. This was apparently a main course - a large piece of fish, stacked with chargrilled aubergine and various other elements; the tomato - semi-dried and speared with a sprig of thyme - had great flavour, but it was a very heavy dish - with a meat course still to come. Oh and somewhere in there a sorbet (not mentioned on the menu) appeared, with a huge sugar cage on top - a dashing dessert.... Bear in mind that this menu is designed as a complete meal and the diner relies on the chef's judgment for the correct balance of choices. Next came another main course, a complex dish of loin of lamb wrapped in leeks with ratatouille, spinach, pesto cous-cous, tapenade and a sweet pepper emulsion. The spinach base was a simple, fresh green, but there were so many elements stacked on top (more and more kept emerging during the deconstruction) that, delicious as individual ones may have been, the overall effect was confusion. The best was yet to come - a superb lemon tart, crisp-based with a deep creamy filling, just enough bite to be interesting, a light dusting of icing sugar and a gorgeous raspberry sorbet in a crisp tart-shaped 'tuile' - but, alas, who could face dessert after what had gone before? And there was more; with the coffee (1/2 cup, served with hot milk) came no less than eight petits fours.Then, of course, the bill - with even the most modest wine choices an evening here will be very expensive indeed. Is it worth it? Perhaps it depends who's paying. **Seats 110** (private room, 60). L 12:30-2:30 daily. D 6:30-10:30 daily. Set L £23. Set D from £23, Menu Prix Fixe £45, Gourmet menu £65. A la carte also available. House wine £15. Toilets wheelchair accessible. No-smoking area. Air conditioning. SC discretionary. Closed Sun. **Christophers:** The hotel's all-day brasserie-style mezzanine restaurant "Christopher's", is also operated by Gallagher. **Seats 80.** Breakfast 7-10:30, L 12:30-2:30, D 6:30-10:30

Dublin 2   *Fitzwilliam Park*

5 Fitzwilliam Square Dublin
ACCOMMODATION   Tel: 01 662 8280 Fax: 01 662 8281 email: info@fitzpark.ie

Mary Madden has recently opened this elegant Georgian house after extensive renovation and refurbishment, yet retaining many of the original features. It's a big house – one of the largest and oldest buildings on the eastern side of the garden square (private, but residents have access) – with a fine back stone staircase. The Grand Salon, a lofty and opulent room on the first floor with fine antiques, paintings and objets d'art, is where a hearty Irish breakfast is served in splendid surroundings. The bedrooms – the higher you go, the smaller they become – are well-appointed and furnished, with tiled bathrooms, satellite TV, radio and direct-dial telephone. Business travellers will find plenty of desk space and can also make use of a boardroom on the ground floor. Secure free parking behind the building via Lad Lane. Conference (35). Secretarial services. Wheelchair access. Children welcome (Under 3s free in parents' room; cots available). Pets by arrangement. **Rooms 20** (all en-suite, 2 mini-suite, 16 executive rooms, 4 for disabled).Lift. B&B £60pps, ss £25. Closed 23-28 Dec. Amex, Diners, MasterCard, Visa.

Dublin 4 ❄ 🏨   *The Four Seasons Hotel*

Simmonscourt Road Dublin
HOTEL   Tel: 01 269 6446 Fax: 01 269 6453

The imminent arrival of a Four Seasons Hotel in Dublin (due to open "early 2000") has created great excitement and there has been a noticeable flurry of activity at the top of the market to upgrade and refurbish the hotels which will find themselves in competition with this giant of the hospitality industry. The exemplary standards of service for which the Four Seasons is renowned will no doubt have a similar ripple effect - which should all be good news for visitors to Dublin. The new hotel is set in its own grounds in a quiet location near the RDS, close to the city centre and all bedrooms will have expansive views as well as excellent facilities for business and leisure. Public areas will be impressively spacious, dining arrangements promise to be very interesting and and the entire hotel is designed with both the private and business guest in mind, for relaxing and conducting business. Conference/banqueting (350/400). Business centre. Secretarial services. Leisure centre (indoor swimming pool). Hairdresser. Garden. Wheelchair access. Parking. Children welcome (Under 12s free in parents' room; cots available). Pets in certain areas. **Rooms 254** (all en-suite, 33 suites, 40 mini-suite, 15 executive rooms, 125 no-smoking, 14 for disabled). Prices not available at the time of going to press. Lift. Open all year. Amex, Diners, MasterCard, Visa.

Dublin 2 — *Les Frères Jacques*

74 Dame Street Dublin
RESTAURANT
Tel: 01 679 4555 Fax: 01 679 4725

One of the few genuinely French restaurants in Dublin, Les Freres Jacques opened beside the Olympia Theatre in 1986, well before the development of Temple Bar made the area fashionable. The staff are all French, the atmosphere is French – and the cooking is definitely French. Seasonal menus are wide-ranging and well-balanced but – as expected when you notice the lobster tank just beside the door on entering – there is a definite bias towards fish and seafood, all of it from Irish waters; there is also game in season. Lunch at Les Freres Jacques is a treat (and good value) but dinner is a feast. The 4-course set dinner offers soup (sea food minestrone perhaps) and three choices on the other courses – smoked chicken & pigeon salad with pine kernels and hazelnut dressings, for example, or roast Wicklow lamb and juices. Poached pear & Roquefort sauce and soup of summer red fruits with pistachio ice cream are all typical examples. Suggestions from the à la carte are also made on the dinner menu; thus west coast oysters (native and rock), grilled lobster, turbot with girolles & roasting juices, individually priced. There are cheeses or beautifully presented desserts, as in a dramatic crème caramel in a sugar cage, with cappuccino cream. Service is efficient and discreet. Children welcome. **Seats** 60 (private room, 15). L 12-1:30 daily. D 7-11 daily. Set L £13.50. Set D £21, à la carte available. House wine £11. No-smoking area. Air conditioning. SC 12.5%. Closed Sundays, 24 Dec-2 Jan. Amex, Diners, MasterCard, Visa.

Dublin 4 — *Furama Chinese Restaurant*

Anglesea House Donnybrook Road Donnybrook Dublin
RESTAURANT
Tel: 01 283 0522 Fax: 01 668 7623

In the sleek black interior of Rodney Mak's long-established restaurant Freddie Lee, who has been head chef since the restaurant opened in 1989, produces terrific food with an authenticity which is unusual in Ireland. Even the menu does not read like other Chinese restaurants – dishes aren't numbered, for a start, and they are also presented and described with great individuality. Thus, starters of soft shell crab in spicy salt and pepper or sweet and sour sauce; king size mussels in rich garlic sauce or spicy chilli sauce; lobster on shell (various ways), stir fried oyster with ginger and scallion, and much more. They do offer Set Dinners, which are more predictable – and many traditional Chinese dishes on the à la carte menu – but the option is there to try something different. Service, under the supervision of Rodney Mak and manager Stephen Lee, is friendly and efficient. Parking. No children after 8pm. **Seats 100** L 12:30-2 Mon-Sat. D 6-11:30 Mon-Sat. Sun 1:30-11. Set L £12. Set D £25. A la carte available. House wine from £11. No-smoking area. Air conditioning. SC 10%. Closed 24-26 Dec & Good Fri. Amex, Diners, MasterCard, Visa.

Dublin 4 — *Glenogra House*

64 Merrion Road Dublin
GUESTHOUSE   Tel: 01 668 3661 Fax: 01 668 3698 email: glenogra@indigo.ie

This comfortable Ballsbridge guesthouse is run by Seamus and Cherry McNamee, who make a point of providing personal service and very good breakfasts. Old and new are carefully combined to create a homelike atmosphere and three new rooms were added last year. Conveniently located for the RDS and within 3 minutes walk of the Sandymount DART station. Parking. Children welcome (Under 10s free in parents' room; cots available). No pets. **Rooms 12** (all en-suite, 2 shower only, all no-smoking). B&B £37.50pps, ss £7.50. Closed Xmas. Amex, Diners, MasterCard, Visa.

Dublin 4 ˣ — *Glenveagh Townhouse*

31 Northumberland Road Ballsbridge Dublin
ACCOMMODATION
Tel: 01 668 4612 Fax: 01 668 4559

A warm welcome and courteous service are the hallmarks of this fine period guesthouse, which has been renovated to a high standard and provides a comfortable base for both business guests and tourists. Although just off the centre of the city, on a fine day it's a pleasant 10-15 minute walk to Trinity College and the Grafton Street area. Bedrooms (which include three suitable for disabled guests) vary – they include singles, twins and family rooms, but all are well-furnished, with a high standard of amenities including complimentary mineral water and toiletries. There's a guest sitting room and facilities for small conferences (14). No dogs. Acc££ Closed 18-28 Dec.

Dublin 2 ˣ   *Good World Chinese Restaurant*

18 South Great Georges Street Dublin
RESTAURANT   Tel/Fax: 01 677 5373

One of a cluster of interesting ethnic restaurants around Wicklow Street and South Great George's Street, the Good World opened in 1991 and is owner-managed by Thomas Choi. It has always been a favourite of the local Chinese community, because of its large selection of Dim Sum, which is served daily. The restaurant also prides itself on an especially full range of other Chinese dishes, suitable for both Chinese and European customers and Thomas Choi makes a welcoming and helpful host. L£ & D££ daily. Closed 25-26 Dec.

Dublin 2   *Gotham Café*

8 South Anne Street Dublin
RESTAURANT   Tel: 01 679 5266   Fax: 01 679 5280

A lively, youthful café-restaurant just off Grafton Street, the Gotham does good informal food: Specialities include Caesar salad, baby calzone, Persian chicken and mini salmon pizza. Sunday brunch is a speciality (12-4.30pm). Children welcome. **Seats 65.** No-smoking area. Air conditioning. Open all day 12pm-12am Mon-Sat. Sun L 12-4:30, Sun D 5-10:30. Menu à la carte. House wine £9.75. SC discretionary (10% on parties of 6+). Closed 2 days Xmas & Good Fri. Amex, MasterCard, Visa.

Dublin 2   *Grafton Plaza Hotel*

Johnsons Place Dublin
HOTEL   Tel: 01 475 0888   Fax: 01 475 0908   email: info@graftonplaza.ie

In a prime city centre location just a couple of minutes walk from Grafton Street, this attractive hotel offers particularly well furnished rooms and good amenities (including fax/modem) at prices which are not unreasonable for the area. Rooms are also available for small conferences, meetings and interviews. The popular 'Break for the Border' nightclub next door is in common ownership with the hotel and offers guests live entertainment on Wednesday-Saturday nights. Small conference (25). Secretarial services. Wheelchair access. Parking by arrangement with nearby carpark. Children welcome (Under 12s free in parents' room; cots available). Pets in certain areas. **Rooms 75** (all en-suite, 4 mini-suite, 30 executive rooms, 5 no-smoking, 4 for disabled). B&B £80pps. Lift. Closed 24-27 Dec. Amex, Diners, MasterCard, Visa.

Dublin 1   *The Gresham*

O'Connell Street Dublin
HOTEL   Tel: 01 874 6881   Fax: 01 878 7175   email: ryan@indigo.ie

First opened in 1817, the hotel has always been at the centre of society in the centre of Dublin, and is now considered one of the city's finest business hotels – with a variety of meeting rooms (max 300) and a 24-hour business centre. However, at the same time it's still a favourite meeting place and the lobby lounge is renowned for its traditional afternoon tea, while the Gresham and Toddy's Bars are popular rendezvous for a pint. The Aberdeen Restaurant has been expanded to cope with the additional guests, and a small fitness room allows guests to work off those extra pounds. Recently added air-conditioned bedrooms are spacious with smart furniture and colourful fabrics and the added benefit of separate walk-in shower in the well-equipped bathroom, but all the other bedrooms, including six penthouse suites, (one occupied for several months by Elizabeth Taylor and Richard Burton many years ago), offer the same facilities including voicemail and fax/modem points. The hotel prides itself on the quality of its staff, particularly the concierge. Conference/banqueting (300/250). Business centre. Secretarial services. Video conferencing. Wheelchair access. own parking. Children welcome (Under 2s free in parents' room; cots available). No pets. **Rooms 288** (all en-suite, 8 suites, 2 mini-suite, 150 executive rooms, 50 no-smoking, 2 for disabled).Lifts. B&B from £95pps, ss £30. Open all year. Amex, Diners, MasterCard, Visa.

Dublin 2   *The Grey Door Irish Restaurant/Guesthouse*

22/23 Upper Pembroke Street Dublin
Tel: 01 676 3286 Fax: 01 676 3287
RESTAURANT/GUESTHOUSE   email: info@greydoor.ie

P J Daly and Barry Wyse's opened The Grey Door in 1979 and now also own several hotels, including the Hibernian Hotel in Ballsbridge and the McCausland in Belfast – see separate entries). The original Grey Door Restaurant changed its style quite dramatically a year or two ago; guests who remember it as a grand, classically elegant place featuring Russian specialities may be surprised to find a sleek, contemporary restaurant serving modern Irish food. *Down in the basement, under the Grey Door, Pier 32 is quite different, with an Irish country atmosphere and traditional "home-made" food – soda breads, simple seafood, farmhouse cheeses and pints of stout convey the feeling, and it's all good fun as well as good eating. **Seats 40** (private room, 70). No-smoking area. D 6-10:45 Mon-Sat. Set D from £25, early bird menu £12 6-7pm. A la carte available. House wine £12.95. SC 12.5%. Closed Sundays, Bank Hols & 24-27 Dec. **Residence:** Above the Grey Door, accommodation is offered in seven rooms, furnished to a high standard with sitting areas and private bathrooms. Conference/banqueting (40/70). Children welcome (Under 2s free in parents' room; cots available). No pets. **Rooms 7** (all en-suite, 2 mini-suite). Room rate £95. Closed 24-27 Dec. Amex, Diners, MasterCard, Visa.

Dublin 7   *The Halfway House*

Navan Road Ashtown Dublin
PUB   Tel: 01 838 3358 Fax: 01 868 3088

A well-supported local and handy meeting place just off the West-Link motorway, this well-known pub is very large, well-run and offers good quality popular bar food. Wheelchair access. Parking. No children after 7pm. Bar food everyday 12-8. Closed 25 Dec & Good Fri. Amex, Diners, MasterCard, Visa.

Dublin 1 *✗*   *The Harbourmaster*

Custom House Docks Dublin
BAR/RESTAURANT   Tel: 01 670 1688 Fax: 01 670 1690

In a waterside setting at Dublin's financial services centre this old Dock Offices building has genuine character and makes a fine restaurant and bar. The bar is pleasant and very busy at times, but it's now more of a restaurant than a pub at meal times and most tables have an interesting (and increasingly attractive) view of the development outside. For fine weather there's also a decked outdoor area overlooking the inner harbour and fountain, with extra seating. The restaurant underwent a major extension programme recently and the extra space gained is in sympathy with the original building and, with waterside views, of great benefit to diners. Open weekdays from 7.30am, Sat & Sun 12pm £-££ o Closed 25 Dec & Good Fri.

Dublin 2 *✗*   *Harcourt Hotel*

60 Harcourt Street Dublin
HOTEL   Tel: 01 478 3677 Fax: 01 475 2013

This small, comfortable hotel lays claim to a unique distinction – it was, for several years, the home of George Bernard Shaw, writer, dramatist and wit. GBS would probably still be keen to stay, since the rooms are comfortable (though not large) and the atmosphere friendly. Being a strict teetotaller he might not approve of the two bars, but they are both very congenial, with the larger bar playing host to some of the best traditional Irish musicians and music, and the more intimate, panelled Barney Google's bar more suitable for quiet conversation or contemplation. GBS was also not known as an habitué of night clubs, but if he was he would be perfectly placed for visiting both the well-known POD (Place of Dance) and other clubs just a short walk away. The rooms have recently been refurbished and there is the recently opened GB Shaw Restaurant serving Irish and Mediterranean dishes. Acc££-£££ Closed 24-25 Dec.

Dublin 2   *Harrington Hall*

69/70 Harcourt Street Dublin
Tel: 01 475 3497 Fax: 01 475 4544
ACCOMMODATION   email: harringtonhall@eircom.net

Opened in March 1998 and conveniently located close to St Stephen's Green, this is a guesthouse (once the home of a former Lord Mayor of Dublin) of grand Georgian splendour. It has been sympathetically and elegantly refurbished, retaining many original features, especially the ornamental ceilings and fireplaces in the well-proportioned ground and first floor rooms, which include a peaceful drawing room. Comfortable and practical bedrooms havedecent bathrooms. Given the need for some finishing touches – a few pictures here and there, and double-glazing installed in the rooms facing the busy street so that guests can enjoy an uninterrupted night's sleep – this is a welcome and considerably cheaper alternative to a city-centre hotel, with the huge advantage of free parking behind the building. Secretarial services. Wheelchair access. Parking. Children welcome. No pets. **Rooms 28** (all en-suite, 3 shower only, 3 suites, 5 executive rooms, all no-smoking, 1 for disabled).Lift. B&B £55pps, ss £30. Open all year. Amex, MasterCard, Visa.

Dublin 2 ✗
CAFÉ/BAR

Harvey's Coffee House
14-15 Trinity Street Dublin
Tel: 01 677 1060

Just off Dame Street, this busy daytime café offers great coffee every-which-way and lots of lovely things to go with it – from toast, bagels and scones in the morning, through to lovely big open sandwiches and other more filling fare at lunchtime. There are also pastries and desserts to take your fancy later. Sunday brunch is a speciality. Open all day £

Dublin 4

Herbert Park Hotel
Ballsbridge Dublin
Tel: 01 667 2200 Fax: 01 667 2595
email: reservations@herbertparkhotel.ie

HOTEL

This very large, striking hotel is near the RDS and the public park after which it is named. It is approached over a little bridge, which leads to an underground carpark and, ultimately, to a chic lower ground foyer and the lift up to the main lobby. Public areas on the ground floor are impressively light and spacious, with excellent light meals and drinks provided by efficient waiting staff. The bright and modern style is also repeated in the bedrooms – stylishly designed and well-finished with a high standard of amenities. Conference/banqueting (100/140). Business centre. Secretarial services. ISDN lines. Air conditioning. Fitness centre. Wheelchair access. Parking. Children (Under 12s free in parents' room in existing beds; cots available). No pets. **Rooms 153** (all en-suite, 2 suites, 1 mini-suite, 27 executive rooms, 20 no-smoking, 7 for disabled). B&B £111pps, ss £62.50. Lift. Open all year. Amex, Diners, MasterCard, Visa.

Dublin 4

The Hibernian Hotel
Eastmoreland Place Ballsbridge Dublin
Tel: 01 668 7666 Fax: 01 660 2655
email: info@hibernianhotel.com

HOTEL/RESTAURANT

The Hibernian Hotel feels as if it's in a peaceful backwater, yet this splendid Victorian building is only yards from one of Dublin's busiest city centre roads. It's very friendly, with a country house feeling in the size and proportions of its rooms and an elegant decorative style with warm country colours. The names of the rooms evoke a homely atmosphere too – the drawing room, the library and so on. Bedrooms are all individually decorated to a high standard with excellent bathrooms featuring a wide range of amenities. Service is exemplary. Small conference/private parties (20/20). Business centre. Secretarial services. Small garden. Wheelchair access. Parking. Children (Under 2s free in parents' room; cots available). No pets.*Refurbishment of public areas and bedrooms was due to start shortly after the Guide went to press. **Rooms 40** (all en-suite, 3 shower only, 10 mini-suite, 14 no-smoking, 2 for disabled). Room rate from £150. Lift. Closed 24-27 Dec. Amex, Diners, MasterCard, Visa. **The Patrick Kavanagh Room:** In keeping with the rest of the hotel, the restaurant is well-appointed, with elegance and charm. David Foley, who has been head chef since 1994, presents lunch and dinner menus that change weekly, in addition to an evening à la carte and a separate vegetarian menu. Global influences are certainly at work here, but David takes great pride in using the best of Irish produce to advantage as, for example, in a dish of cannon of Wicklow lamb stuffed with a pancetta farce served with a broccoli tartlet and quenelles of champ potato. Desserts tend to be based more closely on classical dishes and Irish farmhouse cheeses are an option. Service is friendly and efficient. **Seats 45** L 12:30-2:30 Mon-Fri. D 6:30-10 Mon-Sat. Sun D 7-9 residents only. Set L £17. Gourmet dinner menu £35. Dinner à la carte available. House wine £14.50. Toilets wheelchair accessible. No-smoking area. SC 12.5%. Closed Bank Hols & 24-27 Dec.

Dublin 2   *Hilton Dublin*

Charlemont Place Dublin
Tel: 01 402 9988 Fax: 01 402 9852
HOTEL/RESTAURANT   email: reservations@dublin.stakis.co.uk

Overlooking the Grand Canal, this fairly new hotel (previously Stakis), is just a few minutes walk from the city centre and caters for all the needs of the modern day guest.Each double-glazed bedroom provides a worktop with modem point, swivel satellite TV, individual heater, tea/coffee-making facilities, trouser press, hairdryer and compact bathroom (club rooms also offer a bathrobe, additional toiletries and chocolates). Every floor has a vending machine operated and billed by the room key card. A large underground car park has direct access to the hotel. Conference/banqueting (400/260). Secretarial services. Wheelchair access. Parking. Children (Under 5s free in parents' room; cots available). No pets. **Rooms 189** (all en-suite, 100 no-smoking, 4 for disabled). B&B £95pps. Lift. Closed 25-28 Dec. Amex, Diners, MasterCard, Visa.

Waterfront Restaurant: This well-appointed restaurant offers a buffet-style breakfast and, since the arrival of Gavin McDonagh as head chef in June 1998, it rates as a serious choice among Dublin dining destinations. The glass-walled kitchen provides entertainment for guests who are not overlooking the canal, and food – in the modern Irish idiom – is imaginative, well cooked and well presented. **Seats 104** (private room, 250) No-smoking area. Air conditioning.L 12:30-2:30 daily. D 6-10:30 daily, Sat to 11. L&D à la carte. House wine £11. SC discretionary.Toilets wheelchair accessible. Closed Sun lunch.

Dublin 7   *Hole in the Wall*

Blackhorse Lane Phoenix Park Dublin
PUB   Tel: 01 838 9491 Fax: 01 868 5215

PJ McCaffrey's remarkable pub beside the Phoenix Park is named in honour of a tradition which existed here for around a hundred years – the practice of serving drinks through a hole in the wall of Phoenix Park to members of the army garrison stationed nearby. Today the Hole in the Wall also claims to be the longest pub in Ireland – and it is certainly one of the most interesting, best-run and most hospitable. They do good food too – a buffet lunch every day, 12-3pm. Wheelchair access. Parking. Children welcome. Pets in certain areas. Bar food served daily 12-8. Closed 25 Dec & Good Fri. Amex, Diners, MasterCard, Visa.

Dublin 2   *Il Primo*

16 Montague Street Dublin
RESTAURANT   Tel/Fax: 01 478 3373

Dieter Bergman's cheery little first floor restaurant was way ahead of current fashions when it opened in 1991. It's simple (some would say spartan) but the essentials are right: warm hospitality and excellent, imaginative, freshly cooked modern Italian food. Then there's the wine, which is Dieter's special passion: all wines below £36 are available by the millilitre – customers drink as much as they want and that's the amount they pay for: brilliant. Dieter also organises regular wine tastings and dinners. Children welcome. **Seats 30.** No-smoking area. Air conditioning.L 12-3 Mon-Fri. D 6-11 daily. L&D à la carte. House wine £12.80 per litre. SC 10%. Closed Sat & Sun lunch. Amex, Diners, MasterCard, Visa.

Dublin 2   *Imperial Chinese Restaurant*

12A Wicklow Street Dublin 2
RESTAURANT   Tel: 01 677 2580 Fax: 01 677 9851

Mrs Cheung's long-estabished city centre restaurant has enjoyed enduring popularity with Dubliners and has also a clear vote of confidence from the local Chinese community, who appreciate the authenticity of head chef Mr Yim's cooking, especially dim sum which is a speciality on Sunday.The Imperial was our Oriental Restaurant of the Year in 1999. Children welcome. **Seats 180.** Open daily 12:30-11:45 Fri & Sat to 12:45am. Closed 25-26 Dec. Amex, MasterCard, Visa.

Dublin 14   *Indian Brasserie*

Rathfarnham Dublin 14
RESTAURANT   Tel/Fax: 01 492 0260

Samir Sapru's Indian Brasserie is just a minute's walk from Rathfarnham Castle, at the Butterfield Avenue end of the village. The restaurant, which is run as a buffet, offers freshly prepared wholesome food, aiming to make it the nearest to home cooking that can be achieved in a restaurant. The selection usually includes around eight starters, five or six salads and seven or eight main courses, with each dish individually prepared from scratch and the selection worked out so that all the dishes complement each other. Breads – which are baked quickly at a very high temperature – are cooked to order. The hospitality is intended to make each guest feel as if they are visiting a private house – customers are encouraged to try a little of everything that has been prepared on the night. Own parking. No children after 7pm. **Seats 50.** No-smoking area. Air conditioningD 5-10:30 daily. Sun L only 12:30-3. Set S L £10.50. Set D £15, early bird menu £10.95 5:30-7:30pm. House wine £10.95.SC discretionary. Toilets wheelchair accessible. Closed 25-26 Dec. Amex, Diners, MasterCard, Visa.

Dublin 2 *Jacob's Ladder*

4 Nassau Street Dublin

RESTAURANT   Tel: 01 670 3865 Fax: 01 670 3868

Adrian and Bernie Roche opened this smart restaurant overlooking the playing fields of Trinity College in 1997 and it was an immediate success. The modern decor provides an appropriate backdrop for Adrian's cooking which is in the New Irish style with international influences. He presents well-balanced seasonal menus, which always include some vegetarian dishes (marked on the menu), and there is a welcome heartiness about his food. Typical starters might include sauté of duck livers & confit with parfait and a citrus salad and one of the half dozen main courses on the dinner menu could be roast woodpigeon with vegetable cobbler and Colcannon dumplings. Seafood features strongly in a saute of scallops with beetroot & spiced lentils, for example. To finish, choose between Irish farmhouse cheeses and tempting desserts such as a lemon brûlée with orange ice. Parking by arrangement with nearby carpark. Children welcome. **Seats 80** (private room, 50) No-smoking area.L 12:30-3 Tue-Sat. D 6-10 Tue-Sat. Set D £25. Gourmet menu £32. Early bird menu £16.50 6-7:15pm. L&D à la carte available. House wine £12. SC discretionary. Closed Sun & Mon, and 1 wk August, 3 wks Xmas. Amex, Diners, MasterCard, Visa.

Dublin 1 *Restaurant Jam*

Irish Music Hall of Fame 57 Middle Abbey Street Dublin 1

RESTAURANT   Tel: 01 874 9066

Entered via the Irish Music Hall of Fame and down a corridor, this is a large, funky bistro-style restaurant in a modern bare-brick basement with a long, thick wooden bar, exposed stainless steel pipes and well spaced out eating area with functional wooden tables and chairs.Get this far and you'll be treated to some excellent friendly service and an inexpensive menu of ambitious fast food. The place has a happy, trendy buzz and a set lunch menu which is a steal at £7 for two courses. They do a great Caesar salad - a huge mound of crisp cos lettuce, glistening with just the right amount of dressing and plenty of crispy croutons. Tortilla chips with guacamole, salsa and soured cream is also good and Thai chicken noodles with lemongrass are cooked until the noodles are just crispy underneath - no mean feat. "Jamburgers" are a speciality - 8 oz prime beef pattie on focaccia with corn relish and fries - and cooked to perfection. The only downside is that generous portions may leave no room for dessert. As well as brunch dishes and afternoon teas, there's also a range of open-style sandwiches and pasta dishes.The bar is well stocked, with a good range of cocktails and offers 'The Big Chill' Mon-Fri 5-8pm, when all pints and a cocktail of the day are only £2.00 - now there's good value! **Seats 95.** No smoking area; air conditioning. Open daily 12-11, L 12-5, D 6-11. Set L from £6.95, Set Sun L £10.95, D A la carte, house wine £11, sc discretionry (10% on parties of 6+). Closed 25 Dec, 1 Jan. Amex, Diners, Mastercard, Visa.

Dublin 8 *X* *Jurys Christchurch Inn*

Christchurch Place Dublin

HOTEL   Tel: 01 454 0000 Fax: 01 454 0012

The Jurys Inn chain provides competitively priced middle range accommodation throughout Ireland. Jurys Christchurch Inn is particularly well placed for both tourist and business travellers, with a location close to attractions such as Dublin Castle and Dublinia (the museum of medieval Dublin). Temple Bar and the central city are also close by. There is a large multi-storey car park at the rear with convenient access to the hotel. Rooms are confortable and spacious (though occasionally in need of greater attention to upgrading and maintenance), with large, well positioned work desks. Acc££. Closed 25-26 Dec

Dublin 1 ✗   *Jurys Custom House Inn*

Custom House Quay Dublin
HOTEL   Tel: 01 607 5000 Fax: 01 829 0400

Right beside the financial services centre, overlooking the Liffey and close to train and bus stations, this hotel meets the requirements of business guests with better facilities than is usual in budget hotels. Large bedrooms can sleep up to four and have all the usual facilities, but also fax/modem lines and a higher standard of finish than earlier sister hotels; fabrics and fittings are better quality and neat bathrooms are more thoughtfully designed, with more generous shelf space – although bath tubs are still tiny. As well as a large bar, there is a full restaurant on site, plus conference facilities for up to 100 and a staffed business centre. No room service. No private parking but there is a 400-space multi-storey park with direct access to the hotel. Acc££ Closed 24-26 Dec. Amex, Diners, MasterCard, Visa.

Dublin 4 ⛪   *Jurys Hotel Dublin and The Towers*

Pembroke Road Ballsbridge Dublin
Tel: 01 660 5000 (Jurys) Tel: 667 0033 (Towers)
HOTEL   Fax: 01 660 5540 (Jurys & Towers) email: enquiry@jurys.com

Jurys is quite a Dublin institution – centrally located in the Ballsbridge area, always busy, it has achieved the distinction of being both an international hotel providing high levels of service to business and leisure guests while remaining a popular local hotel for Dubliners. Rooms are of a very high standard in both Jurys (the front section of the hotel which has undergone a major refurbishment) and The Towers (the quieter, more exclusive section of the hotel located to the rear). Business and corporate guests are well looked after and constant maintenance and upgrading, plus a high level of service from a committed and well-trained staff keep this hotel - which was our Business Hotel of the Year 1999 - up with the leaders in an increasingly competitive market. The Dubliner Bar, The Coffee Dock and Raglan's restaurant look after the inner man and visitors have the benefit of a well-stocked newsagent and shop, a swimming pool, fitness centre and cabaret with highly popular and long-running show. Conference/banqueting (850/650). Business centre. ISDN lines. Video conferencing. Leisure centre (semi-indoor swimming pool). Hairdresser. Wheelchair access. Parking. Children welcome (under 12s free in parents' room; cots available). No pets. **Jurys: Rooms 300.** B&B from £91pps. Lift. Open all year. Amex, Diners, MasterCard, Visa. **The Towers: Rooms 100.** B&B from £136pps. Lift. Open all year. Amex, Diners, MasterCard, Visa. **Raglans: Seats 120.** No-smoking area. Air conditioning. Open for L&D daily. Toilets wheelchair accessible. .

Dublin 9   *John Kavanagh*

1 Prospect Square Glasnevin Dublin
PUB   *No Phone* email: antokav@gofree.indigo.ie

John Kavanagh's lays claim to being the oldest family pub in Dublin – it was established in 1833 and the current family are the 6th generation in the business. Also known as "The Gravediggers" because of its location next to the Glasnevin cemetery and its attached folk history, this is a genuine Victorian bar, totally unspoilt – and it has a reputation for serving one of the best pints in Dublin. Theme pub owners eat your hearts out. Parking. No children after 7pm. Pets by arrangement. Bar food served weekdays 12-2. Closed Good Fri & Xmas. No credit cards.

Dublin 2   *Kilkenny Restaurant & Café*

6 Nassau Street Dublin
RESTAURANT/CAFÉ   Tel: 01 677 7066 Fax: 01 670 3715

Situated on the first floor of the shop now known simply as Kilkenny, with a clear view into the grounds of Trinity College, the refurbished Kilkenny Restaurant is one of the most pleasant places in Dublin to have a bite to eat – and the food matches the view. It looks good and the experience generally matches the anticipation. Ingredients are fresh and additive-free (as are all the products on sale in the shop's Food Hall) and food has a home-cooked flavour. Salads, quiches, casseroles, home-baked breads and cakes are the specialities of the Kilkenny Restaurant and they are very good. For quicker bites the shop has a second eating place, Kilkenny Café, where the same principles apply. A range of Kilkenny preserves and dressings – all made and labelled on the premises – is available in the shop. Children welcome. **Seats 190.** Open all day 9-5, Thur to 7. Sun 11-5. Set

L £6.95. Set D £20, early evening menu £10 6-7 pm only. A la carte available. Licensed. No-smoking area. Air conditioning. Closed 25 Dec & 1 Jan. Amex, Diners, MasterCard, Visa.

Dublin 22   *Kingswood Country House*

Old Kingswood Naas Road Clondalkin Dublin
RESTAURANT + COUNTRY HOUSE   Tel/Fax: 01 459 2428

Just off the Naas Road and very close to the industrial estates around Newlands Cross, the country house atmosphere of this guesthouse and restaurant comes as a very pleasant surprise. The restaurant has a lovely cosy atmosphere and a loyal following, for service and atmosphere as well as the food. This is an interesting combination of classic French and traditional and new Irish styles. Ingredients are top quality and the policy is to use as much local and free range produce as possible. Private rooms are available for groups and small business meetings. Small conference/private parties (30). Garden. Parking. Children welcome. **Seats 100** (private room, 30) No-smoking area.L 12:30-2:30 daily. D 6:30-10:30 Mon-Sat. SC 12.5%. Open on Bank Hols. Amex, Diners, MasterCard, Visa. **Accommodation:** Guest rooms, like the rest of the house, have an old-fashioned charm. **Rooms 7** (all en-suite, 4 shower only, some no-smoking). Closed 25-26 Dec & Good Fri.

Dublin 4   *Langkawi*

46 Upper Baggot Street Dublin
RESTAURANT   Tel: 01 668 2760   email: hosey@indigo.ie

Malaysian cuisine is a synthesis of three main distinct national cuisines – Malay, Chinese and Indian – and the result is a distinctive mix that offers something for everyone, from hot, fiery dishes through to more subtle flavours. The now very popular Langkawi sets out to do all styles justice, but there is an understandable emphasis on Malay dishes since this is the rarer cuisine in Ireland. Satays make a good start for the more timid. For the more adventurous diner there is plenty to choose from (with clear menu guidance on heat levels). Chef Alex Hosey uses genuine imported ingredients to achieve an authentic Malaysian taste. Well worth visiting for a lunch or dinner that is out of the ordinary. Wheelchair access. Children welcome. **Seats 60.** No-smoking area. Open all day (10-5) L 12:30-2:00 Mon-Sat. D 6-11:30 daily. Set L £10.95. Set D £20, early evening menu £10 6-7 pm only. Dinner à la carte available. House wine from £10. SC 12.5%. Open Bank Holidays for Dinner. Closed Sundays & Xmas week. Amex, Diners, MasterCard, Visa.

Dublin 4   *Lansdowne Manor*

46-48 Lansdowne Road Ballsbridge Dublin
Tel: 01 668 8848   Fax: 01 668 8873
GUESTHOUSE   email: lansdownemanor@eircom.net

Situated in the heart of "embassyland", Lansdowne Manor comprises two early Victorian mansions which have been recently refurbished and decorated in period style. It now offers some of the most comfortable guesthouse accommodation in the city.Small conference/private parties (15). Wheelchair access. Parking. Children welcome. Pets by arrangement. **Rooms 22** (all en-suite, 5 shower only, 5 suites, 2 mini-suite, 4 executive rooms, 1 for disabled). B&B £50pps, ss £5. Closed 23-27 Dec. Amex, MasterCard, Visa.

Dublin 3 ✳   *Liaison Restaurant*

318 Clontarf Road Dublin
RESTAURANT   Tel: 01 833 6759   Fax: 01 833 6651

A very welcome addition to the northside dining scene, this chic new restaurant is just opposite the wooden bridge across to Bull Island and brings a genuine intention to offer this area a fine dining option for the first time. Although small, wisely chosen neutral shades bring a sense of spaciousness as well as contemporary elegance and, for the most part, the food matches this style. Our visit was made shortly after the restaurant opened and any slight teething problems will almost certainly have been speedily resolved. Wheelchair access. Parking. Children welcome. **Seats 40.** No-smoking area. Air conditioning.L 12-2:30 Tue-Sat. D 6:30-10 Tue-Sat. Set L £12.50. Dinner à la carte. House wine £13.85. Toilets wheelchair accessible. Closed Sun & Mon , & 3 wks in Jan. MasterCard, Visa.

Dublin 2 ˣ   *Little Caesar's Palace*

Balfe Street Dublin
RESTAURANT   Tel: 01 671 8714

This genuine little pizza place is just a stone's throw from the door of the Westbury Hotel – fresh, tasty and inexpensive pizzas (with good crisp bases) cooked before your very eyes could be the perfect antidote to too much luxury, or too much shopping. Open 12noon-midnight. Closed 25 Dec & Good Fri. Amex, Diners, MasterCard, Visa.

Dublin 2   *Lloyds Brasserie*

20 Merrion Street Upper Dublin
Tel: 01 662 7240/1/2 Fax: 01 662 7243
RESTAURANT   email: conradgallagher@eircom.net

Conrad Gallagher is one of the city's best known chef/restaurateurs and this, his second eaterie, is much more casual than his serious Peacock Alley restaurant (see entry). Lloyds is open seven days a week for lunch (brunch at weekends - a speciality) and dinner; additionally, bar food is served all day and there's usually a lively crowd in the piano bar on Thursday, Friday and Saturday evenings from 9pm- 2am. The basement restaurant is minimalist in the extreme, very chic, with red banquettes, marble-topped tables cheek by jowl, aluminium chairs, tiled floor and blue walls. It's a modern restaurant, serving excellent modern food, with golba; influences. There's a good and reasonably priced wine list with a decent showing from the New World. Not suitable for children. **Seats 100** (private room, 16). No-smoking area. Sat & Sun brunch 1-4. L 12:30-2:30 Mon-Fri. D 6-11 daily. Set L £15.50. Early bird menu £15.50 6-7pm. L&D à la carte available. SC discretionary. Closed 25-26 Dec, 1 Jan & Good Fri. Amex, Diners, MasterCard, Visa.

Dublin 4 ˣ   *The Lobster Pot*

9 Ballsbridge Terrace Ballsbridge Dublin
RESTAURANT   Tel/Fax: 01 668 0025

Situated in a conspicuous position on the first floor of a redbrick Ballsbridge terrace, this long-established restaurant has lost none of its charm or quality over the years. How good it is to see old favourites like dressed Kilmore crab, home-made chicken liver pâté and fresh prawn bisque on the menu, along with fresh prawns Mornay and, that good old friend, Coq au Vin. All this and wonderfully old-fashioned service too. Long may it last. L£ Mon-Fri, D££ Mon-Sat. Closed 25 Dec, 1 Jan & Good Fri.

Dublin 8   *Locks Restaurant*

1 Windsor Terrace Portobello Dublin
RESTAURANT   Tel: 01 454 3391 Fax: 01 453 8352

Locks Restaurant is a very special place, in an old building with a lovely canalside setting. Inside it is furnished and decorated in a warm country house style and has a soothing atmosphere – soft lighting, open fires and a feeling that it has evolved rather than being designed by a decorator. Food and service echo that feeling – the short set menus for lunch and dinner offer the kind of food that might be served in a good country house; the seasonal à la carte menu is more ambitious in scale, but offers a similar combination of classic and country French and New Irish cooking; for example, a starter of Locks fish soup with aioli & croutons, and main courses such as roast loin of lamb with dauphinoise potatoes, caramelised onions, mushrooms & rosemary sauce. The cooking is sure, presentation very much in a house style and service professional.Wheelchair access. Children welcome. **Seats** 60 (private room, 30) No-smoking area.L 12:15-2:15 Mon-Fri. D 7:15-11 Mon-Sat. L&D à la carte available. House wine from £13.50. SC 12.5%. Closed Bank Hols, 2 wks during summer, 24 Dec-6 Jan. Amex, Diners, MasterCard, Visa.

Dublin 2   *Longfields Hotel*

9/10 Fitzwilliam Street Lower Dublin
Tel: 01 676 1367 Fax: 01 676 1542
HOTEL/RESTAURANT   email: lfields@indigo.ie

Located in a Georgian terrace right in the heart of Georgian Dublin, this hotel is more like a well proportioned private house, furnished with antiques in period style. Public areas are elegant and comfortable and bedrooms individually furnished, all with en-suite bath/shower. They vary considerably in size as rooms are smaller on the upper floors.

Staff are friendly and there is 24 hour room service. Morning coffee and afternoon tea are served in the drawing room. Children welcome (under 12s free in parents' room; cots available). No pets. **Rooms 26** (all en-suite, 13 shower only, 2 mini-suite, 6 executive rooms). Room rate £62.50 (max 2 guests). Lift. Closed 25-27 Dec. Amex, Diners, MasterCard, Visa. **No 10 Restaurant:** In the basement, with direct access from the hotel or the street, this compact well-appointed restaurant makes a popular venue for both lunch and dinner. Imaginative menus are based on seasonal local ingredients and cooks in a style combining French and Irish influences. French and Irish cheeses are offered, and a choice of coffee/speciality tea. **Seats 40** (private room, 20). L 12:30-2 Mon-Fri. D 6:30-10 Mon-Fri. Sat to 11. Sun D 7-9. Set L £14.95. Set D £28.95. Gourmet menu £50. L*D à la carte available. House wine £13.50. Toilets wheelchair accessible. SC 12.5%. No children after 8pm. Closed 24-26 Dec.

Dublin 8   *The Lord Edward*

23 Christchurch Place Dublin
RESTAURANT   Tel/Fax: 01 454 2420 email: ledward@indigo.ie

Dublin's oldest seafood restaurant is on three floors of a tall, narrow building overlooking Christchurch cathedral. Traditional in a decidedly old-fashioned way, The Lord Edward provides a complete contrast to the wave of trendy restaurants that has taken over Dublin recently, which is just the way a lot of people seem to like it. There are a few non-seafood options – traditional dishes like Irish stew, perhaps or corned beef and cabbage – and the seafood can be excellent. Simplest choices are usually best.Children welcome. **Seats 40.** L 12-3 Mon-Fri. D 6-10:45 Mon-Sat. Closed 24 Dec from dinner to 2 Jan. Amex, Diners, MasterCard, Visa.

Dublin 2✳ ✫   *Mange Tout*

112 Lower Baggot Street Dublin
RESTAURANT   Tel: 01 676 7866 Fax: 01 676 7821 email: tcremin@indigo.ie

This is a very friendly spot with quite a small formal dining room with subtle wall lighting; it attracts a lot of regulars and it's easy to see why.This is serious food, executed with a lot of confidence. Weekly set lunch and à la carte dinner menus have a classic base but manage plenty of modern twists. Starters might include the sweetest crab meat salad on a layer of marinated beetroot with curry crème fraîche and the most perfectly dressed Caesar style salad with smoked chicken and quail's eggs. A well flavoured sorbet follows, then main courses like perfectly cooked roast monkfish served on crushed new potatoes with a drizzling of chorizo oil or a super dish of roast supreme of chicken filled with black pudding and foie gras, served on an onion tart tatin and lightly bathed in tarragon. Mange tout also has a very decent wine list which manages to be interesting and offer good value. Classic deserts or an excellent selection of cheese to finish, all in impeccable condition. Staff are professional, charming and helpful. Children welcome. **Seats 30.** L 12:30-2:15 Tue-Fri. D 7-11 Tue-Sat. Set L from £10.50. Dinner à la carte. House wine from £13.50. SC discretionary. Closed Sat lunch, Sun & Mon, Bank Hols. Amex, MasterCard, Visa.

Dublin 2   *Café Mao*

2 Chatham Row Dublin
RESTAURANT   Tel: 01 670 4899 Fax: 01 670 4999

In simple but stylish surroundings, Café Mao brings to the Grafton Street area the cuisines of Thailand, Malaysia, Indonesia, Japan and China – about as "Asian Fusion" as it gets. The atmosphere at Mao is bright and very buzzy – having a queue at the door, as has happened here from the start, probably zips up the atmosphere a notch or two. Interesting food is based on seasonal ingredients, the standard of cooking is consistently good and so is value for money, although the bill can mount up quickly if you don't watch the number of Asian beers ordered. The "no reservations" policy seems to be working well for the restaurant, although it puts off some potential customers.Wheelchair access. Children welcome. **Seats 120.** No smoking area; air conditioning. Open daily. L 12-3. D 5:30-11. Menu à la carte. House wine from £10.95. SC discretionary (10% parties 6+). Closed Good Fri, Xmas, 1 Jan. MasterCard, Visa.

Dublin 13   *Marine Hotel*

Sutton Cross Dublin

HOTEL   Tel: 01 839 0000   Fax: 01 839 0442   email: info@marine.ie

This attractive, well-maintained hotel is on the sea side of a busy junction, with ample car parking in front and a lawn reaching down to the foreshore at the rear. Public areas, which have all been recently renovated, give a good impression; they include a smart foyer and adjacent bar, an informal conservatory style seating area overlooking the garden and a well-appointed restaurant. Refurbishment of bedrooms, some of which have sea views, is ongoing and 12 new executive rooms were due for completion by late autumn 1999. A popular venue for conferences and social gatherings, especially weddings – capacity up to 200. Banqueting (180). Indoor swimming pool. Garden. Wheelchair access. Parking. Children welcome (Under 4s free in parents' room; cots available). No pets. **Rooms 51** (all en-suite, 3 shower only, 23 executive rooms, 5 no-smoking). B&B £80pps, ss £20. Lift. Closed 24-27 Dec. Amex, Diners, MasterCard, Visa.

Dublin 4   *McCormack's Merrion Inn*

188 Merrion Road Dublin

PUB   Tel: 01 269 3816   Fax: 01 269 7669

The McCormacks are a great pub family (see separate entry for their Mounttown establishment) and this attractive contemporary pub on the main road between Dublin and Dun Laoghaire has always had a good name for food. At lunchtime chef John Teegan puts up an excellent buffet, with a choice of four hot main courses – a roast and a fish dish plus two others – as well as a wide range of salads; it's a well-organised operation and details (such as having chilled drinks to hand) are well-planned. In the evening the style moves up a notch or two, with a menu including the likes of warm crispy bacon & crouton salad, pastas, stir-fries and serious main courses such as medallions of fillet beef (chargrilled and served with a choice of sauces and salads). There are always a few good fish dishes and vegetarian options, and homely desserts always include homemade apple tart. Wheelchair access. Bar food served daily 12-10. Closed 25 Dec & Good Fri. Amex, Diners, MasterCard, Visa.

Dublin 2 ✻   *The Mercer Hotel*

Lower Mercer Street Dublin

Tel: 01 478 2179   Fax: 01 478 0328

HOTEL/RESTAURANT   email: mcrcsi@iol.ie

Tucked away behind the Royal College of Surgeons, this small, intimate hotel is a stone's throw away from Stephen's Green and Grafton Street. It aims to create a clubby home-from-home feel; bedrooms have comfortable, undemanding decor and facilities that would be expected of much larger hotels, including air conditioning, CD players, a fridge for your complimentary mineral water and bathrobes as standard. The 'Green Room' makes a good business venue too, for meeting and private dining for 1-120 people.Conference/banqueting (110/80). Business centre. Secretarial services. ISDN lines. Video conferencing. Wheelchair access. Parking. Children welcome (Under 3s free in parents' room; cots available). Pets by arrangement. **Rooms 21** (all en-suite, 21 executive rooms, 4 no-smoking, 1 for disabled). B&B £66pps, ss £34. Lift. Open all year. Amex, Diners, MasterCard, Visa. **Cusack's:** Comfortable and relaxed surroundings, unpretentious good cooking cheerfully served and well presented - no surprises here, the food comes just as it is described and is just a delight. Oak smoked Irish salmon with mixed leaves and pickled red onion and a seasonal salad with smoked chicken breast and toasted sesame seeds both make good starters and vegetarians are well looked after with the likes of home-made tagliatelle tossed in garlic cream, broccoli and blue cheese. Char-grilled pork chop, with pesto mash and herb jus would be a typical main course, well balanced and well cooked. But Cusack's is perhaps best at puddings - good, traditional desserts like warmed pecan pie with maple syrup and chocolate hazelnut torte with white chocolate sauce. Cusacks serves good food at reasonable prices and deserves to be better known. **Seats 40** (private room, 60). No-smoking area. Air conditioning.. L 12:30-2:30 Mon-Sat. D 6-10 Mon-Sat. Set L £11.95. Set D £25, early bird menu £14.50 6-7:30pm only. L&D à la carte available. House wine £10.50. SC discretionary.Toilets wheelchair accessible. Closed Sun.

Dublin 2   *La Mère Zou*

22 St Stephen's Green Dublin

RESTAURANT   Tel/Fax: 01 661 6669 email: merzou@indigo.ie

Situated in a Georgian basement not far from the Shelbourne Hotel, Eric Tydgadt's French/Belgian restaurant has been open since 1994 and just gets on with doing what it does best, without the fuss and flurry so many other restaurants are prone to at the moment. Although there are some concessions to current cuisine (especially on the lunch menu), this establishment's reputation is based on French country cooking, as in terrine of wild rabbit with pistachio nuts (albeit with a raspberry & onion compote), grilled chicken chasseur (with a mushroom, tomato & white sauce) and specialities such as steamed mussels (various ways) with French fries and even traditional Alsatian sauerkraut with four meats. Prices are reasonable, a policy carried through to the wine list too [* The associated business, Supper's Ready - an enlightened takeaway doing real food like coq au vin - operates from 51, Pleasant Street, Dublin, 8. Tel: 01-475 4556.] **Seats 55** (private room, 8) No-smoking area. L 12:30-2:30 Mon-Fri. D 6-10:30 daily, Sun to 9:30. Set L £10.50. Early bird menu £12.50 6-7:30pm only. L&D à la carte available. House wine £10.80. SC discretionary. Closed L Sat & Sun, 25 Dec-6 Jan. Amex, Diners, MasterCard, Visa.

Dublin 2   *Mermaid Café*

69-70 Dame Street Dublin

RESTAURANT   Tel: 01 670 8236 Fax: 01 670 8205 email: mermaid@iol.com

Interesting decor and imaginative American-inpired cooking are to be found at this restaurant on the edge of Temple Bar. Small, but with every inch of space used with style, owner-chef Benedict Gorman's cooking is among the best in the area and his front-of-house partner, Mark Harrell, is a quietly solicitous host. Examples to indicate the style include starters like New England crab cakes with piquant mayonnaise and smoked mackerel rillette with scallion and tomato salad. Terrific vegetarian main courses such as pumpkin & red onion tart with cumin & parmesan are to be found beside the likes of hearty home-made venison & port sausage with celeriac & elderberry gravy and 'Giant Atlantic Seafood Casserole', a speciality which changes daily depending on availability. Irish cheeses are imaginatively served and in good condition. Espresso and cappuccino arrive with crystallised pecan nuts. Wines are imported privately and are exclusive to the restaurant. Wheelchair access. Children welcome. **Seats 50** (private room, 24) No-smoking area. Air conditioning. L 12:30-2:30 daily, Sun to 3:30. D 6-11 daily, Sun to 9:30. Set D £22.50. L&D à la carte available. House wine from £12.95. SC discretionary (12.5% on parties of 6+) Toilets wheelchair accessible. Closed Xmas week. MasterCard, Visa.

Dublin 4   *Merrion Hall*

54-56 Merrion Road Ballsbridge Dublin

GUESTHOUSE   Tel: 01 668 1426 Fax: 01 668 4280 email: merrionhall@iol.ie

This spacious guesthouse opposite the RDS has recently been taken over by Pat Halpin, proprietor of Aberdeen Lodge, Dublin and Halpin's Hotel, Kilkee (see entries). Bedrooms are finished to a good standard, there's a comfortable roomy sitting room and some off-street parking. Small conference/private parties (50/50). Garden. Parking. Children welcome. No pets. **Rooms 24** (all en-suite, 4 suites, 20 executive rooms). B&B £40pps, ss £25. Open all year. Amex, Diners, MasterCard, Visa.

Dublin 2 🏛🚆   *The Merrion Hotel*

Upper Merrion Street Dublin

Tel: 01 603 0600 Fax: 01 603 0700

HOTEL/RESTAURANT   email: info@merrionhotel.com

Set in the heart of Georgian Dublin opposite the Government Buildings, the main house of this luxurious hotel comprises four meticulously restored Grade 1 listed townhouses built in the 1760s and restored to their former glory over two years; behind them, a contemporary garden wing has been added, overlooking two private period and formal landscaped gardens. Inside, Irish fabrics and antiques reflect the architecture and original interiors with rococo plasterwork ceilings and classically proportioned windows. The elegant and spacious Front Hall, with marble columns, features a series of murals for the neo-classical main stairwell by Martin Mooney, one of Ireland's foremost young artists (indeed, the hotel boasts one of the most important private collections of 20th-century art throughout), while the three interconnecting drawing rooms (one is the cocktail bar with a log fire), have French windows giving access to the gardens. The elegant and gracious bedrooms with individually controlled air-conditioning, have been beautifully designed by Alice Roden, and incorporate the very latest technology, ranging from three telephones, personalised voice-mail with remote access, fax/modem and ISDN lines and video conference facilities. In addition to the usual amenities there is a mini-bar and safe (VCRs and CD players are available on request). Sumptuous Italian marble bathrooms, with a separate walk-in shower, pamper guests to the extreme. The six meeting/private dining rooms combine state-of-the-art technology and Georgian splendour, contrasting with the arched and rough stone-walled Cellar Bar, originally the wine vaults. On the other hand, the splendid leisure complex, The Tethra Spa, with classical mosaics, is almost Romanesque. Staff, under the excellent direction of General Manager Peter MacCann, are quite exemplary and courteous, suggesting standards of hospitality from a bygone era. Complimentary underground valet parking. Restaurant Patrick Guilbaud (see separate entry) is also on site. Conference/banqueting (60/50). Secretarial services. ISDN lines. Video conferencing. Leisure centre. Garden. Wheelchair access. Parking. Children welcome. No pets. **Rooms 145** (all en-suite, 20 suites, 80 no-smoking, 6 for disabled). Room rate £250. Lift. Open all year. Amex, Diners, MasterCard, Visa. **Mornington's:** Executive chef Ed Cooney's dishes reflect the contemporary style of the elegant dining-room, combining fine Irish ingredients with Mediterranean cooking influences. An inexpensive table d'hôte lunch menu contrasts with more choices in the evening, but nonetheless shows off competent and precise cooking, backed up by excellent service. The wine list is grand, but prices are not over the top for such an illustrious establishment. **Seats 60** L 12:30-2 Sun-Fri. D 6-10 daily. Set L from £13. Pre-theatre menu from £16 6-7pm. Dinner à la carte. House wine £15. Toilets wheelchair accessible. No-smoking area. Air conditioning. Closed Sat lunch.

Dublin 4   *Mespil Hotel*

Mespil Road Dublin

HOTEL   Tel: 01 667 1222 Fax: 01 667 1244 email: mespil@leehotels.ie

This fine modern hotel enjoys an excellent location in the Georgian district of the city, overlooking the Grand Canal and within easy walking distance of the city centre. Public areas are spacious and elegant in an easy contemporary style and generously-sized bedrooms are comfortably furnished with good amenities. Facilities are also available for meetings and small conferences (up to 50) and banquets (110). Special breaks offer good value. Sister hotel to Sligo Park Hotel (see entry). Small conference (50). Wheelchair access. Parking. Children welcome (Under 12s free in parents' room; cots available). **Rooms 153** (all en-suite, 3 shower only, 11 executive rooms, 30 no-smoking, 8 for disabled). Room rate £85 (max 3 people). Lift. Closed 24-26 Dec. Amex, Diners, MasterCard, Visa.

Dublin 2   *Milano*

38 Dawson Street Dublin

RESTAURANT   Tel: 01 670 7744 Fax: 01 679 2717

This stylish modern restaurant at the top of Dawson Street is best known for its wide range of excellent pizzas (it's owned by the UK company PizzaExpress), but it's more of a restaurant than the description implies. They run a very popular crèche facility on Sunday afternoons (12-6) and live jazz on Monday evenings. A second branch opened in Temple Bar more recently and they have a jazz duo at Sunday lunchtime (2-4). Children welcome. **Seats 60.** No-smoking area. Air conditioning. Open 12pm-12am daily. Menu à la carte. House wine £10.95. SC discretionary (10% on parties of 10+). Closed Xmas. Amex, MasterCard, Visa.

Dublin 2   *Mont Clare Hotel*

Merrion Square Dublin

HOTEL   Tel: 01 607 3800 Fax: 01 661 5663 email: montclares@ocallaghanhotels.ie

A few doors away from the National Gallery, the Mont Clare is in common ownership with the nearby Davenport and Alexander Hotels. It has recently been totally renovated and refurbished and now has all the amenities expected of a good modern hotel. It is imaginatively decorated in contemporary style – except the old stained glass and mahogany Gallery Bar, which has retained its original pubby atmosphere. Compact bedrooms are well furnished and comfortable, with full marbled bathrooms and good amenities, including a personal safe. There are no on-site leisure facilities but guests have a complimentary arrangement with a nearby fitness centre. Conference/banqueting (120/120). Business centre. Secretarial services. Video conferencing. Parking. Children welcome (Under 2s free in parents' room; cots available). No pets. **Rooms 74** (2 mini-suite). B&B from £50ps, ss £50. Lift. Open all year. Amex, Diners, MasterCard, Visa.

Dublin 2 ❀   *Montys of Kathmandu*

28 Eustace Street Temple Bar Dublin

RESTAURANT   Tel: 01 670 4911   Fax: 01 495 0074   email: montys@eircom.net

The food here has real character at agreeably low prices. The room has the fast-food look, wipe-clean tables, black and white interior and a view into the kitchen so that you can get a glimpse of the food being cooked. The chefs are all from Nepal and although all the familiar dishes are represented there are definite undertones of Nepalese cooking throughout the menu. Friendly staff are more than happy to offer suggestions or choose a well balanced meal for you. Don't skip the appetisers - sheek kebabs are great and samosas are well spiced and crisp. Tandoori butter chicken is everything that it should be ; moist pieces of tender, tandoori chicken off the bone, cooked in a well balanced creamy masala sauce. If a problem ever arises, keenly attentive staff are at pains to rectify the situation - something that happens less often than it should. Wheelchair access. Children welcome. **Seats 60** (private room, 30) L 12-2:30 Mon-Sat. D 6-11:30 daily, Sun to 11. Early bird menu £10.50 6-7pm only. L&D à la carte available. House wine from £9.95. Closed Sun lunch, 25-26 Dec & Good Fri. Amex, MasterCard, Visa.

Dublin 2   *The Morgan*

10 Fleet Street Temple Bar Dublin

HOTEL   Tel: 01 679 3939   Fax: 01 679 3946   email: morganht@iol.ie

Situated in deepest Temple Bar, this unusual boutique hotel is characterised by clean simple lines and uncluttered elegance. Bedrooms have 6' beds in light beech, with classic white cotton bedlinen and natural throws. Standard bedroom facilities include satellite TV and video,CD/hi-fi system, mini-bar, safe, voicemail and internet access. There's a residents lounge, fitness room, masseuse and airconditioned meeting room. The All Sports Café next door also belongs to the hotel. Small conference (20). Wheelchair access. Children welcome (Under 12s free in parents' room; cots available). **Rooms 61** (all en-suite, 1 suite, 1 mini-suite, 20 no-smoking, 1 for disabled). Room rate £127 (max 3 guests). Lift. Closed 24-26 Dec. Amex, Diners, MasterCard, Visa

---

Dublin 1 ❀   *Morrison*

Lower Ormond Quay Dublin

Tel: 01 887 2400   Fax: 01 887 2499

HOTEL/RESTAURANT   email: info@morrisonhotel.ie

Located on Ormond Quay near the Ha'penny Bridge, this stunning new hotel is a first for Dublin. Created by the internationally renowned designer, John Rocha, east meets west here in an explosion of ideas which, however unlikely, seem to make perfect sense in such a confident pair of hands. Thus a simple, cool bedroom design - the essence of orderly thinking - does not seem at all at odds with the dramatic (some might say flamboyant) style of the public areas. It is interesting that this highly original hotel should be on the north quays, until recently neglected but the probable site of Dublin's most interesting developments during the coming decade. Wheelchair access. Parking by arrangement with nearby carpark. No children after 6pm. No pets. **Rooms 95** (all en-suite, 1 suite, 7 mini-suite, 42 no-smoking, 3 for disabled).Lift. B&B £87.50pps, no. Open all year. Amex, Diners, MasterCard, Visa. **Halo:** High drama comes into its own in the restaurant, which is on two levels, with angled mirrors giving a sense of unity (albeit depriving diners of precious privacy) and acres of curtains - notably a rich purple velvet - falling the full height. Regimented tables are too close together for comfort (or anything but the most mundane of polite conversation), service can be painfully slow and the cooking uneven although, at its best, it can be very good. Fish is a wise choice - the sushi plate is a good bet, for example - while a vegetarian special (papardelle with a little asparagus and not much else) is probably best avoided, although it must be said that the hotel was very recently opened on our visit. Prices are quite reasonable, however, and lunch, especially, offers good value. **Seats 80.** No-smoking area. Air conditioning. L 12:30-2 daily. D 7-10:30 daily. Set L £14.50. Set D £20, early bird menu £10 6-7pm only. L&D à la carte available. SC discretionary.Toilets wheelchair accessible.

Dublin 2 — *Muscat*

RESTAURANT

64 South William Street Dublin
Tel: 01 679 7699

Brian Cornish and Bernadette Doherty's tiny restaurant is in a very old building a couple of steps down from the street, and while the logistics of the operation are, theoretically, impossible (and it's fascinating to watch how they do actually work) the hospitality is warm and they hope to have some pavement seating for the 2000 season and to serve "interesting options' during the day in addition to the exisiting menus. Janice Timothy took over as head chef last winter and specialities include home-baked breads, notably cumin bread, and a starter of smoked chicken and caramelised onion spring roll with sesame seed crème fraîche & chilli jam and a main course of beef fillet infused with fresh herbs, served with a red onion dauphinoise and beetroot. and They even have very nice little loos with extras normally associated with much grander places. Children over 8 welcome. **Seats 38.** No-smoking area.L 12:30-2:15 Tue-Fri. D 6-11 Tue-Sat. Menu à la carte. House wine £12.95. SC 10%. Closed Sat lunch, Sun & Mon, 2 wks mid-September, 10 days after Xmas. Amex, MasterCard, Visa, Laser.

Dublin 8 ✻ [PUB★] — *Nancy Hands*

RESTAURANT/PUB

30-32 Parkgate Street Dublin
Tel: 01 677 0149 Fax: 01 677 0187

This remarkable pub is a sister establishment to the Hole in the Wall (see entry) and the proprietor, Martin McCaffrey, has done a great job on it, creating a new pub based on tradition but far from being a theme pub. Food is a priority, their menus are wide-ranging and imaginative - and, not surprisingly, Nancy Hands has already won some major awards for achievements in that area. It should go without saying that a good pub will stock an extensive selection of drinks but that, alas, is far from being the case - so raise a cheer to Nancy hands for its selection, which not only includes a wide choice of wines (including about 10 by the glass and two wines of the week) but also vodkas, whiskies and cocktails. Children welcome. **Seats 140.** No-smoking area. Air conditioningL 12-3 daily, Sun to 5. D 6-10:30 daily, Sun to 10. Set L £13. Early bird menu £13 5:30-7:30pm. Dinner à la carte. House wine £12. Toilets wheelchair accessible. SC discretionary. Closed 25 Dec & Good Fri. Amex, Diners, MasterCard, Visa.

Dublin 2 ✻ ✗ — *Nude Food*

RESTAURANT

21 Suffolk Street Dublin 2.
Tel: 01 672 5577

Nude is a new concept in fast food, providing fantastic organic (whenever possible) food in an ultra-cool environment. Just off Grafton Street it's a great place for a quick snack, with plenty of room to sit down at long canteen-style tables. The crowds and high turnover at this busy one-stop food shop mean the food is really fresh. Queue up MacDonald's style, order and pay at the till, then either your food is ready straight away or they'll bring it down to wherever you are sitting. Choose from a selection of soups (seafood chowder, mushroom or Thai chicken) served with freshly baked breads, hot wraps (chicken masala or potato & courgette) and panini (club nude or chicken & cashew) or try the chill cabinet for salads (Caesar, tomato & mozzarella), wraps (hummus, spinach & peppers or Cajun salmon) or soft bread rolls (smoked salmon & cream cheese). They also make freshly squeezed juices and smoothies - a shake-like concoction consisting of fresh fruits, juices and yoghurt blended with ice, with 25p a hit for nutritional boostings like ginseng, bee pollen and vitamin C complex to name but a few. While the portions may be small and the prices a little higher, you'll find yourself returning again and again.

Dublin 2 ☆ — *One Pico Restaurant*

RESTAURANT

1 Upper Camden Street Dublin
Tel: 01 478 0307 Fax: 01 475 7905
email: eamonnoreilly@ireland.com

Eamonn O'Reilly's elegant country house-style restaurant has a separate entrance although it is attached to the Camden Hall Hotel, which he also owns. Perhaps surprisingly, given the traditional surroundings, the cooking is distinctly contemporary, with worldwide leanings - and sophisticated, technically demanding dishes are executed with confidence and flair. Eamonn bases his menus on first class ingredients and it is their flavours that stand out, together with the precision of the cooking. Dishes typical of the global-influenced area of his culinary palette include tempura of native oysters may come with sesame, soy and lime and marinated rack of prime Irish lamb with semi-dried tomato, black olive & basil. At the other end of the spectrum - but with the same flair and attention to detail, New Irish Cuisine is represented in dishes like smoked loin of pork with champ mash, crispy onions, honey & poitin jus. Classic desserts are beautifully presented and also farmhouse cheeses, in tip-top condition, for those without a sweet tooth. Service is solicitous, the wine list agreeable. Own parking. Children welcome. **Seats 52** (private room, 30) No-smoking area. L 12-3 daily, Sun to 4. D 6-11 daily, Sun & Mon to 10. L&D à la carte. House wine £12. SC 10%. Early bird menu £14.50 6-7pm. Closed Xmas. Amex, Diners, MasterCard, Visa.

Dublin 2   *O'Neill's Public House*

2 Suffolk Street Dublin

PUB   Tel: 01 679 3656   Fax: 01 679 0689   email: mikeon@indigo.ie

A striking pub with its own fine clock over the door and an excellent corner location, it has been in the O'Neill family since 1920 and is equally popular with Dubliners and visitors alike. Students from Trinity and several other colleges nearby home into O'Neill's for its wide range of reasonably priced bar food, which includes a carvery with a choice of five roasts and an equal number of other dishes (including traditional favourites such as Irish Stew) each day. Wheelchair access. No children after 6pm. Bar food served 10:30-7 daily. Closed 25 & 26 Dec, Good Fri. Amex, Diners, MasterCard, Visa.

Dublin 8   *The Old Dublin*

90/91 Francis Street Dublin

RESTAURANT   Tel: 01 454 2028   Fax: 01 454 1406   email: olddub@indigo.ie

Eamonn Walsh's oasis of civilised dining is one of Dublin's longest-established fine restaurants. The standard of cooking is high and the food is lively, with new dishes regularly taking their place alongside established favourites. The dining area is broken up into several domestic-sized rooms with special features – a marble fireplace, some very good pictures – creating a cosy old-world atmosphere. While most famous for its Russian and Scandinavian specialities like blini (buckwheat pancake with cured salmon, prawns and herrings), and planked sirloin Hussar, which still feature on the à la carte, recent menus have been noticeably modern, with starters such as seared duck liver crostini followed by main courses like baked fillet of monkfish wrapped in speck, tomato and coriander dressing. Desserts include good home-made ices and a trio of farmhouse cheeses, served plated. A vegetarian menu is offered, also a reasonable early-bird 2-course dinner. Hospitable, thoughtful service. Children welcome. **Seats 65** (private room, 28) No-smoking area.L 12:30-3 Mon-Fri. D 6-11 Mon-Sat. Set L £10. Set D £21.50, early bird menu £12.50 6-7:30pm. A la carte D available. House wine £13.25. Closed Sat L, Sun, Bank Hols. Amex, Diners, MasterCard, Visa.

Dublin 7   *The Old Jameson Distillery*

Bow Street Dublin

RESTAURANT + PUB   Tel: 01 807 2355   Fax: 01 807 2369   email: rdempsey@iol.ie

While most visitors to Dublin will visit the recently restored Old Jameson Distillery to do the tour (which is fascinating), it's also a good spot for a bite to eat. There are special menus for groups (including evening functions, when the Distillery is not otherwise open) but The Still Room Restaurant is also open to individuals – light food served all day and lunch, featuring Irish specialities like bacon & cabbage soup and John Jameson casserole - and the standard of cooking is high. Wheelchair access. Children welcome. **Seats 100** (private room, 120) Food served daily from 9am. L 12-2:15 daily. D by arrangement for groups only, £21. Set L £8, à la carte available. House wine £10.95. Toilets wheelchair accessible. No-smoking area. Air conditioning. Closed 25 Dec & Good Fri. Amex, Diners, MasterCard, Visa.

Dublin 2   *The Old Stand*

37 Exchequer Street Dublin

PUB   Tel: 01 677 7220   Fax: 01 677 5849

This fine traditional pub, which is a sister establishment to Davy Byrnes, off Grafton Street and equally well-run, occupies a prominent position on the corner of Exchequer Street and St Andrew Street. It has a loyal following amongst the local business community, notably from the "rag trade" area around South William Street. They do a good line in reliable no-nonsense bar food at reasonable prices. A blackboard at the door proclaims daily specials as well as a selection of regulars from the menu – steaks (with or without sauce), grilled salmon steak, omelettes and chips, Irish stew and a vegetarian pasta dish of the day are all typical. Children over 7 welcome. Bar food served daily 12-9. Closed 25-26 Dec & Good Fri. MasterCard, Visa.

Dublin 2   *Pasta Fresca*

2, 3 & 4 Chatham Street Dublin

RESTAURANT   Tel: 01 679 2402 Fax: 01 668 4563

This chic Italian wine bar-delicatessen is just off the Grafton Street shopping area. The popular all-day menu is based on good home-made pastas, interesting vegetarian options and a wide range of salads with well-made dressings. Evening menus offer more choice. Children welcome. **Seats 80** (private room, 20). No-smoking area. Air conditioning.Open 11am-12am daily, Sun 1-9. Menu à la carte. House wine £11.SC discretionary. Toilets wheelchair accessible. Closed 25-26 Dec. Amex, Diners, MasterCard, Visa.

Dublin 2 ✳   *The Pembroke*

31 Lower Pembroke Street Dublin

PUB   Tel: 01 676 2980 Fax: 01 676 6579

There was consternation amongst traditionalists when this fine old pub was given a complete makeover a couple of years ago, creating the bright and trendy bar that it is now. But, even if the open fires and cosiness of old has now gone for ever, the spacious new bar that has been created has character of its own and, along with some striking design features (notably lighting), the atrium/ conservatory area at the back brings the whole place to life. Meeting the needs of those who get in to work before the traffic builds up, bar food begins with breakfast **Seats 300.** Food served 7am-10 pm, Mon-Sat; carvery lunch,12-2:30. Closed 25-26 Dec & Good Fri. Amex, Diners, MasterCard, Visa.

Dublin 2 ✳   *The Pembroke Restaurant*

31 Lower Pembroke Street Dublin

RESTAURANT   Tel: 01 6762994

Climb the narrow stairs beside the pub and you will reach the dining room which also has a small bar area - thankfully, the zeal for reinvention that radically changed the atmosphere of the bar below has not reached the first floor and The Pembroke remains a very cosy, comfortable restaurant where they greet all their customers like old friends. It has an intimate, almost club-like feel with a welcoming turf fire glowing in the hearth.The room seems to almost be in a time warp and looks a bit like someone's dining room. Manager/chef Margaret Hyland's food is bistro-style with plenty of daily specials to whet the appetite. Steaks are excellent and shellfish is cooked to perfection. However, crockery is old-fashioned in the wrong sense of the word and fails to do justice to the food - a comment which could also apply to using a couple of limp lettuce leaves as garnish. But, beyond such details, please don't change it - there are not many places like this left and The Pembroke knows how to take care of people and it's easy to imagine that dinner here could easily run into the early hours of the morning. No children after 7pm. **Seats 70** (private room, 35). L 12.30-3 Mon-Fri, D 6-11; Set D £23.95; early bird £10.95 6-7.30. House wine from £11.50. SC 12.5%. Closed Sun. Amex, Diners, MasterCard, Visa.

Dublin 2 ✗   *Pizza Stop*

6-10 Chatham Lane Dublin

RESTAURANT   Tel: 01 679 4769

This cheap and cheerful little restaurant has been doing good pizzas in style since the late '80s. Just the place to meet up with the family for a tasty meal that won't break the bank. Also good for nightbirds since it stays open until 2 am every day. o Meals£ daily o

Dublin 6 ✗   *Poppadom*

91a Rathgar Road, Dublin

RESTAURANT   Tel: 01 490 2383

Attractively modern and airy, with mustard seed yellow walls, cushioned linen-clad tables and brightly coloured, comfortable chairs, this restaurant menu promises to show just how exquisite and diverse Indian cooking can be. The menu offers some appealingly unusual dishes although, on a recent visit, the standard of cooking was surprisingly inconsistent. Chimbori vada (crispy crab cakes), for example, failed to make the promised impact, while Laddakh chlena, described as a warm goat's cheese fondue set on a flaky 'Taftaan' (layered bread from the northern frontier) was an odd concoction that had no place on an Indian restaurant menu. On the plus side, Gulla kebab (paupiettes of chicken stuffed with pine nuts and sultanas cooked in a spicy fenugreek yoghurt crust) and Chowpatty onda (savoury potato dumplings topped with 'coconut gunpowder') had authenticity on their side - but would have been more enjoyable had they been cooked to order. Shorshey bata maachh, a classical Bengalese red snapper curry was the most interesting dish and one worth going back for, but a very strange sickly-sweet Korma shirazi let the side down again. Service, however, was excellent and a replacement dish, Chicken karahi, was immediately offered; this was delicious and very well spiced and Limbu bhaat, lime rice was an interesting, if subtle change from the standard boiled rice.The masala tea was exceptionally good, made with leaf tea and cardamom pods. Overall, in a city where authentic Indian cuisine is hard to find, this restaurant is worth a journey. Children welcome. **Seats 46.** No-smoking area. Air conditioning. D 6-11:45 daily. Menu à la carte. House wine from £10. SC discretionary.Toilets wheelchair accessible. Closed 25-26 Dec. Diners, MasterCard, Visa.

Dublin 6W   *Popjoys Restaurant*

4 Rathfarnham Road Terenure Dublin

RESTAURANT   Tel: 01 492 9346 Fax: 01 492 9293

Chef-proprietor Warren Massey opened this neighbourhood restaurant in August '96 and is now running it with his brother Denis, who is also a chef. The dining room is comfortable and well-appointed, cooking is based on the best of local and seasonal ingredients – and these qualities, plus good service, have attracted a loyal following. Children welcome. **Seats 70** (private room, 35) No-smoking area. Air conditioning. L 12:30-3 Tue-Sun, Sun to 4. D 6-10:30 Tue-Sat. Set L from £8.50. Set D £30, early bird menu £15 6-7pm. L&D à la carte available. House wine £13. SC discretionary. Closed Sun D, Mon, Tues after Bank Hols,1 wk Xmas, first 2 wks August. Amex, Diners, MasterCard, Visa.

Dublin 2 [PUB★]   *The Porterhouse*

16-18 Parliament Street Temple Bar Dublin

PUB   Tel: 01 679 8847 Fax: 01 670 9605 email: porterh.indigo.ie

When this stunning pub opened in 1996, it changed Dubliners' perception of what a pub could be, opening up a whole new range of possibilities that simply hadn't been considered before. It was Ireland's first micro-brewery pub and, although several others have since set up and are doing an excellent job, The Porterhouse started this admirable new trend in the brewing of beer. Ten different beers are brewed on the premises, several of which have won international awards, and beer connoisseurs can sample a special "tasting tray" selection of plain porter (a classic light stout), oyster stout (brewed with fresh oysters, the logical development of a perfect partnership), Wrasslers 4X (based on a west Cork recipe from the early 1900s, and said to be Michael Collins' favourite tipple), Porter House Red (an Irish Red Ale with traditional flavour), An Brain Blasta (dangerous to know) and the wittily named Temple Brau. But you don't even have to like beer to love The Porterhouse. The whole concept is an innovative move away from the constraints of the traditional Irish pub and yet it stays in tune with its origins – it is emphatically not just another theme pub. The attention to detail which has gone into the decor and design is a constant source of pleasure to visitors – the bottles in glass cases that line the walls, the brewing-related displays in glass-topped tables – and the food, while definitely not gourmet, is a cut above the usual bar food and, like the pub itself, combines elements of tradition with innovation. This is a real Irish pub in the modern idiom and was a respected winner of our Pub of the Year award in 1999. No children after 7pm. Bar food served 12:30-9:30 daily. Closed 25 Dec & Good Fri. MasterCard, Visa. The original Porterhouse is located on Strand Road on the seafront in Bray, Co Wicklow, and like its sister pub in Temple Bar, it offers bar food daily from 12:30-9:30. No children after 7pm. Closed 25 Dec & Good Fri. MasterCard, Visa.Tel/Fax: 01 286 1839.

Dublin 2 ✳   *QV2 Restaurant*

14-15 St Andrew Street Dublin
RESTAURANT   Tel/Fax: 01 677 3363

Handy to Grafton Street and all the city centre attractions, this popular restaurant accurately describes itself as offering "International cuisine with an Irish twist." Eoin McDonnell, head chef since 1991 builds his menus around fresh seasonal produce and hits just the right note on interesting menus that also give good value, especially for lunch and the early bird dinner. Specialities incluse Eoin's Fish Pie - lots of big chunks of fish in a white wine & parsley sauce, with a crispy filo crust - and Fillet of Lamb Daniel Patrick, with fresh mint mash and a honey & mint mayonnaise. The street level room has more atmosphere, but the basement improves as it fills up. Nice, helpful staff; reasonably priced wine list. Children welcome. **Seats 140** (private room, 40) No-smoking area. Air conditioning. L 12-3 Mon-Sat. D 6-12:30 Mon-Sat. Set L £16. Set D £24. L&D à la carte available. House wine £11.50. . SC discretionary (10% on parties of 8+). Closed Sun, 2 Bank Hols, Xmas & Good Fri. Amex, Diners, MasterCard, Visa.

Dublin 4   *Raglan Lodge*

10 Raglan Road Ballsbridge Dublin
GUESTHOUSE   Tel: 01 660 6697 Fax: 01 660 6781

Helen Moran's elegant mid19th-century residence is peacefully situated near the US embassy, yet convenient to the city centre, which is only a 10-15 minute walk away. Well-proportioned, high-ceilinged reception rooms are reminiscent of more leisurely times and the en-suite bedrooms are exceptionally comfortable, with all the necessary amenities. Having been restored and converted to its present use in 1987, Raglan Lodge is now one of the city's most desirable guesthouses – not only for the high level of comfort and service provided, but most particularly, for outstanding breakfasts. Theatre reservations can be arranged.Parking. Children welcome. **Rooms 7** (all en-suite, 2 no-smoking). B&B £50pps, ss £10. Closed 22 Dec-6 Jan. Amex, Diners, MasterCard, Visa.

Dublin 2   *Rajdoot Tandoori*

26 Clarendon Street Dublin
RESTAURANT   Tel: 01 679 4280 Fax: 01 679 4274

A member of a small UK chain of restaurants specialising in subtle, aromatic North Indian cuisine, this restaurant has had a fine reputation for its food and service since it opened in 1984. Tandoori dishes are the main speciality, based on a wide range of ingredients authentically cooked. Set price daily menus include a keenly priced 4-course lunch (£7.95).Wheelchair access. Children over 6 welcome until 7pm. **Seats 92** L 12-2:30 daily. D 6:30-11:30 daily, Sun to 10:30. Set L £8.95. Set D from £18, early bird menu £15 6:30-7:30pm. House wine £11. No-smoking area. Air conditioning. SC discretionary. Closed 25-26 Dec, 1 Jan & Good Fri. Amex, Diners, MasterCard, Visa.

Dublin 6   *Rathmines Plaza Hotel*

Lower Rathmines Road Rathmines Dublin
HOTEL   Tel: 01 496 6966 Fax: 01 491 0603

Secure parking across the road is a distinct advantage for this modern hotel a few minutes' drive from the city centre in the characterful Rathmines district. Spacious bedrooms, each with a good tiled bathroom, offer above-average facilities including fax and computer points, and breakfast is taken in a rustic themed restaurant/bar (that can get very lively at night). Notably friendly staff. Wheelchair access. Parking. Children (Under 12s free in parents' room; cots available). No pets. **Rooms 54** (29 shower only, 3 for disabled). B&B £45pps. Lift. Closed 24-26 Dec. Amex, Diners, MasterCard, Visa.

Dublin 22   *Red Cow Moran's Hotel*

Red Cow Complex Naas Road Dublin
HOTEL   Tel: 01 459 3650 Fax: 04 459 1588 email: sales@morangroup.ie

Strategically located close to the motorway and known as a pub for many years, the Red Cow is now an impressive hotel. A grand staircase sweeping up from the marble lobby gives an indication of the style to follow and, although it will only be of interest to private guests, this is definitely a location to check out if you are considering visiting the area on business or wish to organise conferences or meetings. Bedrooms are all of executive standard, with excellent amenities for business guests including voice mail and fax/modem lines. The purpose-built conference centre offers a wide range of facilities and ample car parking. Conference/banqueting (720/550) Secretarial services. Video conferencing. Wheelchair access. Parking. Children welcome (Under 2s free in parents' room; cots available). No pets. **Rooms 123** (all en-suite, 8 suites, 115 executive rooms, 44 no-smoking, 5 for disabled). B&B £85pps, ss £20. Lift. Closed Xmas. Amex, Diners, MasterCard, Visa.

Dublin 2 ★   *Restaurant Patrick Guilbaud*

RESTAURANT

21 Upper Merrion Street Dublin
Tel: 01 676 4192 Fax: 01 661 0052

The capital's premier French restaurant occupies an elegant ground-floor restaurant in the Main House of The Merrion Hotel, opening on to a terrace and landscaped garden (with al fresco eating in fine weather). Although access can also be gained via the hotel, the main entrance is through the original front door to the 1760s Georgian townhouse. Fine works by Irish artists (Roderic O'Connor, Mary Swanzy, Louis le Brocquy and William Scott, to name but a few – look out especially for Harry Kernoff's 'Jammet's Restaurant', probably Dublin's finest restaurant in the Sixties) are a major decorative feature, making a very fine setting for one of Ireland's most renowned restaurants. Head chef Guillaume Le Brun presides over a fine kitchen and presents wide-ranging à la carte and set menus - the table d'hôte lunch is a snip at £22 and the £75 menu surprise is just that – you are only told what the dishes are, as they are served. Contemporary French cooking is what you get, albeit with a nod to traditional Irish influences, so the best of Irish ingredients, combined with the precision and talents of a team of gifted chefs, produces dishes of dexterity, appeal and flavour. Desserts are particularly interesting – a Nougatine Millefeuille served with an amazing caramelised Fennel Confit is an unlikely-sounding but superbly successful dish and a worthy winner of our Dessert of the Year Award in 1999. Cheeses come from Philippe Olivier, breads are home-made, and the mostly French wine list includes some great classics, with some reasonably-priced offerings. Service is immaculate. Children welcome. **Seats 85** (private room, 24) No-smoking area. Air conditioning. L 12:30-2 Tue-Sat. D 7:30-10:15 Tue-Sat. Set L £22. Gourmet menu £75. L&D à la carte available. House wine from £18. SC discretionary. Toilets wheelchair accessible.Closed Sun & Mon, 25- 6 Jan. Amex, Diners, MasterCard, Visa.

Dublin 18 ❊   *Rodney's Bistro*

RESTAURANT

Cabinteely Village Dublin
Tel: 01 285 1664

Busy, buzzy with closely packed tables, great atmosphere - this little neighbourhod restaurant could be described as the definitive bistro. Friendly service and very good cooking explain its great popularity with the locals. Fish is a particularly strong point - monkfish, plaice, cod and even lobster could be among the daily specials and game comes onto the menu in season. An informative wine list is a little short. Not suitable for children. **Seats 38** D 7-10 Tue-Sat. Menu à la carte. House wine £11.50. Air conditioning. SC 10%. Closed Sun & Mon, 2 wks July, 2 wks Jan. Amex, MasterCard, Visa.

Dublin 4 ✗   *Roly's Bistro*

RESTAURANT

7 Ballsbridge Terrace Ballsbridge Dublin
Tel: 01 668 2611 Fax: 01 660 8535

A smash hit since the day it opened, a visit to this bustling Ballsbridge bistro invariably begins with a warm welcome – usually from Roly Saul or his partner John O'Sullivan (on duty at the desk). Aperitifs at the table are quickly followed by a selection of breads and the menu. Head chef Colin O'Daly is one of Ireland's most highly regarded chefs and has been part-owner of the restaurant since it opened in 1992. He presents imaginative, reasonably priced menus at lunch and an evening à la carte menu, all changed fortnightly. The style is based on Colin's classical French experience but it also gives more than a passing nod to Irish traditions and world cuisines. Thus, starters of grainy Clonakilty Black Pudding wrapped in Brioche served on a well-reduced glaze and pleasingly runny, crisp-coated Deep-fried Brie served with a complementary Braised Red Cabbage & Apple Salad. Similarly, main courses of Roast Loin of Pork with Cajun Spices and Dublin Bay Prawns Newberg, which have become something of a speciality and come with a tian of mixed long grain and wild rice. Wholesomely delicious puddings are worth saving a space for: Pear & Apple Bake with Cinnamon Cream, perhaps, or dark chocolate and apricot slice. Service is generally efficient but discreet.

Dublin 2   *Royal Garden Chinese Restaurant*

Westbury Centre Clarendon Street Dublin

RESTAURANT   Tel: 01 679 1397 Fax: 01 626 7643

Since the early 1980s this well-appointed Chinese restaurant at the back of the Westbury Hotel has been pleasing a loyal local clientele and visitors to the city with its authentic Cantonese cooking and excellent service. Children welcome. **Seats 70.** Air conditioning.L 12:30-2:30 daily, Sun to 4. D 6-12am. Set L from £7, Set Sun L from £8. L&D à la carte available. House wine £10. SC discretionary (12.5% on dinner). Toilets wheelchair accessible.Closed 25-26 Dec & Good Fri. Amex, Diners, MasterCard, Visa.

Dublin 8 ✗   *Ryans of Parkgate Street*

28 Parkgate Street Dublin

PUB   Tel: 01 671 9352 Fax: 01 671 3590

Ryans is one of Ireland's finest and best-loved original Victorian pubs. Its most distinguishing feature is its atmosphere, but there is also magnificent stained glass, original mahogany bar fixtures and an outstanding collection of antique mirrors. Good bar food is available at lunch time and in the evening, and there's a separate restaurant upstairs. Meals£-££ Closed first 2 wks Jan & Bank Hols.

Dublin 2   *Saagar Indian Restaurant*

16 Harcourt Street Dublin

RESTAURANT   Tel: 01 475 5060/5012 Fax: 01 475 5741 email: saagar@iol.ie

Saagar, Meera and Sunil Kumar's basement restaurant just off St Stephen's Green, is one of the most authentic and highly-respected ethnic restaurants in Ireland. The restaurant offers a wide range of speciality dishes, all prepared from fresh ingredients and thoughtfully coded with a range of one to four stars to indicate the heat level. Thus Malai Kabab (chicken marinated in traditional spices) is a safe one-star dish, while traditional Lamb Balti and Lamb Aayish (marinated with exotic spices and cooked in a cognac-flavoured sauce) is a three-star and therefore pretty hot. The vegetarian selection is good, as is to be expected of an Indian restaurant, and the side dishes, such as Naan breads which are made to order in the tandoori oven, are excellent. The Kumars also have restaurants in Athlone and Mullingar. Children welcome. **Seats 70.** L 12:30-2:30 Mon-Fri. D 6-11:30 daily. Set L from £6. Gourmet menu £40. L&D à la carte available. House wine £11. Toilets wheelchair accessible. No-smoking area. SC discretionary. Closed Sat & Sun L, 24-27 Dec. Amex, Diners, MasterCard, Visa.

Dublin 4   *The Schoolhouse Hotel*

2-8 Northumberland Road Ballsbridge Dublin

HOTEL   Tel: 01 667 5014 Fax: 01 667 5015

Dating back to its opening in 1896 as a school, this building beside Mount Street Bridge has seen many changes lately, culminating in its opening in 1998 as one of Dublin's trendiest small hotels. The Inkwell Bar is always a-buzz with young business people of the area. Rooms are finished to a high standard, with air conditioning, power showers and the usual amenities expected of a quality hotel. Small conference (20). Wheelchair access. Parking. Children welcome (Under 4s free in parents' room; cots available). No pets. **Rooms 31** (all en-suite, 15 no-smoking, 2 for disabled). B&B £139pps, no ss. Lift. Closed 24-27 Dec. Amex, Diners, MasterCard, Visa.

Dublin 2   *Shalimar Indian Restaurant*

17 South Great Georges Street Dublin

RESTAURANT   Tel: 01 671 0738 Fax: 01 677 3478 email: anwar@iol.ie

Just across the road from the Central Hotel this welcoming, well-appointed basement restaurant serves generous portions of a wide-range of Indian dishes. Balti dishes are a speciality – diners are invited to mix and match items on the menu to suit individual tastes – and there's also a wide choice of Tandoori and Biryani basmati rice dishes. This is a friendly, relaxing restaurant and prices are reasonable.Wheelchair access. Parking by arrangement with nearby carpark. Children welcome. **Seats 100** (private room, 50) L 12-2:30 daily. D 5-12 daily. Open 12pm-12am all day Sun. Set L £7.95, Set Sun L £8.95. Set D from £15. Gourmet menu £25. Early bird menu £10.95 5-7:30pm. L&D à la carte available. House wine £10.95. No-smoking area. Air conditioning. SC 10%. Closed Xmas & Good Fri. Amex, Diners, MasterCard, Visa.

Dublin 2 🏛🏛   *Shelbourne Hotel*

27 St Stephen's Green Dublin
Tel: 01 676 6471 Fax: 01 661 6006
HOTEL/RESTAURANT   email: info@shelbourne.ie

One of Ireland's most historic buildings – the Irish Constitution was drafted here – this opulent 18th-century hotel is still central to Dublin life today, and the many improvements which have recently taken place ensure its ranking among the world's great hotels. Overlooking Europe's largest garden square, St Stephen's Green, the hotel has retained all its grandeur, and the entrance creates a strong impression with its magnificent faux-marble entrance hall and Lord Mayor's Lounge, a popular meeting place for afternoon tea. The Shelbourne Bar on Kildare Street is relatively new but the Horseshoe Bar, renowned as a meeting place for local politicians and theatrical society, is nothing short of a Dublin institution. Under the direction of general manager Jean Ricoux, who joined the hotel in 1997, major renovation has taken place. As it is an old building, accommodation varies somewhat. The best rooms and suites are very luxurious, but new rooms have recently been added and all rooms are well-appointed, with good bathrooms, bathrobes, mini-bars and three telephones as standard. In 1998 a Health, Fitness & Relaxation Centre was opened, with 18 metre swimming pool, sauna, jacuzzi, steam room, aerobics and state-of-the-art workout equipment, with individual tv screens and headphones.The hotel has two restaurants, No 27 The Green (see below) and The Side Door At The Shelbourne (12-10:45 daily) which has a separate entrance from Kildare Street and, with its striking minimalist decor and Cal-Ital menus, provides a complete contrast to the ultra-traditional atmosphere of the hotel. The Side Door can also be reached via The Shelbourne Bar.(Bar food Mon-Fri 11-11. Closed Sun.) Valet parking. A 15% service charge is added to all bills. Conference/banqueting (400/320). Business centre. Fitness centre (indoor swimming pool). Wheelchair access. Parking. Children. Pets permitted. **Rooms 190** (all en-suite). B&B from £175pps, SC 15%. Lift. Open all year. Amex, Diners, MasterCard, Visa. **No 27 The Green:** This elegant and lofty dining-room offers some very good cooking, combining the best of Irish produce with some traditional/continental flair and expertise. Alongside the daily-changing table d'hôte menus (four choices of starter and main course with dinner providing an additional soup course), there's a substantial à la carte. Specialities, which are strongly seasonal, typically include the best Irish beef in cote de bouef, prime seafood such as Lobster and Dublin Bay prawns and game in season. All in all, this is a well-run restaurant, serving excellent food. Several breads are offered with butter or, as a healthy option, a dish of raw diced vegetables. Service is ultra-professional. **Seats 65.** No-smoking area. L 12:30-2:30 Sun-Fri. D 6:30-10:30 Mon-Sat, Sun 6-10. Set Sun L £19.50. Set D £28.50. L&D à la carte available. House wine from £14.SC 15%. Toilets wheelchair accessible. Closed Sat lunch.

Dublin 1 ✗   *The Stag's Head*

1 Dame Court Dublin
PUB   Tel: 01 679 3701

In Dame Court, just behind the Adams Trinity Hotel, this impressive establishment has retained its original late-Victorian decor and is one of the city's finest pubs. A recent visit was disappointing - dusty and sticky surfaces suggested a lack of routine housekeeping - but it is to hoped this was only a temporary lapse as it's a really lovely pub. Closed 25 Dec & Good Fri.

Dublin 2   *La Stampa*

35 Dawson Street Dublin
RESTAURANT   Tel: 01 677 8611 Fax: 01 677 3336 email: dine@lastampa.ie

Reminiscent of a grand French belle epoque brasserie, this is one of Ireland's finest dining rooms – high-ceiling, large mirrors, wooden floor, Roman urns, statues, busts, candelabra, Victorian lamps, plants, flowers and various bits of bric-a-brac, the whole noisily complemented by a constant bustle, the staff's bright waistcoats, and the sight of food being whirled into place. On entering, there's a small bar with a few comfortable seats where you can sip a drink while studying a menu that encompass dishes from around the world. Typical examples might include: fresh oysters with shallot vinegar or French onion soup with Gruyere croutons and main courses such as fillet of turbot with champ, green pea and herb sauce and fillet of beef Rossini with spinach and Dauphinoise potatoes. A classic tarte tatin might be served with yoghurt ice cream, or a duo of strawberry and coconut mousse with a lemon sorbet. Good coffee and some excellent wines on an inexpensive list, including several by the glass.This is a fun and lively place, offering international food in delightful surroundings. At the time of going to press La Stampa was about to open an hotel next door. No children after 9pm. **Seats 150** L 12:30-2:30 Mon-Fri. D 5:30-12am Mon-Fri, 6-12:30am Sat, 6:30-11:30 Sun. Early bird menu from £14.50 5:30-7pm Mon-Fri. L&D à la carte available. No-smoking area. Air conditioning. SC discretionary (10% on parties of 6+). Closed Sat & Sun L, 25-26 Dec, Good Fri & Easter Sunday. Amex, Diners, MasterCard, Visa.

Dublin 2   *Stauntons on the Green*

83 St Stephen's Green Dublin
GUESTHOUSE   Tel: 01 478 2300   Fax: 01 487 2263   email: hotels@indigo.ie

Well-located with views over St Stephen's Green at the front and its own private gardens at the back, this guesthouse – which is in an elegant Georgian terrace and has fine period reception rooms – offers moderately priced accommodation of a good standard, with all the usual amenities.It's in the heart of the business and banking district and the Grafton Street shopping area is just a stroll across the Green. Meeting rooms are available, with secretarial facilities on request.Children welcome. No pets. **Rooms 36** (all en-suite, 20 shower only). B&B £55pps, ss £15. Closed 24-27 Dec. Amex, Diners, MasterCard, Visa.

Dublin 2 ✳   *Stephen's Green Hotel*

St Stephen's Green Dublin
Tel: 01 607 3600   Fax: 01 661 5663
HOTEL   email: stephensgreenres@ocallaghanhotels.ie

This new hotel on a corner site overlooking St Stephen's Green opened just as the Guide was going to press and is the latest in the O'Callaghan Hotels group (Alexander, Davenport, Mont Clare - see entries). Public areas include an impressive foyer and, in memory of the writer George Fitzmaurice who used to live here, "Pie Dish" restaurant and "Magic Glasses" bar - both named after titles from his work. Guestrooms have exceptionally good facilities, particularly for business travellers, including airconditioning, writing desk, voice mail and modem line as standard. (Small conference (25). Business centre. Secretarial services. ISDN lines. Video conferencing. Leisure centre. Wheelchair access. Children (Under 2s free in parents' room; cots available). No pets. **Rooms 75** (all en-suite, 11 suites, 30 no-smoking). B&B from £80pps. Lift. Open all year. Amex, Diners, MasterCard, Visa.

Dublin 2 ✳   *Tante Zoes*

1 Crow Street Temple Bar Dublin
RESTAURANT   Tel: 01 679 4407   Fax: 01 670 7559   email: robbief@indigo.ie

Tante Zoe's is a dark, relaxing place, kitted out in dark wood, bamboo and cloth covered tables, with old posters and signs from the deep south on the walls and equally suitable for a romantic dinner à deux or a group of pals out for the night. A first time visitor asking for recommendations might begin with Cajun popcorn - a huge mound of juicy baby shrimps coated in crispy spiced breadcrumbs and served with a Marie Rose-style sauce or crab cakes, set on a beautifully decorated plate, glistening with zigzags of different coloured dressings. For mains, Shrimp Creole with (unexciting) rice comes with a well seasoned spicy tomato sauce with plump jumbo shrimps and succulent, crisp-coated blackened chicken has a spiced cream sauce. Side dishes include a Moroccan version of gratin Dauphinois and Maque choux (sweetcorn cooked with peppers, onion and tomato). Genuinely attentive waiting staff contribute to the relaxed atmosphere - and make informed suggestions - bread pudding with whiskey sauce is dead on, a cross between a light Christmas pudding and the best bread & butter pudding ever. Not suitable for children under 10. **Seats 160** (private room, 100) No-smoking area. Open daily 12 noon-midnight, closed 4-5 Sun. Set L £15. Early bird menu £12 6-7pm. L&D à la carte available. SC discretionary (10% on parties of 6+). Closed Xmas & Good Fri. Amex, Diners, MasterCard, Visa.

Dublin 7   *Ta Se Mahogani Gaspipes*

17 Manor Street Stoneybatter Dublin
Tel: 01 679 8138   Fax: 01 670 5353
RESTAURANT   email: kinsley@gofree.indigo.ie

In a small American-style restaurant in Stoneybatter, a very pleasant neighbourhood of the city near Phoenix Park, away from the bustle of Temple Bar (in the "undiscovered"

Dublin). Drina Kinsley prepares an eclectic menu strong on spicy fare like Prawns pingelo with crunchy noodles, mangetout, snow peas & black bean sauce. There's a fresh fish special daily - John Dory withwith home-made breadcrumbs, baked in a lemon balm & butter sauce, perhaps - and a late night jazz menu. Not suitable for children under 7 after 9pm. **Seats 50.** No-smoking area.L 12-3 Tue-Sat. D 6-10 Tue-Th, 6-12 Fri-Sat.Early bird menu £11.95 6-8pm. L&D à la carte available. House wine from £10.95. SC 10%. Closed Sun & Mon, Bank Hols & 25-26 Dec. Diners, MasterCard, Visa.

Dublin 2 — *Temple Bar Hotel*

Fleet Street Temple Bar Dublin

HOTEL — Tel: 01 677 3333 Fax: 01 677 3088

This pleasant hotel is handy for both sides of the river. Spacious reception and lounge areas create a good impression and bedrooms are generally larger than average, almost all with a double and single bed and good amenities. Neat, well-lit bathrooms have over-bath showers and marble wash basin units. No parking, but the hotel has an arrangement with a nearby car park.Conference/banqueting (90/80). Wheelchair access. Children welcome. No pets. **Rooms 130** (all en-suite, 1 suite, 30 no-smoking, 2 for disabled). B&B £65pps, ss £45. Lift. Closed 24-26 Dec. Amex, Diners, MasterCard, Visa.

Dublin 2 ✗ — *Thomas Read*

Parliament Street Dublin

CAFÉ/BAR — Tel: 01 677 1487

This bustling café-bar was one of the first of its type and it is still one of the best. Attracting a wide variety of customers – including literary types from Trinity College and nearby newspapers – it serves a good cup of coffee, with (or without) light food. Its corner position and large windows looking down to Dame Street make this a fine place to sit and watch the world go by. Closed 25 Dec & Good Fri.

Dublin 8 — *Thornton's*

1 Portobello Road Dublin

RESTAURANT — Tel: 01 454 9067 Fax: 01 453 2947

Seriously good cooking in a seriously good restaurant is to be found in this corner premises overlooking the canal. Muriel Thornton and her team of French waiting staff set the tone from the outset, providing a highly professional service to complement Kevin Thornton's superb cooking. There is a small reception bar downstairs (from which guests can see into the kitchen) and a private dining-room, with the main dining areas (candle-lit at night) upstairs in two rooms. Decor is modern and understated with muslin drapes, "distressed" painted tiles and a tall vase of flowers catching the eye. Service is impeccable, from the moment a basket of breads (fennel rolls, tomato and basil, walnut etc) arrive to the final presentation of assorted petits fours accompanying coffees and teas. In between, typical offerings might include an amuse-gueule of two plump sautéed prawns in a bisque and truffle sabayon, sauteed foie gras with scallops and cep sauce followed by roast suckling pig with poitin sauce, finally - another speciality - an iced nougat passionfruit pyramid. Alternatively, an entire table can choose the six-course 'surprise' menu at £59 per person. This is creative cooking of the highest class, utilising first-rate seasonal ingredients, perfectly seasoned and beautifully presented. Chef-patron Kevin Thornton, who was the Guide's Chef of the Year in 1999 and remains our only two-star chef, has a perfectionist's eye for detail and a palate to match. The wine list, though concise, provides a good selection, including several New World wines. Children welcome. **Seats 40** (private room, 15).No-smoking area. Air conditioning. L 12:30-1:45 Friday only. D 7-11 Tue-Sat inclusive. Set L £24. Gourmet menu £59. L&D à la carte available. House wine from £14. SC 12.5%. Closed Sun & Mon, 2 wks at Xmas/New Year. Amex, Diners, MasterCard, Visa.

Dublin 2 ✗ — *Toners*

139 Lower Baggot Street Dublin

PUB — Tel: 01 676 3090 Fax: 01 676 2617

One of the few authentic old pubs left in Dublin, Toners is definitely worth a visit (or two). Among many other claims to fame, it is said to be the only pub ever frequented by the poet W.B. Yeats. Closed 25 Dec & Good Fri.

Dublin 2 — *Tosca*

20 Suffolk Street Dublin
RESTAURANT Tel: 01 679 6744 Fax: 01 677 4310

Owned by Norman Hewson, Tosca is one of the most stylish of the smaller café-bars in Dublin and serves excellent "global" food. Strongly recommended are the minestrone soup, served with large chunks of warm home-made bread, and Mick's Salad, a vibrantly coloured concoction which is a meal in itself. The front window seats are great for people-watching. Wheelchair access. Children welcome. **Seats 70.** No-smoking area. Air conditioning. L 12-3:30 daily, Sun 1-4. D 5:30-12:30 daily (Sun to 12). Menu à la carte. House wine £11.95. SC discretionary (10% on parties of 6+). Closed Xmas & Good Fri. Amex, Diners, MasterCard, Visa.

Dublin 15 ❋ — *Travelodge*

Auburn Avenue Roundabout Navan Road Castleknock Dublin 15
HOTEL Tel: 01 820 2626

Spacious, inexpensive accommodation for two and adequate space for two or three small children in comfortable, well-furnished rooms with neat bathrooms, TV and tea/coffee-making facilities. Room Rate £44.95-£55.95. Amex, Diners, MasterCard, Visa.

Dublin 2 — *Trinity Lodge*

12 South Frederick Street Dublin
Tel: 01 679 5044 Fax: 01 679 5223
GUESTHOUSE email: trinitylodge@eircom.net

As centrally located as it is possible to get, Trinity Lodge offers a very high standard of accommodation just yards away from Trinity College. Children welcome (Under 3s free in parents' room; cots available). Pets by arrangement. **Rooms 13** (all en-suite, 3 suites, 6 executive rooms, 5 no-smoking). B&B £47.50pps, ss £40. Open all year. Amex, Diners, MasterCard, Visa.

Dublin 2 — *Unicorn Restaurant*

12B Merrion Court Merrion Row Dublin
RESTAURANT Tel: 01 676 2182/668 8552

Lovely, secluded location just off a busy street near the Shelbourne Hotel. The doors open out onto a terrace which is used for guest seating in fine weather. A informal and fashionable restaurant, famous for its buffet hors d'oeuvres selection and "No 5" piano bar. (Weds-Sat 9pm-3 am) Café and Restaurant open Mon- Sat from 9 am. Closed Sundays and lunch on Bank Hols. Wheelchair access. Parking. Children welcome. **Seats 80** (private room, 10) Air conditioning. Open 12:30-11:30 Mon-Sat. House wine £14.50. Toilets wheelchair accessible. SC discretionary. Closed Sun, Xmas week. Amex, Diners, MasterCard, Visa.

Dublin 2 ❋ — *Wagamama*

South King Street Dublin 2
RESTAURANT Tel: 01 478 2152 Fax: 01 478 2154

The new Dublin branch of this justly popular London-based noodle bar is now full of groovy young things, but thankfully the infamous queue around the block has not yet caught on. The interior is a huge basement canteen, simple and functional, but strikingly designed with high ceilings. The service is friendly and efficient. The large portions of noodles consist of ramen, udon or soba served in soups or pan-fried, well seasoned and colourfully decorated with South Asian ingredients. There are a few Japanese dishes such as teriyaki (mouth-watering little kebabs) and edamame (freshly steamed geen soya beans, served sprinkled with salt).There's also an excellent selection of fruit and vegetable juices, some rice dishes and plenty of great vegetarian options. Occasionally the cooking may disappoint: on a recent visit the ravioli-like gyoza, for example, was crudely cooked, burnt on the base and raw on top. If you are won over by the way of the noodle this could be the place for you, but all those fashionable bare surfaces make for quite a din which is not everyone's cup of tea. Multi-storey carpark nearby. Children welome.**Seats 130.** No-smoking restaurant; air conditioning. Open daily, 12 noon-11/12 midnight. A la carte. SC discretionary. Amex, Diners, MasterCard, Visa.

Dublin 4 ❀   *Waterloo House*

8-10 Waterloo Road Ballsbridge Dublin
Tel:01 660 1888 Fax: 01 667 1955
GUESTHOUSE   email: waterloohouse@eircom.net

Two Georgian townhouses have been combined to make a luxurious base in a quiet location very convenient to the city centre and also Lansdowne Road (rugby), RDS (equestrian & exhibitions) and several of the city's most famous restaurants. Equally attractive to the business or leisure traveller. ISDN lines. Conservatory & Garden. Wheelchair access. Own parking. Children welcome. No pets. **Rooms 20** (some no-smoking, some for disabled). B&B £42.50pps, ss £22.50. Lift. Closed Xmas week. MasterCard, Visa.

Dublin 2 ⛫   *Westbury Hotel*

Grafton Street Dublin
Tel: 01 679 1122 Fax: 01 679 7078
HOTEL/RESTAURANT   email: westbury@doylehotels.com

Possibly the most conveniently situated of all the central Dublin hotels, the Westbury is a very small stone's throw from the main shopping street in the city. The Westbury has all the benefits of luxury hotels – notably valet parking – to offset any practical disadvantages of the location. Unashamedly sumptuous, the hotel's public areas drip with chandeliers and have accessories to match – like the grand piano on The Terrace, a popular first floor meeting place for afternoon tea and frequently used for fashion shows. Accommodation is similarly luxurious, with bedrooms that include penthouse suites and a high proportion of suites, junior suites and executive rooms. With conference facilities to match its quality of accommodation and service, the hotel is understandably popular with business guests, but it also makes a luxurious base for a leisure break in the city.Conference/banqueting (220/200). Business centre. Secretarial services. ISDN lines. Wheelchair access. Parking. Children welcome (Under 12s free in parents' room; cots available). No pets. **Rooms 204** (all en-suite, 8 suites, 34 executive rooms, 80 no-smoking, 4 for disabled). Room rate £210pps (max 2 guests). Lift. Open all year. Amex, Diners, MasterCard, Visa. **Russell Room:** After a drink in one of the hotel's two bars – the first floor Terrace bar and the Sandbank Bistro, an informal seafood restaurant and bar accessible from the back of the building – fine dining is available in the Russell Room. Executive Chef Paddy Brady offers a choice of set menus and à la carte dining at both lunch and dinner, plus a separate vegetarian menu. The style is classic French, with some global cuisine and New Irish influences. Each autumn the Westbury hosts an International Gourmet Food Season; the event runs for a number of weeks and features guest appearances by executive chefs of well-known hotels around the world. They present menus typical of their own establishments, with the Russell Room as their venue. **Seats 80** (private room, 14) No-smoking area. Air conditioning. SC 15%.L 12:30-2 daily, Sun to 2:30. D 6:30-10:30 daily, Sun to 10. Set D £28.50. L&D à la carte available. Toilets wheelchair accessible.

Dublin 1 ❀ ⚔   *Wrights Fisherman Wharf Restaurant*

IFSC Custom House Docks Dublin
RESTAURANT   Tel:01 670 1900 Fax: 01 670 1657

There is a buzz about places frequented by people with power and the atmosphere created by the ordinary-looking men and women in business suits who frequent this attractive waterside restaurant is quite noticeable. The food - which has an understandable bias in favour of seafood - is good, the service is terrific (time is money) and the prices match the height of the nearby buildings. To be informed that an otherwise unremarkable maincourse special is £19 is staggering - a full lunch at one of the city's finest restaurants would be in that region. However, Australian chef Fintan O'Malley is doing a good job and, given the location, the price of a meal here probably seems very small beans indeed to the average guest. Just make sure your broker is paying. Parking by arrangement with nearby carpark. **Seats 70** L 12-3 Mon-Fri. D Mon-Sat. SC 12.5%. Closed Sunday. Amex, Diners, MasterCard, Visa.

Dublin 1 ✳   *Zafraan*

RESTAURANT

41 Great Georges Street South Dublin
Tel: 01 677 0999 Fax: 01 677 0979

This bright and roomy restaurant, spanning two floors, is on a corner site with a huge spiral staircase. The menu is best described as 'fusion' Indian food with a twist, with some surprising combinations; a blackcurrant ragout with tiger prawns is an unusual example. Good service initially lacked knowledge of the menu, although an attentive manager may soon sort out any difficulties. Recommendations include Vada (delicious lentil dumplings), beautifully spiced tender Nawabi gousth (crisp fried lamb with soya and red onion vinaigrette) and main course like chicken korma (well executed if a little predictable and freshly cooked, delicately flavoured Malabari jhinga (tiger prawn green curry with turmeric and green mango). Steamed rice and assorted flat breads (with mint, poppy and sesame seeds) make good accompaniments and a passion fruit and mango sorbet could make the perfect ending. This is a delightful restaurant with good food and deserves to be better known. Wheelchair access. Parking by arrangement with nearby carpark. Children welcome. **Seats 90.** No-smoking area. Air conditioning. 12-11 daily, Sun from 2. Set L £7.95. Early bird menu £10 5:30-7pm. L&D à la carte available. House wine £12. Toilets wheelchair accessible. SC discretionary. Closed Xmas, Easter. Amex, MasterCard, Visa.

Dublin ✗   *Zen*

RESTAURANT

89 Upper Rathmines Road Dublin
Tel: 01 497 9428

Denis O'Connor's unusual Chinese restaurant in a converted church has a well-earned reputation for authenticity. Staff are sourced in Beijing and, although there are plenty of popular dishes on their menus, this is one of the relatively small number of oriental restaurants in Dublin where more adventurous diners are rewarded with food that is more highly spiced than normal. D££ daily, L£ Thurs, Fri & Sun. Amex Diners, MasterCard, Visa.

DUBLIN County

Although the growth rates which have made the Irish economy something of a miracle since 1994 are expected to ease during 2000, it is around Dublin that the pressures of success will continue to be most evident. The Greater Dublin area has been developing so rapidly in recent years that, not surprisingly, the citizens of what used to be County Dublin occasionally suffer from a minor identity crisis. For they are now in theory living in three new counties - Fingal in the north, South Dublin in the southwest, and Dun Laoghaire-Rathdown in the southeast. But although Dubliners of town and county alike will happily accept that they're part of a thrusting modern city, equally they'll cheerfully adhere to the old Irish saying that when God made time, He made a lot of it. So most folk are allowing themselves all the time in the world to get used to the fact that they are now either Fingallions, or South Dubliners, or - Heaven forbid - Hyphenators out in Dun Laoghaire-Rathdown.

In this approach, they seem to be supported by An Post, the Irish Post Office, which - in the first year of the 21st century - appears to have a sublime disregard for the creation some years ago of these new counties. For An Post, you're still either in Dublin city or Dublin county, and that's that. All of which is good news for the visitor, for it means that if you feel that the frenetic pace of Dublin city is a mite overpowering, you will very quickly find that nearby, in what used to be and for most folk still is County Dublin, there are still many oases of a much more easy-going way of life waiting to be discovered.

Admittedly the fact that the handsome Dublin mountains overlook the city in spectacular style means that even up in the nearby hills, you can sometimes be aware of the city's buzz. But if you want to find a vigorous contrast between modern style and classical elegance, you can find it in an unusual form at Dun Laoghaire's remarkable harbour, where one of the world's most modern ferryports is in interesting synergy with one of the world's largest Victorian artificial harbours. And should you head northward into Fingal, you'll quickly discover an away from-it-all sort of place of estuary towns, fishing ports, offshore islands alive with seabirds, and an environment of leisurely pace in which it's thought very bad form to hasten over meals in restaurants where portion control is either unknown, or merely in its infancy.

Local Attractions and Information

Balbriggan	Ardgillan Castle 01 849 2212
Donabate	Newbridge House, Park & Traditional Farm 01 843 6534
Dun Laoghaire	American Week (early July) 01 284 1864
Dun Laoghaire	National Maritime Museum Haigh Terrace 01 280 0969
Dun Laoghaire	Tourist Information 01 280 6984/5/6
Lucan Primrose Hill Garden	(house attrib James Gandon) 01 628 0373
Malahide	The Talbot Botanic Gardens, Malahide Castle 01 872 7530
Malahide	Fry Model Railway, Malahide Castle Demesne 01 846 3779
Malahide	Malahide Castle & Demesne 01 846 2184
Sandycove	James Joyce Museum (Martello Tower) 01 280 9265
Sandyford	Fernhill Gardens (Himalayan species; walled garden) 01 295 6000

Blackrock   *Ayumi Ya*

Newpark Centre Newtown Park Avenue Co Dublin
RESTAURANT   Tel: 01 283 1767 Fax: 01 288 0428 email: info@ayumiya.ie

Established in 1983, Ayumi-Ya was the first authentic traditional Japanese restaurant in Dublin and, despite the growing interest in Japanese cooking in mainstream restaurants, Ayumi-Ya and its new sister Aya@Brown Thomas, still reign supreme. It's an exceptionally customer-friendly restaurant: their floral logo is a fusion of the Irish shamrock and Japanese chrysanthemum, encircled by a ring of friendship, symbolising a genuine desire to bring the two cultures together. In practical terms, this is demonstrated by their helpfulness in getting Irish customers to get the best possible experience of Japanese food, and through the food, the caring service and the restaurant's restorative calm, an insight into the culture. Yoishi and his team suggest making a traditional Japanese choice and selecting a variety of starters from a traditional tasting menu, thus experiencing as many tastes, textures and flavours as possible. Alternatively, the set menus have been carefully compiled to include the most popular dishes including yakitori (grilled skewered chicken with teriyaki sauce), tempura (vegetables or fish deep-fried in light batter), sushi (raw fish in vinegared rice), norimaki (vinegared rice wrapped in nori seaweed with fish or vegetable filling). An exceptional choice is available for vegetarians. **Seats 60** (private room, 14) No smoking area; air conditioning. D 6-11 daily Sun only, D5.30-9.45, Set D £21.95, early evening menu £12.95, 6-7pm only; à la carte available, house wine £10.95, sc 10%. Toilets wheelchair accessible. Children welcome before 8 pm. Closed 24-26 Dec, 1 Jan & Good Fri. Amex, Diners, MasterCard, Visa. **Directions:** Between Stradbrook Road at N11. Behind a landmark pub The Playwright.

Blackrock ❋   *Blueberry's*

15 Main Street Blackrock Co. Dublin
RESTAURANT   Tel: 01 2788900 Fax: 01 2788903

A dashing new sister for Morels of Glasthule, this fresh, bright first-floor restaurant has lots of polished wood and classy contemporary table settings - a fitting background for David Crossoir's stylish food. The best fresh ingredients provide a sound foundation for confident, creative cooking that has flair without succumbing to the temptations of over-presentation. Well-balanced menus offer plenty of choice: well-made soups (always a good sign), a fine array of tempting starters (salad of smoked duck with fresh figs, caramelised apples, walnut dressing and mache is typical) and mains that take vegetarian cooking seriously (ricotta & spinach tortellini with saute spinach, char-grilled aubergines, shallot & herb dresing with balsamic syrup). Seafood is a strong option, in daily specials and regular dishes such as medallions of monkfish wrapped in Parma ham and basil mousse, with oven-dried tomato risotto and spiced tomato coulis; served sliced, it's one of the prettiest dishes around (and reminiscent of the national flag). New Irish Cuisine is also well represented in dishes supreme of salmon with truffle mash, saute cabbage, smoked lardons and similarly creative beef and lamb dishes. All this and delicious desserts - or a cheese selection - and friendly, efficient service under the management of Alain Kerloc'H too. This is a fine addition to the Dublin dining scene and is sure to succeed. **Seats 38.** No smoking area. Air conditioning. L 12.30-2.15 (Sun to 2.45), D 5.30-10 (Fri & Sat to 10.30, Sun 6-9). Set Sun L & early evening menu (5.30-7) £13.95. A la carte available. House wine £14.50; no sc. Children welcome before 8. Closed 4 days - Xmas and New Year Amex, Diners, MasterCard, Visa. **Directions:** Above Jack O'Rourke's pub on the Main Street Blackrock.

Blackrock ❋   *Dali's Restaurant*

63-65 Main Street Blackrock Co Dublin
RESTAURANT   Tel: 01 278 0660 Fax: 01 278 0661

A pleasant room, with a chic little bar just inside the door and the dining area at a slightly higher level, a prompt welcome and offer of an aperitif sets the tone for a meal of caring service - restaurant manager Gary Emmet looks after customers with exemplary efficency and it is easy to see why regulars keep coming back. Head chef Karl Lawless's energies are not wasted in the kitchen either. His menus are modishly light and colourful, including zesty first courses like crabmeat & tomato salad with a lime & ginger mayonnaise and monkfish & prawn brochette witha mango, mint & chili salsa, followed by main courses that include several slight variations on old favourites - rack of lamb might come with a lemon & mint butter - and home-made pasta and fish dishes; side dishes are charged extra. Desserts are quite traditional - sticky toffee pudding with vanilla ice cream and caramel sauce is typical, and there's a decent tatsing plate, or cheeseboard. **Seats 70.** No smoking area. L 12-3 Tue-Sat D 6-10.30 Tue-Sat, Set L £8.95, early evening menu £10, 6-7 only; à la carte available; house wine £12.50, sc 10% on parties of 6+. Children welcome, Closed 25-26 Dec & 1 Jan. Amex, Diners, MasterCard, Visa. **Directions:** Opposite Blackrock library

---

Blackrock   *Radisson SAS St Helen's Hotel*

Stillorgan Road Co Dublin
HOTEL/RESTAURANT   Tel: 01 218 6000 Fax: 01 218 6030

Set in four acres of formal gardens just south of Dublin's city centre, with views across Dublin Bay to Howth Head, the fine 18th century house at the heart of this impressive new hotel was once a private residence. Careful restoration and imaginative modernisation have created interesting public areas, including the Orangerie bar and a pillared ballroom with minstrels' gallery and grand piano. A fine formal dining room, Le Panto, has views over the garden (L Tue-Sun, D Tue-Sat) and there's a brasserie, Talavera, which was an immediate success and is open every evening (7-10). Bedrooms, in a new four-storey block adjoining the main building, include ten suites and 16 junior suites; all have garden views (some of the best rooms also have balconies) and air conditioning and are well-equipped for business guests (with desks and fax machines). Rooms are comfortably furnished to a high standard in contemporary style, although less spacious than might be expected in a new development; small bathrooms with economy baths, especially, fail to live up to the opulence that the old house promises. Conference/banqueting (350/220). Business centre. ISDN lines.Garden, snooker. Ample parking. Children (Under 17s free in parents' room; cots available). Pets by arrangement **Rooms 151** (21 suites, 19 executive, 37 no-smoking, 8 for disabled). Room rate £195 (max 3 guests). Open all year. Amex, Diners, Mastecard, Visa. **Directions:** On N11 from city

---

Blackrock ✳   *Ristorante da Roberto*

5 George's Avenue Blackrock Co Dublin
RESTAURANT   Tel: 01 278 0759 Fax: 0404 61507

The decor at this popular Italian restaurant is a little strange - stained glass windows and chandeliers seem at odds with a terracotta-style tiled floor and country kitchen chairs. Experience of proprietor-chef Roberto Morsiani's previous restaurant (the inexpensive little Il Cacciatore at Ashford, where he was chef-partner), perhaps coloured expectations of this new venture, which offers much more ambitious menus at much higher prices. Quite a few house specialities feature - Prawns Roberto's Way, Greedy Man's Ravioli, Chef's Rustic Veal - plus a wide choice of fish (mostly local), a page of pastas and a vegetarian section. A recent visit suggests inconsistency in the standard of dishes (a disappointing salad came totally innocent of dressing, for example); however, the overall experience is enjoyable and provides a good contrast to the chic contemporary restaurants which have also opened in Blackrock recently. The best tables are in the front section; the back room (where non-smokers tend to end up) is very noisy. **Seats 70.** Air conditioning D 5.30-11.30; D1-10 Sun only, à la carte available, house wine £10; sc discretionary Children; Closed Mon & 3 weeks in Oct. MasterCard, Visa. **Directions:** Off the Main street in Blackrock, side road opposite the post office.

Booterstown   *La Tavola*

114 Rock Road Booterstown Co Dublin
RESTAURANT   Tel: 01 283 5101

Easy to find at the lower corner of Booterstown Avenue, Kevin Hart and Philip Davis's friendly, informal restaurant has been providing good popular food at very customer-friendly prices since 1992. Pasta and pizza predominate on value-conscious menus, but they are well-made and there are vegetarian options. Daily blackboard specials offer fresh fish and some extra meat and poultry dishes. **Seats 42.** No smoking area; D 5-11.15 Tue-Sat (Tue to 10.15); à la carte available, house wine £10.95; sc discretionary.Closed Sun, Mon. Amex.

Dalkey ˣ   *Daniel Finnegan*

2 Sorrento Road Dalkey Co Dublin
PUB   Tel: 01 285 8505

An immaculately maintained pub of great character, much-loved by locals and visitors alike. It's bright, comfortable and cosy, with wood panelling and traditional Irish seating in 'snugs'. Food is served at lunchtime only - a full hot bar lunch, including starters such as baked Dalkey crab, brie fritters with apple coulis and main courses like roast stuffed pork steak, honey roast half duck and grilled cod steak, followed by traditional desserts like applie pie and lemon cheesecake. The fresh fish (from the harbour nearby) is excellent, the vegetables predictable but tasty and value good. Booking is advisable to avoid a long wait. Carpark nearby. Closed 25 Dec, Good Fri & & New Year.

Dalkey   *The Queen's*

12 Castle Street Dalkey Co Dublin
PUB   Tel: 01 285 4569 Fax: 01 285 8345 email: queens@clubi.ie

The oldest pub in Dalkey, and also one of the oldest in Ireland, The Queen's was originally licensed to "dispense liquor" as far back as 1745. Recent renovations and improvements have been done with due respect for the age and character of the premises. There are now two restaurants on the premises - La Romana, which has offered good value Italian/Mediterranean food for some years and the new first floor restaurant and piano bar, The Vico, which serves contemporary international food in a more upmarket atmosphere. Good bar food – chowders, casseroles, salads, quiches – is also available every afternoon and can be served to patio areas at the back and front in fine weather. Wheelchair accessible; children welcome at La Romana, up to 7.30. Restaurants both seat 70. Vico D only 6-11 Tue-Sat; L Romana D daily 6-11. Bar food L&D daily. Vico closed Sun, Mon; pub closed 25 Dec & Good Fri. Amex, Diners, MasterCard, Visa. **Directions:** Main Street Dalkey, beside Heritage Centre

Dalkey   *Thai House*

21 Railway Road Dalkey Co Dublin
RESTAURANT   Tel: 01 284 7304 Fax: 01 284 7304

Tony Ecock's restaurant provided a major boost to the Dalkey dining scene when it opened in 1997 and, together with partner/chef Boonma Nilrat, is careful to ensure that standards are maintained. Although quite pricey, a welcoming atmosphere and authentic, interesting food have built up a loyal following – and a reputation for including dishes that are genuinely spicy and do not pander to blander tastes. Begin with the Thai House Special Starter Pack – a tasty sampling plate of six starters: crisp deep-fried dishes like spring rolls, prawns with Thai sauce, marinated skewered pork or chicken satay with sweet and spicy sauce – all well-known dishes but spiced and cooked without compromise. From a choice of soups that include the famous Tom Yam Gung (spicy prawn soup with lemon grass and chilli) Tom Yam Rumit – a spicy soup with prawns, squid, crab and mussels – is perhaps the most interesting. Main courses include a range of curries, fried rice dishes and pan-fried dishes such as Bu Paht Pung Galee – delicious crab fried with spring onions, garlic and sugar in special Thai sauce – although, at £12, it's an expensive course when rice is charged as an extra. Vegetarian dishes are listed separately and there are several set menus for two to six people. Not suitable for children. **Seats 34.** No smoking area. Air conditioning. D 6-11.30 Tue-Sat (Sun 5.30-11.30); Set D £24, house wine £10.50; sc discretionary. Toilets wheelchair accessible Closed Mon & last 2 weeks in Jan. Amex, Diners, MasterCard, Visa. **Directions:** 100 yards from Dalkey Dart station.

Dublin Airport   *Great Southern Hotel*

Dublin Airport Co Dublin
HOTEL   Tel: 01 844 6000 Fax: 01 844 6001 email: res@dubairport.gsh.ie

This large modern hotel opened in the airport complex in 1998 and is just two minutes drive from the main terminal building (with a coach service available). Rooms, which are all double-glazed, are en-suite with proper bathrooms. There's a high proportion of executive rooms (12 of which are designated lady executive) and 24 are non-smoking. Large bar/bistro on the ground floor. Conference/banqueting (400/240); video conferencing; secretarial services; business centre. Children (Under 2s free in parents' room; cots available). Wheelchair accessible. **Rooms 147** (2 mini-suites, 58 executive rooms, 24 no-smoking, 4 for disabled).Lift. Room rate £120, max 3 guests per room. Closed 24-26 Dec. Amex, Diners, MasterCard, Visa. **Directions:** Situated in airport complex.

Dublin Airport ❊   *Posthouse Dublin Airport*

Dublin Airport, Co. Dublin
HOTEL   Tel: 01-808-0500 Fax: 01-844-6002

This big comfortable hotel makes an ideal meeting place and guests may use the extensive facilities of the Airport Sports & Leisure complex free of charge Conference/banqueting (130/130) Parking.Children (Under 4s free in parents' room; cots available). Wheelchair accessible. **Rooms 249** (all en-suite, 103 executive rooms, 101 no-smoking, 3 for disabled) Room rate £157.76, max 2 guests per room; 24hr room service; Closed 24-25 Dec Amex, Diners, MasterCard, Visa. **Directions:** Hotel is in airport complex on right hand side of entrance to airport.

Dun Laoghaire ❊   *The Black Tulip Bistro*

107 Lower Georges St, Dun Laoghaire, Co. Dublin
RESTAURANT   Tel: 01-2805318

The dated 1980s exterior of this town centre restaurant gives no clue to the cosy, welcoming atmosphere and good food that lies behind the dreary frontage. Once through the front door, it is a delight. Proprietor-chef Fiona Anderson presents interesting modern European menus, which offer plenty of choice but , sensibly, are not over-extensive - and everything sampled on a recent visit attracted praise. Starters included smoked chicken with lightly curried crème fraîche, a roast leek & artichoke salad with toasted pumpkin seed dressing and (particularly special) seared scallops with home-dried tomatoes, mixed leaves and a balsamic reduction. Equally good main courses included pan-seared swordfish with wok-fried greens, seasame & soya dressisng and jasmine rice and a more traditional loin of lamb with dauphinoise potato, French beans, confit of garlic and rosemary jus. Consistently creative, accurate cooking, attractive presentation, good service and an interesting wine list mean that, although quite expensive, value is good. **Seats 50** (private room, 20) D 5.30-10pm Tue-Thurs, D5.30-10.30 Fri-Sat; Set D £18.9, early evening menu £12.95 5.30-7.30pm only, à la carte available, No smoking area; closed Mon/Sun; no children; Amex, Diners, MasterCard, Visa. **Directions:** Dun Laoghaire main street, beside St. Michaels Hospital.

Dun Laoghaire ✗   *Bistro Vino*

RESTAURANT

56 Glasthule Road Dun Laoghaire Co Dublin
Tel/Fax: 01 280 6097

This small first floor evening restaurant (up steep stairs) is near the seafront at Sandycove. It pre-dates surrounding establishments in this now fashionable area by a long chalk. But it's still a hit with the locals, who appreciate the moderate prices, unpretentious, good food and informal atmosphere. A la carte except for an inexpensive early set menu (£11.95, 5-7 pm). D£-££ daily Amex, Diners, MasterCard, Visa.

Dun Laoghaire   *Brasserie Na Mara*

RESTAURANT

1 Harbour Road Dun Laoghaire Co Dublin
Tel: 01 280 6767 Fax: 01 284 4649

The old Kingstown terminal building beside the Dun Laoghaire DART station makes a fine location for a harbourside restaurant. The current contemporary decor is stylish (and the bar faces in towards the reception area, so you look out over the harbour with aperitifs while reading the menu) although getting a little tired. The comfort level isn't what it used to be when the decor was more traditional - the hard floor is noisy and small tables and mean chairs do little for the enjoyment of food. However, interesting menus are in a bright, modern style to suit the decor,and include plenty of seafood as one would expect. A recent visit suggests that execution can be a little disappointing, however - Caesar salad made with lolla rossa and oakleaf lettuce rather than cos (and served without croutons), crab claws lacking in flavour and texture, lamb distinctly tough. However, prices are not excessive, service has improved and it is clearly very popular locally.No children under 7. **Seats 90** (private room, 50) No smoking area. L 12.30-2.30 Mon-Fri D 6.30-10 Mon-Sat, à la carte available, house wine £11.45. Toilets wheelchair accessible; sc discretionary. Arrangement with nearby carpark. Amex, Closed Bank Hols, New Years Day, Good Fri, Xmas Day. Diners, MasterCard, Visa. **Directions:** Opposite Dun Laoghaire town hall

---

Dun Laoghaire   *Caviston's Seafood Restaurant*

RESTAURANT

59 Glasthule Road Dun Laoghaire Co Dublin
Tel: 01 280 9120/2715 Fax: 01 284 4054
email: caviston@indigo.ie

Caviston's of Sandycove has long been a mecca for lovers of good food. Here you will find everything that is good, from organic vegetables to farmhouse cheeses, cooked meats to specialist oils and other exotic items. But it was always for fish and shellfish that Caviston's were especially renowned – even providing a collection of well-thumbed recipe books for on-the-spot reference. At their little restaurant next door, they serve an imaginative range of seafood dishes influenced by various traditions and all washed down by a glass or two from a very tempting little wine list. You might even be offered our 1999 Seafood Dish of the Year: Roast Monkfish Fillets, Roast Red Pepper and Olive Oil Dressing. Caviston's food is simple, colourful, perfectly cooked - it speaks volumes for how good seafood can be. Children welcome. **Seats 26.** No-smoking restaurant; air conditioning. L only, 3 sittings Tues-Sat: 12-1.30, 1.30-3, 3-5; all à la carte; sc discretionary. Toilets wheelchair accessible. Closed Sun/Mon & Xmas week to New Year Diners, MasterCard, Visa. **Directions:** Between Dun Laoghaire and Dalkey, 5 mins. Walk from Glasthule DART Station.

Dun Laoghaire ❋ ✗   *Eagle House*

18 Glasthule Road Dun Laoghaire Co Dublin
PUB   Tel: 01 280 4740

This fine traditional establishment is full of interest and a great local. The interior is dark, but has a fascinating collection of model boats, ships and other nautical bric-a-brac and is arranged in comfortably sized alcoves and 'snugs' on different levels. Bar meals, cooked by Morels (who run the restaurant upstairs - see entry) is available at lunchtime and in the evening and can be very good. Inconsistencies were disappointing on a recent lunch visit, however - while starters (crostini and garlic mushrooms) were excellent and served piping hot, enormous traditional main courses (Vienna steak and a fish special, breaded plaice) served with piles of steamed potatoes, carrots and turnips were heavy and uninteresting. Closed 25 Dec & Good Fri.

Dun Laoghaire   *P McCormack & Sons*

67 Lr Mounttown Dun Laoghaire Co Dublin
PUB   Tel: 01 280 5519 Fax: 01 280 0145 email: cormak@iol.ie

This fine pub (and "emporium") has been run by the McCormack family since 1960. It's one of the neatest pubs around, with a landscaped carpark, no less. The garden corner creates a very pleasant outlook for an imaginative conservatory extension at the back of the pub. The main part of the pub is full of traditional character and the whole place has a well-run hum about it. Good bar food includes fresh fish available on the day as well as classics such as beef hot pot, chicken a la king and loads of salads. Evening menus offer tasty light dishes: moules marinières, warm crispy bacon and crouton salad and steak sandwiches. Main dishes include a fish special, a 10 oz sirloin steak (with mushroom and Irish whiskey sauce perhaps) or pasta dishes with fresh parmesan. No children after 4pm. Bar food daily 12-2.30pm & 6-10pm. (pub open to 12.30). Amex, Diners, MasterCard, Visa. closed Xmas day, Good Fri; wheelchair accessible. **Directions:** near Dun Laoghaire at Monkstown end.

Dun Laoghaire ☆   *Morels*

18 Glasthule Road Dun Laoghaire Co Dublin
RESTAURANT   Tel: 01 230 0210 Fax: 01 230 0466

On the first floor of the Eagle House pub (see entry) the bistro is vividly decorated in Mediterranean tones, with seating in three rooms and a seafood tank at the entrance. On a recent visit, the staircase and reception area were in need of renovation, but the standard of food is exceptionally high and Morels remains the benchmark restaurant for the Dun Laoghaire area. Head chef John Dunne presents wide-ranging but not over-extensive contemporary menus, offering a choice of about seven on each course - roast butternut squash & garlic soup and breast of woodpigeon with puy lentils and red onion confit are typical starters and main courses show New Irish Cuisine influences in dishes like fillet of beef with potato boxty, roast garlic, shalllots & wild mushroom fricassee and offer creative vegetarian options such as white bean cassoulet with mediterranean vegetables, plum tomato coulis & parmesan tuile. Dishes attracting special praise include an unusual starter of scrambled free range eggs with crabmeat, oysters & prawn coulis and a superb fish special of the day - John Dory, with parmesan crisp and beans in a balsamic dressing. Good-value wines with interesting £11 and £15 sections, in addition to the regular list. Irish-French service is friendly and swift. Limited parking at Eagle House carpark. Children welcome before 8 pm *Morels has a sister restaurant at Stephens Hall Hotel in Dublin city. **Seats 120** (private room, 30).No smoking area Air conditioning D 5.30-10 daily (Sun 6-9); L Sun only 12.30-2.45, Set Sun L £13.50. Tasting D (on request)£29.50; early evening menu 5.30-7 only £13.50; also à la carte; house wine £11.50. Closed 25-27 Dec & 1 Jan Amex, Diners, MasterCard, Visa. **Directions:** In centre of Glasthule village, above the Eagle House pub

Dun Laoghaire   *Royal Marine Hotel*

Marine Road Dun Laoghaire Co Dublin
HOTEL   Tel: 01 280 1911 Fax: 01 280 1089 email: ryan@indigo.ie

Overlooking Dublin Bay and the ferry port, this grand old Victorian hotel has ample parking and extensive landscaped gardens (perfect for weddings), and yet is only a twenty minute DART ride to the centre of Dublin. On entering the marble floored foyer a few steps take you up and through arched columns into the Bay Lounge (popular for afternoon teas) and the Powerscourt Restaurant. Eight bay-windowed suites have four-poster beds and freestanding antique furniture, but most rooms have fitted furniture and offer standard facilities, including decent bathrooms; those on the executive floor that provide extras for the business traveller. Conference/banqueting (400/300); video conferencing; secretarial services. Business centre. Own parking. Wheelchair accessible. No pets. **Rooms 103** (8 suites, 2 mini-suite, 60 executive rooms, 0 no-smoking, 2 for disabled). Lift. B&B £75pps, ss £25; sc 15%. Open all year Amex, Diners, MasterCard, Visa. **Directions:** opposite Dun Laoghaire ferry port

---

Glencullen [PUB★] *Johnnie Fox's Pub*

The Dublin Mountains Glencullen Co Dublin
PUB   Tel: 01 295 5647 Fax: 01 295 8911

Nestling in an attractive wooded hamlet in the Dublin Mountains, south of Dublin city, Johnnie Fox's has numerous claims to fame. Undoubtedly one of County Dublin's best-loved pubs in present times, it can also claim to be one of the oldest, with a history going back to the eighteenth century. Daniel O'Connell, who lived in Glencullen at one time, was a regular apparently, and it's "undoubtedly" the highest pub in the land. More to the point, however, is the fact that it's a warm, friendly and very well run place just about equally famous for its food – the "Famous Seafood Kitchen" – and its music – "Famous Hooley Nights" (booking advisable). Unlike so many superficially similar pubs that have popped up all over the world recently, it's also real. Kitsch, perhaps, but real nonetheless – the rickety old furniture is real, the dust is real and you certainly won't find a gas fire here – there's a lovely turf or log fire at every turn. It's a pleasant place to drop into at quieter times too, if you're walking in the hills or just loafing around. Reservations recommended for food.Own parking Children welcome before 7 pm. **Seats 250** (private room, 45). Open all day (12-10, Sun 4-10); all food à la carte, house wine £11 sc discretionary. Closed 25 Dec & Good Fri. Amex, Diners, MasterCard, Visa **Directions:** In Dublin Mountains, 30 mins drive from Dublin city centre.

Howth *Abbey Tavern*

Abbey Street Howth Co Dublin
Tel: 01 839 0307/01 832 2006 Fax: 01 839 0284
PUB/RESTAURANT   email: info@abbeytavern.ie

Just 50 yards up from the harbour, part of this famous pub dates back to the 15th century, when it was built as a seminary for the local monks (as an addition to the 12th century Chapter House next door). Currently owned by James and Eithne Scott-Lennon – James' grandfather bought it in 1945 – the entire establishment was refurbished in 1998 but this well-run and immaculately maintained pub retains all the authentic features that have always made the Abbey special – open turf fires, original stone walls, flagged floors and gas lights. Bar food – Howth seafood chowder, smoked salmon with home-made brown bread, a hot traditional dish such as corned beef and cabbage, a ploughman's salad – is available at lunchtime. In 1960 the Abbey started to lay on entertainment and this, more than anything else, has brought the tavern its fame: it can cater for groups of anything between two and 200 and the format, which now runs like clockwork, is a traditional 5-course dinner followed by traditional Irish music. It's on every night but booking is essential, especially in high season. Banqueting for 200. **Abbot Restaurant:** In 1956 a restaurant was opened, quite a novel move in a pub at the time; since the recent redevelopment it has been named The Abbot and has its own separate entrance. Attractively and comfortably refurbished in keeping with the building, with open turf fires at both ends of the room, it makes a fine setting for well-cooked and not over-complicated food. **Seats 100** (private room, 40) No smoking area Air conditioning L 12-3.30 daily D 7-10.30 Mon-Sat, all à la carte, house wine £10.50 Toilets wheelchair accessible sc discretionary Children welcome before 8 pm No private parking - carpark on harbour. Closed 25-26 Dec & Good Fri Amex, Diners, MasterCard, Visa. **Directions:** 9 miles from Dublin, in centre of Howth.

Howth ^X *Bloody Stream*

14 West Pier Howth Co Dublin
PUB/RESTAURANT   Bar Tel: 01 839 5076 Restaurant Tel: 01 839 5078

This characterful pub and restaurant is part of Howth DART station, the result of sympathetic and imaginative restoration of areas of the building which had been disused for many years. It's named after a nearby stream, which still occasionally gets out of hand after heavy rain and causes flooding - fortunately the stone floors don't come to much harm. Food is served upstairs in an informal little restaurant which, on a recent visit, provided very acceptable food although the service was inexplicably slow. Closed 25 Dec & Good Fri.

Howth ✗ *Casa Pasta*

12 Harbour Road Howth Co Dublin
RESTAURANT   Tel: 01 839 5608

Atmosphere in spades is what sets this first floor restaurant overlooking Howth harbour apart, and although this was partly due to its tiny size, doubling it in 1998 doesn't seem to have diminished its appeal – it's still notoriously hard to get into, especially at weekends. (However ventilation in the new section can be a problem - book into the original room if possible.) The secret of Casa Pasta's success is entertainment – paper tablecloths and crayons provided for budding artists (of all ages), great jazz and other live music most nights (usually from 9 pm); interesting modern pictures; swift young servers; and blackboard menus featuring youthful international food (lots of pastas and salads) that is neither over-ambitious nor over-priced. Regulars that locals happily order without even consulting the menu include runny deep-fried brie with spicy chutney, big Caesar salads (possibly with slivers of chicken breast), home-made tagliatelle with mixed seafood in a creamy wine sauce – and desserts like gooey, boozy tiramisu and sticky banoffi pie. Wines are not quite as cheap and cheerful as might be hoped given the style of food and surroundings. * There are sister restaurants in Clontarf at 55 Clontarf Road, Dublin 3. Tel/Fax: 01 833 1402 and Donnybrook at Eirpage House, Donnybrook, Dublin 4 Tel: 01 2608108. Open daily 12.30-11 for Lunch & Dinner Set L £9.95, à la carte available, sc discretionary. Children welcome. Open all year. Amex, Visa

---

Howth ✗ *Citrus*

1 Island View House, Harbour Road Howth Co Dublin
RESTAURANT   Tel: 01 832 0200

Along the front a little from Casa Pasta, and in the same ownership, John Aungier has once again achieved atmosphere in spades at this stylish 2-storey restaurant. It has a little chrome-seated outdoor eating area at the front, a buzzy ground-floor café/bar where live jazz attracts a regular crowd and a slightly more formal first-floor dining room . The food is zappy global cuisine with the emphasis on Thai influences which, on the whole, is done well and without pretension. Appetisers like fishcakes with chilli sauce/lime and coriander mayonnaise, seafood wontons, rumaki (monkfish and chestnuts rapped in bacon) and vegetable tempura all come in at £3-4, and main courses like chicken and hot garlic sauce with rice, sole with coriander and chilli sauce and Thai Green and Red curries are mostly well under £10 – these prices plus good service and friendliness make the atmosphere all the more enjoyable. A shortish list of world wines is well-pitched for the style of the place, although more informative tasting notes would be helpful. L£ & D££ daily

---

Howth *Deer Park Hotel & Golf Courses*

Howth Co Dublin
Tel: 01 832 2624 Fax: 01 839 2405
HOTEL/RESTAURANT   email: sales@deerpark.iol.ie

Set high up on the Hill of Howth, in the midst of Ireland's largest golf complex, the Deerpark Hotel enjoys wonderful views across Howth demesne (of which it is part) to the islands of Ireland's Eye and Lambay and, on a clear day, right up the coast to the distant Mournes. Although golf breaks are a particular attraction, especially in summer, the hotel makes a comfortable base for anyone visiting the area and rooms have extra large beds, a sofa or armchairs and, in some cases, not just a kettle and tray for making drinks, but a kitchenette with fridge and toaster too. New rooms (27) and a large indoor swimming pool, sauna and steam room plus two all-weather tennis courts were recently added. At the time of going to press, twelve old rooms are to be demolished and 20 new ones ready for June 2000. Conference/banqueting (95/100) Parking. Children welcome (under 12s free in parents' room; cots available). Wheelchair accessible. No pets. **Rooms 78** (all en-suite) B&B £49pps, ss £17. Closed 24-26. Dec. Amex, Diners, MasterCard, Visa. **Restaurant:** The restaurant is situated at the front of the hotel, with sea views, and is well-appointed with comfortable chairs and white linen. Set 3-course lunch and dinner menus are not adventurous but are based on good ingredients, competently cooked and offer good value

– in short, menus read as traditional hotel food, but the food on the plate is above average. **Seats 75** (private room, 60) L 12-2.30 & D 6-9.30 daily. Set L £13.50. Set D £23; house wine from £10.50; sc 12.5%. Toilets wheelchair accessible. **Directions:** Follow coast road via Clontarf and Sutton – on right hand side before Howth Harbour.

Howth   *King Sitric Fish Restaurant & Accommodation*

East Pier Howth Co Dublin.

RESTAURANT   Tel: 01 832 5235   Fax: 01 839 2442   email: info@kingsitric.ie

Named after an 11th century Norse King of Dublin who had close links with Howth and was a cousin of the legendary Brian Boru, The King Sitric is one of Dublin's longest established fine restaurants. Perfectly situated at the end of the East Pier, owner-chef Aidan MacManus can keep an eye on his lobster pots in Balscadden Bay on one side and the fishing boats coming into harbour on the other. Each day's menu depends completely on the availability of fresh seafood landed that day, which is one of the many good reasons for adding game to the repertoire in winter (when gales can keep the boats in harbour for days at a time). House specialities include shellfish of all kinds, notably crab and lobster, a particularly good Irish farmhouse cheese trolley, the dessert 'Meringue Sitric' (which was invented to make use of all the egg whites left over after making yolk-rich sauces for fish) and one of the best brown bread recipes in the country, handed down through generations of Aidan's family and made personally by his mother until quite recently. Courteous, efficient service from long-serving staff, under the direction of Joan McManus, adds greatly to the enjoyment of Aidan's fine food. Exceptional wine list. At the time of going to press complete reconstruction of the building is almost complete and the restaurant is expected to open in December 1999. Children welcome. **Rooms 8** (2 mini-suites, all no-smoking, 1 for disabled). Stair Lift. B&B £45pps, ss £20. **Seats 65** (private room, 10/20) No smoking area. Air conditioning. L 12.30-2.15 Mon-Sat D 6.30-10.30 Mon-Sat Set D £32, à la carte available; house wine £12.50; sc discretionary. Toilets wheelchair accessible. Closed Xmas 3/4 days. Amex, Diners, MasterCard, Visa. **Directions:** At east pier on Howth Harbour.

Howth ✗   *The Waterside & The Wheelhouse Restaurant*

Harbour Road Howth Co Dublin

PUB /RESTAURANT   Tel: 01 839 0555 Fax: 01 839 3632

The ground floor of this attractive premises overlooking the harbourfront is one of the pleasantest bars in the area - well-run comfortable and full of character. **The Wheelhouse:** On the first floor over the Waterside, this is a friendly and welcoming place, with a cosy ambience and good, moderately priced food. Head chef Colm Hennessey is doing a good job, offering a wide choice on menus that naturally include a large selection of local fish dishes - but they're also renowned for steaks and dishes specialities include rack of Kildare lamb with honey & mustard crust, so non-fish eaters will be well looked after too. **Seats 60.** Air conditioning. D only (in restaurant) 6.30-10.30 daily (Sun to 9.30). Bar Food served daily 12.30-8.30. Children welcome. Car parking nearby. Closed 25 Dec. Amex, Diners, MasterCard, Visa.

Killiney   *Fitzpatrick Castle Dublin*

Killiney Co Dublin

HOTEL   Tel: 01 284 0700   Fax: 01 285 0207

Half an hour's drive from the city centre, this imposing castellated mansion overlooking Dublin Bay dates back to 1741. It is surrounded by landscaped gardens and, despite its size and grand style, has a surprisingly relaxed atmosphere. Bedrooms combine old-world charm with modern facilities. Spacious bedrooms include four junior suites and the 40 executive rooms have e-mail sockets. Extensive facilities include two large lounges, two restaurants, a basement disco, a conference suite for up to 400 delegates and a new Library Bar, opened in 1998. Five championship golf courses, including Druid's Glen, are nearby. Secretarial services. Business centre. Leisure centre – swimming pool Own parking. Children welcome (under 2s free in parents' room; cots available). Wheelchair accessible. No pets. **Rooms 113** (9 suites, 40 executive rooms, 25 no-smoking) B&B £74.50pps, Lift Closed 25 Dec Amex, Diners, MasterCard, Visa. **Directions:** Well signposted in Killiney area

Leixlip   *Becketts*

HOTEL

Cooldrinagh House Leixlip Co Dublin
Tel: 01 624 7040 Fax: 01 624 7072

A handsome house on the Co Dublin side of the river that divides Leixlip, Becketts is an unusual country house offering a special kind of service aimed specifically at business guests: from the moment you arrive a butler looks after all your needs, whether it be dining, laundry, limousine facilities or specific requirements for meetings or conferences. Imaginatively converted to its present use, luxurious accommodation includes four boardroom suites and six executive suites, all furnished to a high standard in a lively contemporary style. All have a workstation equipped for computers, including modem/internet connection and audio visual equipment, private fax machines etc are also available on request. Public areas, including a bar and a stylish modern restaurant, have a far less business-like atmosphere and would make an interesting outing for non-residents with no special business in mind, especially those who appreciate wine – this unusual establishment is, after all, the brainchild of John O'Byrne, proprietor of the distinctive Dublin restaurant Dobbins. Cooldrinagh House overlooks the Eddie Hackett-designed Leixlip golf course, for which golf tee off times may be booked in advance. Conference/banqueting (350/250) Business centre/secretarial services. Wheelchair accessible. No pets. **Rooms 10** (4 suites, 6 executive rooms) B&B £65pps Closed 25 Dec & Good Fri Amex, Diners, MasterCard, Visa. **Directions:** Take N4, turn off at Spa Hotel, next left after Springfield Hotel

---

Lucan   *Finnstown Country House Hotel*

HOTEL

Newcastle Road Lucan Co Dublin
Tel: 01 628 0644 Fax: 01 628 1088

Very much the hub of local activities, this fine old manor house set in 45 acres of woodland is impressive, but also full of charm. A welcoming open fire in the foyer sets the right tone. All of the large, well-proportioned reception rooms – drawing room, restaurant, bar – are elegantly furnished in a traditional style well-suited to the house. Although quite grand, there is a comfortable lived-in feeling throughout. Bedrooms include studio suites, with a small fridge and toaster in addition to the standard tea/coffee making facilities, and all rooms have good facilities including full bathrooms (with bath and shower). The hotel has six rooms to suit meetings of various sizes and The Library, a large new room on the ground floor, for conferences and banqueting. In addition to indoor leisure facilities (including a lovely swimming pool) within the grounds, the hotel has its own nine hole golf course and residential golf breaks are a speciality.

Conference/banqueting (80/100) Business centre. Leisure centre. Tennis, golf (9/18), fishing, Own parking. Wheelchair accessible. Children (Under 3s free in parents' room; cots available).Pets permitted. **Rooms 51** (26 suites, 10 no-smoking, 1 for disabled) B&B £65pps, ss £30 Open all year Amex, Diners, MasterCard, Visa. **Directions:** Off main Dublin-Galway road (N4): take exit for Newcastle off dual carriageway.

Malahide   *Bon Appetit*

RESTAURANT

9 St James Terrace Malahide Co Dublin
Tel/Fax: 01 845 0314

Patsy McGuirk's well-established basement restaurant is in a Georgian terrace near the marina. Attractive, recently renovated decor is enhanced by a collection of local watercolours and there's a welcome emphasis on comfort. Patsy offers a shortish, well-balanced lunch menu and and a 5-course dinner menu, daily specials and "chef's recommendations" in addition to a full à la carte. The style tends to be classic French, sometimes tempered by Mediterranean and modern Irish influences. Seafood, mostly from nearby Howth, predominates but steaks, Wicklow lamb, farmyard duckling and ostrich, which is farmed nearby, also feature. Fresh prawn bisque with cognac is a regular and a long-established house speciality is Sole Creation McGuirk (a whole boned black sole, filled with turbot and prawns, in a beurre blanc sauce – now a classic) while simple sole on the bone is presented whole at the table, then re-presented bone-free and neatly reassembled. Pretty desserts: fresh strawberries in a crisp filo basket, sliced and sprinkled with Grand Marnier is typical, or there's an Irish cheese platter. A fine wine list has its heart in France; there are helpful tasting notes and a special selection, as well as six house wines.Children over 12 welcome. **Seats 60** (private room, 20) No smoking area. Air conditioning. L 12.30-2 Mon-Fri, D 7-10.30 Mon-Sat; Set L £15, Set D £28, also à la carte; house wine from £11.50; sc discretionary. Closed Sun, Bank Holidays & Xmas week Amex, Diners, MasterCard, Visa. **Directions:** In a period terrace, on a slip road opposite the tennis club.

Malahide   *Grand Hotel*

Malahide Co Dublin

HOTEL   Tel: 01 845 0000 Fax: 01 845 0987 email: info@thegrand.ie

Just 8 miles from Dublin airport, and set in six acres of gardens, this seaside hotel is well-situated for business and pleasure. Many of the bedrooms have sea views, the beach (tidal estuary) is just across the road and there are numerous golf courses nearby. A new wing, including 50 new executive rooms was completed in June 1999. Conference/banqueting (700/800) Business centre. Leisure centre (21 metre swimming pool). Tennis, golf (9/18) and fishing nearby. Own parking. Wheelchair accessible. Children welcome (under 12s free in parents' room; cots available). No pets. **Rooms 150** (7 suites, 2 mini-suites, 39 executive rooms, 15 shower only, 25 no-smoking, 1 for disabled) Lift B&B £90pps, ss £30 Closed 25-26 Dec Amex, Diners, MasterCard, Visa. **Directions:** Centre of Malahide, 10 mins from Dublin Airport and 30 mins from Dublin city centre.

Malahide ❉   *Les Visages Restaurant*

9 Marine Court The Green Malahide Co.Dublin

RESTAURANT   Tel: 01 8451233 Fax: 01 8460892

Sinead McGowan's pleasant first-floor restaurant overlooks a little of the "old Malahide" where small boats are beached alongside a couple of old cottages - a glimpse of life as it was here only a few years ago before the massive marina complex (which is inevitably also in view) changed Malahide for ever. Window tables are preferable, of course, but the restaurant is arranged to include convivial booths and all tables seem quite comfortable. A warm welcome and friendly, helpful service make a good start and the food - from menus which are imaginative but not over-ambitious - is generally of an admirably high standard, although details like repeating garnishes on consecutive dishes, can spoil an otherwise good impression. **Seats 60.** D 5-10.30 Tues-Sat, L12.30-3.45 Sun only, Set SunL £12.95 Set D £15.95, early evening menu 5-6.30 only £12.95, à la carte available, house wine £10.95 No smoking area Air conditioning sc discretionary Children welcome Closed 25-28 Dec Amex, Diners, MasterCard, Visa. **Directions:** Turn left at traffic lights in centre of Malahide, then right at next lights. Restaurant is on right on first floor overlooking estuary and marina.

Malahide   *Siam Thai Restaurant*

Gas Lane Malahide Co Dublin

RESTAURANT   Tel: 01 845 4698 Fax: 01 478 4798 email: siames@tinet.ie

Handily located in a laneway close to the marina (although parking can be tricky), this large, well-appointed restaurant was well ahead of the wave of global and Pacific Rim restaurants that has hit the Dublin area recently and it is holding its own in the face of growing competition. Suracheto Yoodsang, head chef since 1996, presents menus that offer many of the Thai classics on an extensive à la carte as well as the set menus. The balance of ingredients is "true Thai" and dishes not only have variety – in textures as well as flavours – but there's a willingness to vary the spiciness according to personal preference. Dishes attracting praise on a recent visit include Siam Combination Appetizers (a selection for two, including chicken satay, spring rolls, special coated prawns, marinated pork ribs, prawns wrapped in ham and bags of golden wonton with plum sauce) and main courses of Ghung Phad Phong Garee (a generous quantity of Tiger prawns with scallions, mushrooms and basil leaves and a good kick to the sauce) and Ped Makham (succulent boneless crisp-skinned duck with crispy noodles and plum sauce). Incidentally, no monosodium glutamate is used in the food (something we applaud). A sister restaurant, Siam Thai Restaurant, Monkstown, Co Dublin (Tel: 01 284 3308) is run on identical lines. **Seats 96** D 6-12 daily Set D from £20, à la carte available, house wine £11.95 Toilets wheelchair accessible Non-smoking restaurant Air conditioning sc 10% Children welcome before 8 pm Closed 25 Dec & Good Fri Amex, Diners, MasterCard, Visa. **Directions:** Down laneway off Strand Street and at bottom of Old Street, near the marina.

Monkstown ✗   *Empress Restaurant*

Clifton Avenue Monkstown Co Dublin

RESTAURANT   Tel: 01 284 3200 Fax: 01 284 3188

Since opening in 1992 owner-chef Burt Tsang has built up a strong local following for this first-floor restaurant just off Monkstown Crescent. He offers regional Chinese dishes

– Sichuan, Shandong and Beijing – plus Thai and Vietnamese cuisine, in set dinners for varying numbers in addition to an à la carte. Specialities include Beijing duck, carved at the table and served with fresh vegetables and hoi sin sauce on pancakes, which requires 24 hours notice. A good choice of vegetarian options is always available; typically Thai vegetable curries. Charming service. D££ 6-12 Mon-Sat; Sun open from 3pm.

Monkstown · *The Purty Kitchen*

Old Dunleary Road Monkstown Co Dublin
PUB · Tel: 01 284 3576

Established in 1728 – making it the second oldest pub in Dublin (after The Brazen Head) and the oldest in Dun Laoghaire – this attractive old pub has seen some changes recently, but its essential character remains. It has retained the dim atmosphere that seems to be a constant feature of the best old Irish pubs and is well set up for enjoyment of the bar food, for which it has earned a good reputation. Meals£-££

Portmarnock ▥ · *Portmarnock Hotel & Golf Links*

Strand Road Portmarnock Co Dublin
Tel: 01 846 0611 Fax: 01 846 2442
HOTEL/RESTAURANT · email: reservatins@portmarnock.com

Originally owned by the Jameson family, of Irish whiskey fame, Portmarnock Hotel and Golf Links enjoys a wonderful beachside position overlooking the islands of Lambay and Ireland's Eye. Very close to the airport, and only eleven miles from Dublin city centre, the hotel seems to offer the best of every world – the peace and convenience of the location and a magnificent 18 hole Bernhard Langer-designed links course. Public areas, including an impressive foyer, are bright and spacious, with elegant modern decor and a relaxed atmosphere. The Jameson Bar, in the old house, has great character and there's also an informal Links Bar and Restaurant next to the golf shop. Accommodation is particularly imaginative, designed so that all rooms have sea or golf course views. Rooms – including some in the original house which are furnished with antiques, two suites with four-posters and private sitting rooms and executive rooms with balconies or bay windows – are all furnished to a very high standard of comfort and have excellent bathrooms. Conference/banqueting (350/220) Business centre/secretarial services. Golf(18), Own parking. Wheelchair accessible. Children welcome, cots available). No pets. **Rooms 103** (2 suites, all en-suite). Lift. B&B £102pps, ss £38 Open all year Amex, Diners, MasterCard, Visa. **The Osborne Restaurant:** Named after the artist Walter Osborne, who painted many of his most famous pictures in the area including the view from the Jameson house, the restaurant has been a major addition to the north Dublin dining scene since the hotel opened in 1996. Eric Faussurier, who has been executive chef from the outset, makes full use of local ingredients – especially seafood from the nearby fishing port of Howth – in a classic style with New Irish Cuisine influences. **Seats 110** (private room, 20) No smoking area. D 7-10.30 Tues-Sat, Set D £32.50, à la carte available; house wine from £13.75; sc discretionary. Toilets wheelchair accessible **Directions:** From Malahide, take coast road for 2km; on left hand side.

Rathcoole · *An Poitin Stil*

Rathcoole Naas Rd Co Dublin
PUB/RESTAURANT · Tel: 01 458 9244 Fax: 01 4588091

An imposing thatched pub on the Naas dual carriageway, the Poitin Stil looks like a contemporary superpub from the road, but although it has changed a lot in recent years, it was actually established in 1643. Once inside this famous sporting pub, its daunting first impression is quickly forgotten as it is broken up into several quite different bars, all likely to be packed with punters from the nearby racecourses. A sense of history is a genuine part of its charm: there is a fine old copper still, from which the pub takes its name, and a lot of fascinating original 'Arkle' memorabilia. Good traditional bar food is available from the carvery at lunchtime and there's limited food throughout opening hours. Traditional music also draws the crowds at weekends. Own parking Children welcome. **Seats 120** (private room, 30) No smoking area. Open all day (12-11) Bar food served 12-11 daily, L 12.30-3.30, all à la carte. Toilets wheelchair accessible. Amex, Diners, MasterCard, Visa. Closed 25 Dec & Good Fri. **Directions:** Prominent premises on the Naas Road from Dublin (N8).

Skerries

The Redbank Restaurant & Lodge

7 Church Street Skerries Co Dublin
Tel: 01 849 1005 Fax: 01 849 1598
RESTAURANT/ACCOMMODATION
email: redbank@tinet.ie

There's a double-entendre to the name of Terry and Margaret McCoy's restaurant - there is a sandbank of the same name nearby, but it's also in a converted banking premises, which makes a restaurant of character and practicality - even the old vault had its uses: as a wine cellar. Margaret provides a warm welcome, serving aperitifs and crudites in an elegantly furnished bar/reception area and overseeing service in the comfortable, traditional restaurant (where smoking is only allowed if a private party takes over a room). One of the great characters of contemporary Irish cooking – and currently President of the Restaurants Association of Ireland – Terry is an avid supporter of local produce and suppliers and is always experimenting to make the most of them. Fresh seafood from Skerries harbour provides the backbone of his menus, but without limiting the vision – this is a man who goes out at dawn with a bucket to gather young nettles for soup. Dishes conceived and cooked with generosity are often named after key points on the local land- and sea-scape, or are related to history – thus grilled goats cheese St Patrick is a reminder that the saint once lived on Church Island off Skerries. The dessert trolley is legendary (perhaps the traditional adjective "groaning" should apply to the diners – a large space should be left if pudding is to be part of your meal). Should the sauces and accompaniments prove too much, plainly cooked food is gladly provided and dishes suitable for vegetarians are marked on the menu. **Seats 50.** D 6-9.30 daily L12.30-4.30 Sun only £15.75, Set D £26, à la carte available, house wine £12.75 No smoking area sc discretionary Children welcome before 8 pm Closed 24-25 Dec Amex, Diners, MasterCard, Visa. **Directions:** Heading north from Dublin on N1, turn off at Blake's Cross and follow road to Skerries. Accommodation is offered in comfortably furnished bedrooms and there are facilities for meetings/small conferences (max 10). **Rooms 12** (all en-suite, 7 no-smoking, 1 for disabled) B&B £35pps, ss £10

Stillorgan

China-Sichuan Restaurant

4 Lower Kilmacud Road Stillorgan Co Dublin
RESTAURANT
Tel: 01 288 4817 Fax: 01 288 0882

Five miles south of Dublin city centre, David and Julie Hui's China-Sichuan Restaurant is rather unique – it has been run in co-operation with the cultural exchange programme of the state-run China Sichuan Catering Service Company since opening in 1986. While it looks much the same as any other Chinese restaurant, its chefs and special spices are supplied direct from Sichuan province, and it quickly gained recognition for its authentic oriental food and refusal to "bland-down" the style to suit local tastes (although spicy and chilli-hot dishes are clearly identified on menus). "Bon Bon Chicken" for example, is a dish of cold chicken shreds in a hot and spicy sauce – but the kitchen is flexible enough to alter the spicing to suit individual tastes. While set menus are relatively limited (especially at lunch time), the à la carte offers plenty to tempt the most jaded palate. Poultry is a strength – smoked duckling in Sichuan style, for example, which is smoked over bay leaves, black Chinese tea leaves and camphor wood then deep-fried, producing a crisp-skinned and succulent dish with a delicate, subtle smoky flavour. Beef, lamb and especially pork marry well with traditional flavourings, and seafood dishes offer much more than the usual king prawns – black sole, monkfish, scallops and squid all feature – and there's a hot seafood combination in garlic. A separate vegetarian menu also includes plenty of hot and spicy dishes, and interesting vegetable side dishes include a choice of stir-fried vegetables (one choice from a list – the Chinese don't mix them all up as Westerners do) and fried long beans, flavoured with chopped Chinese radish. Children welcome before 8 pm. **Seats 60.** Air conditioning. L 12.30-2 & D 6-10.30 daily. Set L £8, Set D £20, à la carte available; house wine £11.50; sc 10%. Toilets wheelchair accessible. Closed 24-26 Dec & Good Fri. Amex, MasterCard, Visa. **Directions:** 5 miles from city, through Stillorgan main road, turn right from Lower Kilmacud Road

Stillorgan

Stillorgan Park Hotel

Stillorgan Co Dublin
HOTEL   Tel: 01 288 1621 Fax: 01 283 1610 email: sales@stillorganpark.com

Since coming under new management in 1994 this hotel on the Stillorgan dual carriageway has had a complete makeover and is now remarkable for a dashing modern style throughout. Public areas include the stylish reception and lounge areas that are visible from the road and must be a great draw to passers by. Bedrooms - some with views of Dublin Bay - are spacious, attractively decorated in a bright contemporary style and have well-finished bathrooms. Good facilities for business guests include work space and fax/modem lines in rooms. Conference/banqueting (180/140) Business centre/secretarial services. Own parking. Wheelchair accessible. Children (Under 2s free in parents' room; cots available).No pets. **Rooms 100** (2 suites, 6 mini-suites, 92 executive rooms, 10 no-smoking, 4 for disabled) Lift. B&B £65pps, ss £34 Open all year Amex, Diners, MasterCard, Visa.

The Purple Sage Restaurant: An attractive, informal restaurant with seating in several areas, there is a distinctly continental feel to the stylishly decorated Purple Sage, and it certainly doesn't have that "hotel dining room" atmosphere. Staff are welcoming and charming and head chef Enda Dunne's menus are imaginative and appealing in the contemporary global style. Vegetarian dishes are especially tempting and the hotel regularly runs special themed dining weeks, including one when "healthy options" are highlighted on the menu and a Healthy Hint given each day such as "Poach fish and experiment with different herbs". The cooking is good and the real effort made to please and interest customers is commendable. Children welcome. **Seats 50.** No smoking area. Air conditioning. L 12-2.30 & D from 5.45 daily. Set L £13.95, Set Sun L £14.95, Set D £21.95, à la carte available; house wine £10.50; sc discretionary. Toilets wheelchair accessible. **Directions:** Situated on main N11, 2 miles from Dublin city centre

---

Swords ✗   *Lukas*

River Mall Main Street Swords Co Dublin
RESTAURANT   Tel/Fax: 01 840 9080

Kate Gibbons' informal first-floor restaurant – on the river side of the main street in Swords – is an atmospheric little place serving modern food at reasonable prices. Home-made pastas take pride of place on head chef Denis Murnane's eclectic menus, typically offering a choice of spaghetti, penne or tagliatelle served with accompaniments and sauces, such as chicken and blue cheese or tomato, basil and garlic. There are also the more traditional pesto and carbonara sauces. Spicier cuisines influence some of the starter choices – quesadillas, for instance, or chicken wings Tex-Mex style, and there are several Mexican/Cajun main courses plus a list of daily blackboard specials. Live music on some nights. D£-££ daily

---

Swords   *The Old Schoolhouse*

Coolbanagher Church Road Swords Co Dublin
RESTAURANT   Tel: 01 840 2846   Fax: 01 840 5060   email: sincater@indigo.ie

In a quiet riverside site close to the Northern Cross motorway, and only 5 minutes from the airport, this 18th century stone school building has been restored by the Sinclair family to make a attractive country-style restaurant. Mojor renovations during 1999 have seen the dining room restored to its original 20' height, with exposed beams and the garden and conservatory upgraded for al fresco dining. Personal service and good home cooking are the aims; all ingredients are locally sourced and fresh every day, which allows for a seasonal à la carte and table d'hôte menus that change about twice a week (plus daily blackboard specials which include a lot of seafood). à la carte menus offer starters such as Westport mussels with garlic, shallots and white wine and an unusual Old Schoolhouse-style chowder, with big chunks of fish, whole crab claws and generous juices rather than soup – filling and excellent. Main courses include classics such as black sole on the bone meunière (faithfully rendered) and less usual options like wild boar with figs. Children welcome. **Seats 80** (private room, 10/20) No smoking area Air conditioning. L 12.30-2.30 & D 6.30-10.30 Mon-Sat. Set L £12.95, Set D £25.95; early bird menu £16.95 Mon-Fri till 7.30; à la carte also available;house wine £11.50; sc discretionary. Closed Sundays, Xmas-New Year, Easter weekend. Amex, Diners, MasterCard, Visa. **Directions:** From Dublin, turn left after Lord Mayor's Pub

CARLOW

When you are surrounded by counties as famous as Kildare, Wicklow, Wexford and Kilkenny, then you have to make a special effort, and Carlow punches way above its weight. For although it is Ireland's second smallest county, it confidently incorporates such wonderful varieties of scenery that it has been memorably commented that the Creator was in fine form when He made this enchanting place. Whether you're lingering along the gentle meanderings of the waterway of the River Barrow, or savouring the soaring lines of the Blackstairs Mountains as they sweep upwards to the 793 m peak of Mount Leinster, this gallant little area will have you in thrall. There's history a-plenty if you wish to seek it out. But for those who prefer to live in the present, the county town of Carlow itself buzzes with student life and the energetic trade of a market centre, while a more leisurely pace can be enjoyed at riverside villages such as Leighlinbridge and Bagenalstown. The tidy little town of Borris is a charmer, one of Ireland's better kept secrets, typical in fact of Carlow county, a place cherished by those who know it well.

Local Attractions and Information

Carlow Town,	Tourist Information 0503 31554
Tullow	Altamont Gardens 0503 59128

Ballon ❄   *Ballykealey Country House*

Ballon Co Carlow

COUNTRY HOUSE HOTEL   Tel: 0503 59288 Fax: 0503 59297 email: bh@iol.ie

Seat of the Lecky family for three centuries, the present house was designed by Thomas A Cobden (designer of Carlow cathedral) and built in the 1830s as a wedding present. Gothic arches and Tudor chimney stacks take you back to the architectural oddities of the time, but the house is set in well-maintained grounds and has recently been extensively refurbished. Large, comfortably furnished reception rooms have a friendly atmosphere and quite impressive individually designed rooms are in keeping with the character of the house but with the necessary modern amenities, including direct-dial phones, tea/coffee trays and TV. The Garden Room restaurant overlooks the grounds; head chef James Murray recently moved from Kilkea Castle. Small conferences (35); secretarial service. No wheelchair access; not suitable for children under 12. No pets. **Rooms 12** (2 shower only, 4 executive, 4 non-smoking). B&B £45pps, ss £20 +10% sc. Restaurant **Seats 38** (private room 25/30), Open Tues-Sun, D 6.30-9.30pm, Set D £28.50. Closed 23 Dec-7 Feb. MasterCard, Visa. **Directions:** N80 from Carlow, about 10 miles on right 1 mile before Ballon.

Bagnelstown   *Lorum Old Rectory*

Kilgreaney Co Carlow

COUNTRY HOUSE   Tel/Fax: 0503 75282 email: lorum@lorum.com

Pet Friendly Establishment

This historic country house is close to many places of interest, including medieval Kilkenny, New Ross (where river cruises are available), Kildare's National Stud and Japanese Gardens. Close by is Gowran Park racecourse and activities such as golf and a riding school (offering both outdoor and indoor tuition). Elegant, spacious and very comfortable accommodation includes a lovely drawing room for guests and a bedroom with a four-poster (at a small supplement); all rooms have phones and tea/coffee trays. But it is Don and Bobbie Smith's hospitality that keeps bringing guests back. Euro-Toques member Bobbie prepares good home cooking based mainly on organic ingredients. Dinner for residents is served at a long mahogany table (book by 3 pm). This is a really relaxed family-friendly and pet-friendly place - children enjoy swings in the orchard and there are many interesting resident animals - so it is hardly surprising that this is a place where guests are welcome to bring their own dogs too, by arrangement. Private parties/small conferences (10). Own parking. **Rooms 5**, all en-suite. B&B £35pps, ss £10. Dinner £22.50. Closed 22-30 Dec. Amex, MasterCard, Visa. **Directions:** On the R705, 4 miles from Bagnelstown.

Borris ❊ — *The Step House*

66 Main Street Borris Co Carlow
ACCOMMODATION   Tel: 0503 73209 Fax: 0503 73395

Cait Coady's attractive old house has undergone extensive renovation and has been stylishly decorated and furnished in period style, with antiques throughout. Well-proportioned reception rooms include a fine dining room (used for breakfast); a matching drawing room that overlooks the back garden was being redesigned at the time of our visit and a putting green is planned for 2000. The Coadys also own the bar next door and have recently taken over one of Ireland's finest classic pubs, Tynans Bridge Bar, in Kilkenny city. NB - there are several flights of stairs, including steps up to the front door. Children over 12 welcome. Pets permitted by arrangement. Own parking. **Rooms 6** (5 shower only). TV. No wheelchair access. Closed 20 Dec-18 March. MasterCard, Visa. **Directions:** From main Carlow-Kilkenny road, take turning to Bagnelstown.

Carlow — *Barrowville Townhouse*

Kilkenny Road Carlow Co Carlow
ACCOMMODATION   Tel: 0503 43324 Fax: 0503 41953

Guesthouse of the Year

Ex-hoteliers Marie and Randal Dempsey have run this exceptionally comfortable and well-managed guesthouse just a few minutes walk from the town centre for ten years. Although immaculately maintained the house is old, so bedrooms vary in size and character, but all are comfortable and attractively furnished with a mixture of antiques and fitted furniture, plus direct dial phones, tea/coffee trays and TV. Good housekeeping and generous, thoughtfully designed and well-finished bathrooms contribute greatly to a generally high standard of comfort. Marie Dempsey is renowned for excellent breakfasts served in a lovely conservatory (complete with a large vine) overlooking the lovely back garden. There is also a particularly pleasant and comfortable residents' drawing room, with an open fire, grand piano and plenty to read. Private parking. Garden. Children over 12 welcome. No pets. **Rooms 7**, all en-suite & non-smoking. £25 pps, £5 ss. Open all year. Amex, MasterCard,Visa. **Directions:** Southside of Carlow town, on the N9.

Carlow — *Beams Restaurant*

59 Dublin Street Carlow Co Carlow
RESTAURANT   Tel: 0503 31824

Originally a coaching inn, this characterful building has been lovingly restored by the owners, Betty and Peter O'Gorman, who have run it as a restaurant since 1986. They also operate The Wine Tavern off-licence and specialist food shop next door - and Peter's passion for wine is reflected in the wine list which, on a recent visit, included outstanding house wines. Massive wooden beams create a warm atmosphere and are a reminder of the building's long history (it has actually held a full licence since 1760) and, although there are some eccentricities about the restaurant and the way it is run, the essentials are right and many of the country's trendy young restaurateurs would do well to come and learn some basics here. Classic French cuisine is the speciality of French chef Romain Chall, who has been at The Beams since it opened and is deservedly described by Peter O'Gorman as a "master craftsman" He has established a reputation for fine fare, including game (such as wild duck and pheasant in season) and seafood such as scallops and sole, which are often on the dinner menu (at a very small supplement). Vegetarian dishes regularly feature on the menu (seasonal vegetables, many of them grown by Peter, are a delight) and any special dietary requirements can be met at a day's notice. **Seats 40** D only Tue-Sat from 7.30 pm; D £22. Closed Sun & Mon, 1 wk Xmas. MasterCard, Visa. **Directions:** Town centre, on main street.

Carlow ˣ — *Danette's Feast*

Urglin Glebe Carlow Co Carlow
RESTAURANT   Tel: 0503 40817 Fax: 0503 40817

Danette O'Connell and David Milne opened their relaxed country house restaurant in 1994 and have built up a considerable reputation, particularly for the regular musical evenings which have become a special feature. Except when the weather is fine enough for aperitifs in the garden, David welcomes guests with drinks and nibbles in a little drawing room where there is an open fire in winter. Having taken orders from one of Euro-

Toques chef Danette's imaginative menus, diners are escorted through to one of two well-proportioned dining rooms furnished with antiques. Seasonal menus always include some interesting vegetarian options and feature specialist Irish products including bio-dynamically grown produce from west Wicklow and a fine range of farmhouse cheeses. The famous musical evenings take place once a month - a soirée followed by an 8-course Tasting Menu. As both David and Danette are musicians, the background music for each meal is also treated as an important element of the dining experience. Open Weds-Sat D£££ Sun L££. Closed 1 wk Xmas and Bank Hols. MasterCard, Visa

Carlow ❋   *Dolmen Hotel*

Kilkenny Road Carlow

HOTEL   Tel: 0503 42002 Fax 0503 42375 email: reservations@dolmenhotel.ie

Carlow's newest hotel is an obvious choice for large gatherings, provides comfortable accommodation with all the expected amenities (remote multi-channel TV, direct dial phone, tea/coffee tray, trouser press) and also has apartments available for fishing, shooting, horseriding or golf breaks. The site could perhaps have been used to greater advantage (the river view at the back is largely wasted, while the restaurant overlooks the carpark at the front, for example) and the hotel had not quite settled in on our visit, so some changes may be expected. Off-season value breaks. Conferences/banqueting (750/650); secretarial services; video-conferencing on request. Wheelchair access. Ample parking. Garden. Children under 12 free in parents' room; cots available. No pets. **Rooms 40** (all en-suite, 3 suites, 6 non-smoking rooms, 1 equipped for disabled). £52.50pps, ss £12. Closed 25 Dec. Amex, Diners, MasterCard, Visa. **Directions:** 1.5 miles from Carlow on main Kilkenny road.

Leighlinbridge ˣ   *The Lord Bagenal Inn*

Leighlinbridge Co Carlow

PUB   Tel: 0503 21668 Fax: 0503 22639

The Lord Bagenal is a useful place to break a journey and there's a very pleasant walk along the river. A great deal of development has recently taken place and was still continuing (to include accommodation) at the time of going to press. The proprietor, James Kehoe, has taken care to retain some of the best features of the old building - notably the old end bar, with its open fire and comfortably old-fashioned air and the restaurant section beside it - while incorporating many interesting new ideas. The grandest is ongoing work around the harbour area but the most novel is undoubtedly the supervised indoor playroom, which is in the bar but behind glass so that, in time-honoured fashion, offspring can be seen and not heard. The new bar arrangement includes a buffet - bar meals which were disappointing on the Guide's most recent visits but will hopefully return to the high standards for which The Lord Bagenal was famous. Seasonal restaurant meals offer a fairly robust modern Irish style, with local farmhouse cheeses and a strong wine list. Open all day daily meals £, D££. Closed Good Fri & 25 Dec. Diners, MasterCard, Visa.

CAVAN

Cavan town is blossoming in 2000 as it begins to enjoy the benefits of a new by-pass. Because the county's main roads have naturally follows the easiest routes through the least resistant territory, most visitors have an abiding impression of Cavan as a watery place of low-lying rounded little hills, intertwined with many lakes and rivers. And certainly much of the county is classic drumlin country, almost with more water than they know what to do with. But if you take your time wandering through this green and silver land - particularly if travelling at the leisurely pace of the deservedly renowned Shannon-Erne Waterway which has joined Ireland's two greatest lake and river systems - then you'll become aware that this is a place of rewardingly gentle pleasures. And you'll have time to discover that it does have its own mountain, or at least it shares the 667 m peak of Cuilcagh with neighbouring Fermanagh. In fact, Cavan is much more extensive than is popularly imagined, for in the northeast it has Shercock with its own miniature lake district, while in its southeast it takes in all of Lough Ramor at the charming lakeside village of Virginia. It also shares Lough Sheelin, that place of legend for the angler, with Westmeath and Meath, and always throughout its drumlin heartlands you can find many little Cavan lakes which, should the fancy take you, can be called your own at least for the day that's in it.

Local Attractions and Information

Belturbet	Tourist Office 049 22044
Cavan	Tourist Information 049 31942
Co Cavan Ballyjamesduff International Pork Festival (June)	049 44242

Ballyconnell   Slieve Russell Hotel & Country Club

Ballyconnell Co Cavan

HOTEL   Tel: 049 9526444 Fax: 049 9526474 email: slieve-russell@quinn-hotels.com
Close to the attractive town of Ballyconnell, on the recently re-opened canal linking the Shannon and Lough Erne, this is a particularly unspoilt area well known for its myriad lakes and fine fishing. This striking flagship of the Sean Quinn Group is named after a nearby mountain and set amongst 300 acres of landscaped gardens and grounds, including 50 acres of lakes, everything is on a generous scale - and it's very much the social and business centre of the area. In the foyer, generous seating areas are arranged around the marble colonnades and a grand central staircase, flanked by a large bar on one side and two restaurants at the other. All bedrooms have pleasant country views, extra large beds and spacious marble bathrooms as well as the usual amenities (direct dial, phone tea/coffee tray,TV, trouser press Excellent conference and business facilities are matched by leisure facilities in the Golf and Country Club - the championship golf course, which opened in 1992, has become one of the top golfing venues in Ireland and there's a putting green, practice area and nine hole, par 3 course. Off-season value breaks. Conference/banqueting (550). Hairdressing. Leisure centre. Golf, tennis, snooker, garden. Children under 3 free in parents' room; crèche. No pets. **Rooms 151** (10 suites, 3 mini-suites, 3 disabled rooms) £80pps, ss £15. Lift. Open all year. Amex, Diners, MasterCard, Visa. **Directions:** (From Dublin) take N3 to Cavan, to Ballyconnell.

Belturbet   International Fishing Centre

Loughdooley Belturbet Co Cavan

GUESTHOUSE/RESTAURANT   Tel: 049 9522616

Michel and Yvette Neuville's International Fishing Centre offers residential fishing holidays, mainly for continental guests, and they also run a restaurant which is open to non-residents. As well as attracting local diners, the restaurant provides an excellent facility for holidaymakers on river cruises, as there are pontoons at the bottom of the garden - where, with typical French practicality, the menu is clearly displayed. The centre is like a little corner of France, with all signage in French and a very French menu accompanied by a sensible wine selection and a refreshingly reasonable bill. When the weather allows, tables are set out on the terrace. Ample parking. Children welcome up to 9pm. No pets. **Rooms 16** (all en-suite) £24 pp, no ss. No pets. Restaurant **Seats 80** Max preferred table size 8, no children after 9 pm. D 7-9 daily. Set/early D£14 @ 7 pm; Gourmet menu £25; also à la carte. House wine £8. Open all year. MasterCard, Visa **Directions:** From centre of Belturbet, take Ballyconnell direction and turn right off Bridge Street, then right again (past Emerald Star) and next right again to International Fishing Centre.

Blacklion ☆   *MacNean House & Bistro*

Blacklion Co Cavan

RESTAURANT/ACCOMMODATION   Tel: 072 53022 Fax: 072 53404

Nearby attractions include Marble Arch Caves and Florence Court, golf, fishing and hill walking - but it is Neven Maguire's cooking that has put this little border town firmly on the culinary map. Since winning the Baileys Euro-Toques Young Chef competition in 1994 - with a prize giving him experience in a Luxembourg restaurant - Neven's cooking moved into the international class, culminating in his selection to represent Ireland at the world's most prestigious cooking competition, the Bocuse d'Or, in 2001. Here, in a small and distinctly low-key family restaurant, Neven sources the best local produce and prepares menus that reflect international trends rather than local preferences. Lamb, beef, guinea fowl, quail, scallops, langoustine ("Dublin Bay Prawns"), cod, halibut and organic produce from nearby Eden Plants are typical and the choice is wide (and perhaps sometimes over-ambitious) for a small establishment. Desserts have always been a particular passion for Neven and it's a must to leave a little room for one of his carefully crafted confections - the grand finale is just that in this case. Sunday lunch somehow combines elements of the traditional meal with more adventurous choices - and very good value at £12. Friendly service, by family members. Vegetarian dishes are on the main menu and there's a separate vegetarian menu. No children under 10 after 7 pm. Non-smoking restaurant. **Seats 40** D 6-9, Tue-Sun; L Sun only, from 12.30. Gourmet Dinner £32. House wine from £10. Service discretionary. Closed Monday & 24-26 Dec. MasterCard, Visa. Accommodation **Rooms 6** (all en-suite & non-smoking; 2 shower only). £25pps, ss£26. Direct-dial phone, tea/coffee tray & TV in all rooms. Children welcome; cot available. No pets. **Directions:** On N16, main Belfast-Sligo route.

Butlersbridge   *Derragarra Inn*

Butlersbridge Co Cavan

PUB   Tel/Fax: 049 4331003

This well-known thatched inn makes a useful place to break a journey and is easily spotted by the famous collection of agricultural memorabilia around the door - and there's more of the same inside. Recent renovations have improved the existing bar and introduced a new one with extra seating for up to 80. Food has always been reliable - popular bar staples, plus some more ambitious restaurant dishes with the emphasis on steaks and seafood. Wheelchair access. Own parking. Children welcome. **Meals** Mon-Sat 10.30-9.45, Sun 12.30-3 & 7-9.45. Set Sun L £10. Closed 25 Dec & Good Fri. MasterCard, Visa. **Directions:** Parallell to the new by-pass, on the old main road, a few miles north of Cavan town.

Cavan   *Hotel Kilmore*

Dublin Road Cavan Co Cavan

HOTEL   Tel: 049 4332288 Fax: 049 4332458 email: kilmore@quinn-hotels.com

The leading hotel of the area, the Kilmore has an impressive foyer and spacious public rooms and it's the focal point of local business and social activities - also a pleasant place to break a journey. Bedrooms, which include a bridal suite, are comfortable and well-equipped with direct dial 'phones, TV and tea/coffee trays. Leisure activities nearby include golf, fishing and horse-riding Conference/banqueting (100/500) Children welcome (under 2s free in parents' room, cot available). No pets. **Rooms 39** (all en-suite, 2 mini-suites, 2 rooms for disabled). Open all year. Amex, Diners, MasterCard, Visa. **Directions:** N3 Dublin-Cavan road; on right hand side approaching Cavan town.

Cavan   *Lifeforce Mill*

Mill Rock Cavan Co Cavan

CAFÉ/RESTAURANT/VISITOR CENTRE   Tel: 049 4362722 Fax: 049 4362923

The Lifeforce Mill dates back to 1846 and, although the commercial milling operation closed down in the 1950s, it is now enjoying a new lease of life welcoming visitors and producing Lifeforce Stoneground Wholemeal Flour. All of the original machinery has been restored to working order, including what is believed to be the only working McAdam Water Turbine. Designed by Belfast engineer Robert McAdam, the turbine was used to harness the power of the Kennypottle River and drive the great stone wheels instead of the usual, but slower and less efficient, water wheel. The innovative mill tour allows visitors to experience the end result as well as learning about the workings of the mill itself: each visitor makes a loaf of traditional soda bread with the stoneground flour produced by the mill at the beginning of the tour and collects it, hot from the ovens of the coffee shop, on leaving. Wholesome fare is served in the coffee shop/restaurant - which also has a tale to tell. Although Victorian, it is not part of the original mill site - it was transported from Drogheda to avoid demolition during road improvements, then re-erected beside the mill. In addition to the daytime coffee shop, an informal contemporary restaurant, Granario's, is now open four evenings a week. Not suitable for very small children (under 2). Meals: **Seats 65**, Tue-Sat all day, 9-5; D Thur-Sun 6-11 at 'Granario's'; à la carte. Toilets wheelchair accessible. MasterCard, Visa. Closed Mon & 24 Dec-7 Jan. **Directions:** Signed in the centre of Cavan town.

Cloverhill ✳   *The Olde Post Inn*

Cloverhill Co Cavan
Tel: 047 55555 Fax: 047 55111
RESTAURANT/BAR/ACCOMMODATION   email: oldepostinn@tinet.ie

This old stone building in a neatly landscaped garden served as a post office until 1974 and has now been renovated and converted to make an attractive inn. There's a proper bar to enjoy your pre/post-prandial drinks and the restaurant is furnished in an appropriately old-world style, with bare walls and beams, country furniture - comfortably rustic. On a recent visit, service was friendly and efficient, the menu imaginative and the cooking, in a contemporary Irish style, sound. Local produce features strongly - typically locally farmed venison (on a bed of caramelised red onions with a gin & juniper sauce) and duckling (maple-roasted with a rosti stuffing, citrus & vodka sauce) - although, surprisingly, no pork- for which Cavan is famous. Accommodation is quite comfortable, although not as luxurious as the brochure implies. Ample parking. Wheelchair access (restaurant/ground floor only). Children welcome. Restaurant **Seats 70** Private room (25); no smoking area. D 6.30-8.30 (daily Mar-Sep) Set D £29; also à la carte. L £14.50 Sun only, from 12.30. Closed all Mon & Feb15-Mar1; Sun D 1 Oct-1 Mar. MasterCard, Visa. **Rooms 6** (4 en-suite, 2 shower only), £30 pps, ss £5. 1 family room; children free in parents' room up to 12. No pets. **Directions:** 5 miles north of Cavan town on N54 to Monaghan.

Kingscourt   *Cabra Castle Hotel & Golf Club*

Kingscourt Co Cavan
HOTEL   Tel: 042 9667030 Fax: 042 9667039 email: cabrach@iol.ie

Formerly known as Cormey Castle and renamed Cabra Castle in the early 19th century, this impressive hotel is set amidst 100 acres of garden and parkland, with lovely views over the Cavan countryside, famous for its lakes and fine fishing. (The nearby Dun A Ri Forest has many walks and nature trails on land once part of the Cabra estate.) Although initially imposing, with its large public rooms and antique furnishings, the atmosphere at Cabra Castle is relaxing. Due to the age of the building, the bedrooms vary in size and outlook, but all are comfortable and individually decorated. Accommodation includes some ground floor rooms suitable for less able guests, four suites and, in addition to rooms in the main building, the newer rooms in an extension are particularly suitable for families. There are also some romantic beamed rooms, in a courtyard that has been converted to provide modern comforts without sacrificing character. A special combination of formal background and easy ambience make this a good venue for private and business functions; it is popular for both weddings and conferences but special interest breaks such as golf, fishing and horse-riding are also a great attraction. Conferences/banqueting (300); secretarial services. Garden, golf (9), fishing. Off-season value breaks. Ample parking. Wheelchair accessible. Children welcome; pets permitted. **Rooms 70** (incl 2 suites, 2 mini-suites, 8 executive rooms, 1 disabled room) B&B £60 pps, ss£20. Closed 24-26 Dec. Amex, Diners, MasterCard, Visa. **Directions:** 1.8 miles outside Kingscourt on Carrickmacross Road.

Kingscourt ✗   *Gartlans Pub*

Main Street Kingscourt Co Cavan
PUB   Tel: 042 9667003

This pretty thatched pub is a delightfully unspoilt example of the kind of grocery/pub that used to be so typical of Ireland, especially in country areas. Few enough of them remain, now that the theme pub has moved in, but this one is real, with plenty of local news items around the walls, a serving hatch where simple groceries can be bought, all served with genuine warmth and hospitality. The Gartlans have been here since 1911 and they have achieved the remarkable feat of appearing to make time stand still. Closed 25 Dec & Good Fri.

Mountnugent ✗   ### Ross House & Castle

Mountnugent Co Cavan

COUNTRYHOUSE   Tel/Fax: 049 8540218 email: rosshouse@tinet.ie

In mature grounds on the shores of Lough Sheelin, Peter and Ulla Harkort's old manor house enjoys a very lovely location and offers a good standard of accommodation at a modest price. Bedrooms, which are distinctly continental in style, have telephone, TV and tea/coffee trays and some unusual features: three have their own conservatories, four have fireplaces (help yourself to logs from the shed) and all have an unfamiliar type of shower not likely to be seen elsewhere in Ireland. Peace and relaxation are the great attraction, and there's a fine choice of activities at hand: a pier offers boats (and engines) for fishermen to explore the lake, there's safe bathing from a sandy beach, tennis and a sauna. At the castle nearby, Peter and Ulla's daughter Viola Harkort provides most unusual accommodation (it is a very real castle) and organises pony trekking and horse-riding. Ulla cooks for everyone, making packed lunches, sandwiches and High Tea (£3-£10) and a 4-course dinner (£14/£18). Children and pets welcome. Acc£-££. Open all year. MasterCard, Visa. **Directions:** From Dublin: N3 Navan-Kells, then Oldcastle-Mountnugent, where signposted.

CLARE

While America's First Lady may have been officially visiting Galway city when she came to Ireland in the summer of 1999, the people of Clare move into the new century entertained by knowing that Mrs Clinton and her entourage were seen one afternoon having themselves a fine old time one afternoon across the bay in County Clare. There's a heroic quality to this western county which other places deny at their peril. This, after all, is "The Banner County" of Gaelic sporting legend. This is the homeland of some of the finest traditional music in the land. This is a larger-than life county which is bounded by the Atlantic to the west, Galway Bay to the north, the Shannon and Lough Derg to the east, and the Shannon Estuary to the south. And it's typical of Clare that, even with its boundaries marked on such a grand scale, there is always something extra added. Thus the Atlantic coasts include not only the astonishing and majestic Cliffs of Moher, but also one of Ireland's greatest surfing beaches at Lahinch on Liscannor Bay. As for that Galway Bay coastline, it is where The Burren, the fantastical North Clare moonscape of limestone which is home to so much unexpectedly exotic flora, comes plunging spectacularly towards the sea around the attractive village of Ballyvaughan. To the eastward, Lough Derg is one of Ireland's most handsome lakes, but even amidst its generous beauty, we find that Clare has claimed one of the most scenic lake coastlines of all. As for the Shannon Estuary, well, Ireland may have many estuaries, but needless to say the lordly Shannon has far and away the biggest estuary of all. Yet despite the heroic scale of its geography, the urban centres of Clare such as the county town of Ennis and and the increasingly busy recreational port of Kilrush, together with smaller places like Ennistimon, Milltown Malbay, Corofin and Mountshannon - they all have a very human and friendly dimension. For this is a county where the human spirit defines itself as being very human indeed in the midst of scenic effects which at times seem to border on the supernatural.

Local Attractions and Information

Ballyvaughan	Aillwee Cave, 065 7077036
Bunratty	Bunratty Castle & Folk Park 061 361020
Cliffs of Moher	(Tourist Information) 065 7081171
Ennis	World Irish Dancing Championships (March) 01 4752220
Kinvara	Dunguaire Castle (medieval banquets etc) 061 360788
Quin	Craggaunowen Project (Celts &Living Past) 061 360788
Shannon Airport	Tourist Information 061 61664 / 61565

Ballyvaughan | *Aillwee Cave*

Ballyvaughan Co Clare

CAFÉ/VISITOR CENTRE | Tel: 065 7077036 Fax: 065 7077107

Visitors to this 2-million-year-old cave will see more than the amazing illuminated tunnels and waterfalls, for there is much of interest to foodlovers as well. Driving up to the entrance, look out for the sign to the cheese-making demonstrations - for it is here that the local Burren Gold cheese is made. Even if the process is in a quiet phase at the time of a visit, there is still plenty to see - and buy - as the cheesemaking takes place alongside a well-stocked food shop. Just inside the entrance to the cave there is a souvenir shop with a good book section (including travel and cookery books of Irish interest) and a café/restaurant serving inexpensive, wholesome fare - typically baked potatoes with Burren Gold cheese Children welcome. Cafe **Seats 58** No-smoking area. Toilets wheelchair accessible Meals all day Mon-Sun. Closed 25 Dec. Amex, MasterCard, Visa **Directions:** 5 miles south-west of Ballyvaughan; well-signposted throughout the area.

Ballyvaughan | *An Fear Gorta (Tea & Garden Rooms)*

Ballyvaughan Co Clare

RESTAURANT | Tel: 065 7077023 / 065 7077127

Approached from the harbourfront through a lovely front garden, Katherine O'Donoghue's delightful old stone restaurant dates back to 1790, when it was built as a residence for 'coast security officers'. Having been rebuilt by the present owners in 1981, it is now just the spot for a light bite to eat. In fine weather the beautiful back garden or the conservatory can be idyllic; otherwise the homely dining room offers comfort and shelter, with its informal arrangement of old furniture and a tempting display of home-baked fare. This is the speciality of the house - all laid out on an old cast-iron range and very reasonably priced - beginning at only 90p for scone, butter & home-made jam. Speciality teas are available as well as savoury choices including farmhouse cheeses, home-baked ham and Tea Room Specials including Open Smoked Salmon Sandwich on Brown Bread. 2-3 course lunch specials are available at £6/£7 and there's even home-made jam and marmalade to take away. Open 11-5.30 (L 12-4.30.) Mon-Sat June-Sept; Closed Oct-May. No credit cards. **Directions:** On the harbour front in Ballyvaughan, beside Monks pub.

Ballyvaughan 🏛

COUNTRYHOUSE HOTEL & RESTAURANT

Gregans Castle

Ballyvaughan Co Clare
Tel: 065 7077005 Fax: 065 7077111
email: res@gregans.ie

Gregans Castle has a long and interesting history, going back to a tower house, or small castle, which was built by the O'Loughlen clan (the region's principal tribe) between the 10th and 17th centuries and is still intact. The present house dates from the late 18th century and has been continuously added to, up to the present day. The present owners, Peter and Moira Haden, opened Gregans Castle as a country house hotel in 1976 and (true to the traditions of the house) have continued to develop and improve it (recently with their son Simon-Peter who is now Manager). The exterior is grey and stark, in keeping with the lunar landscape of the surrounding Burren, serving only to heighten the contrast between first impressions and the warmth, comfort and hospitality to be found within. Spacious accommodation, which includes four suites and two mini-suites, is furnished to a very high standard and rooms all have excellent bathrooms and lovely countryside views. Peace and quiet are the dominant themes - the otherwise luxurious rooms are deliberately left without the worldly interference of television. Yet this luxurious hotel is not too formal or at all intimidating; non-residents are welcome to drop in for lunch or afternoon tea in the Corkscrew Bar - named after a nearby hill which, incidentally, provides the most scenic approach to Ballyvaughan. In fine weather guests can sit out beside the Celtic Cross rose garden and watch patches of sun and shade chasing across the hills. Children welcome (no concessions, but cot available @ £10). No pets. **Rooms 22** (4 suites, 2 mini-suites) B&B £68 pps; ss£40. No service charge. Hotel closed late Oct-early April. Amex, MasterCard, Visa. **The Dining Room** is elegantly furnished in keeping with the rest of the house and has recently been extended to include a new bay window area and beautifully redecorated in a rich country house style. Most tables now have lovely views over the Burren (which on fine summer evenings enjoys very special light effects as the sun sets over Galway Bay) and dinner is often gently accompanied by a pianist or harpist. Head chef John Hughes, who joined the hotel in April 1999, cooks confidently in the modern Irish style with some French influence and offers a wide choice of dishes based on the best of local produce, including organic vegetables. There is always a selection of local cheeses, with homemade biscuits. **Seats 50** (Private Room, 30). No smoking area. Children welcome (not under 10 after 7.30). Toilets wheelchair accessible. D 7-8.30, 5-course D £36, any 2 courses £25. House wines from £14.50. Service discretionary. Corkscrew Bar: L 12-3 daily (short à la carte). **Directions:** On N67, 3.5 miles south of Ballyvaughan.

Ballyvaughan

HOTEL

Hyland's Hotel

The Square Ballyvaughan Co Clare
Tel: 065 7077037 Fax: 065 7077131 email: hylands@tinet.ie

Open fires, comfortable well-crafted furniture and sympathetic lighting create a welcoming atmosphere that is carried through into all areas of this delightful family-run hotel, which dates back to the 18th century and ownership is currently in the capable hands of 7th and 8th generation family members Marie & Deirdre Hyland. Food served is based on excellent local produce - locally caught seafood, Burren lamb, farmhouse cheeses, organic vegetables and herbs. New bedrooms have recently been added and all are very comfortable, with good amenities (direct dial phone, tea/coffee tray, TV). Off-season value/special interest breaks. Children under12 free in parents' room, cots available. No pets. **Rooms 30** (15 non-smoking,one for disabled). B&B £46.50 pps. Closed mid Dec-14 Feb. Amex, Diners, MasterCard,Visa. **Restaurant: Seats 50** D 7-9.15 daily, à la carte. House wine £10.50. Service discretionary. Bar Meals 12.30-9.30 daily; à la carte. **Directions:** In centre of Ballyvaughan, beside the harbour.

Ballyvaughan [PUB★]

Monks Bar & Restaurant

The Quay Ballyvaughan Co Clare
PUB/RESTAURANT
Tel: 065 7077059

Michael and Bernadette Monks' famous pub is an informal, cottagey kind of a place with several small bars well set up for the comfortable consumption of delicious informal meals, especially seafood. It's been drawing people along to the pier at Ballyvaughan since 1981 and, now the next generation is also having its say as David and Jennifer Monks have taken on an active management role, there's an even stronger emphasis on food. They do their own special version of seafood chowder and fishcakes are also a speciality, or you can have real prawn cocktail or mussels steamed in garlic, or open prawn or salmon sandwiches. If you want to splash out a bit and spend more than a fiver, there's a seafood platter (or, for the faint-hearted, a half platter) and, after 6pm, an extensive menu including poached fresh salmon, lobster, steak, chicken, lamb and more, served with hot vegetables. There's always a vegetarian dish of the day and a nice choice of wines to wash it all down with. Live music (Tue/Wed night traditional, Sat modern). **Seats 80** No smoking area. Toilets wheelchair accessible. L 12-3.45 (Sun to 5), D 6-8.45 (Sun to 8). A la carte. House wine £11.50. Closed 25 Dec, Good Fri. MasterCard, Visa. **Directions:** In Ballyvaughan village, beside the pier.

Ballyvaughan

Rusheen Lodge

Knocknagrough Ballyvaughan Co Clare
ACCOMMODATION   Tel: 065 7077092 Fax: 065 7077152 email: rusheen@iol.ie

Since they first welcomed guests to Rusheen Lodge in 1991, Rita and John McGann have built up an enviable reputation for hospitality. Generously proportioned, well-appointed bedrooms, good bathrooms and spacious public rooms make this a very comfortable place to stay. Breakfast - whether traditional Irish or continental- is a major feature of a stay. Evening meals are not provided, but the pubs and restaurants of Ballyvaughan are only a few minutes walk. It was John McGann's father, Jacko McGann, who discovered the Aillwee Cave, an immense network of caverns and waterfalls under the Burren which is now a major attraction in the area. Wheelchair access. Parking, Children welcome, under 2 free in parents' room. No pets. **Rooms 8** (2 suites, 6 executive rooms, all no-smoking). B&B £30 pps, ss£10. Closed Dec & Jan. Amex, MasterCard, Visa. **Directions:** Just south of Ballyvaughan village on the N67.

Ballyvaughan

Whitethorn Restaurant

Ballyvaughan Co Clare
RESTAURANT   Tel: 065 7077044 Fax: 065 7077155email: whitethorne@tinet.ie
Wine List of the Year

Sarah and John McDonnell's restaurant is beautifully located on the sea side of the road and, as they also run a fine craft shop and a visitor centre, "Burren exposure" where visitors learn about the formation of the Burren rockscape, its history and the amazing diversity of flora which brings so many visitors to the region in early summer. The restaurant has magnificent sea views and offers excellent home-made self-service fare throughout the day (which visitors can take indoors or out depending on the weather and inclination): home-made soups including chowder and a daily special - carrot & lovage perhaps, smoked salmon quiche and stuffed char-grilled aubergine are all typical and all modestly priced. On Fridays and Saturdays in July and August, evening brings a more formal dining arrangement, but offers the same good cooking and excellent value in imaginative menus based on local produce. Tempting vegetarian dishes, nice homely desserts - and, of course, an especially interesting wine list. John's passion for wine got him involved with running The Australian Wine Bureau in Ireland, but the restaurant wine list travels much further afield and the pleasure with which he has sourced Whitethorn's liquid offerings is tangible in the reading. What's more, he makes out individual wine suggestions to match specific dishes on the dinner menus - and even sits down with guests while they're considering the menu, to help with making the best choices to suit the food, individual taste and the mood of the moment. All this is done with the lightest possible touch - and John's sheer enthusiasm is infectious. Self-service Meals 12-4.30 daily, average main course £5.95 Restaurant, **Seats 120** D Fri & Sat; à la carte,average main course £13.95. House wine £9.95. Closed Nov-Mar Diners, MasterCard, Visa. **Directions:** 0.25 miles from Ballyvaughan on Galway road, N67.

Bunratty ❈ ✗
Bunratty Castle Hotel
Bunratty Co Clare

HOTEL   Tel: 061-364116 Fax: 061 364891

This new hotel on a rise just beside Bunratty Castle has been quite attractively designed to reflect its Georgian origins. Comfortable, traditionally furnished rooms have all the modern comforts, including air conditioning. **Rooms 60** B&B from £40 pps. Closed 25 Dec. Amex, Diners, MasterCard, Visa.

Bunratty
Durty Nelly's
Bunratty Co Clare

PUB/RESTAURANT   Tel: 061 364861

Although often seriously over-crowded with tourists in summer, this famous and genuinely characterful old pub in the shadow of Bunratty Castle somehow manages to provide cheerful service and above-average food to the great numbers who pass through its doors. All-day fare is served downstairs in the Oyster Restaurant daily 12-10.30; L 12-3; D 6-10.30) upstairs there is a more exclusive restaurant, The Loft, open in the evening only (Mon-Sat, 6-10). Both areas offer à la carte menus. Closed 25 Dec, Good Fri. Amex, Diners, MasterCard, Visa. **Directions:** Just off the N18 Limerick-Galway road, beside Bunratty Castle.

Bunratty
Fitzpatrick Bunratty Hotel
Bunratty Co Clare

HOTEL   Tel: 061 361177 Fax: 061 471252 email: info@fitzpatrick.com

Conveniently located just ten minutes from both Shannon International Airport and Limerick city, Fitzpatrick Bunratty is in wooded grounds beside Bunratty Castle and Folk Park and offers good facilities for both business and leisure guests. The style of the building is typical of many hotels established in the 1960s, but the Fitzpatrick Hotel Group have been energetic in their efforts to update facilities. Public areas are quite impressive, as are recent additions, including a fine fitness centre with 20 metre swimming pool and an excellent conference & banqueting centre with state-of-the-art facilities. Bedrooms are well-equipped, with the facilities expected of a hotel of this calibre, and considerable improvements have been undertaken during the past year - 30 bedrooms, a new gallery lounge and PJ's restaurant have all been refurbished and work was due to continue on further bedrooms during the winter of 1999. (As this is incomplete at the time of going to press it may still be advisable in the meantime to inquire about the decorative state of bedrooms when booking.) Off season breaks offer good value. Conference/banqueting (1000/500); video-conferencing; secretarial services. Leisure centre. Garden. Children under12 free in parents room; cots available. Wheelchair accessible. **Rooms 115** (6 suites,10 no-smoking rooms, 13 for disabled). £74.95 pps, ss £20. Closed 25 Dec. Amex, Diners, MasterCard, Visa. **Directions:** Just off the N18 Limerick-Galway road, beside Bunratty Castle

---

Clarecastle 🏛
Carnelly House
Clarecastle Co Clare

COUNTRYHOUSE   Tel: 065 6828442 Fax: 065 6829222 email: rgleeson@iol.ie

Conveniently located for Shannon airport and for touring the west of Ireland,Dermott and Rosemarie Gleeson's fine redbrick Georgian house is set on 100 acres of farm and woodland and offers discerning guests very special accommodation. Reception rooms include an impressive drawing room with Corinthian pillars, Francini ceiling, grand piano and a striking panelled dining room where communal dinners are taken at 8 pm. (Residents only, except groups for lunch or dinner by arrangement.) Bedrooms are large and furnished to a very high standard, with antiques, canopied king size or twin beds and luxurious private bathrooms. Yet the grandeur is not at all daunting and Carnelly - which is also well-placed for a wide range of country pursuits, including many of the country's most famous hunts - has been described as "one of the warmest, friendliest and most entertaining houses in Ireland". Not suitable for children under 10. There is also a gate lodge, which is available by the night, week or month. Pets permitted by arrangement. **Rooms 5** (all executive, 2 no -smoking) £87.50 pps, ss£32.50. Closed mid Dec-mid Mar Amex, Diners, MasterCard, Visa. **Directions:** On N18, one mile south of Clarecastle.

Corofin ✣   *Caherbolane Farmhouse*

Caherbolane Corofin Co Clare
FARMHOUSE   Tel: 065 6837638

Holiday makers often complain that farmhouses aren't what they used to be - there's no real sense of being on a farm. Well, Sinead Cahill's quite ordinary-looking roadside farmhouse **is** real and you're quite likely to meet your hostess in green wellingtons, busying herself around the farm between looking after the house and making dinner. Families will feel at home immediately. Children welcome. No pets. **Rooms 3** (1 ensuite); B&B £17.50, ss £5. Dinner by arrangement. Closed 31 Oct-16 May. No credit cards. **Directions:** Signposted from Corofin - 5 Km on the Gort road.

Corofin ✣   *Clifden House*

Corofin Co Clare
COUNTRY HOUSE   Tel/Fax: 065 6837692

This unusual early Georgian manor on the shore of Lough Inchiquin was found "slipping gracefully into ruin" 20 years ago by Jim and Bernadette Robson who, while conceding that "the work is not yet finished nor will it be twenty years hence", have gone a considerable way towards restoration "following the criteria of respecting its tradition of hospitality and the comfort of our friends and guests". Bedrooms are highly individualistic (one bathroom in particular even more so), stylish and comfortable - do not be concerned that certain areas, including the stairs and landing, are only partially restored. Hospitality is king here and the Robsons enjoy their food, in every sense of the word - organic meats come from a nearby farm, fish and game are also local and vegetables and fruit from their own walled garden - Bernadette enjoys cooking (ask to see her collection of old cookery books) and everybody enjoys the results. There is a short wine list and guests are also welcome to bring their own. Accommodation is also offered in two 3- and 4-bedroom holiday houses in a stable wing, with cobbled yard and riverside lawn; they can be either self-catering or serviced. Gardens, walking, fishing (boats available). Children welcome (cot available). No pets. **Rooms 4** (all en-suite, 1 shower only). £35 pp (no ss). Communal dinner at 8 pm, £20. Closed mid Dec-mid Mar. **Directions:** Two kilometres west of Corofin.

Corofin ✣   *Fergus View*

Kilnaboy Corofin Ennis Co Clare
FARMHOUSE   Tel: 065 6837606 Fax: 6837192 email: deckell@indigo.ie

Mary Kelleher runs a very hospitable house and the care taken to ensure guests enjoy their visit to the full is shown in details like the the information packs on the area compiled by her and left in each bedroom - and an interesting breakfast menu that includes home-made yogurt, freshly squeezed juice, home-made muesli, local cheese and a wide range of teas as well as cooked breakfasts with free range eggs. Rooms are comfortable although a little on the small side, as often happens when family homes are converted to include en-suite facilities. But refurbishment is an ongoing buisness and there is also a lovely stone cottage next door, Tigh Eamon, which has been charmingly converted for self-catering accommodation. Children welcome (cot available). No pets. **Rooms 6** (5 en-suite, all shower only). £22pps (£20 without shower); ss £11 (£8 without shower). Dinner 6.30 Mon-Fri £16.50; wine licence. Closed 1 October-Easter. No credit cards. **Directions:** 2 miles north of Corofin on Kilfenora road; first house on left after Kilnaboy medieval church.

Cratloe   *Bunratty View*

Bunratty Co Clare
ACCOMMODATION   Tel: 061 357352 Fax: 061 357491

A modern house, providing comfortable, spacious accommodation conveniently close to Bunratty Castle and Shannon Airport. Rooms have double and single beds, phone, tea/coffee facilities, satellite TV, hairdryers and en-suite bathrooms which vary somewhat (some shower only). There's a comfortable residents' lounge with an open fire and bright dining room, where good breakfasts are served. **Rooms 6** (all en-suite, 3 no-smoking, 2 suitable for less able guests); B&B £20 pps, ss £5. Closed 24-30 Dec MasterCard, Visa. **Directions:** Signed off the N18 (1st left after Bunratty Castle, coming from the airport).

Doolin ✗   *Aran View House Hotel*

Coast Road Doolin Co Clare

HOTEL   Tel: 065 74061 Fax: 065 74540

Just outside Doolin, and commanding dramatic sea views across to the islands, the Linnane's family-run hotel makes a good base for a family holiday - it is only a mile to a good beach, there is sea-angling and golf nearby and, of course, there is the traditional music for which Doolin is world famous. Public rooms include a comfortable bar for all weathers - it has a sea view and an open fire. Bedrooms vary considerably in size and outlook due to the age and nature of the building: rooms at the front are most desirable - several at the back have no view, but are otherwise pleasant. A high proportion - six rooms - are suitable for disabled guests and there are two extra large ones and two singles; six are non-smoking. All are en-suite with over-bath showers, tea/coffee trays and TV (local stations) Children are welcome - outdoor play area and children's menu provided. There is a restaurant (open to non-residents) with very reasonably priced set menus (£10 at lunch and dinner) available as well as an à la carte offering local produce, including lobster. **Rooms 19** (all en-suite); B&B £45 pps. Closed 31 Oct-1 April. Amex, Diners, MasterCard, Visa. **Directions:** Just outside Doolin, on the left approaching on the coast road from Ballyvaughan.

Doolin ❊   *Doolin Crafts Gallery*

Ballyvoe Doolin Co Clare

RESTAURANT   Tel: 065 7074309 Fax: 065 7074511

This delightful place could keep you happily occupied for longer than you think - Hillary Clinton spent four hours here on her recent visit to the west of Ireland and it's easy to see why. The shop is jam-packed with terrific, quality crafts and clothing - some of them exclusively available here - and the Flagship Restaurant will tempt you to linger over what is, with unusual accuracy, described as "simple home cooking, using local produce, and home baking": grilled local goats cheese with pesto on garden salad, Lisdoonvarna smoked salmon plate, fresh salmon mayonnaise on brown bread, Kerry apple pie. Ah, if only there were more places like this. The garden is quite charming too, and very typical of Clare. **Seats 40** (+ 20 in garden) No-smoking restaurant. Open 10-6 daily. Closed 1 Oct-Good Fri. A la carte. House wine £10. Service charge discretionary. **Directions:** Beside the cemetery, just outside Doolin.

Doolin ✗   *O'Connor's Pub*

Doolin Co Clare

PUB   Tel: 065 74168 Fax: 065 74668

Famous world-wide for its nightly traditional music, song and dance, O'Connor's pub has brought many people to Doolin. Although the pub has changed hands recently, its reputation for music remains the incentive for many people to travel to this small fishing village. Closed 25 Dec & Good Fri. **Directions:** In the centre of Doolin village

Ennis ✗   *Auburn Lodge Hotel*

Galway Road Ennis Co Clare

HOTEL   Tel: 065 21247 Fax: 065 21202

This pleasant modern hotel just 20 minutes from Shannon airport is built around a central courtyard containing a soothing garden, creating a peaceful atmosphere throughout the building. Quite spacious rooms have good facilities and include some larger executive suites and a pretty bridal suite. Acc££. Amex, Diners, MasterCard, Visa.

Ennis   *The Cloister*

Club Bridge Abbey Street Ennis Co Clare

BAR/RESTAURANT   Tel: 065 6829521 Fax: 065 6824783

This remarkable pub and restaurant has been run by Jim and Annette Brindly since 1991, and although improvements have been made - including the addition of a conservatory a couple of years ago - they have been careful to retain the character of the building, which is actually built into the walls and garden of the adjacent 13th-century abbey. The food style tends towards traditional dishes such as Irish stew and fish pie on the bar menu with more classical dishes in the restaurant. The character of the place -

stone walls and floors, open fires - and nightly traditional music sessions are a great attraction. 'Wine vault at the Cloister' tastings/sales by the case by arrangement. Parking arrangement with nearby carpark. Children welcome Restaurant **Seats 60**. No smoking restrictions. L Mon-Sat 12.30-2.45, D Mon-Sun 6-8.45 (Sun to 8.30). Set D £14. House wine £12. Closed 24-28 Dec. **Directions:** In town centre - turn right at Maid of Erin roundabout.

Ennis
Queen's Hotel & Cruise's Pub

Abbey Street Ennis Co Clare
HOTEL/PUB   Tel: 065 6828963 Fax: 065 6828628

Recent refurbishment has given this centrally located hotel a contemporary feel, especially in its Cafe Bar and Bistro. Bedrooms are more traditional and have all the necessary amenities - ISDN lines as well as direct dial phone, tea/coffee tray, satellite TV with video channel. Cruises pub, next door and in common ownership, has a real sense of history as it's right beside the ruins of the Ennis Friary and dates from 1658. Although quite recently renovated it has retained original features and avoided the "theme pub" atmosphere. Nightly traditional music sessions are a major feature and there's a medieval room, "The Sanctuary", available for folklore evenings and private functions for up to 200 guests. Children under 4 free in parents' room; pets permitted by arrangement. **Rooms 52** (all en-suite, 4 shower-only, some non-smoking). Wheelchair accessible. Lift. Meals Brasserie open all day, eg Irish stew, steak sandwiches. Closed 25 Dec & Good Fri. Amex, Diners, MasterCard, Visa. **Directions:** In centre of town.

Ennis
Garvello's

Clareabbey Limerick Road Ennis Co Clare
RESTAURANT   Tel: 065 6840011 Fax: 065 6840022

'More than just good food' is an appropriate motto for Gay and Jean O'Hara's well-appointed restaurant on the outskirts of Ennis. It is unusual for the area, not least for its very striking modern style - incorporating a bright bar/reception area, wooden floors and very special individual carpets throughout. Head chef Jorg Gerlach uses local produce in contemporary dishes - typically Liscannor Bay scallops with roast celeriac mash, spaghetti of vegetables and a trio of sauces. The menu changes weekly and a vegetarian menu is also available. **Seats 70**. D 6.30-10, Mon-Sat. Set D £25. Service discretionary. No-smoking area. Toilets wheelchair accessible. Own parking. Closed Sun & Mon, Bank Hols, 24-25 Dec & 1 Jan, 1st 2 weeks November. Amex, Diners, MasterCard, Visa. **Directions:** On the right just as you enter Ennis from Limerick direction.

Ennis ✳
Newpark House

Ennis Co Clare
FARMHOUSE   Tel: 065 6821233 email: newparkhouse.ennis@tinet.ie

Strange as it may seem to find a genuine farmhouse in a country setting within easy walking distance of the pubs and restaurants of Ennis, the Barron family home is the exception that defies easy description. It's an old house of great historic interest with large homely rooms, furnished with old family furniture and an hospitable, relaxing atmosphere. Bedrooms vary in size and character, as old houses do, but are comfortable and full of interest. Children may stay free in their parents' room up to 3; pets permitted. Communal dinner £17 at 6.30, book by 3 pm. **Rooms 6** (all en-suite). B&B £25pps, ss £10. **Directions:** Going into Ennis on the R352, turn off opposite the Roselevan Arms.

Ennis
Old Ground Hotel

O'Connell Street Ennis Co Clare
HOTEL/RESTAURANT   Tel: 065 6828127 Fax: 065 6828112 email: oghotel@iol.ie

This ivy-clad former manor house dates back to the 18th century and, set in its own gardens, creates an oasis of calm in the centre of Ennis. One of the country's best-loved hotels, the Old Ground was bought by the Flynn family in 1995 and has been imaginatively extended and renovated by them in a way that is commendably sensitive to the age and importance of the building. Despite the difficulties of dealing with very thick walls in an old building, major improvements were made to existing banqueting/conference facilities in 1996/97, then an extra storey was added to provide new rooms. Again, this has been a sensitive development and, as the famous ivy-clad frontage continues to thrive, the external changes are barely noticeable to the casual observer. Major refurbishment has also taken place throughout the interior of the hotel, including all bedrooms - which have good amenities and well-designed bathrooms - the O'Brien Room restaurant and a traditional style bar, Poet's Corner (bar menu 12.30-9) features traditional music on Wednesday, Thursday and Friday nights. A new bistro is due to open in January 2000. **Rooms 83** (all en-suite.7 mini-suites, 20 executive rooms & 20 non-smoking rooms) B&B £58pps; ss £32. Closed 25-26 Dec. Amex, Diners, MasterCard, Visa

O'Brien Room Restaurant

The hotel's formal dining room is at the front of the hotel and has great character. Head chef Gerry Walsh, who has been with the hotel since 1977, takes pride in using local produce in imaginatively presented dishes such as roast rack of Burren lamb with apricot & almond stuffing or a trio of local seafood. **Seats 80** (private rooms available for 30-275 guests). L12.30-3. D 6.30-9.30 daily. Set L £11.95, Set D £19.95. **Directions:** From N18 (Limerick/Galway road), follow signs to the hotel from the outskirts of Ennis.

Ennis   *Temple Gate Hotel*

The Square Ennis Co Clare

HOTEL   Tel: 065 6823300 Fax: 065 6823322 email: templegh@iol.ie

Built in the centre of Ennis town, to a clever design that makes the best possible use of the site, this family-owned hotel opened to some acclaim in 1996. While retaining the older features (including a church which was first used as a pub and is now the Great Hall Banqueting/Conference room, seating up to 200), existing gothic themes have also been successfully blended into the new, creating a striking modern building which has relevance to its surroundings in the heart of a medieval town. Since then it has succeeded in providing the comfort and convenience expected by today's travellers at a reasonable price. The hotel was soon extended to add 40 new deluxe rooms, two new state-of-the-art syndicate/conference rooms for up to 100 people, and a new "Preachers Bar" replacing the original one in the church. At the time of going to press the restaurant was undergoing extension and redesign, on the same theme as Preachers Bar. Conference/banqueting (220/265); business centre, video-conferencing, secretarial services, ISDN lines. Own parking. Garden. Children under 5 free in parents' room; cot available. Pets allowed in some areas. **Rooms 74** (2 suites, 4 mini-suites, 4 executive rooms, 12 non-smoking & 1 disabled). B&B £50 pps, ss £20. Closed 25-26 Dec. Amex, Diners, MasterCard, Visa. **Directions:** Follow signs for town centre hotels; next door to the tourist office.

Ennis   *West County Conference & Leisure Hotel*

Clare Road Ennis Co Clare

HOTEL   Tel: 065 6828421 Fax: 065 6828801 email: cro@lynchotels.com

Business Hotel Award - Lynch Hotels

Recently extended and refurbished, this modern hotel 5 minutes walk from the centre of Ennis town is not only a well-located and comfortable base for holidaymakers but also renowned for its exceptional conference facilities. The hotel's Island Convention Centre can seat 1,650 delegates in a range of four conference rooms and five meeting rooms that are almost infinitely variable. There is also video-conferencing, full business/office support services and an impressive Health and Leisure Club in which to wind down or shape up. Bedrooms include interconnecting rooms, mini-suites, family rooms and 43 recently added Premier standard rooms with ISDN lines. Off-season value breaks. Children under 3 years free in parents' room. No pets. Ample parking. **Rooms 152** (1 executive, 29 non-smoking, 2 for disabled). B&B £59 pps, ss £15. Lift. Open all year. Amex, Diners, MasterCard, Visa. **Directions:** On the edge of Ennis town on the N18, main Limerick-Galway road.

Ennis ✳   *Woodstock Hotel & Golf Club*

Shanaway Road Ennis Co Clare

HOTEL   Tel: 065 6844777 Fax: 065 6844888 email: woodstock.ennis@tinet.ie

This latest hotel in the Barry Wyse/PJ Daly portfolio (Hibernian Hotel & Grey Door Dublin, McCausland Hotel Belfast) is due to open in March 2000. It is built around a 19th century manor house on around 200 acres, now mostly utilised by the golf course. Bedrooms feature ISDN lines, air conditioning and safe, in addition to the usual amenities. Children are welcome (free in parents' room up to 2; cots available; playroom & crèche provided) and there will be a health and fitness club on the premises and an equestrian centre half a mile away. Conferences/meetings (up to 200); video conferencing, buusiness centre, Given the track record of the team involved, this promises to be a high quality development. **Rooms 65.** (Prices not available at time of going to press). Lift. Closed 24-27 Dec. Amex, Diners, MasterCard, Visa. **Directions:** From Ennis, take main N18; at the first roundabout take N85 to Lahinch for 1/2 mile, then turn left and continue 1/2 mile to hotel.

Kilbaha   *Anvil Farm Guesthouse*

Kilbaha Loop Head Co Clare
ACCOMMODATION   Tel: 065 9058018 Fax: 065 9058133

In a house beside the family's clifftop farm at the end of the Loop Head peninsula, Maura Keating provides comfortable accommodation in one of the country's most remote and unspoilt areas. Rugged cliff scenery, angling, diving, bird watching and walking are some of the attractions that bring visitors to this wild and windblown beauty spot - the perfect antidote to city life. There is plenty to visit in the area too -Maura has all the details for her guests - and good local food for dinner, including Aberdeen Angus beef from their own farm, locally caught Atlantic salmon and local Inagh and Cratloe cheeses. Visitors may also visit the farm, which has a variety of animals and a special interest in Irish sport horse breeding. **Rooms 5** (4 shower-only) B&B £20, ss£5. D by arrangement. Closed1 Nov-1 March **Directions:** Take Loop Head road from Kilkee; Anvil Farm is 2 miles after Cross village.

Kilfenora   *Vaughan's Pub*

Kilfenora Co Clare
PUB   Tel: 065 7088004

One of the most famous music centres in the west of Ireland, traditional Irish music and set dancing at Vaughan's pub and (previously thatched) barn attract visitors from all over the world. In the family since about 1800, John and Kay Vaughan have worked hard since the mid-70s to ensure that visitors to this attractive old pub have the best possible time and it is now being taken over by Mark and Orla Vaughan and moving into a new generation. The pub is warm and homely, with an open fire in the front bar and a garden set up with tables at the back. Kay still personally supervises the food, which has become an important part of the operation over the years: traditional Irish menus (bacon & cabbage, beef & Guinness casserole) are based on good local ingredients, including organic meats, seafood and North Clare cheese. **Seats 50** food served 12-9 daily,Closed 25 Dec & Good Fri. MasterCard, Visa. **Directions:** 18 miles from Ennis on the main street of Kilfenora.

Kilkee ❋   *Halpins Hotel*

Erin Street Kilkee Co Clare
HOTEL   Tel: 065 9056032 Fax: 065 9056317 email: halpins@iol.ie

Adapting the original Victorian building of the Halpin family's small townhouse hotel to provide en-suite bathrooms has meant that bedrooms are neat rather than spacious, but they are comfortable and well-appointed with direct-dial phone, TV, hospitality tray with mineral water as well as tea/coffee-making facilities and a laundry service. There's a characterful basement bar with an open fire where visitors, including the many who come to play the adjacent Kilkee Golf Course get together after dinner at the hotel's restaurant, Vittles. In common ownership with Aberdeen Lodge and Merrion Hall (see Dublin entries.) Conference/banqueting (50), secretarial service. Own parking. Off-season value breaks. Children welcome (cots available). No pets. **Rooms12** (2 suites, 10 executive, 4 non-smoking) B&B £50 pps, ss£10. Closed 15 Nov-15 March. Amex, Diners, MasterCard,Visa. **Directions:** In centre of Kilkee

Kilkee ❋   *Ocean Cove Golf & Leisure Hotel*

Kilkee Bay Kilkee Co Clare
HOTEL   Tel: 065 9083111 Fax: 065 9083123 email: cro@lynchotels.com

This newly built member of the Lynch Hotel group opened in July 1999. Well-located, with views over Kilkee Bay and a wide range of facilities for both business and leisure, it should prove an asset to this traditional family holiday and golfing area.

Conference/banqueting (50); video-conferencing, business centre, secretarial services. Leisure centre. Off season value breaks. Parking (100). Children welcome (under 3s free in parents' room); children's playroom. No pets **Rooms 50** (13 non-smoking) B&B £45 pps, ss £15 (Room rate only available, @ £49, max 2 adults, 2 children). Lift. 24 hr room service. **Directions:** Located in Kilkee town (N67 from Ennis).

Lahinch
Aberdeen Arms Hotel

Lahinch Co Clare

HOTEL   Tel: 065 7081100 Fax: 065 7081228 email: aberdeenarms@tinet.ie

The Aberdeen Arms is the oldest golf links hotel in Ireland, with a history going back to 1850. Since Gerry Norton, the current owner, took over in 1995 a major refurbishment and extension programme has been completed, including the construction of a health centre, renovation of public areas and the addition of banqueting and conference facilities. Public areas are spacious and comfortably furnished, including the lively Klondyke Bar (named after Lahinch's famous 5th hole) and an all-day grill room. Bedrooms are generously sized with good bathrooms and quality furniture. Most have views of the golf links and the long sandy beach which brings large numbers of keen surfers to ride the waves. Children welcome (under 5s free in parents' room). No pets. **Rooms 55.** B&B £49 pps, ss £11. Closed 22-29 Dec. Amex, Diners, MasterCard, Visa. **Directions:** In centre of Lahinch, at top of main street on the left.

Lahinch
Barrtra Seafood Restaurant

Lahinch Co Clare
Tel: 065 7081280

RESTAURANT

Paul and Theresa O'Brien have been providing fine food and hospitality at their traditional, whitewashed restaurant on the cliffs just outside Lahinch for over a decade. A couple of years ago they added a conservatory to the side of the original cottagey building, which has made it lighter and brighter and opened up the whole area to make a more spacious atmosphere. The decor has remained appealingly simple and the views of Liscannor Bay - which can be magic from window tables on a fine evening - are mercifully unchanged. Theresa's good, unfussy cooking predictably highlights seafood, but also offers a wide choice (including a vegetarian menu). Paul provides warm and easy hospitality (and maintains good service). Main courses include lobster, when available, and a wide range of other local seafood as well as alternatives such as steak and vegetarian dishes. An interesting and keenly priced wine list, good cheeseboard, home-baked breads and good cafetiere coffee show an attention to detail in tune with an overall high standard which we have found consistently enjoyable over the years. Children welcome before 7 pm. **Seats 32** (Private room available for 6) D only Tue-Sun 5-10 D £24 (Early/Tourist D,5-6.30 £15), also à la carte. House wines £10-£11. Closed January & Mondays except July & August. Amex, MasterCard, Visa. **Directions:** 2 miles south of Lahinch, on Miltown Malbay road.

Lahinch
Mr Eamon's Restaurant

Kettle Street Lahinch Co Clare
Tel: 065 7081050 Fax: 065 7081810

RESTAURANT

Mr Eamon's is the longest established fine dining restaurant in the area. The ambience is cosy and welcoming, with excellent home-baked breads presented along with a menu that promises tasty starters and vegetarian dishes (such as grilled St Tola cheese with tapenade, local Bonina black pudding or courgettes stuffed with stir-fried vegetables) and a wide range of main courses including steaks (and, on winter menus, spiced beef) and rack of lamb. It is especially strong on local seafood. Hot buttered lobster is a speciality, also fresh crab, monkfish and turbot, which might be served with a classic sauce soubise. Good vegetables, farmhouse cheeses, simple well-made desserts and freshly brewed coffee to finish. **Seats 34** D only, 7-9.30 (Sun to 9) Set D £26. Closed Mondays and all February (phone ahead in winter) Toilets wheelchair accessible. Amex, Diners, MasterCard, Visa. **Directions:** In centre of Lahinch, close to beach and golf course.

Lisdoonvarna
Ballinalacken Castle Hotel

Lisdoonvarna Co Clare
Tel/Fax: 065 7074025

HOTEL

Well away from the bustle of Lisdoonvarna, and with wonderful views of the Atlantic, Aran Islands, Cliffs of Moher and the distant hills of Connemara, Ballinalacken is easily identified by the 15th century castle still standing beside the hotel. In the O'Callaghan family ownership since its establishment in 1940, and currently managed by Marian O'Callaghan, Ballinalacken has retained a Victorian country house atmosphere with its welcoming fire in the hall and well-proportioned public rooms comfortably furnished with antiques. The drawing room and recently extended dining room both enjoy magnificent views. Additions and renovations are undertaken on an on-going basis at Ballinalacken, although the 1980s style in some areas now feels dated. Bedrooms are all en-suite, varying according to age and location in the building - some have double and single beds, some are shower only; the best are large with seating areas and sea views and the worst is a dark one at the back with a shower area clumsily fitted into the corner. Children welcome (under 4s free in parents' room). Pets permitted by arrangement. The restaurant is now open to non-residents and the head chef is Frank Sheedy, formerly of Sheedy's Spa View Hotel. **Rooms 13.** B&B £40 pps, ss£20. Closed 5 Oct-20 Apr. Amex, Diners, MasterCard, Visa. **Directions:** On the coast road, 2 miles north of Doolin.

Lisdoonvarna
Sheedy's Hotel & Restaurant

Lisdoonvarna Co Clare

HOTEL/RESTAURANT   Tel: 065 7074026 Fax: 065 7074555 email cmv@indigo.ie

Characterised by a high standard of maintenance indoors and out, attractive furnishings, warm ambience (in every sense - the sunny foyer has a comfortable seating area and an open fire for chillier days) and friendly hands-on management, it is not surprising that Sheedy's is one of the west of Ireland's best loved small hotels. John and Martina Sheedy took up the reins of family business in 1998 and, while the esssential qualities of comfort, good food and hospitality - and, indeed, the basic character of this old hotel - remain, they have been busy putting their youthful imprint on the decor and overall style. This may not necessarily meet with universal approval from regular visitors, but it has been done with such irresistible warmth and enthusiasm that even the curtainless status of the restaurant (which does actually feel a bit bleak) may soon seem a normal state of affairs. Bedrooms vary in size, but are all en-suite, neatly decorated and well-equipped - updating them is the challenge which is currently taxing Martina's imagination. Children welcome (under 10s free in parents' room, cot available). No pets. Own parking. **Rooms 11** (all en-suite, 2 shower only). B&B £30 pps, ss £10. Closed 30 Sep-Easter. Amex, MasterCard, Visa.

Sheedy's Restaurant

John Sheedy - who had been working at Ashford Castle as Chef de Cuisine since 1989 - took on the family kitchen in 1998 and, despite the modern makeover that the restaurant has received (including a change of name from "The Orchid" to "Sheedy's"), there is a reassuring sense of continuity in John's menus, which make creative use of local produce in a contemporary international style. **Seats 35**. D only 6.30-9. A la carte, also early menu 6-7, £15.95. Seafood Bar The cosy bar beside the foyer (previously open only at night) is now an informal Seafood Bar, serving dishes like seafood platters, crab claws in garlic butter, crab salad and open sandwiches. Bar Meals 12-2.30 & 6-9; à la carte; eg hot dish of the day £6.50. **Directions:** In the town centre; from the square follow directions to Sulphur Well.

Miltown Malbay
Berry Lodge

Annagh Miltown Malbay Co Clare
Tel: 065 7087022 Fax: 065 7087011

COUNTRYHOUSE/RESTAURANT   email: ritameade@esatclear.ie

Near the coast of west Clare, between Kilkee and Lahinch, Berry Lodge is a pleasant Victorian country house and the family home of Rita Meade, who has run it as a guesthouse and restaurant since 1994. Comfortable accommodation is provided in bedrooms furnished with an attractive mixture of old and new, including Irish craft items. Cookery classes - given by Rita in her own kitchen - are a special feature of Berry Lodge. Information, including a short breaks brochure, is available on request. Children welcome. No pets. **Rooms 5** (1 suitable for disabled guests, all shower only) Closed 16 Jan-14 Feb. MasterCard, Visa. **Restaurant:** Rita cooks evening meals for guests and non-residents (booking advised) D Mon-Sat high season 6.30-9.39 A la carte; also Early Bird Menu £13.50. L Sun only 1-3, Set L £12.95. Closed Sun D all year and open weekends only off season, except by arrangement. **Directions:** On the N67, between Quilty and Miltown Malbay.

New Quay

PUB

Linnane's Lobster Bar

New Quay The Burren Co Clare
Tel: 065 7078120

Right on the rocks - with a sliding door opening up in summer, the better to enjoy views clear across Galway Bay - the Linnane family's unpretentious pub has a great reputation for good pints of stout and seafood, especially lobster. In winter there's a cosy turf fire and a more limited selection of food - chowder and homebaked bread perhaps, or crab salad. A phone call is advised to check times of opening and whether food is available off-season. **Meals** 12-8 daily (weekends only Oct-Easter). MasterCard, Visa. **Directions:** Halfway between Kinvara and Ballyvaughan.

Newmarket-on-Fergus

COUNTRYHOUSE HOTEL

Carrygerry Country House

Newmarket-on-Fergus Co Clare
Tel: 061 363739 Fax: 061 363823

Only 10 minutes from Shannon airport and in a beautiful rural setting, Carrygerry is a lovely residence dating back to 1793. It overlooks the Shannon and Fergus estuaries and, peacefully surrounded by woodlands, gardens and pastures, seems very distant from an international airport. After sensitive restoration in the late 1980s, Carrygerry has been run by the present owners, Marinus and Angela van Kooyk, as a country house hotel since 1996. Reception rooms are elegantly furnished with antiques and are very comfortable, with open fires. Bedrooms are all non-smoking and include three suitable for disabled guests. Rooms in the main house are spacious and furnished to a high standard in period style, with all the amenities and those in the coachyard are also comfortably furnished, although with rather less style. All the bedrooms have been recently refurbished and bathrooms are due for improvement in the winter of 1999/2000. Small conferences/banqueting (max 60). Children under 12s free in parents' room. Pets permitted. The hotel's restaurant, L'Orangerie, offers dinner 6 days, 7-9.30 (à la carte). **Rooms 12** (4 shower-only; 3 suitable for disabled guests; all no-smoking.) B&B £49 pp, ss £11. Closed Jan & Feb. Amex, Diners, MasterCard, Visa. **Directions:** Very close to Shannon airport; after Shannon Aerospace, turn right, hotel at the end of that road.

Newmarket-on-Fergus

HOTEL

Clare Inn

Dromoland Newmarket-on-Fergus Co Clare
Tel: 061 368161 Fax: 061 368622 email: cro@lynchotels.com

Business Hotel Award - Lynch Hotels

Built in the grounds of Dromoland Castle, this 1960s hotel overlooks the Shannon estuary and shares the Castle's golf course. Spacious, well-maintained public areas include a leisure centre with 17-metre pool, gymnasium and sauna, while banqueting/conference facilities (400) include back-up secretarial services, business centre and video-conferencing. Bedrooms are generally quite large and well-appointed, including some extra features including free movies, ISDN lines and an in-room safe. Children welcome (under 3s free in parents' room, cot available; playroom, creche). No pets. Ample parking. **Rooms 183** (1 suite, 22 executive rooms, 4 non-smoking). B&B £45pps, ss£15 (Room-only Rate also available @ £59 for 2 adults & 3 children). Lift. Open all year. Amex, Diners, MasterCard, Visa. **Directions:** On N18, main Limerick-Galway road, 10 minutes drive from Ennis.

Newmarket-on-Fergus 🏛

HOTEL/RESTAURANT

Dromoland Castle Hotel

Newmarket-on-Fergus Co Clare
Tel: 061 368144 Fax: 061 363355

Sommelier of the Year Award

Dromoland is one of Ireland's grandest hotels, and also one of the best-loved. The ancestral home of the O'Briens, barons of Inchiquin and direct descendants of Brian Boru, High King of Ireland, it is one of the few Irish estates tracing its history back to Gaelic royal families. Today, the visitor is keenly aware of this sense of history, but will not find it daunting. Under the warm and thoughtful management of Mark Nolan, who has been General Manager since 1989, Dromoland is a very relaxing hotel, where the grandeur of the surroundings - the castle itself, its lakes and parkland and magnificent furnishings - does not overpower but rather enhances the pleasure for guests. It is an enchanting place, where wide corridors lined with oak panelling are hung with ancient portraits and scented with the haunting aroma of woodsmoke. Public areas are very grand, with all the crystal chandeliers and massive antiques to be expected in a real Irish Castle, but the atmosphere suggests that a lot of fun is to be had here too. Bedrooms are all furnished to a very high standard, with luxurious bathrooms. The Brian Boru International Centre brought a new dimension to the Castle's activities a few years ago and can accommodate almost any type of business gathering, including exhibitions, conferences and banquets. Child under 12 free in parents' room. Pets permitted by arrangement. **Rooms 100** (6 suites, 11 mini-suites), Room Rate £254 (2 adult guests). Lift. Open all year. Amex, Diners, MasterCard, Visa.

Earl of Thomond Restaurant ★

The most beautiful room in the castle, the Earl of Thomond Dining Room is magnificent, with crystal, gilding and rich fabrics - and has a lovely view over the lake and golf course. Guests ease into the experience of dinner with an aperitif in the Library Bar, overlooking the eighth green, before moving through to beautifully presented tables and gentle background music provided by a traditional Irish harpist. In the evening a wide choice includes a table d'hôte menu (£36), vegetarian menu (£29.50 - on a recent visit we found this to be an especially attractive option) and an à la carte beginning with Head Chef David McCann's Dromoland signature dish, a "New Irish Cuisine" spectacular of traditional black pudding and buttermilk pancake topped with pan-fried foie gras and glazed apple; a superb dish and well worth trying. The à la carte continues in similar vein, offering a wonderful selection of luxurious dishes. The table d'hôte is more down-to-earth - a little less glamorous than the carte but with the same quality of ingredients and cooking - and possibly, we felt on a recent visit, agreeably more Irish in tone. David McCann bases his menus on the best of local produce, all the little niceties of a very special meal are observed and service, under restaurant manager Tony Frisby, is excellent. Briefer lunch menus offer a shortened à la carte and a Chef's Suggested Lunch (£17.50) with a choice of three on each course. The wine list - about 250 wines, predominantly French - is under the constant review of sommelier Pascal Playon, the worthy winner of our Sommelier of the Year Award, who is not only knowledgable, but an exceptionally thoughtful and helpful wine host.(House wines from £17). A 15% service charge is added to all prices. Non-smoking Restaurant. Toilets wheelchair accessible. L12.30-1.30 £19.50; D £36; à la carte also available.* Beside the castle, the Dromoland Golf and Country Club incorporates not only an 18-hole parkland course, a gym, a Health Clinic offering specialist treatments, but also the Green Room Bar and Fig Tree Restaurant, which provide informal alternatives to facilities in the castle, including all day bar food. **Directions:** 15 miles from Limerick by the Ennis road; 2 miles from Newmarket on Fergus.

Shannon   *Oakwood Arms Hotel*

Shannon Airport Shannon Co Clare
HOTEL   Tel: 061 361500 Fax: 061 361414 email: oakwoarm@iol.ie

John and Josephine O'Sullivan opened this mock-Tudor red brick hotel in 1991 and it created a good impression from the start, with its high standard of maintenance and neatly laid-out flower beds. The lounge bar and function room both have aviation themes: the bar honours the memory of the pioneer female pilot Sophie Pearse, who came from the area, and the restaurant is named after The Spruce Goose, Howard Hughes' famous flying boat. Public areas are quite spacious and comfortably furnished and there is ample evidence of a well-run establishment. Although not individually decorated, rooms have all the necessary comforts and are double-glazed, with air-conditioning. A new wing (26 rooms) and a fitness centre were recently added. Conference/banqueting (300/250) facilities are good, with video-conferencing and back-up secretarial services available. Food in The Spruce Goose restaurant is moderately priced, fresh and homely. Under 3s free in parents' room; cots available. No pets. **Rooms 101** (8 suites, 22 executive rooms, 12 non-smoking, 3 disabled) £48 pps, ss£22. 12.5% service added to bills. Closed 25 Dec. Amex, Diners, MasterCard, Visa. **Directions:** On the main Limerick-Shannon road, on the right hand side approaching from Limerick.

Shannon   *Shannon Great Southern Hotel*

Shannon Airport Shannon Co Clare
HOTEL   Tel: 061 471122 Fax: 061 471982 email: res@shannon.gsh.ie www.gsh.ie

Just two minutes walk from the main terminal building at Shannon Airport, the Shannon Great Southern offers unbeatable convenience for travellers recovering from or preparing for international flights. The hotel is fully sound-proofed and bedrooms, all of which have been recently refurbished and upgraded, are spacious and comfortable, with all the amenities expected of a good modern hotel. Activities available include snooker and a recently completed mini-gym for residents, and there is golf and horseriding nearby. Day trips can be arranged to local sites, such as the Cliffs of Moher or the Aillwee Caves, including admission and full day transport. The hotel also has good conference facilities for groups of 12 to 200 (banqueting 140), backed up by a private business centre with full secretarial services. **Rooms 115** Room Rate £100 (up to 3 guests) 1 mini-suite, 58 executive rooms, 36 non-smoking rooms. Closed 24-26 Dec. Amex, Diners, MasterCard, Visa. **Directions:** At Shannon airport, 2 minutes walk from terminal building.

Tulla

Flappers Restaurant

Main Street Tulla Co Clare

RESTAURANT

Tel: 065 35711

Run by Patricia and Jim McInerney, this simple little split-level restaurant (the lower part is non-smoking) has little decoration except for a pair of striking pictures and fresh flowers on the tables. Lunchtime sees the emphasis on fairly hearty food and good value, although you could easily work up to a rather smart 3-course meal too. In the evening the mood changes dramatically and, in addition to a set 2 or 3-course menu, there's an ambitious à la carte offering the likes of roast quail with raisin and pinenut couscous and deep fried calamari with spicy marinara sauce, followed by main courses like roast rack of lamb with basil pesto mash and port sauce or grilled salmon with vodka cream sauce and green peppercorns. Desserts are equally impressive and there's a fine and very fairly priced wine list. What's more, the locals even have a take-away service - a boon for holidaymakers self-catering in the area. **Seats 38** No-smoking area; air conditioning. Wheelchair access to toilets. L 12-3, D 6.30 (7 in winter)-9.30. A la carte. House wine £10.50. Service charge discretionary (10% on groups of 8+). Closed Sunday, Monday, all bank holidays. Also closed, evenings only: first 2 weeks Nov & 1 week end Jan. Amex, MasterCard, Visa. **Directions:** On the main street of Tulla village, on the right hand side going up the hill.

CORK City

A city flowing in milk and honey

Of all Ireland's cities, it is Cork which most warmly gives the impression of being a place at comfort with itself through being set in the midst of a land flowing in milk and honey. Cork is all about the good things in life. While it may be stretching things a little to assert that the southern capital has a Mediterranean atmosphere, there's no doubting its Continental and cosmpolitan flavour, and the Cork people's relaxed enjoyment of it all.

Trading in life's pleasanter commodities has always been what Cork and its famous "merchant princes" are all about. At one time, the city was known as "the butter capital of Europe". The way in which sea and land intertwine throughout the wonderfully sheltered natural harbour, and through the lively old city itself, has encouraged waterborne trade in farm produce and a sea-minded outlook. Thus today Cork is at the heart of Ireland's most nautical area, a place world-renowned for its dynamic interaction with the sea both for business and pleasure.

It's an area noted, too, for the entertaining and individualistic quality of its branded products. Just eastward of the city is Midleton, home to the Jameson Heritage Centre, and home as well to Irish Distillers manufacturing headquarters where they create products as various as Jameson, Powers and Paddy whiskey - to name only three of their whiskey brands - as well as Huzzar Vodka and Cork Dry Gin.

In the city itself, we find two Irish stouts being brewed - Murphy's and Beamish's. Each has its own distinctive flavour, each in turn is different from Guinness, and it is one of life's pleasures in one of Cork's characterful pubs to discuss and compare their merits. Also the subject of inevitable discussion is another product of the area, and an instantly famous one it is too. Viagra is produced at the Pfizer plant at the ferryport of Ringaskiddy south of the city. If the thought of that leaves you speechless, you can always head northwest of the city, where the Blarney Stone in Blarney Castle is just waiting to make you eloquent and able to take on the Cork people's delightful line in deflationary and quirky humour.

Local Attractions and Information

CORK

Cork Tourist Information	021 273251
Guinness Cork Jazz Festival (late October)	021 278979
Cork International Choral Festival (April/May)	021 308308
Cork International Film Festival (October)	021 271711
Crawford Gallery, Emmett Place	021 966777

The English Market (covered, speciality food stalls Mon-Sat)

Cork   **Bully's**

40 Paul Street Cork Co Cork
RESTAURANT   Tel: 021 273555

A small, buzzy and inexpensive restaurant in one of the busiest little shopping streets in the city centre, Bully's has built up a strong reputation over the years for good food at reasonable prices. A speciality is pizzas, which had ultra light, crisp bases long before they began to show up in fashionable restaurants; the dough is made on the premises every day using Italian flour. But their No.10 pizza (£6.99) is a Cork Special, with ham, sausage, black and white pudding as well as tomatoes and mozzarella. They serve lots of other things too - freshly made burgers, steaks, omelettes, chicken dishes and pasta - and there's a short, reasonably priced wine list. **Seats 40** Open all day Mon-Sun. Closed 25-26 Dec & 1 Jan. Amex, MasterCard, Visa. **Directions:** In Cork city centre, next to Paul Street shopping centre. Branches at: Bishopstown, Cork (021-546838),Douglas, Cork (021-892415) & Fermoy (025-33947).

Cork   *Café Paradiso*

16 Lancaster Quay Western Road Cork Co Cork
RESTAURANT   Tel: 021 277939 (Bookings)/021 274973 Fax: 021 307469
Vegetarian Dish of the Year

Cafe Paradiso has been a great success since it opened six years ago and 1999 saw the philosophy of this mould-breaking vegetarian restaurant reach a far wider public with the publication of the lovely Cafe Paradiso Cookbook. Here you will find (amongst many other culinary gems) the recipe for our Vegetarian Dish of the Year: goats' cheese, pinenut and oven-roasted tomato charlotte, served with wilted greens and puy lentils in basil oil. This dish is a good example of the reason why vegetarian food never seems the same after eating at Café Paradiso - this is exciting mainstream cooking and even the most committed carnivores love every mouthful. Any chef with a goat cheese starter on the menu should take a look at Denis Cotter's goats' cheese charlotte and see how it lightens up an ingredient which can be too heavy to make a successful first course and is often a great disappointment. The restaurant itself is a lively place with a busy atmosphere and the staff, under the direction of Bridget Healy, are not only friendly and helpful but obviously enthusiastic about their work. Seasonal menus, topped up by daily specials, might include asparagus gratin with a tangy Gabriel cheese crust; peperonata with olive-grilled ciabbatta, basil & parmesan; fresh tagliatelle in basil oil with mangetout, broad beans, cherry tomatoes and parmesan. Lovely desserts too - pear & almond frangipani with blackcurrant coulis perhaps - and some organic wines on a seriously global list. **Seats 45** No Smoking area. Toilets wheelchair accessible. L12.30-3, D 6.30-10.30 Tues-Sat. A la carte. House wines £10-13. Service discretionary. Closed Sun, Mon, Xmas wk, last 2 wks Aug. MasterCard, Visa. **Directions:** On Western Road, opposite Jurys Hotel.

Cork ✗   *Clarion Hotel Morrisons Quay*

Morrisons Quay Cork Co Cork

HOTEL   Tel: 021 275858 Fax: 021 275833

Very central and right on the river bank, this compact hotel aims to provide the luxury of hotel suites but at an affordable price. The richly coloured foyer, although small, makes a good impression with its oriental rugs. Of the 42 rooms, 28 are suites, each well-equipped with its own lobby and kitchenette in addition to a bedroom with seating area or separate sitting room. Simple modern decor is pleasant and quality materials have been used throughout. **Rooms 42** (28 suites). Acc£££. Closed 25 Dec & 1 Jan. Amex, Diners, MasterCard, Visa. **Directions:** Head to the city centre; drive through Patrick Street and Grand Parade to South Mall; turn right after the pedestrian lights - the hotel is on the right.

Cork   *Crawford Gallery Café*

Emmet Place Cork Co Cork

RESTAURANT   Tel: 021 274415

This fine 1724 building houses an excellent collection of 18th- and 19th-century landscapes - and it's also home to the Crawford Gallery Café, one of Cork city's favourite informal eating places. An outpost of Ballymaloe House at Shanagarry (since 1988), the menu offers Ballymaloe breads and many of the other dishes so familiar to Ballymaloe fans. The menu changes weekly, but the style - a judicious mixture of timeless country house fare and trendier international dishes featuring lots of roasted vegetables - remains reassuringly constant. Interesting choice of drinks includes homemade lemonade, fresh orange juice, Cappoquin apple juice and a house wine. **Seats 80** No smoking area. Meals 10-5 Mon-Sat, L 12.30-2.30. Set L £12.50; also à la carte. House wine £10. Service discretionary. Closed Sun, 24 Dec-6 Jan. Diners, MasterCard, Visa. **Directions:** In the Crawford Municipal Gallery, next to the Cork Opera House.

Cork   *Dan Lowrey's Tavern*

13 MacCurtain Street Cork Co Cork

PUB   Tel: 021 505071

This smashing pub just across the road from Isaacs was established in 1875 and has been run by Anthony and Catherine O'Riordan since 1995. Long before the arrival of the "theme pub", Lowrey's was famous for having windows which originated from Kilkenny Cathedral, but it also has many of its own original features, including a fine mahogany bar. Good bar food has become a point of pride under the current ownership, with Catherine O'Riordan and Eleanor Murray in the kitchen, so it's a good place for an inexpensive tasty meal. There's also a nice little quarter-bottle wine list representing France, Chile, Italy and Romania, all at £2.60. Meals 12.30-3 daily. Closed 25 Dec & Good Fri. No credit cards. **Directions:** Halfway along MacCurtain Street, opposite Isaacs Restaurant.

Cork ❋   *ECO Douglas*

1 Eastville Douglas Village Cork Co Cork
RESTAURANT   Tel: 021 892522 Fax: 021-895354 email: mail@eco.ie

This busy, contemporary restaurant is understandably popular, as it combines interesting menus with good cooking and reasonable prices - a winning formula by any standards, so booking ahead is wise. Space is limited and the decor on the dark side, but the lively buzz compensates for lack of natural light and tables are reasonably spaced, although the small reception area can be a bit disorganised if your table isn't ready on arrival. And while service is friendly and helpful, delays do occur. Perhaps the choice offered - on an interesting international menu with vegetarian dishes considerably highlighted in green - is a bit over-ambitious. Good wine list - over 80 reasonably priced wines from all over the world, including Argentina and Uruguay. Children welcome up to 7 pm. Street parking (can be difficult) **Seats 75** No-smoking area; air conditioning. Open 12-11 Mon-Sat, D 5-10.30 Sun & bank hols. Evening menu from 5 pm. A la carte. House wine £10.95. Service discretionary Closed Good Fri, 25-26 Dec. Amex, MasterCard,Visa. **Directions:** In Douglas village - 3 miles out from city centre, 1 mile from airport.

Cork ✗   *Farmgate Café*

Old English Market Princes Street Cork Co Cork
CAFE/RESTAURANT   Tel: 021 278134 Fax: 021 632771

A sister restaurant to the Farmgate Country Store and Restaurant in Midleton, Kay Harte's Farmgate Café shares the same commitment to serving fresh food - and, as it is located above the English Market, where ingredients are purchased daily, it doesn't come much fresher than this. They serve traditional food, including some famous old Cork dishes with a special market connection - tripe & drisheen and corned beef & champ with green cabbage. Another speciality is "the freshest of fish". All this and home-baked cakes and breads too. Meals£-££ daytime Mon-Sat. Diners, MasterCard.

Cork   *Fitzpatrick Cork Hotel*

Tivoli Cork Co Cork
HOTEL   Tel: 021 507533 Fax: 021 507641

Situated in 25 acres of landscaped gardens about five minutes drive from the city centre (courtesy coach service all day), this modern tower block hotel has an eye-catching external glass lift and overlooks the River Lee. Spacious bedrooms are furnished to a high standard, with good bathrooms. Self-contained conference/banqueting suites can each accommodate up to 700 guests & there's a business centre. A well-equipped leisure centre has indoor tennis and squash, as well as a 25-metre pool - and there's even a 9-hole golf course. Children welcome (under 5s free in parents' room, cots available, creche). Pets permitted by arrangement. **Rooms 109** (3 suites, 2 mini-suites, 29 executive rooms, 16 no-smoking rooms and 5 for disabled). B&B £50 pps, ss £20. Closed 25-26 Dec. Amex, Diners MasterCard, Visa. **Directions:** At the Tivoli flyover above the main Cork Dublin road and clearly signed off it. (From Cork, take first left then right at the flyover.)

Cork ✗   *Flemings*

Silver Grange House Tivoli Cork Co Cork
RESTAURANT/ACCOMMODATION   Tel: 021 821621 Fax: 021 821178

Clearly signed off the main Cork-Dublin road, this large Georgian family house is set in well-maintained grounds, including a kitchen garden which provides most of the fruit, vegetables and herbs required for the restaurant during the summer. The light, airy double dining room is comfortably furnished and, in contrast to the current wave of designer decor, has a pleasant air of faded gentility. Well-appointed linen-clad tables provide a suitable setting for Michael Fleming's classical cooking. Seasonal table d'hôte and à la carte menus offer a good selection of classics, slightly influenced by current international trends - a vegetarian dish of crispy vegetable wontons with tossed leaf salad, Atlantic prawns & scallops with grilled polenta & a sweet pepper jus - but the main thrust of the cooking style is classical French. Vegetables are imaginative in selection and presentation, desserts include a beautiful tasting plate. Lunch and dinner are served every day. **Accommodation:** There are four spacious en-suite rooms, comfortably furnished in a style appropriate to the age of the house (£35 pps/£14 single supplement). Closed 25 Dec. Amex, Diners, MasterCard, Visa. **Directions:** Next to Lotamore House; well-signed up to the left off Cork-Dublin road as you are leaving the city

Cork ✗   *Harold's*

Tramway House Douglas Village East Cork Co Cork
RESTAURANT   Tel: 021 361613 /891155 Fax: 021 891155

When Euro-Toques chef Harold Lynch and front-of-house partner Beth Haughton opened this stylish little place just off the busiest shopping area of Douglas in August 1993 it was an immediate hit. The interesting modern interior sets the right tone for Harold's lively Cal-Ital influenced food. On a sensibly limited, moderately priced à la carte menu, old favourites like twice-baked cheese souffle jostle for space with starters such as tapas or warm salad of smoked chicken with sundried tomatoes, pinenuts, parmesan shavings and balsamic dressing. Main courses range from reassuringly familiar, perfectly cooked noisettes of spring lamb with warm mint dressing through to fish of the day - a gleaming white fillet of John Dory, perhaps, on a light buttery sauce - or a flavoursome vegetarian option like fettucine with wild and fresh mushrooms. Desserts favour classics with a modern twist - crème brûlée with plum salad, perhaps - and there's always a selection of Irish farmhouse cheeses. Delicious brown soda bread, good coffee by the cup. L£ Sun Sep-Apr only, D££ Tue-Sat. Closed 25 Dec. MasterCard, Visa.

Cork 🏨   *Hayfield Manor Hotel*

Perrott Avenue College Road Cork Co Cork
HOTEL   Tel: 021 315600 Fax: 021 316839 email: enquiries@hayfieldmanor.ie

Set in two acres of gardens next door to University College Cork, Hayfield Manor Hotel provides every comfort and a remarkable level of privacy and seclusion just a mile from the city centre. Although newly built - it only opened in 1996 - it has the genuine feel of a large period house. Conference rooms of varying sizes include a library/boardroom beside the drawing room that doubles as a private dining room. Spacious bedrooms vary in decor, are beautifully furnished to a very high standard with antiques and have generous marbled bathrooms with individual tiling, heated towel rails and quality toiletries. Accommodation is of a very high standard and housekeeping is immaculate. Conference facilities for up to 120 delegates; secretarial services. Tennis, golf and fishing nearby. Beauty and massage therapies by arrangement. Under 7s free in parents' room (cots available). No pets. **Rooms 87** (4 suites, 9 mini-suites, 70 executive rooms; 20 no-smoking, 4 for disabled). Open all year. Amex, Diners, MasterCard, Visa

The Manor Room

This well-appointed, traditional dining room overlooks the walled garden at the back of the hotel, giving it a quiet, serene atmosphere. Head chef Robert Cowley, who has been with the hotel since 1997, makes good use of local produce, often with a contemporary twist even to traditional dishes such as oak smoked salmon (with crispy vegetables and Meyer lemon sauce) or grilled sirloin steak (with truffled creamed potatoes and thyme jus). Informal meals are also available all day, in the bar. **Seats 80** L12.30-2.15 Sun-Fri, D 7-9.15 daily. Set L £19.50. Set D £19.50; à la carte also available. House wine £16. Service discretionary. Closed Sat L. **Directions:** From Cork city, N22 for Killarney. Turn left at university, then right at the top of the road; take the next left - the hotel is at the top of the avenue.

Cork ✗   *Hotel Isaacs*

48 MacCurtain Street Cork Co Cork
HOTEL/RESTAURANT   Tel: 021 500011 Fax: 021 506355

Opposite the theatre and approached through a cobbled courtyard, this is a simple hotel offering basic comforts at a reasonable price. The bedrooms have attractive polished stripped wood floor and free-standing pine furniture - some rooms over the street can be noisy. No lift. Car park nearby. Rooms 36. Closed 3 days Xmas. Diners, MasterCard, Visa.

Greene's Restaurant

Opening a restaurant next door to Isaacs (with the confusion of the hotel's similar name) was bound to lead to comparisons and Greene's has certainly not been the winner. A novel waterfall feature is quite impressive but they got off to quite a shaky start last year. However,although menus are still perhaps over-ambitious, a recent dinner indicates considerable improvement. Starters such as deep-fried crab claws in beer batter - nicely presented on mayonnaise with a mixed salad in the centre - and Peking style breast of duck on ginger stir-fried vegetables with noodles and a jus were more than adequately cooked and a dessert of summer fruits in a pastry cup with Baileys Cream sabayon went down a treat. Friendly, well-paced service and a fairly priced wine list enhanced the good all-round impression.

Cork ✗   *Imperial Hotel*

South Mall Cork Co Cork
HOTEL   Tel: 021 274040 Fax: 021 275375

This thriving hotel in Cork's main commercial and banking centre was taken over by the Flynn family in 1998. It dates back to 1813 and has a colourful history - Michael Collins spent his last night here, no less, and that suite now bears his name - although most guests are more impressed by its convenient location, near the river and just a couple of minutes walk from the Patrick Street shopping area - equally suited to business or pleasure and with free car parking available for residents. Rooms are all en-suite, with a mixture of furnishings, and there are attractive weekend rates. Conference/banqueting (350/300). Private car park. Children under 12 free in parents' room, cots available. Pets permitted by arrangement. **Rooms 88** (all en-suite, 5 shower-only). B&B £55pps, ss£20. Closed 24-27 Dec Amex, Diners, MasterCard, Visa. **Directions:** City centre, 3 minutes from main shopping area, Patrick's Street.

Cork ☆   *Isaacs Restaurant*

48 MacCurtain Street Cork Co Cork
RESTAURANT   Tel: 021 503805 Fax: 021 551348

New Irish Cuisine Award - Michael Ryan

This large, atmospheric modern restaurant in an 18th-century warehouse is one of the great restaurant success stories, not just in Cork but throughout the country. The co-owners, Michael and Catherine Ryan together with partner/head chef Canice Sharkey, make a magnificent team. Canice's cooking is consistently excellent in tempting, colourful dishes which cleverly combine sunny Mediterranean influences and comforting Irish traditions - a comforting potato and leek soup sits easily on the menu alongside tempura of prawns with soya and ginger and a traditional seafood chowder might come with garlic croutons. Although it has been done in a quiet, low-key way, this restaurant has played a leading role in the culinary revolution that has been overtaking Ireland. Isaacs' exciting blend of Irish and international themes, together with a policy of providing great food and good value in an informal, relaxed ambience has proved irresistible since they day they opened and it is greatly to their credit that standards of both cooking and creativity have remained so high. New Irish Cuisine is a term coined in 1996 when, recognising that the essential Irishness of our food was in danger of being lost in the current tidal wave of international influences, the Restaurants Association of Ireland and Bord Bia got together to encourage Irish chefs to consider the regionality of the dishes on their menus. New Irish Cuisine describes updated traditional Irish food, seen in dishes that have their roots in the past and their heads in the present - dishes that utilise traditional and native ingredients in a colourful, contemporary style. It would be hard to think of a better example than Michael Ryan to demonstrate the potential vitality of the concept: a Cork man, who rightly takes great pride in the produce and specialities of his native city and county, Michael has a knack of including both the produce and the dishes in an international repertoire that brings Irish food bang up to date - and downright irresistible to the dining public. Importantly, through his special talent as a demonstrator and communicator, Michael's energetic and inspiring pursuit of excellence and respect for Irish culinary traditions within the framework of international trends, has allowed the philosophy of this unique restaurant to reach wider audiences, both in Ireland and abroad. **Seats 120**. Open all day. L 12.30-2.30 Mon-Sat, D 6.30-9.30 daily. Short à la carte and daily blackboard specials; vegetarian dishes highlighted. House wine £10.50. Service discretionary. Toilets wheelchair accessible. Closed Xmas wk. Amex, Diners, MasterCard, Visa. **Directions:** Halfway along MacCurtain Street, opposite Dan Lowrey's pub.

Cork   *The Ivory Tower*

Exchange Buildings Princes Street Cork Co Cork
RESTAURANT   Tel:021 274665

Seamus O'Connell, a talented and creative cook, runs this unusual restaurant upstairs in an early Victorian commercial building. Very best quality ingredients, creative menus (asparagus, pumpkin & shitake tempura, loin of lamb with spiced vegetable tagine, couscous & sauce maltaise), excellent details like delicious home-baked breads, imaginative presentation - are the hallmarks of The Ivory Tower. Service can be slow but this is an interesting establishment and the food is worth waiting for. Imaginative vegetarian dishes are always a feature. Children over 3 welcome. **Seats 35** D daily 6-10.

Set menus £30 & £45; also à la carte. service charge discretionary. MasterCard, Visa.
Directions: On the corner of Oliver Plunkett Street and Princes Street.
*A seasonal sister restaurant, The Sea Urchin, has recently opened in Goleen, West Cork.

Cork ✳   *Jacobs on the Mall*

                                                                     30A South Mall Cork Co Cork
RESTAURANT   Tel: 021 251530 Fax: 021 251531

This restaurant has caused quite a stir since opening in December 1998, partly because
of the location in a former Turkish bath has created a highly unusual and atmospheric
dining space but also because the head chef, Mercy Fenton, moved over to Cork after
working in some very prestigious UK establishments, including Stephen Bull's Blandford
Street restaurant in London. Given the background it's hardly surprising that Modern
European cooking is the promise and that's what you'll get, along with the oriental
influences that have recently become de rigeur on every European menu. Tempting and
well-balanced menus that change daily are strong on vegetarian dishes (considerately
marked with a V) and there's a good scattering of buzz words - couscous, bruschetta,
risotto - and some indulgences like duck liver parfait with plum chutney and toasted
brioche, although the cooking had not settled down to a consistently high standard at the
time of going to press. Desserts tend to be quite traditional - date & butterscotch pudding
with bourbon cream, brown sugar meringue with bananas and hot fudge and farmhouse
cheeses, always so good in Cork, are served with digestive biscuits and oatcakes. Good,
relaxed service. Children welcome. **Seats 150** (Private rooms, 20 each). No smoking
area. Toilets wheelchair accessible. L 12.30-2.30, D 6.30-10, Mon-Sat; Set L £16, Set
D £24; A la carte. House wine £12.50. L service discretionary (10% added at D). Closed
Sun. Amex, MasterCard, Visa. **Directions:** Beside Bank of Ireland, at the Grand Parade
end of South Mall.

Cork   *Jacques Restaurant*

                                                                       9 Phoenix Street Cork Co Cork
RESTAURANT   Tel: 021 277387 Fax: 021 270634

An integral part of Cork life since 1982, this delightful restaurant has changed with the
years, evolving from quite a traditional place to a dashing Mediterranean-toned bistro.
Jacqueline Barry's menus - lunch, early dinner and dinner - are based on carefully
sourced ingredients from a network of suppliers built up over 18 years. They are
refreshingly short, allowing her to concentrate on the delicious cooking that is her forte.
There are starters such as organic spinach with beetroot jelly, Orla cheese & walnut
dressing, main courses like roast breast of duck with confit of leg, apricot sauce & potato
stuffing. Desserts could be lemon tart or almond cake with plums in red wine &
mascarpone cheese. This is really good cooking - and excellent value too, especially the
early dinner. **Seats 50** No-smoking area; air conditioning. L 12-3, Mon-Fri, D 6-10 Mon-
Sat. Set L £10.90, Set D £21.90; early D 6-7, £11.90. Also à la carte. House wine
£11.90. Service discretionary. Closed Sat L, Sun, Bank Hols & 1 week from 24 Dec.
Amex, MasterCard, Visa. **Directions:** Just around the corner from the GPO, off Pembroke
Street.

Cork ✗   *Jurys Cork Inn*

                                                                   Anderson's Quay Cork Co Cork
HOTEL   Tel: 021 276 444 Fax: 021 276144 email: margaret_nagle@jurys-hotel.ie

In a fine central riverside site, this budget hotel has all the features that Jurys Inns have
now become well known for: room prices include accommodation for up to four (including
a sofa bed) and there is space for a cot (which can be supplied by arrangement). No room
service. Limited parking (22 spaces), plus arrangement with nearby car park. **Rooms 133**
(7 suitable for disabled guests). Café/restaurant 7-10am, 6-9.30pm. The Inn Pub bar
serves lunch every day and there's a late bar (residents only) every night. (Bar closed on
Good Friday). Acc£-££. Closed 25 Dec. Amex, Diners, MasterCard, Visa.

Cork ✗   *Jurys Hotel*

                                                                    Western Road Cork Co Cork
HOTEL   Tel: 021 276622 Fax: 021 274477

Consistently popular with both business and leisure guests since it opened in 1972, this
comfortable hotel has a relaxed atmosphere and is in an attractive riverside setting half

a mile from the city centre. Bedrooms include 20 designed for disabled guests, four suites/mini-suites and 30 executive rooms, 10 of which are designated lady executive. All rooms are a good size and have both double and single beds. Acc£££££. Closed 25 Dec & 1 Jan. Amex, Diners, MasterCard, Visa.

Cork — *Lotamore House*

Tivoli Cork Co Cork

ACCOMMODATION   Tel: 021 822344 Fax: 021 822219 email: lotamore@iol.ie

This large period house is set in mature gardens and, although not grand, it was built on a generous scale. Big, airy rooms have phones, tea/coffee trays, TV and a safe and they're comfortably furnished to sleep three, with room for an extra bed or cot and full bathrooms. A large drawing room has plenty of armchairs, an open fire and, although only breakfast and light meals are offered, Fleming's Restaurant (see entry) is next door. Children welcome (Under 5s free in parents' room, cots available, baby-sitting by arrangement). Wheelchair access. Own parking. **Rooms 20** (all en-suite, 5 no-smoking, 1 for disabled). B&B £32, ss £12. Closed Christmas week. Amex, MasterCard, Visa. **Directions:** On N8, clearly signed from the main Dublin/Waterford road out of Cork, 5 minutes drive from Cork city centre.

Cork — *Lovetts Restaurant & Brasserie*

Churchyard Lane off Well Road Douglas Cork Co Cork

RESTAURANT/BAR   Tel: 021 294909 Fax: 021 294024 e-mail: lovetts@indigo.ie

Home to both the restaurant and the Lovett family since 1977, this fine restaurant is in a late Georgian house situated in mature grounds. Committed to serious cooking, using the best of fresh, free range and local products, head chef Marie Harding is a talented and creative cook and has been a finalist in the Restaurants Association of Ireland/Bord Bia "New Irish Cuisine" competition. The restaurant has many sides to its character, including a fully licensed bar (the extensive wine list is Dermod Lovett's particular passion), private dining in the 'Wild Geese' Room and, in addition to the main restaurant, more informal dining in the Brasserie. Marie's lunch and dinner menus are consistently interesting and always offer a separate vegetarian menu. **Seats 60.** (Private room 8-24). No-smoking restaurant. L 12.30-2, D 7-9.45 Tues-Sat. Set L £15.50, D à la carte. House wine £12.75. Service discretionary. *Bar meals 12.30-2, Tue-Fri Brasserie 7-9.45 Tue-Fri. Closed Sun & Mon, bank hols, Xmas week, 1 wk Aug. Amex, Diners, MasterCard, Visa. **Directions:** Close to south Cork city: from Douglas Road take turning to Mahon and Blackrock and go through a roundabout. Take the fourth turn on the left, Wells Road; Lovetts is off it in Churchyard Lane.

Cork 🏛 — *Maryborough House Hotel*

Maryborough Hill Douglas Cork Co Cork

HOTEL   Tel: 021 365555 Fax: 021 365662 email: maryboro@indigo.ie

The Maryborough House Hotel has at its heart a fine country house set in its own grounds and gardens and has been developed with sensitivity. The original house, which is beautifully proportioned, has many fine features, restored with care and furnished in period style with antiques. The main entrance is via the original flight of steps up to the old front door and, although there is no conventional reception area, guests receive a warm welcome at the desk just inside the front door. The new section of the hotel is modern and blends comfortably with the trees and gardens surrounding it. The new part (which has already had an extra 22 rooms added, less than two years after opening) includes excellent leisure facilities and accommodation which is exceptionally good in terms of design - simple, modern, bright, utilising Irish crafts. Rooms are generously-sized, with a pleasant outlook, good amenities and extras including complimentary mineral water. Bathrooms are well-finished and well-lit, with plenty of marbled shelf space, generous towels and a robe; they have environmentally friendly toiletries and suggestions on saving water by avoiding unnecessary laundry. There were settling in problems in the bar and restaurant areas in the early stages, but more recent visits indicate that these seem to be considerably improved. Conference/banqueting (500/350). Leisure centre. Children welcome (under 2s free in parents room, cots available). No pets. **Rooms 79** (2 suites, 5 mini-suites, 10 executive rooms, 6 no-smoking, 4 for disabled). Lift. B&B £85pps, ss £20. Closed 25-26 Dec. Amex, Diners, MasterCard, Visa. **Directions:** At Douglas village, go to the N28 roundabout, follow sign up Maryborough Hill; 2 minutes on the left.

Cork ✳   *No 5 Fenns Quay Restaurant*

5 Fenns Quay Sheares Street Cork Co Cork

RESTAURANT   Tel: 021 279527

Partially in a 250-year old listed building (the entrance and front part of the restaurant are in an extension), this is a bright, busy restaurant with a welcoming atmosphere and simple decor enlivened by striking modern paintings. Smallish à la carte lunch and dinner menus offer plenty of interesting choices, including several vegetarian options, and there are always several daily specials. Fresh, locally sourced ingredients are cooked well in contemporary style - typically duck spring roll with oriental dipping sauce, warm crab and wilted cabbage salad, lamb kebabs with couscous & minted yogurt dressing - and attractively presented. The wine list, while not extensive, offers variety at reasonable prices - good value is a feature of both food and drink. Despite recent refurbishment, the age of the building has made it difficult to provide wheelchair access. Children welcome before 8 pm. On street parking can be difficult. **Seats 45** No-smoking area; air conditioning. Open all day Mon-Sat 10-5; L 12.30-3, D 6.30-10. Set L £8, Set D with wine £21. House wine £11. Service discretionary. Closed Sun, bank hols. MasterCard, Visa. **Directions:** Central city - 2 minutes from the Courthouse.

Cork   *Metropole Ryan Hotel & Leisure Centre*

MacCurtain Street Cork Co Cork

HOTEL   Tel: 021 508122 Fax: 021 506450 email: enq@metropoleh.com

This imposing city-centre hotel next door to the Everyman Palace and backing on to the River Lee, celebrated its centenary in 1998. Many of the original features remain, such as the marble facade, outside carved stonework and plaster ceilings inside. Always popular with those connected with the arts and entertainment industry, there are many displays (photos and press cuttings) of stars past and present in the public areas and the atmospheric, traditionally-styled Met Tavern. The hotel has recently completed a refurbishment programme, noticeably in the bedrooms that now combine a period feel with modern facilities. Unusually for an old city-centre hotel, there's a splendid leisure club with a large (and unconventionally shaped) indoor swimming pool, overlooked by the Waterside Café and also a gym. Extensive conference facilities (for up to 350). Children under 2 free in parents' room, cots available. No pets. **Rooms 113** (all en-suite, 3 mini-suites, 30 executive rooms, 10 no-smoking, 1 for disabled). B&B £55pps. ss £25. Open all year. Amex, Diners, MasterCard, Visa.

Cork   *Proby's Bistro*

Proby's Quay Crosses Green Cork Co Cork
Tel: 021 316531 Fax: 021 316523

RESTAURANT/ACCOMMODATION   e-mail: probys@deanshall.com

This restaurant, which was extensively refurbished in late summer 1999, is handier to the city centre than it first appears and is a pleasant spot for a bite to eat during the day (tables outside for fine weather) as well as in the evening, when a piano bar is an added attraction. The style - established before the current wave and competently executed - is global cuisine, with an emphasis on things Mediterranean. Accommodation arrangements are unusual, in that rooms occupied by students at the adjacent Deanshall during the academic year become available for visitors in summer (and consequently Proby's is open for breakfast from June to September). Children welcome. **Seats 120** (private room 20). Air conditioning, no-smoking area, toilets wheelchair accessible. Open from 10 am Mon-Sat. L 12-6, D 6-10. A la carte, also early D 6-7.30, £8.95. House wine £11. Closed Sun & 4 days Xmas. Amex, MasterCard, Visa. **Directions:** Between St Finbarre's Cathedral and Beamish & Crawford.

Cork   *Rochestown Park Hotel*

Douglas Cork Co Cork

HOTEL   Tel: 021 892233 Fax: 021 892178

Formerly a home of the Lord Mayors of Cork, this attractive hotel stands in lovely grounds and the original parts of the building feature gracious, well-proportioned public rooms. Facilities include excellent conference/banqueting facilities (recently extended up to 700/450 respectively; video-conferencing available) and a fine leisure centre with a Roman style 20-metre swimming pool and a Thalasso Therapy Centre. All rooms are furnished to a high standard with all the comforts, including air conditioning and safe as well as direct dial phones, tea/coffee trays and TV; business guests are well looked after - there's an executive wing, business centre and secretarial sevices. Since opening in 1989 the hotel has seen many changes under the watchful eye of General Manager Liam Lally - the latest plan is for 45 additional rooms. Wheelchair accessible. Children are welcome (under 6s stay free in parents' room; cots available). No pets. **Rooms 115** (1 suite, 4 mini-suites, 55 executive rooms, 3 disabled). Lift. B&B £45pps, ss £15. Open all year. Amex, Diners, MasterCard, Visa.

Cork   *Seven North Mall*

7 North Mall Cork Co Cork

ACCOMMODATION   Tel: 021 397191 Fax: 021 300811 email: sevennorthmall@tinet.ie

Angela Hegarty runs one of the city's most pleasant guesthouses, on a tree-lined south-facing mall overlooking the River Lee. Rooms in this 1750s townhouse are all spacious, individually furnished in keeping with the house (with new bathrooms skillfully incorporated) and good amenities, including ISDN lines and a safe. Some rooms have river views and there is a ground floor room specially designed for disabled guests. Excellent breakfasts. Secure parking. Many of the city's best restaurants, pubs, museums, galleries and theatres are within a short walk. Not suitable for children under 12. **Rooms 7** (1 for disabled, shower only). B&B £35 pps, ss £10 Closed Christmas week. MasterCard, Visa. **Directions:** On south facing mall overlooking north channel of the River Lee, between North Gate (Griffith) Bridge and pedestrian bridge.

Cork   *Travelodge*

Frankfield Road South Ring Road Cork Co Cork

HOTEL   Tel: 021 310722

Excellent , well-maintained budget accommodation - generous sized bedrooms, with an extra sofabed, TV and decent bathrooms. No service, but tea/coffee-making in the room and breakfast available at the adjacent Little Chef. Room rate £49.95 (£39.95 Nov-Apr). **Directions:** Just over a mile from Cork city centre and a mile from Cork airport on the main airport road.

Cork *x*   *Victoria Lodge*

Victoria Lodge Victoria Cross Cork Co Cork

ACCOMMODATION   Tel: 021 542233 Fax: 021 542572

This unusual guesthouse is about five minutes' drive from the city centre. It was built early this century as a Capuchin monastery and opened as a guesthouse in 1988. The refectory, which still has its panelling and benches intact, is used for breakfast and the old common room has become a television lounge for guests. Comfortably furnished bedrooms, which are generously sized, with en-suite bath and shower, have been recently renovated. Ample private parking. Children welcome (under 3s free in parents' room; cots available). Pets permitted by arrangement. **Rooms 30** (15 executive rooms, 1 for disabled, 4 no-smoking). B&B £30pps, ss £8. Closed 23-28 Dec. Amex, MasterCard, Visa. **Directions:** Take the western exit from Cork city - Western Road/N22, turning left at Victoria Cross (Crows Nest pub); Victoria Lodge is directly opposite the next left-hand turn. (Map available).

Cork *x*   *The Wine Vault*

Lancaster Quay Western Road Cork Co Cork

PUB   Tel: 021 275751

Situated just across the road from the entrance to Jurys Hotel, Reidy's Wine Vault is a stylish contemporary pub and makes a convenient meeting place or a good choice for an informal bite to eat. Originally a wine warehouse, it has been imaginatively converted to its present use, with a high vaulted ceiling and an attractive mixture of old and new fixtures and furnishings. Noelle Reidy supervises the food personally and early visitors will be greeted by the aroma of bread baking at the back, shortly followed by soups, pies and casseroles (shepherd's pie, Irish stew) for lunch, all marked up on the blackboard as they come on stream. Seafood choices are particularly strong but don't overlook the home-cooked Cork spiced beef, which is a local speciality. Closed 25 Dec, Good Fri. Amex, Diners, MasterCard, Visa.

CORK County

Cork stylishly achieved much sporting and cultural success during 1999. For the travelling visitor in 2000, one of the most encouraging of the many achievements was the county's dominance of the Tidy Towns Awards, which saw the bright and cheerful town of Clonakilty take first prize overall, while the tiny village of Rathbarry nearby - a neat place in every sense of the word - was a close runner-up, and outright winner of the tidiest village section. Cork is Ireland's largest county, so it's not surprising that it seems like a small country in its own right. Its highly individualistic people will happily go along with this distinction as they reflect on the variety of a large territory which ranges from the rich farmlands of East Cork, away westward to the handsome coastline of West Cork where the mighty light of the famous Fastnet Rock swings across tumbling ocean and spray-tossed headland. Like Cork city itself, the county is a repository of the good things of life, and the county is a treasure chest of the finest farm produce and the very best of seafood. But it isn't all work by any means. As Ireland's most southerly county, Cork enjoys the mildest climate of all, and it's a place where they work to live, rather than live to work. The arts of living, in fact, are probably seen at their most skilled in County Cork, and they are practised in a huge territory of such variety that it is difficult to grasp even if you devote your entire vacation to this one county. But when you remember that your mind has to absorb the varieties of experience offered by, for instance, the stylish sophistication of Kinsale as set against the lively little ports further west, or the bustle of Clonakilty as matched with the remote and peaceful mountains above Guagan Barra in the northwest of the county, then you really do begin to wonder that so much can be crammed into this one place called County Cork.

Local Attractions and Information

CO CORK

Ballylickey	Mannings Emporium (specialist food products)	027 50456
Bantry	Bantry House,	027 50047
Bantry	Irish International Morris Minor Week (July)	023 44864
Bantry	Murphy's International Mussel Fair (May)	027 50360
Blarney	Blarney Castle	021 385252
Cape Clear Island	International Storytelling Festival (early Sept)	028 39157
Carrigtwohill	Fota Estate (Wildlife Park, Arboretum)	021 812728
Castletownroche	Annes Grove (gardens)	022 26145
Cobh	The Queenstown Story,	021 813591
Glandore	Glandore Regatta (mid July)	021 543333
Glanmire	Riverstown House (Lafrancini plasterwork)	021 821205
Glengariff	Garinish Island	027 63040
Glounthane	Ashbourne House Gardens	021 353319
Kinsale	Gourmet Festival (October)	
Kinsale	Vintage Classic International Rally	021 774362
Kinsale	Charles Fort	021 772263
Kinsale	Desmond Castle	021 774855
Midleton	Jameson Heritage Centre	021 613594
Mizen Head	Signal Station	028 35591
Shanagarry	Ballymaloe Cookery School Gardens	021 646785
Shanagarry	Stephen Pearse's pottery and nearby 'Emporium'	
Skibbereen	Creagh Gardens	028 22121
Youghal	Myrtle Grove	024 92274

Ahakista

Ahakista Bar

Ahakista nr Bantry Co Cork

PUB

Tel: 027 67203

Just across the road from the Shiro Japanese Dinner House, Anthony and Margaret Whooley run one of the most relaxed bars in the country. Known affectionately as "the tin pub" because of its corrugated iron roof, it has a lovely rambling country garden going down to the water at the back, where children are very welcome to burn off excess energy. Margaret does light snacks (soup and sandwiches from "lunchtime to 6 pm"). It's been in the family for three generations now and, although finally succumbing to the telephone after years of resistance, it's a place that just doesn't change. Normal pub hours don't apply in this part of the world, but they're open afternoon and evenings all year, except Xmas Day and Good Fri. No credit cards.

Ahakista   *Hillcrest House*

Ahakista Durrus nr Bantry Co Cork
FARMHOUSE   Tel: 027 67045

Agnes Hegarty's traditional farmhouse attracts many types of visitor, including walkers, who revel in the 55 mile "Sheep's Head Way" - and hospitality comes first at this working farm overlooking Dunmanus Bay, where guests are welcomed with a cup of tea and home-baked scones on arrival. Families are very well catered for as there's a large games room, swing and a donkey on the farm - and comfortably furnished rooms are big enough for an extra child's bed. There is also a ground-floor room suitable for less able guests, with parking at the door and direct access to the dining room. **Rooms 4** (3 en-suite, 2 shower only) B&B £17 pps, ss £6.50 (Under 2s free in parents' room, cot available, £5). High tea £11, or evening meals by arrangement (7 pm; £14); light meals also available. Closed 1 Nov-1 Apr. No credit cards. **Directions:** "Hillcrest Farm" sign in Durrus; also signed on main road shortly after Ahakista.

Ahakista   *Shiro Japanese Dinner House*

Ahakista Durrus nr Bantry Co Cork
RESTAURANT   Tel: 027 67030 027 67206

Since Kei and Werner Pilz first opened their unique restaurant in 1982, a visit to Shiro Japanese Dinner House has always been a very special treat. Though Japanese food has become more familiar in recent years, this serene experience is as different from city restaurants as could be imagined. Shiro is in a beautifully maintained Georgian house overlooking Dunmanus Bay. Although it has grown somewhat - almost double the size of a few years ago, when it could only seat 12 guests in two groups of five and seven - this is still a very small restaurant, perfectly in keeping with the very detailed, fine nature of Kei's authentic classical Japanese cuisine. First there will be zensai (seasonal appetizers with azuke-bachi, egg and sushi snacks), then suimono (a seasonal soup, served in a traditional lidded bowl topped with a little origami bird). A choice of about seven main courses will probably include tempura (seasonal fish and vegetables, lightly-battered and deep-fried) beef teriyaki (gently cooked strips of steak, with teriyaki sauce and fresh vegetables), sashimi (finely sliced raw fish, served with soy sauce and wasabi, a very hot green mustard used for dipping) and combinations such as tempura-sashimi which provide an opportunity to try a wider range if the group is small. It is most interesting to choose as wide a variety as possible, including the sushi (raw fish and vegetables rolled with rice in dried seaweed, served sliced with wasabi and soy sauce for dipping). Presentation of food follows a precise pattern and is very beautiful. The meal is rounded off by a selection of home-made ice creams, colourfully garnished with fresh fruit and arranged dramatically against black plates, followed by a choice of teas and coffees. No children under 8. Self-catering accommodation is available in a traditional cottage in the grounds (£50-£60 for two). **Seats 20** (private room, 5) D daily, 7-9.30; set D £43 + 10%. Closed Jan-Feb. Amex, Diners, MasterCard, Visa. **Directions:** From Bantry, take the road to Durrus, then follow the sign to Ahakista.

Ballinadee   *Glebe Country House*

Ballinadee Bandon Co Cork
COUNTRY HOUSE   Tel: 021 778294 Fax: 021 778456 email: glebehse@indigo.ie

Church records provide interesting detail about this charming old rectory near Kinsale which dates back to 1690 (when it was built for £250; repairs and alterations followed at various dates, and records show completion of the present house in 1857 at a cost of £1,160). More recently, under the hospitable ownership of Gillian Good Bracken, this classically proportioned house has been providing a restful retreat for guests since 1989. The house, which is set in large, well-tended gardens (including a productive kitchen garden) has spacious reception rooms and large, stylishly decorated bedrooms with phone and tea/coffee making facilities. Dinner for residents is at 8 pm by arrangement (please book by noon). Although unlicensed, guests are encouraged to bring their own wine. The whole house may be rented by parties by arrangement and several self-catering apartments are also available. Children welcome (under 5s free in parents' room, cots available). Pets permitted by arrangement. **Rooms 4** (2 shower only, all no-smoking), B&B £30 pps, ss £15. Closed 24-28 Dec. MasterCard, Visa. **Directions:** Take N71 west from Cork to Innishannon; turn sharp left after the bridge and drive 5 miles to Ballinadee.

Ballycotton   *Bayview Hotel*

Ballycotton Co Cork
Tel: 021 646746 Fax: 021 646075
HOTEL/RESTAURANT   email: bayhotel@iol.ie

Overlooking Ballycotton Harbour, Bayview Hotel enjoys a magnificent location on the sea side of the road and with a path to the beach through its own gardens. Since 1971 the hotel has been owned by John and Carmel O'Brien, who completely rebuilt it - fairly low, and sympathetic to the traditional style and scale of the surrounding buildings and harbour - in the early 1990s. Comfortable, homely public areas are complemented by spacious well-furnished bedrooms with good bathrooms; they open on to small balconies and include two corner suites (with jacuzzi) and some particularly cosy top floor rooms. Small conferences/banqueting available for 40/80 people respectively. Children up to 12 free in parents' room. No pets. **Rooms 35** (2 suites, all en-suite, 5 wheelchair accessible). B&B £67.50 pps, ss £20. No service charge. Closed end Oct-Easter. Amex, Diners, MasterCard, Visa

Capricho at the Bayview

Although the name of the restaurant has changed, head chef Ciaran Scully has been at the Bayview since 1995 and his daily menus remain creative modern Irish, developed from a classic French base with contemporary international overtones. He is especially to be complimented on offering dishes which provide a refreshing change to the menus in most of even the best contemporary restaurants - such as a starter of braised pigs cheek with turnip puree, crispy potato cake, honey and clove sauce, or a main course of rabbit with a chanterelle and veal mouseline, served with garlic potatoes and a creamy tarragon sauce. This kind of variety - in addition to a wide selection of seafood, more usual meats and vegetarian dishes - in the sure hands of a talented chef, makes for an interesting and satisfying dining experience, especially when complemented by an elegantly appointed restaurant with lovely sea and harbour views and good service. In fine weather, light meals may be served in the garden. **Seats 70** (private room 40) D 7-9 daily, L Sun only, 1 2. Set D £28, Set Sun L £14. A la carte also offered. (Bar meals available 12.30-6.30 daily). **Directions:** From the N25 (main Cork-Waterford road) take R632 to Garryvoe at Castlemartyr; from Garryvoe, follow signs to Shanagarry & Ballycotton.

Ballycotton   *Spanish Point Seafood Restaurant*

Ballycotton Co Cork
RESTAURANT/ACCOMMODATION   Tel: 021 646177 Fax: 021 646179

Halfway through the village of Ballycotton you suddenly come upon the entrance to Spanish Point, an attractive old building on the seaward side of the road with a clear view across the bay. John and Mary Tattan have been running this relaxed seafood restaurant since 1991 and have built up a considerable reputation locally. Mary takes pride in using local produce, especially fish, to produce creative but not over-elaborate meals. In a little lounge/bar at the back or the sun lounge recently added for residents and diners, aperitifs are served and orders taken from interesting menus that change weekly and offer a good choice - majoring on local seafood, of course, but also several meat and poultry dishes. Lunch menus are shorter; vegetarian options are usually available - ask if this is not mentioned on the menu. The restaurant is in two rooms overlooking the harbour - a fitting setting for good food, cooked and presented with care, and with service to match. The wine list includes an interesting house selection. Small conferences (30) by arrangement. **Seats 60.** No smoking area. L 12.30-2, D 7-9.30 daily, Set L £12.95, Set D £20, House wine £12.50. A la carte also offered. Service discretionary. Low season open weekends only. Closed Jan-mid Feb. MasterCard, Visa. **Accommodation** Comfortable, well-furnished bedrooms all have sea views and good amenities including phone, TV and tea/coffee trays. Children welcome (free in parents' room under 4). Pets permitted. **Rooms 5** (all shower only) B&B £25 pps, ss £5. **Directions:** Off the N25 (main Cork-Waterford road): at Castlemartyr take R632 to Garryvoe, then follow signs to Shanagarry & Ballycotton.

Ballydehob   *Annie's Restaurant*

Main Street Ballydehob Co Cork
RESTAURANT   Tel: 028 37292

Anne and Dano Barrie have been running their tiny cottagey restaurant since 1983 - and, for many, a visit to west Cork is unthinkable without a meal here. Annie makes a great host, welcoming everybody personally, handing out menus - and then sending guests over to Levis' pub across the road for an aperitif. Annie then comes over, takes orders and returns to collect people when their meals are ready. Annie's does have a wine licence but there certainly isn't any spare room for 'reception' and this famous arrangement works extremely well. As to the food at Annie's, everything is freshly made on the day, using local ingredients - fish is delivered every night, meat comes from the local butcher (who kills his own meat), farmhouse cheeses are local and all the breads, ice creams and desserts for the restaurant - and for 'Clara' (see below) - are made on the premises. As for the cooking, it is simple and wholesome, the nearest to really good home cooking you could ever hope to find in a restaurant. Dano cooks fish like a dream. This place is magic. Children welcome, but not after 9 pm. Street parking only. Not convenient for wheelchairs. **Seats 24.** D Tue-Sat 7-9.30, Set D from £22.50, à la carte also offered. House wine £12. Service discretionary. Closed Sun, Mon & all Oct-Nov. MasterCard, Visa.

***Cafe Clara** - Annie's sister restaurant up the road is a cafe/bookshop and is, in Annie's own true words: "Cheep & cheerful - honest to god soups, sandwiches and daily specials". **Seats 26.** Open 10.30-5.30 Mon-Sat. Closed Sun and 24-26 Dec.

Ballydehob ✗   *Levis' Bar*

Corner House Main Street Ballydehob Co Cork
PUB   Tel: 028 37118

Julia and Nell Levis have run this 150-year-old bar and grocery for as long as anyone can remember. It is a characterful and delightfully friendly place, whether you are just in for a casual drink or using the pub as the unofficial 'reception' area for Annie's restaurant across the road. Closed 25 Dec & Good Fri.

Ballylickey   *Ballylickey Manor House*

Ballylickey Bantry Bay Co Cork
Tel: 027 50071 Fax: 027 50124
COUNTRY HOUSE/RESTAURANT   email: ballymh@tinet.ie

Built some 300 years ago by Lord Kenmare as a shooting lodge and home to the Franco-Irish Graves family for four generations, Ballylickey Manor enjoys a stunning, romantic setting overlooking Bantry Bay, with moors and hills behind. There are ten acres of gardens, through which the Ouvane river (trout and salmon fishing) flows. Choose between the elegant and grand bedrooms in the Manor, all lavishly furnished, or more rustic accommodation in the garden - cottages and chalets, some grouped around the outside swimming pool. Residents can dine either in the house or at the poolside restaurant. Garden, outdoor heated swimming pool. Family accommodation "on application" (cot available, £10) Pets permitted by arrangement. Private parking. **Rooms 7** (4 en-suite) B&B £65 pps. Closed Nov-Apr. Amex, Diners, MasterCard, Visa.

Le Rendez-Vous

This weatherboard building next to the pool is remarkably comfortable and smart inside, with an entrance lounge and colourful dining room, decorated and furnished in a pleasing country house style with a chic French flavour. The menu, whether à la carte or table d'hôte, is unashamedly French, almost classical, featuring starters such as foie gras with a Sauternes jelly, clear consommé with mushroom ravioli, or a salad of Bantry Bay prawns flambe with gin. For a main course, roast rack of west Cork lamb, fillet of beef with a marrow crust or steamed turbot with a beurre blanc should satisfy, and when available, lobster Thermidor. For dessert, a French apple tart, baked cream scented with China tea or, alternatively, a local farmhouse cheese selection. No children under 5 after 7.30 pm. **Seats 30.** No smoking restaurant. L12.30-2 Thurs-Tues, D 7-9 daily; Set L £15, Set D £30. 10% sc. Closed Wed L. **Directions:** On N71 between Bantry & Glengariff

Ballylickey

Larchwood House

Pearsons Bridge nr Bantry Co Cork

RESTAURANT/ACCOMMODATION

Tel: 027 66181

The gardens are a special point of interest in themselves here, complementing the restaurant, which is in a relatively modern house with both the traditionally-furnished lounge (where afternoon tea and scones are served) and dining room enjoying lovely views. Sheila Vaughan, a Euro-Toques chef, presents very accomplished six-course dinner menus priced according to the choice of main course, with a typical selection being smoked salmon with citrus salad, an unusual soup such as carrot & peach, pear and melon cocktail, loin of lamb with lemon and mint, and carrageen with mango coulis - wonderful food and in very generous quantities, all the more enjoyable for the garden setting. Here Aidan Vaughan has done everything himself in the last ten years, from building the summer house, paths and bridges to planting trees and shrubs. There are acres to explore, river boulders to cross and nothing prettier than the wild bluebell wood in spring. **Seats 25.** D 7-9.30 Mon-Sat, £25. House wine £12. Service discretionary. Closed Sun & Xmas wk. Amex, Diners, MasterCard, Visa. **Accommodation:** Comfortable en-suite bedrooms vary in situation and outlook: there are two upstairs, two in an adjacent building; those at the back overlook the garden. There are tentative plans to convert an old cowshed on the other side of the hill to make extra rooms. Excellent breakfasts offer a wide choice, including several fish options and a local cheese plate. **Rooms 4** (all en-suite) B&B £25 pps. **Directions:** Take the Kealkil Road off N71 at Ballylickey; after 2 miles signed just before the bridge.

Ballylickey

Sea View House Hotel

Ballylickey Bantry Co Cork

HOTEL/RESTAURANT

Tel: 027 50462 Fax: 027 51555

Personal supervision and warmth of welcome are the hallmarks of Kathleen O'Sullivan's renowned country house hotel close to Ballylickey Bridge. Peacefully located in private grounds, with views over Bantry Bay, it makes a very restorative base for business or pleasure. Spacious, well-proportioned public rooms include a graciously decorated drawing room, a library, cocktail bar and television room, while generously-sized bedrooms - some with sea views - all have good bathrooms and are individually decorated. Family furniture and antiques enhance the whole hotel and standards of maintenance and housekeeping are consistently high. Children welcome (under 6s free in parents' room , cots available). Pets permitted by arrangement. **Rooms 15** (2 mini-suites, 1 ground floor room suitable for less able guests -no lift). B&B £50 pps, ss£15. Closed 15 Nov-15 Mar. Amex, Diners, MasterCard, Visa. **Restaurant:** Overlooking the garden, with views over Bantry Bay, the restaurant is elegant and well-appointed with antiques, fresh flowers and plenty of privacy. Set five-course dinner menus change daily and offer a wide choice on all courses, with the emphasis firmly on local produce, especially seafood, in dishes like simple Irish oak smoked salmon, blackberry sorbet, brill in a light wine sauce or roast rack of lamb with rosemary. Choose from classic desserts - Baileys cream mousse, strawberry shortcake - or local cheeses to finish. Tea or coffee and petits fours may be served out of doors on fine summer evenings. **Seats 50.** No-smoking restaurant. Toilets wheelchair accessible. D 6.45-9 daily, L Sun only 12.45-2; Set D £24, Set Sun L £15. House wines from £12.10% sc. **Directions:** On N71, 3 miles from Bantry, 7 miles from Glengarriff.

Baltimore

Baltimore Harbour Resort Hotel & Leisure Centre

Baltimore Co Cork

HOTEL

Tel: 028 20361 Fax: 028 20466 email: info@bhrhotel.ie

Since the Cullinane family took over this old hotel, they have done a prodigious amount of work, beginning with the complete refurbishment of the original building prior to re-opening in 1995. Most recently, they added on a block of suites (incorporating the traditional arch which now leads through to the carpark) and a new leisure centre, which has a wide range of facilities including a 16-metre swimming pool and gymnasium. The hotel enjoys a lovely position overlooking Roaring Water Bay and is well located for deep sea fishing and visits to nearby islands, including Sherkin and Cape Clear. Modern furnishings, with plenty of light wood and pastel colours, create a sense of space in public areas and the accommodation includes family rooms, junior suites and the new luxury suites. All rooms are comfortably furnished, with neat bathrooms and sea views, and the larger ones have double and single beds. A lift is badly needed however. Public areas include a bar that can be reversed to serve the Sherkin Room (banqueting/conferences for 140) and a bright semi-conservatory Garden Room for informal meals and drinks. Children are well looked after - there's a playroom, a children's club in school holidays and under 3s are free in parents' room (cots available). Off-season breaks are good value. No pets. **Rooms 64** (all en-suite, 12 suites, 1 mini-suite). B&B £52 pps, ss £18. Closed mid Dec-mid Feb. Amex, Diners, MasterCard, Visa. **Directions:** Signposted on the right as you enter Baltimore on the R595 from Skibbereen.

Baltimore [PUB★]   *Bushe's Bar*

PUB/ACCOMMODATION

The Square Baltimore Co Cork
Tel: 028 20125

Pub of the Year

Everyone, especially visiting and local sailors, feels at home in this famous old bar - which is choc-a-bloc with genuine maritime artefacts such as charts, tide tables, ships' clocks, compasses, lanterns, pennants et al - but it's the Bushe family's hospitality that makes it really special. Since Richard and Eileen took on the bar in 1973 it's been "home from home" for regular visitors to Baltimore, for whom a late morning call is de rigeur (in order to collect the ordered newspapers that are rolled up and stacked in the bar window each day). Now there's a new generation of Bushes involved with the business, so all is humming nicely. Simple, homely bar food starts early in the day with tea and coffee from 9.30, moving on to home-made soups and a range of sandwiches including home-cooked meats (ham, roast beef, corned beef), salmon, smoked mackerel or - the most popular by far - open crab sandwiches, served with home-baked brown bread. And all at around a fiver or less. This is a terrific pub, at any time of year, and a very worthy recipient of our Jameson Pub of the Year Award. Bar closed 25 Dec & Good Fri. MasterCard, Visa. **Accommodation:** Over the bar, there are some big, comfortable bedrooms, all with a double and single bed, bath & shower, TV and a kitchenette with all that is needed to make your own continental breakfast. There are also showers provided for the use of sailors and fishermen. **Rooms 3** B&B £17.50 pps. **Directions:** In the middle of Baltimore, on the square overlooking the harbour.

Baltimore   *Casey's of Baltimore*

HOTEL

Baltimore Co Cork.
Tel: 028 20197 Fax: 028 20509 email: caseys@tinet.ie

With dramatic views over Roaring Water Bay to the islands beyond, this attractively developed hotel has grown from the immaculately maintained bar/restaurant that the Caseys had run for twenty years. The old back bar and restaurant have been ingeniously developed to extend the ground floor public areas and to make best use of the view and bedrooms are spacious and well-furnished, with neat bathrooms and views. The staff are always friendly and helpful, there's a relaxed atmosphere and, in addition to a fine dining room overlooking the bay, there are well-organised outdoor eating areas for fine weather. On less favoured days, the open fires are very welcome - and there's traditional music at weekends. Children are welcome (cots available, £5), but not in public areas after 7 pm. No pets. **Rooms 14** (13 en-suite, 1 shower only) B&B £46.50 pps, ss £18.50 Meals. Bar meals daily 12.30-2.30 & 6.30-7.30. Restaurant (**seats 65**): L 12.30-2.30, D 6.30-9.30 daily. Set L (Sun) £12.50, Set D £25. House wine from £10; à la carte also available; service discretionary. Closed 19-25 Feb, 1-14 Nov, 21-27 Dec. Amex, Diners, MasterCard, Visa. **Directions:** On the right as you enter Baltimore on the R595 (Skibbereen) road.

Baltimore   *Chez Youen*

RESTAURANT

The Pier Baltimore Co Cork
Tel: 028 20136 Fax: 028 20495 email: chezyouen@youenjacob.com

Since 1979, Youen Jacob's Breton restaurant has been a major feature in Baltimore. Although other eating places have sprung up around him, Youen is still doing what he does best: simple but dramatic presentation of seafood in the shell. Lobster is very much a speciality and available all year round. The Shellfish Platter is a sight to behold: a complete meal of Dublin Bay Prawns, crab and often velvet crab as well as lobster - all served in shell. Only minor concessions are made to non-fish eaters - starters of leek and potato soup at lunch or melon with port on the dinner menu and, correspondingly, roast lamb or steak with green peppercorn sauce for main course, although vegetarians are willingly catered for. **Seats 40.** No smoking area. D daily 6-10, L Sun from noon. Set D from £18.50, Set Sun L £18.50; à la carte also offered. House wine £12.50. Service 10%. Closed 15 Feb-15 Mar. Amex, Diners, MasterCard, Visa. **Directions:** Just beyond the square, overlooking the harbour.

Baltimore   *La Jolie Brise*

RESTAURANT/ACCOMMODATION

The Square Baltimore Co Cork
Tel: 028 20600 Fax: 028 20495

Just along from Bushe's Bar, La Jolie Brise has brought a breath of fresh air to eating out in Baltimore. Run by Youen Jacob the younger, this cheerful continental-style café spills out on to the pavement and provides holiday-makers with good, inexpensive meals to be washed down with moderately priced wines. Breakfast menus include regular continental and full Irish breakfast and several fish choices, including hot smoked salmon, plus a range of drinks including hot chocolate. Generous, well-made pizzas (also available to take away) and pastas are available and for lunch and dinner there are "European & Irish" specialities like traditional mussels & chips and char-grilled sirloin steaks with salad & chips. Great youthful, contemporary special - 2 main courses and a bottle of wine for £20. **Seats 40.** Smoking unrestricted. Open 8.30 am-10.30 pm daily; à la carte & special menus. House wine £9.50. Service discretionary. Open all year. MasterCard, Visa. **Accommodation:** Above the restaurant the Jacobs have eight very attractive, well-equipped bedrooms in their "Baltimore Bay" guesthouse overlooking the harbour. Everything in it is big - the rooms, the beds, the bathrooms. Amenities are good - direct-dial phones, tea/coffee-making facilities, TV with Video. Furniture is modern, with a light sprinkling of Georgian and Victorian pieces and, in addition to a good sitting area in each room, there's a comfortable residents' lounge. Children up to 4 free in parents' room (cot available). Pets permitted by arrangement. No private parking. **Rooms 8** (7 en-suite, 1 shower only, 1 for wheelchairs). B&B £32 pps, ss £18. Open all year. MasterCard, Visa. **Directions:** Right in the middle of Baltimore, on the square.

Baltimore ❋   *Customs House Restaurant*

RESTAURANT

Baltimore Co Cork
Tel: 028 20200

Susan Holland and Ian Parr's uncluttered contemporary restaurant has made a lot of friends over the last few years and it's easy to see why. They don't take credit cards, do Sunday lunch or allow young children. But they do use only the freshest of local produce in season and they do great daily menus - blackboard menus that highlight local seafood, especially, which is cooked by Susan with flair, served by Ian with unflappability - and give outstanding value for money. The couple, who are Australian, have been running the Customs House as a seasonal restaurant since 1995, then - and this seems to be the secret of the restaurant's dramatic improvement in a few short seasons - use the winter months to travel and gain experience in some very distinguished kitchens indeed. Superb ingredients, presented with deceptive simplicity in classic French and Italian dishes, are often given the lightest of twists to freshen familiar themes: wonderful organic salads, classics include steamed fillets of brill with beurre blanc or brandade de morue with roasted red pepper; simple, perfectly cooked organic side vegetables could be new potatoes and spinach. Then those unbeatable timeless desserts - hazelnut meringue with strawberries and crème anglaise, tarte tatin with house vanilla ice cream, or (very) local cheese - Cooleeney, Gubbeen, Carraig goat - in perfect condition. All this is complemented by an interesting, highly informative and keenly-priced wine list and Ian Parr's efficient, refreshingly low-key service. **Seats 30.** No smoking area. D Tue-Sat, 7-10; Set D £15 (3-course, no choice) & £19 (choice of five on each course); house wines £10. Vegetarian dishes on request; no children under 10. No credit cards (cheques, incl sterling cheques, accepted). Closed Sun/Mon and Nov-Mar. **Directions:** Situated on the hill, just up behind the square in Baltimore.

Baltimore   *The Mews*

RESTAURANT

Baltimore Co Cork
Tel/Fax: 028 20390

Owner-chef Lucia Carey runs this well-appointed restaurant on the ground floor and adjacent conservatory of an attractive stone building. Menus are contemporary and the cooking combines the admirable qualities of generosity and lightness. Meals start off with freshly-baked breads and tapenade and prompt service means that starters like Thai seafood chowder of prawn, crab and coriander parcels will not be far behind. Main courses could include a variation on traditional themes such as rack of lamb with a redcurrant & port sauce and minted onion. There will always be a delicious vegetarian dish on the menu such as oriental vegetable parcels with roasted pepper sauce, all served with imaginative and well-cooked vegetables. Good home-made ices are among the desserts, or you could finish with a local cheese plate and freshly brewed coffee. **Seats 30.** No smoking area. D Tues-Sun, 6-10; à la carte (average main course £15), Closed Oct-May. No credit cards. **Directions:** The Mews is hidden in a laneway just behind the square - start up the hill and turn first right.

Bandon   *The Munster Arms Hotel*

Oliver Plunkett Street Bandon Co Cork
HOTEL   Tel/Fax: 023 41562 email: kingsley@tinet.ie

This substantial town-centre hotel has spacious public areas and, unlike many of the hotels in the area, is as popular with business guests and locals as it is with holiday-makers. It is well-situated for touring the area and there is plenty to do, including angling and riding (there is an equestrian centre nearby). Bedrooms are generally quite big and well-furnished with generous beds and stylish, well-fitted bathrooms (four of the older ones are shower only), providing a good standard of comfort and amenities at a reasonable rate. Conference/banqueting (300/240) with secretarial services available. At the time of going to press there are plans for a large (100-seater) bistro. No private parking, but safe street parking is available beside the hotel. Children free in parents' room up to 12; cot available. Pets permitted by arrangement. **Rooms 30** (all en-suite, 5 no-smoking) B&B £35, no ss. Closed 25 Dec. Amex, Diners, MasterCard, Visa. **Directions:** In the centre of Bandon town; coming from Cork, turn left at the bridge and left again into Oliver Plunkett Street.

Bantry   *O'Connor's Seafood Restaurant*

The Square Bantry Co Cork
RESTAURANT   Tel: 027 50221

Approaching town from the south on the N71, Matt and Ann O'Connor's seafood restaurant is right on the main square (site of the annual early-May mussel festival). Long established, with a front room, booths and a seated bar in the back (note the seafood tapas selection displayed here), all decorated in a nautical theme, there's also a lobster and oyster fish tank by the entrance door. Mussels, cooked all ways, are a speciality - a starter of them grilled with herbs and lemon butter fits the bill perfectly, followed perhaps by fresh scallops and salmon mornay in shells, served with an abundance of vegetables, or else mussels marinière with a fish pie as a main course. There are some non-fish dishes available, such as local lamb, beef and chicken, and at lunchtime you can have soup and a sandwich or daily-changing dishes off the blackboard. At the time of going to press the owners' son, Mark, is about to take over the running of the restaurant, but there will be no immediate changes. No children after 6 pm. **Seats 44.** No smoking area. Mon-Sat L12-5.30, Mon-Sun D 6-10; house wine from £11.50; service charge 10% Closed Sun L Apr-Oct, all Sun Nov-Mar. Telephone to confirm opening times off-season. MasterCard, Visa. **Directions:** In the centre of Bantry, overlooking the square.

Bantry   *The Westlodge Hotel*

Bantry Co Cork
HOTEL   Tel: 027 50360 Fax: 027 50438

Easily spotted on an elevated site above the main road into Bantry, the Westlodge Hotel seems to have thought of all the possible requirements to make a family holiday successful, regardless of weather conditions. A wide range of outdoor activities can be organised, including golf, water sports, horse riding and pony trekking. But - and this is the hotel's greatest strength - there's also plenty to keep energetic youngsters happy if the weather should disappoint, including a 16m swimming pool in the leisure centre. Bedrooms have all been fairly recently refurbished and there is 24-hour room service. The restaurant is well-positioned to take advantage of the view of the bay. Banqueting/conference facilities (400/300) with back-up secretarial services and video-conferencing available on request. **Rooms 95** (3 suites, 4 disabled). Lift. B&B £60 pps, ss £10. Open all year. Amex, Diners, MasterCard, Visa. **Directions:** On the edge of town, on the main Cork-Bantry road.

Bere Island

Lawrence Cove House

Lawrence Cove Bere Island nr Bantry Co Cork
Tel/Fax: 027 75063 email: cove@indigo.ie

RESTAURANT

Mike and Mary Sullivan have built up a loyal following at the seafood restaurant they have run since 1995 on Bere Island, just a short ferry ride from Castletownbere. Since the marina opened, sailing people often tailor their cruising plans to fit in a comfortable and well-fed overnight stay. Mike is the fisherman who supplies many of the country's top restaurants with fresh West Cork fish and shellfish so, although the menu is not over-long, it embraces a wide range of fish and seafood, including some unusual varieties unlikely to be found elsewhere, such as grouper and coryphene ("sunfish"), when in season. And the service even extends to transport, as Mike will bring guests over to the restaurant in his fishing boat and deliver them back to the mainland after dinner if the ferry times aren't convenient. Lawrence Cove was our Seafood Restaurant of the Year in 1999. Not suitable for children under 12. **Seats 40.** Mon-Sun D 6.30-9.30. Set D £25-£35. Closed Oct-Apr. MasterCard, Visa. **Directions:** Regular ferries from Castletownbere. Bere Island Ferry Service (15 cars): Tel: 027-75009

* Simple, hospitable accommodation on the island is available at "Harbour View" B&B. Contact: Ann Sullivan : 027-75011

At the time of going to press the new accommodation hoped for in the Lawrence Cove area for the 1999 season had not materialised; contact the restaurant for information.

Blarney

Blairs Inn

Cloghroe Blarney Co Cork
Tel: 021 381470 Fax: 021 385323 email: blair@tinet.ie

PUB/RESTAURANT

John and Anne Blair's delightful riverside pub is in a quiet, wooded setting just outside Blarney yet, sitting in the garden in summer, you might see trout rising in the Owennageara river (or see a heron out fishing), while winter offers welcoming open fires in this comfortingly traditional country pub. It's a lovely place to drop into for a drink or a session - there's traditional music on Sunday nights all year round and on Mondays from April to October - and the Blairs have built up a special reputation for their food. Anne supervises the kitchen personally, and care and commitment are evident in menus offering a wide (but not over-extensive) range of interesting but fairly traditional dishes based on seafood (from Kenmare and Dingle), local lamb, beef and poultry, and game in season. A la carte menus are available in the bar from lunchtime onwards; lunch and dinner can be booked in the candlelit Snug or Pantry dining areas. Children welcome until 7.30 pm. **Seats 40/50** (restaurant/bar) & 60 in garden. No-smoking area. Bar menu 12.30-9.30 daily. Restaurant L 12.30-3, D 6-9.30. A la carte. House wine £11.50. Service discretionary. Closed 25 Dec & Good Fri. Amex, Diners, MasterCard, Visa. **Directions:** 5 minutes from Blarney village, on the R579.

Blarney

Blarney Park Hotel

Blarney Co Cork
Tel: 021 385281 Fax: 021 381506 email: info@blarneypark.com

HOTEL

Blarney may be best known for its castle (and the famous Blarney Stone) but for many people this modern hotel is the reason for the visit. There is always something going on at Blarney Park and its excellent facilities for both conferences and leisure are put to full use. Close proximity to Cork city (just half an hour on the Limerick road) makes this a very convenient location for business. The hotel also attracts steady all-year business through an energetic programme of short breaks and special interest holidays covering a wide range of topics (such as matching wine and food, learning to swim, rambling and the ever-popular golf). It's a bright, friendly hotel with open fires in spacious public areas and overlooking pleasant grounds. Very family-friendly rooms are arranged with doubles along one side of corridors and smallish twins more suitable for children opposite. Children's rooms have fun packs and excellent back-up services, including an all-year crèche, make this a very relaxing place for a family break. And, of course, everyone loves the leisure centre which has a 40-metre water slide. Conference/banqueting (270/250); business centre, secretarial services, video-conferencing. **Rooms 91** (12 shower only; 1 mini-suite, 17 executive rooms, 2 no-smoking, 2 disabled). Lift. B&B £62 pps, ss £16; no service charge. Closed 25 Dec. Amex, Diners, MasterCard, Visa. **Directions:** In centre of Blarney, on left on entering town from Cork.

Butlerstown   *Atlantic Sunset*
Dunworley, Butlerstown, Co Cork
ACCOMMODATION   Tel: 023 40115

Just along the road from Katherine Noren's Dunworley Cottage Restaurant, Mary Holland provides comfortable accommodation and a genuinely warm welcome in her neat modern house with views down to the sea at Dunworley. The house is wheelchair accessible and the ground floor rooms are suitable for less able guests. The breakfast room and some bedroom windows have sea views and, weather permitting, the sight of the sun setting over the Atlantic can indeed be magnificent. Sandy beaches and coastal walk nearby. **Rooms 4**, 2 en-suite (shower only). B&B £17 pps (£19 en-suite). Closed 20 Dec-1 Jan. No credit cards. **Directions:** From Bandon, follow signs for Timoleague, then Butlerstown, then Dunworley.

Butlerstown   *Butlerstown House*
Butlerstown Bandon Co Cork
ACCOMMODATION   Tel: 023 40137

Elisabeth Jones' classic late eighteenth century house is set in ten acres of private grounds with long views over the rolling west Cork countryside to the Dunmanway Mountains. Guests are welcomed on arrival with tea in the drawing room, allowing a little time to wind down to the pace appropriate to a house characterised by peace and tranquillity. Elegant reception rooms are comfortably furnished in period style; the drawing room opens on to south facing gardens, and if the weather should disappoint there are open fires throughout. The staircase is a fine example of Georgian craftsmanship, leading to four bedrooms that include a master bedroom with four-poster bed. Breakfast is a major event ("a neglected repast we consider as the principal meal of the day") and is taken in style at the "Butlerstown Table" in the dining room. Full catering facilities are available for house parties and small conferences, ie parties of up to 10 people for 2-3 nights. Not suitable for children under 12. Pets permitted by arrangement. **Rooms 4** (3 en-suite, 1 şhower only, all no-smoking) B&B £45pps, ss £10. Open all year. MasterCard, Visa. **Directions:** From Bandon, take N71; bear left after Maxol Station, then R602 to Timoleague

Butlerstown   *Dunworley Cottage Restaurant*
Dunworley Butlerstown Bandon Co Cork
RESTAURANT   Tel: 023 40314

The warmth of Katherine Noren's uniquely Swedish style of hospitality (and the cosiness of open fires when required) contrasts magnificently with the windswept coastal location of her famous west Cork restaurant. The quality of food at Dunworley is, in Katherine's own words, "defined by two principles - the best raw materials have to be used and the preparation has to be performed by a highly skilled cook". These principles are adhered to with admirable consistency by Katherine and her team: all ingredients are sourced locally and as many as possible are organic or wild - that means no intensively farmed fish on the menu, for instance, and much of the fresh produce comes from their own organic garden, which is patrolled by ducks to keep the slugs down. Catering for special dietary requirements is a matter of routine at Dunworley and children can choose from their own menu or have dishes from the à la carte menu at half price. Cooking skills are always of the highest quality at Dunworley, making even the simplest dishes special - the Swedish meatballs, for example, which were originally intended for children but were moved to the main menu by popular demand, and also the nettle soup, which has become a signature dish. Ultra fresh seafood, salads that sing with vitality and delicious home-made breads all contribute to the very special experience at Dunworley. Self-catering holidaymakers can also book ready-made dinners to take away. Scandinavian languages, German and French spoken. Children welcome, but not after 8 pm. **Seats 60.** Reservations essential L12.30-2, D 7-9 Wed-Sun. A la carte. House wines from £10.50. 10% service charge. Closed Mon/Tues and Oct-Mar. Diners, MasterCard, Visa. **Directions:** From Bandon, follow signs for Timoleague (where the restaurant is signposted), then Butlerstown, then Dunworley.

Butlerstown   *O'Neill's*
Butlerstown Bandon Cork
PUB   Tel: 023 40228

Butlerstown is a pretty pastel-painted village, with lovely views across farmland to Dunworley and the sea beyond. Dermot and Mary O'Neill's unspoilt pub is as pleasant and hospitable a place as could be found to enjoy the view - or to admire the traditional mahogany bar and pictures that make old pubs like this such a pleasure to be in. Closed 25 Dec & Good Fri

Carrigaline ✳   *Carrigaline Court Hotel*

Carrigaline Co Cork

HOTEL   Tel: 021 371300 Fax: 021 371103 email: carrigcourt@tinet.ie

This newly built hotel has brought badly needed amenities to the area for business visitors, private and corporate functions and locals who particularly appreciate the leisure facilities. The spacious foyer creates a good first impression and the hotel has attractive features throughout, with interesting contemporary furniture in both public areas and bedrooms, which are stylishly decorated and well-equipped with work desks and ISDN lines. All rooms have king size beds as well as all the more usual amenities, although the bedding selected reduces the comfort afforded - heavy coverlets and the brick-like pillows which have become a feature in too many new hotels - and lighting could also be improved. Marbled bathrooms are quite luxurious, with good quality toiletries. Conference/banqueting facilities (350/275), also smaller meeting rooms, business centre, secretarial services and video-conferencing. Leisure centre. Some parking. Children welcome (under 12s free in parents' room, cot available). Off-season budget breaks. Pets permitted by arrangement. **Rooms 52** (2 suites, 1 disabled). Lift. B&B £45 pps, ss £15. Closed 25 Dec. Amex, Diners, MasterCard, Visa. **Directions:** From Cork city, the hotel is on the right-hand side as you enter Carrigaline.

Carrigaline   *Glenwood House*

Ballinrea Road Carrigaline Co Cork

ACCOMMODATION   Tel/Fax: 021 373878

This excellent, professionally run guesthouse is in purpose-built premises, very conveniently located for Cork airport and the ferry. Comfortable, well-furnished rooms (including one designed for disabled guests) have all the amenities normally expected of hotels, including well-designed bathrooms. Very good breakfasts too. Under 10s free in parents' room. **Rooms 8** (all en-suite). B&B £30pps, ss £10. Closed 24 Dec-2 Jan. Diners, MasterCard, Visa. **Directions:** Follow signs to Ringaskiddy car ferry. Entering Carrigaline, turn right at roundabout; the guesthouse is signed on the right.

Carrigaline   *Gregory's Restaurant*

Main Street Carrigaline Co Cork

RESTAURANT   Tel: 021 371512

Owner-chef Gregory Dawson and his partner and restaurant manager Rachelle Harley opened here in 1994 and the restaurant was an immediate success. Bright, comfortable and friendly, with plenty of buzz, the restaurant provides a good setting for Gregory's sensibly short à la carte menus which change monthly and include some tempting vegetarian options. Typical dishes from a summer menu might include carrot and coriander soup or fresh crab salad to start, then fish of the day or Madras lamb curry with basmati rice and accompaniments. Desserts could include tangy lemon and lime tart or meringue roulade with strawberries and cream - or there's an Irish cheese plate. Home-baked breads, good coffee and helpful service complete a very good all-round package. **Seats 40.** No-smoking area. Air conditioning. Toilets wheelchair accessible. D Tues-Sat 6.30-10, L Sun 12.30-3; D à la carte, Set Sun L £12; house wine £10.95. No service charge. Closed D Sun & Mon, bank hols, Christmas & 2 weeks Oct. Amex, MasterCard, Visa. **Directions:** In the centre of Carrigaline, just on the right as you leave the square heading towards Kinsale.

Castlelyons ⛪   *Ballyvolane House*

Castlelyons Co Cork

COUNTRY HOUSE   Tel: 025 36349 Fax: 025 36781 email: ballyvol@iol.ie

Jeremy and Merrie Greene's gracious mansion is surrounded by its own farmland, magnificent wooded grounds, a recently restored trout lake and formal terraced gardens, all carefully managed and maintained to a high standard - a major replanting of 400 rhododendrons, azaleas and specimen trees is the current project. The Italianate style of the present house - including a remarkable pillared hall with a baby grand piano and open fire - dates from the mid 19th century when modifications were made to the original house of 1728. This is a very lovely house, elegantly furnished and extremely comfortable, with central heating and big log fires; bedrooms are varied, but all are roomy and, like the rest of the house, are furnished with family antiques and look out over attractive gardens and grounds. Ballyvolane has private salmon fishing on 15 km of the renowned River Blackwater, with a wide variety of spring and summer beats. Fishing is Merrie's special enthusiasm (a brochure is available outlining the fishing services she provides) and she's also a great cook, providing guests with delicious country house dinners which are served in style around a long mahogany table (no smoking in the dining room). There is much of interest in the area - the beautiful Blackwater valley is well worth exploring, with its many gardens and historic sites, and Lismore, the Rock of Cashel and Waterford Crystal are among the many interesting places which can easily be visited nearby. The standard of hospitality, comfort and food at Ballyvolane are all exceptional, making this an excellent base for a peaceful and very relaxing break. French is spoken. Pets permitted by arrangement. **Rooms 6** (1 shower only, 1 for disabled). B&B £50pps ss£12. Residents D £25 from 8pm (no-smoking dining room); menu changes daily. House wine £12.50. Closed 23-28 Dec. Amex, Diners, MasterCard, Visa. **Directions:** From Cork, turn off N8 onto R628. Follow four house signs.

Castletownbere   *MacCarthy's*

The Square Castletownbere Co Cork
PUB   Tel: 027 70014

Dating back to the 1870s, and currently run by Adrienne MacCarthy, this famous old pub and grocery store really is the genuine article. Fortunately, it shows no signs of changing. Atmosphere and live traditional music are the most obvious attractions but the grocery is real and provisions the local fishing boats. Simple bar food - seafood chowder, open seafood sandwiches - is available from 9.30am-9.30pm. Closed 25 Dec & Good Fri. No credit cards. **Directions:** In town centre, near the ferry slip.

Castletownbere   *The Old Presbytery*

Brandy Hall House Castletownbere Co Cork
ACCOMMODATION   Tel: 027 70424 Fax: 027 70420

On the edge of Castletownbere and well-signposted from the road, this very pleasant old house on 4 acres is in a magnificent position - on a little point with the sea on two sides and clear views of Berehaven Harbour. The house dates back to the late 1700s and has been sensitively restored by the current owners, David and Mary Wrigley. The five bedrooms vary in size and outlook but all have phone, tea/coffee tray and TV and are furnished to a high standard, in keeping with the character of the house. Breakfast - which includes a vegetarian menu - is served in a pleasant conservatory overlooking the sea. Children welcome (under 5s free in parents' room, cot available); pets permitted by arrangement. **Rooms 5** (all shower only). B&B £20, ss £5. MasterCard, Visa. **Directions:** Turn left as the road narrows by Brandy Hall bridge and follow the sign.

Castletownshend   *Bow Hall*

Casteltownshend Co Cork
ACCOMMODATION   Tel: 028 36114

A very comfortable 17th century house, with a pleasant outlook, excellent home-cooking and a warm welcome by enthusiastic hosts, Dick and Barbara Vickery, a visit to this lovely home is a memorable experience. The cuisine is imaginative; seasonal menus, based on home-grown and local produce, change daily and breakfasts are a highlight, with home-baked breads and muffins, home-made preserves among the delights. Non-smoking house. No pets. Closed Xmas wk. **Rooms 3** (1 en-suite, 2 with private bathrooms), B&B £35, ss £5; min 2 night stay preferred. Advance bookings essential, especially in winter. Residents' dinner at 8 pm (no wine licence). No credit cards. **Directions:** On the right hand side as you drive down into the village, just before the trees in the middle of the street.

Castletownshend [PUB★]   *Mary Ann's Bar & Restaurant*

Castletownshend nr Skibbereen Co Cork
PUB/RESTAURANT   Tel: 028 36146 Fax: 028 36377 email: golfer@indigo.ie

Mention Castletownshend and the chances are that the next words will be 'Mary Ann's', as this welcoming landmark has been the source of happy memories for many a visitor to this picturesque west Cork village over the years. (For those who have come up the hill with a real sailor's appetite from the little quay, the sight of its gleaming bar seen through the open door is one to treasure.) The pub is as old as it looks, going back to 1846, and has been in the energetic and hospitable ownership of Fergus and Patricia O'Mahony since 1988. Even the best old bars need a bit of attention occasionally, however, but any refurbishments at Mary Ann's have left its original character intact. The O'Mahony's have built up a great reputation for food at the bar and in the restaurant, which is split between an upstairs dining room and The Vine Room, which can be used for private parties. Seafood is the star, of course, and comes in many guises, usually along with some of the lovely home-baked brown bread which is one of the house specialities. Another is the Platter of Castlehaven Bay Shellfish and Seafood - a sight to behold, and usually including langoustine, crab meat, crab claws, and both fresh and smoked salmon. Much of the menu depends on the catch of the day, although there are also good steaks and roasts, served with delicious local potatoes and seasonal vegetables. Desserts are good too, but local west Cork cheeses are an excellent option. Bar food 12-2.30 & 6-9.15 daily. Restaurant **Seats 30** D daily £22.95; L Sun only in winter. House wine £11.95. Service discretionary. Closed 25 Dec & Good Fri. MasterCard, Visa. **Directions:** Half way up the steep hill in the village, just below the trees.

Clonakilty   *An Sugan*

Strand Road Clonakilty Co Cork

RESTAURANT/BAR   Tel: 023 33498

The O'Crowley family has owned An Sugan since 1980 and they have done a great job: it's always been a really friendly, well-run place and their reputation for good food is well-deserved. Now mainly a restaurant rather than a bar, the menu changes daily and is very strong on seafood - fish specials could include a choice ten, ranging from cod on a bed of champ to lobster salad. **Seats 48.** L12.30-3 & D 6-9 daily. A la carte; set Sun L £12.90. House wine £12. Service discretionary. Closed 25-26 Dec & Good Fri. MasterCard, Visa. **Directions:** On the left hand side as you enter the town from Cork.

Clonakilty   *Dunmore House Hotel*

Muckross Clonakilty Co Cork

HOTEL   Tel: 023 33352 Fax: 023 34686 email: dunmorehousehotel@tinet.ie

The magnificent coastal location of Jeremiah and Mary O'Donovan's family-owned and managed hotel has been used to advantage to provide sea views for all bedrooms and to allow guests access to their own stretch of foreshore. Comfortable public areas include a bar and lounges; bedrooms are furnished to a high standard and the numerous leisure activities in the area include angling and golf - green fees are free to residents on the hotel's own (highly scenic) nine hole golf course - cycling, horse-riding and watersports; packed lunches are provided on request. Conference/banqueting 250. Wheelchair accessible. Children welcome (under 4s free in parents' room; cot available). Pets permitted by arrangement. **Rooms 23** (2 mini-suites,1 room for disabled). B&B £45pps, ss£10. Closed 23-27 Dec and all Feb. Amex, Diners, MasterCard, Visa. **Directions:** Left turn signposted from the Skibbereen by-pass at Clonakilty.

Clonakilty   *Emmet Hotel*

Emmet Square Clonakilty Co Cork

HOTEL   Tel: 023 33394 Fax: 023 35058

The Emmet Hotel is hidden away in the centre of Clonakilty on a lovely serene Georgian square that contrasts unexpectedly with the hustle and bustle of the nearby streets; it's a most attractive location, although parking is likely to be difficult. The standard of furnishing and comfort is high throughout, with management in the capable hands of Tony and Marie O'Keeffe (who ran their own successful restaurant in Cork for a number of years). Marie is responsible for both restaurant and bar food; her cooking is based on the best of seasonal local produce, much of it organic, and The Bistro has earned a reputation for good, creative cooking. Conference/banqueting for 150. Children welcome (cots available). Pets permitted by arrangement. **Rooms 20** (all en-suite, 3 mini-suites) B&B £35 pps, ss £10. Meals 12.30-2.30 (Sun 2.45) and 6.30-9.30 (10 in summer). Set L £12.95, Set D £18. House wine £12. Service discretionary. Closed 25 Dec. Amex, Diners, MasterCard, Visa. **Directions:** In centre of Clonakilty - turn left into Emmet Square at the Catholic church.

Clonakilty ❊ *Fionnuala's Little Italian Restaurant*

30 Ashe Street Clonakilty Co Cork
RESTAURANT Tel: 023 34355

Fionnuala Harkin's charmingly higgledy-piggledy restaurant is usually packed, although it has actually grown considerably recently as an extra two dining rooms and a small wine bar were added last year, along with an overall raising of standards. Toilets - previously a long climb up the stairs - are now on the ground floor. The reasons for this little place's popularity are simple: good home-cooked food, reasonable prices and friendly service. Vegetarian dishes. Children welcome. Toilets wheelchair accessible. **Seats 50** D only 5.30-10 daily (from 6.30 in winter). Set D £13.50. A la carte. House wine £9.95. Closed 24-26 Dec. MasterCard, Visa. **Directions:** In Clonakilty town centre - on the left as you enter the town through Ashe Street.

Clonakilty *The Lodge & Spa at Inchydoney Island*

Clonakilty, Co Cork
Tel: 023 33143 Fax: 023 35229
HOTEL/RESTAURANT email mkj@inchydoneyisland.com

First sight of this luxurious hotel may be disappointing - on the whole the building is architecturally uninspired and the sight of a large car park between any hotel and the sea is depressing. However, some features - such as keeping the function area quite separate from the rest of the hotel - are clearly sensible and, once inside the hotel (as opposed to the Dunes Pub, which has a more down to earth atmosphere) that pampered feeling soon takes over. Public areas are spacious and impressive, there's a lovely big residents' lounge and library (with a piano) and the bedrooms, all furnished and decorated to a high standard in an uncluttered contemporary style, have ISDN lines, safes - and wonderful views. Health and leisure facilities include a superb Thalassotherapy Spa, which offers a range of very special treatments. Special breaks are a major attraction - the fishing, equestrian, golf or simply an off-season weekend away - and Conferences/banqueting (300/200); secretarial service, video-conferencing. Leisure centre. Wheelchair access. Children welcome (under 12s free in parents' room; cots available, £5). Pets permitted by arrangement. **Rooms 67** (1 suite, 3 mini-suites, 63 executive rooms; 17 non-smoking; 2 for disabled). B&B £100pps, ss £20. Service 10%. Open all year. Amex, Diners, MasterCard, Visa.

Gulfstream Restaurant

Located on the first floor, with panoramic sea views from the (rather few) window tables, this elegant restaurant offers fine dining in a broadly Mediterranean style, utilising organic produce where possible. Menus change monthly, include vegetarian options and willingly cater for special dietary requirements. **Seats 80** Private room (40) Smoking: "Courtesy of Choice" policy. Toilets wheelchair accessible. D daily 6.30-10, L Sun only 12-2.30. A la carte; Set Sun L also available, £16. House wines £14. Service 10%. [*Informal bar meals also available 12-9 daily.]. **Directions:** N 71 from Cork; signed from Clonakilty (2 miles).

Cloyne *Barnabrow Country House*

Cloyne Midleton Co Cork
COUNTRY HOUSE/RESTAURANT Tel/Fax: 021 652534 email: barnabrow@tinet.ie

It takes a brave person to open a country house just down the road from Ballymaloe House, but John O'Brien - a competent professional with a keen knowledge of the local market - is just the man for the job. His sensitive conversion of an imposing seventeenth century house makes good use of its stunning views of Ballycotton, and the decoration is commendably restrained. Innovative wooden furniture (commissioned from local craftsmen) is a point of interest, spacious bedrooms are comfortable and the service is discreet but efficient. Children welcome (cots available £5). Pets permitted. **Rooms 19** (all en-suite & no-smoking; suites 2). B&B £35pps, ss £10. Closed 22-27 Dec. Diners, MasterCard, Visa.

Mór Chlúana Restaurant

At the restaurant, Mór Chlúana (in a courtyard behind the main house) head chef Eamon Harty - who previously worked at Ballymaloe - features local produce in starters like Shanagarry oak smoked salmon with capers and crème fraîche and main courses such as honey glazed loin of pork with apple sauce, poached salmon on a bed of spinach with hollandaise sauce and tomato fondue. The four course Sunday Lunch is particularly good value. **Seats 50**. D 6.30-9, L 12.30-2.30 Set L £12.50; early dinner (5-7) £18. House wine £11.50. Service discretionary. **Directions:** From Cork, turn right off N25 at Midleton; after 3 miles turn left for Cloyne. Barnabrow is 1.5 miles from Cloyne, on the Ballycotton road.

Cobh
Mansworth's

Cobh Co Cork

PUB

Tel: 021 811965

Cobh's oldest established family-owned bar dates back to at least 1895 and is currently in the capable hands of John Mansworth, who is a great promoter of the town. Bar snacks are available but it's really as a character pub that Mansworth's is most appealing. It's a bit of a climb up the hill to reach it but well worth the effort, especially for anyone with an interest in the history of Cobh as a naval port - the photographs and memorabilia on display here will provide hours of pleasure. Closed 25 Dec & Good Fri

---

Courtmacsherry
Courtmacsherry Hotel

Nr Bandon Co Cork

HOTEL/RESTAURANT

Tel: 023 46198 Fax: 023 46137

Family-run by Terry and Carole Adams since 1973, this unpretentious homely hotel offers simple comfort and a relaxed atmosphere. Spacious, pleasantly old-fashioned public rooms provide plenty of places for guests to relax. By comparison, bedrooms are on the small side, but they have direct-dial phones, satellite TV and tea/coffee trays. Traditional family holiday activities are well catered for, with boats and bikes available nearby, lawn tennis in the grounds and there is also Carole Adams' riding school which is on the premises and offers riding and qualified instruction for all ages. Children welcome (under 5s free in parents'room; cot available) Pets permitted in some areas. **Rooms 10** (1 shower only). B&B £40 pps. No ss. MasterCard, Visa. Closed Oct-Easter. **Restaurant:** Overlooking Courtmacsherry Bay, the restaurant is in a pleasant traditionally furnished room. Local fish is the speciality and cooking is supervised personally by Terry Adams. The wine list, which offers over 100 wines from throughout the world, from over a dozen suppliers, is a particular source of pride - regular visits are made to vineyards. **Seats 90** D 7.30-9.30 Mon-Sun, L Sun only,12.45-2.15. Set D £20, Set Sun L £13. Service discretionary. Closed Oct-Easter. **Directions:** From Cork, take the N71 to Bandon and Timoleague, then the R601 to Courtmacsherry.

Hotel may change hands in 2000.

Crookhaven
O'Sullivans

Crookhaven Skibbereen Co Cork

PUB

Tel: 028 35319

This long-established family-run bar is in an attractive location right on the harbour at Crookhaven, with tables beside the water - when it's not too busy, it can be heaven on a sunny day. Angela O'Sullivan personally supervises all the food served in the bar - home-made soups and chowders, shrimps, open sandwiches, home-baked bread, scones and desserts - all good homely fare. Closed 25 Dec & Good Fri. Visa. **Directions:** From Cork, take the N71 and turn left on to the R591 just before Bantry.

Crosshaven ✗
Whispering Pines

Crosshaven Co Cork

HOTEL

Tel: 021 831843 Fax: 021 831679

A particular favourite of fishing people and the sailing community, this hospitable, laid-back family-run hotel is in a sheltered position overlooking the Owenabue River. Accommodation is modest but comfortable and reasonably priced. The hotel owns three boats, custom-built for sea angling. Acc£ Closed Dec. Amex, Diners, MasterCard, Visa.

Durrus
Blairs Cove House

Durrus Co Cork

Tel: 027 61127 Fax: 027 61487

RESTAURANT/ACCOMMODATION

e-mail: blairscove@tinet.ie

At the head of Dunmanus Bay, Blairs Cove enjoys a stunning waterside location. Although additions over the years have enlarged the restaurant considerably - and now include the option of enjoying the view from an elegant conservatory while you dine - the original room at Sabine and Philippe de Mey's remarkable restaurant is lofty, stone-walled and black-beamed: but, although characterful, any tendency to rusticity is immediately offset by the choice of a magnificent chandelier as a central feature, gilt-framed family portraits on the walls and the superb insouciance of using their famous grand piano to display an irresistible array of desserts. They have things down to a fine art at Blairs Cove - and what a formula: an enormous central buffet groans under the weight of the legendary hors d'oeuvre display, a speciality that is unrivalled in Ireland. Main course specialities of local seafood or the best of meat and poultry are char-grilled at a special wood-fired grill right in the restaurant and, in addition to those desserts, full justice is done to the ever-growing selection of local farmhouse cheese for which West Cork is rightly renowned. This place is truly an original. **Seats 80.** D 7.30-9.30 daily Set D £30; service discretionary. Closed Nov-Mar. MasterCard, Visa. **Accommodation:** 3 Suites. Three small apartments, offered for self-catering or B&B, are furnished in very different but equally dashing styles and there is also a cottage in the grounds. Children welcome, cot available; pets permitted in certain areas. B&B £60 pps, ss £10; no service charge. **Directions:** From Durrus, take the Mizen Head road; after 1.5 miles, look for a blue gate on the right hand side.

Fermoy   *La Bigoudenne*

28 MacCurtain Street Fermoy Co Cork
RESTAURANT   Tel: 025 32832

At this little piece of France in the main street of a County Cork town, Noelle and Rodolphe Semeria's hospitality is matched only by their food, which specialises in Breton dishes, especially crêpes - both savoury (made with buckwheat flour) and sweet (with wheat flour). But they do all sorts of other things too, like salads that you only seem to get in France, soup of the day served with 1/4 baguette & butter, a plat du jour and lovely French pastries. Even the bill is a pleasant surprise. **Seats 18.** L12.30-4.30 Tues-Sat, D 7-10 Tues-Sun. Set D £19.95 Gourmet menu £22, also à la carte. Closed Mondays & Jan. Amex, MasterCard, Visa. **Directions:** On the main street, opposite ESB.

Fermoy   *Castlehyde Hotel*

Castlehyde Fermoy Co Cork
HOTEL/RESTAURANT   Tel: 025 31865 Fax: 025 31485 email: cashyde@iol.ie

In a beautifully restored 18th century courtyard building, with all the original features preserved, Erik Speekenbrink's delightful hotel is retained within the original buildings. Bedrooms, which are individually furnished to a high standard with antiques, have a private home feeling and there is a heated outdoor swimming pool. Small conferences (30). No pets. **Rooms 19.** (5 cottage suites, 10 no-smoking , 1 for disabled). B&B £57.50 pps, ss £27.50. Amex, Diners, MasterCard, Visa. **Restaurant:** A conservatory extension helps make the most of the restaurant's pleasant situation, overlooking a lawn and mature woodland. Head chef Clive O'Connor presents both lunch and dinner menus in a creative Irish international style - good breads and soups (always a positive sign), and some unusual dishes, such as rabbit & thyme pie with mustard cream. He's doing a good job and this restaurant deserves to be better known. **Seats 65.** (Private room, 14). L Sun only 12.30-2.30,,D 6.30-9; Set Sun L £14, D à la carte. House wine £14. Service discretionary; air conditioning. Toilets wheelchair accessible. **Directions:** At Fermoy, turn off the N8 and take the N72 (Mallow direction) for about 2 miles.

Glandore [PUB★]   *Hayes' Bar*

Glandore Co Cork
PUB   Tel: 028 33214 / 021 293308

Hayes Bar overlooks the harbour, has outdoor tables - and Ada Hayes' famous bar food. The soup reminds you of the kind your granny used to make and the sandwiches are stupendous. Everything that goes to makes Hayes' special - including the wines and crockery collected on Declan and Ada's frequent trips to France (which also affect the menu, inspiring the likes of Croque Monsieur) - has to be seen to be believed. Just order a simple cup of coffee and see what you get for £1.10. Wine is Declan's particular passion and Hayes' offers some unexpected treats, by the glass as well as the bottle, at refreshingly reasonable prices. Great reading too - from Paul Levy's essay on Great Sandwiches of the World ("Pastrami is chic.") to a lot of background on the wines in stock. By any standards, Hayes' is an outstanding bar. Meals 12-6, Jun-Aug & weekends. Closed weekdays Sep-May except Xmas & Easter. No credit cards

Glandore ✗   *The Rectory*

Glandore Co Cork

RESTAURANT   Tel: 028-33072 Fax: 028-33600

In a prime location overlooking Glandore harbour, this fine Georgian residence makes an impressive family-run restaurant. Michelle O'Brien heads up a friendly and efficient front of house team while her brother Shane is in the kitchen, working alongside Ciaran Woods who has been head chef since 1995. Spacious reception rooms along the front of the house have converted stylishly to make a fine dining area, leading from a linking bar/reception room. Interesting dishes on well-balanced seasonal menus could include irresistible starters like pan-fried foie gras with caramelised granny smiths and truffle flavoured sauce or - from a wide selection of local seafood - ravioli of lobster on a bed of spinach with a shellfish vinaigrette. Main courses, also rich in seafood choices, might include a millefeuille of salmon & monkfish, served on a colourful red pepper vinaigrette and more unusual fish, such as red mullet, typically with saffron potatoes and a sundried tomato sauce flavoured with basil and imaginative meat dishes might include lamb fillet with butterbean & puy lentils with garden herbs. Tempting though the desserts may be, farmhouse cheeses are at their best in west Cork, so leave room if you can. All this, plus good home-made breads, particularly good soups and generous portions all add up to a restaurant that attracts guests back for a return visit. D££-£££ Mon-Sun. Closed Nov-Apr.

Glanmire ✗   *The Barn Restaurant*

Glanmire nr Cork Co Cork

RESTAURANT   Tel: 021 866211 Fax: 021 866525

Just outside Cork, on the old Youghal road, this long-established neighbourhood restaurant has a devoted local clientele. It is comfortably old-fashioned, with uniformed waiters and food with a real home-cooked flavour. Dinner menus offer a wide choice on all courses - roast fillet of local salmon with sorrel sauce indicates the style. Vegetarians are well looked after, saucing is good and accompaniments are carefully selected. Finish with Irish cheeses or something from the traditional dessert trolley. Sunday lunch is very popular and menus are similar in style. Car parking is available behind the restaurant. L£ Sun, D££ Mon-Sun. Amex, Diners, MasterCard, Visa.

Glanworth ❄   *Glanworth Mill Country Inn*

Glanworth Co Cork

Tel: 0254 38555 Fax: 025 38560

ACCOMMODATION/RESTAURANT/CAFE   email: glanworth@iol.ie

Beside a Norman castle on the banks of the River Funcheon, this imaginatively converted old stone mill - complete with the old mill wheel which has been restored, encased in glass and worked into the interior design - makes an unusual place to stay or just stop for a bite to eat along the Blackwater Valley. The whole restoration programme has been undertaken with commendable vision and to a high standard throughout. Public areas include a restful sitting room and the Mill Tea Rooms, where informal meals are served (12 noon-9.30 pm). Bedrooms - all highly individual, with good en-suite bathrooms (and styled on the era and taste of the writer each is named after, including Anthony Trollope, Elizabeth Bowen and William Trevor), phones and complimentary water and fruit. At the time of the guide's visit, landscaping of the riverside garden area was in progress. Small conferences/private parties(46). No pets. **Rooms 10** (1 mini-suite, all no-smoking). B&B £42.45pps, ss £10, Children under 2 free in parents' room. Diners, MasterCard,Visa. More formal meals are served in the Fleece'n'Loom Restaurant, which includes a conservatory area. **Seats 50** D Mon-Sat 7-9.30 à la carte, House wine £11, sc 10%. Closed Sun, Dec 24-28, Good Fri. **Directions:** Take N8 Cork-Dublin Road between Mitchelstown and Fermoy; take Glanworth Road at major Kilworth/Glanworth junction for 5 miles - mill faces you at narrow bridge.

Goleen Harbour   *The Heron's Cove*

Harbour Road Goleen nr Skibbereen Co Cork

Tel: 028 35225 Fax: 028 35422

RESTAURANT/ACCOMMODATION   email: suehill@tinet.ie

When the tide is in and the sun is out there can be few prettier locations than Sue Hill's restaurant overlooking Goleen harbour. She does tasty, inexpensive day-time food - which can be served on a sunny balcony - like hearty soups and home-baked bread, home-cooked ham, farmhouse cheeses and seafood specials. Delicious desserts - tangy lemon tart or a wicked chocolate gateau - are also available with afternoon tea (also freshly brewed coffee). The Heron's Cove philosophy is to use only the best of fresh, local ingredients - typically in wholesome starters like fisherman's broth or warm duckling salad and main courses such as Goleen lamb cutlets with a port & redcurrant sauce. Lobster and Rossmore oysters are available fresh from a tank and prices are refreshingly reasonable. Children welcome at owner's discretion. **Seats 30** Open all day, 12-9.45. L 12-5 (Sun L 1.30-3), D 5-9.45. Set L £12.50 (Set Sun L £10.50) Set D £22; à la carte also available. Closed Nov-May. Amex, MasterCard, Visa. **Accommodation:** Good-sized en-suite rooms have bathrooms, satellite TV, phones, tea/coffee-making facilities and hair dryers. The three doubles have private balconies with sea views and two smaller rooms have a woodland view. Garden. No pets. **Rooms 5.** B&B £25 pps, ss £6.50. Open for dinner, bed & breakfast all year except Christmas week, but it is always advisable to book, especially when the restaurant is closed. **Directions:** Turn left towards the harbour in the centre of Goleen village.

Gougane Barra

Gougane Barra Hotel

Gougane Barra Ballingeary Macroom Co Cork
HOTEL   Tel: 026-47069 Fax: 026-47226 email: gouganebarrahotel@tinet.ie

In one of the most peaceful and beautiful locations in Ireland, this delightfully old-fashioned family-run hotel is set in a Forest Park overlooking Gougane Barra Lake (famous for its monastic settlements). The Lucey family has run the hotel since 1937, offering simple, comfortable accommodation as a restful base for walking holidays. Rooms are comfortable but not over-modernised, all looking out on to the lake or mountain. There are quiet public rooms where guests often like to read; breakfast is served in the lakeside dining room. No weddings or other functions are accepted. Children welcome (under 12s free in parents' room.) No pets. **Rooms 28** (all en-suite). B&B £40pps, ss £10. Closed mid-Oct-mid Apr. Amex, Diners, MasterCard, Visa **Directions:** Situated in Gougane Barra National Forest, well signposted.

Heir Island

Island Cottage

Heir Island Skibbereen Co Cork
RESTAURANT   Tel/Fax: 028 38102 email: islandcottage@tinet.ie

Just a short ferry ride from the mainland yet light years away from the "real" world, this place is unique. Hardly a likely location for a restaurant run by two people who have trained and worked in some of Europe's most prestigious establishments - but, since 1990, that is exactly what John Desmond and Ellmary Fenton have been doing at Island Cottage. Everything about it is different from other restaurants, including the booking policy: a basic advance booking for at least six people must be in place before other smaller groups of 2 to 4 can be accepted - not later than 3pm on the day; changes to group numbers require 24 hours notice and a booking deposit of £5 per head is required to reserve a table. The no-choice 5-course menu (£19) depends on the availability of the fresh local, organic (where possible) and wild island ingredients of that day. A vegetarian dish can be accommodated with advance notice. An early autumn menu that earned special praise for John at a Irish Restaurants Association/Bord Bia "New Irish Cuisine" competition will give an idea of his attachment to the island and the kind of meal to expect: roast duck legs on a bed of turnip with duck jus (using hand-reared ducks "of exceptional quality" from Ballydehob), Cape Clear turbot with shrimp sauce on a bed of sea beet or spinach (the turbot is farmed on Cape Clear Island and the shrimp is caught by local fishermen; sea beet is a wild foreshore vegetable, rather like spinach) and a classic terrine of vanilla ice cream with meringue served with a blackberry sauce, using berries picked by children holidaying on the island. Cookery courses and demonstrations can be arranged, also private dinner parties (October-May). Details of cottages for rent also available from the restaurant. **Seats 24** (max table size 10). D £19. Wed-Sun, 8 pm; one sitting served at group pace. L by arrangement only, groups of 20+. Closed Mon & Tues and 15 Sep-1 June. No credit cards. **Directions:** From Skibbereen, on Ballydehob road, turn left at Church Cross, signposted hare Island and Cunnamore. Narrowwinding road, pass school, church, Minihan's Bar. Continue to end of road, Cunnamore car park. Ferry departs Cunnamore pier @ 7.55 returns @ 11.55 (Journey: 4 minutes.)

Innishannon

Innishannon House Hotel

Innishannon Co Cork
Tel: 021 775121 Fax: 021 775609
email: inishannon@tinet.ie

HOTEL/RESTAURANT

The O'Sullivans call Innishannon House "the most romantic hotel in Ireland", and both the riverside location and the early 18th century house certainly have great charm. Public rooms include a residents' bar and sitting room , all very comfortably furnished but mainly remarkable for the family's astonishing collection of Irish and international paintings. Bedrooms include one suitable for disabled guests and all have en-suite bath and shower. They vary in shape and character but are all individually decorated with antiques; the best rooms have river views, while others overlook the lovely gardens and all have original wooden shutters and are thoughtfully furnished. Children welcome (under 3s free in parents' room; cots available). Garden, fishing, boating. Off-season value breaks. Pets permitted. **Rooms 13** (1 spacious suite) Closed Jan-mid Mar. B&B £65 pps, ss £15. Closed mid Jan-mid Mar. Amex, Diners, MasterCard, Visa. **Restaurant:** Conal and Vera O'Sullivan's son, Pearse, returned to Innishannon after gaining experience in kitchens abroad - including a 2-star restaurant in Brussels - and with Michael Clifford in Cork. Since 1997 he has been head chef and is doing a fine job, presenting classical French/new Irish menus at lunch and dinner every day, and also an imaginative bar menu. Afternoon teas are served in the drawing room (or in the garden) from 3-7pm daily. Patchy service on a recent visit marred an otherwise enjoyable meal. **Seats 40** L 12-2.30, D 7-9.30 daily, Set L £15, Set D £27.50-35, à la carte available, House wine £13.50, sc 10%. **Directions:** On N71, 14 miles from Cork

---

Kanturk

Assolas Country House

Kanturk Co Cork
Tel: 029 50015 Fax: 029 50795 email: assolas@tinet.ie

COUNTRY HOUSE

Natural Food Award

Home to the Bourke family for generations, this gracious 17th century manor house was first opened to guests in 1965 by Hugh and the late Eleanor Bourke. Although still very much involved, day-to-day management has passed to their son Joe, who now runs the house jointly with his wife Hazel, the genius in the kitchen. Generous, thoughtful hospitality, impeccable housekeeping and wonderful food are three of the many attractions that bring guests back to Assolas. Rooms vary according to their position in this lovely old house - some are very spacious and overlook the garden and river and there are some courtyard rooms which are especially suitable for families. A lovingly maintained walled kitchen garden, a little river with tame swans and a couple of boats for guests to potter about in all add to the charm - even boots kept beside the front door for the use of anyone who may feel like looking up the local otters at dusk. Hazel Bourke is a Euro-Toques chef and renowned for imaginative and skilled use of produce from their own garden and the surrounding area, offered in a daily residents' dinner menu, served in a lovely dining room - high-ceilinged and elegantly proportioned with deep red walls, antique furniture and crisp white line - which is not over-decorated, providing an appropriate setting for food that is refreshingly natural in style. Her wonderful Warm Salad of New Potatoes with Kenmare Mussels wowed the judges at the 1999 Wedgwood Chef & Potter Competition, for its simplicity, superb flavours and remarkable aptness on blue and white plate reminiscent of traditional country kitchen ware. Hazel is the winner of the Guide's first Euro-Toques Natural Food Award, and very deservedly so. The wine list concentrates on European wine, notably Maison Guigal, which has supplied the house wines since 1983. The famous Blackwater Valley Reichensteiner, made locally by Dr Billy Christopher, is also listed. **Rooms 6** (all en-suite). B&B £45 pps, ss £10. Dining room **Seats 18**. Residents' D£28, 7-8 pm. Closed Nov-Mar. MasterCard, Visa.

Kanturk

The Vintage

O'Brien Street Kanturk Co Cork
Tel: 029 50549 Fax: 029 51209

PUB

Stephen Bowles has been running this fine pub since 1985, and the experienced pub visitor will quickly recognise all the signs of a well-run establishment. The attractive, well-maintained exterior draws people in and, once through the door, the comfortable, pleasingly traditional interior keeps them there. Be sure to stay for a pint or a quick bite of bar food, even if it's only a bowl of home-made soup. Other regulars include steaks done various ways, fish of the day, eg fillet of lemon sole with tartare sauce and something special for vegetarians, as well as freshly prepared sandwiches. Meals 12.30-9.30 Mon-Sat, 6-10 Sun. Closed 25 Dec & Good Fri. MasterCard, Visa. **Directions:** In a terrace of houses alongside the river in Kanturk village.

Kilbrittain   *Casino House*

Coolmain Bay Kilbrittain Nr Kinsale Co Cork

RESTAURANT   Tel: 023 49944 Fax: 023 49945

While Kerrin and Michael Relja's delightful restaurant is just a few miles west of Kinsale, it's one of the country's best kept secrets. The couple's cool continental style makes a pleasing contrast to their lovely old house, and the warmth of Kerrin's hospitality is matched only by the excellence of Michael's food. Michael cooks with verve and confidence, in starters such as saddle of rabbit in potato pastry with sage butter or risotto of lobster. Well-balanced main course choices include meats - fillet steak with a burgundy sauce, lamb with spinach dumplings on a bayleaf jus or breast of Ballydehob duck on a juniper berry sauce, served with a tomato tartlet - but also imaginative seafood dishes like monkfish wrapped in turnip spaghetti on a red paprika sauce, all with their own vegetable garnish and simple seasonal side vegetables. Their attention to detail is outstanding and perfectionism in every aspect of the restaurant is admirable. Local cheeses are handled with particular respect, earning the restaurant the Guide's 1999 Farmhouse Cheese Award. **Seats 35** (private room 22). D Mon-Tues/Thurs-Sun 7-9, Sun L 1-3, à la carte only, house wine £11.90-12.50, sc discretionary. Closed 1 Jan-17 Mar. MasterCard, Visa. **Directions:** on R600 between Kinsale and Clonakilty.

Killeagh   *Ballymakeigh House*

Killeagh Youghal Co Cork

FARM STAY   Tel: 024 95184 Fax: 024 95370 email: ballymakeigh@tinet.ie

Winner of our Farmhouse of the Year Award last year, Ballymakeigh House provides an exceptional standard of comfort, food and hospitality in one of the most outstanding establishments of its type in Ireland. Set at the heart of an east Cork dairy farm, this attractive old house is immaculately maintained and run by Margaret Browne, who is a Euro-Toques chef and author of a recent cookery book. The house is warm and homely with plenty of space for guests, who are welcome to use the garden and visit the farmyard. The individually decorated bedrooms are full of character and equally comfortable and Margaret's hospitality is matched only by her energetic pursuit of excellence - ongoing improvements and developments are a constant characteristic of Ballymakeigh. Equestrian centre, tennis, garden, children's playground. Off-season value breaks. Children welcome (under 3s free in parents' room, cots available). Pets permitted. **Rooms 6** (all en-suite). B&B £35pps, ss £10, Closed Nov-May, MasterCard, Visa

Browne's Restaurant

Non-residents are welcome to sample Margaret's excellent cooking, which is a personal blend of traditional and new Irish cuisine with international influences, all based on the very best of fresh local ingredients. Margaret's latest project was a major extension to the restaurant and its opening hours, completed in 1999, which means casual daytime callers can now drop in for an informal bite in addition to the more formal meals served in the evening and at Sunday lunchtime. Children welcome; vegetarian menu available. **Seats 70** (private room, 60) L 12-5 daily, D 6-9 daily, Set Sun L £14, Set D £10, house wines £11-12, sc discretionary, Closed at Xmas. **Directions:** Take M25 to Killeagh village, signposted at Old Thatch Pub.

Kinsale   *1601*

Pearse Street Kinsale Co Cork

PUB   Tel: 021 772529

Named in honour of the battle of Kinsale - the story is chronicled on the walls inside the pub - James Gahan took over the pub in 1989 and has since earned a reputation for good food which draws people from far around. Like many other establishments in the area, the 1601 specialises in seafood - oysters, mussels, real scampi, Kinsale salmon (fresh and smoked). But they also look after vegetarians, with quiches and stir-fries, and use other local produce imaginatively - Clonakilty black pudding, for example, is presented unusually in a salad. Live music is also a feature - details from the pub. Wheelchair accessible. Children welcome. Meals 12-8 daily. Closed 25 Dec & Good Fri. MasterCard, Visa. **Directions:** In centre of Kinsale, opposite Blue Haven Hotel.

Kinsale   *Actons Hotel*

Pier Road Kinsale Co Cork

HOTEL   Tel: 021 772135 Fax: 021 772231 email: actons@indigo.ie

Overlooking the harbour and standing in its own grounds, this attractive quayside establishment is Kinsale's most famous hotel, dating back to 1946 when it was created from several substantial period houses. It has recently undergone extensive renovations. The leisure facilities are possibly the best in the area and there are also good conference/banqueting facilities for up to 300. Bar food available daily, 12-9. Wheelchair access. Lift. Children welcome (under 12s free in parents' room, cots available.) No pets. **Rooms 76** (3 mini-suites,2 for disabled). B&B £60pps, ss £25. Open all year. Amex, Diners, MasterCard, Visa. **Directions:** On the waterfront, short walk from town centre.

Kinsale   **The Blue Haven Hotel**

3 Pearse Street Kinsale Co Cork

HOTEL   Tel: 021 772209/06 Fax: 021 774268 email: bluhaven@iol.ie

Shortly before the Guide went to press, this attractive hotel at the heart of Kinsale was bought by Brian Greene, who also owns the Greenhills Hotel, Limerick (see entry). Eight deluxe bedrooms had recently been added and a major refurbishment programme had been completed, so all the bedrooms are new or redone, with double glazing offsetting the street noise that is inevitable with a central location. Both the well-appointed rooms and their neat bathrooms make up in thoughtful planning anything they lack in spaciousness. Due to the nature of the building, public areas are also quite compact, but the lounge/lobby and the bar areas are well-planned and comfortable. Children welcome (unders 4s free in parents' room, cots available). No pets. Street parking. **Rooms 18** (16 en-suite, 2 shower). B&B £80pps, ss £20. Closed 4-27 Jan. Amex, Diners, MasterCard, Visa. Restaurant **Seats 70** (private room, 40) D 7-9.30 daily, Set D £27.50, à la carte available, House wine £16.50, sc 10%. **Directions:** In the centre of town

---

Kinsale   *The Bulman*

Summercove Kinsale Co Cork

PUB/RESTAURANT   Tel: 021 772131 Fax: 021 773359

The emphasis at The Bulman has shifted more towards food since the first floor restaurant was opened, but it is still very much a pub. The bar is characterful and maritime (though this is definitely not a theme pub) and a great place to be in fine weather, when you can wander out to the seafront and sit on the wall beside the carpark. Bar food - crab claws, steaks, salmon salad - is available from 12.30-6.45 daily. The first floor restaurant, The Bistro, specialises in seafood and all fish dishes are based on locally caught and speedily delivered fresh fish. Menus are under constant review but the contents of the lobster tank are much in demand and king prawns are also a particular speciality. Vegetarian dishes available. Wheelchair access. Own carpark. **Seats 50.** No smoking area. D 6.45-10 daily, Sun L 12.30 on, à la carte, sc discretionary, Closed 25 Dec & Good Fri. MasterCard, Visa. **Directions:** Beside Charles Fort, short distance from Kinsale

---

Kinsale ❋   *Crackpots*

3 Cork Street Kinsale Co Cork
Tel: 021 772847 Fax: 021 773517

RESTAURANT/POTTERY   email: crackpts@iol.ie

This attractive and unusual restaurant has a lot going for it - not only can you drop in for a glass of wine at the bar as well as the usual meals but, if you take a fancy to the tableware, you can buy that too. Menus are imaginative and considerate, with plenty for vegetarians and, although there is no shortage of fish, the range of dishes offered provides some contrast in an area that naturally specialises heavily in seafood. International influences are at work - sushi, risotto, linguine, toastad and curry might all be on the same menu - and that's all part of the fun. An interesting wine list features "Wine Geese" labels (a visit to nearby Desmond Castle will tell you all about this) and house wines are keenly priced, starting at an exceptionally modest £7.50. Children welcome until 7pm. **Seats 50.** No smoking area; air conditioning. D 6.30-10.30 daily, Sun L 1-3, all à la carte, house wine £7.50. Closed Nov. Diners, MasterCard, Visa. **Directions:** Between Garda Station and Wine Museum.

Kinsale *Man Friday*

Scilly Kinsale Co Cork
RESTAURANT   Tel: 021 772260   Fax: 021 772262

High up over the harbour, Philip Horgan's popular, characterful restaurant is housed in a series of rooms. It has a garden terrace which makes a nice spot for drinks and coffee in fine weather. Abdu LeMarti, who has been head chef since 1985, presents seasonal à la carte menus that major on seafood but offer plenty else besides, including several vegetarian choices and duck, steak and lamb. While geared to fairly traditional tastes, the cooking is sound and can include imaginative ideas. Simple, well-made desserts include good ice creams. Service is cheerful and efficient. **Seats 100** (private room, 50) No smoking area; air conditioning. Toilets wheelchair accessible. D Mon-Sat 6.45-10.30, only à la carte, house wine £12.90, sc discretionary. Closed Sun, Dec 24-26. Amex, Diners, MasterCard, Visa. **Directions:** 10 minutes walk from town centre, overlooking Harbour at Scilly near the Spaniard Pub.

Kinsale *Max's Wine Bar*

Main Street Kinsale Co Cork
RESTAURANT   Tel: 021 772443

Max's was one of the original Kinsale Good Food Circle restaurants, the places that once earned the town the title of "Gourmet capital of Ireland". While that title may now be challenged by several other culinary hotspots, it is both sad to see those who did so much for the town hang up their aprons - and encouraging to see young energetic replacements moving in. Max's has been taken over by a young couple, Anne Marie Galvin, who supervises front of house, and chef Olivier Queva, who previously worked nearby at The Vintage. The interior is much the same, with varnished tables and lots of plants, and the menu structure is similar too, with a light snack lunch and Early Bird offered as well as the main dinner menu. Olivier's classical background shows in his use of fresh stocks, soups and home-made chutneys, but there are plenty of international influences too and he likes to use less favoured ingredients such as crubeens and oxtail as well as seafood from the pier - langoustines, oysters, mussels, black sole, salmon, ray etc - which is always so much in demand. Vegetarian dishes are always on the menu too. Children welcome until 7.30. **Seats 32.** No smoking area. L 12.30-3 Mon-Sat, Sun L 1-3, D 6.30-10.30 daily Sun L 1-3, Set L £12.50, Early Bird D 6.30-7.30 daily £12.50, à la carte available, house wine £11.50, sc discretionary. Closed Nov-Mar. MasterCard, Visa. **Directions:** Easily found on Main Street.

Kinsale *The Moorings*

Scilly Kinsale Co Cork
ACCOMMODATION   Tel: 021 772376   Fax: 021 772675

Pat and Irene Jones' superbly appointed, purpose-built guesthouse has its own car park (a very big plus in Kinsale). Spacious well-equipped bedrooms have air-conditioning as well as phone, TV and tea/coffee tray, good en-suite bathrooms (bath and shower) and balconies with views across the marina - and there's even a 2-room apartment. Downstairs, a large conservatory is used for breakfast (although room service is available) and just lounging around harbour-watching. There is wheelchair access and one bedroom equipped for disabled guests. Not suitable for children under 12. Pets permitted. **Rooms 8** (all en-suite). B&B £60pps, ss £40, Wheelchair access. Closed December. Amex, Diners, MasterCard, Visa. **Directions:** 1/2 mile from town centre, next door to Spinnaker Pub.

Kinsale *The Old Bank House*

11 Pearse Street Kinsale Co Cork
ACCOMMODATION   Tel: 021 774075   Fax: 021 774296

Marie and Michael Riese's townhouse in the middle of Kinsale has earned a high reputation for quality of accommodation and service - it has an elegant residents' sitting room, a well-appointed breakfast room and comfortable country house-style bedrooms with good amenities, antiques and quality materials. In 1999, the Old Bank House expanded into the Post Office next door, to include a further seven bedrooms and - this is a major improvement - they now have a lift. All rooms are now furnished and decorated to the same high standard, with lovely bathrooms, phone, TV and 24 rooms service for coffee, tea, wine, mineral water etc (which may also be served in the sitting room) ISDN line and safe available at reception. No smoking in public areas. "Very quiet small babies and well-behaved children" and small dogs are welcome by arrangement. No wheelchair access. Lift. Street parking. **Rooms 17** (1 suite, 1 shower only). B&B £60pps, ss £35. Closed 23-26 Dec. Amex, MasterCard, Visa. **Directions:** At the start of Kinsale town, on the right hand side next to the Post Office.

Kinsale   *The Old Presbytery*

43 Cork Street Kinsale Co Cork

ACCOMMODATION   Tel: 021 772027 Fax: 021 772166 email: info@oldpres.com

This old house in the centre of the town has provided excellent accommodation for many years and the current owners, Philip and Mary McEvoy, have recently completed the construction of three new self-catering suites, each with two en-suite bedrooms, sitting room, kitchenette and an extra bathroom. The new rooms are well-proportioned and furnished in the same style and to the same high standard as the original refurbished bedrooms (with stripped pine country furniture and antique beds); they can be taken on a nightly basis, sleeping up to six adults. The top suite has an additional lounge area leading from a spiral staircase, with magnificent views over the town and harbour **Rooms 6** (3 suites, all no-smoking). B&B £35pps, ss £15. Closed Xmas. MasterCard, Visa. **Directions:** Down Pearse Street, turn left at junction, take second right turn at the Garda Station. House is on the right.

Kinsale   *The Old Rectory*

Rampart Lane Kinsale Co Cork

ACCOMMODATION   Tel/Fax: 021 772678

Set in large secluded gardens overlooking the town, Martha and Dave Pringle's fine Georgian house offers luxurious accommodation in very spacious bedrooms (all no-smoking). It is an unusual set-up for Kinsale, being very quiet and private, with plenty of parking and lots of space. The reception rooms are very big too, and there's even a wine bar, which contributes to the informal atmosphere. Not suitable for children under 10. No pets. **Rooms 3** (1 en-suite, 2 with private non-connecting bathrooms, all no-smoking) B&B £55pps, ss £20. Closed Xmas. No credit cards. **Directions:** Keep left after St. Multose Church, then first left after St. Multose Walk.

Kinsale 🏛   *Perryville House*

Long Quay Kinsale Co Cork

ACCOMMODATION   Tel: 021 772731 Fax: 021 772298 email: sales@perryville.iol.ie

One of the prettiest houses in Kinsale, Laura and Andrew Corcoran's characterful house on the harbour front has been renovated to a very high standard and, under the management of Barry McDermott, provides luxuriously appointed accommodation. Gracious public rooms are beautifully furnished, as if for a private home. Spacious, individually decorated bedrooms vary in size and outlook (ones at the front are most appealing, but the back is quieter) and all have extra large beds and thoughtful extras such as fresh flowers, complimentary mineral water, quality toiletries, robes and slippers. Accommodation includes seven suites, all with exceptionally well-appointed bathrooms (4 shower only). Breakfasts include home-baked breads and local cheeses. Morning coffee and afternoon tea are available to residents in the drawing room and there is a wine licence. No smoking establishment. Own parking. Not suitable for children. No pets. **Rooms 22** (7 mini-suites, all no-smoking, 4 shower only). B&B Room Rate £150pps, sc discretionary. Closed 1 Nov-13 Mar. Amex, Diners, MasterCard, Visa

Directions: Central location overlooking marina

Kinsale   *Sovereign House*

Newman's Mall Kinsale Co Cork
Tel: 021 772850 Fax: 021 774723

ACCOMMODATION   e-mail: sovereignhouse@tinet.ie

In the heart of old Kinsale, the McKeown family's Queen Anne townhouse dates from 1708. It offers a high level of comfort in elegant and fascinating surroundings. Fourposter beds are at home in this historic house, but so too are the modern amenities - good bathrooms, direct dial phones and tea & coffee trays. The house also has a reading room and a full size snooker room. And, if Mrs McKeown isn't too busy, ask to see the workshop at the top of the house. No pets. **Rooms 4** (all en-suite, 1 suite, all no-smoking). B&B £65pps, ss £10. Closed Xmas. Amex, MasterCard, Visa. **Directions:** Turn left at White House, take second right at roundabout, take second right at Desmond Castle, then turn left.

Kinsale ✗ *The Spaniard*

Scilly Co Cork

PUB   Tel: 021 772436 Fax: 021 773303

Who could fail to be charmed by The Spaniard, that characterful and friendly old pub perched high up above the town? Although probably best known for music (nightly), they do a good job on the food side too. Much of their wholesome, tasty fare is traditional but it occasionally strays into the international zone - Cajun chicken and peppers, for example - and, of course, local seafood is especially important. There's a daily special for vegetarians and evening meals are quite elaborate affairs - sirloin steak with three pepper sauce, or farmhouse duckling with plum brandy sauce for instance. Meals£. Closed 25 Dec & Good Fri. Diners, MasterCard, Visa.

Kinsale *Trident Hotel*

World's End Co Cork

HOTEL   Tel: 021 772301 Fax: 021 774173 email: info@tridenthotel.com

This blocky, concrete-and-glass 1960s waterfront building enjoys one of Kinsale's finest locations and, under the excellent management of Hal McElroy, is a well-run, hospitable and comfortable place to stay. The pubby Fisherman's Wharf bar is a good meeting place and Gerry O'Connor, head chef for the main restaurant, also has responsibility for the bar food (12-9 daily). Bedrooms include two suites, with private balconies directly overlooking the harbour. Conference/banqueting (220/220); business centre, secretarial services; video-conferencing on request. Wheelchair access. Children welcome. No pets. **Rooms 58** (all en-suite, 2 suites, 2 for disabled). B&B £65pps, ss £20, Wheelchair access. Lift. Closed 24-26 Dec. Amex, Diners, MasterCard, Visa.

Savannah Waterfront Restaurant

While it is difficult for a hotel restaurant to compete with the exceptional number and variety of restaurants in Kinsale, the Savannah - which is named after the first steam-powered vessel to cross the Atlantic from west to east - does a good job. The restaurant is well-located on the first floor with views over the harbour - which also makes it an exceptionally pleasant room for breakfast - has plenty of atmosphere. The food is good and especially welcome in winter, when many of the smaller restaurants are closed **Seats 80.** D 7-9.30 daily, Sun L 1-2.30, Set Sun L £12, Set D £20, à la carte D available, sc discretionary. Toilets wheelchair accessible. Closed Dec 24-26. **Directions:** Take the R600 from Cork to Kinsale - the Hotel is at the end of Pier Road

---

Kinsale *The Vintage Restaurant*

50 Main Street Kinsale Co Cork

RESTAURANT   Tel: 021-772502 Fax: 021-774828 email: vintage@indigo.ie

Raoul and Seiko de Gendre have put a lot of work into The Vintage without spoiling its traditional cottagey style. Raoul supervises the kitchen in an unusually democratic way, allowing a number of chefs of equal standing take turns. But, whoever is cooking, the best of Irish ingredients are used in dishes that tend towards the classical but are also influenced by world cuisine. Wide-ranging, à la carte menus tend to be especially strong on seafood in summer and game in the winter - main course examples from a summer menu might include whole black sole meuniere (£20), roast rack of lamb with a herb crust and flageolet beans provencale (£19.90) or lobster various ways (£21 per lb). Details are good - tasty little amuse-bouches are served with aperitifs, tables are beautifully appointed, service professional. Wine appreciation evenings and other special events are held regularly. Private dining room available. Wheelchair accessible (but not toilets). **Seats 52.** No-smoking area; air conditioning. D Tues-Sat 6.30-10 (open 7 days May-Sept) all à la carte, house wine £16.50, sc discretionary. Closed Sun/Mon off season, Jan-Feb Amex, Diners, MasterCard, Visa. **Directions:** From the Post Office, turn left at the Bank of Ireland - restaurant is on the right.

Macroom *The Castle Hotel*

Main Street Macroom Co Cork

HOTEL   Tel: 026-41074 Fax: 026-41505 email: castlehotel@tinet.ie

The neat frontage of this hotel conceals major changes that have been taking place recently. In the ownership of the Buckley family since 1952, it is currently under the management of Don and Gerard Buckley, who are maximising its potential; first through gradual refurbishment and, more recently, through thoughtfully planned reconstruction. Public areas gleam welcomingly, and the bar and dining room, especially, are most attractive - no doubt they will be even more so soon, as this is the area due for major change in 2000. Bedrooms are on the small side but all have recently been refurbished; there are slight variations - some older rooms are shower-only, newer ones have trouser presses - but all have phone, TV and tea/coffee trays. An impressive 2-storey extension at the back has a new leisure centre on the ground floor (with fine swimming pool, updated gym and adjacent carpark) and new bedrooms above it. Conferences/banqueting (60/60). Off-season value breaks. Children welcome (under 4s free in parents' room, cots available). No pets. **Rooms 42** (all en-suite,12 shower only; 16 executive rooms). B&B £45pps, ss £10. Closed 25-27 Dec. Amex, Diners, MasterCard, Visa. **Directions:** On the main street of Macroom - N22, main Cork-Killarney road.

Macroom   *The Mills Inn*

Ballyvourney Macroom Co Cork
Tel: 026 45237 Fax: 026 45454
PUB/ACCOMMODATION   email: info@millinn.ie

One of Ireland's oldest inns, The Mills Inn is in a Gaeltacht (Irish-speaking) area and dates back to 1755 - it seemed appropriate on the Guide's most recent visit that a thatcher was enjoying a well-earned lunch break in the bar and was up on the roof of an outbuilding again as we left. The inn was traditionally used to break the journey from Cork to Killarney - and still makes a great stopping place as the food is good and freshly cooked all day - but is now clearly popular with locals as well as travellers. It has old-world charm (despite the regrettable conversion of real fires to gas) and there is a real sense of hospitality. Toilets wheelchair accessible. Meals 40 L 12.30-2.30 daily, D 6-9 daily, Sun L 12.30, Set Sun L £12.95, D à la carte, house wine £12, sc discretionary. Closed 25 Dec. Diners, MasterCard, Visa. **Accommodation:** Rooms vary considerably due to the age of the building, but all are comfortably furnished with neat bathrooms and good amenities. Superior rooms even have jacuzzi baths, and there is a large, well-planned ground-floor room suitable for less able guests (who can use the residents' car park right at the door - in a courtyard shared with a vintage car and an agricultural museum). Full room service is available for drinks and meals. Small conferences/banqueting (20/60), secretarial services. Off season value breaks. Children are welcome (under 12s free in parents' room, cots available). Pets permitted. **Rooms 13** (7 executive rooms, 3 shower only, 1 for disabled). B&B £35pps, ss £5, Wheelchair access. **Directions:** On N22, 20 minutes from Killarney

---

Mallow ♨ ★   *Longueville House*

Mallow Co Cork.
Tel: 022 47156 Fax: 022 47459
HOTEL/RESTAURANT   email: info@longuevillehouse.ie

Hotel of the Year

When Longueville House opened its doors to guests in 1967, it was one of the first Irish country houses to do so. Its history is wonderfully romantic, "the history of Ireland in miniature", and it is a story with a happy ending. Having lost their lands in the Cromwellian Confiscation (1652-57), the O'Callaghans took up ownership again some 300 years later. The present house, a particularly elegant Georgian mansion of pleasingly human proportions, dates from 1720, (with wings added in 1800 and the lovely Turner conservatory - which is still in good order and due shortly to take on a new lease of life as an extension to the dining room - in 1862) overlooks the ruins of their original home, Dromineen Castle. Many things make Longueville special, most importantly the warm, informal hospitality and charm of the O'Callaghans themselves - Michael and Jane, now joined by their son (and talented chef) William and his wife Aisling. The location, overlooking the famous River Blackwater, is lovely. The river, farm and garden supply fresh salmon in season, the famous Longueville lamb and all the fruit and vegetables. In years when the weather is kind, the estate's crowning glory (and Michael O'Callaghan's great enthusiasm) is their own house wine, a light refreshing white fittingly named "Coisreal Longueville". Graciously proportioned reception rooms include a bar and drawing room both elegantly furnished in country house style - yet they are next in line in the endless rota of refurbishment which keeps this lovely old house in tiptop condition. Accommodation is equally sumptuous and bedrooms - which include a suite, six mini-suites and six rooms designated non-smoking - are spacious, superbly comfortable and stylishly decorated to the highest standards (under the personal supervision of Jane O'Callaghan). As well as being one of the finest leisure destinations in the country, this all adds up to a good venue for small conferences and business meetings (max 30; banqueting 70). A range of back-up services is available to business guests. Children welcome (under 4s free in parents' room, cots available). Pets permitted by arrangement. **Rooms 22.** (1 suite, 6 mini-suites, 6 no-smoking). B&B £62.50pps, ss £32.50 Closed mid-Dec-mid Feb. Amex, Diners, MasterCard, Visa

Presidents' Restaurant ★

Named after the family collection of specially commissioned portraits of all Ireland's past presidents, which made for a seriously masculine collection until the addition of Mary Robinson, this is the main dining room and opens into the conservatory - and there is a smaller, inner room for those who wish to smoke. William O'Callaghan's well-balanced dinner menus (£32) offer a sensibly limited choice of four or five dishes on each course, plus an intriguing Tasting Menu (£45) for complete parties. Local ingredients star, in a starter of Ardrahan cheese in puff pastry pastry with a garden salad, for example, followed by fish of the day (which might be Blackwater salmon, or a sea fish such as haddock, coated with tomato and herb breadcrumbs and served with a star of anis sauce). Longueville lamb comes in many guises - roast loin filled with parsley purée, perhaps, with a mint & chive sauce or with pot barley risotto, spinach and hyssop sauce. Garden produce influences the dessert menu too, as in gooseberry tart with elderflower ice cream (a magic combination) and it is hard to resist the local farmhouse cheeses. Home-made chocolates and petits fours come with the coffee and service, under Jane or Aisling O'Callaghan's direction, is excellent. A fine wine list includes many wines imported directly by Michael O'Callaghan **Seats 54** D 7-9.30 daily, Set D £32-45, Bar Food 1-5 daily, house wine £14, sc discretionary. Toilets wheelchair accessible. Amex, Diners, MasterCard, Visa. **Directions:** 3 miles west of Mallow via N72 to Killarney

---

Midleton *✗*   *The Clean Slate Restaurant*

Distillery Rd Midleton Co Cork
RESTAURANT   Tel/Fax: 021 633655

Chef-proprietor Colm Falvey opened this striking modern restaurant close to the Jameson Heritage Centre in spring 1998. He presents interesting and very reasonably priced à la carte lunch menus - which include simple things such as open sandwiches as well as stuffed mussels and salade tiede of lamb's kidneys - and more adventurous and wide-ranging evening menus, which are also à la carte. Although the cooking style is international, local produce features strongly - Kenmare Bay sea trout, Rossmore mussels, Ardsallagh goats cheese. Desserts are very tempting, service friendly and the wine list wide-ranging but not overlong (with most wines under £20). L£ & D££ daily, except Sun low season. MasterCard, Visa.

Midleton *✗*   *The Farmgate*

Coolbawn Midleton Co Cork
RESTAURANT   Tel/Fax: 021 632771

This unique shop and restaurant has been drawing people to Midleton in growing numbers since 1985 and it's a great credit to sisters Marog O'Brien and Kay Harte. Kay now runs the younger version at the English Market in Cork while Marog looks after Midleton. The shop at the front is full of wonderful local produce - organic fruit and vegetables, cheeses, honey - and their own super home baking, while the evocatively decorated, comfortable restaurant at the back, with its old pine furniture and modern sculpture, is regularly transformed from bustling daytime café to sophisticated evening restaurant (on Friday and Saturday) complete with string quartet. Meals all day Mon-Sat, D££ Fri & Sat. Closed Bank Hols. MasterCard, Visa.

Midleton *✗*   *Finins*

75 Main Street Midleton Co Cork
PUB   Tel: 021-631878 Fax: 021 633847

Finin O'Sullivan's thriving bar in the centre of the town has long been a popular place for locals to meet for a drink and to eat some good wholesome food. An attractive, no-nonsense sort of a place. L£ & D££ daily. Closed 25-26 Dec. Amex, Diners, MasterCard, Visa.

Midleton ❊   *Glenview House*

Midleton Glenview House Ballinaclasha Midleton Co Cork
COUNTRY HOUSE   Tel: 021-631680 Fax: 021-634680

When Ken & Beth Sheppard bought their lovely Georgian house near Midleton in 1963 it was virtually derelict. Two years later, Ken bought the entire contents of the Dublin Georgian buildings infamously demolished to make way for the new ESB offices - and today this well-tended, comfortable and elegantly furnished house is the richer for that act of courage. Now, with a welcoming fire in the hall and two well-proportioned reception rooms on either side, it's hard to imagine it any other way. Except for one adapted for wheelchair users, bedrooms in the main house are on the first floor, all comfortably furnished with en-suite bathrooms (one has an old bath with a highly original - and practical - shower arrangement built in), hair dryers and tea/coffee-making facilities. The latest phase of restoration has created some delightful self-catering accommodation in converted outbuildings - with the agreeable arrangement of dinner in the main house as an option. Dinner is cooked by Beth and served at a communal table (8pm, usually residents only; book by noon). Garden, terrace, croquet, lawn tennis, forest walks. Children welcome (under 2s free in parents' room, cot available, £4). Wheelchair friendly; guide dogs (only) welcome. **Rooms 7**, 4 shower-only; (4 in main house, 1 fully wheelchair accessible; 3 in converted coach house, 1 fully wheelchair accessible). B&B £40pps, ss £8. Open all year. Amex, MasterCard, Visa. **Directions:** Take L35 from Midleton to Fermoy for 2.5 miles, take left for Watergrasshill and then immediately right. Glenview is signposted from the road.

Midleton   *Old Midleton Distillery*

Midleton Co Cork
Tel: 021 613594 / 021 613642
VISITOR CENTRE/ CAFÉ/BAR   email: amcenery@idl.ie

The Old Midleton Distillery is a fascinating place to visit - that such visiting can be thirsty work is acknowledged at the door (a whiskey tasting is part of the tour) but it can also be hungry work. Sensibly, the Centre has a nice informal restaurant where you can get simple country style food - typically, freshly-made sandwiches such as Irish Cheddar and homemade chutney or baked ham & wholegrain mustard. Alternatives are ploughman's lunches or quiche and salad. There are also afternoon teas with tempting home-made cakes and scones & jam. **Seats 160.** No-smoking area; air conditioning. L 12-3, all à la carte. Restaurant closed Apr-Oct (Distillery closed only 25 Dec, Good Fri). Toilets wheelchair accessible. Amex, Diners, MasterCard, Visa. **Directions:** 15 miles east of Cork on main Waterford (N25) road.

Midleton   *Midleton Park Hotel*

Old Cork Road Midleton Co Cork
HOTEL   Tel: 021 631767 Fax: 021 631605 email: info@midletonparkhotel.ie

This pleasant hotel close to the Old Midleton Distillery is roomy with good business facilities. Recently refurbished bedrooms - which are all en-suite with tea/coffee facilities, TV, video, phone, hair dryer and trouser press - include 8 rooms suitable for disabled guests and 6 non-smoking rooms as well as a 'presidential suite' for VIP guests. Although it is used a lot by the business community, the hotel also makes a good base for touring east Cork - Fota Island wildlife park, Cobh harbour (last port of call for the Titanic) are nearby and golf packages are arranged. Banqueting/conferences 400/350. Secretarial services. Children welcome (under 14s free in parents' room; cots available). No pets. Ample parking. **Rooms 40** (1 suites, 1 mini-suite, 6 no-smoking, 8 for disabled). B&B £50pps, ss £15, Wheelchair access. Closed 25 Dec. Amex, Diners, MasterCard, Visa. **Directions:** 12 miles east of Cork City on N25

Midleton ❊   *Rathcoursey House*

Ballinacurra Midleton Co Cork
RESTAURANT/ACCOMMODATION   Tel: 021 613418

Just as we were going to press we heard that Rathcoursey House had been bought by best-selling food writer and former restaurateur Beth Hallinan, who has recently been working at Delphi Lodge, Co Mayo (see entry). The Guide has not yet visited, but it certainly sounds promising. Dinner, £25, B&B £45 pps.

Monkstown   *The Bosun*

The Pier Monkstown Co Cork
PUB/ RESTAURANT/ACCOMMODATION   Tel: 021-842172 Fax: 021-842008

Nicky and Patricia Moynihan's waterside establishment close to the Cobh car ferry, has grown a lot over the years, with the restaurant and accommodation now more important features than the original bar and another 12 new rooms planned. Bar food is still taken seriously, however; seafood takes pride of place and the afternoon/evening bar menu includes everything from chowder or garlic mussels through to real scampi and chips, although serious main courses for carnivores such as rack of lamb and beef stroganoff are also available. Next to the bar, a well-appointed restaurant provides a more formal setting for wide-ranging dinner and à la carte menus - and also Sunday lunch, which is especially popular. Again seafood is the speciality, ranging from popular starters such as crab claws or oysters worked into imaginative dishes, and main courses that include steaks and local duckling as well as seafood every which way, from grilled sole on the bone to medallions of marinated monkfish or a cold seafood platter. There's always a choice for vegetarians and vegetables are generous and carefully cooked. Finish with home-made ices, perhaps, or a selection of Irish farmhouse cheeses. **Rooms 15** (9 shower only). B&B £30pps, ss £15, Wheelchair access. Lift. Children under 2 free in parents' room. Closed 24-26 Dec. Amex, Diners, MasterCard, Visa. **Meals 80** (private room, 25). No-smoking area; air conditioning. Bar Food 12-9.30 daily, Sun L 12-2.30, D 6.30-9.30, Set D £24, à la carte available, house wine £12.75, sc discretionary. Toilets wheelchair accessible. Amex, Diners, MasterCard, Visa. **Directions:** On sea front, beside the Cobh ferry.

Oysterhaven   *Finders Inn*

Nohoval Oysterhaven Co Cork
RESTAURANT   Tel/Fax: 021 770737

Very popular with local people (but perhaps harder for visitors to find) the McDonnell family's characterful restaurant is in a row of traditional cottages above Oysterhaven, en route from Crosshaven to Kinsale. It is a very charming place, packed with antiques and, because of the nature of the building, broken up naturally into a number of dining areas (which gives it an air of mystery). Seafood stars, of course - smoked salmon, Oysterhaven oysters, bisques, chowders, scallops and lobster are all here, but there are a few other specialities too, including steaks, lamb and lovely tender crisp-skinned duckling with an orange-sage sauce. Good desserts, charming service and a great atmosphere. Well worth taking the trouble to find. Not suitable for children under 8 after 8 pm. **Seats 90** (private room, 70). D Mon-Sat 7-9.30, sc discretionary. Toilets wheelchair accessible. Closed Xmas week. Diners, MasterCard, Visa. **Directions:** From Cork, take Kinsale road, turn left at The Huntsman roadhouse, follow Oysterhaven road and, at crossroads, go straight ahead towards the water.

Rathpeacon *✗*   *Country Squire Inn*

Old Mallow Rd Rathpeacon Co. Cork
PUB   Tel: 021 301812

The County Squire is just a couple of miles outside Cork city on the Old Mallow road, the N20. It's a very old pub, dating back to the early 1800s. Pat and Regina bought it in 1987 and converted it into half a pub, half a restaurant. It's an immaculately kept place and full of character, with old Singer sewing machine tables (and stools). Pat likes to cook a blend of traditional Irish and classic French food, and the bar food is quite ambitious - garlic mussels, stuffed sole, salmon with prawns and fillet and sirloin steaks are all typical, with vegetarian food available on request. In the evening, similar food is presented more formally in the cosy little restaurant. L£ Mon-Sat, D££ Mon-Sun. Closed Good Fri & 25 Dec. Amex, MasterCard, Visa.

Rosscarbery   *Celtic Ross Hotel*

Rosscarbery Co Cork
HOTEL   Tel: 023 48722 Fax: 023 48723 email: info@celticrosshotel.com

Opened in 1997, this contemporary hotel is close to the sea, overlooking Rosscarbery Bay (although not on the sea side of the road). It's an attractive modern building with an unusual tower feature containing a bog oak, which is quite dramatic. Public areas are attractive and spacious, with the restaurant (and many of the bedrooms) overlooking the sea. It is also well placed as a base for touring west Cork, and offers facilities in the leisure centre for alternative activities if the weather should disappoint. Conference/banqueting (250/220); business centre. Well-equipped bedrooms have phones, tea/coffee trays and TV and children under 3 may stay free in their parents' room (cots available). Dogs allowed in some areas. **Rooms 67** (3 suites, 3 for disabled). B&B £70pps, ss £15. Wheelchair access. Lift. Open all year. Amex, Diners, MasterCard, Visa. **Directions:** Take N71 from Cork to Inishannon to Bandon to Clonakilty and then Rosscarbery

---

Rosscarbery ❈   *O'Callaghan-Walshe*

The Square Rosscarbery Co Cork
RESTAURANT   Tel: 023-48125

This unique restaurant on the square of the old village (well off the busy main west Cork road) has a previous commercial history that's almost tangible - and the atmosphere is well-matched by both proprietor-host Sean Kearney's larger-than-life personality and the exceptional freshness and quality of the seafood, although steaks share the billing. Menus change weekly but specialities to look out for include a superb Fruits de Mer platter (available as small. £9.50 or large, £24.50 but, in the Guide's experience, the small one is very large indeed with an exceptional range and quality of fish and shellfish included). The famous Rosscarbery Pacific oysters feature, of course, char-grilled prime fish such as turbot, steamed lobster with lemon butter. Ultra-freshness, good attention to detail in breads and accompaniments, all add up to make this place a delight. Not suitable for children after 7 pm. **Seats 40** D 6.30-9.15 daily, all à la carte, house wine £12.50, sc discretionary. Open only at weekends in winter. Diners, MasterCard, Visa. **Directions:** On the square in town, behind the Celtic Ross Hotel.

Schull   *Adèle's*

Main Street Schull Co Cork
RESTAURANT   Tel: 028 28459   Fax: 028 28865   email: adeles@schull.net

Adèle Connor's bakery and coffee shop in Schull works like a magnet - if you happen to be in Schull early in the morning, you'll find it hard to squeeze in to buy some of her wonderful home bakes, never mind trying to find a table for a cup of coffee and a home-baked scone. There are delicious savoury things too, such as ciabatta specials served with small tossed salads - traditional and smoked Gubbeen with chutney perhaps - or an omelette with roasted red pepper and garlic. In the evening Simon Connor presents a different kind of menu in the first floor restaurant; a set menu or a short à la carte might include a roast tomato, fennel and mozzarella salad, roasted marinated wild rabbit with saffron potatoes and baby white turnips, then a tossed salad, followed by luscious puddings such as rum soaked raisins with mascarpone. Officially, they say bookings are 'accepted'; 'advised' might be wiser. Times of opening vary according to the season. Children welcome. No wheelchair access. **Seats 40.** Open daily from 9.30, D 7.30-10.30, Sun L 11-5, Set L £7, Set D £17, à la carte available, house wine £11, sc discretionary. Closed Nov-Xmas/Jan-Easter. Amex, MasterCard, Visa. **Directions:** Turn off N71 at Ballydehob for Schull - in town centre.

Schull ✗   *The Bunratty Inn*

Schull Co Cork
PUB   Tel: 028 28341

This comfortable pub serves home-cooked bar food and there is outside eating in summer. Call ahead off-season. Closed 25 Dec & Good Fri. MasterCard, Visa.

Schull   *La Coquille*

Schull Co Cork
RESTAURANT   Tel: 028 28642   Fax: 028 28573

Jean-Michel Cahier's chic little restaurant is situated in the main street, convenient to the harbour. Unlike the majority of restaurants in the area, it sets seafood in context on a wide-ranging menu that includes more red meats and poultry than most places. Competently handled classics are the main feature, in starters like smoked salmon and crab mayonnaise, well-made soups and main courses such as half roast duck with orange sauce and scallops with a brandy cream. Desserts include an excellent tarte tatin and M.

Cahier's cheeseboard does full justice to the quality of local produce. Professional service is provided by French staff. **Seats 35.** No smoking area. D 7-10, Wed-Mon. Set D £20, Gourmet Menu £30. House wine from £10. Service 10%. Closed Tues & all Nov. Amex, Diners, MasterCard, Visa.

Schull
Corthna Lodge Country House

Schull Co Cork

ACCOMMODATION   Tel: 028 28517 Fax: 028 28032

Situated up the hill from Schull, commanding good countryside and sea views, Loretta Davitt's roomy modern house has been one of the best places to stay in the area since opening in 1991. All of the rooms are suitable for disabled guests, all are non-smoking and, although they are all shower-only, the bedrooms are very comfortable with good amenities. The atmosphere is hospitable and easy-going, with plenty of space for guests to sit around and relax (both indoors, in a pleasant and comfortably furnished sitting room and outdoors, on a terrace overlooking the lovely garden towards the islands of Roaring Water Bay). Children welcome (cots available). Pets permitted. **Rooms 6** (all no-smoking). B&B £25pps, ss £10. Wheelchair access. Closed Nov-Mar Amex, MasterCard, Visa. **Directions:** Through village, up hill, left at the V on hill, first right - house is signposted.

Schull
East End Hotel

Main Street Schull Co Cork

HOTEL   Tel: 028 28101 Fax: 028 28012

The future of this hotel, on the main street overlooking Schull harbour, is uncertain as we go to press as it may shortly change hands. To date it has been family-run and modest but very friendly. Non-resident sailors and fishing people have always been welcome to come and have showers. Most bedrooms have en-suite facilities (some shower only) and all have direct dial phones. A large paved area at the back of the hotel makes a pleasant, sheltered place to sit away from the road. **Rooms 17** (13 shower only). B&B £27.50pps, ss £17.50, Wheelchair access. Closed Xmas week. Amex, Diners, MasterCard, Visa. **Directions:** Take N71 from Skibbereen, pass through Ballydehob - hotel is on right as you enter Schull.

Schull
The Restaurant In Blue

Crookhaven Road Schull Co Cork

RESTAURANT   Tel/Fax: 028 28305

Burvill Evans and Christine Crabtree's Restaurant in Blue has thick walls, small windows and homely antique furnishings, all creating a relaxed cottagey atmosphere. The dining room is divided between a high room that was originally a barn and an adjoining conservatory which overlooks a very natural garden. Burvill's ingredients are carefully sourced and he is adamant about the care to be taken: local seafood stars on the menu with all fish bought on the bone and filleted by him; similarly, breast of local free-range chicken is also bought whole and boned out then, perhaps, rolled and stuffed with spring onions and oyster mushrooms, and served with delicious organic vegetables. Finish with local cheeses or a scrumptious dessert such as spiced rhubarb brûlée & brûlée of poached pear. Accommodation is also available in one en-suite room; £50 pps. * As we go to press, plans are afoot to open a larger bistro-style sister restaurant "Blues" in Skibbereen, to be open daily for breakfast, lunch & dinner from November 1999. Further details from this number. **Seats 50.** D Wed-Sun 7-9.45, Set D £23-26, also à la carte, house wine £13, sc discretionary. Closed Mon/Tues, Nov-May. MasterCard, Visa. **Directions:** About two miles outside Schull on the R592 to Toormore.

Schull ❊
Stanley House

South Schull Co Cork

ACCOMMODATION   Tel: 028 28425 / 028 28649 email: watersideinn@tinet.ie

Nancy Brosnan's modern guesthouse provides a west Cork home from home for her many returning guests. Compact bedrooms are comfortably furnished with tea/coffee making facilities and there's a pleasant conservatory running along the back of the house, with wonderful sea views over a field where guests can watch Nancy's little herd of deer and sometimes see foxes come out to play at dusk. Good breakfasts too. Children welcome (under 3s free in parents' room, cots available). No pets. Own parking. **Rooms 4** (all shower only, all no-smoking). B&B £18pps, ss £7. Closed 31 Oct-1 Mar. MasterCard, Visa. **Directions:** Through village to top of Main Street, first left at junction - house signposted.

Schull ✗

T J Newman's

Corner House Main Street Schull Co Cork
PUB   Tel: 028 28223

Just up the hill from the harbour, this characterful and delightfully old-fashioned little pub has been a special home-from-home for visiting sailors as long as anyone can remember. During the past year Kitty Newman has caused consternation by offering the premises for sale - but, at the time of going to press it seems that no drastic change is imminent, so perhaps the danger has receded. Closed 25 Dec & Good Fri. No credit cards.

Shanagarry 🏛 ★

Ballymaloe House

Shanagarry Midleton Co Cork
Tel: 021 652531 Fax: 021 652021
COUNTRY HOUSE/RESTAURANT   email: bmaloe@iol.ie

Ireland's most famous country house hotel, Ballymaloe was one of the first country houses to open its doors to guests when Myrtle and her husband, the late Ivan Allen, opened The Yeats Room restaurant in 1964. Accommodation followed in 1967 and since then a unique network of family enterprises has developed around Ballymaloe House - including not only the farmlands and gardens that supply so much of the kitchen produce, but also a craft and kitchenware shop, a wine company, a company producing chutneys and sauce, the Crawford Gallery Café in Cork city and, of course, Tim and Darina Allen's internationally acclaimed Cookery School. Yet, despite the fame, Ballymaloe is still most remarkable for its unspoilt charm: Myrtle - now rightly receiving international recognition for a lifetime's work "recapturing forgotten flavours, and preserving those that may soon die"- is ably assisted by her children and now their families too. The house, modestly described in its Blue Book entry as "a large family farmhouse" is in the middle of the family's 400 acre farm, but the description fails to do justice to the gracious nature of the original house, or the sensitively designed later additions. The intensely restorative atmosphere of Ballymaloe is still as strong as ever; there are few greater pleasures than a fine Ballymaloe dinner followed by the relaxed comforts provided by a delightful, thoughtfully furnished (but not over decorated) country bedroom. Groundfloor courtyard rooms are suitable for wheelchairs. Children welcome. Special winter breaks offered. **Rooms 33** B&B £85pps, ss £20. Service discretionary. Closed 24-27 Dec Amex, Diners, MasterCard, Visa

Restaurant ★

A food philosophy centred on using only the highest quality ingredients is central to everything done at Ballymaloe, where much of the produce comes from their own farm and gardens. The rest, including seafood from Ballycotton and Kenmare, and meats from the trusted local butcher, comes from leading local producers. Rory O'Connell (who is Darina Allen's brother) has been head chef at Ballymaloe since 1995 and has proved himself supremely suited to translating the Ballymaloe philosophy into cooking which takes account of international trends but is utterly true to itself. Although based on skilful interpretations of classic French and Irish country cooking, the style is light and colourful, occasionally witty; presentation is creative but not over-complicated, allowing the beauty of the food to speak for itself. The restaurant is in a series of domestic-sized dining rooms (some for non-smokers) and guests are called to their tables from the conservatory or drawing room, where aperitifs are served. Rory presents a daily 5-course dinner menu, with vegetarian dishes given a leaf symbol. A good beginning in early summer might be Ballycotton crab soup with rouille and croutons, while second courses might include classics like lobster mayonnaise and asparagus with hollandaise sauce - local lobster, home grown asparagus and skilfully made sauces based on free range eggs. Then, half a dozen main courses will include two or three imaginative fish dishes plus, perhaps, succulent, crisp-skinned roast duck (from a local farmyard) with a Madeira sauce and wonderful fresh peas. There is always a strong vegetarian choice, typically courgette blossoms stuffed with Ardsallagh goats cheese & parsley pesto. Lovely simple side dishes - Shanagarry new potatoes, young carrots and a green salad - accompany. A cheese course follows - Irish farmhouse cheeses, of course, in excellent condition - then the famous dessert trolley is wheeled to the table, laden with irresistible things like lemon souffle, fresh raspberries, chocolate hazelnut tart and praline ice cream (served from the ice bowl - a Ballymaloe invention). Finish with coffee or tea and home-made petits fours, served in the drawing room - and perhaps a drink from the small bar before retiring contentedly to bed. Children welcome at lunchtime and by arrrangement at dinner. Children's high tea 5.30. **Seats 100.** L 12.30-2, D7-9.30 daily; Set L £18, Set D £34.50. House wine £16. Service discretionary. Reservations essential. **Directions:** From Cork, take N25 to Midelton, then Ballycotton road via Cloyne. From Waterford, take N25 to Castlemartyr, then follow signs for Ballymaloe.

Shanagarry
The Garden Café

RESTAURANT

Ballymaloe Cookery School Shanagarry Co Cork
Tel: 021 646422 Fax: 021 646909

This colourful little addition to the Ballymaloe empire has been popular ever since it opened in 1998 - simple, well-prepared food (with the Ballymaloe imprimatur) at rock bottom prices is a great recipe for success. In addition to the many other visitors, the café also has a captive market of students from the famous cookery school nearby. The menu takes its cue from the wonderful gardens which surround the café and school (open April-October; there is a £3 entry charge if you want to tour them). Organic fruit and vegetables feature prominently, while meat and fish are sourced locally and cooked in a wood burning oven. For breakfast there are plenty of freshly squeezed fruit juices and a superb selection of Frittatas. Pizzas from the woodburning oven are a particular speciality - there's a choice of about ten, many inspired by and starring local produce. Home-made elderflower cordial makes a delicious accompaniment, although there is also a short wine list including some half- and quarter-bottles. Service is excellent. There is a lovely rural view over the fields where Darina' free-range pigs happily forage. **Seats 80.** Open daily, non-smoking restaurant, L 12.30-3, D 7-9, Set L £14.50, also à la carte, house wine £11, sc discretionary. Toilets wheelchair accessible. Closed Oct 1-Easter. MasterCard, Visa. **Directions:** 1/4 mile from Shanagarry - signposted.

Skibbereen ✳
Kalbo's Bistro

RESTAURANT

48 North Street Skibbereen Co Cork
Tel: 028 21515 email: kalbo@tinet.ie

This bright, buzzy town-centre restaurant is an understandably popular meeting place. It's informal but there's an air of quality about it - staff are quick and helpful and the food is wholesome and flavoursome in a light contemporary style - good soups, pastas, baguettes, tortillas and salads at lunchtime and more serious dishes of local seafood, rack of lamb, steaks and so on in the evening. Home-made burgers come with a choice of toppings sand vegetarian options are imaginative. **Seats 40.** Open daily, L 11.30-4.30, D 6.30-9.30, Sun L 12-2.30. A la carte only; house wine £10.95, sc discretionary. Closed 24-29 Dec & Good Fri. Amex, MasterCard, Visa. **Directions:** In town centre.

Skibbereen ✳
Liss Ard Lake Lodge

HOTEL

Skibbereen Co Cork
Tel: 028 40000 Fax: 028 40001 email: lissardlakelodge@tinet.ie

This Victorian lodge opened in 1994 as a most unusual small luxury hotel. It is set in extensive gardens (which are open to the public) and has been designed and renovated with oriental simplicity, thereby enhancing the garden and water views framed by every window. Rooms - all suites except 1 double - combine clean-lined simplicity with unexpected amenities: mini-bars, TV units with video, and hi-fi. Equally unusual bathrooms are finished to a very high standard. On two recent visits, the house has been closed for major refurbishment. A telephone call is advised. D£££ Wed-Mon. Acc££££. Closed Jan & Feb. Amex, Diners, MasterCard, Visa.

Timoleague
Lettercollum House Restaurant

RESTAURANT/ACCOMMODATION

Timoleague Co Cork
Tel: 023 46251 Fax: 023 46270
email: conmc@iol.ie

Con McLoughlin and Karen Austin's restaurant is in the Chapel of their Victorian house. The Chapel retains its stained glass windows, providing a striking contrast to the lively modern food for which the restaurant has earned its reputation, both locally and further afield. Carefully sourced ingredients include organic produce from their own walled garden as well as the best of local meats and seafood, cooked and presented in a style that is accurately described as "based on classical French cuisine but with strong ethnic and vegetarian influences." The result is exciting food. Karen also runs cooking classes and there are all sorts of special events, including theatre and music nights. Small conferences/banqueting (20/50). **Seats 40.** Open daily D 7-9.30, Sun L 1-3, Set Sun L £13.50, Set D £24, sc discretionary. Toilets wheelchair accessible. Closed Dec-Mar. Amex, Diners, MasterCard, Visa. **Accommodation:** The very roomy bedrooms are furnished and decorated in a homely way which is ideal for families - who will have great fun at Lettercollum. Children up to 3 are free in parents' room; cots available. No pets. The best bedroom has the only bath (the rest are all shower only) **Rooms 9** (8 shower only). B&B £24pps, ss £6,. **Directions:** N71 Cork-Bandon, then R602 to Timoleague

---

Goleen   *Fortview House*

Gurtyowen Toormore Goleen Skibbereen Co Cork
FARMHOUSE   Tel/Fax: 028 35324

Violet & Richard Connell's remarkable farmhouse in the hills behind Goleen is immaculate. It is beautifully furnished, with country pine and antiques, brass and iron beds in en-suite bedrooms (that are all individually decorated) and with all sorts of thoughtful little details to surprise and delight. Violet loves cooking, and provides guests with a great choice at breakfast, including Tom & Giana Ferguson's Gubbeen cheese, made down the road. No pets. **Rooms 5** (all en-suite). B&B £25pps, ss £10. Closed Nov-end Feb. No credit cards. **Directions:** 2km from Toormore on main Durrus-Bantry road (R591)

Union Hall   *The Baybery*

Union Hall Glandore Bay Co Cork
RESTAURANT   Tel/Fax: 028 33605 email: baybery@iol.ie

Francis and Kathleen Broadbery opened this stylish little restaurant in a 120 year-old building in Union Hall village in the spring of 1998. It's a pleasant room, informal, with interesting slightly crafty furniture, fresh flowers, good tableware and a welcoming open fire on a chilly day. Their second season demonstrated growing confidence, with wider-ranging menus offering an impressive combination of simple and more ambitious dishes. Highlighting the goodness of local and organic produce, especially seafood, remains a primary aim in lively Mediterranean/Asian dishes that are very competently cooked and attractively presented. Service is charming and helpful and there's a pleasant relaxed atmosphere. Theme nights, wine tasting evenings and so on held off season have become a major feature - and they do a very tempting Irish Country Christmas menu for the Festive Season. An interesting and informative wine list includes half a dozen by the glass and a number of organic wines. **Seats 36.** D 6.30-9.30 daily, à la carte, Early Bird menu £15.95. House wine £12, sc 10%. Toilets wheelchair accessible. Closed 25 Dec (Phone ahead off-season to check opening hours). MasterCard, Visa. **Directions:** Off the N71 between Leap and Skibbereen

---

Union Hall   *Shearwater*

Keelbeg Pier Union Hall Co Cork
ACCOMMODATION   Tel: 028 33178 Fax: 028 34020

Adela Nugent's B&B is located close to Keelbeg pier, on an elevated site overlooking Glandore harbour and the surrounding countryside. All bedrooms are good-sized and comfortably furnished with en-suite facilities (only one with bath); most rooms overlook the harbour. The breakfast room and TV room also have views, and there's a patio for guests' use in fine weather. Children welcome (under 2s free in parents' room). No pets. **Rooms 4** (3 shower only). B&B £19pps, ss £9. Closed Nov-Mar. Amex, Diners, MasterCard, Visa. **Directions:** Off N71 between Clonakilty and Skibbereen.

Youghal ⚏   *Aherne's Seafood Restaurant*

163 North Main Street Youghal Co Cork
Tel: 024 92424 Fax: 024 93633
RESTAURANT/ACCOMMODATION   email: ahernes@eircom.net

Now in its third generation of family ownership, one of the most remarkable features of Aherne's is the sheer warmth of the FitzGibbon family's hospitality and their enormous enthusiasm for the business which, since 1993, has included seriously luxurious accommodation. It is for its food - and, especially, the ultra-fresh seafood that comes straight from the fishing boats in Youghal harbour - that Aherne's is best known, however. While John FitzGibbon supervises the front of house, his brother David reigns over a busy kitchen. Bar food (weekends only 12-10) tends towards simplicity - oysters, chowder, smoked salmon (all served with the renowned moist dark brown yeast bread) - its sheer freshness tells the story. Restaurant meals are naturally more ambitious and include some token meat dishes - rack of lamb with a rosemary jus, char-grilled fillet steak with mushrooms and shallot jus - although seafood is still the undisputed star of the show and David is not afraid of simplicity when it is merited. Specialities like prawns cooked in garlic butter or fresh crab salad can make memorable starters, for example, and hot buttered Youghal Bay lobster are all, in a sense, simple dishes yet they have plenty of glamour too. Nage of prawns and monkfish with vermouth & vegetables is a more complex speciality, and equally tempting. A wine list strong on classic French regions offers a fair selection of half bottles and half a dozen champagnes. **Seats 65.** No smoking area; air conditioning. D 6-9.30 daily, Sun L 12.30-2, Set Sun L £16, Set D £28.50, à la carte available, house wine from £13.50, sc discretionary. Toilets wheelchair accessible. Closed Xmas 5 days. Amex, Diners, MasterCard, Visa.

Rooms 🏛

The stylish rooms at Aherne's are generously sized and individually decorated to a very high standard; all are furnished with antiques and have luxurious, beautifully finished bathrooms. Housekeeping is exemplary and excellent breakfasts are served in a warm and elegantly furnished residents' dining room. Newer rooms, recently added, are equipped to give the option of self-catering if required. Children under 2 free in parents' room. No pets. **Rooms 12** (all executive rooms, all no-smoking) B&B £60pps, ss £20. Wheelchair access. **Directions:** On N25, main route from Cork to Waterford.

DONEGAL

Any gourmet map of Ireland would have needed additions in Donegal during 1999, as centres of creative cuisine developed in this northwest county, particularly in Letterkenny and Inishowen. Donegal is big country. It may not have Ireland's highest mountains, it may not be Ireland's biggest county, but there's a largeness of spirit about this northwesterly corner which lingers long and fondly in the memory of those who visit it. For many folk, particularly those from Northern Ireland, Donegal is the holiday county par excellence.

But in recent years, despite the international fluctuations of trading conditions, there has been development of modern industries and the strengthening of the fishing, particularly at the hugely busy port of Killybegs. This has led to a more balanced economy which actually makes a Donegal a more attractive place for today's visitor. But much and all as Donegal county is increasingly a place where people live and make a living, nevertheless it is still a place of nature on the grand scale, a place assaulted by the winds and weather of the Atlantic Ocean if it is given the slightest chance. But that is part of Donegal's enduring attraction, the fact that in some of Ireland's most rugged territory you will find many sheltered and hospitable little places whose comforts are emphasised by the challenging nature of their broader environment. And needless to say, it is simply startlingly utterly beautiful as well.

Local Attractions and Information

Glenveagh National Park (castle, gardens, parkland)		074 37088
Carrick	Carr Memorial Traditional Music w/e (June)	073 39009
Donegal Highlands	Hillwalking/Irish Language (adults)	073 30248
Church Hill Letterkenny	Glebe House & Gallery	074 37071

Annagry   *Danny Minnie's Restaurant*

Annagry The Rosses Co Donegal

RESTAURANT/ACCOMMODATION   Tel/Fax: 075 48201

Atmospheric Restaurant of the Year

The O'Donnell family has run Danny Minnie's since 1962, and a visit is always a special treat. There's nothing about the exterior as seen from the road to prepare first-time visitors for the atmosphere of this remarkable restaurant: hidden behind a frontage of overgrown creepers a surprise awaits when, after a warm welcome from Terri O'Donnell, guests are suddenly surrounded by antiques and elegantly appointed candle-lit tables. The menu is presented in both Irish and English (but not the wine list, mercifully) and Brian O'Donnell's cooking is a good match for the surroundings - fine, with imaginative saucing, but not at all pompous. On a wide-ranging à la carte menu, seafood stars in the main courses - lobster and other shellfish, availability permitting, and baked fillet of turbot with prawn sauce and pesto, perhaps, or monkfish and courgette with a ginger & herb cream. There is also a strong selection of meats including Donegal mountain lamb, typically served with caramelized onions, blackcurrant & mint jus and Donegal beef, served various ways including classic Beef Wellington. Vegetables are a strength and gorgeous desserts such as crepes suzette with orange and Grand Marnier can be relied on to create an appropriately dramatic finale. Under Terri's direction, helpful service from attentive waitresses is another bonus. [Accommodation is also offered in eight non-smoking rooms, five of them en-suite and one suitable for disabled guests]. **Seats 80** (private room, 30). No smoking area; air conditioning. Open all day. L 12-3 daily, D 6-10 daily, Sun L bar food, all à la carte, house wine £12; sc10%. (Phone ahead to check opening hours, especially for lunch off peak season) Closed 31 Oct -Easter. Diners, MasterCard, Visa. **Directions:** R259 off N56 - follow Airport sign.

Ardara   *Nancy's*

Front Street Ardara Co Donegal

PUB   Tel: 075 41187

This famous pub, in the village renowned for its tweeds and handknits, is a cosy, welcoming place, with five or six small rooms packed with bric a brac and plenty of tables and chairs for the comfortable consumption of good home-made food, especially seafood. The renowned soups - chowder in summer and a wonderful vegetable broth in the colder months - head up a good choice of food, including mussels, smoked salmon, oysters, excellent burgers (made by the local butcher), vegetarian choices like ploughman's or veggie-burgers - and home-made apple pie & cream for pudding. Live music too. Bar food served daily 12-9.30 (from Easter to Oct 31) Wheelchair access. Closed 25 Dec & Good Fri. No credit cards. **Directions:** Beside bridge in centre of village.

Ardara ❈ *The Green Gate*

Ardvally Ardara Co Donegal
ACCOMMODATION   Tel: 075 41546

Paul Chatenoud's amazing little B&B is a one-off. Above Adara, up a steep and twisting boreen that will reward you with a stunning view on arrival, Paul offers simple but comfortable accommodation in his unspoilt traditional cottage and converted outbuildings. It's a far cry from the Parisian bookshop he once ran, but this little place is magic. In the morning (or whenever you wake up - he will be working around his lovely garden and is happy to stop at any time it suits his guests), he cooks up a slightly eccentric breakfast. Forget about freshly squeezed orange juice and all that scene - even the coffee is out of a jar, which is quite a shock coming from a Frenchman - but he fries up a tasty little number in double quick time while you take in the laid-back homeliness of his cosy cottage sitting room. Just be glad you found it, because he's probably right - it may well be "the most beautiful place anywhere in Ireland". Children welcome (Under 10s free in parents' room, cot available). Pets permitted. **Rooms 4** (all en-suite). B&B £20pps, ss £10. Wheelchair access. Open all year. No credit cards. **Directions:** off Donegal Road, one mile from Ardara, on the hill.

Ardara ❈ *Woodhill House*

Ardara Co Donegal
Tel: 075 41112 Fax: 075 41516
COUNTRYHOUSE/BAR/RESTAURANT   email: yates@iol.ie

Formerly the home of Ireland's last commercial whaling family, John and Nancy Yates' large country house is set in its own grounds overlooking the Donegal Highlands and the hard restoration work they have put in over more than a decade is now bearing fruit. This hospitable house has a full bar where light lunches are served and unusual accommodation in the main house and nearby converted outbuildings - rooms are all en-suite but vary greatly in position, size and character so it is worth spending a few minutes discussing your preferences when booking. (The ones outside specially took the Guide's fancy). There's also a restaurant (booking recommended as it's very popular locally) where head chef Tim Dewhurst presents quite traditional menus based on local ingredients at reasonable prices: specialities include oysters, Donegal mountain lamb, duck off the bone and carrageen pudding. Gradually restoring the garden is perhaps Nancy's greatest challenge and it's turning out beautifully, not only on the kitchen garden side but as a pleasure garden too. Upgrading the main house continues on an ongoing basis and six extra rooms are planned in the near future. Children welcome (free in parents' room up to "5 or 6"). Pets permitted by arrangement. **Rooms 9** (all en-suite). B&B £25pps, ss £10. Open all year. Amex, Diners, MasterCard, Visa. Restaurant: **Seats 40** (private room, 15). No smoking area. D 6.30-10 daily, Set D £20, house wine £10; sc discretionary. Closed 1 Nov -15 Mar. Amex, Diners, MasterCard, Visa. **Directions:** 1/4 mile from Ardara and well signed.

Ballybofey ❈ *Jackson's Hotel*

Lifford Ballybofey Co Donegal
HOTEL   Tel/Fax: 074 31021

Although very central, this attractive family-run hotel is set in its own gardens and enjoys a tranquil location alongside the River Finn. The spacious, elegantly furnished foyer creates a good first impression and this is followed through in other public areas including the restaurant, which overlooks the garden. Bedrooms, all recently refurbished to a high standard, are very comfortable with direct-dial phones, tea/coffee trays and TV with video channel and the best have river views. Conference/banqueting (400/600); business centre, ISDN lines, secretarial services. Leisure centre (22m pool). Children welcome (under 2s free in parents' room, cots available). Bank Holiday Special Breaks throughout the year offer particularly good value. Pets permitted in some areas. **Rooms 88** (2 suites, 4 executive rooms). B&B £45pps, ss £15. Wheelchair access. Lift. Open all year. Amex, Diners, MasterCard, Visa. **Directions:** Beside the river, in the centre of town.

Ballybofey   *Kee's Hotel*

HOTEL/RESTAURANT

Stranorlar Ballybofey Co Donegal
Tel: 074 31018 Fax: 074 31917

This centrally located, all-year hotel has an unusually long line of continuous family ownership, having been in the Kee family since 1892. Public areas have recently undergone radical renovations, including a new foyer, meeting rooms and a lift, all completed in 1998. Bedrooms are regularly refurbished and most are very comfortable with good bathrooms; newer rooms include a suite, a mini-suite, one suitable for disabled guests and 20 executive rooms. Those at the back of the hotel, with views of the Blue Stack Mountains, are most desirable and avoid the problems caused by through traffic which can be disturbing in front bedrooms. Residents have direct access from their rooms to the hotel's excellent leisure facilities. Conference/banqueting (150/250). Children are welcome under 3s free in their parents' room; cots and high chairs available, crèche at certain times in the leisure centre. Special breaks offered by the hotel include a novel "Post Christmas Recovery Break". **Rooms 53** (1 mini-suite, 31 executive rooms,1 for disabled). B&B £50pps, ss £8. Wheelchair access. Lift. Open all year. Amex, Diners, MasterCard, Visa

The Looking Glass

Hand-worked tapestries decorate this pleasant warm-toned restaurant, which is in two areas with plenty of alcoves for privacy. Since his arrival in 1994, head chef Frederic Souty has made big changes to what was a country hotel menu. His stylish, confident cooking is seen through seasonal menus, plus daily specials which particularly emphasise seafood. A typical main course might be roast rack of Donegal mountain lamb with roast aubergine and petal tomatoes with garlic jus or the catch of the day which, if you're lucky, might be grilled shelled lobster with a lemon cream and baby vegetables. There's a cheese trolley and desserts include a "Tasting Plate", the perfect choice for the undecided [Bar meals also available daily 12.30-3 and 5.30-9.30.] **Seats 74** (private room, 60). D 6.30-10.30 daily, Sun L 12.30-2, Set Sun L £13.50, Set D £25, à la carte available, house wine £12. toilets wheelchair accessible. No smoking area. sc discretionary. Closed 25 Dec & Good Fri. Amex, Diners, MasterCard, Visa. **Directions:** On the main street in the village

Ballyliffin ❊   *Rossaor House*

ACCOMMODATION

Ballyliffin Inishowen Co Donegal
Tel/Fax: 077 76498

Brian and Anne Harkin's very pleasant and hospitable house is in a beautiful area that deserves to be better known and it has amazing views down over two golf courses to Pollen Strand and Malin Head. Bedrooms are furnished to a very high standard (generous beds, direct dial phone, tea/coffee facilities and TV) and luxuriously decorated - an aspect of the business in which Anne clearly takes particular pleasure. Spacious, comfortably furnished public rooms include a large sitting room, which takes full advantage of the view, and a conservatory breakfast room considerately situated away from the full blast of morning sunshine. There is also self-catering accommodation on the property - details from the Harkins. Children welcome (cot available). No pets. **Rooms 4** (all en-suite). B&B £25pps, ss £5. Closed Xmas. MasterCard, Visa. **Directions:** N2 Dublin to Aughnacloy, A5 to Derry Cross bridge as you enter Derry. Take signs to Buncrana, then Clonmany. Ballyliffin is 1 mile to the right.

Bruckless   *Bruckless House*

FARMHOUSE

Bruckless Co Donegal
Tel: 073 37071 Fax: 073 37070 email: bruc@iol.ie

Although on a working farm, and registered as a farmhouse, the term doesn't do justice to Clive and Joan Evans' lovely 18th-century home, which is set in 19 acres of woodland and gardens overlooking Bruckless Bay - an ideal place for people who enjoy quiet countryside and walking. Family furniture collected through a Hong Kong connection add an unexpected dimension to the elegant reception rooms and generous, comfortably furnished bedrooms. Bedrooms include two single rooms and there is a shared bathroom. Pets permitted by arrangement. **Rooms 5** (2 en-suite, 1 shower only, all no-smoking) B&B £30pps, no ss. Closed Oct-Mar. Amex, MasterCard, Visa. **Directions:** On N56, 12 miles west of Donegal town.

Bunbeg   *Ostan Gweedore*

Bunbeg Co Donegal

HOTEL   Tel: 075 31177 Fax: 075 31726 email: boyle@iol.ie

Although its architectural style may not be to today's taste, Ostan Gweedore was built to make the most of the view - and this it does very well. Most of the comfortable if rather dated bedrooms (plus three suites) and all the public areas, including the recently refurbished restaurant and the Library Bar ("the most westerly reading room on the Atlantic seaboard") have superb views over the shoreline and Mount Errigal. It's ideal for families, with its wonderful beach and outdoor activities, including tennis, pitch & putt and day visits to nearby Tory Island. Wet days are looked after too, with indoor leisure facilities, including a 17-metre swimming pool, jacuzzi and gym, all supervised by qualified staff. This romantic setting means weddings are popular (conferences/banqueting up to 300) and the hotel offers an imaginative "Flybreak", including a return flight Dublin to Donegal, overnight stay and dinner "on the edge of a continent', at a very competitive rate. Check for latest offers. Under 5s free in parents' room. No pets. **Rooms 39** (3 suites). B&B £42.50pps, ss £12.50. Closed Nov-Mar. Amex, MasterCard, Visa. **Directions:** 45 minutes from Letterkenny, close to Carrickfinn Airport

Bundoran   *Le Chateaubrianne*

Sligo Road Bundoran Co Donegal

RESTAURANT   Tel/Fax: 072 42160

Since opening here in 1993, Brian and Anne Loughlin have established this welcoming and very professionally run establishment as the leading restaurant in the area. Brian's cooking is classic French with New Irish overtones and he is a strong supporter of local produce. Imaginative dinner menus offer a well-balanced selection with local seafood well represented, also game in season, with interesting vegetarian options available. Sunday lunch provides something for everyone by offering a clever combination of traditional roasts and more adventurous fare; the same high standard of cooking applies and the meal will be nicely finished off with coffee and petits fours. **Seats 56** (private room, 16). No-smoking restaurant. D 6-10 Tues-Sat (& Sun in summer), Sun L 12.30-3, Set Sun L £14.50, Set D £24, house wine £12; sc discretionary. Toilets wheelchair accessible. Closed Mon, 23-27 Dec, all Jan & Bank Hols. Amex, MasterCard, Visa. **Directions:** On left hand side entering Bundoran from Sligo.

Carndonagh ✳   *Corncrake Restaurant*

Main Street Carndonagh Inishowen Co Donegal

RESTAURANT/Cookery School   Tel: 077 74534

It is difficult to describe Brid McCartney and Noreen Lynch's restaurant adequately because, although it is just the front room of a fairly ordinary house on the main street of a small town, that is where any sense of being "ordinary" ends. The room is not large, but it has a confident, professional air and its low-key decor creates an unlikely spaciousness. Tables are well-appointed, with gleaming glasses and quality cutlery giving a hint to the philosophy at work in the kitchen. It is significant that Brid and Noreen have made a conscious decision to live and work in this lovely (and, so far, unspoilt) part of the country, that they relish it and take pleasure in the produce of the area - and in their work. This is perhaps best seen through their decision to run off-season residential cookery courses at the restaurant, together with Rossaor House (see entry) who provide the accommodation element. Back at the restaurant, local produce appears typically in mussels in a tarragon cream or main courses (£9.50-£13) like roast rack of Donegal mountain lamb with rosemary jus and, endearingly, house specialities like fresh wild salmon coulibiac, with grilled hollandaise appear alongside dear old coq au vin - and all main dishes are served with that wonderful northern speciality, champ. An extra charge for fresh vegetables - although only £1 - is the only wrong note on the Corncrake menu. No children after 7 pm. **Seats 26** (private room, 4) No smoking area. D 6-10, à la carte only, house wine £10;sc discretionary. Open 7 nights June-Sept, Fri/Sat in Mar-May & Oct-Dec, Closed Xmas-17 Mar. No credit cards. **Directions:** On the main street of the town

Clonmany ✳   *The Rusty Nail*

Crossconnell Clonmany Inishowen Co Donegal

PUB   Tel: 077 76116

This terrific pub a short distance from Ballyliffin is just the spot for a bite to eat and it's not just your average pub grub either - they do a mouthwatering blackboard menu of seriously tempting meals. This place is the business. **Seats 60.** Meals Fri-Sun 5-9.30 (everyday in high season) and 12.30-2 Sun only. Open all year. MasterCard. Visa. **Directions:** 2 miles from Clonmany Village, towards the Gap of Mamore.

Donegal   *St Ernan's House Hotel*

Donegal Town Co Donegal

Tel: 073 21065 Fax: 073 22098

COUNTRYHOUSE HOTEL   email: info@sainternans.com

Set on its own wooded island connected to the mainland by a causeway, tranquillity is the main characteristic of Brian and Carmel O'Dowd's unique country house hotel. Spacious public rooms have log fires and antique furniture and, while they vary in size and outlook, the individually decorated bedrooms are furnished to a high standard. All are en-suite (2 shower only) and have good amenities including (surprisingly perhaps) television, while most also have lovely views. Not suitable for children under 6. No pets. **Rooms 12** (2 shower only) B&B £76pps, ss on request. Closed end Oct-mid Apr. MasterCard,Visa. **Restaurant:** The dining room is mainly intended for resident guests, but reservations may be taken from non-residents if there is room. Gabrielle Doyle has been Head Chef since 1992 and produces daily 5-course country house-style dinner menus based on local produce. Vegetarian dishes on request. **Seats 24.** No smoking restaurant. D 6.30-8.30 daily, Set D £17-29, à la carte available, house wine £13 Closed 24-26 Dec & Good Fri. Amex, Diners, MasterCard, Visa. **Directions:** One mile south of Donegal Town

---

Dunkineely   *Castle Murray House Hotel*

St. John's Point Dunkineely Co Donegal

HOTEL/RESTAURANT   Tel: 073 37022 Fax: 073 37330

Thierry and Clare Delcros' beautifully located clifftop hotel has wonderful sea and coastal views over the ruined castle after which it is named. Since they opened in 1991, the Delcros have made numerous improvements, including the addition of a little bar and a residents' sitting room. More recently, the seating for summer meals was extended by the addition of a large verandah complete with awning. Bedrooms are all quite large and fairly comfortably furnished with a mixture of utilitarian modern units and a sprinkling of antiques; all have a double and single bed, most have sea views and there are extra beds and cots available for families on request. Pets permitted. Good breakfasts are served in bedrooms or in the restaurant. Off-season value breaks. **Rooms 10** (all en-suite). B&B £30pps, ss £6. Closed first 2 weeks Feb, Mon-Tues in low season. MasterCard, Visa. **Restaurant:** The restaurant is on the seaward corner of the hotel and maximises the impact of the dramatic view, including the castle (which is floodlit at night). Tweed curtains and an open fire make for real warmth in this exposed location, even in winter. Owner-chef Thierry Delcros' multi-choice menus (basically 3-course, plus options of soup and sorbet), are sensibly priced according to the choice of main course and offer a wide choice, including vegetarian dishes. Seafood is the speciality of the house in the summer months; in winter there are more red meats, poultry and game. **Seats 50.** No smoking restaurant. D 7-9.30 daily (high season), Wed-Sun (low season), Sun L 3-5.30, Sun D 6-7.30, all à la carte, house wine £9.50; sc discretionary. **Directions:** Just a mile off the main Killybegs-Donegal road.

May change hands in 2000.

Fahan   *St John's Country House & restaurant*

Fahan Inishowen Peninsula Co Donegal

RESTAURANT/COUNTRYHOUSE   Tel: 077 60289 Fax: 077 60612

Host of the Year Award

Since 1980, to growing acclaim, Reggie Ryan and Phil McAfee have run Restaurant St John's in their substantial period house overlooking Lough Swilly and it is one of the most hospitable houses in Ireland. Reggie has a way with guests which must be pretty well unrivalled, making each one feel especially welcome and - oh joy of joys - making the whole occasion relaxed and fun, a time when it is no crime to let your hair down a little after dinner. Restaurant St John's has hosted many an international figure and we are in no doubt that he has had the same effect on them all, welcoming them with warmth and leaving each with memories that will always be treasured. The conservatory extension has allowed for Lough views in addition to the original cosy inside rooms, all a fit setting for Phil's cooking, which combines a respect for tradition and understanding of the value of simplicity with a willingness to experiment, ensuring that the many guests who regularly return always have a meal that is both stimulating and relaxing. Given the location, seafood is very popular but Phil's table d'hôte and à la carte menus are based on a wide range of local ingredients, including game in winter. Donegal mountain lamb, which she cooks in many different ways is an established favourite (earning Restaurant St John's the Guide's Irish Lamb Award in 1999 for her "Rack of Donegal Mountain Lamb with Rosemary and Mascarpone Risotto"). A fairly priced wine list includes nine house wines, a special seasonal selection and a good choice of half bottles. Banqueting (80). **Seats 80** (private room, 10) No smoking restaurant; air conditioning. D 7-9.30 daily, Sun L 1-3, Set Sun L £13.20, Set D £22, house wine £11.95; sc discretionary Toilets wheelchair accessible. Closed Jan-Feb. Amex, Diners, MasterCard, Visa. **Accommodation:** Comfortably rooms furnished with antiques, were recently added. Children welcome (under 3s free in parents' room, cot available). Pets permitted. **Rooms 5** (1 suites, all en-suite, all no-smoking) B&B £35pps, ss £10. Wheelchair access. **Directions:** In Fahan village on R238 Derry-Buncrana Road.

Greencastle — *Kealys Seafood Bar*

The Harbour Greencastle Co Donegal
PUB/RESTAURANT   Tel/Fax: 077 81010   email: kealys@iol.ie

Under-stated quality seems a fair description of the tone of James and Tricia Kealy's excellent seafood restaurant, which has always valued simplicity. Since 1989 the restaurant has been a key establishment in a major fishing port and still retains the original bar at its heart. Lunch menus are shortish and the dishes offered simple; however the choice is very adequate and the quality of food and cooking consistently good. Dinner is more ambitious and, in addition to a wide selection of ultra-fresh seafood, James includes a fair selection of meat and poultry - steaks, Inishowen lamb, duck - as well as vegetarian dishes. James bakes a variety of breads and uses local organic vegetables and farmhouse cheeses - typically Gubbeen, St Killian, Boilie and Cashel Blue. Not suitable for children after 8 pm. **Seats 65.** No smoking area. L 12.30-3 Tues-Sun, D 6-10 Tues-Sun, bar food 12.30-5, Set D £20, L&D also à la carte, house wine £9.60. Toilets wheelchair accessible. Closed Mondays, 1 wk Apr, 1 wk Nov, 25 Dec & Good Fri. Amex, Diners, MasterCard, Visa. **Directions:** West bank of Lough Foyle to the harbour at Greencastle.

Killybegs — *The Fleet Inn*

Bridge Street Killybegs Co Donegal
PUB/ACCOMODATION/RESTAURANT   Tel: 073 31518 Fax: 073 31664

Marguerite Howley's pleasant establishment just off the main thoroughfare is an inn in the real sense, offering food, drink and shelter - although, admittedly, bar food is not part of the package which might sometimes be disappointing to visitors. Rooms are a mixture of sizes, ranging from singles to family rooms, all cheerfully decorated, with direct dial phones and TV Not very suitable for children. No pets. **Rooms 10** (all en-suite, 5 no-smoking). B&B £23 pps, ss£3. Restaurant: The upstairs restaurant is open in the evening only and offers a short but appealing menu. It's predictably strong on seafood - Donegal Bay prawns tossed in garlic butter, seared scallops with fresh herb risotto and garlic & tomato sauce - but offers a vegetarian choice such as leek & red pepper tartlet and a few meat dishes, including chargrille steak and, perhaps, venison served roast garlic, braised red cabbage & port jus. **Seats 40** (private dining area, 12). No smoking area. D only, 7-10 daily in summer (Nov-Feb closed Mon & Tue). A la carte; house wine £10; sc discretionary. **Directions:** In the centre of Killybegs - a right turn just after the harbour.

Letterkenny — *Castle Grove Country House*

Ballymaleel Letterkenny Co Donegal
COUNTRYHOUSE HOTEL/RESTAURANT   Tel: 074 51118 Fax: 074 51384

Parkland designed by "Capability" Brown in the mid 18th-century creates a wonderful setting for Raymond and Mary Sweeney's lovely period house overlooking Lough Swilly.

The last few years have seen major changes, including a new conservatory and a larger new restaurant. Most recently, the adjoining coach house has been developed to make seven new bedrooms and a small conference room (max 30), and the original walled garden is under restoration. Bedrooms (all now non-smoking) are generally spacious and furnished to a high standard, although several have shower only. Good breakfasts include a choice of fish as well as traditional Irish breakfast, home-made breads and preserves. There is a high standard of maintenance and housekeeping and staff are friendly and helpful. Two boats belonging to the house are available for fishing on Lough Swilly. Banqueting for up to 60 guests. Not suitable for children under 12. No pets. **Rooms 14** (1 suite, 2 executive rooms, all no-smoking) B&B £45pps, ss £10. Wheelchair access. Closed 23-28 Dec. Amex, Diners, MasterCard, Visa. **Restaurant:** Pascal Desnet has been head chef at Castle Grove since 1998. He offers several menus -table'd'hôte, à la carte and vegetarian - at dinner, plus 2 or 3-course set lunch menus. The style is "New Irish Cuisine" with international overtones and menus are based on local ingredients, including home grown herbs, vegetables and soft fruit, as well as local seafood including wild salmon and Swilly oysters. **Seats 60** (private room, 18) No smoking restaurant. L 12.30-2.30 Mon-Sat, D 6.30-9.30 daily, Set L £11, Set D £18-30, à la carte available, house wine £9.50; sc discretionary. Toilets wheelchair accessible. Closed 24-26 Dec & Good Fri. Amex, Diners, MasterCard, Visa. **Directions:** North from Letterkenny via Rathmelton/Rathmullan road.

Letterkenny ❋

Metropolitan Bar & Restaurant

106 Lr Main St Letterkenny Co Donegal
Tel: 074 20800 Fax: 074 20803
email: conradgallagher@tinet.ie

BAR/RESTAURANT

As the Guide was going to press, news reached us that super chef Conrad Gallagher has just opened this contemporary Bar and Restaurant in his home county. It is reputedly an instant smash-hit and full all the time.

Kincasslagh ❋

Iggy's Bar

Kincasslagh Co Donegal
Tel: 075 43112

PUB

Just a short walk up from the harbour - it's also called the Atlantic Bar - Ann and Iggy Murray have run this delightfully unspoilt pub since 1986 and it's an all year home-from-home for many a visitor. As in all the best country pubs, well-behaved dogs are allowed to accompany their owners and the television isn't usually on unless there's a match. Ann makes lovely simple food for the bar, mainly seafood - home-made soups, delicious crab sandwiches and Rombouts coffee. No children after 7 pm. Meals Light food available noon-6pm daily. Closed 25 Dec & Good Friday. No credit cards. **Directions:** On the corner of the main street, where the road turns off to the harbour.

Lough Eske

Ardnamona House

Lough Eske Co Donegal

COUNTRYHOUSE   Tel: 073 22650 Fax: 073 22819 email: ardnamon@tempoweb.com

The glorious gardens, which were first planted by Sir Arthur Wallace in the 1880s, are central to the special atmosphere of Kieran and Annabel Clarke's secluded Victorian house overlooking Lough Eske and it's hard to credit that it's only a couple of miles from Donegal town. It's a gentle, hospitable house and draws people who value its peace and beauty. Front rooms have lovely views over the Lough to the mountains beyond, but all are individualistic with private bathrooms (and a peaceful outlook through rhododendrons and azaleas which have received international acclaim). Gardeners will enjoy doing the garden trail (guide leaflet provided and all plants labelled) and special interest groups are welcome to visit the gardens by arrangement. There are also miles of walks through ancient oak forests full of mosses and ferns and private boating and fishing on the Lough. Except on Sundays, communal dinner is available for residents, by reservation, at 8.30 pm.(£20; wine licence). Children welcome; dogs allowed by arrangement. **Rooms 6** (all with en-suite or private bathrooms). B&B £47, ss £10. Amex, MasterCard, Visa. **Directions:** From Donegal, follow signs to Harveys Point Country Hotel, then pick up sign to Ardnamona.

Lough Eske   *Harvey's Point Country Hotel*

Lough Eske Co Donegal
Tel: 073 22208 Fax: 073 22352
HOTEL/RESTAURANT   email: harveyspoint@tinet.ie

In a stunning location on the shores of Lough Eske, this unusual hotel has a distinctly alpine atmosphere, with chalet-style buildings, pergolas and covered walkways joining the residential area to the main bars and restaurant. Maintenance is immaculate and the atmosphere can be deeply peaceful. Rooms, which have all been refurbished recently, with four-posters, are based on a Swiss design; they have good amenities and direct access to verandah and gardens. Conferences/banqueting (100/250). Dinner dances and special breaks are often offered at Harvey's Point; telephone for details. Not suitable for children. Pets permitted. **Rooms 20** (4 executive rooms, all en-suite). B&B £55pps, ss £15. Open weekends only Nov-Mar. Amex, Diners, MasterCard, Visa. **Restaurant:** Original paintings by a talented family member, well-appointed tables and the beautiful view make a promising start to the meal, and Marc Gysling's cooking - which is based on Swiss training with Irish influences - does not disappoint. Menus are imaginative but not over-fussy, local produce is used to good effect, the saucing is good and so are details - for example farmhouse cheeses, which are served plated, come with a delicious home-made nut bread. Service is attentive and professional. The wine list includes a range of 'everyday easy drinking' wines (all under £20) and a good selection of half bottles. **Seats 65** (private room, 50) No smoking restaurant; air conditioning. L 12-2 daily, D 6-9.30 daily, Sun L 12-4, Set L £12.50, Set Sun L £12.95, Set D £30, house wine £12.50; sc discretionary. Toilets wheelchair accessible. **Directions:** 6km from Donegal town - well-signed.

Portsalon   *Croaghross Cottage*

Portsalon Letterkenny Co Donegal
ACCOMMODATION   Tel/Fax: 074 59548 email: jkdeane@iol.ie

John and Kay Deane's new single-storey house was purpose built and this latter-day country house enjoys a lovely location on the Fanad peninsula, overlooking Lough Swilly. It's within 5 minutes walk of a great beach - and the renowned 100-year old Portsalon Golf Course - and very convenient to Glenveagh National Park. Three bedrooms open onto a sun terrace, while the two side rooms overlook a landscaped rock garden - one of them is especially suitable for wheelchair users, who can park close to the room. Residents' dinner is, like breakfast, based on local ingredients and good home cooking, with home-made breads and farmhouse cheeses always available (£15, please book ahead; very reasonable short wine list). Barbecues are sometimes arranged when the weather is favourable and, although officially closed in winter, bookings can be made by arrangement. This is an attractive option for a group, as the house is centrally heated throughout and the living room has a big open fire. The Deanes also have a 3-bedroom self-catering cottage available nearby. Children welcome (under 6s free in parents' room, cot available). Pets permitted. **Rooms 5** (all en-suite, 1 for disabled). B&B £30pps, ss £5. Wheelchair access. Closed Oct-mid Mar. MasterCard, Visa. **Directions:** Letterkenny- Ramelton- R246 (Milford direction) through Kerrykeel to Portsalon; opposite golf course, turn left up hill.

Rathmullan   *Fort Royal Hotel*

Rathmullan Letterkenny Co Donegal
HOTEL   Tel: 074 58100 Fax: 074 58103 email: fortroyal@tinet.ie

Overlooking the sea, and with easy access to sandy beaches, the Fletcher family's attractive Victorian hotel is set in 19 acres of lawn and woodland above Lough Swilly. Public rooms, which include a recently refurbished bar, are spacious, well-proportioned and comfortably furnished in country house style, with big armchairs and open fires. Well-appointed bedrooms (all en-suite, most with bath and shower, a few bath only) are designed for relaxation and enjoy a pleasant outlook over wooded grounds. Much of the food at Fort Royal comes from the hotel's own walled gardens and is cooked by Robin and Ann Fletcher's son, Timothy, who has been head chef since 1995. Fort Royal also has croquet, tennis, squash and golf on the premises and activities such as riding and fishing nearby. It's a good base for family holidays or visiting places of local interest, including Glenveagh National Park and Glebe House, the artist Derek Hill's former home, which has a museum and gallery next door. Pets permitted by arrangement. **Rooms 15** (4 executive rooms, all en-suite). B&B £61.50pps, ss £24.50. Closed 1 Nov-31 Mar. Amex, Diners, MasterCard, Visa. **Directions:** R247 from Letterkenny, through Ramelton - hotel signposted on entry to Rathmullan village.

Rathmullan   *Rathmullan House*

Rathmullan Co Donegal
HOTEL/RESTAURANT   Tel: 074 58188 Fax: 074 58200 email: rathhse@iol.ie

Built as a summer house by the Batt banking family of Belfast in the 1800s, Rathmullan has been run as a country house hotel since 1961 by Bob and Robin Wheeler who have now semi-retired and is now managed by their sons William and Mark and daughter-in-law Mary. Set in lovely gardens on the shores of Lough Swilly, this gracious early nineteenth century house remains friendly and informal. Although on quite a large scale and furnished to a high standard, the public areas, which include three elegant sitting rooms, are not too formal - and there's a delightful cellar bar which can be very relaxed. Bedrooms vary in decor, facilities and cost to suit different requirements and budgets - there are luxurious garden suites (close to the swimming pool and leisure facilities) as well as the unpretentious old-fashioned comforts of family rooms at the top of the house. Donegal has an other-worldliness that is increasingly hard to capture in the traditional family holiday areas, and the laid-back charm of Rathmullan House - albeit given invisible backbone by the professionalism of the Wheeler family and their staff - somehow symbolises that special sense of place. Small conferences (20). Children welcome; cot £10. No pets. **Rooms 24** (11 suites, 1 room for disabled). B&B £50pps, ss £10.20. Wheelchair access Closed Jan-mid Feb. Amex, Diners, MasterCard, Visa. **Restaurant:** The dining room with its unusual tented ceiling makes the most of the garden outlook and provides a fine setting for Seamus Douglas's country house cooking as well as the tremendous breakfasts for which Rathmullan is justly famous. [*There's also a less formal Cellar Restaurant (chef Ronnie Blake) open Wed-Sun evening in summer, Fri & Sat off season.] **Seats 70.** No smoking restaurant. L 1-2.45 Mon-Sat, D 7.30-8.45 daily, Sun L 1-2, Set Sun L £15, Set D £27.50, early bird £6 5.30-7.30 Jul/Aug, house wine £10, sc 10% Toilets wheelchair accessible. **Directions:** Letterkenny to Ramelton - turn right to Rathmullan at the bridge, through village and turn right to hotel.

Rossnowlagh   *Sand House Hotel*

Rossnowlagh Co Donegal
HOTEL/RESTAURANT   Tel: 072 51777 Fax: 072 52100 email: info@sandhouse-hotel.ie

Mary and Brian Britton's famous crenellated hotel is perched on the edge of a stunning sandy beach two miles long. The wonderful sea views and easy access to the beach are great attractions of the Sand House. Many of the bedrooms have a superb outlook and all are very comfortable, with good bathrooms - and everyone can enjoy the view from the sun lounge (known as the Atlantic Conservatory). Immaculate maintenance and a high standard of furnishing have always been a special feature, and a major refurbishment of the ground floor, including reception, bars and lounges, will be completed for the 1999 season. But it is nevertheless the hospitality of the Britton family and staff (not to mention Mary Britton's reputation for exceptional housekeeping) which is the real appeal of this remarkable hotel. Small conference (100). Children welcome (under 2s free in parents' room; cots available). Pets permitted by arrangement. **Rooms 45** (1 suite, 4 shower only, all no-smoking). B&B £55pps, ss £15. Closed Oct-Easter. Amex, Diners, MasterCard, Visa.

Restaurant

The restaurant is rather unexpectedly at the front of the hotel (and therefore faces inland) but is well-appointed, in keeping with the rest of the hotel. Sid Davis, Head Chef since 1993, presents 5-course dinner menus that change daily. It is wholesome fare and simplest choices are usually the wisest; meals finish well with a choice of Irish cheeses or desserts that include very good fruit pies. **Seats 80.** No smoking restaurant. D 7-9 daily, Sun L 1-3, Set Sun L £14.50, Set D £25, house wine £10.50; sc discretionary. **Directions:** South of Donegal town on coast road.

Rossnowlagh   *Smugglers Creek Inn*

Rossnowlagh Co Donegal
PUB/RESTAURANT   Tel: 072 52366 Fax: 072 51578

High up on the cliffs, overlooking Donegal Bay and the Blue Stack Mountains, this inn actually dates back to 1845. Most of what you see today is due to the efforts of the present owner, Conor Britton, who has undertaken a major refurbishment and extension programme since he took over in 1991. (And the development continues - as we go to press he's about to build a new 60-seater restaurant upstairs and ten bedrooms) Developments to date have been very sympathetically done, with stonework, stone-flagged floors and open fires providing both atmosphere and comfort. Comforting traditional bar food - chowder, home-baked bread, garlic mussels - has always been good. However, items served in the bar (12.30-4.30 &6.30-9 daily) - moules marinières, home-made pâté with hot toast - are also on the restaurant menu which is predictably strong on seafood but also provides a decent choice for carnivores and vegetarians too. Children welcome up to 9 pm. **Seats 60** (private room, 35). L 12.30-3 daily, D 6.30-9 daily, à la carte, house wine £10.50; sc discretionary. Closed Mon & Tues, Oct-Easter, 25 Nov-26 Dec. MasterCard, Visa. **Directions:** 6 miles north of Ballyshannon on coast road, 10 miles south of Donegal town.

Tory Island   *Ostan Thoraig (Hotel Tory)*

West End Tory Island Co Donegal

HOTEL   Tel: 074 35920 Fax: 074 35613 email: hoteltory@tinet.ie

The Gaeltacht (Irish-speaking) island of Tory lies 5 miles off the north-west corner of Donegal and, in spite of its exposed position, has been inhabited for four thousand years. Perhaps not surprisingly, this other-worldly island managed quite well without an hotel until recently, but once Patrick and Berney Doohan's Ostan Thoraigh was built in 1994 it quickly became the centre of the island's social activities - or, to be more precise, The People's Bar in the hotel quickly became the centre. The hotel is beside the little harbour where the ferries bring in visitors from mainland ports. Although simple, it provides comfortable en-suite accommodation with telephone and television. A special feature of the island is its 'school' of primitive art (founded with the support of well-known artist Derek Hill of nearby Glebe House and Gallery, Church Hill). It even has a king as a founder member: the present King of the Tory is Patsy Dan Rogers, who has exhibited his colourful primitive paintings of the island throughout the British Isles and in America. A tiny gallery on Tory provides exhibition space for the current group of island artists. Small conferences. Children welcome (cot available, £3). Pets permitted by arrangement. **Rooms 14** (1 for disabled) B&B £30pps, ss £10. Wheelchair access. Closed Oct-Easter. MasterCard, Visa. **Directions:** Tory is accessible by ferry (subject to weather conditions) from several mainland ports - telephone 075-31320 for details, or ask at the hotel.

GALWAY

Can Galway be as good in 2000 as it was in 1999? For it enjoyed some sensationally good weather last summer, with the famous Galway Races at the end of July being a fun-filled sun-filled festival for its entire week of devotion to horse racing.

Well, if it can be managed at all, then Galway will do it, for this has to be Ireland's most generous county. You get two counties for the price of one, neatly divided by the handsome sweep of island-studded Lough Corrib. And as a bonus, where the Corrib tumbles into Galway Bay, you get one of Ireland's liveliest cities, a bustling place which cheerfully sees itself as being linked to Spain and the great world beyond the Atlantic. However much the Spanish links may have been romanticised as they filter through the mists of time, the fact is that today Galway city is a place confident of itself. Its strength in the west, when seen in the national context, is a welcome counterbalance to the inevitable domination of the greater Dublin area on the east coast. For although Galway city's population is only a fraction of Dublin's total, nevertheless the western capital is more than ready to stand fair square for the pride of Connacht and a positive assertion of the qualities of life beyond the Pale and west of the Shannon. It does so with pleasure and in the diversity of its territory. Lough Corrib is both a geographical and psychological divide. East of it, there's flatter country, home to hunting packs of mythic lore. West of the Corrib - which used itself to be a major throughfare and is now as ever place of angling renown - you're very quickly into the high ground and moorland which sweep up to the Twelve Pins and other splendid peaks, wonderful mountains which enthusiasts would claim as the most beautiful in all Ireland. Their heavily indented coastline means this region is Connemara, the Land of the Sea, where earth, rock and ocean intermix in one of Ireland's most extraordinary landscapes. Beyond, to the south, the Aran Islands are a place apart, yet they too are part of the Galway mix in this fantastical county which has its own magical light coming in over the sea.

And yet all its extraordinary variety happens within very manageable distances. For instance, in the western part of Galway city, the mature and leafy suburb of Taylor's Hill speaks eloquently of a quietly comfortable way of life which has been established for well over a century. Yet much less than an hour's drive away, whether along the shores of Galway Bay or taking the Corrib route via Oughterard, you'll quickly find yourself in the rugged heart of Connemara, where the scatter of cottages bespeaks a different way of life, an austere way of life which is every bit as significant a part of that remarkable Galway tapestry which enchants Galwegians and visitors alike.

Local Attractions and Information

Galway City

Galway Arts Festival (July)	091 583800
Island Ferries Teo	(Aran Islands from Rossaveal) 091 568903 / 561767
O'Brien Shipping Ltd	(Aran Islands ferries) 091 567283
Tourist Information	091 563081
Town Hall Theatre	091 569755

Co Galway

Aran Islands	Inis Mor, Ionad Arann (heritage centre) 099 61355
Aughrim	Ballinasloe, Battle of Aughrim Centre 0905 73939
	565201
Clifden	Connemara Pony Show (mid August) 095 21863
Gort	Thoor Ballylee (Yeats' Tower) 091 631436
	563081
Tuam	Little Mill (last intact cornmill in area) 093 25486

Aughrim	*Aughrim Schoolhouse Restaurant*
	Ballinasloe Co Galway
RESTAURANT	Tel: 0905 73622

Just off the main Galway road, this charming country restaurant is well-located for people visiting the nearby Battle of Aughrim site. Since Christophe and Caroline Pele took over the restaurant in March 1998, it has taken on a distinctly French tone and, as regular travellers will have noticed from the road, it has not only thrived but grown considerably too. House specialities include tournedos of salmon with a herb crust topped with a beurre blanc and an assiette gourmande - a sample of all their home-made sweets on one plate. **Seats 60** (private room, 15). No smoking area L 12-3 Tues-Sun, D 6.30-9.30 Tues-Sun, Sun L 12-5, Set L £11.50, Set Sun L £12.50, Set D £20, à la carte available, house wine £11.50; sc discretionary. Toilets wheelchair accessible. Closed Mondays, 25 Dec-1 Jan. MasterCard, Visa. **Directions:** 4 miles from Ballinasloe on Galway road (N6)

Ballinasloe — *Haydens Gateway Business & Leisure Hotel*

Dunlo Street Ballinasloe Co Galway
HOTEL
Tel: 0905 42347 Fax: 0905 42895

Now in the ownership of the Lynch family (who have hotels in Ennis, Limerick and Kilkee) Haydens is a long-established and much-loved hotel, very much the centre of local activities in and around Ballinasloe - conference and wedding facilities are good (300/350), with a particularly pleasant banqueting room overlooking the courtyard garden at the back. It's also about halfway between Dublin and Galway, making it a handy place to break the journey although, on the Guide's most recent visit housekeeping in the public areas was not up to its usual high standard. Great improvements have been taking place at the hotel lately however, including the imaginative redevelopment of the bar area, which now extends into the building next door. Bedrooms, all recently refurbished and with neat en-suite bathrooms, are comfortably furnished. Staff are friendly and helpful and there's plenty of free parking. Special breaks, notably golf breaks, are worth inquiring about. Children under 3 free in parents' room. **Rooms 48** (7 executive rooms, 2 no-smoking, 1 for disabled). B&B £45pps, ss £15. Wheelchair access, Lift. Open all year. Amex, Diners, MasterCard, Visa. Bar Food 2.30-6.30 daily, buffet. **Directions:** N6 Galway-Dublin road, on main street of town.

Ballyconneely — *Erriseask House Hotel*

Ballyconneely Clifden Co Galway
Tel: 095 23553 Fax: 095 23639
HOTEL/RESTAURANT
email: erriseask@connemara-ireland.com

This beautifully located shoreside hotel and restaurant seven miles south of Clifden has a low-key, continental atmosphere. With the notable exception of Christian and Stefan Matz's collection of extraordinary Gertrude Degenhardt pictures, the overall decorative approach in the hotel is - like their thoughtful hospitality - understated, allowing the wildness and the raw beauty of the surroundings to take centre stage. There is much light wood, in polished floors and furniture (but the black stuff on draught in the lounge) and a generally low-key approach throughout most of the ground floor and the original bedrooms. These quite simply decorated rooms with en-suite showers were refurbished in 1999. There are also five very unusual newer rooms on the ground floor, with excellent bathrooms and a mezzanine level sitting area with stunning views over untamed fields to the sea and land beyond. Not suitable for children. No dogs. **Rooms 12** (5 mini-suites, 7 shower only) B&B £40pps, ss £15. Closed Oct-May.Amex, Diners, MasterCard, Visa.

Restaurant ★

The restaurant has always been the heart of this unusual hotel. Overlooking fields running down to the white coral strand, it is well-appointed in classical style, with an open fire for chilly evenings, crisp linen, fine glasses and an attention to detail which complements the exceptionally fine food that Stefan Matz prepares for guests. Christian makes a fine host, quietly ensuring that no small detail is overlooked and explaining the wonderful menus - a Menu Degustation (for complete tables), a carte du jour, a table d'hôte and a vegetarian menu, none of them overlong but all changed almost daily. Using the best of local ingredients, Stefan enjoys working on the traditional themes of his adoptive country and brings a continental sophistication to the dishes he creates. His menus are always beautifully balanced and regularly feature an abundance of local seafood and Connemara lamb, as well as Irish beef. (He was the Guide's Bord Bia Irish Beef Award Winner last year, to mark a consistently creative approach, and particularly for his wonderful dish of Fillet of Beef Freshly Smoked on Turf served with Potato Pancakes and Glazed Autumn Vegetable which owed its inspiration to the Connemara landscape and was part of a menu that earned this talented and dedicated chef the title 'New Irish Cuisine Chef of the Year' in 1997). The wine list, which is interesting and far from static, includes a strong selection of half bottles. Not suitable for children under 10. **Seats 36.** No smoking area. D 6.30-8.30 daily (except Wed), Set D £19.50-27.50, à la carte available, house wine £13;o sc discretionary. Closed Wed for non-residents (except Jul-Aug). **Directions:** Follow coast road from Clifden to Ballyconneely.

Cashel 🏛

Cashel House Hotel

Cashel Co Galway
Tel: 095 31001 Fax: 095 31077
email: info@cashel-house-hotel.com

COUNTRYHOUSE HOTEL/RESTAURANT

Dermot and Kay McEvilly were among the pioneers of the Irish country house movement when, as founder members of the Irish Country Houses and Restaurants Association (now known as The Blue Book) they opened Cashel House as an hotel in 1968. The following year General and Madame de Gaulle chose to stay for two weeks, an historic visit of which the McEvilly's are justly proud - look out for the photographs and other memorabilia in the hall. The de Gaulle visit meant immediate recognition for the hotel, but it did even more for Ireland by putting the Gallic seal of approval on Irish hospitality and food. Comfort abounds here, even luxury, yet it's tempered by common sense, a love of gardening and the genuine sense of hospitality that ensures each guest will benefit as much as possible from their stay. The gardens, which run down to their own private beach, contribute greatly to the atmosphere, and the accommodation includes especially comfortable ground floor garden suites, which are also suitable for less able guests (wheelchair accessible but no special grab rails etc in bathrooms). Relaxed hospitality combined with professionalism have earned an international reputation for this outstanding hotel and its qualities are perhaps best seen in details - log fires that burn throughout the year, day rooms furnished with antiques and filled with fresh flowers from the garden, rooms that are individually decorated with many thoughtful touches. Service (with all day room service, including all meals) is impeccable and breakfast includes an interesting selection of home-made produce, from soda bread and marmalade to black pudding. Not suitable for children under 5 except small babies(cots £10). Pets permitted. **Rooms 32** (13 suites, 9 superior rooms, 1 shower only, 16 no-smoking). B&B £25pps, ss £10. Wheelchair access. Closed 4 Jan-4 Feb. Amex, Diners, MasterCard, Visa. **Restaurant:** A large conservatory extension enhances this well-appointed split-level restaurant. Dermot McEvilly has overseen the kitchen personally since the hotel opened, providing a rare consistency of style in five-course dinners that make imaginative use of local produce and seafood - lobster, oysters, fresh and home-smoked wild salmon, mussels, turbot, monkfish - is a great strength. Local meats include Connemara lamb and another, more unusual, speciality is roast stuffed crown of pork. Garden produce is also much in evidence throughout, in soups, salads, side dishes, fine vegetarian dishes and desserts, such as rhubarb tart or strawberries and cream. Farmhouse cheeses come with home-baked biscuits and a choice of coffees and infusions is offered to finish. Service, under the personal supervision of Kay McEvilly, is excellent. An interesting wine list includes four House Wines (£15.95). Lunch (12.30-2.30) and afternoon tea (2.30-5) are served daily in the bar. **Seats 70.** No smoking area. D 7.30-8.30 daily, Set D £32-34, à la carte L available. House wine from £15; sc discretionary. Toilets wheelchair accessible. **Directions:** South off N59 (Galway-Clifden road) 1 mile west of Recess

---

Cashel

Zetland Country House Hotel

Cashel Bay Connemara Co Galway
HOTEL   Tel: 095 31111 Fax: 095 31117 email: zetland@iol.ie

On an elevated site, with views over Cashel Bay, Zetland House Hotel was originally built as a sporting lodge in the early 19th century - and still makes a good base for fishing holidays. This is a charming house, with a light and airy atmosphere and an elegance bordering on luxury, in both its spacious antique-furnished public areas and bedrooms. The latter are individually decorated in a relaxed country house style. The gardens surrounding the house are very lovely too, greatly enhancing the peaceful atmosphere of the house. Small conferences/banqueting (20/60). Special breaks. Tennis, billiards. Children welcome (under 4s free in parents' room; cot available). Pets permitted in some areas. **Rooms 20** (4 mini-suites, 6 executive rooms). B&B £55pps. Wheelchair access. Closed 1 Nov-1 Apr. Amex, Diners, MasterCard, Visa. **Directions:** N59 from Galway. Turn left after Recess

---

Claddaghduff

Acton's Guesthouse

Leegaun Claddaghduff Co Galway
ACCOMMODATION   Tel: 095 44339 Fax: 095 44309

In one of the most stunning away-from-it-all locations in Ireland, this wonderful, professionally run guesthouse has direct access to a sandy beach and uninterrupted views of the sea and islands. It can be just heavenly. The house - a modern bungalow -

is neat and homely, with seven comfortable en-suite rooms (4 shower-only, 1 with jacuzzi bath), tea/coffee trays, phones and satellite TV. There's a cosy sitting room with a turf fire, and Rita Acton's home cooking to enjoy in the dining room (which is placed to take full advantage of the view). Rita's imaginative set menu dinners could include Connemara salmon with strawberries and lemon dressing, rack of Connemara lamb with fresh herb crust, and vegetarian dishes such as Castle Farm goats cheese in filo pastry with red onion and raisin relish. Children under 4 free in parents' room. No pets. **Rooms 7** (4 shower only, all no-smoking). B&B £30pps, ss £5. Set D £22, 7-9 Tues-Sat. Wheelchair access. Closed 1 Oct-1 Apr. Amex, Diners, MasterCard, Visa. **Directions:** N59 from Galway fro 2 miles. Turn left on to Claddaghduff road for 4 miles

---

Clarenbridge *Oyster Manor Hotel*

Clarenbridge Co Galway
HOTEL   Tel: 091 796777 Fax: 091 796770

Family-owned by Ned and Julianne Forde, this new hotel on the edge of Clarenbridge is popular for conferences and family celebrations (400/500 respectively; secretarial services available) and the large bar at the back makes a focal point, with live music most nights. Rooms have all the necessary amenities and are comfortably furnished with modern amenities. Children free in parents' room up to 10; cots available. No pets. **Rooms 26** (1 suite, 3 executive rooms, 3 no-smoking). B&B £65pps, ss £25. Wheelchair access. Closed 24-25 Dec. Amex, Diners, MasterCard, Visa. **Directions:** Main Limerick Road, South East of Galway City.

Clarenbridge *Paddy Burkes*

Clarenbridge Co Galway
PUB   Tel: 091 796226 Fax: 091 796016

Established in 1650 and still going strong, Paddy Burkes' internationally famous pub and seafood bar is home to the Clarenbridge Oyster Festival - September 1999 saw its 45th birthday. Extensive renovations have recently brought many improvements. Although most famous for its seafood, this characterful old pub serves much else besides, including stir-fries, curries, steaks and vegetarian dishes, both on the regular bar menu and as daily specials. The visitors book reads like a Who's Who - an unbelievable array of the rich and famous. And that's not including the ones who "prefer not to be named". **Bar Meals** 12.30-10 daily no smoking area; air conditioning; wheelchair access. Closed 24-25 Dec & Good Fri. Amex, Diners, MasterCard, Visa. **Directions:** Seven miles south of Galway city on Limerick Road.

Clifden ✗ *Abbeyglen Castle*

Sky Road Clifden Co Galway
HOTEL   Tel: 095 21201 Fax: 095 21797 email: info@abbeyglen.ie

Set romantically in its own parkland valley overlooking Clifden and the sea, Abbeyglen is family-owned and run in a very hands-on fashion by Paul and Brian Hughes. It's a place that has won a lot of friends over the years and it's easy to see why: it's big and comfortable and laid-back - and there's a generosity of spirit about the place which is very charming. Public areas include a spacious drawing room for residents and a relaxing, pubby bar with open peat fire. Bedrooms (all with good bathrooms) are quite big and have been recently refurbished, as part of an ongoing improvement programme. Acc££-£££. Amex, Diners, MasterCard, Visa. **Directions:** About 300 yards out of Clifden on the Sky Road, on the left.

Clifden *Ardagh Hotel & Restaurant*

Ballyconneely Road Clifden Co Galway
Tel: 095 21384 Fax: 095 21314
HOTEL/RESTAURANT   email: ardaghhotel@tinet.ie

Beautifully located on the Ballyconneely road, overlooking Ardbear Bay, Stephane and Monique Bauvet's family-run hotel is well known for hospitality, comfort and good food. It has style, too, in a gentle sort of way - not "decorated" but furnished in a homely style with good fabrics and classic country colours. Turf fires, comfortable armchairs and a plant-filled conservatory area upstairs all indicate that peaceful relaxation is the aim here. Bedrooms vary according to their position but they are all well-furnished, with all the amenities required for a comfortable stay. (Not all have sea views - single rooms are at the back with a pleasant countryside outlook, and have shower only.) Bedrooms include some extra large rooms, especially suitable for families. **Rooms 21** (3 suites, 4 shower only). B&B £55pps, ss £15. Closed end Oct-end Mar. Amex, Diners, MasterCard, Visa. **Restaurant:** The well-appointed restaurant is on the first floor and set up to take full advantage of the view, providing a fitting setting for Monique's fine cooking, which specialises in local seafood. She makes imaginative use of local ingredients, including organic vegetables, in nightly 5-course dinner menu offering plenty of choice - typically in dishes like king prawn brochette with wild rice & Pernod sauce, fresh Atlantic bouillabaisse with garlic croutons & rouille and pot roast loin of Connemara lamb oated with fresh basil pesto, served with rosemary & thyme lamb jus. **Seats 55.** No smoking area. L 12.30-3 daily, D 7.15-9.30 daily, Set D £26.50, house wine £12.95; sc 12.5%. **Directions:** 2km south of Clifden on Ballconneely-Roundstone Road, on left hand side.

Clifden | *Destrys Restaurant*

Main Street Clifden Co Galway
CAFÉ/RESTAURANT | Tel: 095 21722

This wacky little restaurant was opened by Paddy and Julia Foyle a few years ago and, in addition to normal custom, head chef Dermot Gannon provides dinners for residents at their other establishment Quay House (see entry). It's a fun, buzzy restaurant; Dermot's new-wave cooking is superb and prices are reasonable, so a good time is sure to be had by all. At night they do an à la carte menu (main courses about £8.95-£14.95) and there's a lighter selection at lunchtime. Examples of Dermot's style include specialities like monkfish roasted on the bone with garlic & thyme, lime hollandaise and a vegetarian choice such as salad of goats cheese & pickled vegetables with apricot & dill. Home baking is a strong point, and they make great brown yeast bread as well as foccacia. Not suitable for children after 7 pm. [*Dermot's sister and her husband run Wings, an unusually authentic Chinese restaurant up the road.] **Seats 30** (private room, 8) D 6-10 Tues-Sun, Sun L 12-3, all à la carte, house wine £12.95; sc discretionary. Toilet wheelchair accessible. Closed Nov-17 Mar. MasterCard, Visa. **Directions:** Main Street, centre of town

---

Clifden | *O'Grady's Seafood Restaurant*

Market Street Clifden Co Galway
RESTAURANT | Tel: 095 21450

O'Grady's was the first place to give Clifden a reputation as a good food town. In season (April-October) they're open for lunch and dinner an they certainly know how to cook seafood. Although the classics are still in there somewhere, the menu has undergone some modernisation of late, possibly to bring the style more into line with its trendy sister restaurants Kirwan's Lane (Galway city) and Kirwan's on the Mall (Westport). Typical dishes include starters like confit of duck leg with caramelised plum sage mash and soy jus, and main courses such as cumin spiced monktail with coriander & citrus couscous and crispy eggplant, or roast duck breast with white pudding & mango stuffing and a smoked garlic jus. **Seats 90** (private room, 10) No smoking area L 12-2.30 Mon-Sat, D 6.30-10 Mon-Sat, all à la carte, house wine £12.50; sc discretionary. Closed Nov-Apr. MasterCard,Visa. **Directions:** Right in the centre of Clifden

---

Clifden ⚏ | *The Quay House*

Beach Road Clifden Co Galway
ACCOMMODATION | Tel: 095 21369 Fax: 095 21608 email: thequay@iol.ie

In a lovely location - the house is right on the harbour, with pretty water views when the tide is in - The Quay House was built around 1820. It has the distinction of being the oldest building in Clifden and has also had a surprisingly varied usage: it was originally the harbourmaster's house, then a convent, then a monastery, was converted into a hotel at the turn of the century and finally, since 1993, has been enjoying its most recent incarnation as specialist accommodation in the incomparable hands of long-time hoteliers, Paddy and Julia Foyle. Accommodation is in a growing number of airy, wittily decorated and sumptuously comfortable rooms, which includes not only two wheelchair-friendly rooms but a whole new development alongside the original house - seven stunning new studio rooms with small fitted kitchens and balconies overlooking the harbour. As in the older rooms, excellent bathrooms all have full bath and shower. Evening meals are no longer served at Quay House, but guests can be booked into the Foyles' restaurant, Destrys, just up the road. Breakfast, including delicious freshly-baked breads and scones straight from the Aga, is served in the conservatory (Open to non-residents). Although officially closed in winter it is always worth inquiring. Children under 12 free in parents' room (cots available). No pets. **Rooms 14** (all en-suite, 2 for disabled). B&B £40pps, ss £10. Wheelchair access. Closed Nov-Mar. Amex, MasterCard, Visa. **Directions:** Overlooking Clifden harbour - follow sign to the Beach Road

Clifden — *Rock Glen Country House Hotel*

Ballyconneely Road Clifden Co Galway
HOTEL/RESTAURANT   Tel: 095 21035 Fax: 095 21737 email: rockglen@iol.ie

Built in 1815 as a shooting lodge for Clifden Castle, Rock Glen is now run by the Roche family as a delightful hotel - beautifully situated in quiet grounds well away from the road, it enjoys views over a sheltered anchorage. The public rooms and some of the bedrooms have the full advantage of the view, but the whole hotel is very restful and comfortable, with a pleasing outlook from all windows. Rooms are furnished in country house style, with good bathrooms (all have a full bath and over-bath shower) and amenities - some, such as tea/coffee trays, are not in the rooms but available on request. In addition to local activities - fishing, pony trekking, golf - there's a putting green on site, also all-weather tennis and croquet; indoors there are plenty of places to read quietly and a full size snooker table. Children welcome - under 4s free in parents' room, cots available. Pets permitted by arrangement, in some areas. **Rooms 26** (1 suite, 2 mini-suites). B&B £60pps, ss £30. service 12.5%. Wheelchair access, lift. Closed 24-26 Dec & Good Fri. Amex, Diners, Visa. **Restaurant:** John Roche, who has been in charge of the kitchen for many years, now has more assistance with this side of the hotel. Considerately, five-course menus are also available as individually priced courses (ie semi à la carte); local ingredients, especially seafood, play a major role in an updated country house style and classics like roast rack of Connemara lamb with ratatouille, green beans and rosemary jus are still very much on the menu. A typical seafood dish might be halibut and brill served as a duo, with sauteed spinach, red onion compote & tarragon butter sauce. Finish with tempting desserts - biscotti of poached nectarine, perhaps, with mascarpone cream & glazed meringue - or Irish farmhouse cheese & biscuits. Service is friendly and efficient and an excellent breakfast is served in the restaurant. **Seats 60:** No-smoking restaurant. D 7-9 daily, all à la carte, house wine £12.50; sc 12.5%. Toilets wheelchair accessible. **Directions:** N57from Galway, 1.5 miles from Clifden on Ballyconneely road.

Clifden — *Station House Hotel*

Clifden Co Galway
HOTEL   Tel: 095 21699 Fax: 095 21667

Built on the site of the late lamented railway station this large new hotel comes complete with leisure centre and conference/banqueting facilities 250/180). Public areas are impressively spacious and modern, while bedrooms are a good size, contemporary in style and comfortably furnished with ISDN lines as well as more usual amenities such as direct-dial phones, tea/coffee making and TV. The old Station House has become a themed bar and restaurant and the complex includes a wide range of shops and boutiques. Children welcome (under 12s free in parents' room; cots available). Pets permitted by arrangement. **Rooms 78** (10 executive rooms, 1 shower only, 48 no-smoking, 3 for disabled) B&B £25pps, ss £10. Wheelchair access. Closed 25 Dec. Amex, Diners, MasterCard, Visa. **Directions:** Follow N59 from Galway city

Clifden — *O'Grady's Sunnybank House*

Clifden Co Galway
ACCOMMODATION   Tel: 095 21437 Fax: 095 21976

Set in its own mature gardens, with panoramic views, Sunnybank is owned and run by the O'Grady family, of O'Grady's restaurant. They offer exceptional facilities (including ISDN lines as well as phone, tea/coffee-making and TV with video channel) at reasonable prices: as well as very comfortably appointed en-suite bedrooms and day rooms for guests' use. There is also a heated swimming pool, sauna and tennis court. Not suitable for children under 7; no pets. **Rooms 8** (all en-suite, 4 no-smoking, 2 for disabled guests), B&B £30 pps, ss £10. Closed Nov-Mar MasterCard, Visa. **Directions:** From Galway - right at Esso station & left after RC church; from Wesport - right before church.

Costello 🏛   *Fermoyle Lodge*

Costello Co Galway
COUNTRYHOUSE   Tel: 091 786111 Fax: 091 786154

One of Ireland's best-kept secrets, Nicola Stronach's delightful sporting lodge seems to enjoy the best of all possible worlds. Although only 29 miles from Galway, it's hidden from the road in one of the wildest and most remote parts of Connemara. Protected by mature woodland and shrubs, it has stunning lake and mountain views, with both salmon and sea trout fishing on the doorstep. All this and creature comforts too. The spacious, well-proportioned house has been sensitively renovated and beautifully furnished and decorated. Nicola has used the best of materials wisely, in a warm, low-key style that allows for every comfort without detracting from the wonderful setting that is its greatest attribute. Bedrooms are all very comfortable, with private bathrooms. A set dinner (£25) is served at 7.30 - 24 hour notice is required and any particular dislikes or allergies should be mentioned on booking. **Rooms 6** (all en-suite). B&B £45pps, ss £10. Closed Nov-Mar. MasterCard, Visa. **Directions:** From Galway, take N59 to Clifden. At Oughterard turn left just before the bridge signed Costello - Lodge is 11 miles along this road on right.

Craughwell 🏛   *St Clerans*

Craughwell Co Galway
COUNTRYHOUSE   Tel: 091 846555 Fax: 091 846600 email: stcleran@iol.ie

Previously the home of John Huston, St Clerans is a magnificent manor house beautifully located in rolling countryside. It has been carefully restored by the current owner, the American entertainer Merv Griffin, and decorated with no expense spared to make a sumptuous, hedonistically luxurious country retreat, operating under the management of Elizabeth O'Mahony. The decor, which is for the most part elegant, with some regard for period tastes, does occasionally go right over the top - as evidenced in the carpets in the hall and drawing room. But there's a great sense of fun about the furnishing and everything is of the best possible quality. As to the accommodation, each room is individually decorated and most are done in what might best be described as an upbeat country house style. Others - particularly those on the lower ground floor, including John Huston's own favourite room, which opens out onto a terrace with steps up to the garden - are restrained, almost subdued, in atmosphere. All are spacious, with luxuriously appointed bathrooms (one has its original shower only) and a wonderful away-from-it-all feeling. Small conferences/private parties (25). Children under 12 free in parents' room. No pets. **Rooms 12** (all en-suite) B&B £112.50pps, ss £112.50. Wheelchair access. Open all year. Amex, MasterCard, Visa. **Restaurant:** The restaurant, which is open to non-residents by reservation, provides an elegant setting for Japanese head chef Hisashi Kumagai's cooking. Menus change daily but the style is an unusual mixture of Japanese and international cuisine - is seen in specialities such as millefeuille of panfried shark with risotto, sundried tomato citrus beurre blanc & sevruga caviar, while local ingredients like farmed venison are seen in dishes like noisette of venison with woodland mushroom ragout and madeira sauce. **Seats 24** (private room, 24). D 7-9.30 daily, Set D £34, house wine £16.50; sc discretionary. **Directions:** 5 minutes off main Dublin-Galway road (N6), just outside village of Craughwell.

Craughwell   *Raftery's, The Blazers Bar*

Craughwell Co Galway
BAR   Tel: 091 846708 Fax: 091 846004

Donald and Theresa Raftery's famous family-run establishment is on the main Galway-Dublin road and is the meeting place for the well-known Galway Blazers Hunt, who are kennelled close by. It can make a handy stopping place: bar food is served every day - house specialities are seafood chowder, smoked salmon and home-made brown bread. Bar Food: 10.30-8 Mon-Sat (Sun to 6.30). Closed 25 Dec & Good Fri. Amex, MasterCard, Visa. **Directions:** On N6 between Loughrea and Galway

Furbo   *Connemara Coast Hotel*

Furbo Co Galway
HOTEL   Tel: 091 592108 Fax: 091 592065 email: sinnott@iol.ie

Like the other Sinnott hotels - Connemera Gateway and Brooks Hotel in Dublin - this beautifully located hotel is an attractive building which makes the best possible use of the site without intruding on the surroundings. Set on the sea side of the road, in its own extensive grounds, it is hard to credit that Galway city is only a 10 minute drive away. An impressive foyer decorated with fresh flowers sets the tone on entering, public areas are spacious and facilities are particularly good - a fine bar, two restaurants, a children's playroom and a leisure centre (which now has a Canadian hot tub) among them. A programme of upgrading bedrooms is underway and a new executive/bridal suite is to be included. Conference facilities for up to 450 delegates, with business centre/secretarial back-up and video conferencing on request. A range of special breaks is available. Children under 2 free in parents' room; cots available. No pets. **Rooms 112** (1 suite, 9 executive rooms). B&B £75pps, ss £25. Wheelchair access. Closed 25 Dec. & Good Fri. Amex, Diners, MasterCard, Visa. **Directions:** 6 miles from Galway city on Spiddal road

---

Galway   *Ardawn House*

31 College Road Galway Co Galway
ACCOMMODATION   Tel: 091 568833 Fax: 091 563454 email: ardawn@iol.ie

Mike and Breda Guiloyle's hospitable guesthouse is easily found, just a few minutes walk from Eyre Square. Accommodation is all en-suite and rooms are comfortably furnished, with good amenities. But it's Mike and Breda who make Ardawn House special - they take great pride in every aspect of the business, (including an extensive breakfast) and also help guests to get the very best out of their visit to Galway. Children welcome (unders 2s free in parents' room). No pets. **Rooms 8** (8 shower only, all no-smoking). B&B £40pps, ss £15. Closed 22-26 Dec Amex, MasterCard, Visa. **Directions:** Off N6, take city last exit; follow signs to city centre. First house on right after greyhound track.

Galway   *Ardilaun House Hotel*

Taylor's Hill Galway Co Galway
HOTEL   Tel: 091 521433 Fax: 091 521546 email: ardilaun@iol.ie

Ardilaun House Hotel is convenient to the city but its wooded grounds give it a country feeling. Friendly, helpful staff make a good impression on arrival and everything about the hotel - which has recently been extensively renovated, extended and refurbished - confirms the feeling of a well-run establishment. Public areas are spacious, elegantly furnished and some - notably the dining room - overlook gardens at the back. Bedrooms are furnished to a high standard (and have ISDN lines), current in-house leisure facilities include billiards and a new leisure centre opened in 1999. Purpose-built conference facilities offer a wide range of options for large and small groups (max 450), with back-up business services. Attractive banqueting facilities are especially suitable for weddings (up to 270 guests). Children welcome (cots available). Pets permitted. **Rooms 89** (1 suite, 2 mini-suites, 4 executive rooms, 6 shower only, 4 no-smoking, 3 for disabled). B&B £65pps, ss £15. Wheelchair access. Lift. Closed 23-28 Dec. Amex, Diners, MasterCard, Visa. **Directions:** Take signposts for Salthill

---

Galway   *Brennan's Yard Hotel*

Lower Merchants Road Galway Co Galway
HOTEL   Tel: 091 568166 Fax: 091 568262

Located close to Spanish Arch, in a characterful stone building, Brennans Yard first opened in 1992 and a second phase of the development was due to go ahead a couple of years later. It is an interesting hotel - all rooms were individually designed with country pine antiques and Irish craft items, giving the hotel special character. A major expansion and renovation programme saw 25 new rooms added in 1999 and original rooms were refurbished to the same standard, the restaurant was also redecorated, a new bar built and, finally the long-promised new reception and lobby area completed. Children under 12 free in parents' room; cots available. Parking in nearby carpark. **Rooms 45** (10 no-smoking, 1 for disabled). B&B £47.50pps, ss £12.50. Wheelchair access, Lift. Closed 24-28 Dec. Amex, Diners, MasterCard, Visa. **Directions:** In Galway city centre, beside Spanish Arch

---

Galway   *Corrib Great Southern Hotel*

Dublin Road Galway Co Galway
HOTEL   Tel: 091 755281 Fax: 091 751390

This large modern hotel overlooks Galway Bay and has good facilities for business guests and family holidays (ask about their Weekend Specials). Public areas include O'Malleys Pub, which has sea views, and a quieter residents' lounge; in summer evening entertainment and crèche facilities are laid on. Bedrooms vary considerably; the best are spacious and well planned, with stylish bathrooms. An excellent business/convention centre has facilities for groups from 8 to 750, with video-conferencing and back-up facilities available; banqueting for up to 550. Children under 2 free in parents' room, cots available, children's teas (5-6pm) creche. Leisure centre. No pets. Own parking. **Rooms 180** (suites 4, mini-suites 3, executive 60, no-smoking 19, disabled 2). B&B £80 pps, ss £22. Lift. Closed 24-26 Dec. Amex, Diners, MasterCard, Visa. **Directions:** Off main Dublin road into Galway city.

Galway   *Galway Ryan Hotel & Leisure Club*

                                Dublin Road Galway City East Co Galway
HOTEL   Tel: 091 753181 Fax: 091 753187

Only a mile or so from the city centre, this hotel makes a useful base for business or leisure. En-suite bedrooms have baths and showers and are of a good standard throughout. There is desk space for business guests and 24 hour room service. Meeting rooms (for up to 3 people) are available and there is an exceptional leisure centre. Friendly staff and good facilities for children (under 2s free in parents room, cots available) make the Ryan an excellent base for a family holiday. No pets. Own parking. **Rooms 94** (10 executive rooms, 10 no-smoking, 1 for disabled). B&B £55pps, ss £25. Wheelchair access, Lift. Open all year. Amex, Diners, MasterCard, Visa. **Directions:** On Galway-Dublin road, just outside Galway city.

Galway   *Glenlo Abbey Hotel*

                                Bushypark Galway Co Galway
HOTEL   Tel: 091 526666 Fax: 091 527800 email: glenlo@iol.ie

Originally an eighteenth century residence, Glenlo Abbey is just two and a half miles from Galway city yet offers all the advantages of the country - the hotel is on a 138-acre estate, with its own golf course and Pavilion. It enjoys views over Lough Corrib and the surrounding countryside. The scale of the hotel is generous throughout, public rooms are impressive and bedrooms are well-furnished with good amenities and marbled bathrooms. The old Abbey has been restored to provide privacy for meetings and private dining, and there is a fully equipped business service bureau to back up seminars, conferences and presentations; (conference/banqueting 250/170). For indoor relaxation there's the Oak Cellar bar (where light food is served) and, in addition to the classical River Room restaurant, the hotel operates an historic Pullman train carriage as a restaurant in the hotel grounds - it's in beautiful order, has a great atmosphere and, needless to say, makes a meal here a memorable event. No pets. Own parking. **Rooms 46** (2 suites, 2 mini-suites, 2 shower only). B&B £109.50pps, ss £52.50. Wheelchair access, Lift. Open all year. Amex, Diners, MasterCard, Visa. **Directions:** 2.5 miles from Galway city on N59 in direction of Clifden

---

Galway   *Great Southern Hotel*

                                Eyre Square Galway Co Galway
HOTEL   Tel: 091 564041 Fax: 091 566704 email: res@galway.gsh.ie

Overlooking Eyre Square right in the heart of Galway, this historic railway hotel was built in 1845 and has retained many of its original features and old-world charm which mixes easily with modern facilities. Public rooms - notably the foyer - are quite grand. There's a country style bar, O'Flahertys Pub, down in the basement (with access from the Square or the hotel) in addition to the hotel cocktail lounge. Bedrooms, which vary somewhat but are generally spacious and comfortable, are traditionally furnished with dark mahogany and brass light fittings. Conference/banqueting (350/300); back-up business facilities and video-conferencing. Indoor swimming pool. Children under 2 free in parents' room, cots available. No pets. Arrangement with nearby carpark. **Rooms 116** (3 suites, 20 executive rooms, 8 no-smoking, 1 for disabled). B&B £87.50pps, ss £22. Wheelchair access, Lift. Closed 24-26 Dec. Amex, Diners, MasterCard, Visa. **Directions:** In centre of city overlooking Eyre Square

---

Galway ✗   *Jurys Galway Inn*

                                Quay Street Galway Co Galway
HOTEL   Tel: 091 566444 Fax: 091 568415 email: tara-flynn@jurys.com

Jurys Galway Inn is magnificently sited to make the most of both the river - which rushes past almost all the bedroom windows - and the great buzz of the Spanish Arch area of the city (just outside the door). Like the other Jurys room-only 'inns', the hotel offers a good standard of basic accommodation without frills. Rooms are large (sleeping up to four people) and well finished, with everything required for comfort and convenience - ample well-lit work/shelf space, neat en-suite bathroom, TV, phone - but no extras. Beds are generous, with good-quality bedding, and open wardrobes are more than adequate. Neat tea/coffee-making facilities are built into the design, but there is no room service. Public areas include an impressive, well-designed foyer with seating areas, a pubby bar with good atmosphere and self-service cafeteria. Arrangement with next door car park. Acc££. Closed 25 & 26 Dec. Amex, Diners, MasterCard, Visa.

Galway ✗   *K C Blakes*

10 Quay Street Galway Co Galway
RESTAURANT   Tel: 091 561826 Fax: 091 561829

K C Blakes is named after a stone Tower House, of a type built sometime between 1440 and 1640, which stands as a typical example of the medieval stone architecture of the ancient city of Galway. The Casey's new restaurant, with all its sleek black designer style and contemporary chic could not present a stronger contrast to such a building. The head chef is John Casey, previously the chef at his family restaurant Westwood Bistro - which recently became the new Westwood Hotel, under new ownership. True to form, he sources ingredients for K C Blakes with care and cooks with skill to produce dishes ranging from traditional Irish (beef and Guinness stew), new Irish cuisine (black pudding croquettes with pear & cranberry sauce), classical French (sole meunière) to Global cuisine (a huge choice here - let's say chicken fajita). It's a remarkable operation, aimed at a wide market and keenly priced. No parking. L£ Mon-Fri, D££ daily. Closed 25 Dec. Amex, MasterCard, Visa.

Galway 🏛   *Killeen House*

Bushypark Galway Co Galway
Tel: 091 524179 Fax: 091 528065
COUNTRYHOUSE   email: killeenhouse@ireland.com

Catherine Doyle's delightful house really has the best of both worlds. It's on the Clifden road just on the edge of Galway city yet, with 25 acres of private grounds and gardens reaching down to the shores of Lough Corrib, offers all the advantages of the country, too. The house was built in 1840 and has all the features of a more leisurely era, when space was plentiful - not only in the reception rooms, which include an elegant dining room overlooking the gardens (where delicious breakfasts are served in style), but also the bedrooms. These are luxuriously and individually furnished (1 shower only), each in a different period, e.g. Regency, Edwardian and (most fun this one) Art Nouveau. Not suitable for children under 12. No pets. Garden. Own parking. **Rooms 5** (1 shower only). B&B £45pps, ss £20. Lift. Closed Xmas week. Amex, Diners, MasterCard, Visa. **Directions:** On N59 between Galway city and Moycullen village.

Galway ✗   *Kirbys of Cross Street*

Cross Street Galway Co Galway
RESTAURANT   Tel: 091 569404 Fax: 091 569403

One of a trio of establishments situated (the others are two of Galway's leading pubs, Busker Browne's and The Slate House), this dashingly informal two-storey restaurant offers contemporary cuisine in specialities like grilled black & white seafood pudding on a seafood vegetable salad. No-smoking area; air conditioning. Children over 7 welcome. No parking. **Seats 80.** L&D daily. Closed 25 Dec. Amex, Diners, MasterCard, Visa. **Directions:** City centre - on corner of Cross Street and Kirwan's Lane.

Galway   *Kirwan's Lane Restaurant*

Kirwan's Lane Galway Co Galway
RESTAURANT   Tel/Fax: 091 568266

Clifden man Michael O'Grady is the chef-proprietor at this classy contemporary restaurant in a laneway just beside the Hotel Spanish Arch. It's been open since 1996, but it's been such a success that it was doubled in size last year. Menus offer a wide choice of international dishes based on local ingredients - tian of crab, lemon & coriander monktail - sometimes with a pleasing leaning towards New Irish Cuisine. Evening menus are slightly more formal, but in both cases à la carte menus which are not overlong are offered and the style is similar. Live piano playing sometimes adds to the atmosphere -

don't forget that booking is strongly advised, as this is one of Galway's most popular restaurants. Not suitable for children under 7. No parking (multi-storey carpark nearby). **Seats 50.** No smoking area; air conditioning. L 12.30-2.30, D 6.30-10.30 Mon-Sat, all à la carte, house wine £12.95; sc discretionary. Toilets wheelchair accessible. Closed Sun & 24-30 Dec. Amex, MasterCard, Visa. **Directions:** Just off Cross Street and Quay Street

Galway   *The Malt House*

Old Malt Shopping Mall High Street Galway Co Galway
RESTAURANT   Tel: 091 567866 Fax: 091 563993

The Cunningham's welcoming old restaurant and bar in a quiet cul-de-sac laneway off High Street has great character and a friendly attitude. There's a lunchtime bar menu with soups and salads, served with good home-made bread, popular hot seafood dishes - baked garlic mussels, panfried crab claws - steaks and vegetarian dishes; a nice note - they will serve the restaurant menu in the bar if required. Dinner menus are more formal but the emphasis is still on fairly traditional dishes - and none the worse for that. The Malt House has a loyal and well-deserved local following and plans are in progress to extend the restaurant into the courtyard at the front. No parking. **Seats 50.** No smoking restaurant; air conditioning. L 12.30-2.30, D 6.30-10.30 Mon-Sat also Bar Food, Set L £13.50, Set D £13.95-22.50, à la carte available, house wine £10.95; sc discretionary. Toilets wheelchair accessible. Closed Sundays & Xmas week. Amex, Diners, MasterCard, Visa. **Directions:** Restaurant is in an alleyway to the left off High Street towards Spanish Arch.

Galway   *McDonagh's Seafood House*

22 Quay Street Galway Co Galway
RESTAURANT   Tel: 091 565001 Fax: 091 562246

This unusual restaurant is a fish shop during the day - they buy whole catches from local fishermen and have it on sale in the shop within a couple of hours of leaving the boat. Buying the whole catch guarantees the wide variety the shop is famous for. Then, when it comes to the cooking, there's the fish & chips operation - select your variety and see it cooked in front of you. On the other side of the shop is the Seafood bar, a more formal restaurant where an extensive range of dishes is offered. They even do their own smoking on the premises and fish caught by anglers can be brought in and smoked to take home - and they do party food, too. The family also owns the dashing Hotel Spanish Arch (091 569600) a couple of doors up the street. Arrangement with nearby carpark. **Seats 42.** No smoking area; air conditioning. L 12-2.30 daily, D 5-10 Mon-Sat, Set L £8.75, Set D £15-25, à la carte available, house wine £10.50; sc discretionary. Toilets wheelchair accessible. Closed Xmas-New Year. Diners, MasterCard, Visa. **Directions:** Near Jury's Hotel, Spanish Arch.

Galway ˣ   *Nimmo's*

Spanish Arch Long Walk Galway Co Galway
RESTAURANT   Tel: 091 563565 Fax: 091 846403

Stephan Zeltner-Healy, chef-proprietor at this extraordinarily old waterside restaurant just through the Spanish Arch, is a very fine chef indeed, as regular visitors to his previous tiny restaurant over Tigh Neachtain pub may remember. Here he is in another tiny restaurant, presenting the same inscrutable menus. Other chefs over-write menus, giving lengthy descriptions for every dish - with Stephan every order is an adventure. It all sounds quite ordinary, so be prepared! Everything is based on carefully sourced seasonal local ingredients - and Stephan's cooking is excellent. D££ Mon-Sat & Sun Bank Hol wkends. Closed 25 Dec & 1 Jan, Mon low season. Amex, MasterCard, Visa.

Galway   *Norman Villa*

86 Lower Salthill Galway Co Galway
ACCOMMODATION   Tel/Fax: 091 521131 email: normanvilla@oceanfree.net

Dee and Mark Keogh's guesthouse is exquisite. It's a lovely old house, immaculately maintained and imaginatively converted to make the most of every inch, ensuring guest comfort without spoiling the interior proportions. It's dashingly decorated, with lovely rich colours. A great collection of modern paintings looks especially magnificent juxtaposed with antique furniture. Dee and Mark are dedicated hosts, too. The only catch is that Norman Villa's well-deserved popularity makes it necessary to book well in advance, which does involve planning a long time ahead, but is well worth the effort.(But cancellations can occur, so do call for an impulse break anyway.) Not suitable for children under 2. Garden. No pets. Own parking. **Rooms 5** (all shower only, all no-smoking) B&B £35pps, ss £5. Closed early Jan-mid Feb. MasterCard, Visa. **Directions:** Follow signs from Galway city centre to Salthill, then Lower Salthill - house is beside P. J. Flaherty's Pub.

Galway ❋ *Park House Hotel*

Forster Street Eyre Square Galway Co Galway
HOTEL   Tel: 091 564924 Fax: 091 569219 email: parkhousehotel@tinet.ie

This attractive, owner-run hotel just off Eyre Square is furnished to a high standard and warmly decorated throughout. Providing a high level of personal service is a particular point of pride, making this an especially comfortable base for visitors on business or leisure. There are facilities for small conferences and banqueting (40/50) and one of the hotel's greatest assets in this busy city is a private residents' car park. Children welcome (under 12s free in parents' room, cots available). No pets. **Rooms 57** (all en-suite, 1 for disabled). B&B £57.50pps, ss £22.50. Wheelchair access, Lift. Closed 24-26 Dec. Amex, Diners, MasterCard, Visa. **Directions:** City centre, off Eyre Square

Galway *Tigh Neachtain*

Cross Street Galway Co Galway
PUB   Tel: 091 568820

Tigh Neachtain is one of Galway's oldest pubs - the origins of the building are medieval - and it has been in the same family for a century. Quite unspoilt, it has great charm and a friendly atmosphere - the pint is good and there's bar food. But perhaps the nicest thing of all is the way an impromptu traditional music session can get going at the drop of a hat. Closed 25 Dec & Good Fri. No credit cards.

Galway *Westwood House Hotel*

Dangan Upper Newcastle Galway Co Galway
HOTEL   Tel: 091 521442 Fax: 091 521400 email: westwoodhotel@tinet.ie

This new hotel was just opening as we went to press. It is in the same group as the Schoolhouse Hotel in Dublin and the Station House Hotel, Clifden (see entries). Well located, on the edge Galway and convenient to both the city and Connemara, it's set well back from the road and offers a high standard of accommodation for business and leisure at fairly reasonable prices. Conference facilities (400) with back-up services; ISDN lines in bedrooms. A range of 2-3 night leisure breaks offers particularly good value. Children welcome (under 2s free in parents' room, cots available). Pets permitted in some areas. Own parking. **Rooms 58** (6 suites, 8 executive rooms). B&B £49pps, ss £20. Wheelchair access, Lift. Closed 24-25 Dec. Amex, Diners, MasterCard, Visa. **Directions:** On edge of Galway city, take the Clifden road

Headford *Lisdonagh House*

Caherlistrane Headford Co Galway
COUNTRYHOUSE   Tel: 093 31163 Fax: 093 31528 email: lisdonag@iol.ie

Situated about 15 minutes drive north of Galway city in the heart of hunting and fishing country, Lisdonagh house is on an elevated site with beautiful views overlooking Lake Hackett. It is a lovely property, with large well-proportioned reception rooms, a fine staircase and luxurious bedrooms, furnished with antiques and decorated in period style, with marbled bathrooms to match. A 4-course residents' dinner (choice limited to one of two main courses), £25, is served between 7.30 and 9.30. House wine £12. Small conferences/private parties for up to 30. Children welcome (under 2s free in parents' room, cots available). Pets permitted. **Rooms 10** (6 executive rooms, 3 shower only, 5 no-smoking, 3 for disabled) B&B £60pps, ss £20. Wheelchair access. Closed 1 Dec-1 Mar. Amex, MasterCard, Visa. **Directions:** From Oranmore roundabout, through Claregalway on to N17 for 16 miles, turn off at R333 through Belclare to Caherlistrane.

Inishbofin *Day's Hotel*

Middle Quarter Inishbofin Island Co Galway
HOTEL   Tel: 095 45809 Fax: 095 45803

This modest, but hospitable family-run hotel beside the harbour has been first (and last) port of call for many visitors to the island over the years. Plans are currently afoot to upgrade the hotel substantially. Off-season, inquire about the availability of food and drink on the island. No pets. **Rooms 14** (8 en-suite). B&B £30.35pps, no ss. Wheelchair access. Closed Oct-Mar. Amex, MasterCard, Visa. **Directions:** Ferries to the island run regularly from Cleggan, with ticket offices in Clifden (regular buses between Clifden and Cleggan) and also at Kings of Cleggan. For bookings and enquiries, phone: 095 4464 or 095 21520. Credit card bookings are accepted.

Kilcolgan [PUB★]   *Moran's Oyster Cottage*

The Weir Kilcolgan Co Galway
PUB/RESTAURANT   Tel: 091 796113 Fax: 091 79650

This is just the kind of Irish pub that people everywhere dream about. It's as pretty as a picture, with a well-kept thatched roof and a lovely waterside location (with plenty of seats outside where you can while away the time and watch the swans floating by). It's also brilliantly well-run by the Moran family - and so it should be, after all they've had six generations to practise. They're famed throughout the country for their wonderful local seafood, especially the native oysters (from their own oyster beds) which are in season from September to April. Willie Moran is an ace oyster opener, a regular champion in the famous annual competitions held in the locality. Farmed Gigas oysters are on the menu all year. Then there's chowder and smoked salmon and seafood cocktail and mussels and, perhaps best of all, delicious crab sandwiches and salads. Morans was our 1999 Seafood Pub of the Year Meals 11.30-10.30 daily. House wine £11. Closed 25 Dec & Good Fri. Amex, MasterCard, Visa. **Directions:** Just off the Galway-Limerick road, signed between Clarenbridge and Kilcolgan.

Kinvara ✗   *Merriman Hotel*

Main Street Kinvara Co Galway
HOTEL   Tel: 091 638222 Fax: 091 637686

Claiming to be the largest thatched building in Ireland, the Merriman Hotel is in the main street of Kinvara and has filled a gap by providing good middle-range accommodation in the area. They are working hard to ensure standards of service and accommodation are as high as possible. Special breaks are sometimes offered- an inquiry is worthwhile. Acc££. Closed Jan & Feb. Amex, Diners, MasterCard, Visa.

Kinvara ✗   *Tully's*

Kinvara Co Galway
PUB   Tel: 091 637146

Definitely a spot for traditional music, this is a real local pub in the old tradition, with a little grocery shop at the front and stone-floored bar at the back. Tully's has a fine old stove in the bar for cosy winter sessions, which is always a good sign (They also have a small enclosed garden with a few parasoled tables for fine weather.) Not a food place, although sandwiches, teas and coffees are always available. Normal pub hours. Closed 25 Dec & Good Fri. No credit cards.

Kylemore   *Kylemore Abbey Restaurant*

Kylemore Co Galway
RESTAURANT   Tel/Fax: 095 41146   email: enquiries@kylemoreabbey.ie

Kylemore Abbey, with its stunning mountain and waterside setting, would make a dramatic location for any enterprise. But what the Benedictine nuns are doing here is truly astonishing. The abbey is not only home for the nuns but is also run as an international girls' boarding school. In addition, the nuns run a farm and a restored walled garden, which is open to the public. A short walk further along the wooded shore leads to the Gothic church, a miniature replica of Norwich cathedral. In a neat modern building beside the carpark is one of the country's best craft shops - and an excellent restaurant. Everything at this daytime self-service restaurant is made on the premises, and the range of wholesome offerings includes a good selection of hot and cold savoury dishes, including several vegetarian options - typically black-eye bean casserole or vegetarian lasagne. Home baking is a special strength and big bowls of the nuns' renowned home-made jams are set up at the till, for visitors to help themselves. Beside them are neatly labelled jars to buy and take home. Wheelchair accessible (including toilets). [*Opening in spring 2000: the Garden Tea House, in the restored walled garden, will be open Easter-October,10-4.30.] **Seats 230.** Meals daily 9.30-5.30; Closed Nov-mid Mar. MasterCard, Visa. **Directions:** 2 1/2 miles from Letterfrack, on the N59.

Leenane

Delphi Lodge

Leenane Co Galway

COUNTRYHOUSE Tel: 095 42222 Fax: 095 42296 email: delfish@iol.ie

One of Ireland's most famous sporting lodges, Delphi Lodge was built in the early 19th-century by the Marquis of Sligo. It is beautifully located in an unspoilt valley, surrounded by the region's highest mountains (with the high rainfall dear to fisherfolk). Owned since 1986 by Peter and Jane Mantle - who have restored and extended the original building in period style - the lodge is large and impressive in an informal, understated way, with antiques, fishing gear and a catholic selection of reading matter creating a stylish yet relaxed atmosphere. The dozen guest rooms are all quite different, but they are en-suite (with proper baths) and very comfortably furnished (with lovely lake and mountain views). Dinner, for residents only, is taken at a long oak table. It is cooked by Frank Bennett, who has "a range of dishes that is vast and eclectic - some traditional, some 'nouveau', some oriental - and some Arabic" The famous Delphi Fishery is the main attraction, but people come for other country pursuits, or just peace and quiet. A billiard table, the library and a serious wine list can get visitors through a lot of wet days. Just across the road, four restored cottages offer self-catering accommodation. Small conferences/banqueting (20/26). Not suitable for children. No pets. **Rooms 12** (all en-suite). B&B £50.60pps, ss £20. Closed mid Dec-mid Jan MasterCard, Visa. **Directions:** 8 miles north of Leenane on the Louisburgh road.

Leenane ✻

Killary Lodge

Leenane Co Galway

ACCOMMODATION Tel: 095 42276 / 095 42314 email: lodge@killary.com

Jamie and Mary Young opened their famous Little Killary Adventure Centre, six miles away, in 1981 then, in 1990, they developed the business a stage further to include the accommodation at Killary Lodge. Since then, the standard of accommodation has been steadily upgraded and it now offers a very comfortable place to stay in a beautiful location - and, although those with an interest in outdooor pursuits will get particular enjoyment from the many activities operating from here and Little Killary, it also makes an excellent base for visitors who simply wish to enjoy the area. Conferences and corporate activities (team building etc) are among the many programmes offered at this unusual establishment - contact the manager for further details. **Rooms 21** (all en-suite). B&B £37pps, ss £20. Closed Dec-Mar. MasterCard, Visa. **Directions:** 4km outside Leenane on Clifden road (N59)

Leenane

Portfinn Lodge

Leenane Co Galway
Tel: 095 42265 Fax: 095 42315

RESTAURANT/ACCOMMODATION email: rorydaly@anu.ie

There are few views in Ireland to beat the sight of the sun sinking behind the mountains over Killary harbour. On a good evening that's something you can look forward to at Rory and Brid Daly's seafood restaurant, Portfinn Lodge. The dining area is in a room of the main house and an adjoining conservatory. The lobster tank at the entrance bodes well for a good meal - 90% of the menu will be seafood: prawns, salmon, brill, turbot and many of their cousins make a nightly appearance. There is plenty else to choose from, however, including local lamb in various guises and two vegetarian dishes daily. Good brown bread comes with country butter, which is quite a feature in these parts, and there's always an Irish cheeseboard. Not suitable for children under 12. **Seats 35.** No smoking area. D 6.30-9 daily, Set D £17.50, house wine £10; sc 10%. Closed 31 Oct-1 Apr. Diners, MasterCard, Visa. **Guesthouse:** Modest but comfortable accommodation is offered in eight neat purpose-built en-suite rooms, all sleeping three and one with four beds; one room has wheelchair access. Pets permitted. **Rooms 8** (all en-suite). B&B £22pps, ss £18, 10% sc. **Directions:** Midway between Westport and Clifden.

Letterfrack

Rosleague Manor

Letterfrack Co Galway

COUNTRYHOUSE/RESTAURANT Tel: 095 41101 Fax: 095 41168

A lovely pink-washed Regency house of gracious proportions and sensitively handled modernisation, Rosleague looks out over a tidal inlet through gardens planted with rare shrubs and plants. Although the area offers plenty of activity for the energetic, there is a deep sense of peace and it's hard to imagine anywhere better to recharge the soul; or the body, for that matter - breakfast, especially, is a feast of memorable wholesomeness, based on local and home-made speciality produce. Although more sophisticated, dinner - for which non-residents are welcome by reservation - shares the same respect for home-grown and local ingredients, including seafood straight from Cleggan harbour and, of course, the famous Connemara lamb. They grow their own basic vegetables, herbs and typical 'cottage garden' fruit like gooseberries and rhubarb, while more sophisticated produce, including Irish farmhouse cheeses, comes from Patrick Perceval's famous old-fashioned van delivery service. Pets permitted by arrangement. **Rooms 20** (4 mini-suites). B&B £60pps, ss £20 D £28.00. Licensed. Wheelchair access. Closed Nov-Easter. Amex, MasterCard, Visa. **Directions:** Entrance on N59 Main Road, 7 miles north of Clifden.

Moyard   *Garranbaun House*

Moyard Co Galway
COUNTRYHOUSE   Tel/Fax: 095 41649

In a spectacular position overlooking Ballynakill Bay, the Finnegans' imposing 19th century Georgian-style manor has wonderful views of the Twelve Bens, Diamond Hill and the Maam Turks - and there is a trout lake, Lough Garraunbaun, attached to the estate. Delia Finnegan is a most hospitable host, keeping her beautifully furnished house immaculate without spoiling the relaxed atmosphere. Books, turf fires and a grand piano say a lot about the things that bring people here - and Delia's cooking, of course. The organic garden, free range chicken and eggs provide an excellent base for her dinners; also wild local lobster, oysters, shrimps, scallops, salmon and Connemara lamb. Cheeses served are all Irish and baking of bread and scones is a daily event. Not suitable for children under 12. No pets. **Rooms 3** (2 en-suite, all no-smoking). B&B £35pps, no ss. Open all year. Visa. **Directions:** From Clifden, take Westport road - 6 miles on, there's a sign on the left.

Moyard   *Rose Cottage*

Rockfield Moyard Co Galway
FARMHOUSE   Tel/Fax: 095 41082 email: conamara@indigo.ie

This long-established farmhouse is situated on a working farm in a scenic location surrounded by the Twelve Bens mountains. It has moved into a new generation since Patricia O'Toole took over in 1997. Obviously already well prepared for the job (the family has always helped here), Patricia is full of energy and enthusiasm. Expect simple (but increasingly) comfortable accommodation and good home cooking (especially baking) and you won't be disappointed. There's a sitting room with an open turf fire (and television), a dining room for guests (separate tables) and bedrooms have tea/coffee making trays and hair dryers. Nearby attractions include sandy beaches, scenic walks, fishing, island trips, traditional Irish music, horse riding and golf. No pets. **Rooms 8** (6 shower only). B&B £20pps, no ss. Closed Nov-Mar. MasterCard, Visa. **Directions:** 6 miles from Clifden on Westport road.

Moycullen   *Moycullen Country House & Restaurant*

Moycullen Co Galway
Tel:091 555621 Fax: 091 555566
COUNTRYHOUSE/RESTAURANT   email: moycullenhouse@iol.ie

Overlooking Lough Corrib, and set peacefully in 30 acres of rhododendrons and azaleas, Moycullen House was built as a sporting lodge in the arts and crafts style at the beginning of the century. Large bedrooms furnished with antiques all have private baths and there's a spacious residents' sitting room with an open log fire. Children welcome; under 5s free in parents' room, cot/extra bed available; baby-sitting by arrangement. **Rooms 3** (1 min-suite, all no-smoking). B&B £40 pps, ss£15. Closed 23-27 Dec & mid Jan-1 Mar. Amex, Diners, MasterCard, Visa.

Moycullen House Restaurant

Richard and Louise Casburn added a new name to the list of must-visits in Moycullen in 1998 when they opened this very professionally run restaurant. A great deal of thought and work went into getting the changes right, and the effort has paid off handsomely. Louise looks after front-of-house. Richard's menus are ambitious but he offers a sensibly short à la carte with daily extras, eg seafood. The style is modern - dishes like prawn & crab tabbouleh salad with chive dressing; roast loin of lamb with a grain mustard crust and lightly minted jus convey the style. Presentation is not overworked and cooking is excellent. **Seats 40** D from £25, from 7 pm Thurs-Tues. **Directions:** N59 Galway to Moycullen; at cross roads, take left turn onto Spiddal road. Signed on left after about 1.5 Km.

Moycullen

RESTAURANT

White Gables Restaurant
Moycullen Village Co Galway
Tel: 091 555744 Fax: 091 556004

Kevin and Ann Dunne have been running this attractive cottagey restaurant on the main street of Moycullen since 1991 and it's now on many a regular diner's list of favourites. Open stonework, low lighting and candlelight (even at lunch time) create a soothing away-from-it-all atmosphere. Kevin sources ingredients with care and offers weekly-changing dinner and à la carte menus and a set Sunday lunch (which is enormously popular and has two sittings). Cooking is consistently good and, to indicate the style, you can expect hearty, wholesome dishes in specialities such as black and white pudding with wholegrain mustard sauce, good soups, roast half duckling with orange sauce and a range of seafood including lobster from their own tank. Beef as served for Sunday lunch is like no other. Good ices, soft fruit in season; friendly, efficient service. **Seats 45.** No smoking area; air conditioning. D 7-10 (daily in high season), L Sun only 12.30-2.30. Set Sun L £13.95 Set D £23.50. House wine £13; service discretionary. Toilets wheelchair accessible. Closed Mon low season & 23 Dec-14 Feb. Amex, Diners, MasterCard, Visa. **Directions:** On N59 in Moycullen village, 8 Km from Galway city.

Oranmore

HOTEL

Galway Bay Golf & Country Club Hotel
Renville Oranmore Co Galway
Tel: 091 790500 Fax: 091 790510/792510 email: gbaygolf@iol.ie

This rather handsome modern hotel, just eight miles from Galway city, looks out over an 18-hole championship golf course (designed by Christy O'Connor Jnr.) towards Galway Bay. It has a wide range of facilities for both business and leisure. Public areas include an impressively spacious lobby, large bar and a well-appointed restaurant with imaginative decor - all have views. Generous-sized bedrooms, which include six for wheelchair users and a high proportion of executive suites, are furnished to a high standard with well-designed bathrooms. A number of special packages are offered by the hotel, giving good value on both golf and non-golfing breaks. Conference/banqueting (120/200) with secretarial back-up. Children welcome (under 6s free in parents' room; cots available). No pets. **Rooms 92** (all en-suite, 53 suites, 6 rooms for disabled). Closed 25 Dec. B&B £45 pps, ss £15. Amex, Diners, MasterCard, Visa. **Directions:** Take Oranmore road from Galway city; hotel is 2 miles from Oranmore.

Oranmore

HOTEL

Quality Hotel & Leisure Centre
Oranmore Co Galway
Tel: 091 792244 Fax: 091 792246

This large new hotel is easy to find (a big plus for business locations) and offers a high standard of accommodation. Excellent leisure facilities include a 20-metre pool - and there's a selection of meeting rooms including a fine one on the top floor, overlooking the pool. Rooms 90 (20 no-smoking, 3 for disabled). B&B £45pps, ss £15. Annual Closures TBC. Amex, Diners, MasterCard, Visa. **Directions:** at the Oranmore roundabout on the main (N6) road.

Oughterard

HOTEL

Connemara Gateway Hotel
Oughterard Co Galway
Tel: 091 552328 Fax: 091 552332 email: sinnott@iol.ie

An attractive building set well back from the road, this low, neatly designed hotel creates a good impression from the outset. The large foyer has lots of comfortable seating in country-look chintz fabrics. Open turf fires are welcoming and an abundance of fresh and dried flower arrangements bring colour and add interest throughout, as does the work of local artists and sculptors. Bedrooms are variable (reflecting the hotel's origins as a 1960s motel) but all are comfortable, with considerate details (like a little washing line in the bathroom) and some have access to the garden at the back. No rooms designed for wheelchairs, but all are ground floor. There's quite a characterful public bar, used by locals as well as residents, a good leisure centre and a children's games room. Children under 2 free in parents' room; cots available. No pets. **Rooms 62.** (all en-suite, 1 mini-suite). B&B £60 pps, ss £17.50. Closed Amex, Diners, MasterCard, Visa. **Directions:** On the R336-approaching from Galway, the hotel is on the left just before Oughterard.

Oughterard

ACCOMMODATION

Corrib Wave
Portacarron Oughterard Co Galway
Tel: 091 552147 Fax: 091 552736

A fisherman's dream, Michael and Maria Healy's unpretentious waterside guesthouse offers warm family hospitality, comfortable accommodation (all en-suite), an open turf fire to relax by and real home cooking. All rooms have a double and single bed and some are suitable for families. Best of all at Corrib Wave is the location - utter peace and tranquillity. Golf and horseriding nearby and everything to do with fishing organised for you. **Rooms 10** (all en-suite). B&B £25, ss £8. Closed 1 Nov- 15 Mar. Diners MasterCard, Visa. **Directions:** From Galway, signed from N59, 1 Km before Oughterard.

Oughterard   *Currarevagh House*

Oughterard Co Galway
COUNTRYHOUSE   Tel: 091 552312 Fax: 091 552731

Tranquillity, trout and tea in the drawing room - these are the things that draw guests back to the Hodgson family's gracious, but not luxurious early Victorian manor overlooking Lough Corrib. Built in 1846, with 150 acres of woodlands and gardens and sporting rights over 5,000 acres, Currarevagh has been open to guests for over half a century. The present owners Harry and June Hodgson, are founder members of the Irish Country Houses and Restaurants Association (known as the Blue Book). Yet, while the emphasis is on old-fashioned service and hospitality, they are adamant that the atmosphere should be more like a private house party than a hotel, and their restful rituals underline the differences: the day begins with a breakfast worthy of its Edwardian origins, laid out on the sideboard in the dining room; lunch may be one of the renowned picnic hampers required by sporting folk. Then there's afternoon tea, followed by a leisurely dinner. Fishing is the ruling passion, of course - notably brown trout, pike, perch and salmon - but there are plenty of other country pursuits to assist in building up an appetite for June's simple cooking, all based on fresh local produce. Not suitable for children. Pets permitted by arrangement. Garden, tennis. **Rooms 15** (all en-suite). B&B £54 pps, ss £17.50. 10% service charge. Closed Nov-Mar. No credit cards.

Oughterard ✗   *Sweeney's Oughterard House*

Oughterard Co Galway
HOTEL   Tel: 091 091 552207

The Higgins family have owned and run this attractive creeper-clad old hotel for several generations. Prettily situated opposite the river and surrounded by mature trees (on the Clifden side of the town), it is genuinely old-fashioned with comfortable, cottagey public rooms furnished with antiques. Bedrooms vary considerably - some have four-posters. Fishing is the main attraction, but there are plenty of other outdoor pursuits including the gentle pleasure of taking tea on the lawn. Acc££-£££. Closed 22 Dec-mid-Jan.

Portumna   *Shannon Oaks Hotel & Country Club*

Portumna Co Galway
HOTEL   Tel: 0509 41777 Fax: 0509 41357 email: sales@shannonoaks.ie

Situated by the shores of Lough Derg, this attractive, privately-owned hotel opened in 1997. The interior is spacious, original and striking - echoing the themes of river and woodland. A large lobby sets the tone, with polished wooden floor, faux-marble pillaring featuring a winter treescape and ample, well-spaced seating in contemporary style. Public rooms include a warm-toned restaurant (the recent arrival of a highly-respected chef, Tommy Donovan, in summer 1999 bodes well for standards of the hotel's food), which can be opened up in summer, and a cosy, pub-like bar. Bedrooms are designed and finished to an exceptionally high standard, with air conditioning and fax/modem lines as standard. Thoughtful planning has also gone into the design of the conference and banqueting facilities (600/400) and there is a fine leisure centre with air-conditioned gymnasium. Children welcome (free in parents' room up to 16). No pets. **Rooms 63** (3 suites, 4 for disabled). B&B £55pps ss £20. Open all year. Amex, Diners, MasterCard, Visa. **Directions:** On St Joseph's road, Portumna.

Recess   *Ballynahinch Castle Hotel*

Recess Co Galway
HOTEL   Tel: 095 31006 Fax: 095 31085 email: bhinch@iol.ie

This crenellated Victorian mansion enjoys a most romantic position in ancient woodland on the banks of the Ballynahinch River. Renowned as a fishing hotel, it is impressive in scale and relaxed in atmosphere. This magic combination, plus a high level of comfort and friendliness (and an invigorating mixture of residents and locals in the bar at night) all combine to bring people back. Renovations and extensions have recently been undertaken, with great attention to period detail, a policy also carried through successfully in furnishing both public areas and bedrooms. Most bedrooms and some reception rooms - notably the dining room - have lovely views over the river. Facilities for small conferences (12). Garden, tennis. Children welcome (under 5s free in parents' room; cots available). No pets. **Rooms 40** (all en-suite, suites 3, executive 12) B&B £65 pps, ss £20. Bar meals12.30-3 & 6.30-9.30 daily. Closed Xmas week, Feb & Bank Hol. Amex, Diners, MasterCard, Visa.

Recess   *Lough Inagh Lodge Hotel*

Recess Connemara Co Galway

HOTEL   Tel: 095 34706   Fax: 095 34708   email: Inagh@iol.ie

Maire O'Connor's former sporting lodge on the shores of Lough Inagh is now a small hotel with a country house atmosphere. It has large, well-proportioned rooms, interesting period detail and lovely fireplaces with welcoming log fires, plus all the modern comforts. Public areas include two drawing rooms, each with an open fire, a lovely dining room (the Finigglen Room) with deep green walls and graceful spoonback Victorian mahogany chairs (non-residents welcome when there is room) and a very appealing bar (with a big turf fire and its own back door and tiled floor for wet fishing gear). Bedrooms, some with four-posters, are all well-appointed and unusually spacious, with views of lake and countryside. Walk-in dressing rooms lead to well-planned bathrooms and tea/coffee-making facilities are available in rooms on request. While it has special appeal to sportsmen, Lough Inagh is only 42 miles from Galway and makes a good base for touring Connemara. Golf and pony trekking nearby. Off-season breaks offer especially good value. Children welcome (under 3s free in parents' room, cots available). Pets permitted in some areas, by arrangement. **Rooms 12** (all en-suite); B&B £68.20 pps, ss £22. Bar meals 12.30-9 daily. Closed Dec-Feb. Amex, Diners, MasterCard, Visa.

Roundstone   *O'Dowd's*

Roundstone Co Galway

PUB   Tel: 095 35809   Fax: 095 35907   email: odowds@indigo.ie

The O'Dowd family have been welcoming visitors to this much-loved pub overlooking the harbour for longer than most people care to remember - and, although there are some new developments from time to time, the old bar is always the same. It's one of those simple places, with the comfort of an open fire and good pint, where people congregate in total relaxation. A reasonably priced bar menu majoring in seafood offers sustenance or, for more formal meals, the restaurant next door does the honours. The O'Dowds also have a coffee shop, Espresso Stop, as part of the same building, where they do full Irish breakfast, all day food from the bar menu and speciality teas and coffee with scones, croissants and Danish pastries. Own parking. Meals 11.30-9.30 daily. Closed 25 Dec, 3-6pm in winter & some Bank Hols. Amex, MasterCard, Visa. **Directions:** On harbour front in Roundstone village.

Tuam   *Cre na Cille*

High Street Tuam Co Galway

RESTAURANT   Tel/Fax: 093 28232

Cathal and Sally Reynolds' consistently excellent restaurant in Tuam makes a fine stopping place en-route to Galway city or Connemara but, as it is deservedly popular with the locals both at lunchtime and in the evening, booking is strongly advised. Evenings are a little more formal and the setting softer, but the common link is Euro-Toques chef Cathal Reynolds' confident use of local ingredients in generous food at remarkably keen prices. From wide-ranging menus - set lunch, early evening special, set dinner and à la carte - offering a wide range of seafood, meats, poultry and game in season come starters like John Begley's black pudding with apple and onion in a balsamic sauce, main courses like herb-crusted rack of Connemara mountain lamb in red wine jus or a vegetarian dish of the day - a vegetarian crumble perhaps. A customer-friendly wine list with a special £11 cellar. Arrangement with nearby carpark. Children welcome to 8 pm. **Seats 47.** No-smoking area. L&D Mon-Sat, Set L £9, Early D £12.50 (6-7pm). À la carte also available at L&D. House wine from £11, Service discretionary. Closed Sun, 25 Dec 1 Jan & all bank hols. MasterCard, Visa. **Directions:** In the town centre - take the N17 direction from the square; about 100 yards down. on the right.

KERRY

Even with the turning of the Millennium, there's a continuing timelessness about Kerry that gives it a unique quality. What can we say about this splendid place that the Kerrymen (and women) haven't said already? And we can only agree that it's all absolutely true. This magnificent county really is the Kingdom of Kerry. Everything is king size. For not only has Kerry mountains galore - more than anywhere else in Ireland - but the Kingdom also has the highest of all, in Carrantuohill. By international standards, this loftiest peak of MacGillicuddy's Reeks (try pronouncing it "mackil-cuddy") may not seem remarkable at just 1038 m. But when you sense its mysterious heights in the clouds above a countryside of astonishing beauty, its relative elevation is definitely world league. And that beauty of the lower countryside sweeps out into Kerry's fabulous coastline, and up into Kerry's mountains as well. They're beautiful, and remarkably varied with it. So in the upland stakes, Kerry has quantity and quality. Thus it's no surprise to find that, when the enthusiastically visiting Victorians were grading scenery in the early days of tourism, Kerry frequently merited the "sublime" rating. This meant that the county, and particularly the area around Killarney, became a visitors' mecca. At one stage, this was a distinct drawback, with some truth to accusations of tackiness. But in modern times, the entire tourism business in Kerry has put itself through a bootstraps operation, so that by and large they now have - if you'll excuse the expression - a very classy product. And through it all, the Kingdom has a timeless glory, which suits man and beast alike. For the folk in Kerry are renowned for their longevity, particularly in the area along the coast from the lovely little town of Kenmare. Down there, along towards Sneem, you'll hear of Big Bertha, the world's longest-lived cow. She lived productively to the remarkable age, in bovine terms, of 37. She was a great milker, and ancestress in her own lifetime of a veritable herd of progeny. Don't doubt her existence even for a nano-second because, as with everything else in Kerry, it's all absolutely true and then some.

Local Attractions and Information

Beaufort	Hotel Dunloe Castle Gardens 064 44583
Castleisland	Crag Cave 066 41244
Dingle	Oceanworld 066 52111
Glencar	Into the Wilderness Walking Tours (May-Sept) 066-60104
Kenmare	Easter Walking Festival (1st of season) 064 41034
Kenmare	Heritage Centre (lacemaking, history etc) 064 41233
Killarney	Muckross House, Gardens & Traditional Farm 064 31440
Killorglin	Puck Fair (old festival) mid-August 066 62366
Lauragh	Killarney, Derreen Garden 064-83103
Listowel	St John's Art Centre (monthly programme) 068 225662
Listowel	Writers Week (June) 068 21074
Oughterard	Tourist Information 091552808
Tralee	Kerry The Kingdom (3 multi-image, audio-visual attractions) 066 27777
Tralee	Rose of Tralee International Festival (late August) 066 23227
Valentia Island (near Portmagee)	The Skellig Experience 066 76306

Annascaul ˣ

The South Pole Inn

Annascaul Co Kerry

PUB

Tel: 066 57388 /57477

Annascaul, on the Dingle peninsula, is one of the most-photographed villages in Ireland – mainly because of the brilliantly colourful and humorous frontage painted onto his pub by the late Dan Foley (which appeared on the front cover of at least three international guidebooks last year.) It is still a fine pub, although its theatrical owner is greatly missed since he passed on to the greater stage. Nearby, The South Pole, which is down at the lower end of the street is equally interesting - the name becomes clear when you realise there is a connection with the great Irish explorer Sir Ernest Shackleton. As well as being a delightful, well-run pub, The South Pole is full of fascinating Shackleton memorabilia. Closed 25 Dec & Good Fri.

Ballybunion

The Marine Links Hotel

Sandhill Road Ballybunion Co Kerry
Tel: 068 27139 Fax: 068 27666
email:marinelinkshotel@tinet.ie

HOTEL/RESTAURANT

Close to Ballybunion Golf Club, and looking over the mouth of the Shannon River to the Atlantic Ocean, Sandra Williamson and Rosaleen Rafter run as snug and friendly a little hotel as any golfer could wish to find. The growing collection of golf bag tags from around the world in the Hook and Socket Bar is evidence of many an international visitor and a yarn told in this welcoming place. The informally furnished lounge and restaurant have a relaxed holiday atmosphere. Bedrooms, while quite simple, are bright and have all the necessary comforts, with the bonus of sea views across to the cliffs of Clare. Aside from golf, hot seaweed baths, miles of sandy beaches, cliffwalks, horseriding and fishing are all at hand and Kerry's major scenic attractions are only a short drive away. Good value short breaks; discounts at Ballybunion Golf Club except July-September. Children welcome (cots available; under 16s free in parents' room). **Rooms** 20 (all en-suite). B&B £35pps, ss £15. Closed Nov-mid Mar. Amex, Diners, MasterCard, Visa. **Restaurant:** An informal summery atmosphere and an extensive choice - especially strong on fish - have earned this pleasant restaurant a growing reputation. Try local seafood in a dish with a strong Irish theme, perhaps, such as local oysters fried in a Guinness and herb butter. **Seats** 50 D daily 7-9.30, L Sun only 12.30 -2.30. Set Sun L £10, Set D £20, early evening menu £14.95, 7 pm; à la carte also available; house wine £11.95 **Directions:** On seafront, near the golf club.

Ballybunion ✳

Iragh Ti Connor

Main Street Ballybunion Co Kerry
Tel 068 27112 Fax 068 27787

HOTEL

Previously a pub, this "new" hotel is an admirable development and well worth more than a second glance for John O'Connor's scrupulous attention to detail when planning and sourcing materials for its transformation. Real slates, real wooden windows and real cast-iron baths are just a few of the things that make this place special. It wasn't finished when the Guide visited, but it was one of the most promising building sites we've ever had the pleasure of viewing. Conference/banqueting (80/100); secretarial services. Leisure centre. Garden. Parking Children welcome. No Pets. **Rooms** 17 (all en-suite, 2 mini-suites). B&B £60pps, ss £20. MasterCard,Visa. **Directions:** On the left as you come into the main street from Listowel.

Ballybunion ✳

Teach de Broc

Links Road Ballybunion Co Kerry
Tel 068 27581 Fax 068 27919 email teachdebroc@tinet.ie

ACCOMMODATION

You don't have to play golf to appreciate this highly popular guesthouse, but it certainly must help. Aoife and Seamus Brock offer a high standard of comfort, with direct dial phones, TV and tea/coffee-making in all rooms; an energetic programme of extension and refurbishment was in progress at the time of the Guide's visit, resulting in a new dining room and extra four deluxe rooms - and existing rooms are also being upgraded for the 2000 season. But it's the laid-back and genuinely hospitable atmosphere that really gets them coming back for more! Parking. Not suitable for children. **Rooms** 10 (all en-suite & no-smoking, 6 executive,1 for disabled). B&B £30pps, ss £15. Wheelchair access.Open all year. MasterCard, Visa. **Directions:** Directly opposite Ballybunion golf club.

Caherciveen

Brennan's Restaurant

12 Main Street Caherciveen Co Kerry
Tel: 066 947 2021 Fax: 066 947 2914 email: brenrest@iol.ie

RESTAURANT

Conor and Teresa Brennan run a very smooth operation, serving weekday lunches for visitors doing the Ring of Kerry, a deservedly popular early evening menu and a later wider-ranging à la carte every day. Conor takes pride in using the best of local ingredients and serving them imaginatively but without overdressing so you may expect plenty of seafood - prawns, crabmeat, salmon, hake, turbot - and meats including local mountain lamb to be given contemporary treatment (spicy crabmeat filo parcels might come with a warm raw tomato & basil sauce, for example) without being slavishly fashionable. A good cheese plate (five farmhouse cheeses, with full details of origin and style, served with water biscuits and grapes) and well-made desserts, notably pastry and ices **Seats 55** (private room, 30). L 12-3 Mon-Fri, D 5.30 -10 daily. Early evening menu £10, 5.30— 7 pm only. A la carte also available. House wine £12. Children welcome (not under 10 after 8 pm). Arrangement with local carpark. Closed 24-26 Dec & first Mon Nov for 2 weeks. Amex, Diners, MasterCard, Visa. **Directions:** On right in main street, approaching from Killarney.

Caherciveen [PUB★]   *O'Neills "The Point Bar"*

                                                    Renard Point Caherciveen Co Kerry
PUB   Tel/Fax: 066 947 2165

In the same family for 150 years, Michael and Bridie O'Neill's pub, The Point Bar, is beside the Valentia Island car ferry. Recently renovated in true character, it's as neat as ninepence. A lovely place to drop into for a quick one while you're waiting for the ferry – but even better to stay awhile and make the most of their super fresh seafood, served during the summer. They do have a menu and it's a good starting point, covering everything from a whole range of salads and open sandwiches on brown bread – fresh and smoked wild salmon, smoked mackerel, crabmeat, crab claws – to hot dishes like deep-fried squid and a couple of hake and monkfish dishes with garlic and olive oil. Everything on the menu, bar lobster (market price) has been under a tenner to date but, sadly, price increases are likely "due to scarcity of supply", although it is still expected to be reasonably priced. Not very suitable for children. The Valentia Island ferry runs continuously – i.e. not to a timetable – from April-September inclusive. L Mon-Sat, D daily. Food available only from April to October. No credit cards.

Caherdaniel   *Derrynane Hotel*

                                                    Caherdaniel Co Kerry
HOTEL/RESTAURANT   Tel: 066 9475136 Fax: 066 9475160

If only for its superb location – on the seaward side of the Ring of Kerry road – this unassuming 1960s-style hotel would be well worth a visit, but there is much more to it than the view, or even its waterside position. The accommodation is quite modest but very comfortable, the food is good and, under the excellent management of Mary O'Connor and her well-trained staff, this hospitable, family-friendly place provides a welcome home from home for many a contented guest. Don't leave the area without visiting Daniel O'Connell's beautiful house at Derrynane – or the amazing Ballinskelligs chocolate factory. Garden. Well-behaved small dogs with their own beds may stay with their owners. **Rooms 74** (all en-suite). B&B £45pps, ss £10. Closed mid Oct-mid April. Amex, Diners, MasterCard, Visa. **Restaurant:** Beautifully located, overlooking the heated outdoor swimming pool and the hotel's gardens (which reach down to the shore), the restaurant enjoys stunning sea views on a good day. Head chef Derrick Smith ensures that residents are well looked after – he uses the best of local ingredients in imaginative, very fairly priced four-course dinner menus - and this is a place to consider planning a lunch stop on the Ring of Kerry, as the hotel's new Salad Bar is open from 10am-6 pm daily. **Seats 50** (private room, 20) D 7-9 daily, Set D £25, sc discretionary. House wine £10.50. Non smoking restaurant; air conditioning. **Directions:** Midway between Sneem and Waterville on Ring of Kerry.

Caherdaniel   *Iskeroon*

                                                    Caherdaniel Co Kerry
COUNTRY HOUSE   Tel: 066 9475119 Fax: 066 9475488 email: iskeroon@iol.ie

Geraldine and David Hare's beautiful old house is in a secluded position overlooking Derrynane Harbour. The effort taken to get there makes it all the more restful once settled in. All three of the comfortable and interestingly decorated bedrooms overlook the harbour – and the islands of Deenish and Scarriff – and each has its own private bathroom just across a corridor. Geraldine enjoys cooking dinner for guests – local seafood is her speciality – and there's a big turf fire in the drawing room to relax beside afterwards.(£18 at 8.30 pm; book by noon.) The private pier at the bottom of the garden joins an old Mass Path which, by a happy chance, leads not only to the beach but also to Keatinge's pub (known as Bridie's) where a bit of banter and some good seafood is also to be had in the evenings. Unsuitable for children. Dogs by arrangement. **Rooms 3**, all with private bathrooms. B&B approx 35pps, ss £10. Closed 1 Nov-1 May. Amex, MasterCard, Visa. **Directions:** Between Caherdaniel and Waterville (N70), turn off at the Scarriff Inn, signed to Bunavalla Pier. Bearing left at each bend, go to the pier and left through "private" gate; cross beach and enter through white gate posts.

Caherdaniel ✗

The Stepping Stone

Caherdaniel Co Kerry
Tel: 066 9475444 Fax: 066 9475449
email: thesteppingstone@tinet.ie

RESTAURANT

The Stepping Stone is a delightful little restaurant, just off the Ring of Kerry and a brisk walk up from the harbour at Derrynane. It's a characterful, cottagey little place, with tables necessarily tightly packed and a cheerful, professional atmosphere. Bear with it if service is slow – the kitchen is also tiny – but food is imaginative, well-cooked and definitely worth waiting for. Joint owner-chefs Stephen McIlroy and Sally Walker present carefully considered eclectic menus which please modern tastes while often retaining classic partnerships – thus, for example, confit of duck with roast spiced pear and home-made fruit preserve jus is contemporary but is based on the traditional duck-with-fruit theme. Shortish à la carte menus offer four or five choices in each course but this may be doubled by daily blackboard specials. Regional Irish cheeses are nicely served with sultana & onion marmalade and sesame & oat biscuits. D daily. Closed Nov-27 Dec, 5 Jan-Good Fri. MasterCard, Visa.

Camp

Barnagh Bridge Country Guesthouse

Camp Tralee Co Kerry
Tel: 066 7130145 Fax: 066 7130299

ACCOMMODATION

Snuggled into the hillside overlooking Tralee Bay, Heather Williams' unusual architect-designed guesthouse is in extensive grounds between the mountains and the sea. Attractive and comfortable, it was purpose-built, with five individually furnished guest bedrooms (decor themed on local wild flowers), all with en-suite shower rooms. In the dining room guests can drink in the view of Tralee Bay while doing justice to Heather's breakfasts – fresh juices, newly baked breads and scones, locally made preserves, and Dingle smoked salmon and scrambled eggs or a traditional fry (in addition to daily specials such as kippers or French toast). The stylishly decorated guest drawing room opens onto a patio overlooking the Maharees islands and their spectacular sunsets and the latest improvement is a conservatory, to extend the reception area and dining room - and maximise still further on the wonderful view. Garden, fishing, walking. Not suitable for children under 10. No pets. **Rooms 5** (all en-suite & non-smoking). B&B £25 pps, ss £10. Closed Nov-March . Amex MasterCard, Visa. **Directions:** Take N86 Dingle road from Tralee; after 9 miles, take Connor Pass/Castlegregory road R560; guesthouse is 1 mile on left.

Camp ✗

James Ashe

Camp Tralee Co Kerry
Tel: 066 7130133

PUB

This fine old pub just off the Tralee-Dingle road has been in the family for 200 years and the present owner, Thomas Ashe, has been keeping things running smoothly since 1978. It's a delightful place, full of genuine character and hospitality. Good home-cooked food is served in the bar (lunchtime, Monday-Saturday and 4-8 on Sunday) and restaurant (à la carte 6-9.15 Monday-Saturday and set 3-course lunch Sunday 12.30-2). Bar meals daily. Closed mid Jan-mid March. Amex, Diners, MasterCard, Visa. **Directions:** On the main Tralee-Dingle road, 10 miles from Tralee.

Caragh Lake 🏛

Caragh Lodge

Caragh Lake Co Kerry
Tel: 066 9769115 Fax: 066 9769316
email: caraghl@iol.ie

COUNTRY HOUSE/RESTAURANT

Less than a mile from the Ring of Kerry, Mary Gaunt's lovely Victorian house and gardens nestling on the shores of the startlingly beautiful Caragh Lake is an idyllic place, with views of Ireland's highest mountains, the McGillicuddy Reeks. The house – which is elegantly furnished with antiques but not too formal – makes a cool, restful retreat. Bedrooms include some recently added garden rooms with wonderful views, their own entrance and sitting room (complete with open log fire), and are all sumptuously furnished with lovely bathrooms. In the elegant dining room overlooking the lake (open to non-residents by reservation), Mary's real love of cooking shines through. Local produce (such as freshly caught seafood, often including wild salmon from Caragh Lake, Kerry lamb and home-grown vegetables) takes pride of place. Baking is a particular strength, not only in delicious home-baked breads, but also baked desserts and treats for afternoon tea that includes recipes handed down by her family through the generations. Salmon and trout fishing, boating and swimming are all available at the bottom of the garden and there's tennis too. **Rooms 15** (all en-suite, 8 executive, 1 shower only). B&B £57.50, ss £17.50, service included. D £30, 7-8.30; non-residents welcome by reservation. Licensed. Closed mid Oct— late April. Amex, Diners, MasterCard, Visa. **Directions:** From Killorglin on N70, Glenbeigh direction, take second road signed Caragh Lake; at end of road go left again. The house is on the right.

Caragh Lake   *Hotel Ard-na-Sidhe*

Caragh Lake Nr Killorglin Co Kerry
HOTEL   Tel: 064 31900 Fax: 064 37900 email: khl@iol.ie

Set in woodland and among award-winning gardens, this peaceful Victorian retreat is in a beautiful mountain location overlooking Caragh Lake. Decorated throughout in a soothing country house style, very comfortable antique-filled day rooms provide plenty of lounging space for quiet indoor relaxation and a terrace for fine weather – all with wonderful views. Bedrooms – shared between the main house and some with private patios in the garden house – are spacious and elegantly furnished in traditional style, with excellent en-suite bathrooms. This is a sister hotel to the Hotel Europe and Dunloe Castle (see entries), whose leisure facilities are also available to guests. Dooks, Waterville, Killeen and Mahony's Point golf courses are all within easy reach. Not very suitable for children, although concessions are given. No pets. **Rooms 19** (5 suites, 14 min-suites). B&B £67.50, ss £18.50, service included. Closed 1 Oct-1 May Amex, Diners, MasterCard, Visa. **Directions:** Off N70 Ring of Kerry road. signed 5 Km west of Killorglin.

Castlegregory   *O'Riordan's Café*

Castlegregory Dingle Peninsula Co Kerry
RESTAURANT   Tel/Fax: 066 7139379

Kieran O'Callaghan and Shirley Copeland's smashing little café-restaurant is just the place to take a break on a day out on the Dingle Peninsula, or to have a more serious meal if you're staying nearby. It's cosy and welcoming, everything is spick-and-span and it's the kind of place where children can enjoy finding out more about good grown-up food. Menus change every few days, everything is based on local produce and is home cooked. Brandon Bay seafood, salmon and trout from local rivers feature regularly, as does garden produce in soups, salads and vegetable dishes. Freshly baked breads might include herb and onion, sourdough, rye and tomato and fennel – and there are delicious homely puddings and tarts. Wholesome meat dishes include beef in Guinness and marinated Kerry lamb loin chops grilled and served with apricot sauce while vegetarians do very well too – tempura of vegetable with soy and ginger dip or samosas with carrot salad and raita are typical choices – and there's always a good selection of interesting farmhouse cheese, such as Lavistown, Cratloe and Ardrahan. Children welcome. Wheelchair accessible. **Seats 50** L & D daily, 12-5 and 6.30-9. L from £6.60, D from £19, sc discretionary. Licensed. Closed Oct- early May. MasterCard, Visa. **Directions:** On the Conor Pass road, before turning into Castlegregory.

Castlegregory   *Spillanes*

Maharees Castlegregory Co Kerry
PUB   Tel 066 7139125

Since 1975 Marilyn and Michael Spillane have taken great pride in this traditional pub and have earned a well-deserved loyal following as a result. Seafood stars on the menu - mussels grilled with garlic breadcrumbs, crabclaws served in shell with brown bread and a cocktail dipping sauce, fresh and wild salmon in salads and open sandwiches, scampi made from Dingle prawns - but there's plenty for meat-lovers too, such as chargrilled steaks, several chicken dishes and a little children's menu too. Meals available daily in high season, 12.30 to 9.30, and in the evenings in spring and autumn. MasterCard, Visa. Closed Nov-mid March. **Directions:** 2 miles north of Castlegregory, between Brandon and Tralee bays.

Dingle   *Bambury's Guest House*

Mail Road Dingle Co Kerry

ACCOMMODATION   Tel: 066 9151244 Fax: 066 9151786 email: bernieebb@tinet.ie

Just a couple of minutes walk from the centre of Dingle, Jimmy and Bernie Bambury's well-run, purpose-built guesthouse has spacious rooms (including four suitable for disabled guests) all with en-suite shower rooms, tea/coffee trays, phone, satellite TV, hair dryer and complimentary mineral water. Bernie Bambury's breakfasts include griddle cakes with fresh fruit and honey – a house speciality – and vegetarian breakfasts are offered by arrangement. Not suitable for children under 4; pets allowed in some areas. **Rooms 12.** B&B £30, ss £10.Open all year, including Xmas. MasterCard, Visa. **Directions:** On N86, on the left after the Shell garage on entering Dingle.

Dingle   *Beginish Restaurant*

Green Street Dingle Co Kerry

RESTAURANT   Tel: 066 915 1588 Fax: 066 915 1591 email: patmoore@tinet.ie

Irish Lamb Award

Named after one of the nearby Blasket Islands, and conveniently close to the marina, it should come as no surprise that local seafood features strongly on the menu at Pat and John Moore's elegant restaurant. But Kerry mountain lamb is an equally attractive option and very much a speciality of the house in cooking that is never too clever or pretentious, but always an experience to relish due to the sheer quality of ingredients and an imaginative but disciplined approach. Rack of lamb is as far as most restaurants get with this versatile ingredient which is a pity - delicious as it can be, those on holiday for a fortnight might find it a little monotonous. So three cheers for restaurants like Beginish, where the dish may vary, but you can be sure it will be creative - and their roast loin of lamb with filo wrapped lambs kidney, duxelles and roasted shallot attracted particular praise on a recent visit. It's become quite a house speciality and, as part of their consistently creative approach, earned Beginish our Irish lamb Award this year. Unusually for cottagey Dingle, the restaurant is high-ceilinged and elegant, with a conservatory at the back overlooking the garden – a nice spot for lunch or as a private room for 12 at night, when it is floodlit. Lobster can be a bargain, and the daily specials – John Dory fillet baked with white (butter) beans and served with anchovy vinaigrette , perhaps - and vegetarian options can also be very tempting. Rhubarb souffle tart is an unusual house speciality on the dessert menu or farmhouse cheeses – about half a dozen – are served plated, with water biscuits, and there's a choice of freshly brewed coffee, tea or herbal infusions. [*Accommodation: several exceptionally well-equipped and comfortably-furnished self-catering units are offered for varying numbers, normally for a minimum of 1 week, but overnight lettings are sometimes available.] **Seats 52.** D only, Tues-Sun, 6-10; à la carte. House wine £12.50; sc discretionary Closed mid-Nov-mid Mar. Amex, Diners, MasterCard, Visa **Directions:** Below the Catholic Church, on the opposite side of the street.

Dingle   *The Chart House Restaurant*

The Mall Dingle Co Kerry

RESTAURANT   Tel/Fax: 066 9152255

Jim McCarthy (previously restaurant manager at The Park Hotel Kenmare) opened The Chart House as a brand new restaurant in Dingle in 1997. Informal in furnishing style and general approach, offering fairly moderately priced seasonal, multi-cultural menus based on local ingredients, it has brought a new element to Dingle's dining scene. Thus Annascaul black pudding and apples may be used in a starter – spiced with ginger, wrapped in filo pastry and served in a bacon jus; similarly, local steamed mussels may be served provençale with a hint of chili and main course monkfish is cajun spiced with fricassée of wild mushrooms and a tomato and saffron oil. But there are some themes from closer to home too - spring cabbage accompanies a roulade of pork fillet with apricot and bacon stuffing, for instance. Desserts include some classics like iced hazelnut parfait with compôte of fresh berries, or home-made ice creams – and Irish cheeses are cannily offered, at £7.50, with a glass of vintage port. The wine list has been greatly improved in the last year, with helpful tasting notes as well as a clear layout of country of origin as well as vintages - and, of course, there's a Chateau MacCarthy modestly tucked into the top of page 2 (£25.50). **Seats 45.** No smoking area, air conditioning. Wed-Mon, 6.30-10; à la carte. House wine £11.50 Closed 8 Jan -11 Feb. MasterCard, Visa. **Directions:** On the left at the first roundabout as you approach the town.

Dingle *Cleevaun*

Lady's Cross Milltown Dingle Co Kerry
Tel: 066 9151108 Fax: 066 9152228
ACCOMMODATION
email: cleevaun@iol.ie

A cup of tea or coffee and a slice of home-made porter cake welcomes guests to Charlotte and Sean Cluskey's well-run, recently renovated guesthouse just outside the town. Set in an acre of landscaped gardens overlooking Dingle Bay, it's near enough to Dingle to be handy and far enough away to enjoy the peace that the peninsula promises. Furnishing throughout is in a pleasant country pine style: bedrooms are all non-smoking, have good facilities and are well organised, with quality beds, quilted bedspreads and well-finished en-suite bathrooms (1 shower-only). One bedroom has a separate dressing room. Charlotte's breakfasts – served in a large south-facing dining room overlooking Dingle Bay – are quite a speciality. **Rooms 8.** B&B approx £30. Closed mid-Nov-mid-Feb. MasterCard, Visa **Directions:** Just outside the town, on the Slea Head/Ventry scenic route R559.

Dingle *Dick Mack's*

Green Lane Dingle Co Kerry
PUB
Tel 066 9151960

Once a cobbler's, this old shop-bar still sells an eclectic mixture of modern leather items, wellington boots and patent hangover cures. Definitely not a theme bar it's run by Dick's son, Oliver J MacDonnell, who has had the wisdom to leave well alone. Seating is basic, there's an old gas fire for cold evenings and the cashier's booth is put to good use as a snug. Definitely not a food place but open over lunchtime (12-2.30) and evenings (4-11). **Directions:** A few doors up the street from the Beginish restaurant.

Dingle *Dingle Skellig Hotel*

Dingle Co Kerry
HOTEL
Tel: 066 9151144 Fax: 066 9151501 email: dsk@iol.ie

Although modest-looking from the road, this 1960s hotel enjoys a shoreside location on the edge of the town and has won many friends over the years. It is a particularly well-run, family-friendly hotel, with organised entertainment for children and an excellent leisure centre. Roomy public areas are comfortably furnished with a fair degree of style. Good use is made of sea views throughout, especially in the conservatory restaurant, which has special anti-glare glass. Bedrooms are reasonably large, have been recently refurbished and have small but neat bathrooms. On Monday nights throughout the summer, from June, the hotel runs a Ceili night of traditional music, song, story-telling and dance, featuring highly accomplished local artists. Although best known as a holiday destination, the Dingle Skellig also has excellent conference and business meeting facilities, with full back-up services including French and German translation. Children under 3 free in parents' bedrooms; cots available; crèche, playroom, children's playground. **Rooms 116** (all en-suite; 1 suite, 38 executive & 10 no-smoking bedrooms.) Closed 20-27 Dec & all Jan. Amex, Diners, MasterCard, Visa. **Directions:** On the sea side of the road as you approach Dingle from Tralee.

Dingle *Doyle's Seafood Restaurant & Townhouse*

John Street Dingle Co Kerry
RESTAURANT/ACCOMMODATION
Tel: 066 915 1174 Fax: 066 915 1816

Established by John and Stella Doyle in 1974, Doyle's Seafood Bar (as it was then known) was Dingle's first serious restaurant – and thus the foundation stone for the town's current culinary reputation. It changed hands in 1998, although to the casual observer there are few clues – the flagstone floors and old furniture still give this restaurant lots of character. It is now in the good hands of Sean Cluskey (previously manager of Dingle Skellig Hotel) and his wife Charlotte (who runs Cleevaun guesthouse) and local seafood is still the main attraction. Lobster, selected from a tank in the bar, is a speciality. There are, however, concessions to non-seafood eaters – chicken, steaks and vegetable paella as well as lamb. Puddings are nice and traditional or there's a plated selection of farmhouse cheeses from the Munster region to finish. **Seats 45** D only, Mon-Sat 6-10. No-smoking area; air conditioning. MasterCard, Visa. **Accommodation:** High quality accommodation includes a residents' sitting room as well as eight bedrooms. B&B £40 pps approx.

Dingle   *Greenmount House*

Gortonora Dingle Co Kerry

ACCOMMODATION   Tel: 066 915 1414 Fax: 066 915 1974

Just five minutes walk from the centre of Dingle, John and Mary Curran have run one of Ireland's finest guesthouses since the mid-70s. It's an exceptionally comfortable place to stay, quietly located on the hillside, with private parking and uninterrupted views across the town and harbour to the mountains across the bay. The well-appointed bedrooms (all of which are non-smoking) fall into two groups – half are in the original house and, although smaller than the newer ones, are also furnished to a very high standard. The others are junior suites with generous seating areas and good amenities, including fridges as well as tea/coffee-making trays, phone and TV (and their own entrance and balcony). There's also a comfortable residents' sitting room and a conservatory overlooking the harbour, where outstandingly good breakfasts are served. Not suitable for children under 8. No pets. **Rooms 12** (all en-suite, 7 executive bedrooms); B&B 35; no ss. Closed 21-27 Dec. MasterCard, Visa. **Directions:** Turn right and right again on entering Dingle.

Dingle ✗   *The Half Door*

Mail Road Dingle Co Kerry

RESTAURANT/ACCOMMODATION   Tel: 066 915 1600 Fax: 066 915 1883

Since 1991 chef-proprietor Denis O'Connor has been preparing great seafood at the cottagey Dingle restaurant he runs with his wife Teresa. Menus go with the seasons but, in the Guide's experience, whatever is available is perfectly cooked and generously served without over-presentation. An outstanding speciality of the house is the seafood platter, available hot or cold as either a starter or main course with (depending on availability of individual items) lobster, oysters, Dublin Bay prawns, scallops, crab claws and mussels (attractively presented with garlic or lemon butter). Good puddings or Irish farmhouse cheeses to follow. L & D Mon-Sat. Closed 24-26 Dec. **Directions:** Next door to Doyle's. **Accommodation:** The O'Connors also have accommodation in a separate establishment called the Half Door Waterfront Guesthouse, on the edge of Dingle. Ask at the restaurant or call 066 9151883 for details. Closed 24-26 Dec. Amex, MasterCard, Visa.

Dingle   *James Flahive*

The Quay Dingle Co Kerry

PUB   Tel 066 9151634

They don't make them like this any more - Peggy and James Flahive's welcoming, friendly old pub has been a home from home for many a regular visitor for over 30 years. It's hard to imagine any call for a tailor's shop in Dingle these days, but that's how it started off in the 1890s; more recently it's long been a special favourite of sailing people and has had some very distinguished visitors and photos of many of them adorn the walls - along with several of Dingle's best-loved resident, Fungie the dolphin. No food, but a good pint and good company.

Dingle   *Lord Baker's Seafood Restaurant & Bar*

Main Street Dingle Co Kerry

PUB/RESTAURANT   Tel: 066 915 1277 Fax: 066 915 2174

Believed to be the oldest pub in Dingle, this business was established in 1890 by a Tom Baker. A very popular businessman in the area, a colourful orator, member of Kerry County Council and a director of the Tralee-Dingle Railway, he was known locally as "Lord Baker" and as such is now immortalised in John Moriarty's excellent pub and restaurant in the centre of Dingle. A welcoming turf fire burns in the front bar, where bar food such as chowder and home-baked bread or crab claws in garlic butter is served. At the back, there's a much more sophisticated dining set-up in the restaurant proper (and, beyond it, a walled garden). Seafood stars, as it does everywhere in the area, but there's also a good choice of other dishes – local lamb, of course, also beef, chicken and local duckling – all well-cooked and served in an atmosphere of great hospitality. Sunday lunch in the restaurant is a particularly popular event and very well done (booking strongly advised); on other days the lunchtime bar menu, plus one or two daily specials such as a roast, can be taken in the restaurant. The wine list includes a House Selection of ten wines from around the world at £10.50-£13 and an equal choice of half bottles. **Seats 120.** L & D daily 12.30-2.15, 6-9.45. Set L & light D (6-7.30) £12. Set D £22; à la carte also available. No smoking area. Toilets wheelchair accessible. Closed 24-25 Dec & Good Fri. Amex, Diners, MasterCard, Visa. **Directions:** Town centre, on the main street.

Dingle   *Milltown House*

Dingle Co Kerry
Tel: 066 9151372 Fax: 066 9151095
ACCOMMODATION   email: milltown@indigo.ie

This attractive guesthouse on the western side of Dingle, set in immaculate gardens running down to the water's edge, enjoys beautiful views of the harbour and distant mountains. Day rooms include an informal reception room, a comfortably furnished sitting room and a conservatory breakfast room overlooking the garden. The bedrooms – all very comfortable and thoughtfully furnished with phone, TV and tea/coffee making facilities - include two with private patios. Limited room service is available. Garden. Not suitable for children under 10. No pets. **Rooms 10** (2 shower only, 1 disabled). Closed 23-28 Dec. Amex, MasterCard, Visa. **Directions:** West through Dingle town, 3/4 mile from town centre.

Dingle   *Pax Guest House*

Upper John Street Dingle Co Kerry
ACCOMMODATION   Tel: 066 915 1518 email: paxhouse@iol.ie

Just half a mile out of Dingle, this modern house enjoys what may well be the finest view in the area – and, thanks to the exceptional hospitality and high standards of the owners, Joan Brosnan and Ron Wright, is also one of the most comfortable and relaxing places to stay. Rooms are very thoughtfully furnished and decorated in traditional Celtic themes, with well-finished bathrooms (3 shower only). Breakfast is a major event, featuring fresh Dingle Bay seafood as well as an exceptional range of meats and cheeses. Garden. Children welcome (under 2s free in parents' room, cots available). Well-behaved dogs are welcome by arrangement. **Rooms 13** (all en-suite & no-smoking, 1 suite, 1 executive, 3 shower only). B&B £30 pps, ss £5.Closed Nov-Mar.MasterCard, Visa.

Dingle   *Tigh Mhaire de Barra*

The Pier Head Dingle Co Kerry
PUB   Tel: 066 915 1215

Real hospitality, good food and music are the attractions of Mhaire de Barra and Pat Leahy's harbourside pub. In unpretentious and comfortable surroundings they serve good things like home-made soups with freshly-baked bread, local seafood specials, traditional dishes like boiled bacon and cabbage and Kerry porter cake at lunchtime. Evening meals include an additional range of hot main courses. Dingle Pies, for which the pub is famous, are included in the menu off-season (Oct-March), when the rush of the tourist season has died down. Self-catering accommodation has recently been added to the back of the pub, in a quiet garden setting. Meals daily, 12.30-9 (Sun closed 2.30-4 pm). Closed 25 Dec & Good Fri. MasterCard, Visa. **Directions:** On harbour front in Dingle town.

Fenit   *The Tankard*

Kilfenora Fenit Co Kerry
PUB/RESTAURANT   Tel: 066 713 6164 Fax: 066 713 6516

Easily spotted on the seaward side of the road from Tralee, this bright yellow pub and restaurant has built up a great reputation, especially for seafood. An imaginative bar menu is available from lunchtime to late evening (12.30 -10) serving the likes of "smokeys" and boxty, warm chicken salad and vegetarian choices like mushroom & mozzarella salad. **Restaurant:** Except on Sunday this is an evening restaurant, although lunch is available by arrangement. A phone call is worthwhile to get the best of seafood cooking (which can be exceptional). Beyond seafood there's quite a wide choice, especially steaks in various guises, duckling, Kerry lamb and some strong vegetarian options. There's a great sea view from the restaurant (but not the bar). **Seats 60.** D daily 6-10, à la carte; L Sun only 12.30-2.30, Set Sun L £9.95. House wine from £12.50; sc discretionary Closed 25 Dec & Good Fri. Amex, Diners, MasterCard, Visa **Directions:** From Tralee, 5 miles out on the Fenit road, beyond the Spa.

Fenit   *West End Bar*

Fenit Tralee Co Kerry
BAR/RESTAURANT   Tel: 066 7136246

This family-run pub is exactly seven minutes walk from the marina. Good home cooking is available in the bar and informal restaurant (phone ahead to check times) and there is unpretentious, inexpensive accommodation too (10 en-suite rooms, B&B £19, no ss.) Bar/restaurant Meals 5.30-10 daily in summer. A la carte; house wine £10. Closed Nov-Apr. Bar closed 25 Dec & Good Fri only. MasterCard, Visa. **Directions:** 8 miles from Tralee; on corner as you turn down to the marina.

Glencar
The Climbers' Inn

Glencar Killarney Co Kerry

ACCOMMODATION   Tel: 066 9760101   Fax: 066 9760104   email: climbers@iol.ie

A real inn, The Climbers' is the oldest established walking and climbing inn in Ireland. It specialises in walking holidays and short breaks, with or without guides, and offers every comfort for the traveller, whether arriving on foot, on horseback or, more prosaically, by car. (It may sound less exciting but, whether approaching from Killarney or Sneem, the drives are spectacular.) Established in 1875 and in family ownership for four generations, the current owners are Johnny and Anne Walsh, an energetic young couple who have made big improvements since they took over in 1995. Accommodation comprises budget (hostel) and bed & breakfast (rooms with en-suite showers) and has all been recently refurbished. Rooms are simple, functional and spotlessly clean. Home-cooked dinners are served in the dining area of a bar reminiscent of alpine inns, furnished with old church furniture. A guest chef is invited from a different country each season, so the style of cooking varies accordingly. It will, however, be based on local ingredients, often wild, and will aim to satisfy hearty mountain appetites with big soups, home-baked brown bread and main courses which include Kerry mountain lamb, wild venison or salmon (with plenty of wholesome vegetables and a good pudding). Bar food is also available daily from 12 noon – 6 pm in the summer season. "Into the Wilderness" tours are organised from the inn – details from Johnny Walsh, or any tourist office. Not suitable for children under 10. Pets permitted. **Rooms 8** (all en-suite, shower only & no-smoking). B&B £25 pps, ss £5. D£15. House wine £12; sc 10%. Closed Nov-Mar. Amex, Diners, MasterCard, Visa.

Kenmare
Bean & Leaf

4 Rock Street Kenmare Co Kerry

CAFE   Tel: 064 42363 Fax: 064 42196 email: kburke@mail1.tinet.ie

Up a side lane in the middle of Kenmare is this surprising little cyber-café. Excellent range of coffees (with beans to take home), teas and tisanes, scrumptious food (global with South American leanings – tortilla, burrito, chicken taco, guacamole dip) all somehow assembled and/or cooked in a tiny little kitchen in front of your eyes. Lovely pastries and bakes – and art and music too. They even opened a bookstore last year, featuring Irish and Celtic interest books and monthly magazines. Author readings, jazz and art too; what more could anyone want. Moderately priced à la carte L & D Mon-Sat; Closed 25 Dec, Nov & Feb. MasterCard, Visa. **Directions:** Off the main street,one block up from Quill's.

Kenmare ✗
Café Indigo & The Square Pint

The Square Kenmare Co Kerry

RESTAURANT   Tel: 064 42356 Fax: 064 42358

This colourful first floor restaurant is remarkably minimalist, both architecturally and decoratively, for a converted pub in an historic Kerry town. The menu reflects the trendy surroundings, with modern dishes influenced by many international cuisines. A French bias on the wine list with good house wines. Blinis bar, serving savoury and sweet Russian pancakes from 10.30pm-12.30am. Downstairs, The Square Pint serves a daily-changing lunch menu (spiced lentil soup, Irish stew, seafood pie) and snacky things like mini baguettes or grilled vegetables on toast with tapenade spread. In the evenings there's live music every night. L & D daily. Closed 25 Dec & Good Fri. Amex, Diners, MasterCard, Visa.

Kenmare
Ceann Mara

Kenmare Co Kerry

ACCOMMODATION   Tel: 064 41220 Fax: 064 41220

In a peaceful location just outside Kenmare, Thérèsè Hayes's pleasing modern house is set in lovely gardens that run down to the water. Interesting, comfortable reception rooms are full of family antiques and mementoes and the four bedrooms are all very different, but thoughtfully furnished. Very good breakfasts are served in a lovely dining room overlooking the garden. Dogs allowed by arrangement in some areas. **Rooms 4** (3 en-suite, 1 private, 2 non-smoking). B&B £18 pps. Closed Oct-May. **Directions:** Off Cork road R569, about a mile from Kenmare.

Kenmare ☆ — *d'Arcy's*

RESTAURANT

Main Street Kenmare Co Kerry
Tel: 064 41589

Formerly a bank – you can still make out where the vault used to be – Pat Gath and Martin Wilde took over this well-known restaurant in 1998 and, with chef James Mulchrone, have a great success on their hands. The contemporary menu offers excellent dishes that are well executed – the chef has a sure touch and cooking is spot on. Seasonal local ingredients are cleverly used in dishes with overseas influences, mainly oriental and Mediterranean.Kenmare smoked salmon may be served with potato pancakes and a sharp red onion salsa, and a bruschetta of goat's cheese might come with tapenade and sun-dried tomato pesto. Roast herb-crusted loin of lamb might have a port and mustard seed sauce or seared scallops served with fine pasta and a basil pesto broth. For dessert, look no further than a more traditional rhubarb and ginger fool served in a hazelnut tuile, or crème brûlée. Good wine list, home-made breads, and pleasant service – all in all, a lively and welcoming restaurant with a pleasingly cosmopolitan feel to it. No smoking area. No children after 8 pm. **Seats 35.** D only 6-10 Wed-Mon; à la carte. House wine £11.50; sc discretionary. Closed Tue and mid-Jan-mid-Feb.MasterCard, Visa. **Accommodation:** 5 en-suite bedrooms. B&B £20; ss £5. **Directions:** At the top of the town, near the Park Hotel.

Kenmare — *Dromquinna Manor*

HOTEL

Blackwater Bridge PO Kenmare Co Kerry
Tel: 064 41657 Fax: 064 41791 email: dromquinna@tinet.ie

Built in 1850 in an idyllic location – the hotel is set in 42 acres of wooded grounds and has three quarters of a mile of sheltered south-facing sea frontage – Dromquinna Manor has a number of unusual features including a romantic tree house (a 2-bedroom suite with four-poster and balcony, 15ft up a tree), a safe little sandy beach (beside the informal Boat House Bistro) and a 34ft Nelson Sport Angler with professional skipper for fishing parties and scenic cruises. The interior of the house features an original oak-panelled Great Hall, a traditional drawing room complete with concert grand piano and an unusual Dragon Bar. Bedrooms are all individually decorated to specific themes, with good bathrooms (only two are shower-only). The hotel and surroundings can be very busy at times – they do a barbecue Sunday lunch on the quay with a live band (moving into the Boat House in bad weather) which has become very popular – so reservations are essential. Not surprisingly, weddings are also often catered for, so finding a time when the hotel and grounds are quiet enough to be themselves can sometimes be a matter of luck. Children welcome (under 4s free in parents' room, cots available; playground). Garden. Walking. Tennis. Boating. Pets permitted by arrangement. **Rooms 46** (1 suite, 2 mini-suites, 2 shower only) B&B £45 pps, ss £20. Closed 31 Oct-17 March. Amex, Diners, MasterCard, Visa. **Directions:** 3 miles outside Kenmare on the Sneem road.

Kenmare — *The Horseshoe Bar & Restaurant*

RESTAURANT/PUB

3 Main Street Kenmare Co Kerry
Tel: 064 41553 Fax: 064 42502

Chef-proprietor Irma Weeland's nice old-fashioned bar and restaurant is cosy and well-run – and the good home cooking she offers in the informal oil-cloth-tabled restaurant at the back, with its open fire and original cattle stall divisions, is unpretentious and wholesome. Soups, chowders, chicken goujons, burgers and pies will all be home-made, as will the chips (a rare enough event these days). Seafood and steaks are the key players on evening menus, but there's plenty else to choose from, including strong vegetarian options and local duck (often a good bet in west Cork and Kerry). Classic puddings – crème brûlée, treacle tart – and a short but adequate wine list. No children after 8.30. **Seats 45.** L12-4, D 6-10 daily (Sun D to 11.30); à la carte. House wine £11; sc dicretionary. Closed 25 Dec, Good Fri. Open weekends only Jan-Mar. Amex, MasterCard, Visa

Kenmare — *The Lime Tree*

RESTAURANT

Shelburne Street Kenmare Co Kerry
Tel: 064 41225/42434 Fax: 064 41839
email: benchmark@iol.ie

Built in 1832, Tony and Alex Daly's restaurant is an attractive cut stone building set well back from the road. An open log fire, exposed stone walls, original wall panelling and a minstrels' gallery (which is an upper eating area) all give character to the interior. Menus change with the seasons, and there are always daily specials, including several vegetarian options such as goat cheese potato cake or ragout of mushrooms. Local produce – like Sneem black pudding, local free-range duck and Kerry lamb (oven-roasted, with sweet mint pesto perhaps) – is highly valued, and local seafood such as Killmacallogue mussels appear in delicious dishes such as fruits de mer cassoulet with fettucine and seafood potpourri "en papillotte". Finish, perhaps, with a traditional pudding like warm blackberry and pear fruit crumble. Wheelchair accessible. No-smoking area. No children after 7 pm. **Seats 60.** D daily 6.30-10; à la carte. House wine £11.95; sc discretionary. Closed -Nov-Mar. MasterCard, Visa. **Directions:** Next to The Park Hotel.

Kenmare   *Muxnaw Lodge*
Castletownbere Road Kenmare Co Kerry
COUNTRY HOUSE   Tel: 064 41252

Within walking distance from town (first right past the double-arched bridge towards Bantry), Mrs Hannah Boland's wonderfully cosy and homely house was built in 1801 and enjoys spectacular views across Kenmare Bay. It is very much a home – relax in the TV lounge or outside in the sloping gardens (you can even play tennis on the all-weather court). Bedrooms are tranquil, all en suite and with cleverly hidden tea/coffee-making facilities, and are individually furnished with free-standing period pieces and pleasant fabrics. Notice is required by noon if guests wish to dine – a typical dinner cooked in and on the Aga comprises carrot soup, oven-baked salmon and apple pie, but guests are always asked beforehand what they like. **Rooms 5.** (all en-suite & no-smoking). B&B £24. Closed 25 Dec. No credit cards.

Kenmare   *The New Delight*
18 Henry Street Kenmare Co Kerry
RESTAURANT   Tel: 064 42350

A delightful vegetarian café and restaurant that serves almost wholly organic food. Irish carnivores have traditionally treated such places with deep suspicion, it seems, but happily times have changed and they have embraced this relatively new venture, sampling an array of eclectic dishes (with a more Asian slant in the evening). Typically, you could have a celery soup, warm grilled aubergine with feta cheese and salad, and lemon tart – everything is home-made (bread, scones, carrot cake etc). Enclosed tea garden. **Seats 40.** Open all day; L & D daily. Closed Dec-mid Mar. No credit cards. **Directions:** In the town centre.

Kenmare   *Packie's*
Henry Street Kenmare Co Kerry
RESTAURANT   Tel: 064 41508 Fax: 064 42135

Since Tom and Maura Foley opened this buzzy little restaurant in 1992 it has had a special place in the hearts of many who visit Kenmare. It's stylish but unpretentious, with small tables and a big heart. Great local ingredients, especially organic produce and seafood, mingle with imports from sunnier climes and, in Maura's skilful hands, result in imaginative Ireland-meets-the-Med food that is memorable for its intense flavouring. Although roast pepper salad may come with black olives and pesto, and the impression is somehow of world cuisine, it's not all sun-dried tomatoes and pesto – starters of potato pancakes come with garlic or herb butter and crab cakes with traditional tartare sauce. Red onion and caper salsa may sound like an exotic accompaniment for wild smoked salmon, but it's actually a long-established partnership. Close examination of menus will probably reveal more dishes that have stood the test of time than new ones, but the important factor here is the sheer quality of both food – especially local seafood – and cooking. Puddings include good ices and a nice variation on bread and butter pudding – Moriarty's barm brack and butter pudding with rum – or there are Irish farmhouse cheeses to finish. Interesting and well-priced wine list. **Seats 35.** D only Tues-Sat, 5.30-10; à la carte. House wine £11.50; sc discretionary. Closed Sun & Mon and 1 Nov-30 Mar. MasterCard, Visa. **Directions:** Town centre.

Kenmare   *Park Hotel Kenmare*
Kenmare Co Kerry
HOTEL/RESTAURANT   Tel: 064 41200 Fax: 064 41402 email: phkenmare@iol.ie
Skills Development Award - Francis Brennan

In a lovely location adjoining Kenmare town, with views over sloping gardens to the ever-changing mountains across the bay, this renowned hotel was built in 1897 by the Great

Southern and Western Railway Company as an overnight stop for passengers travelling to Parknasilla, 17 miles away. Since 1985, when Francis Brennan became proprietor and general manager, Park Hotel Kenmare has earned international acclaim for exceptional standards of service, comfort and cuisine. Once inside the granite Victorian building, a warm welcome and the ever-burning fire in the hall begin weaving the Park's special magic: any tendency to formality in the antique furnishings is offset by amusing quirks of taste and despite the constant quest for perfection, it is surprisingly relaxed. Public rooms are not overpoweringly grand and several open onto a verandah overlooking river and gardens. Luxurious bedrooms are spacious, with excellent bathrooms and are furnished to exceptional standards of comfort with all the extras expected of top hotels – fresh flowers, robes, mineral water, quality toiletries – and some less predictable, such as hi-fi systems, which have proved a great success. However, the most remarkable aspect of the Park Hotel is its staff. The exceptional standard of training overseen by Francis Brennan through the years has had a very significant effect on standards not only in the hotel, but as a ripple effect throughout the country (and beyond) as those trained under his management have moved on to other positions. In recognition of his unique contribution in this area - and, particularly, at a time when attracting talented young people to the hospitality industry has become a national priority - the Guide is proud to award Francis Brennan its new Skills Development Award, which will allow him to nominate a promising trainee for a bursary sponsored by Irish Distillers Wines & Spirits. **Rooms 49** (9 suites, 23 min-suites, 23 executive, 4 single, 4 no-smoking, 1 disabled). Children welcome (unders 4s free in parents' room, cots available). Pets permitted in some areas; kennels available. B&B £149 (single occupancy £152). Closed 3 Jan-14 April & 29 Oct-23 Dec. Amex, Diners, MasterCard, Visa. **Directions:** At the top of the town.

Restaurant ★ Service in this elegant dining room is unfailingly outstanding and the views from window tables are simply lovely – a fitting setting for very fine food. A stylishly restrained classicism has characterised this distinguished kitchen under several famous head chefs. Currently Joe Ryan occupies the role, offering a wide choice of dishes on seasonal à la carte and set dinner menus (which are changed daily). There is an understandable leaning towards local seafood, including lobster, but Kerry lamb, beef, pork and local duck feature as well as interesting vegetarian dishes. Typically, an early summer menu might start with marinated fillet of salmon with beetroot and wild asparagus, light horseradish and cucumber sauce, then soup such as a light and cold lobster gazpacho – or a refreshing sorbet. Cannelloni of fresh sole and crab on wild mushrooms with a morel cream sauce is a typical main course. Beautifully presented desserts might include red wine soup with caramelised figs and pistachio ice cream and there's a good choice of local farmhouse cheeses. Excellent service; fine list of over 200 wines (House Wine £18.50) A short à la carte lounge menu is available at lunchtime. Not suitable for children after 8 pm. No smoking area. Toilets wheelchair accessible. **Seats 120.** D only, 7-9 daily; Set D £30, Gourmet menu £40; sc discretionary.

Kenmare   *The Purple Heather*

Henry Street Kenmare Co Kerry
RESTAURANT/BAR   Tel: 064 41016

Daytime sister restaurant to Packie's, this traditional darkwood and burgundy bar gradually develops into an informal restaurant at the rear. Run by the O'Connell family since the mid-1970s, The Purple Heather was among the first to establish a reputation for good food in Kenmare. What they aim for – and achieve, with commendable consistency – is good, simple, home-cooked food. Soups come with home-baked breads, salad is made of organic greens with balsamic dressing. Main courses include a number of seafood salads, vegetarian salads (cold and warm), pâtés – including a delicious smoked salmon pâté– plus a range of omelettes and Irish farmhouse cheeses. **Seats 40.** Food served Mon-Sat, 11.45- 6. Closed Sun, 1 wk Xmas & bank hols. No credit cards **Directions:** Town centre.

Kenmare   *Riversdale House Hotel*

Kenmare Co Kerry
HOTEL   Tel: 064 41299

Set in seven acres of gardens on the shores of Kenmare Bay, this pleasant hotel has a large open-plan lounge with a cluster of chesterfields around an open stone fireplace and a bar, with a long counter, that often provides live Irish entertainment. Best of the bedrooms (those on the ground floor have direct access to the gardens) are obviously those with breathtaking views across the estuary to the hills beyond, and especially worth seeking out are the eaved fifth-floor suites, each with its own patio balcony. But all the rooms are comfortably furnished in contemporary style, providing satellite TV, tea/coffee-making facilities and neat bathrooms. Conference/banqueting 250/350; secretarial services. Garden, walking, fishing. Children up to 3 free in parents' room; cots available. Pets allowed in some areas. **Rooms 110** (4 suites). B&B £52 pps, ss £22.Closed early Nov-20 March. Amex, Diners, MasterCard, Visa. **Directions:** Coming from Killarney, across the double-arched bridge out of town on the N71, the hotel is on the left.

Kenmare   *The Rosegarden*

Kenmare Co Kerry

ACCOMMODATION   Tel: 064 42288   Fax: 064 42305   email: rosegard@iol.ie

Peter and Ingrid Ringlever's guesthouse is set back from the road and has an immaculate garden and pond at the front. The house has a distinctly continental feel about it (hardly surprising since the couple are Dutch) and is spotlessly clean. The centrally-heated bedrooms, all en suite (excellent shower pressure) offer guests satellite TV (including a nightly-changing in-house movie shown at 10pm), tea/coffee-making facilities and biscuits. Dinner (à la carte or nightly-changing table d'hôte) combines local produce with some international touches; witness Kenmare Bay shrimps in a spicy oriental sauce, breaded medallions of pork served with a peppercorn, tomato and basil sauce, finishing with tiramisu. Various breads come with three assorted butters including curry. **Rooms 8** (all en-suite & no-smoking). Restaurant **Seats 26.** D£13.95, 6.30-9 daily. Closed Nov-Mar. Amex, Diners, MasterCard, Visa. **Directions:** Just out of town at the start of the Ring of Kerry road.

Kenmare   *Sallyport House*

Kenmare Co Kerry

COUNTRY HOUSE   Tel: 064 42066   Fax: 064 4206

This renovated country house on the edge of Kenmare is in a quiet and convenient location overlooking the harbour, with fine garden and mountain views at the rear. It is spacious throughout, from the large entrance hall (with welcoming fire) to bedrooms that are thoughtfully furnished with a mixture of antique and good quality reproduction furniture, plus orthopaedic beds, TV, phone and (unusual enough to merit mention) lights and mirrors correctly placed for their function. All rooms have practical, fully-tiled bathrooms with powerful over-bath showers and built-in hair dryers. Delicious breakfasts are served in a sunny dining room overlooking the garden. Ample parking. Not suitable for children under 12. No dogs. **Rooms 5** (all en-suite & no-smoking). B&B £45, ss £20. Closed Nov-Easter. No credit cards. **Directions:** South of town on N71, between town and bridge.

Kenmare 🏛️   *Sheen Falls Lodge*

Kenmare Co Kerry

HOTEL/RESTAURANT   Tel: 064 41600   Fax: 064 41386   email: sheenfalls@iol.ie

This stunning hotel made an immediate impact from the day it opened in April 1991; it has continued to develop and mature most impressively since - and was the Guide's Hotel of the Year in 1999. The waterside location is beautiful and welcoming fires always burn in the elegant foyer and in several of the spacious, elegantly furnished reception rooms, including a lounge bar area overlooking the waterfall. Luxurious rooms all have superb amenities, marbled bathrooms and views of the cascading river or Kenmare Bay. Exceptional facilities for business and private guests include state-of-the-art conference facilities (120), a fine library and an equestrian centre. A recently completed Health Spa includes a pretty indoor plunge pool and, together with an informal bar and bistro ("Oscars", 6-10 daily), has been so carefully landscaped and integrated with the older building that it feels as if it has always been there. But it is the staff, under the guidance of the exceptionally warm and hospitable General Manager, Adrian Bartels, who make this luxurious and stylish international hotel the home from home that it quickly becomes for each new guest. Little Hay Cottage, a luxuriously appointed self-contained two-bedroomed thatched cottage in its own garden, is also available to rent. **Rooms 61** (9 suites, 8 mini-suites, 10 no-smoking bedrooms, 1 disabled). Room rate £258 (up to 2 guests). Leisure centre (swimming pool, jacuzzi, sauna, steam room, massage), snooker, equestrian, walking, fishing, gardens, tennis, cycling. Closed 2 Jan-11 Feb, 29 Nov-23 Dec. Access, Amex, Visa, Diners.

La Cascade Restaurant ★ This beautifully appointed restaurant is arranged in tiers to take full advantage of the waterfalls – floodlit at night and providing a dramatic backdrop for Fergus Moore's superb cooking, which is French with modern Irish overtones.

Unquestionably one of Ireland's most talented chefs, Fergus has been executive chef since the hotel opened and, with the backing of faultless service under restaurant manager Shane Fitzpatrick, has earned great praise for consistently high standards. Both a daily table d'hôte and a separate vegetarian menu are offered and will certainly please even the most discerning diner. Menus favour seafood, but the overall choice is balanced with three meat or poultry dishes on a selection of six. Luxurious starters bursting with flavour might typically include fresh crabmeat with ginger, apple & spring onion flavoured with coconut milk or saute of hot foie gras on toasted brioche with apricot compote & herb oil dressing and main courses are in a similar vein – fillet of turbot with a saute of spinach and oyster mushrooms, perhaps, or, or loin of venison with braised red cabbage and glazed apple and a prune & caraway jus. As to the wine, suffice it to say that the hotel rejoices in having not one, but two superb sommeliers – Alain Bras and David Collard – and that the wine cellar is open for guests to choose their own bottle from nearly 500 wines. Port can also be served in the cellar after dinner. *Light lunches (smoked salmon, club sandwiches etc) are available in the sun lounge, 12-4 daily, followed by afternoon tea, 4-6 pm.daily. **Seats 120.** D only 7.15-9.30. Set D £37.50. House wines £16-20. Service discretionary.

Kenmare ♨   *Shelburne Lodge*

ACCOMMODATION

Killowen Cork Road Kenmare Co Kerry
Tel: 064 41013 Fax: 064 42135

Shelburne Lodge is the oldest house in Kenmare and has all the style and attention to detail that would be expected from Tom and Maura Foley, proprietors of the dashing Kenmare restaurant, Packies. A fine stone house on the edge of the town, the lodge is set back from the road in its own grounds and lovely gardens. Spacious day rooms include an elegant, comfortable drawing room and a large, well-appointed dining room where excellent breakfasts are served. Accommodation, in seven rooms individually decorated to a high standard, is extremely comfortable and everything (especially beds and bedding) is of the highest quality; individual decoration extends to the excellent bathrooms – all with full bath except the more informal conversion at the back of the house, which is especially suitable for families and has neat shower rooms. No evening meals are served, but residents are directed to Packies. Garden, tennis. Own parking. No pets. **Rooms 9** (all en-suite, 2 shower-only). B&B £45, ss £10. Closed 1 Nov- 31 Mar. MasterCard, Visa. **Directions:** 500 yards from town centre, on the Cork road R569.

Killarney   *Aghadoe Heights Hotel*

HOTEL/RESTAURANT

Aghadoe Killarney Co Kerry
Tel: 064 31766 Fax: 064 31345

A few miles out of town and well-signposted off the N22 road (both directions: Tralee and Cork), this low-rise hotel, built in the '60s, enjoys stunning views of the lakes and the mountains beyond and also overlooks Killarney's two 18-hole championship golf courses. It's very luxuriously furnished and decorated, with lots of marble, antiques and good paintings, and the club-like Lake Room with its leather chesterfields and dark wood has always been particularly relaxing. However, all that may soon be history as proprietor Patrick Curran, who took over the hotel in 1997, is about to make major changes. As the Guide goes to print, the hotel is winding down for a long winter closure while the builders get to work. Plans include a new bar, an extension to the famous first-floor dining room, Frederick's Restaurant, the addition of 17 new bedrooms and the extension and refurbishment of all the existing bedrooms. The expected re-opening date is 1st April 2000, then they will be open all year. For further details, contact the hotel direct. Amex, Diners, MasterCard, Visa.

Killarney   *Cahernane House Hotel*

HOTEL/RESTAURANT

Muckross Road Killarney Co Kerry
Tel: 064 31895 Fax: 064 34340
email: cahernane@tinet.ie

Formerly the residence of the Earls of Pembroke, this beautifully situated hotel is set in parkland with wonderful views of Killarney's lakes and mountains. A welcoming fire burns in a large entrance hall (that has probably seen little change since the original house was built in 1877) and, although a large modern wing has added a new dimension, it is the character of the old building that holds the spirit of the hotel. Rooms vary from traditional master bedrooms in the manor house, which are furnished with antiques, to the simpler but spacious and well-appointed rooms with good bathrooms in the new wing. Reduced green fees are available for residents playing the local championship courses; tee-off times can be booked through the hotel. Flying lessons can also be arranged. Garden. Fishing. Tennis. Children welcome (under 5s free in parents room; cots available).Well behaved pets permitted by arrangement. **Rooms 44** (7 mini-suites, 3 shower only). B&B £65 pps, £25ss.

The Herbert Room Restaurant: Friendly staff and a warm welcome get a visit to this spacious and well-appointed restaurant off to a good start. Head chef James Hunt offers appealing menus that incorporate local and seasonal ingredients into a contemporary international style. Details (such as an amuse-bouche of chicken consomme capuccino with crouton) were impressive on a recent visit and starters - warmed asparagus with beetroot remoulade and Black Forest ham, plum tomato timbale with cucumber soup and crab - were also well executed. However inconsistencies in the cooking of main courses (notably wild duck) and disappointing desserts meant that, on this occasion, the meal failed to live up to its early promise. Attentive service from well-trained staff; extensive wine list and wide choice of teas and coffees. **Seats 60** (14 private). D 7-9.30pm. Set D £32; à la carte also available. House wine from £16. Closed Nov-March. Amex, Diners, MasterCard, Visa. **Directions:** 1 mile from Killarney town centre, on road to Kenmare and Muckross House. Acc£££ .Closed Nov-Mar. Amex, Diners, MasterCard, Visa.

Killarney ✳   *Castlerosse Hotel*

Killarney Co Kerry

HOTEL   Tel 064-31144 Fax 064-31031 e-mail castler@iol.ie

This lowrise modern hotel enjoys a lakeside setting with superb lake and mountain views from back rooms, including the restaurant and bar. Major developments, which have transformed it in recent years, include an impressive leisure centre and a well-appointed new wing; older rooms were also refurbished and upgraded to match the new standard at the time. Corridors to some rooms are long, but luggage can be delivered to back rooms by car - and that all have easy access to well-maintained grounds. Conferences / Banqueting (200/200) Garden. Leisure centre.Tennis.Fishing. Children welcome (under 2s free in parents room; cots available). No Pets. **Rooms 110** (all en-suite, 1 mini-suite, 2 for disabled). B&B £52 pps, ss £15. Closed Nov-March. Amex, Diners, MasterCard, Visa. **Directions:** Adjoins Killarney Golf Club.

Killarney   *Celtic Cauldron*

27 Plunkett Street Killarney Co Kerry

RESTAURANT   Tel: 064 36821

This is Ireland's first and reputedly only traditional restaurant, offering authentic fare from the Celtic nations, based on original recipes and medieval cooking methods. The dining-room is reminiscent of a farmhouse kitchen, with lots of bric-a-brac scattered around and, wherever possible, produce is organic and local: typical examples include Irish cockles, mussels and prawns cooked in a cream and mead sauce with herbs and served with potato cakes; Glamorgan sausage, a Welsh vegetarian dish made from cheese, wholemeal breadcrumbs, leeks and herbs; Scottish pheasant and port pâté. Main courses might include braised venison in port and juniper berries or braised beef in a rich ale gravy. Desserts are traditional too; perhaps apple pie or bread and butter pudding. **Seats 40.** D daily 6-10pm. A la Carte. House wine from £6.50. sc discretionary. No-smoking area. Toilets wheelchair accessible. Closed Nov-Mar. **Directions:** Centrally located in Plunkett Street, in the heart of Killarney.

Killarney ✳   *The Cooperage Restaurant*

Old Market Lane Killarney Co Kerry.

RESTAURANT   Tel 064 37716 Fax 064 37716 email chezmart@iol.ie

This striking modern restaurant in an attractively restored town centre premises has brought a breath of fresh air to the Killarney dining scene. A lot of thought has gone into the decor, which is more than just eye-catching and (unlike many contemporary restaurants) the dining space is comfortable as well as visually impressive. A friendly welcome and efficient service from the outset are promising signs, followed through by contemporary menus which suggest an element of simplicity and recognition of seasonality and provenance of ingredients as well as eye appeal. Good first courses might include an excellent Mediterranean soup and a typical fish of the day could be cod, served with perfectly cooked vegetables. Lunch menu are shortish, plus blackboard specials, with more choice in the evening. Apart from a lively (some might say noisy) atmosphere, what you get here is imaginative good food, well prepared at reasonable prices. Shortish fairly priced wine list a bit patchy on vintages. **Seats 70.** No-smoking area; air conditioning. L 12-3, D 6-10 daily. A la Carte. House wine £11.95. Toilets accessible by wheelchair. Parking nearby. Open all Year. MasterCard, Visa. **Directions:** Under the arch at Market cross, Killarney main street.

Killarney   *Fuchsia House*

Muckross Road Killarney Co Kerry

ACCOMMODATION   Tel: 064 33743 Fax: 064 36588

A short walk from the town centre, on the N71 road to Kenmare, this is purpose-built guesthouse is set well back from the road, with a well-maintained rear garden and ample car parking in the front. On arrival in the afternoon you'll be served tea and home-made cake in the drawing room, a prelude to an outstanding breakfast the next morning, with many fresh goodies on show. Spacious bedrooms, very luxuriously furnished with smart co-ordinating fabrics and quality bedding (the beds are especially firm and comfortable), offer facilities more usually associated with expensive hotels, from remote-control satellite TV and direct-dial telephone to a professional hairdryer and power shower in the well-equipped bathrooms. Hosts Tom and Mary Treacy are part of a family of well-known and dedicated Killarney hoteliers (Killarney Lodge, Killarney Park and Ross Hotels), ensuring the house is immaculately run and maintained. A large conservatory has recently been added for guests' use. Garden. Cycling. Wheelchair accessible. Children welcome (under 10s free in parents room; cots available; childrens' playground.) No Pets. **Rooms 10** (all en-suite & no smoking). B&B £40 pps, ss £20. Closed 15 Nov-1st March. Diners, MasterCard, Visa. **Directions:** Located on N71 .75km from town on the right hand side.

Killarney   *Gaby's Seafood Restaurant*

27 High Street Killarney Co Kerry

RESTAURANT   Tel: 064 32519 Fax: 064 32747

One of Ireland's longest established seafood restaurants, Gaby's has a cosy little bar beside an open fire just inside the door, then several steps lead up to the main dining area, which is cleverly broken up into several sections and has a pleasantly informal atmosphere. Chef-proprietor Gert Maes offers well designed seasonal à la carte menus in classic French style – and in three languages. Absolute freshness is clearly the priority – a note on the menu reminds that availability depends on daily landings – but there's always plenty else to choose from, with steaks and local lamb as back-up. Specialities include cassoulet of prawns and monkfish – Dublin Bay prawns and monkfish in a lightly gingered sauce – and Gaby's "Famous Smoked Salmon Pâté", served in a little pot with a salad garnish and crisp hot toast. Lobster is also a speciality and wild Atlantic salmon, in a light chive & lemon sauce perhaps. Lovely desserts – a trio of home-made ices in a crisp tuile basket with blackcurrant coulis is typical – and freshly brewed coffee to finish. **Seats 75.** D only, Mon-Sat 6-10pm. A la Carte available; house wine £16; sc discretionary Toilets wheelchair accessible. Closed Sun, 22 Dec-3 Jan, Mid Feb-Mid March. Amex, Diners, MasterCard, Visa. **Directions:** On the Main Street.

Killarney ˣ   *Hotel Dunloe Castle*

Beaufort Killarney Co Kerry

HOTEL   Tel: 064 44111 Fax: 064 44583 email: khl@iol.ie

Sister hotel to the Hotel Europe (Fossa) and Ard-na-Sidhe (Caragh Lake), Dunloe Castle has many features in common with the larger Europe: the style of the building is similar, the same priorities apply – generous space is allowed for all areas throughout, the quality of furnishing is exceptionally high and both maintenance and housekeeping are superb. The original castle is still part of the development, but the hotel is mainly modern and, like the Europe, the atmosphere is distinctly continental. But Dunloe Castle has some special features of its own, including the park around the hotel, which is internationally renowned for its unique botanical collection, and an equestrian centre. D£££. Acc££. Closed Oct-April. Amex, Diners, MasterCard, Visa.

Killarney ˣ   *Hotel Europe*

Fossa Killarney Co Kerry

HOTEL   Tel: 064 31900 Fax: 064 32118 email: khl@iol.ie

Although now around thirty years old, the Europe was exceptionally well built and has been so immaculately maintained through the years that it still outshines many a new top level hotel. Public areas are very large and impressive, furnished to the highest standards and make full use of the hotel's wonderful location. The leisure facilities – which include a 25-metre swimming pool and seaweed bath, all dating back to the time of the hotel's construction – are also a credit to the vision and wisdom of the original developers. Bedrooms follow a similar pattern, with lots of space, best quality furnishings, beautiful views and balconies all along the lake side of the hotel. Given the high standards and facilities offered, rates are very reasonable, and it is also worth inquiring about special breaks. The hotel's continental connections show clearly in the style throughout but especially, perhaps, when it comes to food -breakfast, for example, is a hot and cold buffet. Excellent conference and meeting facilities include a 450-seat auditorium with built-in microphones and translation system. L££ daily, D£££ daily. Acc£££. Closed Nov-Mar. Amex, Diners, MasterCard, Visa.

Killarney — *Kathleen's Country House*

Madam's Height Tralee Road Killarney Co Kerry
ACCOMMODATION   Tel: 064 32810   Fax: 064 32340

Long before the current rash of purpose-built guesthouses, Kathleen O'Regan Sheppard was offering hotel standard accommodation at guesthouse prices, and this family-run business continues to offer good value, hospitality and comfort in a quiet location – in gardens just a mile from the town centre. All of the individually decorated rooms are non-smoking and furnished to a high standard, with orthopaedic beds, phone, TV, tea/coffee-making facilities and fully tiled bathrooms with full bath and shower. Spacious public areas provide plenty of room for relaxing and include a pleasant dining room where good breakfasts are served overlooking the garden. Special rates are offered off-season. Own parking. Wheelchair accessible. Not suitable for very young children (over 5s welcome).No Pets. **Rooms 17** (all en-suite). B&B £42.50 pps, ss £27.50. Closed 7 Nov-14 Mar.Amex, MasterCard, Visa. **Directions:** Off Tralee road (N 22).

Killarney — *Killarney Great Southern Hotel*

Killarney Co Kerry
HOTEL   Tel: 064 31262   Fax: 064 31642   email: res@killarney.gsh.ie

This classic railway hotel was established in 1854 and its pillared entrance and ivy-clad facade still convey a sense of occasion. Recent refurbishment has been completed with due respect for the age and history of the building, and the spacious foyer, especially, has retained a high level of grandeur. Belying its central position, the hotel is set in 36 acres of landscaped gardens, providing peace and relaxation on the premises. Facilities added over the years include two tennis courts, an indoor heated swimming pool and a leisure centre. Regularly refurbished bedrooms include – unusually these days – 12 single rooms. Conferences/ Banqueting (1,000/650); secretarial services, video conferencing. Business centre. Leisure centre.Garden.Tennis. Hairdresser. Wheelchair accessible. Children welcome (under 2s free in parents room; cots available, crèche, playground). Pets permitted by arrangement. **Rooms 181** (3 suites, 2 mini-suites, 15 exec, 1 for disabled). B&B £74 pps, ss £22; sc 12.5%. Open all year. Amex, Diners, MasterCard, Visa. **Directions:** Right in the centre of Killarney town.

Killarney — *Killarney Lodge*

Countess Road Killarney Co Kerry
ACCOMMODATION   Tel: 064 36499   Fax: 064 31070   email: kylodge@iol.ie

Catherine Treacy's purpose-built guesthouse is set in private walled gardens just a two minute walk from the town centre and has large en-suite air-conditioned bedrooms with all the amenities expected of a hotel room and large public rooms to relax in. Garden. Parking. Children welcome (under 12s free in parents room; cots available). Wheelchair accessible. No pets. **Rooms 16** (all en-suite & no smoking, 2 mini-suites, 14 exec, 1 shower only, 1 for disabled). B&B £42 pps, ss £30. Closed 6 Nov-31 Jan. Amex, Diners, MasterCard, Visa. **Directions:** Two minutes walk from Town centre off Muckross road.

Killarney 🏛 — *Killarney Park Hotel*

Kenmare Place Killarney Co Kerry
HOTEL/RESTAURANT   Tel: 064 35555   Fax: 064 35266

Situated in its own grounds, a short stroll from the town centre, this luxurious, well run and deceptively modern hotel has already undergone a recent transformation, with the refurbishment of all public areas and the leisure centre, and the addition of several new junior suites and a state-of-the-art conference room. Public areas have an elegant Victorian feel, enhanced by the sweeping staircase that leads to bedrooms furnished in contemporary country house style. Sister hotel to the much older Ross Hotel nearby, which is equally delightful.Conferences/ Banqueting (150/120); secretarial services, video conferencing. Business centre. Leisure centre. Snooker.Garden. No Pets. Children welcome (under 2s free in parents room; cots available, playroom). Lift. **Rooms 76** (3 suites, 18 mini-suites, 30 no-smoking, 1 for disabled). B&B £110 pps, ss £110; sc discretionary. Closed 23-26 Dec. Amex, Diners, MasterCard, Visa. **Restaurant:** A large and opulent room with an ornate ceiling, heavy drapes and grand paintings, with a pianist playing popular pieces throughout dinner. A lengthy à la carte menu is available in high season, otherwise a fixed-price menu with several choices is offered. Restaurant seats 120 (40 private). D 7-9.15pm. Sun L 12.30-2pm. Set D £30. House wine £15. Toilets wheelchair accessible. Air conditioning. **Directions:** Located in Killarney town - all access routes lead to town centre.

Killarney ✲   *Killarney Royal*

College Street Killarney Co Kerry
HOTEL   Tel 064 31853 Fax 064 34001 Email royalhot@iol.ie

This older sister to the luxurious Hayfield Manor Hotel in Cork city (see entry) has recently completed a major refurbishment programme and the results, in an elegant period style that is totally appropriate to the age and design of the building, are very impressive. No expense has been spared to ensure the highest quality of materials and workmanship, air conditioning has been installed throughout the hotel and rooms have been individually designed, all with marble bathrooms and sitting areas. Wheelchair accessible. Arrangement with nearby carpark. Children welcome (under 7s free in parents room; cots available). **Rooms 29** (all en-suite, 5 suites, 5 no-smoking). B&B £85 pps, ss £35. Closed 22-28 Dec. Amex, Diners, MasterCard, Visa. **Directions:** Town centre of Killarney on College street off the N22.

Killarney   *The Killarney Ryan Hotel & Leisure Centre*

Killarney Co Kerry
HOTEL   Tel: 064 31555 Fax: 064 32438

This modern hotel on the edge of Killarney is set in 20 acres of grounds and has earned an exceptional reputation for family holidays. In the summer holidays, especially, but also on holiday weekends and special breaks, the facilities and activities available for children from tiny tots to teenagers are outstanding – a supervised crèche, children's entertainment (including a 'club' for older children), indoor and outdoor supervised sports and special menus and meal times. All rooms are comfortably furnished with good facilities. In addition to on-site activities, golf, pitch & putt, riding and fishing are all available nearby. Garden. Tennis. Leisure centre. Own parking. Wheelchair accessible. Children welcome (under 2s free in parents room; cots available, crèche, playground, playroom). No Pets. **Rooms 164** (all en-suite). B&B £55 pps, ss £30. Lift. Closed 6-23 Dec, 4 Jan-4 Feb. Amex, Diners, MasterCard, Visa. **Directions:** On main Cork road, 1 km from centre of Killarney.

Killarney   *Killeen House Hotel*

Aghadoe Killarney Co Kerry
HOTEL   Tel: 064 31711 Fax: 064 31811 email: charhing@indigo.ie

Recognising its potential as "a charming little hotel", Michael and Geraldine Rosney bought this early nineteenth century rectory in 1992. Just 10 minutes drive from Killarney town centre and 5 minutes from Killeen and Mahoney's Point golf courses, the hotel makes a homely base for business or leisure. There's a warm, welcoming atmosphere that is especially noticeable in the pubby little bar, which is popular with locals as well as residents (run as an "honour" bar with golf balls accepted as local tender). Rooms vary in size but all have full bathrooms (one with jacuzzi) and are freshly-decorated, with phone and satellite TV. There's a traditional drawing room for guests, furnished with a mixture of antiques and newer furniture, and an open fire. Major refurbishment was underway on the Guide's most recent visit. Children welcome (free in parents room under 12s ; cots available). Pets permitted by arrangement. **Rooms 23** (all en-suite). B&B £47.50 pps, ss £20. Closed 1 Nov - 1 April. Amex, Diners, MasterCard, Visa. **Directions:** 4 miles from Killarney - just off Dingle road.

Killarney   *Lake Hotel*

Muckross Road Killarney Co Kerry
HOTEL   Tel: 064 31035 Fax: 064 31902 lakehotel@tinet.ie
Coming into town from Kenmare on the N71, the hotel is set well back from the road on
the lake shore, with the ruins of McCarthy Mor Castle within the grounds. The hotel was
built in 1820 and visited by Queen Victoria when she came to Ireland in 1861 (the hotel
still has the original horse-drawn carriage in which she travelled). Recent additions include
a lift, and new suites which have a four-poster bed, spa bath and private balconies
overlooking the lakes. All bedrooms are smartly decorated and furnished and have the
usual modern amenities. Own fishing. Tennis. Children welcome (under 3s free in parents
room; cots available, playroom). Wheelchair accessible. No Pets. **Rooms 70** (12 suites; 2
rooms for disabled; 2 shower only). B&B £40 pps, ss £17. Closed Nov-Mar. Amex, Diners,
MasterCard, Visa. **Directions:** 1 mile from Killarney town on the road to Kenmare.

Killarney *X*   *Muckross Park Hotel*

Muckross Village Killarney Co Kerry
HOTEL   Tel: 064 31938 Fax: 064 31965
Just across the road from Muckross House and Garden, Muckross Abbey and the
Muckross Traditional Farms, this hotel has retained a real "country house" feeling –
despite its close proximity to "Molly's", the hotel's large traditional-style pub/restaurant
(which also has a separate entrance from the car park). The proportions of the building
contribute to the country house feel. There's a spacious, elegant reception area and well-
proportioned day rooms include a residents' sitting room and a restaurant (the
"Bluepool", named after the nearby Cloghreen Blue Pool Nature Trail) overlooking
gardens towards the river. There's also a dining room suitable for private dinner parties
and small conferences (30). Generous bedrooms have large double and single beds,
quality furnishings and well-planned bathrooms. Rear rooms overlook the garden and
front ones, although not as quiet, look over the woodland in Muckross Park. Two unusual
suites are on a separate staircase – one has a gallery sleeping area and the other a
bathroom with original stone walling and a corner bath. In addition to rooms in the main
building, the Muckross Suites offer 48 two-bedroom apartments in a new block just
behind the hotel. No dogs. Banqueting for 150. Acc£££. Closed Nov-Mar. Amex, Diners,
MasterCard, Visa.

Killarney   *Clarion Randles Court Hotel*

Muckross Road Killarney Co Kerry
HOTEL   Tel: 064 35333 Fax: 064 35206 email: randles@iol.ie
Within easy walking distance of the town centre, but also convenient to attractions such
as Muckross House and Killarney National Park, this attractive house was originally built
in 1906 as a family residence and underwent extensive refurbishment before opening as
an hotel in 1991. Although it has grown a little since then it has retained the domesticity
and warmth of the family home. Period features, including fireplaces and stained glass
windows, have been retained. Comfortably furnished public rooms include a small bar, a
large drawing room with log fire, tapestries and antiques and an elegant restaurant
opening onto a sheltered patio. Spacious bedrooms are furnished to a high standard, with
direct dial telephones, satellite television, radio, hair dryers and well-appointed
bathrooms. Own parking. No pets. **Rooms 50** (2 suites, 12 mini-suites, 1 for disabled).
Closures & prices unconfirmed at time of going to press. Amex, Diners, MasterCard, Visa.

Killarney   *Torc Great Southern Hotel*

Park Road Killarney Co Kerry
HOTEL   Tel: 064 31611 Fax: 064 31824 email: res@torc.gsh.ie
On the main Cork road, this modern hotel set in gardens is just 5 minutes walk from the
town centre. Well-run, with views of the Kerry Mountains, it makes a good base for a
holiday in the area. Very handy for Killarney's championship golf courses - special breaks
available. Pets permitted by arrangement. Garden. Tennis. Indoor swimming pool.
Parking. Children welcome (under 2s free in parents room; cots available, crèche).
Wheelchair accessible. Pets by arrangement. **Rooms 96** (all en-suite, 1 for disabled).
B&B £53 pps, ss £22. Closed Mid Oct-Mid April. Amex, Diners, MasterCard, Visa.
Directions: On the main Cork road into Killarney town.

Killorglin
Nick's Seafood Restaurant & Piano Bar

Lower Bridge Street Killorglin Co Kerry

RESTAURANT   Tel: 066 976 1219/976 1936 Fax: 066 976 1233

Nick Foley's cooking – classic French with an Irish accent– has earned a particular reputation for his way with local seafood, although there are always other choices, notably prime Kerry beef and lamb. Moules marinière or provençale, lobster thermidor, shellfish mornay and peppered steak in brandy cream sauce are all typical of his classic style. Vegetarians aren't forgotten either – there's a choice of three dishes on the regular menu. Dessert choices are changed daily and there's a good cheeseboard. Aside from providing excellent food, Nick's is also renowned for its music and great atmosphere. Children welcome. **Seats 80** (private room,30). No-smoking area; air conditioning. D Wed-Sun D 6.30-10pm in winter, daily in summer. Set D £28.35. House wine £12.50.; sc discretionary. Closed Mon + Tues, 2 weeks Feb, month of Nov, 24+25 Dec-Easter. Amex, Diners, MasterCard, Visa. **Directions:** On the Ring of Kerry road 20 km from Killarney.

Listowel *
Allo's Bar & Bistro

41 Church Street Listowel Co Kerry

RESTAURANT/PUB   Tel: 068 22880

Named after the previous owner ("Alphonsus, aka Allo") Armel Whyte and Helen Mullane's cafe-bar seems much older than it is – they have reconstructed the whole interior with salvaged materials (the flooring was once in the London Stock Exchange). It is convincingly done with the long, narrow bar divided up in the traditional way. On a visit in spring 1999, we found a huge building job in progress as Armel and Helen have acquired the house next door and were making major alternations to integrate the two. It is unlikely that Armel's cooking will change dramatically however, as he is well-known for his lively combination of traditional and new Irish cooking with some international influences, all based on all the best local ingredients. Meals£-££ Closed 25 Dec & Good Fri. Amex, MasterCard, Visa.

Listowel ✻
Listowel Arms Hotel

The Square Listowel Co Kerry

HOTEL   Tel 068 21500 Fax 068 22524

This much-loved old hotel is rich in history and especially famous as the main venue for the annual Listowel Writers Week. Since 1996 the hotel has been blessed with the energetic and discerning ownership of Kevin O'Callaghan, who has overseen a major extension and overhaul of the whole premises during the last two years. When complete (December 1999) the extension will provide a new restaurant, kitchen, banqueting area and new bedrooms, all overlooking the River Feale. Meanwhile, improvements already made to the existing building have been done with great sensitivity, so greater comfort has been gained without loss of character. Conference/banqueting (500/400); video-conferencing, secretarial services, ISDN lines. Wheelchair accessible. Lift. Children welcome (under 5s free in parents' room, cots available). Pets permitted by arrangement. **Rooms 37** (all en-suite). B&B £40 pps, ss £15 (Higher rates apply to Festival weeks, incl Murphys Irish Open & Listowel Race Week.) **Directions:** In the corner of the historic old square in Listowel town centre.

Moll's Gap ✻
Avoca Handweavers

Moll's Gap Kenmare Co Kerry

RESTAURANT   Tel: 064 34720 Fax: 064 35742

High up at a famous viewing point on the Ring of Kerry, this outpost of the County Wicklow weaving company sells its fine range of clothing and crafts - and offers wholesome, home-made fare to sustain the weary sightseer. Parking. Restaurant **seats 80.** No-smoking area. Food service all day 10-5pm. Toilets wheelchair accessible. Closed 10 Nov -12 Mar. Amex, Diners, MasterCard, Visa. **Directions:** On Ring of Kerry, 14 miles from Killarney, 6 from Kenmare at famous panoramic crossroads.

Parknasilla
Great Southern Hotel

Parknasilla Sneem Co Kerry

HOTEL   Tel: 064 45122 Fax: 064 45323 email: es@parknasilla.gsh.ie

Overlooking Kenmare Bay, set in 300 acres of sub-tropical parkland, this classic Victorian hotel is blessed with one of the most beautiful locations in Ireland. The spacious foyer with its antiques and fresh flowers sets a tone of quiet luxury. Whether activity or relaxation is required there are excellent amenities at hand – including an outdoor swimming pool and Canadian hot tub - and an abundance of comfortable places (including a no-smoking drawing room) for a quiet read or afternoon tea. Public rooms include an impressive restaurant and a library (added in 1995 for the hotel's centenary and available for the use of all guests, although also ideal for meetings and small conferences). Bedrooms vary in size and outlook but all have en-suite bathrooms with bath and shower, direct-dial telephone, radio, TV with in-house movie channel, trouser press and hair dryer. Most also have tea/coffee making facilities. Leisure centre. Golf (9), tennis, snooker, fishing, equestrian, walking. Wheelchair accessible. Children welcome (under 2s free in parents room; cots available; tea 5.30-6). No Pets. **Rooms 84** (all en-suite,1 suite, 8 mini-suites, 13 exec, 1 for disabled). B&B £105.50, ss £22. No sc. Amex, Diners, MasterCard, Visa. **Directions:** 30 miles outside Killarney, past Kenmare en route to Sneem

Portmagee ✗   *Fisherman's Bar*

Portmagee Co Kerry
PUB/RESTAURANT   Tel: 066 77103

Whether for a cup of coffee – very enjoyable taken at an outside table beside the sea on a fine day – or something more substantial from the all-day bar menu, the O'Keefe's comfortable, well-run pub just beside the Valentia Island bridge is always a delightful place to take a break. Local seafood stars – a bowl of chowder, perhaps, or hot crab claws with garlic butter, both served with home-made brown bread – and main dishes include seafood platters and Irish stew. Beside the bar, more formal meals are available in the evening at the attractive Skelligs Restaurant, which also specialises in seafood and is especially highly regarded by sailing folk. Bar food should be available all day in high season; a call to check times is advised. Closed 25 Dec & Good Fri.MasterCard, Visa.

Tahilla   *Tahilla Cove Country House*

Tahilla Sneem Co Kerry
COUNTRY HOUSE   Tel: 064 45204 Fax: 064 45104

This family-run guesthouse feels more like a small hotel – it has a proper bar, for example, with its own entrance (which is used by locals as well as residents). This is a low-key place, with an old country house in there somewhere (which has been much added to) and there is a blocky annex in the garden. It has two very special features, however: the location, which is genuinely waterside, is really lovely and away-from-it-all; and the owners, James and Deirdre Waterhouse. Tahilla has been in the family since 1948, and run since 1987 by James and Deirdre – who have the wisdom to understand why their many regulars love it just the way it is. Comfort and relaxation are the priorities. All the public rooms have sea views, including the dining room and a large sitting room, with plenty of armchairs and sofas, which opens onto a terrace (where there are patio tables and chairs overlooking the garden and the cove with its little stone jetty). Accommodation is divided between the main house and another close by; rooms vary considerably but all except two have sea views, many have private balconies and all are en-suite, with bathrooms of varying sizes and appointments (only one single is shower-only). All rooms have phone, TV, hair-dryer and individually controlled heating. Food is prepared personally by the proprietors and, although the dining room is mainly intended for residents, others are welcome when there is room – simple 4-course country house style menus change daily – and bar food is available from noon to 7 pm. Garden. Walking. Fishing. Wheelchair accessible. Children welcome. Pets permitted in some areas by arrangement. **Rooms 9** (all en-suite, 1 shower only). B&B £40 pps, ss £20. Closed mid Oct-Easter. Amex, Diners, MasterCard, Visa. **Directions:** On the northern side of Kenmare Bay (route N70). Ring of Kerry 11 miles west of Kenmare and 5 miles east of Sneem.

Tralee   *Abbey Gate Hotel*

Tralee Co Kerry
HOTEL   Tel: 066 712 9888 Fax: 066 712 9821

Situated in a relatively quiet corner in the centre of Tralee, this large and rather stylish modern hotel has become one of the area's leading establishments since opening in 1994. A large marble-floored foyer has ample seating space and other public areas include the main Vineyard Restaurant and an enormous traditional-style Market Place pub, where bar food is served all day. Bedrooms are a good size, comfortably furnished in a modern style with usual amenities including phone, satellite TV, tea/coffee-making facilities and well-finished en-suite bathrooms (all with bath and shower). Children are welcome – there's an outdoor playground, informal meals at the Market Place buffet and Tralee's famous Aquadome is nearby. Conferences / Banqueting (350/260); secretarial services; video conferencing. Own parking. Wheelchair accessible. Children welcome (under 2s free in parents room; cots available). **Rooms 100** (14 no-smoking, 1 for disabled). B&B £45 pps, ss £15. Closed 25 Dec. Amex, MasterCard, Visa. **Directions:** Town centre.

Tralee ✗   *The Brandon Hotel*

Princes Street Tralee Co Kerry
HOTEL   Tel: 066 23333 Fax: 066 25019

Overlooking a park and the famous Siamsa Tire folk theatre, and close to the Aquadome, Tralee's largest hotel is at the heart of activities throughout the area. Spacious public areas are quite impressive, and while some bedrooms are on the small side, all have been recently refurbished and have direct-dial phone, radio and TV (no tea/coffee-making facilities) and tiled bathrooms. There's a well-equipped leisure centre and good banqueting/conference facilities. Acc££-££££. Closed 24-28 Dec. Amex, Diners, MasterCard, Visa. *Next door to the Brandon Hotel there is an interesting new restaurant, **Restaurant Uno:** (Tel 066 718950)

Tralee ✲   *Castlemorris House*

Ballymullen, Tralee, Co Kerry.
ACCOMMODATION   Tel 066-718 0060   Fax 066-712 8007

Mary and Paddy Barry's attractive creeper-clad Victorian house makes a lovely place to stay, with good home baking (complimentary afternoon tea in front of the drawing room fire on arrival) and the friendly atmosphere of a family home. Bedrooms are spacious and well-furnished for comfort with style. Breakfast is a speciality and dinner is available by arrangement. Garden. Children over 10 welcome. pets allowed in some areas. **Rooms 6** (all en-suite, 4 shower only). B&B £35 pps, ss £10. Open all year. Amex, MasterCard, Visa. **Directions:** On the edge of Tralee town (Dingle side).

Tralee ✲   *Meadowlands Hotel*

Oakpark, Tralee, Co Kerry.
HOTEL   Tel 066-7180444   Fax 066-7180964

This hotel in a peaceful part of the town was recently demolished and completely rebuilt, finally re-opening in June 1998. First impressions (from the road) may be off-putting; it's all a bit brash and seems like the many "budget" hotels which have mushroomed all over Ireland in the last few years. But the bright colours will mellow and the quality of materials and workmanship that has gone into Meadowlands will stand the hotel in good stead over the years. The interior layout and design are impressive; notably the whole hotel is wheelchair friendly and furniture, commissioned from Irish craft manufacturers, is interesting, well-made and practical. Bedrooms are comfortable, with striking decor and the suites have jacuzzis. Off-season value breaks. Small conferences/ private parties (30/30); secretarial services, video conferencing. Garden. Children welcome (under 5s free in parents room; cots available). Wheelchair accessible. No pets. **Rooms 27** (2 suites, 1 mini-suite, 24 executive, 2 for disabled). Lift. B&B £60 pps, ss £15. Closed 24-26 Dec. MasterCard, Visa. **Directions:** 1 km. From Tralee town centre on the N69. Main Street.

Tralee ✲   *Quality Tralee Court Hotel*

Castle Street Tralee Co Kerry
HOTEL   Tel 066 712 1877   Fax 066 712 2273

Previously the famous (and historic) Benners Hotel, the Tralee Court has been completely refurbished by new owners and offers a high standard of accommodation in the heart of the town. No private parking. No pets. **Rooms 45** (1 suite, 2 mini-suites). Wheelchair accessible. Lift. B&B £45 pps, ss £20. Annual closures TBC. **Directions:** Town centre.

Waterville   *Butler Arms Hotel*

Waterville Co Kerry
HOTEL   Tel: 066 947 4144 Fax: 066 947 4520

One of Ireland's best-known hotels – it is one of several to have strong links with Charlie Chaplin – Peter and Mary Huggards' Butler Arms Hotel dominates the seafront at

Waterville. Like many hotels which have been owner-run for several generations it has established a special reputation for its homely atmosphere and good service. Improvements are constantly being made and public areas, including two sitting rooms, a sun lounge and a cocktail bar, are spacious and comfortably furnished, while the beamed Fisherman's Bar (which also has a separate entrance from the street) provides a livelier atmosphere. Bedrooms vary from distinctly non-standard rooms in the old part of the hotel (which many regular guests request) to smartly decorated, spacious rooms with neat en-suite bathrooms and uninterrupted sea views in a wing constructed in the early '90s. Off season value breaks. Garden; fishing; tennis. Snooker. Wheelchair accessible. Own parking. Children welcome. **Rooms 30** (all en-suite, 2 suites). B&B £62.50 pps, £25. No sc. Closed mid April-mid Oct. Amex, Diners, MasterCard, Visa. **Directions:** N70, 50 miles SouthWest of Killarney in centre of village.

Waterville   *The Huntsman*

Waterville Co Kerry
BAR/RESTAURANT   Tel: 066 947 4124 Fax: 066 947 4560

Raymond and Deirdre Hunt's landmark restaurant has been providing a warm and restoring stop on the Ring of Kerry since 1978. There's always a welcoming turf fire in the bar and tables are set up in both bar and restaurant to maximise some of Kerry's finest sea and mountain views. Raymond specialises in classic French seafood cookery and, although the bar menu is quite extensive and includes popular dishes such as deep-fried fish and fries, Irish stew, omelettes and pasta, as well as classics – grilled black sole and shellfish in garlic butter, the full à la carte menu is also available for bar meals. (Mixing choices from the two menus is also allowed.) Accommodation is available in a luxurious development alongside the restaurant – ask Ray about overnight stays and The Huntsman Club, which is a time-share operation of special interest to golfers. Bar/Restaurant **Seats 90** (private room,18). Food service all day 8-10pm. L from 11.30 & D 6-10 daily. Set D £25. À la Carte available. House wine from £10.75. Advisable to call ahead for reservations, Nov-Mar. Closed 3 days Xmas. Amex, Diners, MasterCard, Visa. **Directions:** As you enter village on seaside opposite Church of Ireland.

Waterville   *The Smuggler's Inn*

ACCOMMODATION/BAR/RESTAURANT   Tel: 066 947 4330 Fax: 066 947 4422

Harry and Lucille Hunt's famous clifftop pub enjoys a remarkable location right beside the world famous championship Waterville Golf Course (and overlooking a mile of sandy beach to the sea and mountain views beyond). It's a real inn, providing food, drink and shelter. A fine place to take a break from the Ring of Kerry on a good day – bar food is available from 11am-10pm daily (snack menu only 3-6 pm), both lunch and dinner are served in the restaurant daily and there are garden tables overlooking the beach for fine summer days. Local ingredients provide the base for Harry's mainly traditional cooking, with seafood (including lobster from their own tank) being the speciality. Non seafood-lovers have plenty of other choices, including Kerry lamb and beef, of course, and there's a separate vegetarian menu available. Accommodation is offered in modest but pleasantly decorated rooms which vary in size, outlook and facilities (and price – one has a balcony) but all are comfortably furnished.There's a first-floor residents' sitting room with sofas and armchairs, books, television–and magnificent sea views. Children welcome (under 5s free in parents' room, cots available). Pets by arrangement. Bar/restaurant wheelchair accessible. **Rooms 17** (all en-suite). B&B £25 pps, ss £18. Closed 14 Nov-1 Mar. Amex, Diners, MasterCard, Visa. **Directions:** Next to Waterville Golf Club.

KILDARE

Kildare is the horse county par excellence. The horse is so central and natural a part of Irish life that you'll find significant stud farms in a surprisingly large number of counties. But it is in Kildare that they reach their greatest concentration in the ultimate equine county. Thus it's ironic that, a mere 400 million years ago, Kildare was just a salty ocean where the only creatures remotely equine were the extremely primitive ancestors of sea horses. However, things have been looking up for the horse in County Kildare ever since, and today the lush pastures of the gently sloping Liffey and Barrow valleys provide ideal country for nurturing champions. Apart from many famous private farms, the Irish National Stud in Kildare town just beyond the legendary gallops of The Curragh is open for visitors, and it also includes a remarkable Japanese garden, reckoned the best Japanese rock garden in Europe, as well as the Museum of the Horse. Once you get away from the busy main roads, Kildare is full of surprises, and in the northwest of the county you enter the awe-inspiring Bog of Allen, the largest in Ireland, across whose wide open spaces the early engineers struggled to progress the Grand Canal on its route from the east coast towards the Shannon. Inevitably, Kildare is feeling an element of commuter pressure from Dublin, and the fact that it is on the main route from the capital to the south and southwest means that it seems to have more miles of motorway per square mile of county than anywhere else. Yet the underlying quality of the land is such that only the shortest diversion from the arterial roads is required to find total rural peace.

Local Attractions and Information

Carbury	Ballindoolin House & Garden Co Kildare 0405 31430
Kill	Goffs Bloodstock Sales (frequent) 045 886600
Straffan	Steam Museum 01 627 3155
Celbridge	Castletown House 01 628 8252
Tully	Irish National Stud 045 21617
Tully	Japanese Gardens 045 21251
Kilcock	Larchill Arcadian Gardens (follies) 01 6287354
Naas	Furness (Palladian House) 045 866815
Straffan	Lodge Park Walled Garden (beside Steam Museum) 01 6288412

Athy

Tonlegee House & Restaurant

Athy Co Kildare
Tel/Fax: 0507 31473
email: tonlegeehouse@tinet.ie

COUNTRY HOUSE/RESTAURANT

This elegant country house just outside Athy was built in 1790 and now combines modern comfort with an element of old-fashioned style. The individually furnished en-suite bedrooms include a junior suite and one single room and all are comfortably furnished to a high standard with phones, TV and complimentary mineral water and well-finished bathrooms. Children welcome. Pets permitted by arrangement. **Rooms 9** (1 mini-suite, 4 executive, 1 shower only). B&B £37.50 pps, ss £17.50; sc discretionary. Closed 2 wks Nov, Xmas, New Year, Good Fri & Bank Hols. Amex, MasterCard, Visa.

Restaurant: Seasonal menus are in a modern European style and based on home-grown and local produce Imaginative menus offer a balanced choice, including house specialities such as quail & wild mushroom pie with Madeira sauce - and local Kildare lamb is an especially strong option, alongside more unusual dishes like roast saddle of rabbit with braised cabbage and tortellini. Tempting desserts might include a thin apple tart with cinnamon cream (cooked to order) or home made ice creams – or make the most of a good Irish farmhouse cheeseboard. **Seats 40.** D only 6-9 pm (Mon & Sun residents only). Set D £19.50; house wine from £12.50; sc discretionary.

Ballymore Eustace [PUB★]

Ballymore Inn

Ballymore Eustace Co Kildare
Tel: 045 864585

PUB/RESTAURANT

It's the food that draws people to the O'Sullivan family's pub and it's wise to book well ahead to get a taste of the wonderful things this country kitchen has to offer, especially at weekends. The outside of the Ballymore Inn gives little away, although the blackboard menu at the door is a hint of what's to come. Inside, the clues begin to add up, especially if you turn right into the more "foodie" side. Unusual furniture, imaginative use of colour and striking fresh flowers and plants all add up to the kind of place where details count so the menu, when it arrives, fits into the pattern. There's lots to choose from, such as delicious soups, Caesar salad with crispy bacon, excellent steaks, pasta dishes – with chicken, tomato and goat's cheese perhaps – and stir fries. Creative modern pizzas that marry artisan Irish food products with traditional methods are a house speciality and they've found that a special pizza oven installed last year has turned out to be a marvel for all sorts of other dishes too. What makes these pizzas special is partly that they have wonderfully light, thin and crisply cooked bases and every ingredient is in tip-top condition and the range includes some wonderful combinations, most of which happen to be vegetarian. You can choose from the likes of Pepperoni, Tomato, Chilli & Mozzarella or Grilled Peppers with Olives and Pesto, or dither between Spinach, Oyster Mushroom and Goat's Cheese and Anchovy, Black Olives, Capers, Red Onion and Cooleeney Cheese. They're all wonderful but best of all, we think, is the Grilled Fennel, Roasted Peppers, Basil and Ardrahan Cheese, which was the winner of our Vegetarian Dish of the Year for 1999. Children welcome. **Seats 40.** No smoking area; air conditioning. Toilets wheelchair accessible. L 12.30-3 & D 6-9 Mon-Sat; No food on Sun; closed 25 Dec & Good Fri.Amex, MasterCard, Visa.

Castledermot   *Kilkea Castle*

Kilkea Castledermot Co Kildare
HOTEL/RESTAURANT   Tel: 0503 45156 Fax: 0503 45187 email: kilkea@iol.ie

The oldest inhabited castle in Ireland, Kilkea dates back to the twelfth century and has been sensitively renovated and converted into a hotel without loss of elegance and grandeur. Rooms, many with lovely views over the formal gardens and surrounding countryside, are splendidly furnished to incorporate modern comforts. Public areas include a hall complete with knights in armour and two pleasant ground floor bars – a cosy back one and a larger one that opens onto a terrace overlooking gardens and a golf course. Some of the bedrooms in the main castle are very romantic – as indeed is the whole setting – making it understandably popular for weddings. The adjoining leisure centre, architecturally discreet, offers state-of-the-art facilities: indoor swimming pool, saunas, jacuzzi, steamroom, well-equipped exercise room and sunbed. Outdoor sports include clay pigeon shooting, archery, tennis and fishing. An 18-hole championship golf course, which has views of the castle from every fairway, opened in 1994, using the River Greese flowing through the grounds as a natural hazard and adding a couple of extra lakes to increase the challenge still further; informal meals are served in the golf club. Special weekend breaks at the castle are good value. Conferences/banqueting (300/500).; secretarial services. Leisure Centre. Garden. Tennis, Golf (18), fishing. Children welcome (under 12s free in parents' room; cots avail, babysitting on request). No pets. **Rooms 36** (1 suite, 9 mini-suites, 8 exec, 3 shower only). B&B £75 pps, ss £35. Closed 23-27 Dec.Amex, Diners, MasterCard, Visa.

De Lacy's Restaurant: Named after Hugh de Lacy, who built Kilkea Castle in 1180, this beautiful first-floor restaurant has a real "castle" atmosphere and magnificent views over the countryside. It also overlooks the delightful formal kitchen garden (source of much that appears on the table in summer) and has a bright, airy atmosphere. The quality of ingredients shines through, with good contrast in flavour and, in specialities such as the roast of the day, there are excellent simpler alternatives available (and certainly no lack of generosity). Roast rack of Kildare lamb is a speciality - coated with herbed breadcrumbs and served with garlic and rosemary flavoured sauce, perhaps – but seafood is not overlooked: typically, grilled fillet of cod might be served on a tasty bed of lightly spiced stir-fry style root vegetables. Guests may take coffee on the terrace in summer and wander around to see the old fruit trees, vegetables and herbs. Restaurant **seats 60** (40 private). L daily 12.30-2.00, Sun to 2.30, D 7.00-9.30. Set L £18.50. Set D £30. House wine £13.50;sc 12.5 %. Toilets wheelchair accessible.

The Curragh ✗   *Martinstown House*

The Curragh Co Kildare
COUNTRY HOUSE   Tel: 045 441269 Fax: 045 441208

Just on the edge of the Curragh, near Punchestown, Naas and The Curragh race courses, this delightful 200 year old 'Strawberry Hill' gothic style house is on a farm, set in 170 acres of beautifully wooded land. It also has a lovely walled garden that provides vegetables, fruit and flowers for the house in season. There are free range hens, sheep, cattle and horses. Meryl Long welcomes guests to this idyllic setting, aiming to offer them "a way of life which I knew as a child (but with better bathrooms!) a warm welcome, real fires and good food." It is a lovely family house, with very nicely proportioned rooms – gracious but not too grand – and bedrooms that are all different, very comfortably furnished with fresh flowers and with their own special character. A stay here is sure to be enjoyable, with the help of a truly hospitable hostess who believes that holidays should be fun, full of interest and with an easy-going atmosphere. Acc££. Closed Easter.Amex, MasterCard, Visa.

Kilcullen   *Berneys Bar & Restaurant*

Kilcullen Co Kildare

PUB/RESTAURANT   Tel: 045 481260 Fax: 045 481877 email: berneys@indigo.ie

Paul and Freda Mullen have been running this welcoming bar on the main street since 1989 – it's a real local, with its own character, a beer garden for summer and a log fire that's a welcome sight on cold days. Freda's cooking is a mixture of Irish and country French, and in addition to a good choice of sandwiches and salads and one or two regulars she offers a short bar menu of 2-3 soups, hot dishes and puddings, changed daily. Evening meals are served in the restaurant, a large L-shaped room beside the bar with warm red walls and interesting pictures. The restaurant menu moves up a few gears and offers a much wider choice and more elaborate dishes. There's always a good choice of seafood and vegetarian dishes as well as popular fare like steaks (various ways), roast venison and duck – although limited bar food such as sandwiches and salads is available until 11 pm. Children welcome before 7pm. Parking. Restaurant **seats 80** (private room, 40). No-smoking area; air conditioning. D Mon-Sat 7-10 (Sun to 9) Set D £30. A la carte also available. House wine £11.50; sc discretionary. Bar Food Mon-Sat 11-11pm. Toilets wheelchair accessible Closed Good Fri + 25 Dec. Amex, Diners, MasterCard, Visa. **Directions:** South of Naas continue on M9 turn right into Kilcullen, in town over the bridge.

Leixlip   *Leixlip House Hotel*

Captain's Hill Leixlip Co Kildare

HOTEL/RESTAURANT   Tel: 01 624 2268 Fax: 01 624 4177

Up on a hill overlooking Leixlip village, this lovely Georgian house is just eight miles from Dublin city centre. Having undergone extensive renovation (it has been furnished and decorated to a very high standard in period style) it opened as a hotel in 1996. Gleaming antique furniture and gilt-framed mirrors enhance thick carpeted public rooms in soft country colours, all creating an atmosphere of discreet opulence. Bedrooms include two suites furnished with traditional mahogany furniture. The strong, simple decor particularly pleases the many business guests who stay here. Attention to detail is good throughout although it is surprising that, while all are en-suite, nine of the fifteen bedrooms have shower-only. The hotel's conference centre has facilities for up to 120 people, can be adapted to suit a wide range of uses and has back-up business services. Hotel guests have complimentary use of a nearby gym. Special dinner and overnight rates are available at certain times; details from Reservations. Secretarial services. Children welcome before 6 pm. No pets. **Rooms 15** (all en-suite, 9 shower only). B&B £60 pps, ss £30. Children welcome (under 12s free in parents' room).

The Bradaun Restaurant: The commitment to quality evident in the hotel as a whole is continued in the restaurant, a bright, high-ceilinged, formally appointed dining room. Head chef Sean Hicks, who has been with the hotel since it opened, offers modern Irish cooking in lunch and dinner menus that change twice weekly. Menus are imaginative, wide-ranging, based on fresh seasonal produce and well executed. Main courses offer a balanced choice, usually with two fish dishes and often including Kildare lamb – loin with glazed shallots and a thyme & garlic sauce perhaps. Desserts are equally good – fresh fruit terrine and a caramelised confit was especially enjoyed on a recent visit, for example, – and all the details are right including good coffee and petits four. No children under 10 after 6pm. **Seats 45.** L 12-2 (Sun 12.30-4) & D 7-10 (Sun to 8.30); early D£16.95,7-8.30. Set L £15 (incl Sun). Set D £25; à la carte also available. House wine from £13; sc discretionary. Toilets wheelchair accessible. Parking. Closed Xmas day. Amex, Diners, MasterCard, Visa. **Directions:** Leixlip exit off M4 Motorway. Take right in Leixlip village at traffic lights.

Maynooth

Glenroyal Hotel & Leisure Club

Straffan Road Maynooth Co Kildare

HOTEL

Tel: 01 629 0909 Fax: 01 6290919

Situated on the outskirts of the university town of Maynooth, and only 20 minutes from Dublin city centre, this large hotel serves the needs of a large area requiring facilities for a wide range of events, notably conferences, corporate events and weddings. Demand is high. It also has extensive leisure facilities. These include a dramatically designed 20 metre pool (with underwater loungers, whirlpool and children's splashpool), a gymnasium and much else besides. Bedrooms, which include one room suitable for disabled guests and 10 executive rooms, are all comfortably furnished – mostly in contemporary style – with all the amenities expected of this kind of hotel and neat en-suite bathrooms (some shower only). Conferences/Banqueting (400/275); secretarial services. Video conferencing. Leisure centre. Children welcome (under 4s free in parents room; cots available). No Pets. **Rooms 57** (10 suites, 7 shower only, 1 for disabled). B&B £45 pps, ss £15. Lift. Wheelchair accessible. Open all year. Amex, Diners, MasterCard, Visa. **Directions:** From Dublin, M4 to Maynooth turn right off slip road to Maynooth.

Maynooth 🏛

Moyglare Manor

Maynooth Co Kildare

Tel: 01 628 6351 Fax: 01 628 5405

COUNTRY HOUSE/RESTAURANT

email: moyglare@iol.ie

Country hedges and workaday farmland give way to neatly manicured hedging, rolling parkland then beautifully tended gardens as one approaches this imposing classical Georgian manor – and it comes as no surprise to find that the owner, Norah Devlin, lavishes her love of beautiful things on the place, with a passion for antiques that has become legendary. Gilt-framed mirrors and portraits are everywhere, shown to advantage against deep-shaded damask walls. The remarkable abundance of chairs and sofas of every pedigree ensures comfortable seating, even when the restaurant is fully booked with large parties milling around before and after dining. First-time visitors sometimes describe it as "like being in an antique shop", but after recovering from the stunning effect of its contents guests invariably reflect on the immaculate maintenance and comfort of the place under the careful stewardship of long-time manager Shay Curran. Spacious bedrooms are also lavishly furnished in period style, some with four-posters or half testers, and include a ground-floor suite; all have well-appointed bathrooms with quality appointments and good attention to detail. All rooms have recently been upgraded to a very high standard and, despite a longstanding aim for peacefulness, the modern world seem to have caught up with Moyglare and TVs have been installed in bedrooms. Small Conferences (30/45); secretarial services. Garden; walking. Children welcome (over 12). No Pets. **Rooms 16** (1 suite, 2 rooms for disabled). B&B £75 pps, ss £20. Closed Sat L, 24-26 Dec. Amex, Diners, MasterCard, Visa. **Restaurant:** Hotel manager Shay Curran personally supervises the formally-appointed restaurant, which is in several interconnecting rooms; the middle ones nice and cosy for winter, those overlooking the garden and countryside pleasant in fine weather. Grand and romantic, it's just the place for a special occasion and there's pianist playing background music in the evening. Jim Cullinane, who has been head chef since 1983, presents daily lunch and dinner menus (plus an à la carte at dinner). He is known for his nicely balanced combination of traditional favourites and sophisticated places, attractively presented, with a vegetarian option always available. There is an emphasis on seafood and game in season – roast pheasant, perhaps, hung long enough to give it a gamey flavour, perfectly cooked and served off the bone accompanied by a nice little serving of green-flecked champ as well as game chips and Cumberland sauce. Lunch menus offer less choice than dinner, but are nevertheless quite formal and convey a sense of occasion. Fine meals are complemented by an exceptional wine list of special interest to the connoisseur – which is why Moyglare Manor was the winner of our 1999 Wine List of the Year Award. Not suitable for children under 12. Restaurant **seats 50** (private room, 20). No smoking area. L Mon-Fri 1-2.30 (& Sun from 12.30); D daily 7-9. Set L £22.50 (incl Sun L). Set D £27.50. A la carte D also available. House wine £18; sc discretionary. Toilets wheelchair accessible. **Directions:** From Dublin to west on N4. Take exit for Maynooth keep right at Catholic Church. 2 miles on, turn left at Moyglare crossroads.

Moone   *Moone High Cross Inn*

Bolton Hill Moone Co Kildare

PUB/ACCOMMODATION   Tel: 0507 24210/24112

The Clynch family has been running this characterful country pub since 1978, although it dates back to the 1870s when it was a pub and grocery shop. It's a warm, welcoming place with open fires in both the bars. The larger one is well set up with rustic tables (including old school desks) for the comfortable service of bar food, where traditional dishes like Irish stew, bacon and cabbage (and often a fresh fish of the day) are served between 11 am and 9.30 pm. Upstairs there are eight simple en-suite letting bedrooms, which are very popular for overflow from weddings at nearby Kilkea Castle as well as normal holiday business. Children welcome. Pets permitted in certain areas. **Rooms 5** (all en-suite). B&B £30 pps, ss £15. Bar food 11-9.30. Visa. Closed Good Fri, 25 Dec. **Directions:** 39 miles south of Dublin, just off the Dublin Carlow-Kilkenny-Waterford road

Naas   *Fletcher's*

Commercial House Naas Co Kildare

PUB   Tel: 045 897328

This great old pub goes back well into the 1800s and has been in the Fletcher family since Tom Fletcher's father ran it in the 1930s. It's the kind of place that puts Irish theme pubs to shame, with its simple wooden floor and long, plain mahogany bar broken up in the traditional way with mahogany dividers and stained glass panels. They did up the back lounge recently, but there's no need to worry – it shouldn't need work for another couple of hundred years. Closed 25 Dec, Good Fri & Bank Hols.

Naas ❊   *Jo Olives Restaurant*

10 Main Street, Naas, Co Kildare

RESTAURANT   Tel: 045 894788 Fax: 045 438283

Above Kavanagh's pub in the centre of Naas, Joe Gray (restaurant manager) and Olivier Valory (head chef) are running a most successful little restaurant that draws its regulars from a wide area around the town. Major changes are due to the dining area (and kitchen) as we go to press, but the style of cooking is unlikely to move away from a format that has proved so successful. Seafood ("prawn kebabs Jo Olives") and game in season are the main areas of speciality (the fish mainly on daily blackboard specials) but you'll also find some less likely soulmates, such as seared kangaroo fillet, which don't quite fit the image of a place that prizes local produce. Still, there's room for experiment in any kitchen, so why should this one be different. We look forward to seeing the new, extended Jo Olive's very shortly. Not suitable for children under 10. **Seats 45.** D only 7-10.30 Tue-Sat; à la carte. House wine £10.95; sc discretionary. Closed Sun, Mon; 4 days Xmas. MasterCard, Visa. **Directions:** Main street Naas.

Narraghmore   *The Pond House*

Narraghmore, Co Kildare

GUESTHOUSE   Tel: 045 485456

No need to explain the name of Nuala Clarke's unusual guesthouse, which will become obvious as soon as you reach it. Although it's in a different county, The Pond House is handy enough to Rathsallagh (see entry, Dunlavin) to be a regular recipient of overflow custom, a system that pleases all concerned - word has got around and some very interesting people stay here. The house is quietly located and spacious (a large patio area at the back was being developed at the time of the Guide's visit), the atmosphere is distinctly laid back and, unusually for a guesthouse, it even has a proper bar where race-goers and wedding guests can enjoy a small one or two before heading upstairs. Bedrooms are pleasant in a country pine way, but by no means luxurious (no phone or TV and they're all shower only.) Nuala is a natural hostess and clearly enjoys making people feel at home. Garden. Not suitable for children. Pets by arrangement. **Rooms 5**, (all shower only). B&B £30 pps, ss £5. Open all year. MasterCard, Visa. **Directions:** 1 mile off main Dublin Carlow road to Narraghmore, next right - sign posted.

Newbridge   *Keadeen Hotel*

Curragh Road Newbridge Co Kildare

HOTEL   Tel: 045 431666   Fax: 045 434402   email: keadeen@iol.ie

Centrally located and easily accessible off the M7 motorway, this family-owned hotel is set in eight acres of fine landscaped garden just south of the town (and quite near the Curragh racecourse). Accommodation is generously sized and furnished to a high standard. A fine romanesque Health & Fitness Club was opened in 1996 with an 18-metre swimming pool and scented aromatherapy room among its attractions, plus a staffed gymnasium with specialist equipment imported from America. Extensive conference and banqueting facilities cater for anything from 15 to 800 people. Secretarial services, video conferencing. Leisure centre. Garden. Parking. No Pets. Children welcome (under 3s free in parents rooms; cots available). **Rooms 55** (1 suite, 3 mini-suites, 20 executive, 1 for disabled) B&B £47.50 pps. Closed 24 Dec-4 Jan. Amex, Diners, MasterCard, Visa.

Newbridge   *The Red House Inn*

Newbridge Co Kildare

HOTEL/RESTAURANT   Tel: 045 431657   Fax: 045 431934

Proprietor-manager Brian Fallon runs a tidy ship at this cosy inn just off the Naas dual carriageway. It has a very relaxed atmosphere, especially in the characterful bar and the restful conservatory and garden at the back. A range of accommodation is offered and all rooms have good amenities. Conference/Banqueting (400/300); secretarial services. Garden. Children under 5 free in parents' room; cots available. **Rooms 12** (1 suite, 1 mini-suite. 2 no-smoking rooms, 1 for disabled). B&B £45 pps, ss£10. No sc. Closed Xmas (3 days), 1-7 Jan. Amex, MasterCard, Visa. **Restaurant:** The dining room is well appointed in a classic style, very suitable for the mainly traditional home-cooked food for which The Red House is known especially prime beef and Kildare lamb although vegetarian options are always given too. Children welcome. **Seats 45** (private room, 25). Air conditioning. L Mon-Sun 12.30-3, D Mon-Sat 6.30-10. Set L £14.50 (inc Sun); Set D £24.95. Early Bird 6.30-7.30, £17. A la carte also available. House wine from £11.50; sc discretionary. Toilets wheelchair accessible. Closed D Sun. **Directions:** on the N7 between Naas and Newbridge.

Straffan 🏛   *Barberstown Castle*

Straffan Co Kildare

Tel: 01 628 8157   Fax: 01 627 7027

HOTEL/RESTAURANT   email: castleir@iol.ie

Barberstown Castle is fascinating; steeped in history through three very different historical periods, it's one of the few houses in the area to have been occupied continuously for over 400 years. The oldest part is very much a real castle – the original keep in the middle section of the building, which includes the atmospheric cellar restaurant, was built by Nicholas Barby in the early 13th century. This was followed by a more domestic Elizabethan house, added in the second half of the 16th century. Hugh Barton (also associated with nearby Straffan House, now the Kildare Hotel & Country Club, with whom it shares golf and leisure facilities) built the 'new' Victorian wing in the 1830s. Most recently, in the current ownership of Kenneth Healy, the property has been thoroughly renovated and appropriately refurbished, in keeping with its age and style, to offer a high standard of modern comfort throughout. Very comfortable accommodation is provided in well-appointed, individually decorated en-suite rooms – some are in the oldest section, the Castle Keep, others are more recent, but all have great style. Public areas, including two drawing rooms and an elegant bar, have been renovated with the same care, and there are big log fires everywhere. Conferences/Banqueting (60/200); secretarial services. Business centre. Garden. Walking. Children welcome (under 6s free in parents' room). Wheelchair accessible. Pets permitted by arrangement. **Rooms 22** (1 suite, 8 executive, 1 for disabled, all no-smoking). B&B £68 pps, ss £15. No sc. Amex, Diners, MasterCard, Visa.

The Castle Restaurant: The restaurant is in a series of whitewashed rooms in the semi-basement of the old Castle Keep, which gives it great atmosphere, heightened by fires and candles in alcoves. The present head chef Ciaran Woods joined the castle in 1999 and is particularly keen on seafood, which tends to be luxurious – lobster, scallops. Local lamb and beef also feature and there's a good selection of Irish farmhouse cheeses. Home baked breads include speciality breads as well as traditional brown soda.

Restaurant **Seats 70** (private room 20/30)). Non-smoking. D only 7-9.30 daily. Set D £31. A la carte also available. House wine £15; sc discretionary. Toilets wheelchair accessible. Closed 24-26 Dec, 1st week Jan. **Directions:** West N4 - turn for Straffan at Maynooth. South N7 - turn for Straffan at Kill.

Straffan 🏨🍴

Kildare Hotel & Country Club

Straffan Co Kildare
Tel: 01 601 7200 Fax: 01 601 7299
email: hotel@kclub.ie

COUNTRY HOUSE/RESTAURANT

International Hospitality Award - Ray Carroll

The origins of Straffan House go back a long way – the history is known as far back as 550 AD – but it was the arrival of the Barton wine family in 1831 that established the tone of today's magnificent building, by giving it a distinctively French elegance. It was bought by the Smurfit Group in 1988 and, after extensive renovations, opened as an hotel in 1991. Set in lush countryside, and overlooking its own golf course, the hotel boasts unrivalled opulence. The interior is magnificent, with superb furnishings and a wonderful collection of original paintings by well-known artists, including William Orpen, Louis le Brocqy, Sir John Lavery and Jack B. Yeats, who has a room devoted to his work. All bedrooms and bathrooms are individually designed in the grand style, with superb amenities and great attention to detail. Under the guidance of Ray Carroll, who has been with the hotel from the outset and was general manager for two years before taking over responsibility for the Golf and becoming Chief Executive of the Resort, it is run with apparently effortless perfection. Ray's illustrious career in the hotel business has taken him from Park Lane in London's West End, to Barbados and Cashel, Co Tipperary - a variety indicative of the range of experience required when it comes to offering international hospitality at the very top of the market. The Kildare Hotel & Country Club has deservedly received many accolades (including the Guide's Golf Hotel of the Year Award last year) and, like the golf course which is host to the Smurfit European Open, has continued to develop and improve. At the time of going to press, Ray's international hospitality skills are due to be energetically exercised, as both the hotel and golf course are on the point of embarking on major developments in preparation for the Ryder Cup, which the K Club will host in 2005. Conferences/ Banqueting (160/160); secretarial services. Leisure centre; specialist therapies. Hairdresser. Golf (18), tennis, garden walking, fishing. cycling, equestrian. Snooker. Pets permitted by arrangement. Children welcome (under 12s free in parents room; cots available). **Rooms 45** (7 suites, 29 executive rooms, some for disabled). Lift. Room rate £310. No sc.

The Byerley Turk Restaurant★ Dramatically draped tall windows marble columns, paintings of racehorses, tables laden with crested china, monogrammed white linen, gleaming modern crystal and silver – these all create an impressive background for the hotel's fine food. Executive chef Michel Flamme, who has been with the hotel since it opened, bases his cooking on classical French cuisine with some traditional Irish influences – in, for example, a starter of pan-fried Clonakilty black and white pudding, colcannon potato and parsley jus. He presents a seasonal à la carte, a daily changing set dinner menu (£55) and a special "Dining Experience" for complete parties (£95); all the menus are very luxurious and notable for a growing number of specialities. These include braised ox cheeks with puréed root vegetables and flatleaf parsley served with a rich claret sauce, poached Galway Bay lobster surrounded by a chilled vegetable salad with parsley oil and mesclun and, to finish, a range of hot speciality souffles. Given the intertwined history of Straffan House and the Barton family, it is appropriate that Bordeaux Reserve from Barton and Guestier should be the label chosen for the hotel's house wine (£17.95) Children welcome. **Seats 80** (private room available).Air conditioning. D 7-9.45. Set D £55. Gourmet Menu £95. House Wine £17.95; sc discretionary. Toilets wheelchair accessible. Amex, Diners, MasterCard, Visa. **Directions:** 30 mins south west of Dublin Airport and city (M50 - N4).

KILKENNY

Where better to be in the first year of a new century and a new millennium than Kilkenny, where the sense of the past in an ancient inland city sharpens our enjoyment of the present. Kilkenny is a land of achingly beautiful valleys where elegant rivers weave their way through a rich countryside spiced by handsome hills. Rivers are the key to the county. Almost the entire eastern border is marked by the Barrow, which becomes ever more spectacularly lovely as it thrusts towards the sea at the tiny river port of St Mullins. The southern border is marked by the broad tidal sweep of the Suir, and this fine county is divided diagonally by the meandering of the most beautiful river of all, the Nore. Invaders inevitably progressed up its tree-lined course towards the ancient site of Kilkenny city itself. They quickly became Kilkenny folk in the process, for this is a land to call home. The monastic and later mediaeval city lent itself so naturally to being an administrative centre that at times it appeared set to become the capital of Ireland. Today, it seems odd at first that this miniature city doesn't have its own university. But after you've enjoyed Kilkenny's time-hallowed streets and old buildings, you'll soon realise that, with a plethora of festivals featuring artistic, theatrical and comedy themes, Kilkenny has its own individual buzz of creativity and energy which many an arid modern university campus might well envy.

Local Attractions and Information

Kilkenny	Cat Laughs Comedy Festival (May) 056 63416
Kilkenny	Rothe House (16th century house, exhibitions) 056 22893
Kilkenny	City Tourist Information 056 51500
Thomastown	Kilfane Glen & Waterfall 056 24558
Thomastown	Mount Juliet (parkland surrounding hotel) 056 24455

Bennettsbridge ✗   *Nicholas Mosse Irish Country Shop*

Bennettsbridge Co Kilkenny
CAFÉ   Tel: 056 27105

One of the best reasons to go just outside Kilkenny city to Bennettsbridge is to visit the Nicholas Mosse Pottery. They have recently moved the whole operation over to the old riverside mill, which now has a new shop and visitor centre where you can see the full range – including handblown glass and table linens as well as acres of the famous spongeware. The new restaurant is on the first floor and was not fully operational at the time of the Guide's visit, but it's sure to offer reasonably priced wholesome fare. Opening times and annual closures unavailable at the time of going to press. Amex, Diners, MasterCard, Visa.

Graiguenamanagh ✳   *Cafe Duiske*

Abbey Street Graiguenamanagh Co Kilkenny
RESTAURANT   Tel 0503 24986 / 8

Even as we were about to recommend Aidan and Marina Power's Cafe Duiske as a new entry in this year's guide, news reached us that they are already on the move. But not too far away, as they have bought the refectory of nearby 13th century Duiske Abbey and will shortly transfer business to The Monks Refectory, a 40-seater à la carte restaurant with disabled access and toilet. Decor will make the most of the building, with local art and hand-thrown pottery. Fresh local produce will feature including game in season and smoked eel (the trading of eel dates back to the Cistercian monks who built the town and weirs on the river and is now being produced again). **Seats 36.** L 12-6, D 6-10 (Sun to 9). Closed Tue. **Directions:** In the village, through an archway off Main Street.

Graiguenamanagh ✳   *Waterside*

The Quay, Graiguenamanagh, Co.Kilkenny
RESTAURANT/GUESTHOUSE   Tel: 0503-24246 Fax: 0503-24733
e-mail: info@waterside.iol.ie

Very attractive old stone warehouses have been converted to make this impressive waterside restaurant and guesthouse. It changed hands in 1998 and the new owners, Brian Roberts and Rita Whelan, are planning to upgrade the accommodation, which is currently quite comfortable but simple. The restaurant is well-appointed and offers modern European food (marinated feta cheese with roasted vegetables and guinea fowl with cranberry & port sauce are typical examples). **Rooms 10** (all shower only) B&B £35pps, ss £10. Restaurant **Seats 38** D Thurs.-Sun, 7-9; L Sun only 12.30 -2.30. Set L £12, Set D £21.80. Closed Mon-Wed. MasterCard, Visa. **Directions:** 17 miles southeast of Kilkenny on banks of River Barrow.

Inistioge   *Berryhill*

Inistioge Co Kilkenny
COUNTRY HOUSE   Tel/Fax: 056 58434

George and Belinda Dyer's delightful country house was built by George's family in 1780 – it has been immaculately maintained by successive generations and stands high above a valley, on the family's 250 acre farm, proudly overlooking the River Nore. Handsomely covered with virginia creeper, it is comfortably big rather than grand, with a homely hall and well-proportioned reception rooms full of lovely old family things. Bedrooms are very spacious – junior suites really, with a dressing/sitting area and room to make tea and coffee – and each has an animal theme. Good home cooking (with some international influences) is the aim for residents' dinner and local produce will be much in evidence – notably Berryhill trout and salmon from their own private stretch of the Nore – and home-produced lamb as well as local cheeses. Breakfast is a speciality – fresh fruits, Nore smoked salmon & scrambled egg and "anything the heart desires" taken at the dining room table in front of a log fire. Not suitable for children under 10. No pets. **Rooms 3** (all mini-suites) B&B £45 ss £10; no service charge. Closed 1 Nov - 30 Apr.MasterCard, Visa . **Directions:** R700 from Thomastown to Inistioge, through Square, bear right over bridge, 1st left, 1st right and 2nd on left.

Kilkenny   *Butler House*

Patrick Street Kilkenny Co Kilkenny
ACCOMMODATION   Tel: 056 65707 Fax: 056 65626 email: res@butler.ie

Located close to Kilkenny Castle, this elegant Georgian townhouse was restored by the Irish State Design Agency in the 1970s.The resulting combination of what was at the time contemporary design and period architecture leads to some interesting discussions. However, the accommodation is very adequate, with all the amenities now expected of good 3-star guesthouse accommodation and the garden has just been landscaped. Conferences (110); Wheelchair accessible. **Rooms 13** (12 shower only) B&B £54.50, ss £20, sc included. Closed 24-29 Dec. Amex, Diners, MasterCard, Visa. **Directions:** City centre opposite Kilkenny Castle.

Kilkenny   *Café Sol*

William Street Kilkenny Co Kilkenny
RESTAURANT   Tel: 056 64987

Eavan Kenny and Gail Johnson opened this fun café-restaurant just off the High Street in 1995 and have now given it a complete refurbishment, which has made the restaurant much more comfortable and cosier, especially for the evening. Good home-cooked all-day food has made their reputation: soups with freshly baked scones, imaginative sandwiches, great vegetarian dishes like warm salad of goats cheese with walnuts and beetroot, light fish dishes like potato cakes with smoked salmon and sour cream, gorgeous salads - Lavistown sausages with mashed potato, mustard mayonnaise and salad. Lots of nice bakes, too – and a good range of drinks to wash them down. Evening menus are more formal, but the same sound principles apply. **Seats 60.** Open 10-5 Mon-Sat, L 12-4.30, Set L from £9; D Wed-Sat 7 -10, Set D £19.50, à la carte menu available.Closed all Sun, D Mon & Tue. 5 days Xmas & Good Fri. MasterCard, Visa. **Directions:** 2nd turn left up High Street from Castle, opposite Town Hall.

Inistioge   *The Motte*

Plas Newydd Lodge Inistioge Co Kilkenny
RESTAURANT   Tel: 056 58655

On the edge of the picturesque village of Inistioge, with views of extensive parklands and the River Nore, The Motte is situated in the classically proportioned Plas Newydd Lodge, named in honour of the ladies of Llangollen, who eloped from Inistioge in the late 18th century. Although small in size, this unique country restaurant is big on personality – of the host, the irrepressible Tom Reade-Duncan, and of the chef, Alan Walton, as conveyed through his imaginative menus and distinctive style of cooking. The pair of them combine a special blend of classical style and wacky artistic inspiration. Menus are sensibly limited to six choices on each course – starters such as galantine of duck with kumquat, for example, and apple or venison sausage on a tagliatelle bed, with tomato & chilli sauce Main courses range from the unconventional – ostrich steak on a bed of rosemary – to the locally popular, as in a perfect sirloin steak with a brandy and green peppercorn sauce. Side vegetables are always imaginative and perfectly cooked.**Seats 32.** D only, Tues-Sat 7-9.30. Set D£22.50. House wine 312; sc discretionary. Closed 1 wk Xmas, 2 wks Oct. Wheelchair access. MasterCard, Visa. **Directions:** From Thomastown, five miles on the right on the New Ross Road.

Kilkenny   *The Hibernian Hotel*

33 Patrick Street, Kilkenny
HOTEL   Tel: 056 71888   Fax: 056 71877   e-mail: info@hibernian.iol.ie

Formerly the Hibernian Bank, this Georgian building has gone a long way to being restored to its former glory to become "The Hibernian" - luxurious guesthouse accommodation in the centre of Kilkenny. At the time of the Guide's visit, building was in progress to create a 40-bedroom hotel, modelled on the style of the original building. Existing accommodation (9 rooms) is particularly spacious and furnished to a very high standard in keeping with the character of the building. The new hotel, due for completion late in 1999, will also have a bar, restaurant, conference suites and private parking. **Rooms** 40 (all en-suite,10 no-smoking) B&B £59pps, ss £20. Wheelchair access; lift . Closed Dec.24-26. Amex, MasterCard, Visa. **Directions:** 100 metres from Castle, facing the Parade, on Lower Patrick Street.

Kilkenny   *Hotel Kilkenny*

College Road. Kilkenny
Tel: 056-6200   Fax: 056-65984
HOTEL/RESTAURANT   e-mail: kilkenny@griffingroup.ie

This sister hotel to the Ferrycarrig Hotel near Wexford (see entry) has just completed a major development and refurbishment programme, including an impressive new health & fitness club with 20 metre swimming pool, refurbishment of all bedrooms the addition of 24 deluxe rooms and a new stone conservatory style bar which greatly enhances the hotel entrance. Bedrooms have been done in an unusual modern classic style, using specially commissioned Irish-made furniture and the result is very pleasing. Conference/banqueting 400/380. Wheelchair access. Children welcome (under 4s free in parents' room; cots available). No pets. **Rooms 103** (all en-suite), 24 executive rooms. B&B £57.50pps, £69 single. Wheelchair access. Amex, Diners, MasterCard, Visa. **Directions:** On ring road at Clonmel roundabout exit.

Kilkenny   *Kilkenny Design Centre*

Castle Yard, Kilkenny
RESTAURANT   Tel: 056 22118   Fax: 056 65905

This first floor self-service restaurant (above the temptations of a different sort on display in the famous craft shop below) is deservedly popular. Wholesome, healthy and absolutely delicious fare is consistently provided at very reasonable prices. Home baking is a strong point, there are hot specials like Guinness casserole and great salads; everything is freshly prepared every day. Improvements for 2000 include the addition of air conditioning and wheelchair access. **Seats 120.** No smoking area. Meals Mon-Sat 9.30-5. Self service main courses from £4.95. Closed Sun, Bank Hols Jan-April. Amex. Diners, MasterCard, Visa. **Directions:** Opposite Kilkenny Castle entrance.

Kilkenny   *Lacken House*

Dublin Road Kilkenny Co Kilkenny
Tel: 056 61085   Fax: 056 62435
RESTAURANT/ACCOMMODATION   email: lackenhs@indigo.ie

Irish Beef Award

Eugene and Breda McSweeney's period house on the edge of Kilkenny city has been the leading restaurant in the area for over 15 years. Eugene is a well-known Euro-Toques chef, who has represented Ireland many times in culinary competition, while Breda was the Guide's 1999 Sommelier of the Year. In line with the Euro-Toques principles of using the best local ingredients, supporting local producers and thus, in the words of Paul Bocuse "defending the ingredients that are the building blocks of good cooking", Eugene is an enthusiastic supporter of local produce. A particular speciality is beef, which is raised by a local farmer known personally to Eugene and always on the menu in a current speciality dish. On a recent visit, Eugene's Fillet of Beef served with Clonakilty Pudding Mash, Crispy Bacon and Wholegrain Mustard Cream turned out to be a dream of a dish. The Clonakilty pudding - enough to add interest without weight - is worked into a creamy, well-flavoured mash, topped with the steak then a single rasher set jauntily alongside, and a slightly crunchy mustard cream around it: admirably simple, with excellent flavour and texture. An example of how successful New Irish Cuisine can be, when traditional elements are developed in a contemporary style. Desserts are always good – or there are Irish farmhouse cheeses from the trolley, served with home-made biscuits. Small conferences by arrangement for up to 12 people. **Seats 30.** Private room for 20, Open Tues-Sat D 6.30-10.30 Set D £25, House Wine £13 .Closed 1 wk Xmas.MasterCard, Visa. **Directions:** On Dublin Road, 6 minutes from Kilkenny Tourist Office. **Accommodation: Rooms 9** en-suite guest bedrooms all have phone TV, tea/coffee-making trays. **Rooms** vary in size and outlook, but were upgraded during 1999. Excellent breakfasts. B&B £30.ss £6.

Kilkenny ✳   *Lautrec's Bistro*

9 St.Kieran Street, Kilkenny
RESTAURANT   Tel: 056-62720

This cheerful restaurant is just around the corner from the Tourist Information Office (which has, most inconsiderately to less able visitors, recently been moved up steep stairs to the first floor while the ground floor is used for commercial offices). Its most attractive feature in sunny weather is that the doors open out onto the pavement and there are tables semi-alfresco. (The pavement is rather narrow). Food, on a recent lunch visit, was mixed - pastas and salads were fine, but pizza (which is quite a speciality) soggy-based and doughy. **Seats 100.** Open daily noon-10.30 L 12-2 , D 6.30 -10.30. MasterCard, Visa. **Directions:** Lane beside TOI.

Kilkenny   *Newpark Hotel*

Castlecomer Road Kilkenny Co Kilkenny
HOTEL   Tel: 056 22122 Fax: 056 61111

Very much at the heart of local activities, this 1960's hotel on the N77 has just completed a huge extension and renovation programme and the makeover - symbolised by an impressive circular foyer which is really striking from the road and even more so on entering - is a revelation. The whole job has been done with such flair and attention to detail that it's hard to see where the original building has got to. Conference and meeting rooms have been particularly imaginatively handled, but the whole project deserves great praise. It includes 33 executive bedrooms, the foyer and atrium features, conference centre/banqueting (500/350) and Scott Dove Bar & Bistro, with entrances from the hotel and carpark. Children welcome. No pets. **Rooms 111.** (16 shower only, 10 no-smoking, 2 for disabled). B&B £60, ss £15. Wheel chair access.Lift. Open all year. Amex, Diners, MasterCard, Visa.

Kilkenny ✳   *Rinuccini Restaurant*

1 The Parade, Kilkenny
RESTAURANT   Tel: 056-61575

This well-established Italian restaurant is in a semi-basement in the impressive terrace opposite Kilkenny Castle and the closely packed tables are an indication of the usual level of business. When empty it looks a little bleak, but the room quickly fills up with a healthy mixture of locals (who clearly have their preferred tables) and tourists. The cooking style is mainly classic Italian, with quite an extensive à la carte evening menu and a much shorter one at lunchtime. Service is prompt, from the time fresh bread and butter is delivered speedily with the menu. Food is characterised by freshness of ingredients and a high standard of cooking: excellent minestrone (a classic test), delicious seafood and memorable pasta. The simple things are right, which is always a good sign. **Seats 56.** L12-2.30, D 6-10.30 daily; à la carte. L from £7, D from £14. House wine selection, £12.95. Closed 26-27 Dec, Good Friday. Amex, Diners, MasterCard, Visa. **Directions:** Opposite Kilkenny Castle

---

Maddoxtown   *Blanchville House*

Dunbell Maddoxtown Co Kilkenny
COUNTRY HOUSE   Tel: 056 27197 Fax: 056 27636 email: info@blanchville.ie

Tim and Monica Phelan's elegant Georgian house is just 5 miles out of Kilkenny city, surrounded by its own farmland and gardens. It's easy to spot – there's a folly in its grounds. The house has an airy atmosphere, with matching well-proportioned dining and drawing rooms on either side of the hall and the pleasant, comfortably furnished bedrooms in period style all overlook attractive countryside. Dinner is available to residents (bookings required before noon) and, like the next morning's excellent breakfast, is taken at the communal mahogany dining table. No wine licence but guests are welcome to bring their own. Not suitable for children under 10. Well-behaved dogs are permitted by arrangement. [*The Phelans have renovated their Coach House to make three self-catering apartments]. **Rooms 6** (all non-smoking, 5 en-suite) B&B £35pps, £5 ss. Closed 1 Nov-28 Feb Amex, MasterCard, Visa. **Directions:** N10 from Kilkenny to Carlow/Dublin 2 miles; first right after Pike Pub, a mile to crossroads (Connolly's Pub), take left, go one mile.

Thomastown ❊   *Silks*

Marshes Street, Thomastown, Co.Kilkenny
RESTAURANT   Tel: 056-54400

This rather dashing contemporary restaurant in a converted schoolhouse on the edge of the town has brought Mediterranean cuisine to Thomastown with a vengeance and it certainly seems to be the place to be seen. There are two rooms - the back one, which overlooks garden and pond, would be pleasant on a summer evening or for Sunday lunch. Rather brusque reception might get a visit off on the wrong foot - there is a bar, but it seems to be the practice to whisk guests straight through to their tables and present menus immediately. There's a choice of menus (it might be worth asking the waiter about set menus if only the carte is offered, or vice versa; main courses on the carte could be as much as a whole set dinner, or you may prefer a more flexible choice). The style, however, is fairly consistent: Mediterranean/global plus some local specialities, such as Lavistown cheese tartlet. Typical starters might include king scallops wrapped in parma ham, roasted and served on a bed of fine green beans with mango sauce and a typical main course is lamb rack with herb crust served with a garlic and tapenade jus. Both cooking and service were uneven on a recent visit, but there were several large groups requiring a lot of attention. Sunday lunch offers particularly good value. **Seats 70.** (private room, 35). DTue-Sun, 7-10. Set D from £12.95 (most à la carte main courses cost more). L Sun only 12-3; Set L £12. Closed Mon; Jan. 7-21. Wheelchair access. Public car park adjacent.MasterCard,Visa. **Directions:** along Mount Juliet Road, Thomastown.

Thomastown 🏛🏛   *Mount Juliet Estate*

Thomastown Co Kilkenny
HOTEL/RESTAURANT   Tel: 056 73000 Fax: 056 73019 email: info@mountjuliet.ie

Built over 200 years ago by the Earl of Carrick, and named in honour of his wife, Mount Juliet House is one of Ireland's finest Georgian houses. Lying amidst 1500 acres of unspoilt woodland, pasture and formal gardens beside the River Nore, it is one of Europe's greatest country estates, with world class sporting amenities and conference facilities. It retains an aura of eighteenth century grandeur. The original elegance has been painstakingly preserved, so that the hand-carved Adam fireplaces, walls and ceilings decorated with intricate stucco work and many other original features can still be enjoyed today. The 32 bedrooms have period decor with all the comfort of modern facilities. Additional bedrooms on the estate are in the Hunters Yard and the Rose Garden two-bedroom lodges. The Jack Nicklaus-designed golf course on the estate went straight into the list of top-ranking courses when it opened in 1991; it hosted the Irish Open for three years consecutively (from 1993 to 1995). Conference/banqueting (200/140). Children welcome. No pets. **Rooms 59**, all en-suite, (13 suites, 44 executive rooms) B&B £82.50pps, £157.50 single. Closed 24 Dec– 2 Jan. Amex, Diners, MasterCard, Visa.

Lady Helen Dining Room: Although grand, this graceful high-ceilinged room, softly decorated in pastel shades and with sweeping views over the grounds, is not forbidding and has a pleasant atmosphere. To match these beautiful surroundings, executive chef Jonathan Baron presents a classic daily dinner menu based on local ingredients, including wild salmon from the River Nore, vegetables and herbs from the Mount Juliet garden and regional Irish farmhouse cheese. Service is efficient and friendly. **Seats 60.** D only 7-9.30. Set D £47.50, House wine £15.50 *Informal dining is available at Hunters Yard, Presidents Bar and also a new contemporary restaurant, Kendals, opened in 1999 for breakfast, lunch & dinner daily. **Directions:** M7 from Dublin, then M9 towards Waterford, arriving at Thomastown on the N9 via Carlow and Gowran.

LAOIS

Laois is a place which celebrates the year 2000 by re-discovering its own sense of identity. With its territory bisected by the rail and road links between Dublin and Cork, it is often glimpsed only fleetingly by inter-city travellers. But as with any Irish county, it is a wonderfully rewarding place to visit as soon as you move off the main roads. And a salutary place to visit as well. For, in the eastern part between Stradbally and Portlaoise, there's the Rock of Dunamase, that fabulous natural fortress which many occupiers inevitably assumed to be impregnable. Dunamase's remarkably long history of fortifications and defences and sieges and eventual captures has a relevance and a resonance for all times and all peoples and all places. But there's much more to Laois than mournful musings on the ultimate vanity of human ambitions. With its border shared with Carlow along the River Barrow, eastern Laois comfortably reflects Carlow's quiet beauty. To the northwest, we find that Offaly bids strongly to have the Slieve Bloom Mountains thought of as an Offaly hill range, but in fact there's more of the Slieve Blooms in Laois than Offaly. And though the River Nore may be thought of as quintessential Kilkenny, long before it gets anywhere near Kilkenny it is quietly building as it meanders across much of Laois, gathering strength from the weirdly-named Delour, Tonet, Gully, Erskina and Goul rivers on the way. The Erskina and Goul rivers become one in Laois's own Curragh, a mysterious place of wide open spaces and marshy territory northwest of Durrow which, in marked contrast, was created as a planned estate town by the Duke of Ormond.

Local Attractions and Information

Ballinakill   Heywood (Sir Edwin Lutyens gardens) 0502 33563
Emo Court   (James Gandon) & Gardens 056 21450

Abbeyleix   *Morrissey's*

PUB
Main Street Abbeyleix Co Laois
Tel: 0502 31281 Fax: 0502 31357

One of Ireland's finest and best-loved pubs, Morrissey's is a fine building on the wide main street of this attractive little town. It's a great place to lift the spirits while taking a break between Dublin and Cork – food is not its strength but a quick cup of coffee and enjoyment of the atmosphere is sometimes all that's needed. Morrissey's has been in the same family since it first opened as a grocery in 1775, when it started life as a thatched one-storey house. In 1880 it was rebuilt as the lofty two-storey premises we see today, with high shelf-lined walls and a pot belly stove to gather round on cold days. The present owner, Patrick Mulhall, is rightly proud of this special place, which is unique in so many ways. They have a list of people who have served their time at Morrissey's since 1850 – and, true to the old tradition, television, cards and singing are not allowed. No children after 7 pm. Closed 25 Dec & Good Fri. **Directions:** In the village, on the right heading south.

Abbeyleix   *Preston House*

RESTAURANT/ACCOMMODATION
Main Street Abbeyleix Co Laois
Tel/Fax: 0502 31432

While Morrissey's pub is a must, if you fancy a bite to eat just walk down the hill a few doors to Michael and Allison Dowling's attractive creeper-clad house, where a sign on the pavement welcomes people to their friendly and informal country-style restaurant Allison's good home cooking starts off with delicious scones, served with coffee and home-made preserves before lunch, at which time the choice widens to a short but tempting à la carte – typically including starters like smoked haddock chowder with freshly-baked brown bread or grilled goat's cheese and side salad. Vegetarians can look forward to colourful, zesty dishes such as ratatouille or spinach crèpe with salad Delicious desserts range from the simple – apple crumble and cream – to sophisticated classics like crème brûlée. Dinner menus are also à la carte and, although more formal and offering a wider choice, the same philosophy applies. A first-floor ballroom runs across the whole width of this substantial building and, with a library area up a few stairs at one end providing comfortable seating for non-participants and a minstrels' gallery at the other, it makes a superb venue for local events. Not suitable for children under 5 afte 6 pm. **Seats 50.** No smoking area. L 12.30-3 Tue-Sun, D 6-9 Tue-Sat, Set L (incl Sun £13. A la carte also available. House wine £11.50; sc discretionary (10% on parties c

6+). Closed D Sun, all Mon, 10 days Xmas.MasterCard, Visa. **Accommodation** Large bedrooms are interestingly furnished with antiques. Unusual en-suite facilities have been cleverly incorporated without spoiling the proportions of these fine rooms – by hiding them in what appears to be a long wardrobe but which opens up to reveal a row of individual facilities – shower, WC etc. Children under 4 free in parents' room; cot available. **Rooms 4** (all shower only & no-smoking). B&B £25, ss £5. **Directions:** In the village, a few doors down from Morrissey's.

Ballacolla ❊ — Foxrock Inn

Clough Ballacolla Co Laois
PUB/B&B — Tel/Fax 0502 38637 email foxrock@tinet.ie

Sean and Marian Hyland run a very friendly, relaxed little place here for lovers of the country life. Hill walking, fishing (coarse and game), golf and pitch & putt are all in the neighbourhood and they'll make packed lunches to see you through the day. Evening meals, an open fire and traditional music make the pub a welcoming place to come back to and there is accommodation just up the stairs, in six modest but comfortable rooms (5 en-suite). B&B £20 pps, ss £5. Closed 25 Dec & Good Fri. Visa. **Directions:** On the R434, which links Durrow (N4) and Borris-in-Ossory (N7).

Mountrath — *Roundwood House*

Mountrath Co Laois
COUNTRY HOUSE — Tel: 0502 32120 Fax: 0502 32711 email: roundwood@tinet.ie

Just a couple of miles off the main Dublin-Limerick road, Frank and Rosemarie Kennan's unspoilt early Georgian house lies secluded in mature woods of lime, beech and chestnut. A sense of history and an appreciation of genuine hospitality are all that is needed to make the most of a stay here – forget about co-ordinated decor and immaculate maintenance, just relax and share the immense pleasure and satisfaction that Frank and Rosemarie derive from the years of renovation work they have put into this wonderful property. Although unconventional in some ways, the house is extremely comfortable and well-heated (with central heating as well as log fires) and all the bathrooms have been recently renovated (all have full bath). The Kennans have also been taking on the outbuildings of late and now have several beautifully converted rooms at the back and further outbuildings, Coach House and Forge Cottage, ready for self-catering. An extraordinary (and historically unique) barn is the next stage; this enterprise defies description, but don't leave Roundwood without seeing it. Children, who always love the unusual animals and their young in the back yard, are very welcome and Rosemarie does a separate tea for them. Residents dinner (8 pm) is based on the best local and seasonal ingredients (notably locally reared beef and lamb); Rosemarie's food suits the house perfectly – good interesting cooking without unnecessary frills – and Frank is an excellent host. **Rooms 10** (all en-suite & no-smoking). B&B £44 pps, ss £12. No sc. Closed 25 Dec & Jan.Amex, Diners, MasterCard, Visa. **Directions:** 3 miles from Mountrath, on R440.

Portlaoise — *The Kitchen & Foodhall*

Hynds Square Portlaoise Co Laois
RESTAURANT/DELICATESSEN — Tel: 0502 62061 Fax: 0502 62075

Jim Tynan's smashing restaurant and food shop is definitely worth a little detour. Delicious home-made food, an open fire, relaxed atmosphere - a perfect place to break a journey or for a special visit. Lovely home-bakes, ready meals, speciality foods and wines in the shop. **Seats 200** (daytime)/50 (evening). Open all day, 9-5.15, Mon-Sat; L from 12.30. D Thur-Sat, 7-9.30. Set L from £5.50, D à la carte. House wine £10.90. Wheelchair access. Closed 24 dec-3 Jan. MasterCard, Visa. **Directions:** In the centre of Portlaoise, beside the Courthouse.

LEITRIM

In this new age of detailed statistical analysis, it's intriguing to find that, of all Ireland's counties, it is Leitrim which has to try hardest. That's official. Because, according to government data, it is Leitrim which has the doubtful distinction of having the poorest soil in the entire country. It's a covering of such low fertility, so we're told, that it is barely capable in some places of growing even the scrubbiest trees. Yet the very fact that Leitrim is thus categorised in the official statistics shows that such general overviews can easily become blunt instruments of analysis. For there are pockets of fertility in Leitrim of such good quality that, for instance, one of Ireland's leading organic horticulture firms is able to grow superb produce in the north of the county. And as for Leitrim lacking in glamorous tourist attractions other than the obvious one of the magnificent inland waterways, well, even that is largely a matter of perception. For Leitrim shares the shores of Lough Gill with Sligo, so much so that Yeat's Lake Isle of Innisfree is within an ace of being in Leitrim rather than Sligo of Yeatsian fame. To the northward, we find that more than half of lovely Glencar, popularly perceived as being one of Sligo's finest jewels, is in fact in Leitrim. As for the notion of Leitrim being the ultimate inland and rural county - not so. Leitrim has an Atlantic coastline, albeit of only four kilometres, around Tullaghan. It's said this administrative quirk is a throwback to the time when the all-powerful bishops of the early church aspired to have ways of travelling to Rome without having to cross the territory of neighbouring clerics. Whatever the reason, it's one of Leitrim's many surprises, which are such that it often happens that when you're touring in the area and find yourself in a beautiful bit of country, a reference to the map produces the unexpected information that you're in Leitrim. So forget about those gloomy soil facts - this is a county of hidden quality which deserves to be better known. And for anyone who seeks the essential Ireland, it's worth noting that the ancient Irish system of bar licences resulted in Leitrim having more pubs per head of population than any other county -148 souls per licence, which barely stands comparison with the Dublin figure of 1,119. This means the Leitrim pubs, like the county itself, have to try harder with all sorts of quaint ancillary trades, and they're all the better for that.

Local Attractions and Information

Carrick-On-Shannon	Tourism Information (May-September) 078 2017C
Rossinver	Eden Plants & The Organic Centre 072 54122

Carrick-on-Shannon

Hollywell

Carrick-on-Shannon Co Leitrim
Tel: 078 21124

COUNTRY HOUSE

After many years as hoteliers in the town (and a family tradition of inn-keeping that goes back 200 years), Tom and Rosaleen Maher moved to this delightful period house on a rise over the bridge, with beautiful views over the Shannon and its own river frontage. It's a lovely graciously proportioned house, with a relaxed family atmosphere. Tom and Rosaleen have an easy hospitality (not surprisingly, perhaps, as their name derives from the Gaelic "Meachar" meaning hospitable), making guests feel at home very quickly and this, as much as the comfort of the house and its tranquil surroundings, is what makes "Hollywell" special. Bedrooms are all individually furnished in period style and it's worth getting up in good time for delicious breakfasts, with freshly-baked bread and home-made preserves. No evening meals, but Tom and Rosaleen advise guests on the best local choices and there's a comfortable guests' sitting room with an open fire to gather around on their return. Garden. Fishing (coarse). Not suitable for children under 12. Pets permitted by arrangement. **Room 4** (4 en-suite, 2 shower only). B&B £30 pps, ss £5-12.50. Closed 10 days Xmas-New Year. MasterCard, Visa. **Directions:** From Dublin, cross bridge on N4, keep left at Gings pub. Hollywell entrance is on left up the hill.

Carrick-on-Shannon ✳

The Landmark Hotel

Dublin Road Carrick-on-Shannon Co Leitrim
Tel 078 22222 Fax 078 2223;

HOTEL

This very large new almost-riverside hotel is aptly named and brings much-needed business and leisure facilities to the area. Conference/banqueting (400/400); secretarial services; business centre. Leisure centre (indoor swimming pool). Golf nearby (9) Children welcome (under 5s free in parents' room; cots available). No pets. **Rooms 60** (4 for disabled). Wheelchair access. Lift.B&B £47.50 pps, ss£15. Closed Xmas. Amex, MasterCard, Visa. **Directions:** On N4, 2 hours from Dublin.

Glencar

Glencar Lodge

CAFÉ

Glencar Co Leitrim (via Sligo)
Tel/Fax: 071 45475 email: glencar@tinet.ie

The drive down the Glencar valley towards Sligo is one of the most beautiful in Ireland and – apart from the well-documented attractions of the lake and waterfalls – Frank Slevin and Helen Crowley's delightful little café/restaurant and craft shop is another good reason to stop along the way. Glencar Lodge was the hunting lodge of Lissadell House and is set in beautiful gardens. They serve home-made soups, salads made from locally grown organic vegetables, quiches, open and toasted sandwiches, delicious Illy coffee and all sorts of irresistible home-made cakes, gateaux and tarts – or you can have a glass of wine with some Irish farmhouse cheeses if you like. During the winter they also cater for private parties and corporate functions, serving modern Irish cuisine. **Seats 30.** Meals 11-6 daily in summer. No-smoking area. Wheelchair accessible. Closed Oct-May. Amex, MasterCard, Visa. **Directions:** Turn off N16 for Glencar.

Keshcarrigan

Canal View House & Restaurant

RESTAURANT/ACCOMMODATION

Keshcarrigan nr Carrick-on-Shannon Co Leitrim
Tel: 078 42056 Fax: 078 42404

A fireside cup of tea and home-baked scones or biscuits in the comfortable residents' lounge (with views of the cruisers passing) welcomes guests on arrival at Jeanette Conefry's immaculate guesthouse and restaurant overlooking the Shannon-Erne Waterway. Bedrooms – some with water views, all with a pleasant outlook – are individually furnished to a high standard. Direct-dial telephones have recently been installed and all have neat en-suite shower rooms. Peace and quiet are an attraction here, but television is available in bedrooms on request. Families are welcome and well looked after.Pets permitted by arrangement. **Rooms 6.** B&B £25 pps, ss£5. Closed 1 wk Xmas. MasterCard, Visa. **Restaurant:** Gerard and Jeanette Conefry opened the restaurant to coincide with the opening of the waterway in 1992, and it has been a great success. Since 1995 they've been ably assisted in the kitchen by Rita Duggan, and there are private mooring facilities so that restaurant guests can stay there on boats overnight. Table d'hôte and à la carte menus are based on the best ingredients, including locally grown organic vegetables and home-grown herbs, plus carefully sourced produce such as Keshcarrigan venison, fish from Killybegs, veal and steak from local farms. There is a generous sprinkling of vegetarian dishes, marked with a leaf symbol. The dessert menu offers a choice of five or six, including home-made ice creams with butterscotch sauce. Farmhouses cheeses are also available. **Seats 40.** (private room, 10). D daily 7-9 (Sun 6.30-8),à la carte; L Sun only 1-3.30, Set L £11.50. House wine £9.50; sc discretionary. Wheelchair accessible. **Directions:** R209 from Carrick-on-Shannon to Keshcarrigan village; 4th house on right after village.

Kinlough ✻

Courthouse Restaurant

RESTAURANT/ACCOMODATION

Kinlough Co Leitrim
Tel 072 42391

Piero and Sandra Melis have converted the old courthouse in the attractive village of Kinlough into a stylish little restaurant. It's a particularly welcoming place and, in addition to good food - contemporary cooking in the Mediterranean style with some more down to earth local influences, especially at lunchtime - the helpful attitude of the staff will make people want to return. Not suitable for children under 4 after 8 pm. **Seats 25.** L12.30-2.30 &D 6.30-9.30 Wed-Mon, (Sat & Sun from 11). Set L £11. D à la carte. House wine £10; sc discretionary. No-smoking area.Closed Tue and 1st 2 weeks Nov, Xmas & 1 week Feb. MasterCard, Visa. **Accommodation:** Neat, freshly decorated bedrooms offer comfortable accommodation at a very reasonable price. **Rooms 4** (all en-suite, shower only). B&B £20 pps, ss £2. **Directions:** Off main Donegal-Sligo road (N15), 5 km towards Sligo from Bundoran. Take turning directly opposite Tullaghan House.

Rooskey ✻

Shannon Key West Hotel

HOTEL

Rooskey Co Leitrim
Tel 078 38800 Fax 078 38811

This large new riverside hotel has brought valuable facilities to the area and is open all year (except Christmas), making it a particularly good venue for off-season short breaks, meetings and conferences. Conference/banqueting (250/220); video conferencing and back-up secretarial services. Business centre. Leisure centre. Children welcome (under

4s free in parents' room, cots available). **Rooms 39**, all en-suite. B&B £48 pp, no ss. Closed 25 Dec. Amex, Diners, MasterCard, Visa. **Directions:** On N4, main Dublin-Sligo route, midway between Longford and Carrick-on-Shannon.

Tullaghan ❊   *Tullaghan House*

Tullaghan Co Leitrim

COUNTRY HOUSE   Tel 072 41515 / 42055 Fax 072 41515

This delightfully unspoilt Georgian residence is set back from the road in its own garden (entrance from a slip road at the back). It's run by the (equally delightful) McCanney sisters: Elizabeth, Cathleen, Suzanne and Rosa, who took over the house in the spring of 1998 and are gradually making improvements, in a gentle way so as not to lose the charming family home atmosphere that is one of its main attributes. The bedrooms are all individually furnished, with very different characters and public rooms are spacious and comfortable, with old family furniture. No evening meals but the Courthouse Restaurant at Kinlough (see entry) is nearby. Children welcome (under 6s free in parents' room). Pets permitted in some areas. **Rooms 6**, all en-suite. Closed 23 Dec-5 Jan. MasterCard, Visa. **Directions:** On main Donegal Sligo road (N15), 1 mile towards Sligo from Bundoran, on right hand side.

LIMERICK

The Millennium is being marked in Limerick with a city-centre waterways development which will transform the heart of the city, with water levels in the Shannon being maintained at a more attractive level by a new weir and sea lock system which is due to be in action by August 2000.

The story of Limerick city and county is to a large extent the story of the Shannon Estuary, for in times past it was the total access and ready availability of the transport provided by Ireland's largest estuary which dictated the development of life along its southern shore and into the River Shannon itself. But as we move inland from the river, the very richness of the countryside soon begins to develop its own dynamic. After all, eastern Limerick is verging into Tipperary's Golden Vale, and the eastern county's Slieve Felim hills, rising to Cullaun at 462 m, reflect the nearby style of Tipperary's Silvermine Mountains.

Southwest of Limerick city, the splendid hunting country and utterly rural atmosphere of the area around the beautiful village of Adare makes it a real effort of imagination to visualise the muddy salt waters of the Shannon Estuary just a few miles away down the meandering River Maigue, yet the Estuary is there nevertheless. Equally, although the former flying boat port of Foynes and the nearby jetty at Aughinish may be expanding to accommodate the most modern large ships, just a few miles inland we find ourselves in areas totally remote from the sea in countryside which lent itself so well to mixed farming that the price of pigs in Dromcolliher (a.k.a. Drumcolligher) on the edge of the Mullaghareirk Mountains used to set the price of pigs throughout Ireland.

Limerick city may have come to international attention in the late 1990s through the popular success of Frank McCourt's moving book "Angela's Ashes", but by the time it appeared the picture it conveyed was long since out of date. Nobody would deny that Limerick can be a gritty place with its own spin on the human condition, but in recent years the growth of the computer industry in concert with the rapid expansion of the remarkably vibrant University has given Limerick a completely new place in Irish life, and the city's energy and urban renewal makes it an entertaining place to visit, while the eclectic collection on stunning display in the unique Hunt Museum sets a style which other areas of Limerick life are keen to match.

That said, Limerick still keeps its feet firmly on the ground, and connoisseurs are firmly of the opinion that the best pint of Guinness in all Ireland is to be had in this no-nonsense city, where they insist on being able to choose the temperature of their drink, and refuse to have any truck with modern fads which would attempt to chill the rich multi-flavoured black pint into a state of near-freezing tastlessness aimed at immature palates.

Local Attractions and Information

Adare	May Fair 061 396894
Glin Castle	Pleasure Grounds & Walled Garden 068 34364
Limerick City	Hunt Museum ,Customs House, Rutland Street 061 312833
Limerick City	King John's Castle 061 411201
Lough Gur	Interpretative Centre (3000BC to present day) 061 360788

Adare ♨♨

Adare Manor Hotel & Golf Club

Adare Co Limerick
Tel: 061 396566 Fax: 061 396124
email: reservations@adaremanor.com

HOTEL/RESTAURANT

The former home of the Earls of Dunraven, this magnificent neo-Gothic mansion is set in 900 acres on the banks of the River Maigue. Its splendid chandeliered drawing room and the glazed cloister of the dining room look over formal box-hedged gardens towards the Robert Trent Jones golf course. Other grand public areas include the gallery, named after the Palace of Versailles, with its unique 15th century choir stalls and fine stained glass windows. Luxurious bedrooms have individual hand carved fireplaces, fine locally-made mahogany furniture, cut-glass table lamps and impressive marble bathrooms with strong showers over huge bathtubs. 1999 saw major changes at the Manor as a new clubhouse was opened and 25 townhouses were completed in the grounds. In total, extra accommodation and facilities include a conference centre plus a bar, restaurant, private dining room and 11 new executive bedrooms. Conference/banqueting (250/200). Leisure centre, Golf (18), Equestrian. Walking. Garden. Fishing. Children welcome. **Rooms 63** (staterooms 13; some rooms for disabled). Room rate £240.Wheelchair access. Lift. Open all year. Amex, Diners, MasterCard, Visa.

Oak Room Restaurant: Gerard Costelloe has been Chef de Cuisine since 1993 and his seasonal menus change weekly. Local produce, including vegetables from the estate's own gardens, is included on menus, and although based on classical French cuisine, the style includes some modern Irish food, as in roast lamb cutlets on colcannon, for example. A separate vegetarian menu is offered. **Seats 70** L 12.30-2, D7-9.30 daily. Set L £21.50, Set D £34.50. House wine from £19; sc 15 %. *Alternatively, food is available from the Clubhouse Bar & Restaurant, 7am-10 pm daily. Open all year. **Directions:** On N21 in Limerick.

Adare · *Carrabawn Guesthouse*

Adare Co Limerick

ACCOMMODATION · Tel: 061 396067 Fax: 061 396925

In an area known for high standards, with prices to match, this immaculate owner-run establishment provides a good alternative to the local luxury accommodation. Bernard and Bridget Lohan have been welcoming guests here since 1984 – and many of them return on an annual basis because of the high level of comfort and friendly service provided. Bedrooms are very well maintained with all the amenities required. In addition to seeing guests off with a good Irish breakfast, light evening meals can be provided by arrangement. Children welcome. Pets permitted. **Rooms 8** (all shower only & no smoking). B&B £30 pps. Closed Xmas. **Directions:** On N21 in Adare.

Adare ✗ ⛪ · *Dunraven Arms Hotel*

Adare Co Limerick

HOTEL/RESTAURANT · Tel: 061 396633 Fax: 061 396541 email: dunraven@iol.ie

Established in 1792, and set in one of Ireland's most picturesque villages, the Dunraven Arms has seen many changes over the last few years and is now a large hotel. It has been developed with commendable discretion and, under the personal management of Bryan and Louis Murphy, somehow manages to retain the comfortable ambience of a country inn. A very luxurious inn nevertheless – the **76 rooms** are all furnished to the highest of standards: there are six suites and 14 junior suites and all the remaining accommodation is in executive rooms. There is also an unusually high proportion of rooms (20) suitable for disabled guests. The furnishing standard is superb throughout, with antiques, private dressing rooms and luxurious bathrooms, plus excellent amenities for private and business guests, all complemented by an outstanding standard of housekeeping. It's an excellent base for sporting activities – equestrian holidays are a speciality and both golf and fishing are available nearby – and also extremely popular for both conferences and private functions, which are held beside the main hotel (with separate catering facilities). A leisure centre has also been recently completed. **Maigue Restaurant:** Named after the River Maigue, which flows through the village of Adare, the restaurant is delightfully old fashioned – more akin to eating in a large country house than in a hotel. Mark Phelan, who has been head chef since 1996, takes pride in using the best of local produce in meals that combine the traditions of the area with influences from around the world. Mark is also responsible for food served in the bar. Across the road, in one of the traditional thatched cottages, head chef Sandra Earl cooks for an informal restaurant, The Inn Between, which is in common ownership with the Dunraven Arms; details of opening times are available at the hotel. Acc£££ L£ & D££ daily. Closed 25 Dec. Amex, Diners, MasterCard, Visa. **Directions:** On right in village coming from Limerick.

Adare · *The Wild Geese Restaurant*

Rose Cottage Adare Co Limerick

RESTAURANT · Tel/Fax: 061 396451 email: wldgeese@iol.ie

In one of the prettiest cottages in the prettiest village in Ireland, Conleth Roche and Serge Soustrain's restaurant has charm that is equally matched by the service they provide. Serge presents mainly French menus based on the best local produce – all transformed into something very special by his highly skilled cooking. Semi à la carte dinner menus are priced by the course, with one or two supplements (Liscannor Bay lobster, Clare oysters). Main courses, offered with a choice of vegetables or salad, are imaginative and well judged and delicious desserts tend to be classic – a good crème brûlée perhaps (served with home-made biscuits) – or you can round off with Irish cheeses. A short à la carte menu is offered at lunchtime in summer and served informally. Not suitable for children under 10 after 7 pm. **Seats 45** (private room,8).No-smoking area. L12-3pm,May-Oct. D 6.30-10 all year. Set L £10. Set D £30. A la carte available. House wine £13. Parking. Closed Sun, Mon & Jan 5-25. Amex, Diners, MasterCard, Visa. **Directions:** At top of Adare village opposite Dunraven Arms Hotel.

Adare   *Woodlands House Hotel*

Knockanes Adare Co Limerick

HOTEL   Tel: 061 396118/605100 Fax: 061 396073 email: woodlands\hotel@iol.ie

Just outside Adare, the Fitzgerald family's hotel has grown quite dramatically since it opened in 1983 and management has now moved into the next generation. The whole hotel has been systematically upgraded and developed over the years – the low, grey-tiled building is set in well-kept gardens and presents a very neat and welcoming appearance from the road. It has always been a popular venue for weddings and is particularly well suited to large gatherings, with spacious public areas throughout, including two bars, and a restaurant and banqueting suite overlooking gardens and countryside. New and upgraded bedrooms have significantly raised the standard of accommodation and a new leisure centre, with 20 metre pool, jacuzzi, sauna, steamroom and gym, was opened in 1999. Conferences/Banqueting (400/350). Leisure centre. Garden. Hairdresser. Children welcome (under 4s free in parents' room; cots available, creche, playroom). Pets permitted by arrangement. **Rooms 92** (5 mini-suites, 45 exec, 10 shower only. 2 for disabled). B&B £43 pps, ss £10. Closed 24-25 Dec.Amex, Diners, MasterCard, Visa. **Directions:** 2 miles from Adare off N21 approaching from Limerick.

Ballingarry 🏛 ☆   *The Mustard Seed at Echo Lodge*

Ballingarry Co Limerick

COUNTRY HOUSE/RESTAURANT   Tel: 069 68508 Fax: 069 68511

One of the country's prettiest and most characterful restaurants, Dan Mullane's famous Mustard Seed started life in Adare in 1985. Having celebrated its first decade it began the next one by moving just ten minutes drive away to Echo Lodge, a spacious Victorian country residence set on seven acres, with mature trees, shrubberies, kitchen garden and orchard. The Mustard Seed's new home offers luxurious accommodation, allowing Dan to provide the thoroughgoing hospitality that comes so naturally to him. Elegance, comfort and generosity are the key features – seen through decor and furnishings which bear the mark of a seasoned traveller whose eye has found much to delight in while wandering the world. Small conferences/banqueting (20/60). Garden. **Rooms 12** (all en-suite, 1 suite, 5 shower only, 6 no-smoking bedrooms, 1 for disabled). B&B £65 pps, ss £25. Closed Feb. Amex, MasterCard, Visa. **Restaurant:** While the accommodation offered at Echo Lodge is exceptional, the main emphasis of the establishment is on food and hospitality, with admirable attention to detail. Drinks, served in the Library, come with a tasty amuse-bouche; fresh flowers are carefully selected to suit the decor in the dining room. Head chef Owen Sherry takes great pride in sourcing his ingredients from the best local producers and suppliers; much of the food carefully prepared in his kitchen is organic, including herbs, vegetables and fruit from their own gardens. Owen's cooking is contemporary country house style, seen in wide-ranging menus with starters like a delicious terrine of chicken breast studded with pigeon on seasonal leaves and chutney juices; a soup course influenced by garden produce, like creamy leek & potato; an imaginative main course, perhaps of lamb – honey glazed shank, with a cassolet of beans and home-grown baby vegetables. A good plated Irish cheese selection or gorgeous puddings (like hot crunchy apple & blackcurrant crumble with a quenelle of calvados cream and caramel sauce) are followed by coffee and irresistible home-made petits fours, served at the table or in the Library. Not suitable for children. **Seats 50.** Non-smoking restaurant. D 7-9.30pm, Set D £31. House wines from £11. Closed Sun & Mon in low season; all Feb. Amex, MasterCard, Visa. **Directions:** From top of Adare Village take 1st turn to left follow signs to Ballingarry - 8 miles.

Castleconnell   *Castle Oaks House Hotel*

Castleconnell Co Limerick

HOTEL   Tel: 061 377666 Fax: 061 377717

Set quietly in 26 acres of wooded countryside on the banks of the Shannon, this attractive hotel is in an idyllic location on the edge of the picturesque village of Castleconnell, just a few miles on the Dublin side of Limerick. The old part of the hotel is a Georgian mansion, with the gracious proportions and elegance that implies, although a new wing provides extra accommodation which makes up in comfort and convenience anything it might lack in character. Rooms include two executive rooms with whirlpool baths (and a romantic bridal suite) and are all en-suite with full bathrooms (bath and shower). One room was specially designed for asthmatics, with hard surfaces and specially chosen fabrics. Private fishing is a particular attraction, and the hotel also offers an unusual venue for conferences and weddings in a converted chapel, which accommodates up to 300 people. Nice, helpful staff and a family-friendly attitude make this a pleasant hotel. Conferences / Banqueting (250/270); secretarial services. Leisure centre (15-metre pool). Garden. Children welcome (under 4s free in parents' room; cots available). No Pets. **Rooms 20** (2 suites, 1 no-smoking room). B&B £44 pps, ss £20.90. Amex, Diners, MasterCard, Visa. Closed Dec 24-26. **Directions:** 5 miles on N7 out of Limerick take left after Finnegans Pub. Hotel 2 miles on left.

Croom

Mill Race Restaurant

Croom Mills Croom Co Limerick

RESTAURANT/VISITOR CENTRE   Tel: 061 397130 Fax: 061 397199

One of the most imaginatively handled restorations of its type, a visit to Croom Mills shows the whole traditional corn milling process from beginning to end – including a sample of freshly baked bread hot from the oven. Many other exhibits illustrate related operations and crafts – the blacksmith, for instance, in his 19th century forge – and several primary power sources are to be seen in action, including the giant 16 foot cast iron waterwheel, built in Cork in 1852. The tour takes about an hour – but there are other attractions here too, notably one of the country's best craft and gift shops and the Mill Race Restaurant. Major improvements have recently been completed, which has added to the comfort - but the food has been excellent from the word go, and would be hard to better. Starting from early morning there's a full breakfast menu available, then a full lunch menu (plus a light lunch menu available for groups) and a great range of home cooked goodies on display all day for lighter bites. Vegetarians are well looked after and there's an outdoor eating area overlooking the millrace. This is good home cooking served in very pleasing surroundings – Mary Hayes and her team deserve great credit. **Seats 150.** No-smoking area. Food served daily 8-5.30. Sun to 6pm. Set Sun L £10. Wine licence. Closed Good Fri, Xmas week. **Directions:** On N20 main Cork Road, just after bridge on left by the River Maigue.

Glin 🏛

Glin Castle

Glin Co Limerick

COUNTRYHOUSE   Tel: 068 34112/34173 Fax: 068 34364 email: knight@iol.ie

The Fitzgeralds, hereditary Knights of Glin, have lived in Glin Castle for 700 years and it's now the home of the 29th Knight and his wife Madame Fitzgerald. The interior is stunning, with beautiful interiors enhanced by decorative plasterwork and collections of Irish furniture and paintings. Guests are magnificently looked after by manager Bob Duff. Accommodation was originally all in suites – huge and luxurious, but not at all intimidating because of the lived-in atmosphere that characterises the whole castle – but additional rooms ("small, friendly, with a family atmosphere") were opened last year. Furnished and decorated in traditional country house style (there was no need for this family to haunt the auctions in order to furnish the new rooms!), everything has been done just right and every room feels as if it has always been that way. Excellent dinners prepared by Bob Duff's wife Rachel Collins, who has been chef since 1997, and have previously been served communally in the beautiful dining room, although separate tables are the coming thing. When the Knight is at home he will take visitors on a tour of the house and show them all his pictures and old furniture. Not to be missed while in Glin is O'Shaughnessy's pub, just outside the castle walls; one of the finest pubs in Ireland it is now in its sixth generation of family ownership and precious little has changed in the last hundred years. The garden and house open to the public at certain times. Non-residents are welcome to dine - reservations are essential. Small conferences (20/30), private parties. Garden. Walking . Tennis. Children welcome (under 5s free in parents room; cots available). Pets by arrangement. **Rooms 15** (3 junior suites, 10 no-smoking rooms). B&B £85 pps, ss £30. Dining Room **Seats 30.** Non-smoking. L 12.30-2.30. D 7-9.30. Set L £15. Set D £27.50. House wine £11.50; sc discretionary. Amex, Diners, MasterCard, Visa. Closed Dec & Jan. **Directions:** 32 M25 West of Limerick city on N69.

Limerick ❋   *Brûlées Restaurant*

21 Henry Street, Limerick City, Co Limerick
RESTAURANT   Tel 061-319931 Fax 061-319931

Just a stroll across from Jurys Limerick Inn, Donal Cooper and Teresa Murphy's well-appointed corner restaurant has a soothing ambience and welcoming spicy cocktail olives and plain black olives to pick at on arrival. Donal quickly follows up with a choice of three freshly-baked breads to get guests off to a good start while reading Teresa's appealing menus. She takes pride in using the finest of ingredients, both local and imported, in a cooking style accurately described as "international with an Irish twist". Imaginative, colourful food is as good as it sounds - tomato, red onion & basil tart and a warm salad of rabbit, for example, made excellent starters on a recent visit. Vegetarian dishes can be a tempting option and fish is likely to be a daily special - typically fillet of John Dory, served on a scrumptious bed of tomato & goats cheese mashed potatoes, with caramelised onions and a creamy fennel sauce - a lovely contemporary dish, perfectly cooked, attractively presented and not too fussy. Simple, attractively prepared and carefully cooked side vegetables are another plus point - and gorgeous puddings include (what else) a perfect crème brûlée. Not suitable for children. **Seats 30.** No smoking area. Wed-Sun D 6.30-10.30. Set D £25. A la Carte available. House wine £11.95. sc discretionary. Closed Xmas day, Mon+Tues each week. MasterCard, Visa. **Directions:** On the corner of Henry Street and Mallow Street, near Jurys Inn roundabout.

Limerick   *Castletroy Park Hotel*

Dublin Road Limerick Co Limerick
HOTEL   Tel: 061 335566   Fax: 061 331117   email: sales@castletroy-park.ie

Although far from enticing from the road, this blocky redbrick hotel has a warm and welcoming atmosphere in all the public areas and, while not individually decorated, the rooms are thoughtfully furnished with special attention to the needs of the business traveller (good desk space, second phone, fax and computer points). Refurbishment of all rooms is underway at the time of going to press. The hotel is much sought after as a conference venue and, after work, The Merry Pedlar pub offers a change of scene. Conferences / Banqueting (450-280); secretarial services. Business centre. Garden. Children welcome (under 12s free in parents room). Pets permitted by arrangement. **Rooms 107** (2 suites, 5 mini-suites, 24 executive, 20 no-smoking, 1 for disabled). B&B £61 pps, ss £41. Lift. Wheelchair access. Open all Year.Amex, Diners, MasterCard, Visa. **Directions:** On main Dublin - Limerick road (N7); 3 miles from Limerick city, 25 minutes from Shannon Airport.

Limerick   *DuCartes at the Hunt Museum*

Hunt Museum Old Custom House Rutland Street Limerick Co Limerick
RESTAURANT/MUSEUM   Tel: 061 312662   Fax: 061 417929

This delightful modern café/restaurant is at the back of the museum, overlooking the river, with tables outside on the terrace in fine weather. As well as providing an appropriately elegant space to restore visitors to the museum, it is a popular lunchtime venue for locals. All ingredients are sourced locally and prepared daily: attractively presented and healthy home-cooked food in the modern idiom should not disappoint. [D, for groups only by arrangement, £35.] **Seats 70.** No smoking area; air conditioning. Meals daily 10-5.L 12-3. Set L £9. House wine £10.50. Closed 2-5 Sun; 25 Dec. MasterCard, Visa .

Limerick ✗   *Green Onion Caffé*

Rutland Street Limerick Co Limerick
RESTAURANT/CAFE   Tel: 061 400710

This popular cafe-restaurant recently moved around the corner into these new premises in the old town hall - an interesting space, on two levels which is a bit like going to the cinema, especially given the funky style and dimly lit tables up in the "gods". It's clearly thriving but, judging by a recent visit, something has gone amiss in the move. The style hasn't changed - daytime menus offer interesting sandwiches (e.g. crab and dill mayonnaise) made to order on homemade brown bread or bap and served with a seasonal salad garnish and salads – Greek, chicken caesar - and pasta dishes - but service can be patchy and the famous air of confidence seems lacking. Evening menus are more extensive. L£ & D££ Mon-Sat. Closed Xmas, New Year & Bank Hols. Amex, Diners, MasterCard, Visa.

Limerick ✗   *Greenhills Hotel*

Ennis Road Limerick Co Limerick
HOTEL   Tel: 061 453033 Fax: 061 453307

Owner-managed by the Greene family since 1969, this friendly hotel is conveniently located just 5 minutes from the city and 20 minutes from Shannon airport. As well as providing a convenient base for touring the west, the hotel makes a useful business location and offers good conference facilities for up to 400 delegates (with back-up business services including French and German translation). Bedrooms include 11 executive rooms, 15 for non-smokers and ten rooms suitable for disabled guests – an unusually high proportion. Bedrooms are comfortably furnished in contemporary style and have full en-suite bathrooms (bath and shower). Excellent health and leisure facilities are a major attraction. Acc££. Closed 25 Dec. Amex, Diners, MasterCard, Visa.

Limerick ✗   *Jurys Hotel*

Ennis Road Limerick Co Limerick
HOTEL   Tel: 061 327777 Fax: 061 326400 email: margaret-holian@jurys.com

Set in a garden site on the banks of the Shannon, the hotel is just two minutes walk from the city centre and 15 minutes drive from Shannon airport. Good-sized rooms are decorated to a high standard with plenty of workspace for business guests and neat, well-lit bathrooms. Unusually for a city centre hotel, Jurys has a good leisure centre and also an outdoor tennis court. Acc£££. Closed 24 & 25 Dec o Amex, Diners, MasterCard, Visa.

Limerick ✗   *Jurys Inn Limerick*

Lower Mallow Street Limerick Co Limerick
HOTEL   Tel: 061 207000 Fax: 061 400966 email: ronan_mcauley@jurys.com

Like other Jurys Inns, this budget hotel enjoys a prime city centre location and has carparking available in an adjoining multi-storey carpark. **Rooms** are large, comfortable and furnished to a high standard, especially considering the moderate cost. Bathrooms are fairly basic but have everything required including a proper (if budget-sized) bath as well as overbath shower. Don't expect high levels of service – that's what keeps the costs down – but there is a restaurant and pub-like bar as part of the development. Traffic noise can be disturbing in front rooms. Acc££. Closed 25 Dec Amex, Diners, MasterCard, Visa.

Limerick   *Limerick Inn*

Ennis Road Limerick Co Limerick
HOTEL   Tel: 061 326666 Fax: 061 326281 email: limerick-inn@limerick-inn.ie

This large low-rise modern hotel a few miles out of town on the Shannon Airport road is owner-run by the Ryan family. Although well-placed as a base for touring, its main strength is as a conference venue – the largest of five conference rooms can accommodate 600 delegates and there are smaller meeting rooms for groups of up to 30; backup secretarial services are available. Bedrooms, all of which have full en-suite bathrooms (bath and shower), include four suites and 30 executive rooms, and there is a fine health and leisure centre. Tennis. Garden. Walking. Hairdresser. Children welcome (under 12s free in parents room; cots available). No Pets. **Rooms 153** (20 no-smoking). B&B £71.50 pps, ss £28.50. Closed Dec 25/26. Amex, Diners, MasterCard, Visa. **Directions:** 2 miles North of Limerick on N18, from Shannon/Galway South on N18.

Limerick 🏨   *Limerick Ryan Hotel*

Ardhu House Ennis Road Limerick Co Limerick
HOTEL   Tel: 061 453922 Fax: 061 326333

Situated on the outskirts of Limerick city, this hotel is built around an attractive old house dating from 1780. The original building is still gracious and has some elegantly proportioned rooms, including a peaceful drawing room. The new wing (1960s vintage) is a completely separate block reached by a corridor. However, it does provide a large number of convenient modern bedrooms (with voicemail phones), and two suites. Conference and business facilities – located in the old house – comprise 11 meeting or private dining rooms catering groups of all sizes, and back-up services are provided by a 24-hour business centre. No leisure facilities on site, but residents have complimentary use of a nearby fitness centre. Conferences/ Banqueting (130/200); secretarial services video conferencing. Own parking. Children welcome (under 12s free in parents room;

cost available). No Pets. **Rooms 178** (2 suites, 30 executive, 20 no-smoking). B&B £55 pps, ss £25. Wheelchair accessible. Lift. Amex, Diners, MasterCard, Visa. **Directions:** On main Limerick to Galway to Shannon route.

Limerick	*Roo's Bistro Bar*

Unit 4 Steamboat Quay Dock Road Limerick Co Limerick

RESTAURANT   Tel: 061 411111 Fax: 061 400111

Well-known Limerick restaurateurs Kieran and Sindy Pollard moved down to the new development on Steamboat Quay in 1998, to relocate their successful restaurant, Quenelle's, in a very upbeat contemporary style. However, given the great sense of change surrounding everything (especially in the hospitality industry) as we approach the millennium, perhaps it should cause no surprise that it's already developed from Quenelle's fine dining to Roo's casual dining. Same chef, same location - just lower prices. Children welcome. **Seats 90** (20 private). No-smoking area; air conditioning. Open daily, 5.30-10.30. Early bird 5.30-7, £9.90. House wine £11.50; sc discretionary. Toilets wheelchair accessible. Amex, MasterCard, Visa. Closed 24-25 Dec, New Years Day. **Directions:** On the waterfront, off Dock road.

Limerick	*South Court Business & Leisure Hotel*

Raheen Roundabout Limerick Co Limerick

HOTEL   Tel: 061 487487 Fax: 061 487499 email: cro@lynchotel.com

Business Hotel Award - Lynch Hotels

Ideally located for Shannon Airport and the Raheen Industrial Estate, the South Court Hotel presents a somewhat daunting exterior, but once inside visitors soon discover that it caters especially well for business guests, both on and off-duty. In addition to excellent conference and meeting facilities, the bedrooms are comfortable, impressively spacious and well equipped, with generous desk areas and the latest technology – including fax/modem/ISDN points – in every room. Executive bedrooms even have a separate work area providing a "mini-office" with a leather desk chair and private fax machine. Local, as well as hotel, residents will value having access to the hotel's excellent leisure facilities and the informal bar and café/restaurant which are an important part of the development. Conferences / Banqueting (200/180); secretarial services, video conferencing. Business centre. Leisure centre. Cycling. Hairdresser. No Pets. Children welcome (under 3s free in parents' room). Wheelchair accessible. **Rooms 65** (all en-suite, 1 suite, 14 executive, 12 no-smoking). B&B £45 pps, ss £25. Amex, MasterCard, Visa. Open all year. **Directions:** Located on the main N20 Cork/Trail road 3 miles from Limerick City.

LONGFORD

Longford will be somewhere to keep an eye on as the 21st century gets into its stride. The good people of Longford have become so accustomed to seeing their county dismissed as "the least interesting territory in all Ireland" in speed-through travel guides that they've adopted a sensibly wry attitude to the whole business. Thus they get on with life in a style appropriate to a quietly prosperous and unpretentious county which nevertheless can spring some surprises.

These are not, however, to be found in the scenery, for Longford is mostly either gently undulating farming country, or bogland. The higher ground in the north of the county up towards the intricate Lough Gowna rises to no more than 276m in an eminence which romantics might call Carn Clonhugh, but usually it's prosaically known as Corn Hill.

Over to the east, where there's more high ground, there's even less pulling of the punches in the name of the little market town in its midst, for Granard - which sounds rather elegant - can actually be translated as "Ugly Height". Yet this suggests a pleasure in words for their own sake, which is appropriate, for Longford produced the novelist Maria Edgeworth from Edgeworthstown, while along towards that fine place Ballymahon and the south of its territory on the Westmeath border, Longford takes in part of the Goldsmith country. Goldsmith himself would be charmed to know that, six kilometres south of the road between Longford and Edgeworthstown, there's the tiny village of Ardagh, a place of just 75 citizens which is so immaculately maintained that it has been the winner of the Tidiest Village in the Tidy Towns awards three times during the past ten years, and on the most recent occasion, in 1998, it won the top award as well.

Over to the west, the scenery becomes more varied as Longford has a lengthy shoreline along the northeast part of Lough Ree. It also has pretty Richmond Harbour west of Longford town at Cloondara, where the Royal Canal - gradually being restored along its meandering track from Dublin - finally gets to the Shannon. And as for Longford town itself, they're working on it, and some day the rest of Ireland will wake up to find that there's life a-plenty going on there, if you just know where to look for it.

Local Attractions and Information

Longford	Tourist Information (seasonal) 043 46566
Longford	Carriglass Manor
	(James Gandon stableyard, lace museum) 043 41026

Granard   *Toberphelim House*

Granard Co Longford

FARMSTAY   Tel/Fax: 043 86568 email: tober@tinet.ie

Dan and Mary Smyth's Georgian farmhouse is about half a mile off the road, on a rise that provides a lovely view of the surrounding countryside. Very much a working farm – cows, beef cattle and sheep plus an assortment of domestic animals and hens – it is a hospitable, easy-going place. Guests are welcome to wander around and walk the fields. ("Rubber boots are a must"). There's a guests' sitting room with television and three bedrooms: two en-suite (shower) with a single and double bed in each and one twin room with a separate private bathroom. All are comfortably furnished and well-maintained, but don't expect amenities like phones and TV in the rooms. Families are welcome – and dinner, light meals and snacks can be arranged as long as notice is given before 12 noon. Cooking is traditional farmhouse fare and meals are taken around a big mahogany dining table. They have a wine licence - and also a Wine Development Board Certificate to help make the most of it. Children welcome. **Rooms 3** (2 shower only, 1 private). B&B £25pps, ss £10. Residents' D £17 at 7 pm (book by noon). Wines £2.60-£13.50. Closed 21 Sep-1 May. Diners, MasterCard, Visa. **Directions:** Take the N55 at the Cavan end of Granard, turn off at the Statoil station making a right at the next junction. The house is situated about half a mile towards Abbeylara, to the left.

Longford   *Longford Arms Hotel*

Main Street Longford Co Longford

HOTEL   Tel: 043 46296 Fax: 043 46244 email: longfordarms@tinet.ie

Located right in the heart of the midlands, this comfortable family-run hotel has recently been renovated to a high standard. The hotel presents a neat face to the street and public areas give a good impression on arrival. Bedrooms are comfortably furnished and particularly convenient for business guests as they have adequate desk space and the amenities required for this type of travel (including trouser presses and irons). All bedrooms have good bathrooms (with both bath and shower). The coffee shop provides good casual daytime food and they do all their baking in-house – a good place to take a break. (Bar/coffee shop food is open all day, 12 -8). Conference/banqueting (500/550).Video-conferencing. Secretarial services; business centre. Children welcome (under 3s free in parents' room; cots available). Wheelchair accessible. Pets permitted by arrangement. **Rooms 66.** (20 no-smoking;ISDN lines available). B&B £44pps, no ss. Own parking. Closed 25 Dec. Amex, Diners, MasterCard, Visa. **Directions:** Centre of Longford town.

LOUTH

It could well be that 2000 is "best year yet" for this big-hearted little county on Ireland's East Coast. Louth may be Ireland's smallest county at only 317 square miles, but it still manages to be two or even three counties in one. Much of it is fine farmland, which is at its best in the area west of the extensive wildfowl paradise of Dundalk Bay, on whose shores we find the attractive village of Blackrock, one of Ireland's better kept secrets. But as well there are the distinctive uplands in the southwest, whose name of Oriel recalls an ancient princedom. And in the north of the county, the Cooley Mountains sweep upwards in a style which well matches their better-known neighbours, the Mountains of Mourne, on the other side of the handsome inlet of Carlingford Lough. As its name suggests, this is one of Ireland's few genuine fjords, and on its Louth shore the ancient little port of Carlingford town used to be one of the country's best-kept secrets, a quiet little place imbued with history. Today, it is happily prospering both as a recreational harbour for the Dundalk and Newry area, and as a bustling visitor attraction in its own right. The county's three main townships of Ardee, Dundalk and Drogheda each have their own distinctive style, and all three have been coming vibrantly to life in recent years. The historic borough of Drogheda is the main commercial port, while the evocatively-named Port Oriel at Clogher Head is an active little fishing harbour. Inevitably, Louth's location plumb on the main east coast corridor between Belfast and Dublin hampered its image in times past, for the trunk road battered its way mercilessly through towns and villages. But now that the M1 is developing to remove the weight of through traffic and speed access throughout the county, Louth is re-discovering its own identity, and it's an attractive one at that.

Local Attractions and Information

Dundalk	Tourist Information 042 35484
Dunleer	White River Mill 041 51141

Ardee

COUNTRY HOUSE

Red House
Ardee Co Louth
Tel/Fax: 041 685 3523

Although it is just off a busy road, Red House is set in parkland that has been well maintained for 200 years. The trees surrounding this lovely Georgian house insulate it so well that it seems in a world apart. It is a beautiful and interesting house, with lovely reception rooms and a mahogany panelled library. The three spacious bedrooms are elegantly proportioned and furnished with antiques, and while one has an en-suite bathroom the others are private but (in true country house style) along a corridor. Linda Connolly runs the house with warmth and efficiency and cooks very acceptable dinners for residents (by arrangement). There is a floodlit tennis court and an indoor heated swimming pool during the summer months. Small conference/private parties (25/40); Children welcome (under 2s free in parents' room; cots available). Pets permitted in some areas. **Rooms 3** (1 en-suite, 2 private, all no-smoking) B&B £45pps, ss £10. Residents D £25 (advance booking necessary); house wine £12; no sc. Closed 15 Dec-15 Jan. Amex, MasterCard, Visa. **Directions:** Situated just north of Ardee on the N52.

Blackrock

PUB/RESTAURANT

The Brake
Main Street Blackrock Co Louth
Tel: 042 9321393 Fax: 042 9322568

Although it may not look especially inviting from the outside, first-time visitors are always amazed by the warmth and country charm of the Brake once they get in the door – all old pine and rural bric-a-brac, it has open fires and friendly staff. It's a great place to stop just for a cup of tea, but even better if you're hungry – it has a well-deserved reputation for good bar meals, with a wide range offered – not just the usual pub staples, but seafood such as smoked mussels, jumbo prawns and even lobster. There are lots of meat dishes, too, especially steaks with a range of sauces and creamy dishes that come with rice, such as prawns provençal, beef stroganoff and pork a la crème. Salads and accompaniments are particularly good, all arranged buffet style. Beware of the unusual opening hours though – this is a late afternoon into evening place.No children under 14. **Seats 130.** No smoking area; air conditioning. D 6.30-10 daily (Sun to 9.30). A la carte; house wine £10; sc discretionary. Toilets wheelchair accessible. Own parking. Closed 25 Dec & Good Fri. MasterCard, Visa. **Directions:** Turn off the main Dublin-Belfast road 3 miles south of Dundalk.It is situated on the seafront in the village.

Blackrock

Clermont Arms

Main St. Blackrock Co.Louth
RESTAURANT/PUB   Tel:042 9322666 Fax:042 9322568

Sister establishment to The Brake, next door, the Clermont Arms has been developed with the same blend of charm and practicality, making it a characterful and relaxing place for a drink or good food. Also like its older sister, The Clermont is open only from late afternoon into evening (from 4pm). For summer, there's a large paved area at the back, sheltered and away from the road. Not suitable for children under 14. **Seats 100.** No smoking area; air-conditioning.D 6-10 daily (Sun to 9).A la carte. House wine £10, sc discretionary.Toilets wheelchair accessible Own parking. Closed 25 Dec & Good Fri.MasterCard, Visa. **Directions:** Turn off the main Belfast-Dublin road 3 miles south of Dundalk. Pub is situated on the seafront in Blackrock village.

Carlingford

Ghan House

Carlingford Co Louth
COUNTRY HOUSE/RESTAURANT   Tel/Fax: 042 9373682 email:ghanhouse@tinet.ie

This 18th century house is an attractive location in its own walled grounds on the edge of Carlingford village. It is of interest both for its accommodation and, more unusually, because the Carroll family run a cookery school on the premises. The accommodation is in four very different country rooms in the main house, each with sea or mountain views (three with well-finished en-suite bathrooms), and eight new bedrooms, which have been finished to a high standard in a separate building. Needless to say dinner is quite a priority – the style is country house. In addition to the cookery school (contact Paul Carroll for the 2000 programme), Ghan House is also a good venue for small conferences and meetings; details of services and rates available on request. Conference/banqueting (55/85).Garden; walking. Children welcome (under 5s free in parents' room; cots available). Pets permitted by arrangement. **Rooms 12** (all en-suite, 3 mini-suite, 1 shower only, all no-smoking) B&B £30-40 pps, no ss. Own parking. Closed 23 Dec-12 Jan. MasterCard, Visa. Restaurant **Seats 35.** No smoking restaurant. D 7-9.30 Fri & Sat (Mon-Thurs, groups by arrangement); L Sun only, Set L £14. Set D from £23; house wine £11.50; sc discretionary Toilets wheelchair accessible. Children over 8 welcome. Non-residents welcome (bookings advised). **Directions:** Take the N1 north from Dublin for 53 miles. Turn right just after Dundalk at main roundabout. Signposts available on left upon entry into the village.

Carlingford

Jordan's Town House & Restaurant

Newry Street Carlingford Co Louth
Tel: 042 9373223 Fax: 042 9373827
GUESTHOUSE/RESTAURANT   email: jordans@iol.ie

Since Harry and Marian Jordan opened their restaurant in the centre of Carlingford in 1984 the village has seen great changes – not least in the number and variety of eating places visitors can now choose from. But the Jordans keep their interest in food alive by taking turn-about in the kitchen and front-of-house and, since they added an accommodation element to the business, they are effectively running a country house, although it operates as a restaurant with rooms. The restaurant has a reception area at the front and, up a few stairs at the end, a long, rather narrow dining room which now seems quite dated. However, fresh local produce provides the basis for everything served – especially seafood, but Carlingford lamb and local beef are not forgotten. Bread is made daily from flour milled by a stone watermill at nearby Dunleer. The style is essentially hearty country house with occasional international influences: expect dishes like caper-baked hake, braised shank of lamb and vegetarian choices such as vegetarian moussaka or wok-fried vegetable hotpot. Louth is renowned for large portions, so make sure of a good appetite. Children welcome (under 4s free in parents' room; cots available). Wheelchair accessible. **Seats 56.** No smoking area. D 6-9 daily.Set D £27.50, early evening menu £15 6-7.30 pm only. L Sun only,12.30-2.30; Set Sun L £15. A la carte D available; house wine £12.75; sc discretionary Children welcome. Own parking. Closed Mon & Tues, Oct-Mar (rest.only); 25 Dec, Good Fri; 3 wks Jan. Amex, MasterCard, Visa. **Accommodation:** Bedrooms are in a converted row of stone fisherman's cottages – attractive, spacious and well-furnished, with good bathrooms (bath and shower in all rooms). **Rooms 5** (all en- suite, 1 for disabled) B&B £45pps, ss £10. **Directions:** Situated in the village of Carlingford.

Carlingford ✗   *MaGee's Bistro*

Tholsel Street Carlingford Co Louth
RESTAURANT   Tel/Fax: 042 73751

Hugh Finegan and Sheila Keiros removed their successful bistro to new premises around the corner last year (just along from PJs /The Anchor Bar) so Sheila's imaginative, contemporary cooking has now reached a much wider audience. The new place is stylish and much bigger; it's in two sections, with a 'cheap'n'cheerful' café/pizza side which can be used on its own in low season, and a slightly more formal restaurant alongside. As predicted, the new open kitchen produces lots of zappy new wave food with heaps of flavour – and Hugh is a star out front, making sure there's lots of fun. Meals£-££ daily in summer – check times of season.Closed Jan. MasterCard, Visa. **Directions:** In centre of village.

Carlingford ✗   *O'Hares*

Carlingford Co Louth
PUB   Tel: 042 73106

Paul McPartland took over this renowned pub a couple of years ago; thankfully, there has been little noticeable change. It's one of those lovely places with a grocery at the front and an unspoilt hard-floored pub with an open fire at the back. Loos (always clean) are in the yard and the food is simple but good. You can have soup and sandwiches if you like, but the speciality is Carlingford oysters – with a pint of stout of course. Closed 25 Dec & Good Fri. **Directions:** In centre of village.

Carlingford   *The Oystercatcher Lodge & Bistro*

Market Square Carlingford Co Louth
RESTAURANT/ACCOMMODATION   Tel: 042 9373922 Fax: 042 9373987

Brian and Denise McKevitt's popular little restaurant with rooms opened on the square in Carlingford village in summer 1998. Seafood is the main offering – Carlingford oysters, of course (several ways), crab puffs and Carlingford Lough mussels with a leek, saffron and wine sauce are all typical first courses. There are half a dozen seafood main courses to match, but carnivores do well too, with local lamb, steaks, duck and pork done in various ways. There are also a couple of vegetarian pastas although, in our experience, vegetarians would do better to take a selection from the excellent range of salads and vegetables which are laid out for self-service with the main course. Prices can add up rather quickly to £20+ per head for 3 courses, which might seem a bit much for the café-style atmosphere but the cooking, especially of seafood, is good. Not suitable for children under 7 after 8 pm. **Seats 40** (private room, 14) No smoking area D 6.30-10 daily (Sun times seasonal L from 12.30 Sun only, Set Sun L £13.50 Set D £19.50, early evening menu £16, 6-7 pm only. House wines £12; sc discretionary. Toilets wheelchair accessible. Own parking. Closed Tue & Xmas week. MasterCard, Visa. Guest rooms are bright, spacious and very clean, with polished floors. **Rooms 8** (all shower only) B&B £35 pps,ss £15. Children (Under 7s free in parents' room; cots available). **Directions:** Turn east at the roundabout north of Dundalk,then continue on for approx. 12 miles

Collon   *Forge Gallery Restaurant*

Church Street, Collon, Co.Louth
Tel: 041 9826272 Fax: 041 9826584
RESTAURANT   email: forggallery@tinet.ie

For the best part of fifteen years Des Carroll and Conor Phelan's charming two-storey restaurant has been providing consistently excellent food, hospitality and service. They've earned a great reputation and a devoted following along the way. It's a most attractive place – the building itself is unusual and has been furnished and decorated with flair, providing a fine setting for food that never disappoints. Des offers weekly menus that combine country French and New Irish styles, with a few other influences along the way – notably Thai. Everything is based on the best possible seasonal produce, much of it local – seafood, game in season, vegetables, fruit – and great home-made breads -white yeast bread, scones or brown bread with thyme perhaps. Typical main courses include a special vegetarian dish such as pillows of filo with leeks and roquefort as well as local meat, such as rack of tender Cooley lamb, and seafood such as prawns and scallops in wine and garlic sauce. But the really good news is that accommodation and private dining facilities are planned "in the coming year". **Seats 60.** No smoking area; air conditioning. D only Tue-Sat, 7-9.30. Set D £27; a l carte also available. House wine £15; sc discretionary (10% on parties of 6+). Own parking. Closed Sun & Mon; 25 Dec & mid 2 wks Jan. Amex, Diners, MasterCard, Visa. **Directions:** On N2, midway between Slane and Ardee, in centre of village.

Drogheda
Black Bull Inn
Dublin Road Drogheda Co Louth
PUB Tel: 041 9837139

This attractive roadside pub is on the left of the hill, just as you leave Drogheda in the Dublin direction. It has built up a considerable reputation for bar food over the years and now has an interesting food shop/delicatessen next door. Children welcome before 7pm. Open all day (10-5) L 12-3 (Sun to 2) & D 6-10, daily. Set L £15 Set D £20; early evening menu £10, 6-7 pm only; à la carte available; house wine £12. Wheelchair accessible. Own parking. Closed 25 Dec & Good Fri. Amex, MasterCard, Visa. **Directions:** On N1, on southern edge of town.

Drogheda
Boyne Valley Hotel & Country Club
Drogheda, Co.Louth
HOTEL Tel: 041 9837737 Fax: 041 9839188

At the heart of this substantial hotel, set in large gardens just on the Dublin side of Drogheda town, lies an 18th century mansion. It is not as obvious as it used to be since recent developments created a completely new entrance, but it is still there and provides some unspoilt, graciously proportioned rooms that contrast well with the later additions. Owner-run by Michael and Rosemary McNamara since 1992, it has the personal touch unique to hands-on personal management and is very popular with locals, for both business and pleasure, as well as visitors using it as a base for touring the famous historic sites of the area. While rooms in the old building have more character, the new ones are finished to a very high standard (and a further 34 new bedrooms will be opening in May 2000). Conference/banqueting (250/260); secretarial services. Business centre.Leisure centre. Tennis, pitch & putt. Parking. Pets allowed in some areas by arrangement. **Rooms 37** (all no-smoking, 8 for disabled) B&B £49.50pps, ss £5.50. Wheelchair accessible/Lift. Open all year. Amex, Diners, MasterCard, Visa. **Directions:** South of Drogheda at edge of town on N1

Dundalk
Ballymascanlon House Hotel
Dundalk, Co.Louth
HOTEL   Tel: 042 9371124 Fax: 042 9371598 email: info@ballymascanlon.com

Set in 130 acres of parkland, this hotel just north of Dundalk has developed around a large Victorian house. Although it has been in the same family ownership since 1948, major improvements have been made over the last few of years. This has been done with great style, and lifted the hotel into a completely different class. Corporate facilities include three versatile meeting rooms and there are back-up business services available. The new leisure facilities, which include a 20 metre deck level pool and tennis courts, are very impressive. Conference/banqueting (250/250); secretarial services. Leisure centre. Tennis, golf (18), garden, walking. Children welcome (under 2s free in parents' room; cots available). **Rooms 74** (3 suites, 2 mini-suites, 54 executive rooms, 1 for disabled) B&B £56pps, ss £15. Wheelchair accessible.Lift. Closed 25 Dec. Amex, Diners, MasterCard, Visa. **Directions:** N1 from Dublin, 3 miles north of Dundalk

Dundalk
Quaglinos
88 Clanbrassil Street, Dundalk, Co.Louth
RESTAURANT Tel: 042 9338567 Fax: 042 9328598

Quaglino's is a long-established and highly regarded restaurant in Dundalk. Here owner-chef Pat Kerley takes great pride in the active promotion of Irish cuisine and uses as much local produce as possible. He operates no less than three menus at this popular restaurant – not just a table d'hôte and an à la carte, but an Italian one too. They all feature local specialities, notably oysters from the beautiful Carlingford Lough and organic vegetables – typically in a tradition-inspired dish like pot-roasted beef with Deerpark organic vegetables. An experienced and successful competition cook, Pat – who has been a finalist in the New Irish Cuisine competition run by the Restaurants Association of Ireland and Bord Bia – is rightly proud of the growing popularity of Irish cuisine in recent years and does all he can to encourage it. The restaurant is run on traditional lines, with good service a priority. As in most Louth restaurants, generosity is the keynote. Children welcome. **Seats 60.** No smoking area; air conditioning. D only, 6.30-11 Mon-Sat. Set D £18.50-£25, à la carte available; house wine £11; sc discretionary. Closed Sun. Amex, Diners, MasterCard, Visa. **Directions:** Town centre, upstairs restaurant.

Termonfeckin

Triple House Restaurant

RESTAURANT

Termonfeckin Co Louth
Tel/Fax: 041 9822616

The pretty village of Termonfeckin provides a fine setting for Pat Fox's attractive restaurant, which is in a 200-year-old converted farmhouse in landscaped gardens surrounded by mature trees. On cold evenings a log fire in the reception area (an alternative to the conservatory used for aperitifs in summer) is very welcome. Pat presents a number of menus, a wide-ranging dinner menu, an à la carte and also blackboard seafood extras from nearby Clogherhead. What they all have in common is a commitment to using the best of local produce – particularly seafood – fresh Clogherhead prawns, Annagassan crab, and a dish he entitles, intriguingly, Port Oriel Pot-Pourri. But locally-reared meats feature too, in rack of local lamb with a herb crust, for example. Vegetarians do well, too, with vegetable filled crêpes – perhaps with a colourful light tomato sauce and cheese topping or fettucine pesto. Finish, perhaps, with a speciality dessert, a dacquoise that varies with the season's fruits or a plated selection of farmhouse cheeses such as Cashel Blue, Cooleeney and Wexford Cheddar. The wine list reflects Pat's particular interests and special evenings are sometimes held for enthusiasts off-season. Children welcome. **Seats 40.** No smoking area. D 6.30-9.30 Tue-Sat; Set D £18.50, à la carte available; early bird menu £12.95, 6.30-7.30 only; L Sun only, 1-3, Set Sun L £12.95. House wine £12.50; sc discretionary.Toilets wheelchair accessible. Closed Mon Sep-May, 26-28 Sep & 2 wks mid-Jan. MasterCard, Visa. **Directions:** 4 miles north-east of Drogheda.

MAYO

A sense of life as it was lived in the distant past is appropriate to a year as significant as 2000, and Mayo can give you this. Mayo is magnificent. All Ireland's counties have their devotees, but enthusiasts for Mayo have a devotion which is pure passion. In their heart of hearts, they feel that this austerely majestic Atlantic-battered territory is somehow more truly Irish than anywhere else. And who could argue with them after experiencing the glories of scenery, sea and sky which this western rampart of Ireland puts on ever-changing display?

Yet among Mayo's many splendid mountain ranges we find pockets of fertile land, through which there tumble fish-filled streams and rivers. And in the west of the county, the rolling hills of the drumlin country, which run in a virtually continuous band right across Ireland from Strangford Lough, meet the sea again in the island studded wonder of Clew Bay. At its head is the delightful town of Westport, one of the most attractive small towns in all Ireland, a cosmopolitan jewel of civilisation set in dramatic country with the holy mountain of Croagh Patrick (762 m) soaring above the bay. Along Mayo's rugged north coast, turf cutting at Ceide Fields near Ballycastle has revealed the oldest intact field and farm system in existence, preserved through being covered in blanket bog 5,000 years ago. An award-winning interpretive centre has been created at the site, and even the most jaded visitor will find fascination and inspiration in the clear view which it provides into Ireland's distant past.

As a contemporary contrast, only a few miles to the southeast the lively town of Ballina is where the salmon-rich River Moy meets the sea in the broad sweep of Killala Bay. It takes a leap of the imagination to appreciate that the sheltered Moy Valley is in the same county as the spectacularly rugged cliffs of Achill Island. But leaps of the imagination is what Mayo inspires.

Local Attractions and Information

Ballina	Street Festival/Arts Week (July) 056 70905
Ceide Fields	Visitor Centre 0996 43325
Foxford	Woollen Mills Visitor Centre 094 56756
Westport	House & Children's Zoo 098 25430 / 27766
Westport	Tourist Information 098 25711

Ballina ❀   *Gaughans*

O'Rahilly Street, Ballina, Co. Mayo

PUB   Tel: 096 70096 email: gaughan@indigo.ie

This is one of the great old pubs of Ireland and has a gentle way of drawing you in, with the menu up in the window and a display of local pottery to arouse the curiosity. Edward and Mary Gaughan have been here since 1936 and everybody loves the way they run the place. And the food is good too - open smoked salmon or crab sandwich, quiche lorraine with salad, ploughman's lunch, lemon meringue pie and pineapple upside down pudding. Great wholesome fare. And, charmingly listed along with the Bewley's tea and coffee, the wine and Irish coffee "Glass of spring water: Free." Now that's style. Pets permitted. Children welcome. Bar food served Mon-Sat, 11am-6pm. Closed 25 Dec & Good Fri. **Directions:** Ballina town centre.

Ballina ❀   *Teach Iorrais*

Geesala, Ballina, Co. Mayo

HOTEL   Tel: 097 86888 Fax: 097 86855 email:teachior@iol.ie

This new hotel in the Gaeltacht has introduced much needed facilities and will be a great asset to the area. Off-season breaks offer especially good value. Conference/banqueting (400/325); secretarial services. Fishing, walking, garden. Pets permitted by arrangement. Children welcome (under 10s free in parents' room; cots available). Wheelchair accessible. **Rooms 31** (all en-suite,1 suite, 10 no-smoking, 1 for disabled).B&B £38pps, ss £15. Open all year. Amex, Diners, MasterCard. **Directions:** Take Geesala Road from Bangor Erris.

Ballina ✗   *Mount Falcon Castle*

Foxford Road Ballina Co Mayo
COUNTRY HOUSE   Tel: 096 21172   Fax: 096 71517   email: mfsalmon@iol.ie

Not really a castle at all, Mount Falcon is a substantial neo-Gothic house, built around 1876. Mrs. Constance Aldridge has personally made guests welcome at her home for over half a century. Connie, as she is affectionately known, has a personality perfectly suited to the house, with its dramatic entrance hall (complete with piano for impromptu late-night sessions), comfortable chintzy drawing room with huge fire fed by logs from the estate, and genuinely old-fashioned bedrooms. Country pursuits really are at the heart of Mount Falcon and their kitchen uses only the best local produce, mostly from the estate farm and walled kitchen gardens. This is wholesome, no-nonsense cooking: salmon is straight from the River Moy and great joints of Aga-roasted local meat take pride of place on the sideboard. Even the butter is home-made. Non-residents are welcome to dinner by reservation. L££ & D££ daily Acc£££ Closed Xmas wk & Feb & Mar.

Castlebar ✣   *Breaffy House Hotel*

Breaffy Road Castlebar Co Mayo
HOTEL   Tel:094 22033   Fax:094 22276   email: Breaffyhotel@anu.ie

This handsome hotel is set in its own grounds and has undergone major renovation and refurbishments over the last few years. The restaurant has recently been completely refurbished and the latest phase is a new leisure complex, to be opened in summer 2000. Conference/banqueting (250/250); secretarial services. Garden.Off season value breaks. Children welcome (under 12s free in parents' room; food only charged; cots available). **Rooms 59** (2 mini-suite, 2 for disabled). B&B £60pps, ss £15. Wheelchair accessible. Lift. Closed 24-26 Dec.Amex, Diners, MasterCard, Visa. **Directions:** Approx. 4km outside Castlebar on Claremorris Road (N60)

Clare Island   *Clare Island Lighthouse*

Clare Island, Westport, Co Mayo
Tel: 098 45120   Fax: 098 45120
COUNTRY HOUSE   email: clareislandlighthous@tinet.i

Should you happen to visit this wondrous place on a fine day it will undoubtedly remain in your heart for ever – and even if the weather gods are less generous, you will be sure of shelter, comfort, good food and companionship which will all add up to a unique experience. Perched 387 feet above the Atlantic, above a sheer cliff, this sturdy lighthouse was in use until 1965 and then lay unused until Robert and Monica Timmerman took on its restoration in 1991. It now makes a wonderful place for a break, and the Timmermans are also promoting it for small seminars, workshops and special groups. If the usual ferry service is too time-consuming they can arrange a water-taxi from the mainland. Best of all, perhaps, they recommend slowing down and taking the scenic route – by train to Westport, where they can arrange collection at the station. Bedrooms are all different but comfortably furnished in an appropriate country style and living areas are spacious, with polished wooden floors, oriental rugs, leather furniture and turf fires. [Details of ferry services are available from Chris O'Grady (086 8515003) and Charles O'Malley (098 25045); in high season, June-August, there is a regular service, at other times it is essential to check.] D£20 @ 7pm (book by 2); wine licence. Not suitable for children. **Rooms 5** (all en-suite, all no-smoking). B&B £45pps, ss £10. **Directions:** Westport-Louisburgh-Roonagh-ferry

Cong 🏰   *Ashford Castle*

Cong Co Mayo
HOTEL/RESTAURANT   Tel: 092 46003   Fax: 092 46260   email: ashford@ashford.ie

Ireland's grandest castle hotel, with a history going back to the early 13th century, Ashford is set in 350 acres of beautiful parkland. Grandeur, formality and tranquillity are the essential characteristics, first seen in the approach through well manicured lawns, in the entrance and formal gardens and, once inside, in a succession of impressive public rooms that illustrate a long and proud history – panelled walls, oil paintings, balustrades, suits of armour and magnificent fireplaces. Accommodation at the castle varies considerably due to the size and age of the building, and each room in some way reflects the special qualities of this unique hotel. The best bedrooms and the luxurious suites at the top of the castle -many with magnificent views of Lough Corrib, the River Cong and wooded parkland - are elegantly furnished with period furniture, some with enormous and beautifully appointed bathrooms, others with remarkable architectural features, such as a panelled wooden ceiling recently discovered behind plasterwork in one of the suites (and now fully restored). A bijou fitness centre has computerised exercise equipment; steam room; sauna and whirlpool, all strikingly designed in neo-classical style. A specialist team backs up impressive conference facilities. The hotel's general manager, Rory Murphy, brings his own natural and easy charm to the job of making guests feel comfortable and relaxed in what might seem rather awesome surroundings, while at the same time managing to ensure that the appropriate standards are continually maintained at this great hotel. Conference/banqueting (110/75); video conferencing; secretarial services. Fitness centre. Tennis, equestrian centre, golf (9), fishing, snooker, cycling. No pets. **Rooms 83** (6 suites, 5 mini-suites). Lift. B&B £158pps, ss £142 (Room rate £284). A 15% service charge is added to all prices. Amex, Diners, MasterCard, Visa.

The Connaught Room★ This is the jewel in Ashford Castle's culinary crown and one of Ireland's most impressive restaurants. Denis Lenihan, who has been Executive Chef at the castle since 1975, oversees the cooking for both this and the George V Dining Room. The style is classical French using the best of local ingredients – Atlantic prawns, Galway Bay sole, Cleggan lobster, Connemara lamb – in sophisticated dishes that will please the most discerning diner. Irish farmhouse cheeses and warm souffles are among the tempting endings for luxurious meals, which are greatly enhanced by a meticulous attention to detail. Service is discreet and extremely professional. An extensive wine list is enhanced by the inclusion of a special selection of Wines of the Month, of varying styles and from several regions, at friendly prices. **Seats 22** D only, 7-9.30 (usually residents only).

George V Dining Room★ Lunch and dinner are served in this much larger but almost equally opulent dining room, and an all-day snack menu is also available. A five-course dinner menu is offered and although the standard of cooking and service equals that of The Connaught Room, there is a more down to earth tone about the menus, which are in English, with a choice of about eight on the first and middle courses. Cleggan mussels baked on the half shell under a provençale crust with a little shaved fennel salad, sauté of river salmon on a julienne of red cabbage, cider and ginger are typical of menus that major in seafood but have plenty of other options to choose from. A separate vegetarian menu has less choice but is more modern and includes some tempting suggestions. Lunch (£23 for the full lunch, £18 for two courses) offers a shortened and somewhat simplified version of the dinner menu. **Seats 50** (private room, 20) No smoking area. L 1-2.30, D 7-9.30. Set L £27.60 Set D £38. A la carte D also available; house wine £22; sc 15%. **Directions:** 1/2 hour drive from Galway city (on R345)

Crossmolina   *Enniscoe House*

Castle Hill, Nr Crossmolina, Ballina, Co Mayo
COUNTRY HOUSE   Tel: 096 31112 Fax: 096 31773 email: enniscoe@indigo.ie

In parkland and mature woods on the shores of Lough Conn, Enniscoe is stern and gaunt, as Georgian mansions in the north-west of Ireland tend to be, but any intimidating impressions of "the last great house of North Mayo" are quickly dispelled once inside this fascinating old place. Built by ancestors of the present owner, Susan Kellett, (they settled here in the 1660s), Enniscoe attracts anglers and visitors with a natural empathy for the untamed wildness of this little known area. The house has great charm and makes a lovely place to come back to after a day in the rugged countryside. Family portraits, antique furniture and crackling log fires all complement Susan's warm hospitality and wholesome dinners, which non-residents are welcome to share by reservation. It is the activities at the back of the house that have attracted special interest lately however: in the old farm buildings since 1992, when the local Historical Society opened a genealogy centre, The Mayo North Family History Research Centre (096 31809) that researches names and families of Mayo origin. Alongside there's a small but growing agricultural museum that houses a display of old farm machinery. Most recently, very exciting major renovations have been taking place in the walled gardens (officially open from autumn 1999), a small conference centre (20) is opening in the courtyard in spring 200, also four self-catering units. Children welcome; dogs are allowed by arrangement. Closed 14 Oct- 1 Apr.Amex, MasterCard, Visa. Small conference (20); Parking. Children (Under 2s free in parents' room; cots available).Garden, walking; D£25, 8pm - non residents welcome by reservation; house wines £10. **Rooms 6** (all en-suite, 2 no-smoking). B&B £56pps, ss £10. **Directions:** 2 miles south of Crossmolina on R315.

Dugort

ACCOMMODATION

Gray's Guest House
Dugort Achill Island Co Mayo
Tel: 098 43244/43315

Vi McDowell has been running this legendary guesthouse in the attractive village of Dugort since 1979, and nobody understands better the qualities of peace, quiet and gentle hospitality that have been bringing guests here for the last hundred years. It is an unusual establishment, occupying a series of houses, and each area has a slightly different appeal. There's a large, traditionally furnished sitting room with an open fire and several conservatories for quiet reading. Bedrooms and bathrooms vary considerably due to the age and nature of the premises, but the emphasis is on old-fashioned comfort; they all have tea & coffee-making trays and there are extra shared bathrooms in addition to en-suite facilities. Children are welcome (under 10s 50%) and there's an indoor playroom and safe outdoor play area plus pool and table tennis for older children. Dogs are allowed by arrangement. It's a nice place to drop into for coffee, light lunch or afternoon tea (which is served in the garden in fine weather) and the dining room is open to non-residents for evening meals by arrangement (7pm). Pets permitted by arrangement. Children welcome before 8pm; (under 3s free in parents' room). Garden, walking, pool table. **Rooms 15** (all en-suite) .B&B £30pps, ss £4, Closed 25 Dec. No credit cards (personal cheques accepted) **Directions:** Castlebar, Newport, Achill Sound, Dugort.

Keel

CAFÉ

The Beehive
Keel Achill Island Co Mayo
Tel: 098 43134 Fax: 098 43018

At their informal restaurant and attractive craft shop in Keel, husband and wife team Patricia and Michael Joyce take pride in the careful preparation and presentation of the best of Achill produce, especially local seafood such as fresh and smoked salmon, mussels, oysters and crab. Since opening in 1991, they have extended the menu each year and now offer an all-day menu daily. Everything is homemade, and they specialise in home-made soups such as seafood chowder, leek and mussel, tomato and basil and carrot and coriander, all served with homemade brown scones. Baking is a speciality, so there's always a tempting selection of cakes, bracks, teabreads, fruit tarts, baked desserts and scones with home-made preserves or you can simply have a toasted sandwich, or an Irish farmhouse cheese plate (with a glass of wine perhaps). For fine weather there are tables on a raised patio, overlooking Keel beach. * The family also has accommodation on the island. **Seats 100** (private room, 45) No smoking area. Meals, 10.30-5.45; à la carte; wine licence. Toilets wheelchair accessible. **Directions:** Situated in the centre of Keel overlooking beach and Minuan cliffs

---

Keel ✳

RESTAURANT

The Boley House Restaurant
Keel, Achill Island, Co. Mayo
Tel: 098 43147 Fax: 098 43427

Noreen McNamara Cooney has run this picturesque, immaculately maintained cottage restaurant for 30 years and there is no sign of its popularity diminishing. Local seafood is of course the star - and this, together with the unique atmosphere, is what keeps bringing people back. Children welcome. **Seats 60.** No smoking restaurant. D only, 6.30-9.15 daily; Set D £20; à la carte also available; house wine £12; sc discretionary Toilets wheelchair accessible. Open all year. MasterCard, Visa.**Directions:** 10 miles from Achill Sound.

Lahardane

PUB

Leonard's
Lahardane Co Mayo

This unspoilt roadside traditonal pub & grocery shop was established in 1897 and the original owners would be proud of it today. If you get hungry, there's the makings of a picnic on the shelves.

Lecanvey

PUB

Stauntons
Lecanvey Westport Co Mayo
Tel 098 64850

Therese Staunton runs this great little pub - genuinely traditional. Not really a food place, but home-made soup and sandwiches. Closed 25 Dec & Good Fri. No credit cards.

Louisburgh ❋   *Durkan's Weir House and Restaurant*

Louisburgh Co Mayo

RESTAURANT/PUB   Tel 098 66140   Fax 098 66324

John and Eileen Durkan's friendly establishment has a welcoming turf fire in the bar, where informal meals are served, and a proper restaurant across the corridor for high summer and winter weekend meals. John takes a serious interest in his cooking, regularly attending courses and keeping up to date with events - but, when it comes to the crunch, it's the quality of the local produce, especially seafood, that has made their reputation. Brill, monkfish, crab, mussels and lobster are always in demand, also steaks - and the house speciality is a 12 oz filet steak served with prawns in the shell and two sauces. Simple home-made soups and freshly baked breads in the bar are, in their way, equally appealing. Children welcome. **Seats 60.** No smoking restaurant D 6.30-9.30; D £25, also à la carte, house wine £10.50; sc discretionary. Toilets wheelchair accessible. Closed 24-26 Dec & Good Fri; restaurant open weekends only Nov-May except Dec. Diners, MasterCard, Visa. *Bar food served daily, 12.30-9.30. **Directions:** : Chapel Street, turn left at centre of town.

Louisburgh ❋   *The River Café*

Bridge Street Louisburgh Co Mayo

CAFE   Tel:098 66518

Real home cooking is the appeal of Clare Hickey's audaciously named little place on the main street of Louisburgh. It's bright and cosy - just the place for tasty home-made soups, fresh salads (avocado, bacon & blue cheese, for example), locally smoked salmon with fresh brown bread. Lovely home-baked cakes and desserts are a speciality; good coffee too. Children welcome **Seats 24-28.** No smoking area. Open 10-5 Tue-Sun. Toilets wheelchair accessible. Closed Mon & Oct-Easter. No credit cards. **Directions:** About 12 miles west of Westport via Murrisk

Newport ⛪   *Newport House*

Newport Co Mayo

COUNTRY HOUSE/RESTAURANT   Tel: 098 41222   Fax: 098 41613

To its many visitors, a stay at Newport House symbolises all that is best about the Irish country house, which was selected as the Guide's Country House of the Year in 1999. Currently in the capable and caring hands of Kieran and Thelma Thompson, Newport has been especially close to the hearts of fishing people for many years, but the comfort and warm hospitality of this wonderful house is accessible to all its guests – not least in shared enjoyment of the club-fender cosiness of the little back bar. The house has a beautiful central hall, sweeping staircase and gracious drawing room, while bedrooms, like the rest of the house, are furnished in style with antiques and fine paintings. Bathrooms, which can be eccentric, work well. The day's catch is weighed and displayed in the hall and the cosy fisherman's bar provides the perfect venue for a reconstruction of the day's sport. **Restaurant:** John Gavin, who has been head chef since 1983, presents interesting five courses menus. Not surprisingly, perhaps, fresh fish is a speciality – not only freshwater fish caught on local lakes and rivers, but also a wide variety of sea fish from nearby Achill. An outstanding wine list includes a great collection of classic French wines – 170 clarets from 1961-1990 vintages, a great collection of white and red burgundies, excellent Rhones – and a good New World collection too. Fishing, garden, walking, snooker. Children welcome (under 2s free in parents' room; cots available). Wheelchair accessible. Pets allowed in some areas. **Rooms 18** (2 shower only, 2 private, 16 en-suite) B&B £82pps, ss £16. Restaurant **Seats 38.** No smoking restaurant; air conditioning. D daily 7-9.30; Set D £32.L Sun only 12.30-2; Set L £14; house wine £13; sc discretionary Toilets wheelchair accessible Non-residents welcome. **Directions:** In town of Newport

Pontoon   *Healy's Hotel*

Pontoon Co Mayo

HOTEL/RESTAURANT   Tel: 094 56443   Fax: 094 56572   email: healyspontoon@tinet.ie

This famous old hotel, loved by fisherfolk, landscape artists and many others who seek peace and tranquillity, changed hands in 1998, and there has since been considerable renovation and refurbishment, without spoiling the old-fashioned qualities that have earned this hotel its special reputation: just a good bit of painting and decorating, some overdue refurbishment in the bar and a general tidy up around the front. At the back, overgrowth has been cleared to re-establish old gardens, and also develop a beer garden. Small conference/private parties (20/68); garden, fishing. Parking. Children welcome (under 3s free in parents' room; cots available). Pets permitted by arrangement. **Rooms 14** (all shower only). B&B £35pps, ss £10. Closed 25 Dec. Restaurant **Seats 68.** No smoking area. D daily 6.30-10, set D £23; L Sun only, 12-4, Set Sun L £12; House wine £13.50; sc discretionary. * Bar food 12.30-9.30 daily. **Directions:** From Dublin take the N4 to Longford switching to the N5. 3 miles from Foxford.

Rosturk
Rosturk Woods

Mulranny Westport Co Mayo
ACCOMMODATION   Tel/Fax: 098 36264 email: stoney@iol.ie

Beautifully located in secluded mature woodland, with direct access to the sandy seashore of Clew Bay, Louisa and Alan Stoney's delightful family home is between Westport and Achill Island, with fishing, swimming, sailing, walking, riding and golf all nearby. It is a lovely, informal house; the three guest bedrooms are all en-suite and very comfortably furnished (one is suitable for disabled guests). Louisa Stoney enjoys cooking for guests, but please book dinner 24 hours in advance. There is also self-catering accommodation available. Garden. Wheelchair accessible. Children (Under 4s free in parents' room; cots available). Pets by arrangement. **Rooms 3** (all en-suite & no-smoking, 1 for disabled).B&B £30pps, ss £5; Closed Dec-Mar. **Directions:** 7 miles from Newport on Mulrany Achill Road

---

Westport
Hotel Westport

The Demesne Newport Road Co Mayo
HOTEL   Tel: 098 25122 Fax: 098 26739 email: sales@hotelwestport.ie

Set in its own grounds on the edge of Westport town centre – which is just a short stroll away – this large modern hotel has recently completed a major expansion. It is the largest hotel in the area and has facilities; the conference and business centre has excellent back-up business services – and the leisure facilities that conference delegates also value highly. The whole hotel is wheelchair-friendly, with no steps or obstacles. Numerous short breaks are offered, including family breaks at times when special children's entertainment is available. Conference/banqueting (500/350); video conferencing; Business centre. Secretarial services. Leisure centre, Swimming Pool, Garden. Parking. Children (Under 3s free in parents' room; cots available). 129 rooms (6 suites, all en-suites, 7 for disabled) Wheelchair accessible. Lift B&B £60pps, ss £25. Open all year.Amex, Diners, MasterCard, Visa. **Directions:** On Castlebar road, turn right onto north mall, then turn onto Newport Street, 1st left & at the end of road.

Westport ❃
Kirwan's on the Mall

South Mall, Westport, Co. Mayo
RESTAURANT   Tel: 098 29077

Michael O'Grady, well-known for Kirwan's Lane in Galway and O'Grady's of Clifden (see entries) has chosen well for his latest venture in the centre of Westport. This buzzy contemporary restaurant only opened in 1999 and was an immediate success - it seems to have been just what Westport was waiting for. **Seats 80.** No smoking, air conditioning. A la carte. House wine from £12.50; sc discretionary.Toilets wheelchair accessible. Closed Sun & 24-31 Dec. Amex, MasterCard, Visa. **Directions:** On the mall in the centre of Westport town

---

Westport ❃
The Lemon Peel

The Octagon Westport Co Mayo
RESTAURANT   Tel: 098 26929 / 098 28558

Proprietor-chef Robbie McMenamin opened this simply-furnished little first-floor restaurant in 1998 and it quickly became a favourite with locals and visitors alike. The atmosphere is buzzy and friendly and, judging by a recent early dinner, the cooking is terrific. Perfectly cooked starters like grilled goats cheese with black olive pate and Manhattan clam chowder, then mains like sea fresh cod steak served on a crab mash with a sweet basil sauce keep tempting people back for more. Vegetables that "have a touch of home" might include a puree of turnips and carrots - hot and well seasoned - and there's a mash "menu": choose from champ, garlic, basil and black olive. Lovely homely puddings like rhubarb & apple crumble and gorgeous chocolate mousse. Good service, good coffee - good place. Not suitable for children under 12. **Seats 34.** No smoking area; air conditioning. D only 5.30-10 (Sun 6-9). Early D £13.95, 5.30-7 only. Also à la carte. House wine £10. sc discretionary. Closed Mon & 1 Feb-7 Mar. MasterCard, Visa. **Directions:** On the Quay road out of Westport.

Westport X

PUB

Matt Molloy's Bar

Bridge Street Westport Co Mayo
Tel: 098 26655

If you had to pick one pub in this pretty town, this soothingly dark atmospheric one would do very nicely – not least because it is owned by Matt Molloy of The Chieftains, a man who clearly has respect for the real pub: no TV (and no children after 9 pm). Musical memorabilia add to the interest, but there's also the real thing as traditional music is a major feature in the back room or out at the back in fine weather. It's worth noting that normal pub hours don't apply – this is an afternoon into evening place, not somewhere for morning coffee. Closed 25 Dec & Good Fri. No credit cards.

Westport

HOTEL

The Olde Railway Hotel

The Mall, Westport Co Mayo
Tel: 098 25166 Fax: 098 25090 email: railway@anu.ie

Once described by William Thackeray as 'one of the prettiest, comfortablist hotels in Ireland', The Olde Railway Hotel was built in 1780 as a coaching inn for guests of Lord Sligo. Attractively situated along the tree-lined Carrowbeg River, on the Mall in the centre of Westport, it is a hotel of character, well known for its antique furniture and a slightly eccentric atmosphere. Certain concessions have been made to the demands of modern travellers, including en-suite bathrooms, satellite television and private car parking. There's a conservatory dining room quietly situated at the back of the hotel and a recently restored function room with original stone walls. The large bar, which is the public face of an otherwise quite private hotel, serves very acceptable bar food - a private garden now supplies organic herbs and vegetables for the hotel. Own parking Garden, fishing, cycling. Children welcome (cots available). No pets. **Rooms 26** (all en-suite & no-smoking) B&B £45pps, ss £20. Open all year. Amex, Diners, MasterCard, Visa. **Directions:** Entering Westport from N5 (Dublin-Westport) road, turn right just before bridge. Hotel is on the mall, overlooking the river.

Westport

RESTAURANT

Quay Cottage

The Harbour Westport Co Mayo
Tel: 098 26412 Fax: 098 28120

Kirstin and Peter MacDonagh have been running this charming stone quayside restaurant since 1984, and it never fails to delight. It's cosy and informal, with scrubbed pine tables and an appropriate maritime decor, which is also reflected in the menu (although there is also much else of interest, including mountain lamb, steaks and imaginative vegetarian options. But seafood really stars, be it in a starter of Quay Cottage chowder special or oysters (plain or grilled). Main courses might include monkfish tandoori (with basmati rice and raita dressing) or pan-fried scallops with a saffron sauce. There are nice homely desserts – or a plated farmhouse cheese selection such as Cashel Blue, smoked Gubbeen and an Irish brie – and freshly-brewed coffee by the cup. There is now a full restaurant licence (allowing draught beers, spirits, liqueurs etc to be served).Children welcome. **Seats 80** (private room, 40) No smoking area; air conditioning. D only, 6-10 daily. Set D £23.50; also à la carte; house wine £10; sc discretionary. Toilets wheelchair accessible. **Directions:** On the harbour front, beside the gate to Westport House.

Westport

HOTEL

Westport Woods Hotel

Quay Road Westport Co Mayo
Tel: 098 25811 Fax: 098 26212 email: woodshotel@anu.ie

Situated in seven acres of woodland just behind Westport House, the Westport Woods hotel has benefited from investment recently. Substantial improvements have been made, including upgrading of the frontage, refurbishment of the lobby and all bedrooms and a new leisure centre, opened July 1999. The hotel is best known for its exceptional range of special breaks: mid-week and weekend breaks, off-peak breaks, golden holidays, family holidays, special interest breaks of every kind – murder mystery, bridge, set dancing, painting, gardening, golf, wine, even one on making a will. If there is a special break to be had, this is where it is most likely to be. Leisure centre. Tennis, garden. Own parking.Wheelchair accessible. Children welcome (under 2s free in parents' room; cots available; playroom, playground.) No pets. **Rooms 111** (all en-suite, 3 suites). B&B £68pps, ss £5-£20 Diners, MasterCard, Visa. **Directions:** 2 minutes from towncentre, towards Louisburgh.

MEATH

Towards the turn of the New Year, the approach of the new millennium is most tellingly marked with the first rays of the dawn at the Winter Solstice illuminating a special chamber of an ancient monument of Royal Meath. Meath of the pastures; Royal Meath...

The word associations which spring so readily to mind perfectly evoke a county which is comfortable with itself, and rightly so. The evidence of an affluent history is everywhere in Meath. But it's a history which sits gently on a county which is enjoying its own contemporary prosperity at a pace which belies the bustle of Dublin just down the road.

That said, anyone with an interest in the past will find paradise in Meath, for along the Boyne Valley the neolithic tumuli at Knowth, Newgrange and Dowth are awe-inspiring, Newgrange in particular having this unique central chamber which is reached by the rays of sun at dawn at the winter solstice. Just 16 kilometres to the southwest is another place of fascination, the Hill of Tara. Royal Tara was for centuries the cultural and religious capital of pre-Christian Ireland. It's fortunes began to wane with the coming of Christianity, which gradually moved the religious focal point to Armagh, but nevertheless Tara was a place of national significance until it was finally abandoned in 1022 AD.

Little now remains of the ancient structures, but it is a magical place, for the approach by the road on its eastern flank gives little indication of the wonderful view of the central plain which the hill suddenly provides. It is truly inspiring, and many Irish people reckon the year is incomplete without a visit to Tara, where the view is to eternity and infinity, and the imagination takes flight.

Local Attractions and Information

Navan	Tourist Information 046 73442
Hill of Tara	Interpretative Centre 041 24824
Trim	Butterstream Garden 046 36017
Newgrange	prehistoric, incl Dowth & Knowth 041 28824

Bettystown
F} RESTAURANT

Bacchus at the Coastguard
Bayview Bettystown Co Meath
Tel: 041 98 28251 Fax: 041 98 28251

Kieran Greenway and Anne Hardy's fine seafood restaurant is right beside the beach, with views over Bettystown Bay where, even at night, it is interesting to see the lights of the ships waiting in the bay to go up the river to the port at Drogheda. The entrance is from the road side (actually the back of the building, as the sea is at the front) and the door opens into a cosy bar where aperitifs are served. The menu majors in seafood, supplied by local fishermen and from the west coast – in starters like croûtes of smoked Donegal salmon with blue cheese set on ginger butter sauce, perhaps, and main courses such as roast monkfish dressed with vegetable julienne on chive beurre blanc. But the choice is far from being restricted to seafood; vegetarian options are included and there's a good selection of poultry and red meaths. This is an excellent restaurant with creative, accurately-cooked food, the cosy ambience and friendly, efficient service. **Seats 60** (private room, 30). No smoking area. D Tue-Sat, 6-10; L12.30-2.30 in summer; Sun L12.30-3, all year. D à la carte; early bird menu £20, 6-7.30; house wine from £10.50; sc discretionary. Closed Mon, 2 weeks Nov, 2 weeks Feb. Amex, MasterCard, Visa. **Directions:** N1 to Julianstown follow coast road through Laytown to Bettystown.

Dunshaughlin
FARM STAY

Gaulstown House
Dunshaughlin Co Meath
Tel/Fax: 01 825 9147

Built in 1829, this fine farmhouse is surrounded by mature trees and set on a working farm. It also overlooks a golf course and is within a short walk of Dunshaughlin village. Spacious en-suite accommodation has all the necessary amenities and good home cooking is Kathryn Delaney's particular interest – be it a really good breakfast to set guests up for the day, afternoon tea on the lawn or – the speciality of the house – dinner for residents, which is served at 6.30pm if booked in advance. Home-reared lamb, local sausages, home-grown vegetables; free range eggs and local honey are all used in everyday cooking. All baking is done in the farm kitchen and an Irish farmhouse cheeseboard is offered at dinner. Traditional dishes like Irish stew and bacon and cabbage are served with pride and there are country puddings such as apple pie. Garden. Children over 12 welcome. No pets. **Rooms 3** (all en-suite, 3 no-smoking) B&B £20pps, ss £6.50.Closed Oct-Mar. MasterCard, Visa. **Directions:** 2km off R125 opposite golf club.

Dunshaughlin   *The Old Workhouse*

Ballinlough Dunshaughlin Co Meath
ACCOMMODATION   Tel/Fax: 01 825 9251 email: comfort@a-vip.com

It's hard to imagine that this striking cut-stone listed building was once a workhouse – it has now been restored by Niamh and Dermod Colgan to make a beautiful old house of great character and charm, with highly individual bedrooms. Each has been furnished and decorated with great attention to detail, using carefully sourced antiques and an ever-growing collection of old plates. Of the five rooms three are officially shower-only but the Colgans have got around the problem of space with ingenuity by installing half-baths instead of shower trays. More power to them for their thoughtfulness (others please take note). Niamh is an enthusiastic cook and lavishes attention on breakfast (and dinner by arrangement, see below), sourcing ingredients with great care. Wheelchair accessible. Children (Under 2s free in parents' room; cots available). **Rooms 5** (1 mini-suite, 4 en-suite, 3 shower only, all no-smoking). B&B £30pps, ss £10-15. Dinner available by arrangement; min 6 people, £25. Closed 1 Dec- 1 Mar. Amex, MasterCard, Visa. **Directions:** 1 mile south of Dunshaughlin village on N3 route

---

Kells   *Boltown House*

Kells Co Meath
FARM STAY   Tel: 046 43605 Fax: 046 43036

Jean and Susan Wilson's family home is a lovely eighteenth century house 4 miles from Kells. Apart from the appeal of endless countryside, hunting, fishing, golfing and touring the historic sites of the area, the real attraction here is the Wilson's exceptional food. Scones appear straight from the Aga when guests arrive and are served with homemade jam and tea from wonderful china cups. Everything served here – especially the baking – is absolutely delicious. Breakfast is a feast of plums stewed with orange zest, home-made brown bread, free range eggs – the works. Accommodation is old-fashioned country – well-worn but immaculately clean throughout; bedrooms have electric blankets, crisp white sheets and lots of towels, but a shared (slightly chilly) bathroom. Absolutely authentic. Golf, fishing, garden Parking. Pets permitted; residents D£24 @8pm (book by noon); **Rooms 3** (all en-suite) B&B £32pps; no ss. Closed Xmas. Amex. **Directions:** Take Oldcastle road from Kells, after Shell petrol station on right, take 2d rd left signed Kilskyre 3km. Boltstown House 3/4 mile on right. Name on gate.

Kilmessan   *Station House*

Kilmessan Co Meath
RESTAURANT/HOTEL   Tel: 046 25239 Fax: 046 25588 email : stnhouse@indigo.ie

Chris and Thelma Slattery's unique establishment is an old railway junction and all the various buildings have been converted to a new use. A major development on the hotel side, including 85 new bedrooms, awaits planning permission at the time of going to press. Our present recommendation is for the restaurant, which is traditionally furnished, overlooking gardens at the back of the station. Wholesome fare is provided by Thelma Slattery, who has overseen the kitchen since 1984 and presents both daily set dinner menus and an à la carte. Both traditional tastes and current food trends are taken into account and there is always an imaginative vegetarian choice. An indication of the style is seen in starters of warm pigeon breast with green salad and juniper berry sauce, or stuffed courgettes with a tomato and herb sauce, then main courses like panfried monkfish with basil pesto dressing, Kilmessan rack of lamb roasted and served with a rosemary jus or mushrooms tortellini with olives, mushrooms and chilli oil. Finish with farmhouse cheeses or desserts such as chocolate and orange parfait or warm lemon tart. Sunday lunch is extremely popular and justifies two sittings but staff remain calm and cheerful throughout. Children welcome. **Seats 85.** No smoking area. L 12.30-3 (Sun to 4.30), D 7-10.30 (Sun to 9.30), Set L £12.95; Set D £21.95, also à la carte; early bird menu £12.95; house wine from £10.95; sc discretionary.Toilets wheelchair accessible.Closed Good Fri & 24 Dec. Amex, Diners, MasterCard, Visa **Directions:** From Dublin N3 to Dunsaughlin turn left; after half a mile, turn right @ fork.

Navan

Ardboyne Hotel

Navan Co Meath
Tel: 046 23119 Fax: 046 22355
email: ardboyne@quinn-hotels.com

HOTEL/RESTAURANT

Standing in its own grounds on the outskirts of town, this modern hotel has a thriving conference and function trade. The entrance and all public areas give a good first impression; all bedrooms have recently been refurbished and two new ones added. However, as has been the case for a number of years, food is particularly good.Conference/banqueting (600/400) Parking. Children under 2 free in parents' room; cots available. Wheelchair accessible. **29 rooms**, 2 suites, all en-suite). B&B £40pps, ss £16 Closed 24-26 Dec o Amex, Diners, MasterCard, Visa.

La Mezzanine: The restaurant was undergoing refurbishment at the time of going to press and new menus are to be introduced. Children welcome **Seats 80** No smoking area; air conditioning. L 12.30-3 & D 6-10 daily. Set L £11.50; Set Sun L £12.75, Set D £19.50, also à la carte, house wine £10, sc discretionary Toilets wheelchair accessible. **Directions:** From Dublin, N3 to Navan, hotel on left approaching town.

Navan

China Garden Restaurant

58 Brews Hill Navan Co Meath
Tel: 046 22621 Fax: 046 29107

RESTAURANT

The Yips take pride in their restaurant's reputation and it shows in good food and quietly attentive service. A fish pond in the seating area at the entrance creates a very soothing atmosphere, a feeling of calm heightened by the dim light of the restaurant interior. A wide choice is offered and the food is good – crispy lemon chicken received particular praise on the Guide's visit – and well-presented. Chinese tea is served with delightful ceremony at the end of the meal. Children welcome. **Seats 95** No smoking area; air conditioning. L 12.30-2.15; Set L from £5.40. D 6-12.30 (Fri & Sat to 1 am) Set D for two, £32. Also à la carte; house wine £10; sc discretionary.Closed L Sun & 24-26 Dec.Amex, Diners, MasterCard, Visa. **Directions:** Centre of Navan

---

Navan

Hudson's Bistro

30 Railway Street Navan Co Meath
Tel: 046 29231 Fax: 046 73382

RESTAURANT

Since Richard and Tricia Hudson's stylish, informal bistro opened in 1991 it has built up a strong following and is now established as a leading restaurant in the area - indeed, due to "popular demand" they are now open every evening. Richard's menus include an exciting à la carte based on wide-ranging influences – Cal-Ital, Mexican, Thai, French and modern Italian. Appealing vegetarian and healthy options are a feature – and, traditionalists will be pleased to hear, the ever-popular sirloin steak has not been overlooked. There are Irish cheeses and/or some very tempting puds to finish. The wine list echoes the global cooking and is keenly priced.Children welcome. **Seats 60** No smoking area. D 5.30-10.30 daily. Set D £25, à la carte also available; early menu £10.50, 5.30-7 pm only. House wine £9.95; sc 10%. Limited toilet wheelchair accessibility. Closed 24-25 Dec & Good Fri. Amex, MasterCard, Visa. **Directions:** Town centre, green-purple building beside Ulster Bank.

Navan

Killyon House

Dublin Road Navan Co Meath
Tel: 046 71224 Fax: 046 72766

ACCOMMODATION

Just across the road from the Ardboyne Hotel, Michael and Sheila Fogarty's modern guesthouse immediately attracts attention, with its striking array of colourful flowers and hanging baskets. The house is furnished stylishly with interesting antiques, and made comfortable by modern double glazing which reduces traffic noise. The back of the house, which leads down to the banks of the Boyne, is unexpectedly tranquil, however, and the dining room overlooks the river, giving guests the added interest of spotting wildlife, sometimes including otters and stoats, along the bank from the window. The Fogartys are extremely hospitable hosts and nothing (even doing a very early breakfast) is too much trouble. The house is very well run and rooms are all en-suite and comfortable, if on the small side and shower-only. There's also a separate guests' sitting room and, although they are too close to the restaurants of Navan to make evening meals a viable option, they do a very good breakfast. Own parking. Children under 5 free in parents' room; cots available. Wheelchair accessible. **6 rooms** (all en-suites, 4 shower only). B&B £20pps, ss £5.Closed 24-25 Dec.MasterCard, Visa. **Directions:** On river, opposite Ardboyne Hotel (N3).

Navan
Newgrange Hotel

Bridge Street Navan Co Meath

HOTEL/RESTAURANT Tel: 046 74100 Fax: 046 73977

This hotel right in the centre of Navan only opened in 1998. It replaced an existing hotel, but was virtually a reconstruction job. Given the constraints of space the results are very stylish and impressive, in both public areas and accommodation. Rooms may not be enormous but they have been furnished with care and decorated with flair; even though space was at a premium, all have well-designed bathrooms with full bath and shower. Double glazing helps ease traffic noise, although this could present problems in hot weather as there is no air conditioning. Conference/banqueting facilities for up to 450. Own parking. Children welcome (under 5s free in parents' room; cots available). No pets. **Rooms 36** (1 suite, all en-suite) B&B £44pps, ss £13.50. Lift. Wheelchair access. Closed 25 Dec. Amex, Diners, MasterCard, Visa. **Restaurant – The Bridge Brasserie:** Like the rest of this impressive new hotel, the restaurant is smartly and quite formally decorated in luxurious fabrics, and the modish neo-gothic theme of the decor seems quite at home in this historic area. Head chef Michael O'Neill presents exciting, contemporary menus at lunch and dinner and there's also an evening à la carte menu. The cooking is good and service both efficient and friendly; although quite expensive for a hotel dining room. There is a real sense of occasion in this restaurant; the adjoining cafe is less formal (and less expensive). *Bar food daily 12.30-7. **Seats 80.** No smoking area; air conditioning. L 12.30-2.30 & D 6-10.30; Set L£12.50 (Sun £13.50); Set D £19.95,à la carte also available; tourist menu £14.50; 6-10.30pm only. House wine £12; sc discretionary. Wheelchair access. **Directions:** Town centre backing onto main N3 (Dublin-Donegal) route.

Skryne
O'Connell's

Skryne nr Tara Co Meath

PUB Tel: 046 25122

Three generations of O'Connell's have been caretakers of this wonderfully unspoilt country pub. The present owner, Mary O'Connell, has been delighting customers old and new for over ten years now. It's all beautifully simple – two little bars with no fancy bits, lots of items of local interest, and a welcoming fire in the grate. What more could anyone want? As for **directions:** – just head for the tower beside the pub, which is visible for miles around. Closed 25 Dec & Good Fri.

Slane
Boyle's Licensed Tea Rooms

Main Street Slane Co Meath

CAFÉ/BAR Tel: 04198 24195

Boyles has been run for the past ten years by Josephine Boyle, the third generation of the family to do so. The tea rooms lie behind a superb traditional black shopfront with gold lettering, with an interior that has barely changed since the 1940s. Visitors from all over the world come here, often after visiting nearby Newgrange – hence the unlikely facility of menus in 12 languages! The food – which is plainly cooked and, true to the era evoked, includes bought-in cakes and shop jam – is not really the point here as people come for the character. Food service all day 11-11 (Sun from 12.30). Closed Tues, 25 Dec & Good Fri. MasterCard, Visa **Directions:** Turn left at square in Slane village from Dublin, 2nd Business House.

Slane ✗
Conyngham Arms Hotel

Slane Co Meath

HOTEL Tel: 041 84444 Fax: 041 24205 email: conynghamarms@tinet.ie

This attractive stone hotel has been owned by the Macken family since 1929. It creates a very good impression with its lovely signage and twin bay trees at the main entrance. Chintzy fabrics and wood panelling create a cosy country feeling in the restaurant and bar areas; the self-service counter in the bar serves lovely traditional home-made food all day (12 noon -8 pm) – roast chicken with stuffing, bacon and cabbage, delicious apple tart – and is good value. All the bedrooms have recently been refurbished; the hotel is popular for weddings and there is one suite. Meals £-££ Acc££ Closed 25 Dec & Good Fri. Amex, Diners, MasterCard, Visa.

MONAGHAN

There may be secrets worth finding in Monaghan's little hills in the 21st Century. They may even find gold... Of all Ireland's counties, it is Monaghan which is most centrally placed in the drumlin country, that strip of rounded glacial hills which runs right across the country from Strangford Lough to Clew Bay. Monaghan, in fact, is all hills. But as very few of them are over 300 m, the county takes its name from Muineachain - "Little Hills". Inevitably, the actively farmed undulating country encloses many lakes, and Monaghan in its quiet way is a coarse angler's paradise. And also looking to water sports is the line of the old Ulster Canal, much of which is in Monaghan.

Once upon a time, it connected Lough Erne to Lough Neagh. It has been derelict for a very long time, but with the success of the restored Shannon-Erne Waterway along the line of the old Ballinamore-Ballyconnell canal, the even more ambitious notion of restoring the Ulster Canal is being given serious consideration, providing us with the vision of cruisers chugging through Monaghan on a fascinating inland voyage all the way from Waterford on the south coast to Coleraine on the north coast.

Vision of a different sort is the theme at Annaghmakerrig House near the Quaker-named village of Newbliss in west Monaghan. The former home of theatrical producer Tyrone Guthrie, it is now a busy centre for writers and artists who can stay there to complete 'work in progress'. In the east of the county at Castleblayney, there's a particularly attractive lake district with forest park and adventure centre Muckno Lough. Meanwhile, north at Clontibret, there's gold in them thar little hills, and the word is that another gold mining operation may be getting under way.

Local Attractions and Information

Annaghmakerrig House	Sir Tyrone Guthrie's writers' centre
Clones	Hilton Park (restored pleasure grounds) 047 56003
Rossmore Forest Park	R189 Newbliss Road

Carrickmacross | *Nuremore Hotel & Country Club*

Carrickmacross Co Monaghan

HOTEL/RESTAURANT   Tel: 042 966 1438 Fax: 960 4261853 email: nuremore@tinet.ie

This fine, well-managed country hotel has prospered and developed over the years and is now an impressive establishment by any standards. Set in a parkland estate with its own 18-hole golf course, the hotel serves the sporting, leisure and business requirements of a wide area very well. The superb country club has a full leisure centre with swimming pool and a good range of related facilities, while new conference centre (opened in 1997) boasts state-of-the-art audio-visual equipment. The hotel gives a very good impression on arrival and this sense of care and maintenance is continued throughout all the spacious areas and the bedrooms. Conference/banqueting (350/500); secretarial services, business centre. Leisure centre, golf, garden, tennis, snooker. Children welcome (playroom). No pets. **Rooms 72** (7 suites, 11 executive, 1 for disabled). B&B 70 pps, ss £20. Open all year.Amex, Diners, MasterCard, Visa. **Restaurant:** The restaurant is elegantly appointed, with a couple of steps dividing the window area and inner tables. Now well established as the leading restaurant in the area, both food and service match the high standards of the rest of the hotel. **Seats 120.** No smoking area; air conditioning. L Sun-Fri, 12.30-2.30; D daily 6.30-9.30. Set L/Sun L £14.50; Set D £26, à la carte also available.House wine £12.50; sc discretionary. Closed L Sat. **Directions:** On N2 Dublin-Derry road, 1 mile south of Carrickmacross.

Clones ⛪ | Hilton Park

Clones Co Monaghan

COUNTRY HOUSE   Tel: 047 56007 Fax: 047 56033 email: hilton@tempoweb.com

Hilton Park, Johnny and Lucy Madden's wonderful 18th century mansion, has been described as a "capsule of social history" because of their collection of family portraits and memorabilia going back 250 years or more. In beautiful countryside, amidst 200 acres of woodland and farmland (home to Johnny's champion rare breed sheep) with lakes, Pleasure Grounds and a Lovers' Walk to set the right tone, the house is magnificent in every sense, and the experience of visiting it a rare treat. Johnny and Lucy are natural hosts and, as the house and its contents go back for so many generations, there is a strong feeling of being a privileged family guest as you wander through grandly-proportioned, beautifully furnished rooms. Four-posters and all the unselfconscious comforts that make for a very special country house stay are part of the charm, but as visitors from all over the world have found, it's the warmth of Johnny and Lucy's welcome that lends that extra magic. International hospitality – with an Irish flavour – at its best - a worthy winner of the Guide's International Hospitality Award in 1999. Not suitable for children under 8. No pets. **Rooms 6** (all en-suite & no smoking).B&B £57.50, ss £10. Residents D £27.50 at 8 pm. House wine £14.75. No sc. Closed Oct-Mar. Amex, MasterCard, Visa. **Directions:** At Scotshouse House on Clones/Ballyhaise Road.

Glaslough

Castle Leslie

COUNTRY HOUSE/RESTAURANT

Glaslough Co Monaghan
Tel: 047 88109 Fax: 047 88256
email: ultan@castle-leslie.ie

Castle Leslie is an extraordinary place, with a long and fascinating history to intrigue guests. Suffice it to say that it is set in a 1,000 acre estate, has been in the Leslie family for over 300 years and has changed very little in that time. There is no reception desk, just a welcoming oak-panelled hall, and there are no phones, television sets or clocks in the rooms, although concessions to the 20th century have been made in the form of generous heating and plentiful hot water. In a charming reverse of circumstances, the family lives in the servants' wing, so guests can enjoy the magnificence of the castle to the full – it has all the original furniture and family portraits. The fourteen bedrooms are all different, furnished and decorated around a particular era, with en-suite bathrooms a feature in their own right. The estate has wonderful walks. Pike fishing, boating and picnic lunches on the estate are available by arrangement. Due to the nature of the castle (and the fact that the Leslies see it as a wonderful refuge from the outside world for adults) this is not a suitable place to bring children. Conferences/banqueting 40/120. **Rooms 14** (13 en-suite, 5 shower only, 1 with private bathroom). **Restaurant:** Good food is an important element of any visit to Castle Leslie and Paul Clarke, previously at the excellent Mizuna restaurant in Belfast, is now head chef: he makes the most of top quality local ingredients in a well-balanced global cuisine characterised by clarity of flavours. Non-residents are welcome to come for dinner, by arrangement, and it is all done in fine old style with pre-dinner drinks in the drawing room (or the Fountain Garden in summer) and dinner served in the original dining room (which has remained unchanged for over a century); the waitresses even wear Victorian uniforms. **Seats 75.** No smoking area. D daily 7-9.15; Set D £28.50. House wine £12.50. **Directions:** Monaghan town-Armagh road-Glaslough.

Monaghan

Andy's Bar & Restaurant

PUB/RESTAURANT

12 Market Street Monaghan Co Monaghan
Tel: 047 82277 Fax: 047 89415

The Redmond family's well-run bar and restaurant in the centre of Monaghan has a strong local following, and it is easy to see why. The high-ceilinged bar is furnished and decorated in traditional Victorian style, with a lot of fine mahogany, stained glass and mirrors. Everything is gleaming clean and arranged well for comfort, with high-backed bar seats and plenty of alcoves set up with tables for the comfortable consumption of their good bar food. Substantial bar meals include a range of mid-day specials on a blackboard as well as a concise written menu. A different, slightly more sophisticated range is offered in the evening, as well as a short children's menu. The upstairs restaurant offers a much more extensive range of popular dishes. Traditional desserts like pavlova, lemon cheesecake, fresh fruit salad and home-made ices are served from a trolley, and there might be something comforting like a hot treacle sponge pudding in cold weather. Bar L Mon-Sat; D daily 6-10. Closed 25 Dec, Good Fri & 1-14 July.MasterCard, Visa **Directions:** Opposite Market House.

Monaghan

Hillgrove Hotel

HOTEL

Armagh Road Monaghan Co Monaghan
Tel: 047 81288

The Hillgrove is the leading hotel in the area, overlooking the town from a fine hillside location. It is impressively well-run and has good conference and banqueting facilities (1200/700).Garden. Children welcome (free in parents' room to 4, cots available). No Pets. **Rooms 44** (4 suites, 5 junior suites, 35 executive, 2 for disabled).B&B £38 pps Open all year. Amex, Diners, MasterCard, Visa .

OFFALY

At the turn of the millennium, Offaly is Ireland's most sky-minded county. Not only is there in Birr the Parsons family's famous 1845-vintage 1.83 m astronomical telescope through which the 3rd Earl of Rosse observed his discovery of the spiral nebulae, but as well in Tullamore there's a thriving amateur Astronomical Society whose members point out that the wide clear skies of Offaly have encouraged the regular observation of heavenly bodies since at least 1057 AD.

Back in Birr meanwhile, the annual Irish Hot Air Balloon meeting has been run with increasing success since 1970. It attracts serious international balloonists who welcome the opportunity for participation in a relaxed fun event where everyone wins a prize, and is equally suitable for beginners as Offaly's bogs provide a soft landing - "there's a bit of give in a bog". Offaly is also historic hunting country. It is home to the Ormonde, which may not be Ireland's largest or richest hunt, "but it's the oldest and undoubtedly the best."

Once upon a time, they invited the neighbouring County Galway Hunt for a shared meet, and afterwards the carousing in Dooley's Hotel in Birr reached such a hectic pitch that the hotel was joyously torched by the visitors. Dooley's was rebuilt to fulfill its central role in Birr, and the hunt from across the Shannon has been known as the Galway Blazers ever since.

The Grand Canal finally reaches the great river at Shannon Harbour in Offaly, after crossing Ireland from Dublin, and on the river itself, waterborne travellers find that Offaly affords the opportunity of visiting Clonmacnoise, where the remains of an ancient monastic university city give pause for thought. In the south of the county, the Slieve Bloom Mountains rise attractively above Offaly's farmland and bogs. These are modest heights, as they attain just 526 m on the peak of Arderin. However, it is their understated charms which particularly appeal, and in the Slieve Blooms we find Ireland's first organised system of gites, the French concept whereby unused farmhouses have been restored to a comfortable standard for self-catering visitor accommodation.

Local Attractions and Information

Birr	Castle Demesne 0509 20336
Clonmacnoise	Monastic settlements/visitor centre 0905 74195
Edenderry	3-day Canal Festival (coarse angling) (June) 0405 32071
Tullamore	Offaly Tourist Council 0506 52566

Annaharvey ✻   *Annaharvey Farm*

Annaharvey, Tullamore, Co Offaly

FARMHOUSE   Tel 0506 43544   Fax 0506 43766   email: annafarm@indigo.ie

Henry and Lynda Deverell's restored grain barn, with pitch pine floors and beams, open fires and comfortable accommodation, provides a good base for a holiday offering all the pleasures of the outdoor life. Equestrian activities are the main attraction (including tuition in indoor and outdoor arenas), but walking, cycling and golfing also lay their claims - and, for the rest days, major sights including Clonmacnoise and Birr Castle are nearby. Conference/banqueting (50/60).Golf, equestrian, walking, garden, snooker, clay pigeon shooting. D 7-9.30; set dinner £20; house wine £10.95; toilets wheelchair accessible. Children welcome (under 3s free in parents' room; cots available). No pets. **Rooms 6** (all en-suite & no-smoking). B&B £25pps, ss £5. Closed mid Dec-1 Feb. MasterCard,Visa. **Directions:** 3 miles from Tullamore on Portarlington Road.

Banagher   *J. J. Hough's*

Main Street Banagher Co Offaly

PUB   Tel: 0509 51893

Hidden behind a thriving vine, which threatens to take over in summer, this charming 250-year old pub is soothingly dark inside – making a fine contrast to the cheerful eccentricity of the current owner, Michael Hough. Very much a local, it's also popular with people from the river cruisers, who come up from the harbour for the pints and the craic. Traditional music every night.Wheelchair access.Children and pets welcome.Closed 25 Dec & Good Fri. **Directions:** On Main Street, Lower Town.

Banagher ✗   *The Vine House*

Banagher Co Offaly
PUB/RESTAURANT   Tel/Fax: 0509 51463

At the bottom of the village, very close to the harbour, this bar and restaurant is well worth knowing about (especially if you are staying overnight in a cruiser). It's an attractive place (with an interesting history too) and both food and hospitality are good. D daily from about 6.30-9.30. £-££. Closed 25 Dec & Good Fri. MasterCard, Visa.

Birr ✗   *Dooly's Hotel*

Emmet Square Birr Co Offaly
HOTEL   Tel: 0509 20032 Fax: 0509 21332

A good holiday centre with plenty to do locally – Birr Castle gardens are very near, also golfing, fishing, riding and river excursions, This attractive, old-fashioned hotel is one of Ireland's oldest coaching inns, dating back to 1747 and is right on Emmet Square, the centre of Georgian Birr. Public rooms, including two characterful bars, are traditional in furnishing style but have all been refurbished recently. Bedrooms have recently been upgraded and now include a junior suite and an executive room; all are en-suite with full bathrooms (bath and shower). When there's a function on, the hotel tries to allocate quiet rooms if possible. Meals £-££. Acc££. Closed 25 Dec.Amex, Diners, MasterCard, Visa.

Birr   *Spinners Town House & Bistro*

Castle Street Birr Co Offaly
ACCOMMODATION/BISTRO   Tel/Fax: 0509 21673

Joe and Fiona Breen's unusual establishment in the centre of Birr runs through five Georgian townhouses, restored and refurbished throughout in a simple contemporary style. In addition to their own sitting room and breakfast room, guests have the use of an enclosed courtyard garden. Bedrooms include family rooms, doubles and twins, all with en-suite or private bathrooms. Children (Under 2s free in parents' room; cots available). Wheelchair accessible. **Rooms 10.** B&B £20pps, ss £5. Closed Christmas. Amex, MasterCard, Visa. **Spinner Bistro**, which offers eclectic menus based on fresh ingredients, local wherever possible, is open to non-residents. **Seats 45** D5-10; daily in summer/5 nights a week winter; à la carte; sc discretionary; licensed. Toilets wheelchair accessible. No children under 12 welcome after 7.30 pm. **Directions:** Down Birr Main street (one way system), take a right at the bottom of the square - last 5 houses on right.

Birr   *The Stables Restaurant & Townhouse*

Oxmantown Mall Birr Co Offaly
RESTAURANT/ACCOMMODATION   Tel: 0509 20263 Fax: 0509 21677

The Boyd family's characterful establishment in a lovely old Georgian house overlooking the tree-lined mall. It has a strong local following. The restaurant is in the converted stables and coach house and has lots of atmosphere, with attractive exposed bricks and stonework, arches and an open fire in the period drawing room (which is used as a bar and reception area). The cooking style is quite traditional – a blend of Cordon Bleu and traditional Irish – and hearty country portions are to be expected. **Seats 65** D 6.30-9.30.Tue-Sun. L Sun only 12.30-3; Set Sun L £12; à la carte also available at D, house wine £9.95; sc discretionary. No smoking area; toilets wheelchair accessible. Own parking; children welcome. Closed Mondays, Ash Wednesday, Good Fri. Amex, Diners, MasterCard, Visa. **Accommodation:** Old world en-suite bedrooms overlook the mall or the courtyard. **Rooms 4** B&B £25pps. **Directions:** Town centre, opposite original gates of Birr Castle.

Birr ✗   *Tullanisk*

Birr Co Offaly
COUNTRY HOUSE   Tel: 0509 20572 Fax: 0509 21783 email: tnisk@indigo.ie

An 18th-century Dower House in the demesne of the Earls of Rosse (still resident at Birr Castle), run by George and Susie Gossip as a private country house. George enjoys producing memorable 'no-choice' dinners, including game in season. The en-suite bedrooms (one with shower only) are large, characterful and comfortable. Delicious breakfasts. Dinner is mainly for residents. D££. Acc££. Closed Xmas. Amex, Diners, MasterCard, Visa.

Crinkle [PUB★]

The Thatch Bar & Restaurant

Crinkle Birr Co Offaly

PUB/RESTAURANT   Tel: 0509 20682 Fax: 0509 21847

This characterful little thatched pub and restaurant just outside Birr shows just how good a genuine, well-run country pub can be. Since 1991 the energetic owner Des Connole has worked tirelessly to improve standards with the help, since June 1995, of head chef James McDonnell. Five-course dinner menus change weekly and include a mixture of traditional dishes such as sirloin steaks with mushrooms in garlic and more interesting things – local pigeon and rabbit terrines, roast duck with vegetable stir-fry, loin of pork with a rhubarb compote. Consistently good cooking and warm hospitality make this one of the best eating places in the area.Children welcome. Parking **Seats 50** (private room, 15-20). D 6.30-9.30 daily, à la carte; L Sun-12.30 & 2.30; Set Sun L £12; early evening bar menu 5.30-7.30, à la carte; house wine £12; sc discretionary. Bar food 12.30-7.30 Mon-Sat. No smoking area; air conditioning.Toilets wheelchair accessible. Closed 25 Dec, Good Fri. Diners, MasterCard, Visa. **Directions:** 1 mile from Birr (Roscrea side).

Dunkerrin ✗

Dunkerrin Arms

Dunkerrin Birr Co Offaly

PUB   Tel: 0505 45377/45399

Set well back from the road, but clearly visible, this large well-managed pub makes a useful break on the Limerick-Dublin road and serves freshly-cooked food all day. Toilets equipped for disabled. Meals £ all day. Closed 25 Dec & Good Fri. Access, Visa.

Kinnity

Kinnity Castle

Kinnity Birr Co Offaly

HOTEL   Tel: 0509 37318 Fax: 0509 37284 email: kinnitycastle@tinet.ie

Recently refurbished in keeping with its dramatic history and theatrical character, this luxurious Gothic Revival castle in the foothills of the Slieve Bloom Mountains is at the centre of a very large estate (accessible for horseriding and walking) with 650 acres of parkland and formal gardens. Public areas – a library bar, Georgian style dining room, Louis XV drawing room and an atmospheric Dungeon Bar – are mainly furnished in the style expected of a castle hotel. The accommodation, however, is slightly different: big, romantic bedrooms have stunning views over the estate (and sumptuous, dramatically styled bathrooms). Medieval-style banqueting/conference facilities for up to 180/220 in a courtyard at the back of the castle; new but atmospheric. Leisure centre. Tennis, fishing, equestrian, garden.Children welcome (Under 12s free in parents' room; cots available). **Rooms 37** (10 suites, 11 mini-suites, 16 executive rooms, 1 shower only). B&B £80pps, ss £15. Open all year. MasterCard, Visa. **Directions:** N7 from Dublin, past Monasterevin; turn right to Emo Court, onto Mountmellick through to Kinnity Village.

Kinnity

Ardmore House

The Walk, Kinnitty, Co. Offaly

B&B   Tel: 0509 37009

Christina Byrne's stone-built Victorian house is set back from the road in its own garden and offers old-fashioned comforts: brass beds, turf fires and home-baked bread for breakfast. Children welcome; pets allowed in certain areas. **Rooms 4** (1 ensuite, 2 shower only). B&B £23-25pps, ss £5-7. Open all year.No credit cards. **Directions:** In village of Kinnitty, 9 miles from Birr.

Tullamore

Tullamore Court Hotel

O'Moore Street Tullamore Co Offaly

HOTEL   Tel 0506 46666 Fax 0506 46677 email:info@tullamorecourthotel.ie

An attractive building, set back from the road a little and softened by trees, this large modern hotel has a large foyer and public areas are bright and cheerful.It serves the local community well, with good conference and banqueting facilities (750/550 respectively) and an excellent leisure centre. An ideal base for business or leisure. Staff are friendly and helpful. Leisure centre, crechè, garden. Children welcome (Under 4s free in parents' room; cots available). Pets permitted by arrangement. **Rooms 72** (3 mini-suites, 9 executive rooms, 4 for disabled). B&B £75pps, ss £15 Wheelchair accessible. Lift.Closed 25 Dec. Amex, Diners, MasterCard, Visa. **Directions:** Turn off main Dublin/Galway road at Kilbeggan/turn off main Dublin/Cork-Limerick road at Monasterevin.

ROSCOMMON

Roscommon welcomes the 21st Century. For Roscommon has been a county much put upon by the counties about it. Or, put another way, to the casual visitor it seemed that just as Roscommon was on the verge of becoming interesting, it became somewhere else. In one notable example - the hotel complex at Hodson's Bay on the western shores of Lough Ree - the location is actually in Roscommon, yet the exigencies of the postal service have given it to Athlone and thereby Westmeath.

But Roscommon is a giving sort of county, for it gave Ireland her first President, Gaelic scholar Douglas Hyde (1860-1949), it was also the birthplace of Oscar Wilde's father, and as well the inimitable songwriter Percy French was a Roscommon man. Like everywhere else in the western half of Ireland, Roscommon suffered grieviously from the Great Famine of the late 1840s, and at Strokestown, the handsome market town serving the eastern part of the county, Strokestown Park House has been sympathetically restored to include a Famine Museum. A visit to it will certainly add a thoughtful element to your meal in the restaurant.

Roscommon town itself has a population of barely 1,500, but the presence of extensive castle ruins and a former gaol tell of a more important past. The gaol was once noted for having a female hangman, today it has shops and a restaurant. Northwestward at Castlerea, we find Clonalis House, ancestral home of the O'Conor Don, and final resting place of Carolan's Harp. In the north of the county, the town of Boyle near lovely Lough Key with its forest park is a substantial centre, with a population nearing the 2,000 mark. Boyle is thriving, and symbolic of this is the restored King House, a masterpiece from 1730. Reckoned to have been the most important provincial town house in Ireland, it is today filled with exhibits which eloquently evoke the past.

Lough Key is of course one on the upper reaches of the inland waterways system, and a beautiful part it is too. In fact, all of Roscommon's eastern boundary is defined by the Shannon and its lakes, but as the towns along it tend to identify themselves with the counties across the river, Roscommon is left looking very thin on facilities. But it has much to intrigue the enquiring visitor. For instance, along the Roscommon shore of Lough Ree near the tiny village of Lecarrow, the remains of a miniature city going back to mediaeval times and beyond can be dimly discerned among the trees down towards Rindown Point.

These hints of an active past serve to emphasise the fact that today, Roscommon moves at a gentler pace than the rest of Ireland - something which is reflected in its pubs to people ratio. It is second only to Leitrim on this scale, as Leitrim has just 148 people for every pub licence, while Roscommon has 170. Slainte!

Local Attractions and Information

Boyle	Josie McDermott Memorial Festival (April/May) 078 47024
Boyle	King House (500 years of Irish life) 079 63242
Boyle	Lough Key Forest Park 079 62363
Castlerea	Clonalis House (ancestral home of Kings of Connaught) 0907 20014
Frenchpark	Dr Douglas Hyde Interpretative Centre 0907 70016
Roscommon	Tourist Information 0903 26342
Strokestown	Park House, Garden & Famine Museum 078 33013

Boyle   *Kate Lavin's*

	St Patrick Street Boyle Co Roscommon
PUB	Tel: 079 62855

Although established in 1889, the survival of Marie Harvey's characterful pub is nothing less than a miracle, as it has been left virtually untouched ever since and closed for around twenty years – the two old ladies who lived here got tired of running it and simply shut the door until a younger relative took up the challenge in the late 'eighties – and had the wisdom to leave well alone. It's one of those magic places with an open fire in the sitting room and the old range in the kitchen – it's lit on St Patrick's Day every year, when a couple of big pots of stew are cooked on it and, believe it or not, served free of charge. Traditional music on Wednesday nights. Open Mon-Thurs 8pm; Fri-Sun 6pm. Children welcome. Pets permitted by arrangement. Closed 25 Dec & Good Fri. No credit cards. **Directions:** In the town centre.

Carrick-on-Shannon ❀   *Glencarne Country House*

Ardcarne, Carrick-on-Shannon Co Roscommon
COUNTRY HOUSE   Tel/Fax: 079 67013

The Harrington family's large Georgian house is set well back from the road, with a large garden in front and farmland behind, so it is easy to find, yet without interference from traffic. Spacious and elegantly furnished with antiques, this is very much a family home and Agnes Harrington has won lots of awards for hospitality and home-cooked food based on their own farm produce. Garden. Children welcome; pets permitted by arrangement. **Rooms** 4 (all en-suite).B&B £22pps, ss £5. Set D £20, 7.30pm (book by 6pm); wine licence.Closed Mid Oct-1 Mar. No credit cards. **Directions:** On the N4, between Carrick-on-Shannon and Boyle.

Castlerea ❀   *Clonalis House*

Castlerea, Co Roscommon
COUNTRY HOUSE   Tel/Fax: 0907 20014

Although the exterior may be daunting, this 45 roomed Victorian Italianate mansion is magic. It stands on land that has been home of the O'Conors of Connacht for 1,500 years and the hospitable owners Pyers and Marguerite O'Conor-Nash enjoy sharing their rich and varied history with guests, who are welcome to browse through their fascinating archive. Amazing heirlooms include a copy of the last Brehon Law judgment (handed down about 1580) and also Carolan's Harp. Everything is on a huge scale: reception rooms are all very spacious, with lovely old furnishings and many interesting historic details, bedrooms have massive four poster and half tester beds and bathrooms to match and the dining room is particularly impressive, with a richly decorated table to enhance Marguerite's home cooking. Fishing, shooting, golf (9). Unsuitable for children. No pets. B&B £52pps, ss £6. Set Residents D £23.50 (24hrs notice necessary) Closed 1 Oct-mid Apr. Amex, MasterCard, Visa. **Directions:** On the N60, west of Castlerea.

Roscommon ❀   *The Abbey Hotel*

Roscommon
HOTEL/RESTAURANT   Tel:0903 26240 Fax:0903 26021

The heart of this pleasant town centre hotel is an old manor house and, although there are more recent extensions - and plans for a leisure centre and new rooms - the atmosphere of the original building prevails. Most bedrooms are modern with the usual facilities - phone, , tea/coffee-making, multi-channel TV, and there's a romantic honeymoon suite with a four-poster in the old house. Banqueting (70) Garden. Children welcome (under 10s free in parents' room; cots available). Wheelchair accessible. **Rooms** 25 (all en-suite). B&B £45pps, ss £10. Closed 24-26 Dec. Amex, Diners, MasterCard, Visa. **Restaurant:** A fairly recent addition, the restaurant is designed on two levels in a semi-brasserie style and makes a popular meeting place, where friendly, helpful staff serve unpretentious wholesome fare. **Seats 70** (private room, 50). L 12.30-3 daily. D 6-9.30 daily. Set L £12.50; Set Sun L £14; à la carte available. No smoking area. Toilets wheelchair accessible. **Directions:** On the Galway road.

Roscommon ❀   *Restaurant Le Chateau*

Old Jail, Stonecourt Centre, Roscommon, Co Roscommon
RESTAURANT   Tel:0903 27616 Fax:0903 73668 email:lechateau@tinet.ie

This new restaurant is in Roscommon's 18th century jailhouse and opened in the summer of 1999, after the Guide's visit. It's a sister establishment to Restaurant Le Chateau in Athlone (our Atmospheric Restaurant of the Year in 1999, see entry) and run by Steven Linehan's brother Cormac, on very similar lines to the Athlone restaurant. **Seats 60** (private room, 30). D 5.30-10 daily (Sun to 9.30). Set D £24, early evening menu £15.50 ,5.30-7 pm only. House wines from £13. No smoking area; air conditioning. Toilets wheelchair accessible.Children welcome. Parking nearby. MasterCard, Visa. **Directions:** In Roscommon town, behind the Bank of Ireland on the main street.

SLIGO

Not now, nor at any time, would you think that Sligo is one of Ireland's smallest counties. Yet such is the case. But there's a stylish confidence to Sligo which belies its small area. Perhaps it's because they know that their place and their way of life have been immortalised through association with two of the outstanding creative talents of modern Ireland, W.B.Yeats and his painter brother Jack. The former's greatness is beyond question, while the latter's star was never higher than it is today.

But whatever the reason for Sligo's special quality, there's certainly something about it that encourages repeat visits. The town of Sligo itself is a fine place, big enough to be reassuring, yet small enough to be comfortable. And the county in which it is set is an area in which nature has been profligate in her gifts. The mountains, with unique Ben Bulben setting the standard, are simply astonishing. The sea is vividly omnipresent, and the beaches are magnificent.

Mankind has been living here with enthusiasm for a very long time indeed, for in recent years it has been demonstrated that some of County Sligo's ancient monuments are amongst the oldest in northwest Europe. Lakes abound, and there are tumbling rivers a-plenty. Yet if you wish to get away from the bustle of the regular tourist haunts, Sligo can look after your needs in this as well, for the western part of the county down through the Ox Mountains towards Mayo is an uncrowded region of wide vistas and clear roads.

Local Attractions and Information

Drumcliffe	Lissadell House 071 63150
Inniscrone	Sea Weed Bath House 096 36238
Sligo	Yeats Memorial Building, Hyde Bridge 071 42693
Sligo	County Library & Museum, Stephen Street 071 2212
Sligo	Tourist Information (June-August) 071 61201

Ballymote   *Temple House*

Ballymote Co Sligo

COUNTRY HOUSE   Tel: 071 83329 Fax: 071 83808 email: guest@templehouse.ie

One of Ireland's most unspoilt old houses, this is a unique place – a Georgian Mansion situated in 1,000 acres of farm and woodland, overlooking the original lakeside castle which was built by the Knights Templar in 1200 A.D. The Percevals have lived here since 1665 and the house was redesigned and refurbished in 1864 – some of the furnishings date back to that major revamp. The whole of the house has retained its old atmosphere, and in addition to central heating has log fires to cheer the enormous rooms. Spacious bedrooms are all furnished with old family furniture and guests have the use of an elegant sitting room with open fires. Deb Perceval's evening meals are served in the very beautiful dining room and are a treat to look forward to – she is a Euro-Toques chef and takes pride in preparing fine meals based on produce from the estate and other local suppliers. NB: Sandy Perceval is seriously allergic to scented products, so guests are asked to avoid all perfumes, aftershave and aerosols. Children welcome (under 2s free in parents' room; cots available). No pets. **Rooms 6** (4 en-suite, 2 shower only). B&B £45pps, ss £10. Residents D £19, 7.30pm (book by 1pm); house wine £9. Children's tea 6.30pm; sc discretionary. Closed Nov 30-Apr 1. Amex, MasterCard, Visa. **Directions:** Signposted 12 miles south of Sligo on the N17.

Castlebaldwin ▥ ★   *Cromleach Lodge*

Castlebaldwin via Boyle Co Sligo

HOTEL/RESTAURANT   Tel: 071 65155 Fax: 071 65455 email: cromleach@iol.ie

Chef of the Year

Set in the hills just above Lough Arrow, Cromleach Lodge enjoys one of the finest views in Ireland. The building, which is uncompromisingly modern in style and occupies a prominent position, has been the source of some controversy – but proprietors Moira and Christy Tighe wanted to maximise the view from both restaurant and rooms and find that their design has served them very well. But it is not architecture that brings people to Cromleach, rather the drive and dedication of Christy and Moira, which translates into high standards of both food and accommodation. Most importantly, they have the magic ingredient of genuine hospitality, doing everything possible to ensure comfort and relaxation for their guests. Spacious bedrooms are thoughtfully furnished with king-size and single beds, excellent bathrooms and every comfort to please the most fastidious of guests. Housekeeping is outstanding (it is one of the few places to provide not only a mini-bar but, more importantly, a jug of fresh milk in the fridge for your tea and coffee). Other extras include a complimentary basket of fruit. Small conferences (14); off-season cookery-class breaks. Children welcome (under 7s free in parents' room; cots available). Pets permitted by arrangement. Rooms 10 (all en-suite, 2 mini-suites, 5 no-smoking) B&B £79pps, ss £30. Closed Nov-Jan. Amex, Diners, MasterCard, Visa. **Restaurant:** The restaurant (which is totally non-smoking) is arranged as a series of rooms, creating a number of individual dining areas for varying numbers of people – a system which works better for groups than couples dining alone. Immaculate maintenance and lovely simple table settings – crisp linen, modern silver and crystal, fine, understated china and fresh seasonal flowers – provide a fit setting for dinner, the high point of every guest's visit to Cromleach. Moira Tighe and her personally trained all-female kitchen team work superbly well together, producing some memorable cooking.They have a growing number of established specialities that are in constant demand (many developed by pastry chef Sheila Sharpe) so menus have to include these as a base, with new dishes added as appropriate. Menus offered include an 8-course Gourmet Tasting Menu (for residents only) and a 5-course table d'hôte which has a minimum charge of £25 (but also flexibility, in that courses are charged individually so you can pick and choose between them if you like). Dishes which especially delighted the Guide recently included a featherlight goats cheese soufflé, loin of lamb served with a barley risotto and an outstanding dessert of iced almond & apricot nougat in a honey tuile leaf. Accessible house wines from around the world, from £12.95 to £22.95, and the dessert menu comes with helpful suggestions of dessert wines and ports. Moira is an exceptional chef and a very worthy recipient of this year's Chef of the Year Award. **Seats 50** (private rooms, 4-24).D only, 6.30-9 daily (Sun to 8) Set D £25/£35, also à la carte; house wines from £12.95; sc discretionary. No smoking restaurant.Toilets wheelchair accessible. **Directions:** Signposted from Castlebaldwin on the N4.

Collooney   *Glebe House*

Collooney Co Sligo
Tel: 071 67787 Fax: 071 30438
COUNTRY HOUSE/RESTAURANT   e-mail: glebehse@esat.biz.com

Brid and Marc Torrades have been running their renowned restaurant with rooms just outside Collooney village since 1990. It is now firmly established as a leading establishment in the area. The house had lain empty for several years before they bought it and started ongoing renovations - a new phase, including an extensive upgrade of both bedrooms and the restaurant, is just about to start as we go to press. Brid is an enthusiastic Euro-Toques chef and takes great pride in sourcing the best of local ingredients for her cooking, which is imaginative without being fussy. She offers an à la carte, and dinner menus that are changed daily always include strong vegetarian choices. Typical dishes might be a duck confit with elderberries and fillet of beef on a herb potato rosti with wild forest mushrooms. Finish with a surprise sweet plate, or an Irish farmhouse cheeseboard. Garden & fishing. Children welcome (under 3s free in parents' room; cots available). Wheelchair accessible. Rooms 6 (all en-suite, 2 shower only). B&B £30pps, ss £5-10. Restaurant **Seats 50** (private room, 35). D 6.30-9.30 daily;(Sun to 9, summer only); Set D £19.95; also à la carte; house wine £10.50; no sc.No smoking area Toilets wheelchair accessible.Limited opening Oct-Mar.Amex, Diners, MasterCard, Visa. **Directions:** Take the N4 to Collooney. At the second roundabout, exit at first left, Ballisodare road; take first left,then second left.

Collooney   *Markree Castle*

Collooney Co Sligo
HOTEL/RESTAURANT   Tel: 071 67800 Fax: 071 67840 email: markree@iol.ie

Sligo's oldest inhabited house has been home to the Cooper family for 350 years. Set in magnificent park and farmland, this is a proper castle, with a huge portico leading to a covered stone stairway that sweeps up to an impressive hall, where an enormous log fire always burns. Everything is on a very large scale, and it is greatly to the credit of the present owners, Charles and Mary Cooper, that they have achieved the present level of renovation and comfort since they took it on in a sad state of disrepair in 1989. They have always been generous with the heating, which made a stay here surprisingly comfortable even in the early days of the restoration programme. Ground floor reception areas include a very comfortably furnished double drawing room with two fireplaces (where light food – including their famous afternoon tea – is served). Conferences/banqueting (60/120). Children welcome (under 4s free in parents' room; cots available). Pets permitted. **Rooms 30** (all en-suite, 5 executive rooms, 1 for disabled). B&B £59.50pps, ss £6.50.Wheelchair accessible.Lift.Closed 24-26 Dec o Amex, Diners, MasterCard, Visa. **Restaurant:** There is a beautiful dining room, where head chef Tom Joyce has been serving very good food since 1993. Non-residents welcome (Reservations recommended). **Seats 80** (private room, 40) D 7.30-9.30 daily;L 1-2.30 Sun only.Set D £22.90, Set Sun L £13.90; house wine £11; no sc. No smoking restaurant. **Directions:** Just off the N4, take the Drumahoire exit at Collooney roundabout.

Enniscrone ❊ *The Tea Rooms*

Kilcullen's Seaweed Baths, Pier Road Enniscrone Co Sligo
CAFE   Tel 096 36238

Tracey Flatley has been running the tearooms at the famous seaweed baths since the summer of 1998 and a very good job she is doing of it. Inexpensive snacks and salads include home-made soups with freshly baked brown bread, quiche & salad or smoked salmon salad with brown bread - and her baking is seriously tempting. She passed the Guide's meringue test with flying colours and it's hard to imagine anyone resisting at least one little bite of lemon meringue pie, or carrot cake, or perhaps a yummy choux bun. Fruit or herbal teas too, if you like. **Seats 45**. Food served 10-9 daily. Closed weekdays Nov-May. **Directions:** Drive into Enniscrone town and take turning to the pier.

Riverstown ⚒ *Coopershill*

Riverstown Co Sligo
Tel: 071 65108 Fax: 071 65466
COUNTRY HOUSE   email: ohara@coopershill.com

Undoubtedly one of the most delightful and superbly comfortable Georgian houses in Ireland, this sturdy granite mansion was built to withstand the rigours of a Sligo winter – but numerous chimneys suggest there is warmth to be found within its stern grey walls. Peacocks wander elegantly on the croquet lawns (and roost in the splendid trees around the house at night) making this lovely place, home of the O'Hara family since it was built in 1774, a particularly perfect country house. Nothing escapes Brian O'Hara's disciplined eye: in immaculate order from top to bottom, the house not only has the original eighteenth century furniture but also some fascinating features – notably an unusual Victorian free-standing rolltop bath complete with fully integrated cast-iron shower 'cubicle' and original brass rail and fittings, all in full working order. Lindy runs the house and kitchen with the seamless hospitality born of long experience, and creates deliciously wholesome, unpretentious food which is served in their lovely dining room (where the family silver is used with magnificent insouciance – even at breakfast). Tennis, boating, fishing, garden, croquet; snooker room. Children welcome (under one, free in parents' room; cots available). No pets. **Rooms 8** (7 en-suite, 1 shower only,1 private) B&B £59pps, ss £10. Residents Dining Room **Seats 16-20** D 8.30 daily; Set D £27, house wines £9-13; sc discretionary. Non smoking restaurant. Closed 1 Nov-31 Mar. Amex, Diners, MasterCard, Visa. **Directions:** Signposted from N4 at Drumfin crossroads.

Rosses Point *Austie's*

Rosses Point Co Sligo
PUB   Tel: 071 77111

This 200 year-old pub overlooking Sligo Bay has always been associated with a seafaring family and is full of fascinating nautical memorabilia. It has a very nice ship-shape feeling about it and friendly people behind the bar. The sea stars on the simple bar menu too, with local seafood in dishes like garlic mussels, seafood chowder and in open sandwiches or salads made with crab, prawns and salmon. If you're going out to Rosses Point specially it's wise to ring ahead and check opening times off-season. Open evenings only (Sept-Mar). **Seats 80**. D 6-9.45 daily; house wine £9.90; sc discretionary. No smoking area. Bar food served 12-11.30 in summer, evenings only off-season. Parking. Closed 25 Dec & Good Fri. MasterCard, Visa.

Sligo

Bistro Bianconi

44 O'Connell Street, Sligo
Tel/Fax: 071 41744

RESTAURANT

This informal restaurant is gentle on the eye, with its terracottas and soft sandy tones, gentle wall lights and large leafy plants. It has never been a restaurant with pretensions but it's a good family-friendly place with food to please all age groups and table service.The idea was based on Italian restaurants in Liège, Belgium, and when they first opened in 1993 menus were strictly Italian – a wide range of pizzas and good pastas and salads – but recent menus are designed rather to suit the modern Irish palate. The menu is now more global – still mainly Italian but also featuring spicier cuisines. **Seats 75.** D 5.30-10.30 daily; house wines £11; sc discretionary(10% on groups of 9+). No smoking area; air conditioning.Toilets wheelchair accessible. Street parking only. Closed 25-26 Dec & Good Fri.Amex, Diners, MasterCard, Visa. **Directions:** Situated on main street.

Sligo

Hargadon's

O'Connell Street Sligo Co Sligo
Tel: 071 70993

PUB

Unquestionably one of Ireland's greatest old pubs, the best time to see Hargadon's properly is early in the day when it's quiet – they'll give you good coffee (and a newspaper to go with it) and you can relax and take in the detail of this remarkable old place. It still has the shelves which used to hold the groceries when it was a traditional grocer-bar, the snugs and the old pot belly stove – and it's still owner-run and unspoilt. Later in the day it gets very busy, especially at weekends – but by then it's time for a bit of craic anyway. **Seats 100.** Food served Mon-Sat, 12-4. No smoking area; air conditioning. Toilets wheelchair accessible.Closed 25 Dec & Good Fri. **Directions:** Situated in town centre on the main street.

Sligo ❋

Garavogue

Rear 15-16 Stephens Street Sligo Co Sligo
Tel 071 40100 Fax 40106

BAR/RESTAURANT

Named after the Garavogue river which flows past the wide paved area outside the front door, this new restaurant opened in 1999 to a rapturous welcome from locals who know their food and relish the sheer style of the place. It's in a particularly attractive new building that maximises the natural advantages of the site - town centre yet with space, light and water around it - and also has a cleverly designed interior, with height and loads of drama giving visual impact. A central bar takes pride of place on the ground floor and is the initial focal point, before the eye is drawn up towards the first floor restaurant area. Snazzy bar food - calamari with Thai dipping sauce, nachos with guacamole, sour cream and salsa - is served here, while main meals are available upstairs and maintain a similar tone. Window tables on the first floor are especially desirable. Outside seating. No children after 8 pm. *At the time of going to press a new bar/restaurant "Bar Eile" was due to open next door. **Seats 120.** L Mon-Sat 12.30-3, D Wed-Sun, 6-10. House wine from £12. sc discretionary. No smoking area; air conditioning. Toilets wheelchair accesssible; lift. Bar menu daily 5-7. Carpark almost adjacent. Open all year. MasterCard, Visa.

Sligo

Sligo Park Hotel

Pearse Road Sligo Co Sligo
Tel: 071 60291 Fax: 071 69556

HOTEL

Set in landscaped gardens and parkland on the edge of Sligo town, this contemporary hotel provides a warm welcome and excellent leisure, conference and banqueting facilities. Leisure centre, tennis, garden, snooker. Children welcome (under 4s free in parents' room; cots available). **Rooms 110** (48 executive rooms, 2 shower only, 6 no-smoking, 2 for disabled).B&B £49.50pps, ss £6.50. Own parking. Closed 23-26 Dec & Good Fri. Amex, Diners, MasterCard, Visa. **Directions:** On the N4,one mile from Sligo.

Sligo ❁

Tower Hotel Sligo

Quay Street Sligo Co Sligo

HOTEL   Tel:071 44000 Fax:071 46888 email: towersl@iol.ie

This neat redbrick hotel is very centrally located and makes a comfortable base for business or leisure. First impressions in the spacious, colourful lobby area are good and the standard of interior design throughout the hotel is high. Conference/banqueting (200/180). Children welcome (under 3s free in parents' room; cots available). No pets. **Rooms 60** (3 suites, 8 no-smoking,1 for disabled) B&B £50pps, ss £15. Lift; wheelchair accessible. Own parking. Closed 25-26 Dec. Amex, Diners, MasterCard, Visa. **Directions:** Located next door to City Hall in the centre of Sligo.

Strandhill

The Strand Bar & Restaurant

Strandhill Co Sligo

RESTAURANT/PUB   Tel: 071 68140 Fax:071 68593

Just ten minutes drive from Sligo, close to the airport and one of Europe's most magnificent surfing beaches, this well-known bar has a big welcoming turf fire, cosy snugs and friendly staff. Planned extensions and alterations had not proceeded at the time of the Guide's most recent visit, but work is now expected to begin in March 2000. No children after 9pm.Bar meals served all day (11-8pm). Toilets wheelchair accessible. Air conditioning. Closed 25 Dec & Good Fri.Visa. **Directions:** Follow signposts to Sligo airport (Strandhill). Strand House is situated at the end, near the beach.

Tubbercurry

Killoran's Traditional Lounge

Main Street Tubbercurry Co Sligo

PUB   Tel: 071 85111 Fax: 071 86300

Killoran's is renowned for its music – traditional Irish nights are held every Thursday from June to September. There's set dancing, ceili music, a traditional fashion show and boxty, colcannon and potato cakes are served to everyone (with samples of their country butter churned by the visitors). Children welcome. All great fun. **Seats 50.** No smoking area; air conditioning. Toilets wheelchair accessible. Closed 25 Dec & Good Fri. Amex, MasterCard, Visa. **Directions:** Situated in the centre of Tubbercurry.

TIPPERARY

In this new millennium, as it has been for thousands of years, the cup of life is overflowing in Tipperary. In this wondrously fertile region, there's an air of fulfilment, a happy awareness of the world in harmony. And the placenames reinforce this sense of natural bounty. Across the middle of the county, there's the Golden Vale, with prosperous lands along the wide valley of the River Suir and its many tributaries, and westwards towards County Limerick across a watershed around Donohill.

The county's largest town, down in the far south under the Comeragh Mountains, is the handsome borough of Clonmel - its name translates as "Honey Meadow". Yet although there are many meadows of all kinds in Tipperary, there's much more to this largest inland county in Ireland than farmland, for it is graced with some of the most elegant mountains in the country. The Comeraghs may be in Waterford, but Tipperary gets the benefit of their view. Totally in southeast Tipperary is Slievenamon (719 m) the "Mountain of the Women". Along the south of the county, the Knockmealdowns soar. Across the valley, the lovely Galtees reach 919 m on Galtymore, and on their northern flank, the Glen of Aherlow is a place of enchantment.

North of the Golden Vale, the Silvermine Mountains rise to 694 m on Keeper Hill, and beyond them the farming countryside rolls on in glorious profusion to Tipperary's own "sea coast", the beautiful eastern shore of Lough Derg. Inevitably, history and historic monuments abound in such country, with the fabulous Rock of Cashel and its dramatic remains of ancient ecclesiastical buildings setting a very high standard for evoking the past. But Tipperary lends itself every bit as well to enjoyment of the here and now. Tipperary is all about living life to the full, and they do it with style in a place of abundance.

Local Attractions and Information

Cahir Castle	052 41011
Clonmel Moortown	(apple/arable farm with walks & maps) 052 41459
Glen of Aherlow	Glenbrook Trout Farm 062 56214
Thurles	Racecourse 0504 22253
Tipperary town	Tourist Information 062 5145

Ballinderry   *Kylenoe*

Nenagh, Co Tipperary
COUNTRY HOUSE/FARMHOUSE   Tel: 067 22015 Fax: 067 22275

Virginia Moeran's lovely old stone house on 150 acres of farm and woodland offers home comfort and real country pleasures close to Lough Derg. The farm is home to an international stud and the woodlands provide a haven for an abundance of wildlife, including deer, red squirrel, badgers, rabbits and foxes. With beautiful walks, riding (with or without tuition), golf and water sports available on the premises or close by, "Kylenoe" provides a real rural retreat. Spacious, airy bedrooms are furnished in gentle country house style, with antiques and family belongings, and overlook beautiful rolling countryside. Downstairs there's a delightful guests' sitting room and plenty of interesting reading. Virginia enjoys cooking – her breakfasts are a speciality – and dinner is available to residents by arrangement. Importantly for people who like to travel with their dogs, this is a place where man's best friend is also made welcome – and Kylenoe was the recipient of our Pet Friendly Establishment Award last year. Children welcome (under 2s free in parents' room; cot available) **Rooms 3** (2 en-suite,all no-smoking) B&B £30pps, ss £5. Wheelchair accessible; chair lift. Residents D £22 8pm (book by noon). Closed 22 Dec-3 Jan.MasterCard, Visa **Directions:** Nenagh-Borrisokane-through Terryglass, 1.5 miles on LHS on the Ballinderry road.

Birdhill   *Matt The Thresher*

Birdhill Co Tipperary
PUB   Tel: 061 379227 Fax: 061 379219

Ted and Kay Moynihan's large roadside pub never ceases to amaze – every year it seems to get bigger and develop more additions to the core business. One of the latest, for example, is self-catering apartments ("Matt's Resting Loft"). But it's all done with such style and confidence, it's kept so scrupulously clean and the new parts are integrated into the older ones so successfully that you can't help but admire it – even if you really prefer smaller, less energetic pubs. The bar food is very acceptable too – interesting but not too adventurous, based on freshly cooked quality ingredients and varied without offering an over-long menu. Soups, home-made breads, seafood – fresh and smoked salmon, crab claws, mussels – and a good range of sandwiches. There are more substantial main meals – steaks and lamb cutlets, for example – in the evenings. Children welcome. Meals Bar food 10am - 10pm daily. Wheelchair accessible. Closed 25 Dec & Good Fri. Amex, Diners, MasterCard, Visa. **Directions:** N7, halfway between Nenagh-Limerick.

Borrisokane   *Ballycormac House*

Aglish Borrisokane Nr Nenagh Co Tipperary
COUNTRY HOUSE   Tel: 067 21129 Fax: 067 21200

John and Cheryleen Lang took over this well-known farmhouse as a going concern in the summer of 1998 and to any casual visitor previously familiar with it there are no obvious changes. It's a charming, cottagey place, delightfully furnished and very comfortable in a laid-back way – all the five bedrooms have their own bathrooms (4 en-suite, one private, and all with full bath) and one of them is a romantic suite with its own fireplace. The main change is that the Langs have their own horses on the premises and equestrian activities are now the biggest attraction. Cheryleen cooks a country house style dinner for guests, based on fresh local ingredients (including produce from their own garden). Non-residents are welcome for dinner by reservation, if there is room. If you have any special dietary requests (including vegetarian meals) please mention them when booking. No smoking in the dining room or bedrooms. Children and well-behaved pets welcome (children under 2 free in parents' room; cot available) **Rooms 5** (1 suite,3 en-suite,1 private). B&B £25, no single supplement, +£5 for the suite). Dining Rooms **Seats 14** (no smoking). Set D £20, 8pm (book by 12pm). Open all year.MasterCard, Visa. **Directions:** Turn right 1/4 mile from Borrisokane on N54 towards Portumna; signposted all the way (approx 3 miles).

Cahir ❊   *Clifford's at The Bell*

Cahir Co Tipperary
RESTAURANT   Tel: 052 43232

Just as the Guide was going to press, the exciting news reached us that Michael and Deirdre Clifford (previously of the renowned Cork restaurant Clifford's) have relocated to open a fine dining establishment at The Bell in Cahir. Available details are scant, but it's bound to be good. D Tue-Sat 7-10.30, L Sun only 12.30-3. D à la carte, sun L Table d'Hote. House wines £12.50.

Cahir   *Kilcoran Lodge Hotel*

Cahir Co Tipperary
HOTEL   Tel: 052 41288 Fax: 052 41994

This former hunting lodge is set in spacious grounds just off the main Dublin-Cork road – it makes a good place for a break when travelling. While it has all the comforts now expected of an hotel and has recently undergone major refurbishment, Kilcoran has retained its old-world character to a remarkable degree and is very welcoming, with open fires and friendly, helpful staff. There's a leisure club on the premises, with indoor pool, gym and solarium. Nearby outdoor activities, iinclude fishing, golf, pony trekking and hill walking. Leisure centre; garden. Wheelchair accessible. Children welcome (under12s free in parents' room; cots available). Pets permitted by arrangement. **Rooms 22** (6 suites, 1 executive room, 2 for disabled). B&B £35pps. Open all year. Amex, MasterCard, Visa. **Directions:** Main Dublin/Cork road N8-4 miles from Cahir on the Cork side.

Cashel ❊   *Ballyowen House*

Cashel Co Tipperary
COUNTRY HOUSE   Tel: 062 61265

This impressive mid 18th century house is set in lovely wooded grounds and has been owned by the McCan family since 1864. The building is listed for its historic and architectural importance and it has provided an interesting and comfortable place to stay since the 1980s. Dinner for residents includes home-produced lamb, fruit and vegetables and the McCans take this part of the operation seriously, having recently attended courses at Ballymaloe Cookery School. Children over 4 welcome. Pets permitted by arrangement. **Rooms 3** (2 en-suite, 1 with private bathroom; all no-smoking). B&B £25, ss £5. Resident's D £15, 7.30-8.30. Closed Nov-mar. No credit cards. **Directions:** Off N8, 4 miles north of Cashel turn at junction signed Dualla -1 mile.

Cashel

Cashel Palace Hotel

Main Street Cashel Co. Tipperary

HOTEL   Tel: 062 62707 Fax: 062 61521 email: reception@cashel-palace.ie

One of Ireland's most famous hotels, and originally a bishop's residence, Cashel Palace is a large, graciously proportioned Queen Anne style house (dating from 1730) set well back from the road in the centre of Cashel town.The beautiful reception rooms and some of the spacious, elegantly furnished bedrooms overlook the gardens and the Rock of Cashel at the rear. The informal Bishop's Buttery restaurant in the basement is a good place for a light bite to eat when travelling. The hotel has changed hands several times recently, with successive owners having contrasting views on how this wonderful building should best be restored and managed. Conference/banqueting (100/90). Secretarial services. Garden. Children welcome (under 12s free in parents' room; cots available). No pets. **Rooms 23** (all en-suite. B&B £65pps, ss £40. Barfood served daily 10am-8pm. Toilets wheelchair accessible. Own parking. Closed 24-26 Dec. Amex, Diners, MasterCard, Visa. **Directions:** In Cashel town centre(on N8).

Cashel ✗

Chez Hans

Rockside Cashel Co Tipperary

RESTAURANT   Tel: 062 61177

Hans-Peter Matthia's dramatically converted Wesleyan chapel is tucked behind the town right under the Rock of Cashel. Although others have since followed suit, the idea of opening a restaurant in a church was highly original when he established it in 1968. The atmosphere and scale – indeed the whole style of the place – is superb and, despite some reservations about reception and front of house management on a recent visit, provides an excellent setting for the fine food which Hans-Peter and his son Jason prepare for appreciative diners (some of whom travel great distances for the treat). The choice of fifteen soups and starters ranges from a simple cream of mushroom soup, through luxurious pâté of chicken liver and foie gras with spiced pear chutney and toasted brioche to light choices such as ogen melon with fresh fruit and a mango sorbet. There is also seafood such as oak smoked wild Irish salmon with pickled cucumber and crème fraîche. Main courses offer an equally wide choice, always including rack of Tipperary lamb, cassoulet of seafood – a selection of half a dozen varieties of fish and shellfish with a delicate chive veloute sauce – and roast duckling with honey and thyme roasted shallots and soy and ginger sauce. D£££ Mon-Sat. Closed 25 Dec, Good Fri, 1st-3 wks Jan. MasterCard, Visa

Cashel

Dowling's

Cashel Co Tipperary

PUB   Tel: 062 62130

On the left of the main street heading towards Cork, Pat and Helen Dowling's unspoilt traditional pub is just the spot if you like things simple. There's an open fire, light bar food – home-made soups, salads and sandwiches – and there may be impromptu music sessions at the weekend. Not suitable for children. Barfood served daily til 8pm. Closed 25 Dec & Good Fri. No Credit cards. **Directions:** The last pub at the end of town on the way to Cork.

Cashel ❄

Legends Guesthouse

The Kiln Cashel Co Tipperary

ACCOMMODATION   Tel: 062 61292 fax 062 62876

Tucked just under the Rock of Cashel, this neat guesthouse provides comfortable accommodation and a good base for visiting the area's many sites. There is also a restaurant, The Kiln (not visited by the guide), serving D Tues-Sat and Sub L; open to non-residents. **Rooms 7** (all en-suite, 3 shower only), B&B £25 pps. ss £10. Amex, MasterCard, Visa.

Cashel

The Spearman Restaurant

97 Main Street Cashel Co Tipperary

RESTAURANT   Tel: 062 61143

David and Louise Spearman run an admirably down-to-earth restaurant, where menus change weekly and include an evening à la carte with about half a dozen starters and a dozen main courses. Pasta features strongly ("fresh parmesan served with all pastas"), there are a few world influences coming through (Thai chicken, for example) but it is mainly sound European cooking. Lunch menus are shorter but include some of the dinner dishes as well as lighter fare and some extra daily specials. This is a great place to break a journey at lunchtime because you can be sure of wholesome food and quick service. Sunday lunch, on the other hand, is the time to see a more leisurely side of The Spearman. Children welcome **Seats 38.** L 12.30-2.30 & D 6-9 daily; (D Sun May-Oct only). Set Sun L £12.95; à la carte also available; house wine from £4.95; sc discretionary. No smoking area Closed all Nov; also D Sun, all Mon (Oct-May). Amex, Diners, MasterCard, Visa. **Directions:** Opposite turn for Clonmel road on the main street.

Clonmel ˣ   *Hotel Minella*

Clonmel Co Tipperary
HOTEL   Tel: 052 22388 Fax: 052 24381

Just on the edge of Clonmel, in its own grounds overlooking the River Suir, the original part of this hotel was built in 1863 as a private residence. It was bought in the early 1960s by John and Mary Nallen and since then has been owner-run by the Nallen family. They have expanded the hotel over the years, to provide extensive banqueting and conference facilities and high quality accommodation. Public areas in the old house, including a cocktail bar, restaurant and lounge areas, have a lovely view over well-kept lawns and the river. Bedrooms, which include three suites with steam rooms, five junior suites with jacuzzis, ten executive rooms and one suitable for disabled guests, are all furnished to a high standard with well-finished bathrooms (three are shower-only) and housekeeping is exemplary. Excellent facilities and the romantic situation make the hotel especially popular for weddings. Leisure centre with 20 metre swimming pool. Acc£££ Closed 24-28 Dec. Amex, Diners, MasterCard, Visa.

Clonmel   *Knocklofty House*

Knocklofty Clonmel Co Tipperary
COUNTRY HOUSE   Tel: 052 38222 Fax: 052 38300

Formerly the country residence of the Earls of Donoughmore, Knocklofty House is set in 105 acres of gardens and parkland with sweeping views over the river Suir (which runs through the demesne). The original house dates back to the 17th century, with additions following in the 18th and 19th centuries. The interior is classic Irish Georgian. Fine reception rooms include a two-storey galleried library and an oak-panelled dining room with extensive views over river and parkland to the Comeragh and Knockmealdown mountains beyond. Spacious bedrooms are decorated in sympathy with the age and style of the house, but with all the modern comforts. It makes a romantic setting for weddings. Conference/banqueting (40/120).Leisure centre.Trout & salmon fishing.Garden,tennis & fishing available. Children (Under 6s free in parents' room; cots available) Pets.permitted. **Rooms 17** (all en-suite, 3 shower only). B&B £55pps, ss £5. Closed 24-26 Dec & Good Fri. Amex, Diners, MasterCard, Visa. Restaurant **Seats 40** (private room, 60/70) L12.30-2.30 & 7-9.30 daily (D Sun 6.30-8.30); Set L £13.25, Set D £25, house wine £13, sc discretionary. Toilets wheelchair accessible. **Directions:** 4 miles outside of Clonmel on Ardfinnon road.

Clonmel   *Mr Bumbles*

Richmond House Kickham Street Clonmel Co Tipperary
RESTAURANT   Tel: 052 29188

Declan Gavigan's large bistro-style restaurant in the centre of town caters for a changing clientele throughout the day and evening, seven days a week. With a stylish seating area at reception, attractively laid tables and plenty of plants, the atmosphere is relaxed and informal. The menus – a light morning and afternoon menu, a fairly short à la carte lunch menu and a choice of à la carte or set dinner in the evening – offer straightforward, popular dishes with an international tone as well as the hearty steaks (char-grilled with green peppercorn sauce) and Tipperary lamb (roasted with rosemary & thyme, served with tarragon champ and its own juices) for which the area is renowned. Lunchtime main courses include home-made burgers, chicken breast (typically with Mediterranean vegetables, basil and sundried tomato pesto) and a roast of the day with hot vegetables. Friendly service and fair pricing help make this cheerful restaurant an asset to the area. **Seats 60** (Private parties, 30). Air conditioning. L 12.30-2.30 daily (Sun 12-3); D 6-10 daily (Sun to 9.30). A la carte; house wine £10; sc discretionary.Closed 24-26 Dec. MasterCard, Visa. **Directions:** Situated beside Superquinn car-park, opposite the Omniplex cinema .

Clonmel [PUB★]
Sean Tierney

13 O'Connell Street Clonmel Co Tipperary

PUB
Tel: 052 24467

What an amazing place this tall, narrow pub is. Warm, welcoming and spotlessly clean in spite of the huge amount of memorabilia and bric a brac filling every conceivable space. No "characterful" dust here; every bit of brass or copper, every glass and bottle glints and gleams to an almost unbelievable degree. The front bar, especially, is seriously packed with "artefacts of bygone days – in short a mini-museum". A giant screen is discreetly hidden around the corner, for watching matches. Upstairs (and there are a lot of them – this is a four storey building) there's a relaxed traditional family-style restaurant. Food starts with breakfast at 10.30 and there are all sorts of menus for different times and occasions. Expect popular, good value food like potato wedges, mushrooms with garlic, steaks and grills rather than gourmet fare, although the evening restaurant menus are more ambitious. Loos are at the very top, but grand when you get there.Children welcome before 8 pm Barfood served daily; Open (Mon-Sat) 10.30-9; Sun 12.30-2;4-9. No smoking area; air conditioning. Street parking only. Closed 25 Dec & Good Fri. Visa. **Directions:** Situated 1/2 way down O'Connell St., on left across from Dunnes Stores.

Garykennedy
Ciss Ryan's Pub

Garykennedy Portroe Nenagh Co Tipperary

PUB
Tel: 067 23364

Garykennedy is one of the most charming little harbours on the inland waterways. It's about six miles from Nenagh but it's really in a world of its own. Ciss Ryan's is a lovely old traditional pub, and although it changed hands in 1998 there have been no major changes. It's well-run, spotlessly clean and serves nice, simple home-made bar food such as chowders and smoked salmon with home-made brown bread, as well as more substantial dishes like bacon & cabbage; homemade burgers are a speciality. Wheelchair accessible. No Pets. Barfood served daily 12-9pm. Children welcome before 9 pm. Own parking. Closed 25 Dec & Good Fri. MasterCard, Visa. **Directions:** 8 miles from Killaloe; turn left at Portroe cross.

Glen of Aherlow
Aherlow House Hotel

Glen of Aherlow Co Tipperary

HOTEL
Tel: 062 56153 Fax: 062 56212 email: aherlow@iol.ie

Originally a hunting lodge, this hotel is romantically located in a forest on the slopes of this famous glen and enjoys stunning views of the surrounding mountains and countryside. The old house is lovely, with well-proportioned rooms furnished in an appealing country house style. The drawing room, bar and dining room are all well-placed to take advantage of the view, and there is a large terrace for fine weather. The bedrooms in the original house also reflect the gracious style, while those recently added have less character, but are comfortably furnished and have all the modern conveniences.1999 saw the construction of fourteen self-catering houses - which unfortunately dominate the site but are quite appealing in a "mountain lodge" style - and also a health and fitness club which offers therapeutic spa baths, aromatherapy treatments, jacuzzi and steam rooms as well as a gym. Conference/banqueting (300/300); secretarial services.Children welcome (under 6s free in parents' room; cots available). Wheelchair accessible. No Pets. **Rooms 29** (all en-suite). B&B £37pps, ss £10. **Directions:** From Tipperary town take the R664 road. Signposted to the right after 4 miles.

Killaloe
Goosers

Ballina Killaloe Co Tipperary

PUB/RESTAURANT
Tel: 061 376791 Fax:061 376244

Just across the road from the river and close to the bridge that links Tipperary and Clare, this pub is chameleon-like in character. At quieter times it is an orderly, welcoming place where the day's blackboard specials (soups with freshly baked brown bread, oysters, mussels, Irish stew and bacon and cabbage are typical), can be enjoyed at leisure in front of an open fire. At other times, however – as on several recent visits – it can get overcrowded and clearing is not always as efficient as it should be. Midweek or off-season visits might be most enjoyable. There is a restaurant at the back which has a separate side entrance and is more civilised at all times – and they do a good Sunday lunch (booking advised). Outdoor seating. Wheelchair accessible (including toilets). **Seats 60** (private room, 10). No smoking area. Barfood served daily, 10.30am-10.pm. L 12.30-3 & D 6-10, daily. Set L £16; à la carte available; house wine £11.50; sc discretionary. Children (not under 4) welcome before 8pm. No car park. Closed 25 Dec & Good Fri. Amex, Diners, MasterCard, Visa. **Directions:** Riverside Ballina

Killaloe   *Waterman's Lodge Hotel*

Ballina Killaloe Co Tipperary
HOTEL   Tel: 061 376333 Fax:061 375445 e-mail:Info@watermanslodge.ie

Views down to Killaloe and across the Shannon are among the pleasant features of this appealing country house hotel and restaurant. It changed hands late in 1998 and has since been undergoing systematic refurbishment, although it has perhaps not completely settled into a professional routine yet. Golf, fishing, horse riding and pony trekking are all available nearby. Wheelchair accessible (including toilets). Pets permitted by arrangement. **Rooms 10** (all en-suite,1 shower only) B&B £55pps, ss£20. Closed 20 Dec-10 Feb. Amex, MasterCard, Visa. **Restaurant:** Head chef Thomas O'Leary's dinner menus are well-balanced and wide-ranging, based on the best of local produce including Ballina beef, seared on the grill and served with wild mushrooms and a shallot confit, perhaps and local cheeses. There are international influences but the style is mainly contemporary country house cooking. Menus change weekly, vegetarian dishes are always available and any other dietary requirements can be met if a day's notice is given. A phone call is recommended to check opening times off-season.Wheelchair accessible. **Seats 40** D 7.30-9.30 daily. Set D £28.50; à la carte available;house wine £12.50; sc discretionary. **Directions:** From Birdhill on the N7,travel to Killaloe and Ballina. After the bridge, on the left.

*Killaloe * News * Just as the guide went to press news reached us that Harry McKeown, until recently head chef at Cooke's Cafe, Dublin (see entry) is opening a new restaurant on the waterfront in Killaloe. It's a purpose-built, chalet style building with, as yet, no name or telephone number. Details available from Harry on his mobile: 087 673 8681.*

Nenagh   *Country Choice Delicatessen & Coffee-Bar*

25 Kenyon Street Nenagh Co Tipperary
CAFÉ/DELI   Tel/Fax: 067 32596

This magic place is a mecca for food-lovers from all over the country, who make sure of building in a visit to Peter and Mary Ward's unique shop when planning a journey anywhere near Nenagh. Old hands head for the little coffee shop at the back first, fortifying themselves with the superb, simple home-cooked food that reflects a policy of seasonality – if the range is small at a particular time of year, so be it. Meats, milk, cream, eggs, butter and flour: "The economy of Tipperary is agricultural and we intend to demonstrate this with a finished product of tantalising smells and tastes." Specialities developed over the years include Cashel Blue and broccoli soup – served with their magnificent home-baked breads (made with local flours) – savoury and sweet pastry dishes (quiches, fruit tarts) and tender, gently-cooked meat dishes like lamb ragout and beef and Guinness casserole.The shop carries a very wide range of the finest Irish artisan produce, plus a smaller selection of specialist products from further afield, such as olive oil. Two specialities deserve special mention: the home-made marmalade based on oranges left to caramelise in the Aga overnight, producing a runny but richly flavoured preserve; secondly – and most importantly – there is Peter's passion for cheese. He is widely credited as the country's best supplier of Irish farmhouse cheeses, which he minds like babies as they ripen and, unlike most shops, only puts on display when they are mature: do not leave without buying cheese. **Seats 40.** No smoking area. Open all day (9.30-5.30); L 12-3 daily, à la carte; house wine from £11.Children welcome. No private carpark. Closed Sundays,Bank Holidays & Good Fri. No credit cards. **Directions:** In the heart of Nenagh town, Kenyon Street is signposted at the market cross end of Pearse Street.

Terryglass   *Tir na Fiuise Farmhouse*

Terryglass Co Tipperary
FARM STAY   Tel/Fax: 067 22041 email: nheenan@tinet.ie

Just a mile or so from the pretty village of Terryglass, Niall and Inez Heenan's neat family farmhouse is on a 125 acre organic farm. Recent additions to the family mean that bed & breakfast will not be available this year, but there are two delightful, recently converted self-catering cottages in old barns behind the main house, offering all the interest of a farm stay with the comfort of well-designed en-suite bedrooms and cosy kitchen/living areas with solid fuel stoves and labour-saving kitchen appliances. Guests are welcome to take part in activities on the farm ("help with the haymaking and let the children feed our pigs!") or lend a hand with the turf-cutting in summer.Granary (1-bedroom) from £120 per week; Stables (2-bedroom), from £190. Weekend breaks also available off-season. Open all year. MasterCard, Visa. **Directions:** Take the road opposite the bridge in Terryglass village.

Thurles   *Inch House*

Bouladuff Thurles Co Tipperary
Tel: 0504 51348/51261 Fax:0504 51754
COUNTRY HOUSE/RESTAURANT   e-mail: inchhse@iol.ie

Built in 1720 by John Ryan, one of the few landed Catholic gentlemen in Tipperary, this magnificent Georgian house managed to survive some of the most turbulent periods in Irish history and to remain in the Ryan family for almost 300 years. John and Norah Egan, who farm the surrounding 250 acres, took it over in a state of dereliction in 1985 and began the major restoration work which has resulted in the handsome, comfortably furnished period house which guests enjoy today. Reception rooms on either side of a welcoming hallway include an unusual William Morris-style drawing room with a tall stained glass window, a magnificent plasterwork ceiling (and adjoining library bar) and a fine dining room which is used for residents' breakfasts and is transformed into a restaurant at night. Both rooms have period fireplaces with big log fires. The five bedrooms are quite individual, (some with rather cramped bathrooms) and are furnished with antiques. Children welcome (under 5s free in parents' room; cot available).No Pets. **Rooms 5** (all en-suite, 2 shower only). B&B £30pps, ss £5. Closed Xmas week. MasterCard, Visa, **Restaurant:** Polished wood floors, classic country house decor and tables laid with crisp white linen and fresh flowers provide a fine setting for dinner, especially when the atmosphere is softened by firelight and candles. Menus are changed weekly and offer a well-balanced choice in a fairly traditional style that combines French country cooking and Irish influences. Anyone with special dietary needs, including vegetarians, should mention this on booking to allow for preparation of extra dishes. Banqueting (45).Not suitable for children under 10 after 7 pm. **Seats 45.** No smoking restaurant. D 7-9.30 daily; Set D £23.50; house wines £11; sc discretionary. Toilets wheelchair accessible Closed Sun & Mon. **Directions:** From Thurles town,take the Nenagh road-drive for 4 miles and it is situated on the left.

Roscrea ✷   *The Waterfront Restaurant*

The Mall Roscrea Co Tipperary
RESTAURANT   Tel: 0505 22431

This characterful old building near the river is full of atmosphere and you can have anything from a snack to break journey - toasted sandwiches, quiche & salad - with a good cup of cafetiere coffee, to a full meal later in the day. Sirloin steak, served in the traditional manner with crispy onions, mushrooms and pepper sauce tops the bill at £13.95 (12 oz). There are lots of steps and little rooms, but one of several dining areas is on the ground floor.Children welcome.Parking nearby. **Seats 70** (private room, 30). No smoking area; air conditioning.Open all day (9.30-9pm); L 12.30-3 daily; D 3-9pm daily;à la carte available;house wine £8.95; sc discretionary. Closed Xmas day. Amex, Diners, MasterCard, Visa. **Directions:** Beside the river, in the centre of Roscrea.

Thurles ✷   *Dwan Brew Pub & Restaurant*

The Mall Thurles Co Tipperary
PUB   Tel: 0504 26007 Fax: 0504 26060

This trendy bar and microbrewery opened in the centre of Thurles in 1998 and has taken off with a vengeance. It's an old building which has been given the contemporary design treatment and this, together with the entertainment value of the in-house brews, means it is understandably popular with a young crowd who like their music very loud. The staff are friendly and helpful, the food style is world cuisine - panfried tiger prawns, cajun chicken are typical, also the ubiquitous steak - and adequately executed although, on the Guide's visit, the tiny table allocated was less than comfortable. Ground floor wheelchair accessible, but toilets are up a metal staircase. Children welcome before 9 pm Barfood served 10.30am-9.30pm (Mon-Sat). Parking nearby. Closed Xmas & Good Fri.MasterCard, Visa **Directions:** Off Liberty Square.

WATERFORD

On the quays of Waterford city, we are witness to a trading tradition which, in 2000, goes back at least 1,147 years. Today's larger ships may berth across the river, but the old quays retain a nautical flavour which is accentuated by a very useful marina facility in the heart of town. The fine port of Waterford was founded in 853 AD when the Vikings - Danes for the most part - established the trading settlement of Vadrefjord. Its strategic location in a sheltered spot at the head of the estuary near the confluence of the Suir and Barrow rivers guaranteed its continuing success under different administrators, so much so that it tended to completely dominate the county of Waterford, almost all of which is actually to the west of the port.

But for many years now, the county town has been Dungarvan, which is two-thirds of the way westward along Waterford's extensive south coast. This spreading of the administrative centres of gravity has to some extent balanced the life of the Waterford region. But even so, the extreme west of the county is still one of Ireland's best kept secrets, a place of remarkable beauty between the Knockmealdown, Comeragh and Monavullagh mountains, where fish-filled rivers such as the Bride, the Blackwater, and the Nire make their way seawards at different speeds through valleys of remarkable variety.

West Waterford is a place of surprises. For instance, around the delightful coastal village of Ardmore, ancient monuments suggest that the local holy man, St Declan, introduced Christianity to the area quite a few years before St Patrick went to work in the rest of Ireland. And across the bay from Ardmore, the Ring neighbourhood is a Gaeltacht (Irish-speaking) area with its own bustling fishing port at Helvick.

Dungarvan itself is in the midst of an attractive revival. It has relinquished its role as a commercial port, but is enthusiastically taking to recreational boating and harbourside regeneration instead. Along the bluff south coast, secret coves gave smugglers and others access to charming villages like Stradbally and Bunmahon. Further east, the increased tempo of the presence of Waterford city is felt both at the traditional resort of Tramore, and around the fishing/sailing harbour of Dunmore East, which devotees would claim as the Number One Enjoyment Centre in all Ireland.

Local Attractions and Information

Dungarvan	Tourist Information 0058 41741
Lismore	Lismore Castle Gardens 058 54424
Waterford city	Tourist Information 051 875823
Waterford	Crystal Glass Factory 051 73311
Waterford	International Festival of Light Opera (September) 051 375437
Waterford	South East Regional Tourist Authority 051 875823

Annestown

COUNTRY HOUSE

Annestown House

Annestown Co Waterford
Tel: 051 396160 Fax: 051 396474
email: annestownhouse@tinet.ie

Half way up the hill on the Tramore-Dungarvan road, John and Pippa Galloway's comfortable home overlooks a small bay, with a private path leading to the beach below. In front of the house are manicured lawns – one for croquet, one for tennis – while inside there are several lounges with log-burning fires and a billiard room with full-size table. Everywhere you look there are books – a catholic collection ranging from classics to thrillers. For the evening meal there will be, typically, dishes such as mushroom soup, roast duck and rhubarb crumble. Annestown also has a wine license. In the morning a hearty Irish breakfast (with excellent breads) will set you up for the day ahead. All the centrally-heated bedrooms are en suite with direct-dial telephone and tea-making facilities (and hot water bottles are thoughtfully provided for those who still feel cold). **Rooms 5** (all en-suite, all no-smoking), B&B £70pps, ss £10. Residents' D Tues-Sun €20, 7.45pm (book by noon). Closed 1 Dec-28 Feb. Amex, MasterCard, Visa. **Directions:** Midway between Tramore and Bunmahon on Coast Road R675

Ardmore ❊   *Whitehorses Restaurant*

Ardmore Co Waterford

RESTAURANT   Tel: 024 9404C

A delightfully bright and breezy café-restaurant on the main street, White Horses is one of those places that changes its character through the day. They're open for all the little lifts that visitors need through the day - morning coffee, afternoon tea - as well as imaginative lunches (plus their traditional Sunday lunch, which runs all afternoon) and a more ambitious à la carte evening menu. Vegetarian dishes feature on both menus - a noodle stir-fry during the day perhaps, and Ardsallagh goats cheese with sesame seed salad in the evening - and there's a good balance between traditional favourites like steaks and more adventurous fare: the daytime fish could be deep-fried plaice with tartare sauce, for example, while its evening counterpart might be Helvick salmon with a crust of cousous, served with a sauce verte. Attractive and pleasant to be in - the use of local Ardmore pottery is a big plus on the presentation side - this is a friendly, well-run place and equally good for a cuppa and a gateau or pastry from the home-made selection on display, or a full meal. **Seats 60**. No smoking area; air conditioning. Open all day (10-11); L 10-4 & D 6-11 daily (Sun D 12-4); Set Sun L £11; D à la carte; house wine £10.50; sc discretionary.Closed Mon (to 6pm).MasterCard, Visa. **Directions:** In centre of Main Street.

Ballymacarbry   *Melody's Nire View Bar*

Ballymacarbry Co Waterford

PUB   Tel: 052 36147

This well-known pony-trekking and horse riding centre in the upper reaches of the Nire Valley has been in the family for over a hundred years - and it's a great place to take a break if you're walking or simply touring the area. When something simple but good is needed, Melody's is just the spot for a bowl of Carmel's home-made soup served with freshly baked brown bread, or a freshly-cut sandwich and a bit of crisp-crusted apple tart The soup might be mulligatawny, mixed vegetable, simple mushroom or carrot & tomato, but it will certainly be made from fresh ingredients that morning and the sandwiches - typically turkey, ham, cheese or salad - are freshly made up to order. Recent renovations and extensions have made the pub brighter and more comfortable without losing its atmosphere and its most important features - genuine hospitality, real open fires and simple good food - remain unchanged. There's live music on Tuesdays, Wednesdays & (usually) Sundays in summer too. Maps are available for a number of walks taking from 11/2-4 hours.Light meals.Closed 25 Dec & Good Fri. No credit cards. **Directions:** On Nire Valley scenic route, R671, between Clonmel and main Dungarvan-Lismore road (N72).

Ballymacarbry ❊   *Glasha Farmhouse*

Glasha Ballymacarbry Co.Waterford

FARMHOUSE   Tel/Fax: 052 36108

Paddy and Olive O'Gorman's spacious farmhouse is set in its own grounds high up in the hills and provides a very comfortable base for a relaxed rural break. Bedrooms have lots of little extras and neat shower rooms; a leaflet is provided outlining the many activities nearby - fishing, walking, pony trekking and golf amongst them. The aim is to give an all-in country break, with a home-cooked dinner at the end of the day - possibly followed by a session at the local pub, which is only 3 minutes walk away. Olive's menus are quite extensive with a choice of three starters, soup, five main courses (including a vegetarian option as well as local meats, fish and poultry) and several desserts or farmhouse cheese - rounding off perhaps with an Irish coffee. There's plenty of lounging room, including a conservatory. Children welcome, cots available. **Rooms 9** (all shower only, all no-smoking) B&B £25pps, ss £6.50. Residents' Dinner £20. Closed Xmas. MasterCard, Visa. **Directions:** Off N672 road between Clonmel and Dungarvan – 3 signs on the N672

Cappagh ❊   *Castle Farm*

Modeligo Cappagh Co.Waterford

FARMHOUSE   Tel: 058 68049   Fax: 058 68099

The Nugent family's unusual farmhouse overlooking the River Finisk is in the 18th century wing of a real 15th century castle. Although most of the house is quite normal inside, it blends into the original building in places - so, for example, the dining room has walls five feet deep and an original castle archway. Comfortable accommodation, meticulous housekeeping, a very pleasant guests' sitting room and fresh flowers everywhere all add up to a very appealing farmhouse indeed and Joan uses their own produce - fruit, vegetables, meats and herbs - in her cooking. Children (Under 2s free in parents' room; cots available). Pets in certain areas. **Rooms 5** (all en-suite). B&B £25pps, ss £6. Dining Room **Seats 20** D from 7 daily Set D £20, house wine £10. Children's tea £8.50 at 6 pm). Closed 1 Nov-1 Mar. Diners, MasterCard, Visa. **Directions:** Off N72 on R671, Nire Valley scenic route.

Cappoquin   *Richmond House*

COUNTRY HOUSE/RESTAURANT

Cappoquin Co Waterford
Tel: 058 54278 Fax: 058 54988

Set in private parkland just outside Cappoquin, the Deevy family's fine 18th century country house and restaurant offers a delightful combination of genuine hospitality, high standards of comfort, thoughtful service and excellent food. Approaching through well-tended grounds, a good impression is made from the outset, a feeling confirmed by the welcoming hall, which has a wood-burning stove and well-proportioned, elegantly furnished reception rooms opening off it. Ten individually decorated en-suite bedrooms vary in size and appointments but are comfortably furnished in country house style with full bathrooms. **Restaurant:** The restaurant is the most important single element at Richmond House, and non-residents regularly make up a high proportion of the guests. Warm and friendly service begins at the front door, then menus are presented over aperitifs, in front of the drawing room fire or in a conservatory overlooking the garden. Herbs, fruit and vegetables are grown on the premises for use in the kitchen and Paul is an ardent supporter of local produce, buying seafood from Dunmore East and Dungarvan, beef, lamb, bacon and sausages from his trusted local butcher and extra organic produce grown nearby. A wide range of local cheeses also features, including Knockanore Smoked, which won an Irish Food Writers Guild Award in 1998 and is produced just a few miles away. Paul constantly seeks ways to improve the range and style offered and there is a sureness of touch in his kitchen, seen in stimulating menus that always include imaginative vegetarian choices and offer a balance between traditional country house cooking and more adventurous dishes inspired by the current trend towards global cuisine. Under Claire's direction, service is excellent and admirably discreet care continues throughout. Ample private parking. Children welcome. No pets. **Rooms 9** (all en-suite). B&B £60pps, ss £10. Restaurant **Seats 40.** No smoking area. D 7-9 Tues-Sat (Sun & Mon residents only); Gourmet D £29, à la carte also available; house wine £12; sc discretionary.Toilets wheelchair accessible. Closed 23 Dec-14 Feb. Amex, Diners, MasterCard, Visa. **Directions:** Half a mile outside Cappoquin on N72.

Cheekpoint   *Jack Meade's Pub*

PUB

Cheekpoint Road Halfway House Waterford Co Waterford
Tel: 051 873187

William and Carmel Hartley's lovely old pub is widely known as "Meade's Under The Bridge" though it was actually established in 1705, thereby predating the bridge by over 150 years. It's been in the Hartley family since 1857, so they know a fair bit about its colourful history. In response to all the questions frequently asked by curious visitors this has all been put down in a useful little brochure. Old-fashioned this pub may be, but it's immaculate inside and out, with pretty roses around the door and everything inside gleaming. Outdoors in extensive waterside grounds there's a mixture of heritage museum – an old lime kiln, ice house, a restored cottage and even an agricultural museum to look at – and also a large beer garden, children's playground, toilets (including wheelchair facilities) and a baby changing room. Food is available all-day in peak season, at lunchtime all year and there are barbecues on summer Sundays and bank holidays. Like any place geared for a crowd, this can be a very busy pub in high season. Quieter types will love it in the winter though, when the fires are on and there's a bit of space to relax in. Children welcome (not after 9pm). No pets.Own parking. Bar Food 12.30-9 daily July/Aug, 12.30-2.30 & 5-9 Sept-Jun, Set L £4.50; house wine £10. Closed 25 Dec & Good Fri. No credit cards. **Directions:** From Waterford, turn left after Reginald's Tower. After hospital, bear left to Cheekpoint. Pub is under bridge on the left.

Cheekpoint   *McAlpin's Suir Inn*

Cheekpoint Co Waterford

RESTAURANT   Tel: 051 382220 email: cheekpoint@eircom.net

This immaculately maintained black-and-white painted inn is 300 years old and has been run by the McAlpin family since 1972. During that time they have earned an enviable reputation for hospitality and good food served at a moderate price, notably local seafood. It's a characterful, country style place with rustic furniture, cottagey plates and old prints decorating the walls. Seasonal menus offer a choice of about six starters (nearly all seafood and all under £5) and ten main courses, including three cold dishes and two vegetarian ones, again all moderately priced. All meals come with brown soda bread, butter and a side salad – and there's a nice little wine list including a special selection of eight good New World wines, "The £11 Cellar". Own parking. No children after 8 pm **Seats 35** No smoking area; air conditioning.D 6-9.45 daily in summer, Wed-Sat in winter; à la carte; sc discretionary. Toilets wheelchair accessible. Closed 2 wks Xmas. MasterCard, Visa. **Directions:** Seven miles east of Waterford

---

Cheekpoint *   *Three Rivers Guesthouse*

Cheekpoint Co Waterford

GUESTHOUSE   Tel: 051 382520 Fax: 051 382542 email: 3rivers@iol.ie

Very nicely located in a quiet position away from the road and overlooking Waterford Estuary, this pleasant guesthouse makes a comfortable base for a golfing holiday (four courses nearby), for fishing, horse riding, watersports, walking or touring the area. Bedrooms are a little dated but have all the necessary amenities and there a spacious residents' lounge and large breakfast room, both with lovely views over the garden to the Estuary. Children welcome (under 12s free in parents' room; cots available). Wheelchair accessible. Pets by arrangement. Garden. **Rooms 14** (all shower only, all no-smoking). B&B £30pps, ss £10 Closed 25-26 Dec. Amex, Diners, MasterCard, Visa. **Directions:** From Waterford, follow signs for Dunmore East, left for Passage East, right for Cheekpoint, turn right after Faithlegg Hotel.

Dungarvan *   *Gortnadiha House*

Ring, Dungarvan, Co Waterford

FARMHOUSE   Tel: 058 46142   Fax: 058 46538 email: ringcheese@ tinet.ie

Eileen and Thomas Harty's home is on a working dairy farm in a lovely setting, with woodland gardens and sea views. In addition to the normal farming activities, this one has a special claim to fame, as they're producers of the characterful Ring Farmhouse Cheese, which is made on the premises. Accommodation in the family home is comfortable, hospitality is warm and breakfasts offer a very wide selection of local and home produce, including fresh fish in season - and, of course, farmhouse cheese. Children welcome. Pets in certain areas. **Rooms 3** (all en-suite).B&B £25pps, ss £10. Closed 15 Nov-15 Mar Visa. **Directions:** On peninsula of Ring 7km from Dungarvan off the N25

Dungarvan *   *King John's Patisserie*

Harbour Mill, Davitt's Quay, Dungarvan, Co.Waterford

RESTAURANT/CAFÉ   Tel: 058 45756 Fax: 058 45854

This little place may be elusive if you're looking for a name but, come coffee time, cruise along the quayside and keep an eye out for the bright blue awning. Just the place for a coffee any-which-way you like it, this light and airy modern café just exudes quality and style with its beech tables and flooring, peppermint green and indigo blue seating, lots of chrome and a selection of newspapers to browse while you sip. A range of fatly-packed freshly-cut sandwiches will catch your eye just inside the door, and the main display offers all kinds of tempting pastries and gateaux - including specialities like "chocolate squidgy cake" - all explained with admirable interest and patience by friendly staff. They also do hearty breakfasts, there's a blackboard menu offering home-made hot dishes at lunchtime (with a glass of wine if you like) and a take-away service.Wheelchair accessible. Children welcome **Seats 40** No smoking area; air conditioning. Open all day (8am-9pm); all à la carte; house wine £9; sc discretionary. Closed 24 Dec (10 days) & Good Fri.MasterCard, Visa. **Directions:** Off main N25 Waterford-Cork road, waterside position in harbour.

Dungarvan ❋ — The Moorings Bar & Bistro

The Quay, Dungarvan, Co.Waterford
RESTAURANT/PUB/B&B
Tel/Fax: 058 41461

Attractively located overlooking Dungarvan harbour, this pleasant bar and informal restaurant has an atmosphere of cheerful efficiency and its well-spaced and neatly laid tables create a good impression on entering. A tempting blackboard menu in the front bar offers a good mixture of traditional and modern fare such as chowder with brown bread, lasagne and salad, some special seafood dishes such as crumbed scallops and salad and baguettes with various fillings, which are served to your table. There's a strong maritime flavour to the decor, especially in the back bar which is imaginatively furnished like an old ship's cabin and leads through to an area used as a wine bar/restaurant in the evening. Food is appetising and nicely presented and staff are capable and friendly. Evening bistro menus are more substantial, including dishes steaks and a selection of fish dishes. The simple accommodation currently available is quite comfortable, but there are plans for refurbishment and/or new rooms. Wheelchair accessible. Children welcome before 7pm. No pets. **Seats 30** (private room, 15) No smoking area. L 12-3 & D 6.30-10 daily; all à la carte; house wine £9.50; sc 12.5%. **Rooms 3** B&B £20pps, ss £10. Closed 25 Dec & Good Fri. No credit cards. **Directions:** Over the bridge at end of Quay

Dungarvan — The Park Hotel

Dungarvan Co Waterford
HOTEL
Tel: 058 42899 Fax: 058 42969

This attractive hotel on the outskirts of Dungarvan is owner-run by the Flynn family, who have many years of experience in the hotel business It has views over the Colligan River estuary and fits comfortably into its surroundings, with mature trees softening the approach. Public areas include a cosy traditional bar with panelled walls and a spacious, elegantly appointed dining room. Bedrooms are furnished and decorated to a high standard, with well-finished bathrooms (full bath and shower) and generous desk space as well as easy chairs. In addition to the many outdoor activities in the area – including tennis, fishing, windsurfing, walking, horseriding, pony-trekking as well as shooting and hunting, in season – there's an aqua and fitness centre with 20 metre pool, separate children's pool and many other features. Conference/banqueting (300). Own parking Leisure centre. Children welcome (under 4s free in parents' room; cots available). Pets permitted by arrangement. **Rooms 39** (all en-suite). B&B £45.50pps, ss £16.50. Lift. Wheelchair accessible. Closed Xmas. Amex, Diners, MasterCard, Visa. **Directions:** Signed on the N25 Cork-Dungarvan road.

Dungarvan ✗ — Seanachai Bar & Restaurant

Dungarvan West Co Waterford
PUB
Tel: 058 46285 Fax: 058 46305

Few could fail to be charmed by this proudly maintained traditional pub just off the main Cork road – it has white-washed walls, a well-kept thatched roof, displays of local memorabilia and a big open fire in the old kitchen complete with crane and cooking pots. Expect warm hospitality and wholesome, simply prepared fresh food offered from a choice of menus, in English or Irish. Local seafood is a speciality. There are vegetarian options and a special "children's corner". Traditional music is a big draw here – with informal sessions every night in summer and a traditional night every Saturday all year – and Set Dancing is so popular that a new wooden floor has had to be built in the restaurant, in addition to the flower-decked courtyard area already in use. Closed 25 Dec & Good Fri. MasterCard, Visa. **Directions:** Just outside Dungarvan, off the main Youghal road.

Dungarvan — Tannery Restaurant

10 Quay Street Dungarvan Co Waterford
RESTAURANT
Tel: 058 45420 Fax: 058 45118

Farmhouse Cheese Award

An old leather tannery has been imaginatively converted to make Paul and Maire Flynn's stylish contemporary restaurant. The kitchen is open to view as guests go upstairs to the first-floor dining area and the tannery theme is echoed throughout the light, clean-lined interior, creating a sense of history that, along with dramatic paintings and fresh flowers, adds greatly to the atmosphere. Paul's colourful, modish dishes are equally contemporary, presented on elegant white plates set against unadorned lightwood tables. Wide-ranging menus inspired by global trends are based mainly on local ingredients: local seafood features in a successful modern rendition of traditional fish chowder, mad with smoked haddock and spring onions and main courses such as a fillet of John Dor served with wild rice, and a morel and parma ham cream. Dashing desserts are temptin but don't miss the cheese. A selection of four farmhouse cheeses is presented in perfec condition and most are usually fairly local: a ripe Cashel Blue will often be included an west Cork will usually be represented - by Durrus or Milleens, perhaps, or if you are luck the West Cork Cheese Company's wonderful mature Gabriel, Desmond or Mizen. Min Gabhar fresh goats cheese may be offered in season (April-October) and they sometime offer a continental cheese such as Pont l'Eveque alongside the Irish ones. Whatever th day's quartet may be, it is very attractively served on a board with a selection of biscuits celery, walnuts and fruit - a very worthy winner of our Farmhouse Cheese Award this yea Lunch is especially good value.Toilets wheelchair accessible. Children welcome befor 8.30pm. **Seats 55** (private room, 30). No smoking area. L 12.30-2.15 Sat & D 6.30-1 Tues-Sat; Sun D 5-9 July/Aug only; all à la carte; house wine £12.50; sc discretionar Closed end Jan- Feb (3 wks). Amex, Diners, MasterCard, Visa. **Directions:** Down lanewa to right of Old Library

Dunmore East   *The Shij*

RESTAURANT

Dunmore East Co Waterfor
Tel: 051 38314

The Prendivilles well-known bar and restaurant is in a Victorian corner house with a pati on the harbour side used mainly for casual lunches in summer. Inside, an atmospheri bar and informal restaurant designed around a nautical theme - and, althougl concessions are made to non-seafood eaters, seafood is emphatically the star. Starter might include an imaginative creation such as cured fillets of monkfish with chervil an dill, served with a sorbet "bloody mary style". Soups will usually include a good bisqu and main courses range from simple pan-fried fish of the day to luxurious dishes such a poached fillets of dover sole and prawns with a lobster and brandy sauce (which migh be garnished rather surprisingly with a goat's cheese lasagne). Tempting desserts tend t be variations on classic themes and there's always an Irish farmhouse cheeseboard. Se Sunday lunch menus offered in spring and autumn are shorter and simpler, but als major on seafood. Children welcome before 9 pm. **Seats 75.** No smoking area; a conditioning.L 12.30-2 & D 7-10 daily. Set Sun L £13.50, à la carte, house win £12.50; sc discretionary. (NB: L Jun-Aug only, except Sun L in Apr-May, Sep-Oct. Close 25 Dec & Good Fri. Amex, Diners, MasterCard, Visa. **Directions:** 11 miles from Waterfor on the Dunmore road

Faithlegg ❊   *Faithlegg House Hote*

HOTEL

Faithlegg, Co.Waterfor
Tel: 058 382000 Fax: 058 38201(

This lovely 18th century house is set in wooded landscape with magnificent views ove its own golf course and the Suir estuary. The house has been sensitively developed as luxury hotel - the tone is set in the reception area, with its original stone floor, classi fireplace and specially commissioned Waterford Crystal chandelier and a simila sensitivity to the essentials of conversion is evident throughout. Public areas are spaciou and elegant and bedrooms, in both the old house and a discreetly positioned new wing are furnished to a very high standard with excellent facilities, including ISDN lines Somewhere along the line an architectural sense of humour has been at work too, a visitors to the snooker room will discover. Conference/banqueting (180/150); secretaria services. Ample parking.Leisure centre, golf, fishing, gardens. Children welcome (unde 3s free in parents' room; cots available). Wheelchair accessible, Lift. No pets. **Rooms 82** (2 suites, 14 master bedrooms, 4 no-smoking, 5 for disabled). B&B £62.50pps, s £32.50. Closed 25-26 Dec.Amex, Diners, MasterCard, Visa. **Directions:** 6 miles east o Waterford city.

Lismore ✗   *Ballyrafter House Hote*

HOTEL/RESTAURANT

Lismore Co Waterfor
Tel: 058 54002 Fax: 058 5305(

Fishing is a big draw to Joe & Noreen Willoughby's welcoming country house hotel, bu a relaxing atmosphere, log fires and good home cooking appeal to a growing number o people who simply enjoy the area and have come to see the unpretentious comforts of Ballyrafter as a home from home. The bar, where informal meals are served, is lined with fishing photographs and an open fire, family antiques and flowers from the garden create a caring atmosphere in the restaurant and the Duke of Devonshire's fairytale castle looks magical from window tables when floodlit at night. Appetising meals are based on local ingredients including, of course, fresh and smoked Blackwater salmon, along with home-produced honey and a trio of local cheeses - Knockanore, Knockalara and Ring - and service is friendly and helpful. Bedrooms are simple and comfortable and a new restaurant, a larger bar food area and five new bedrooms are currently planned for the courtyard area at the back of the hotel. **Rooms** 10 B&B £38 pps (all en-suite, some shower only). Restaurant **Seats 30.** No Smoking Restaurant. D 7.30-9.30 daily (Mon residents only); Set D £22; L Sun only 1-3 pm, Set Sun L £12.50 House Wine: £9.50; sc included. Bar Meals 12-6.30 daily, L 1-2.30. Closed end Nov-early Mar. Amex, Diners, Mastercard,Visa. **Directions:** On the edge of Lismore town, from Cappoquin direction.

Lismore [PUB★]   *Buggy's Glencairn Inn*

PUB/RESTAURANT

Glencairn near Lismore Co Waterford
Tel/Fax: 058 56232

There may be no traditional inn sign outside Ken and Cathleen Buggy's dream of a country pub, but reassuring notices beside the cheerfully painted door ease visitors into the little firelit bar. Ken's artlessly rustic food is the main attraction, however, and everything in this miniscule pub is based on fresh ingredients and "made on the day" so be prepared for limited choice, especially towards the end of service. The menu offers around four dishes per course, served in the bar as well as two little dining rooms charmingly set up with a stylish country informality. Starters like fresh basil and tomato salad or a freshly made soup of the day (with home-made brown soda bread), may be followed by Blackwater wild salmon in lemon butter or venison and beef provençale, all served with crisp little chips, vegetable of the day and a side salad. Finish up with something like bread and butter pudding (with home-made ice cream), or farmhouse cheeses, then cafetière coffee or an Irish coffee. Upstairs there are five delightful en-suite rooms (£30-£35 pps).Off road parking.Toilets wheelchair accessible. No children under 15. **Seats 20** (private room, 16) No smoking area D & Bar Food 7.20-9 daily in summer, Wed-Sun in winter; all à la carte; house wine £11.95; sc 10%. Closed 24 Dec-2 Jan & occasionally throughout the year. (A phone call ahead is wise; dinner reservations advised). MasterCard, Visa. **Directions:** Halway between Tallow and Lismore (R627) on minor road parallel to River Blackwater

---

Lismore [PUB★]   *Madden's Bar*

PUB

Main Street Lismore Co Waterford
Tel: 058 54148 Fax: 058 53343 email: madden@tinet .ie

Due respect is paid to tradition in Owen and John Maddens' delightful pub, yet a distinctly youthful atmosphere prevails behind the neat and colourful face it presents to the world. Many interesting features include a huge fireplace in the dining area (found by accident during renovations) and a smaller one in the back "drinking" bar - and a great deal of the owners' personality is to be seen in attention to detail throughout: careful choice of woods for the two bar areas, for instance, and sunny yellow walls which also have a hint of smoke and age. Similar care with table settings that combine quality with style - and Owen's light, modern menus offer food which is more bistro fare than traditional bar food. A selection of delicious home-made breads comes first and the menus feature local produce (organic where possible) in colourful, zesty modern dishes like spicy chicken baguette with fried potatoes and a tomato salsa or fish of the day with lime tartare sauce & home-made potato chips. Lovely desserts like lemon tart or chocolate fudge cake are irresistible - and there's even a pianist playing at lunchtime. Bar Food12.30-2.30 Mon-Fri. Closed Xmas 2 weeks.MasterCard, Visa. **Directions:**. In town centre.

Lismore   *O'Brien's*

PUB

Main Street Lismore Co Waterford
Tel: 058 54816

Lismore has a great selection of pubs, each with its own special character, but this one is the jewel in the crown. Run by sisters Joan and Mary Casey for "a very long time", it is a completely unspoilt example of how many pubs used to be. The hours are slightly unusual, described by the delightful proprietresses as 10-12 in the morning and 8-10 in the evening "give or take". Go and relish it. Closed 25 Dec & Good Fri. **Directions:** In town centre.

Nire Valley

Hanora's Cottage

ACCOMMODATION/RESTAURANT

Nire Valley Ballymacarbry Co Waterford
Tel 052 36134 Fax 052 36540

Major renovations and extensions were completed at the Wall family's large modern guesthouse in the spring of 1999, but Hanora's still nurtures the spirit of the ancestral home around which it is built. The Walls are very hospitable hosts and this, plus the luxurious accommodation and good food they provide, makes Hanora's a very special place - and especially wonderful for foot-weary walkers. Spacious, thoughtfully furnished rooms are now all new or recently refurbished, most have jacuzzi baths and there are three especially romantic ones for honeymooners. There's also a new conservatory with a spa tub, overlooking the garden with views of the mountains. **Restaurant:** A completely new restaurant and kitchen emerged from the recent building work, to the delight of head chef Eoin Wall and his wife Judith, who is also a chef. Dinner visitors travel from far and wide to mingle with residents at the fireside and choose from imaginative, well-balanced menus, before moving through to the restaurant. An enthusiastic supporter of small suppliers, Eoin uses local produce whenever possible - fresh fish from Dunmore East, free range chickens from Stradbally and local cheeses, for example. Hanora's legendary breakfast buffet gets guests off to a good start and includes more local produce - Crinnaughton Apple Juice from Lismore, home-made preserves and Seamus's delicious freshly-baked breads which are also used in packed lunches provided for residents. Own parking. No pets. Not suitable for children. Hanora's Cottage was the Guide's Guesthouse of the Year in 1999. **Rooms 11** (3 mini-suites); B&B £40.60pps, ss £15; Closed 22-27 Dec; MasterCard, Visa. **Directions:** From Clonmel or Dungarvan via Ballymacarbry

Waterford

Dwyer's Restaurant

RESTAURANT

8 Mary Street Waterford Co Waterford
Tel: 051 877478 Fax: 051 877480

Quietly located in an elegantly converted old barracks, chef-proprietor Martin Dwyer and his wife Sile have been running what is now widely recognised as Waterford's leading restaurant since 1989. Without show or fuss they consistently provide excellence in dishes where low-key presentation of some of the country's finest food is accompanied by discreet, thoughtful service. Martin carefully sources the best seasonal local produce which he prepares in a style which is basically classic French, although with some country French and New Irish influences; he sums up his philosophy with admirable simplicity: "We feel that the basis of good food is taste rather than presentation or fashion". Menus change monthly and main courses lean towards seafood –seared turbot on a bed of fennel, with fennel cream sauce and roast fillet of hake with prawn vinaigrette would both be typical – but there are good choices for carnivores and vegetarians too. Classic desserts are well worth leaving room for and there's always an Irish cheese plate. Espresso and herbal teas are offered as well as regular cafetiere coffee and tea. Like the cooking, the wine list favours France, although Spain, Italy, Germany and the New World are also represented. The early evening menu represents particularly good value. Children welcome before 8 pm. (Major refurbishments are about to begin as we go to press). **Seats 32** (private room, 8). No smoking area. D 6-10 Mon-Sat, Set D £25, early evening menu £15, 6-7 pm only; à la carte also available; house wine £10.50; sc discretionary. No private parking. Toilets wheelchair accessible Closed Sun, Xmas wk & Bank Hols.Amex, Diners, MasterCard, Visa. **Directions:** 50 yards south of Bridge, turn right – 100 yards down road on right.

Waterford

Foxmount Farm

FARM STAY

Passage East off Dunmore East Road Waterford Co Waterford
Tel: 051 874308 Fax: 051 854906 email:foxmount@iol.ie

Foxmount Farm, the Kent family's 17th century country house and working dairy farm, is just 15 minutes drive from the centre of Waterford city. It is a haven of peace and tranquillity. Margaret Kent's hospitality is the key to Foxmount Farm's special magic, but the house is lovely too – classically proportioned reception rooms provide a fine setting for home-cooked food. Dinner, prepared personally by Margaret and based on the farm's own produce,is available for residents by arrangement; vegetarian or other special dietary requirements can be built into menus if mentioned on booking. Margaret is a great baker as guests quickly discover when she serves afternoon tea in the drawing room (or in the morning, when freshly-baked breads are presented with her renowned breakfasts). Thoughtfully furnished accommodation, in five very different rooms, is extremely comfortable and includes some family rooms – but bear in mind that peace and relaxation are the aim at Foxmount, so don't expect phones or TVs in bedrooms. There is a hard tennis court on the premises (plus table tennis).Children welcome, pets by arrangement **Rooms 5** (4 en-suite; 2 private bathrooms, 2 shower-only). B&B £30pps, ss £5 Residents' D £20 at 7pm (book by 6pm) BYO wine. Closed Dec-Feb. No credit cards. **Directions:** From Waterford city take Dunmore East road – after 1.5 km, take Passage East road.

Waterford   *Granville Hotel*

Meagher Quay Waterford Co Waterford
HOTEL   Tel: 051 305555 Fax: 051 305566 email: stay@granville-hotel.ie

One of the country's oldest hotels, this much-loved quayside establishment in the centre of Waterford has many historical connections – with Bianconi, for example, who established Ireland's earliest transport system, and also Charles Stuart Parnell, who made many a rousing speech here. Since 1979 it's been owner-run by the Cusack family, who have overseen significant restoration and major refurbishment. It's a large hotel – bigger than it looks perhaps – with fine public areas and well-appointed bedrooms (all with well-designed bathrooms with both bath and shower).Conference/banqueting (200), video conferencing, secretarial services. Business centre.Leisure centre. Parking nearby. Children (Under 12s free in parents' room; cots available). No pets. **Rooms 100** (1 suite, 3 mini-suites, 96 executive rooms, 10 no-smoking; ISDN lines). B&B £60pps, ss £20. Wheelchair accessible. Lift. Closed 25-26 Dec. Amex, Diners, MasterCard, Visa. **Directions:** In city centre, on the quays.

Waterford   *Henry Downes*

10 Thomas Street Waterford Co Waterford
PUB   Tel: 051 874118

In the same (eccentric) family for five generations, Johnny de Bromhead's unusual pub is one of the few remaining houses to bottle its own whiskey. Although not the easiest of places to find, once visited it will certainly not be forgotten. Large, dark and cavernous – with a squash court on the premises as well as the more predictable billiards and snooker – it consists of a series of bars of differing character, each with its own particular following. It achieves with natural grace what so-called Irish theme pubs would dearly love to capture (and can't). Friendly, humorous bar staff enjoy filling customers in on the pub's proud history – and will gladly sell you a bottle of Henry Downes No.9 to take away.Wine £7 (to drink in pub). Closed 2-4 Sun-Fri, 25 Dec & Good Fri. No credit cards. **Directions:** Second right after Bridge Hotel, halfway up Thomas Street on right.

Waterford *x*   *Jurys Hotel*

Ferrybank Waterford Co Waterford
HOTEL   Tel: 051 832111 Fax: 051 832863

Situated high up over the River Suir, across from the town centre, this 1960s building is set in its own grounds with ample parking space and quite impressive public areas. Bedrooms, which include one suite, all have good views over Waterford city and are comfortably furnished with darkwood furniture and full bathrooms (all have bath and shower).The well-equipped leisure centre is a popular attraction. Conference facilities for up to 800 (banquets 550). Acc£££ Closed 24-26 Dec Amex, Diners, MasterCard, Visa.

Waterford   *Quality Marina Hotel*

Canada Street Waterford Co Waterford
HOTEL   Tel: 051 856600 Fax: 051 856605

This stylish new hotel has an attractive riverside location away from heavy traffic and within a few minutes walk of the town centre. The decor, like the building itself, is bright and cheerful in a budget-conscious style; bedrooms have all the usual modern amenities - phone, TV, tea/coffee-making; some also have lovely river views - there's only a boardwalk/outside seating area between the hotel and the water. Children welcome (under 4s free in parents' room; cots available). No pets. **Rooms 80** (3 suites, 15 no-smoking rooms, 2 for disabled). Lift; wheelchair access. B&B45pps, ss £15 (Room rate only also available, £60 for up to 3 guests without food). Own parking. Closed 25 Dec. Amex, Diners, MasterCard, Visa **Directions:** Opposite Reginald's Tower, take Dunmore road; hotel is on the left.

Waterford   *McCluskey's Bistro*

RESTAURANT
18 High Street Waterford Co Waterford
Tel/Fax: 051 857766

Proprietor-chef Paul McCluskey's colourful bistro near Reginald's Tower is deservedly popular. His menus are carefully thought out, based on the traditional French themes that everyone loves (moules marinières, peppered minute steak with herb tomatoes or garlic butter and Lyonnaise potatoes, daube provençale) lightened with global influences (penne with pesto, aubergine, courgette, parmesan and scallions, roast monkfish with Thai sauce, aoili, butter beans and sauté potatoes). He relies on prime local ingredients (Knockalara cheese, local butcher Tom Phelan's sausages). The quality of ingredients is impressive, the cooking admirably simple and the whole package excellent value for money (notably for the early evening sitting), so it's hardly surprising there's lots of return business. Children welcome.Toilets wheelchair accessible. **Seats 50.** No smoking area.L 12-2.30 & D 6-10 Tues-Sat; à la carte; early evening menu £15.95, 6-7.30 pm only; house wine £11.95; sc discretionary.Closed Sun & Mon. MasterCard, Visa.**Directions:** Near Post Office on High Street, one street back parallel to the Quay

Waterford   *O'Grady's*

RESTAURANT
Cork Road Waterford Co Waterford
Tel: 051 378851 Fax: 051 374062

Off-road parking and a warm reception from the proprietors get guests off to a good start at Sue and Cornelius O'Grady's restaurant in a restored Gothic lodge on the main Cork road. The dining area – which is fresh and bright, with booths and café curtains providing privacy without shutting diners off from the buzz – is well-situated at the rear of the building, away from the road. Menus, which change weekly and always offer tempting vegetarian dishes, include 2/3 course lunch menus, an early-bird menu (before 8 pm) and an interesting, well-balanced à la carte. Starters often include local seafood - straightforward oysters, perhaps - while main courses offer some unusual dishes including specialities such as calves' liver, Alsace bacon, onion gravy and colcannon for example, as well as ever-popular choices like steaks. Farmhouse cheeses are served plated. Children welcome. Own parking **Seats 60** (private room, 12). No smoking area.L 12.30-2.30 & D 6.30-9.30 daily. Set L £14.75 Set Sun L £15.75, D à la carte available, house wine £13; sc 10%. Closed Xmas. Amex, Diners, MasterCard, Visa. **Directions:** On main Cork road, 1 mile from city centre

Waterford   *Waterford Castle Hotel*

HOTEL
The Island Ballinakill Waterford Co Waterford
Tel: 051 878203 Fax: 051 879316 email: info@waterfordcastle.com

This beautiful hotel dates back to the 15th century. It is uniquely situated on its own wooded island (complete with 18 hole golf course) and reached by a little private ferry. Major renovations and building work, to include 36 new bedrooms, a leisure centre, function room and residents' lounge was about to begin as the Guide went to press. Children welcome (under 4s free in parents' room; cots available). Wheelchair accessible. Lift. No Pets. **Rooms 19** (5 suites, 1 mini-suite) Room rate £260. Open all year. Amex, Diners, MasterCard, Visa. **Directions:** Outskirts of Waterford city just off Dunmore East road

Waterford   *The Wine Vault*

RESTAURANT
High Street Waterford Co Waterford
Tel/Fax: 051 853444 email: bacchus@tinet.ie

Situated in the medieval part of the city, in an 18th century bonded warehouse with the remains of a 15th century tower house, David Dennison's informal little wine bar and restaurant includes a vaulted wine merchant's premises and has great atmosphere. Informal, bistro-style menus are international in tone and strong on vegetarian choices and local produce. A special gourmet tasting menu has wines specifically chosen by wine-man David to complement each course. Lunchtime specials and early evening menu (5.30-7.30) are especially good value. Exceptional wine list. Toilets wheelchair accessible. Children welcome **Seats 60** (private room, 25).No smoking area; air conditioning. L 12.30-2.30 & D 5.30-10.30 Mon-Sat.Gourmet D £50 with wine; early evening menu from £13, 5.30-7.30, à la carte available; house wines £13-20; sc discretionary. Closed Sun, 25 Dec, 1 Jan & Good Fri.MasterCard, Visa. **Directions:** On High Street, parallel to Quay, near City Square car park

WESTMEATH

With Athlone re-discovering itself as the cosmopolitan capital of the Shannon inland waterway, while Mullingar to the east finds its own vitality and prosperity, Westmeath's time has come in 2000 and the years ahead. As its name suggests, in the distant past Westmeath tended to be ruled by whoever held Meath itself. But today it is a county so cheerfully and successfully developing its own identity that they should find a completely new name for the place.

For Westmeath is somewhere that makes the very best of what it has to hand. Its highest "peak" is only the modest Mullaghmeen of 258 m, 10 kilometres north of Castlepollard. But this is in an area where hills of ordinary height have impressive shapes which make them appear like miniature mountains around the spectacularly beautiful Lough Derravaragh, famed for its association with the legend of the Children of Lir, who were turned into swans by their wicked step-mother Aoife, and remained as swans for 900 years until saved by the coming of Christianity.

Westmeath abounds in lakes to complement Derravaragh, such as the handsome expanses of Lough Owel and Lough Ennell on either side of the fine county town of Mullingar, where they've been making life even more watery in recent years with schemes to speed the restoration of the Royal Canal on its way through town from Dublin to the north Shannon.

Meanwhile, Westmeath's other main urban centre of Athlone has, like Mullingar, greatly benefitted from having a by-pass built to remove through traffic bound for the west coast. Thus Athlone is confidently developing as Ireland's main inland river town, its Shannonside prosperity growing on a useful mixture of electronics, pharmaceuticals and the healthcare industry. Despite such modern trends, this remains a very rural place - immediately south of the town, you can still hear the haunting call of the corncrake coming across the callows (water meadows).

But Athlone itself has a real buzz, particularly in the compact area around the old castle by the west bank quayside. And north of it, there's Lough Ree in all its glory, wonderful for boating in an area near the delightful village of Glasson, where the Goldsmith country verges towards County Longford, they have a monument to mark what some enthusiasts reckon to be the geographical centre of all Ireland. You really can't get more utterly rural than that.

Local Attractions and Information

Athlone	Youth Festival (April) 0902 73358
Heineken Athlone	River Festival & Regatta (June) 0902 94981
Athlone	All Ireland Drama Festival (May) 0902 72333
Athlone	Tourist Information 0902 94630
Clonmellon	Ballinlough Castle Gardens & Demesne 046 33135

Athlone   *Higgins'*

2 Pearse Street Athlone Co Westmeath
ACCOMMODATION/PUB   Tel: 0902 92519

The Higgins' well-run, hospitable pub is near the Norman castle and provides comfortable inexpensive accommodation in a very central location. Bedrooms range from a single room to a large family room, all with hair dryer, TV and access to tea and coffee-making facilities in the breakfast room. Bedrooms have secondary glazing to reduce the possibility of disturbance at night and there's a residents' lounge, also with television. The pub only does light bar food, but there are several good restaurants nearby including some suitable for inexpensive family meals. Children welcome. No pets. **Rooms 4** (all en-suite, shower-only & no-smoking). B&B £19pps, ss £6. No private parking. Closed 25 Dec & Good Fri. MasterCard, Visa. **Directions:** Town centre, near the main Post Office and castle.

Athlone   *Hodson Bay Hotel*

Hodson Bay Athlone Co Westmeath
HOTEL/RESTAURANT   Tel: 0902 92444 Fax: 0902 92688
email: info@hodsonbayhotel.com

Very much the centre of local activities, this well-located modern hotel adjoins Athlone Golf Club on the shores of Lough Ree, just four miles outside Athlone town. With lovely lake and island views and a wide range of leisure activities on site – including boating and fishing and a fine leisure centre – it's in great demand as a venue for both business and social occasions.The hotel has grown considerably since opening in 1992 - the Waterfront Bar & Buttery have just been expanded and refurbished giving a larger dining area, more elegant and comfortable surroundings; the next stage is a further 20 bedrooms and children's playroom, to be added in the winter of 1999/2000. Bedrooms, which are accessible by lift and include one room designed for disabled guests, are bright and comfortable, with contemporary decor, well-finished en-suite bathrooms and double and single beds in most rooms. Phone, TV, hairdryer, trouser press and tea/coffee trays are standard. Excellent banqueting/conference facilities (600/700); secretarial services, business centre;video conferencing available. Helipad. Leisure centre. Tennis, golf (18), fishing, garden. Ample parking. Children welcome (under 3s free in parents' room; cots available). **Rooms 97** (3 suites, 2 mini-suites, 2 executive rooms, 2 for disabled).B&B £50pps. Open all year. Amex, Diners, MasterCard, Visa.

L'Escale Restaurant: The restaurant is on the lake side of the hotel, well-appointed in traditional style. Head chef Tony Hanevy has been at the hotel since 1992 and recent visits have consistently indicated a standard of cooking which is well above the usual expectation for hotels. In addition to the basic à la carte daily set menus ensure variety for residents. While not adventurous, the quality of ingredients, cooking, presentation and service all ensure an enjoyable meal. Expect popular dishes: steaks may be predictable but this is great beef country and they are well-cooked, with a choice of sauces. The seafood selection can sometimes include lobster, along with several fish. Vegetarians get a choice of three or four dishes (on the carte) and farmhouse cheese is always available in addition to traditional desserts. **Seats 150** (private room, 500) No smoking area; air conditioning. L 12.30-2.30 & D 7-9.30 daily. Set L £11.50 (Sun £13), Set D £21, à la carte available, house wines from £11.50; sc inc.in price. Waterfront Bar & Buttery 10am-9pm daily. Toilets wheelchair accessible. **Directions:** Located off the Rosommon road, just 4 miles from Athlone town. Take the bypass and follow signs for Hodson Bay.

Athlone *The Left Bank Bistro*

Bastion Street Athlone Co Westmeath
Tel 0902 94446 Fax 0902 94509
RESTAURANT e-mail leftbank@isite.ie

Annie McNamara and Mary McCullough's wacky little restaurant on the bohemian side of the river is a great place for a most entertaining evening out. If you can plan a journey across Ireland to suit, it is also a fine place to stop for lunch when travelling. Old stone walls, oil-clothed tables and paper napkins create an informal atmosphere with loads of character – just right for the enjoyment of Annie's lively food. A wide range of delicious-sounding dishes – from menus described as a multicultural mix including contemporary Australian – make choices difficult, but the quality of ingredients and cooking is consistently high. There are always delicious vegetarian specials and fresh fish dishes are on a board, changed daily. Desserts are quite traditional and overlap into the light snacks that are available morning and afternoon.* At the time of going to press we have news that Left Bank Bistro is planning to move to a new site nearer the river; it will be well into 2000 before work on the building is completed. **Seats 42** (private room, 12) No smoking area. Open noon-5 & 6-9.30 daily. Set L £6.50, Set D £22; à la carte also available; house wine £10. Wheelchair accessible. No private parking. Closed Sun, 24 Dec-10 Jan, bank hols. Amex, MasterCard, Visa. **Directions:** Old town - west of the Shannon, near the castle.

Athlone *The Olive Grove*

Custume Place Athlone Co Westmeath
RESTAURANT Tel: 0902 76946

Garry Hughes and Gael Buckley opened their charming little restaurant in the autumn of 1997 and it has quickly built up a following for its pleasant, informal atmosphere (seasoned with a good dash of style), excellent home-cooked food from noon until late (light food in the afternoon) and a great willingness to do anything which will ensure a good time being had by all.The style is vaguely Mediterranean and youthful – as seen in starters such as bruschetta and vegetarian specials like Greek salad – but this is beef country and the speciality of the house is chargrilled steaks.Children welcome. Parking nearby. **Seats 45** No smoking area.L 12-5 & D 5.30-10 daily (Sun 12-5.30); à la carte; house wines £10, sc discretionary. Closed Mon, 25 Dec, 1 Jan, bank hols. Amex, MasterCard, Visa. **Directions:** Travelling from Dublin, take the left before the bridge in Athlone town centre.

Athlone
Restaurant Le Chateau
Athlone Co Westmeath

RESTAURANT   Tel: 0902 94517 Fax: 0902 73668 e-mail: lechateau@tinet.ie

Steven and Martina Linehan's atmospheric quayside restaurant is in a converted Presbyterian church in Athlone town centre. The church, which was closed in the early 1970s, has been magnificently transformed into a two-storey restaurant of great character. As well as the couple's established reputation for excellent food and hospitality, an additional attraction is now the atmosphere created by this dramatic conversion. Designed around the joint themes of church and river, the upstairs section has raised floors at each end, like the deck of a galleon, while the church theme is reflected in the windows – notably an original "Star of David" at the back of the restaurant – and the general ambience, which is extremely atmospheric. Candles are used generously to create a relaxed, romantic atmosphere, notably during their renowned Candlelight Dinners. Additional facilities also now include a full bar. Le Chateau was the Guide's 1999 Atmospheric Restaurant of the Year. **Seats 85** (private room, 30) No smoking area; air conditioning. D 5.30-10 daily (Sun 5.30-9.30);L12.30-3 Sun only. Set D £24, early evening menu £15.50 5.30-7 pm only; Set Sun L £15. A la carte D also available; house wines from £10.50. Toilets wheelchair accessible. Children welcome. Parking nearby. MasterCard, Visa. **Directions:** Heading west, cross the Shannon keeping to the left, turn left at the T junction; 50 yards, on the right beside the Shannon lock gates.

Athlone
Sean's Bar
13 Main Street Athlone Co Westmeath

PUB   Tel: 0902 92358

West of the river, in the interesting old town near the Norman castle (which has a particularly good visitors' centre for history and information on the area, including flora and fauna of the Shannon), Sean Fitzsimons' seriously historic bar claims to be the pub with the longest continuous use in Ireland – all owners since 1630 are on record. Dimly-lit, with a fine mahogany bar, mirrored shelving and an enormous settle bed, the bar has become popular with the local student population and is very handy for visitors cruising the Shannon (who have direct access to the river through the back bar and beer garden). The sloping floor is a particularly interesting feature, cleverly constructed to ensure that flood water drained back down to the river as the waters subsided (it still works). A glass case containing a section of old wattle wall original to the building highlights the age of the bar, but it's far from being a museum piece. Food is restricted to sandwiches, but the proper priorities are observed and they serve a good pint. Closed 25 Dec & Good Fri. **Directions:** On the west quayside, just in front of the castle.

Glasson
Glasson Village Restaurant
Glasson Athlone Co Westmeath

RESTAURANT   Tel: 0902 85001

In an attractive stone building which formerly served as an RIC barracks, chef-proprietor Michael Brooks opened the Village Restaurant in 1986, making his mark as something of a culinary pioneer in the area. On the edge of the village, there's a real country atmosphere about the place, enhanced by old pine furniture and a conservatory which is particularly pleasant for Sunday lunch. As has been the case since they opened, fresh fish features strongly on the menu – Michael takes pride in having introduced fresh seafood at a time when it wasn't popular locally, and aims to maintain the special reputation earned for fresh fish (including shellfish in season and freshwater fish like Lough Ree eel). The cooking style is imaginative and fairly traditional – country French meets modern Irish perhaps. à la carte menus change with the seasons, set menus daily and there are always a couple of vegetarian dishes. Parking. Children welcome. **Seats 50** (private room, 18). No smoking area. D 6.30-10.30 Tue -Sat & bank hol w/e Sun); L12.30-2.30 Sun only.Set D £21; Set Sun L £13; à la carte D available; house wines from £11; sc discretionary. Parking.Toilets wheelchair accessible. Closed 24-25 Dec, Mondays & 3 weeks from mid Oct. Amex, Diners, MasterCard, Visa. **Directions:** Situated 5 miles from Athlone on Longford/Cavan road (N55).

Glasson X

Grogan's Pub

Glasson Athlone Co Westmeath

PUB

Tel: 0902 85158

It's hard to cross the midlands without being drawn into at least a short visit to this magic pub in the "village of the roses". One of those proudly-run, traditional places with two little bars at the front (one with a welcome open fire in winter) and everything gleaming, it was established in 1750 and feels as if the fundamentals haven't changed too much since then. There's an informal bar/restaurant at the back, known as "Nannie Murph's". Closed 25 Dec & Good Fri .

Glasson

Wineport Lakeshore Restaurant

Glasson Athlone Co Westmeath

RESTAURANT   Tel: 0902 85466 Fax: 0902 85471 email: wineport@iol.ie

Since opening Wineport, their wonderful lakeside restaurant in 1993, Ray Byrne and Jane English have worked tirelessly on improvements – the restaurant is now much bigger and includes a private dining room, The Chart Room. Wineport is almost a second home to many of their regulars. Its stunning location and exceptional hospitality draw guests back time and again – guests who return with additions to the now famous Wineport collections (nauticalia, cats) and find the combination of the view, the company and a good meal irresistible. Head chef Feargal O'Donnell is a member of Euro-Toques and presents strongly seasonal menus based on local ingredients including Irish Angus beef, game in season, eels, home-grown herbs, free range eggs and wild mushrooms. There are New Irish Cuisine dishes such as confit of salmon with a black pudding champ, braised lamb shank with a spicy butterbean cassoulet and smoked ham hocks with a sweet mustard scallion béarnaise. Vegetarian dishes are always offered and an Irish cheeseboard, often including smoked Gubbeen, St Killian, Cooleeney and Cashel Blue. Children welcome before 7 pm. Ray and Jane were the Guide's 1999 Hosts of the Year. **Seats 100** (private room, 60). Air conditioning. D 5-9 daily; L 1-3.30 Sun only. Set D £27, Gourmet Menu £40; early evening menu £17.50 (5-7pm), à la carte D also available. Barfood 4-6pm Mon-Sat,Easter-Oct; house wine £12.75; sc discretionary (10% sc on groups of 10+).Toilets wheelchair accessible Parking. Closed Mon &Tue Nov-Easter, 24-26 Dec. Amex, Diners, MasterCard,Visa. **Directions:** Midway between Dublin and Galway take the Longford/Cavan exit off the Athlone relief road; fork left after 2.5 miles at the Dog & Duck; 1 mile, on the left.

Kilbeggan X

Locke's Distillery

Main Street Lower Kilbeggan Co Westmeath

CAFÉ/BAR   Tel: 0506 32154 Fax: 0506 32139 email: lockes@tinet.ie

Founded in 1757, and possibly the oldest licensed pot distillery in the world, Locke's has been imaginatively restored with a museum and bar open to the public all year round, seven days a week. It makes an interesting break en route between Dublin and Galway. The Distillery Kitchen – a characterful stone-walled place with big refectory tables and a welcoming fire – offers wholesome home-cooked food and good coffee. Closed 25 Dec, Good Fri & 1 Jan.MasterCard, Visa. **Directions:** Well signed on N4.

Kinnegad

The Cottage

Kinnegad village Co Westmeath

RESTAURANT

Tel: 044 75284

In the village of Kinnegad, just at the point where the Galway road forks to the left, this delightful homely cottage restaurant is one of Ireland's best-loved stopping places, with comfy traditional armchairs and real home-made food – anything from proper meals with a glass of wine at given times to snacks at any time and a really great afternoon tea. Baking is a speciality, with scones and home-made preserves, a wide variety of cakes and irresistible cookies always available. Home-made soups, hot dishes like poached salmon, quiches and omelettes served with a salad are all typical, along with desserts such as apple pie or gateaux. The only sad thing is that they're closed on Sundays, when so many people have to head back to the East coast after a weekend of sanity out West. Children welcome. **Seats 40** No smoking area. Open all day Mon-Fri, 8am-7pm (Sat to 2 pm); à la carte menus.Toilets wheelchair accessible. Parking. Closed Sun; Xmas week. No Credit cards. **Directions:** On the N4, Dublin-Galway/Sligo road.

Moate
Castledaly Manor

Castledaly Moate Co Westmeath
COUNTRY HOTEL   Tel: 0902 81221 Fax: 0902 81600 email: castledaly@tinet.ie

Extensive renovation and refurbishment of this Georgian manor house in 36 acres of mature woods and parkland has resulted in an impressive country house hotel with useful facilities. Furnished in period style, there's a clubby bar, traditional drawing room and a restaurant (which has opened since our visit) on the ground floor. Large bedrooms are all furnished to a high standard, some with four-posters. Small conference/meeting facilities (40/40). **Rooms 10** (all en-suite & no-smoking, 8 shower-only). B&B £45 pps, ss£24.50. Closed 25 Dec. Amex, Diners, MasterCard, Visa. **Directions:** Off the main N6 Dublin road between Moate and Athlone

Moate
Temple Country House

Horseleap Moate Co Westmeath
Tel: 0506 35118 Fax: 0506 35008
COUNTRY HOUSE   email: templespa@spiders.ie

Relaxation is the essence of Declan and Bernadette Fagan's philosophy at Temple, their charming and immaculately maintained 200 year-old farmhouse in the unspoilt Westmeath countryside. On its own farmland – where guests are welcome to walk – close to peat bogs, lakes and historical sites, outdoor activities such as walking, cycling and riding are all at hand. There are three lovely country style en-suite rooms in the house and a further five in the courtyard. Relaxation programmes and healthy eating have always been available at Temple, but the new Spa has moved this side of the operation into a new phase, offering yoga, hydrotherapy, massage, reflexology and specialist treatments such as Yon-Ka spa facial and seaweed body contour wraps. Temple is a member of the Health Farms of Ireland Association, which means that Bernadette gives special attention to healthy eating guidelines (and caters for vegetarian, vegan and other special diets). She uses the best of local produce – lamb from the farm, their own garden vegetables, best midland beef, cheese and yogurts – in good home cooking. And, although the Spa is a major attraction, you do not have to be a Spa guest to enjoy a stay at Temple. Garden, cycling, sauna, steam room, children's playground. **Rooms 8** (all en-suite, 5 no-smoking) B&B £45 pps, ss £5. Closed Xmas & New Year. Amex, MasterCard, Visa. **Directions:** Just off N6, 1 mile west of Horseleap.

Mullingar
The Austin Friar Hotel

Austin Friar Street Mullingar Co Westmeath
HOTEL   Tel: 044 45777 Fax: 044 45880

Built near the recently discovered ruins of an Augustinian friary, this unusual new hotel right in the middle of Mullingar opened in 1998 and has made quite an impact. The design – which is elliptical and features a central atrium – is very striking, even slightly disorientating at first, but interesting and pleasing once you have a feeling of how the building works. The very close proximity to the supermarket next door – or, for that matter the poky reception area (about to be overhauled) and narrow stairs – do nothing to prepare visitors for the more stylish elements of the hotel, which blossoms into the bright first floor atrium with contemporary seating areas. Bedrooms opening off this area are furnished to a high standard in a sophisticated modern style, with quality fabrics in warm, simple designs and good amenities including air conditioning as well as phone, TV and tea/coffee trays. On the ground floor there is a rather dashing modern restaurant, Austin's. Coference/banqueting (50/50); secretarial services. Children welcome (under 6s free in parents' room; cots available). **Rooms 19** (all en-suite, 16 shower only, 9 no-smoking). B&B £35 pps, ss £5. Open all year. Amex, MasterCard, Visa. **Directions:** Dublin end of Mullingar, on the right.

Mullingar ☆
Crookedwood House

Mullingar Co Westmeath
Tel: 044 72165 Fax: 044 72166
COUNTRY HOUSE/RESTAURANT   email: cwoodhse@iol.ie

Noel and Julie Kenny's handsome former rectory is a set in a lovely area of lush rolling farmland right in the centre of Ireland, with fine views over Lough Derravaragh. The original house, which is almost two centuries old, includes the whitewashed cellars which provide a characterful setting for a restaurant that has earned a reputation for excellence since Noel and Julie set up their home and business at Crookedwood. The house itself has had a noticeable inclination to grow under their energetic stewardship and now has not only eight spacious, thoughtfully planned, en-suite bedrooms, but also a more recent entrance foyer and reception area designed to take full advantage of views over the lake that inspired one of Ireland's great legends, the Children of Lir - and Noel's speciality swan dessert. Noel bases his strong, distinctive cooking on local ingredients such as beef and venison as well as the seafood that has become a hallmark of the best Irish restaurants, all to be found in punchy, colourful dishes that are gimmick-free and unselfconsciously wholesome. Children welcome (under 8s free in parents' room; cots available). Wheelchair accessible. Pets permitted by arrangement. **Rooms 8** (all en-suite). B&B £52.50, ss £10. Restaurant **Seats 70** (private room, 35).No smoking restaurant. D 6.30-9.30 daily (except Sun), L Sun only 12.30-2.30. Early D £16.50, 6.30-7.15 only. Gourmet D £25; sc discretionary. Toilets wheelchair accessible. Closed Sun D,all Mon & 2wks in Jan. Amex, Diners, MasterCard, Visa. **Directions:** From Dublin take the third exit on the Mullingar bypass,(signed Castlepollard). In Crookedwood village turn right at the Wood pub; about a mile, on the right.

Mullingar

The Greville Arms Hotel

HOTEL

Pearse St Mullingar Co Westmeath
Tel: 044 48563 Fax: 044 48052

Right at the heart of Mullingar's shopping area, this privately owned hotel is old-fashioned in the best sense of the word – well-maintained and well-run, with a strong sense of pride, friendly staff and a good deal of natural charm. Renovation and refurbishment have been undertaken on an ongoing basis over the years and housekeeping is of a high standard throughout. Public areas are in excellent order, including a lovely garden (with William Turner athenaeum) and, since 1998, a rooftop garden and conservatory. Bedrooms are comfortably furnished with good amenities and are well organised for the hotel's many business guests; all have full en-suite bathrooms. An attractive, well-run carvery and food bar is open all day, making it a good place to break a journey. Conference/banqueting (200/400).Video conferencing; secretarial services. Business centre.Garden.Children welcome (under 8s free in parents' room; cots available). No Pets. **Rooms 40** (2 suites, all en-suite). B&B £50pps; no sc. Own parking. Open all year. Amex, Diners, MasterCard, Visa. **Directions:** Town centre, on the main street.

Mullingar

Meares Court

COUNTRY HOUSE

Rathconrath Nr Mullingar Co Westmeath
Tel: 044 55112

Nine miles west of Mullingar, Meares Court is a magnificent Georgian mansion set tranquilly in acres of sweeping parkland. It is the kind of place people fall in love with, as Eithne and Brendan Pendred found when they "retired" here after many years in the hotel business. The house was in good order when they took it over, although they have made (and continue to make) many improvements, including the recent installation of lovely bathrooms for the comfortable bedrooms which are furnished with great style. Reception rooms include a large, elegant drawing room, a cosy study at the back of the house and a dining room where residents' dinners are served. Fishing; garden. Children welcome (free in parents' room under 1 year; cots available). Pets permitted in some areas. **Rooms 4** (all en-suite) B&B £30pps, ss £10. Residents D (£20, 7.30 pm; book by noon); no sc. Closed Xmas. MasterCard, Visa. **Directions:** 14km west of Mullingar, off the Ballymahon road.

Multyfarnham

Mornington House

COUNTRY HOUSE

Multyfarnham Co Westmeath
Tel: 044 72191 Fax: 044 72338 email: morning@indigo.ie

Warwick and Anne O'Hara's gracious Victorian house is surrounded by mature trees and is just a meadow's walk away from Lough Derravarragh where the mythical Children of Lir spent 300 years of their 900 year exile. The Lough is now occupied by a pleasing population of brown trout, pike, eels and other coarse fish. It has been the O'Hara family home since 1858 and is still furnished with much of the original furniture and family portraits and, although centrally heated, log fires remain an essential feature. Bedrooms are typical of this kind of country house – spacious and well-appointed, with old furniture (three have brass beds) – but with comfortable modern mattresses. Anne cooks proper country breakfasts and country house dinners for residents and Warwick does the honours front of house. Well-behaved pets allowed by arrangement. Garden; fishing. **Rooms 5** (all en-suite or private, 2 shower only). B&B £35pps, ss £5. Set residents D £22.50, 8pm (book by 2pm). Closed 1 Nov-1 Apr. Amex, Diners, MasterCard, Visa. **Directions:** From M4/Mullingar bypass take R394 for 8km to Crookedwood. Turn left at the Wood pub,then travel 2km to first junction; turn right; 1km, on the right.

WEXFORD

For many people coming to Ireland in 2000, Wexford county is their introduction, as the ferry port of Rosslare is one of the busiest. But for those of us already in Ireland, when we think of Wexford, the thoughts are of beaches, sunshine and opera. The longest continuous beach in all Ireland runs along Wexford's east coast, an astonishing 27 kilometres from Cahore Point south to Raven Point, which marks the northern side of the entrance to Wexford's shallow harbour.

As for sunshine, while areas further north along the east coast may record marginally less rainfall, in the very maritime climate of the "Sunny Southeast" around Wexford the clouds seem to clear more quickly, so the chances of seeing the elusive orb are much improved. As for opera, well, the annual Wexford Opera Festival every October is a byword for entertaining eccentricity - as international enthusiasts put it, "we go to Wexford town in the Autumn to take in operas written by people we've never heard of, and we have ourselves a thoroughly good time."

All of which is fine and dandy, but there's much more to the intriguing county of Wexford than sun, sand and singing. Wexford itself is but one of three substantial towns in it, the other two being the market town of Enniscorthy, and the river port of New Ross. While much of the county is low-lying, to the northwest it rises towards the handsome Blackstairs Mountains, where the 793m peak of Mount Leinster may be just over the boundary in Carlow, but one of the most attractive little hill towns in all Ireland, Bunclody, is most definitely in Wexford. In the north of the county, Gorey is a pleasant and prosperous place, and for connoisseurs of coastlines, the entire south coast of Wexford is a fascinating area of living history, shellfish-filled shallow estuaries, and an excellent little harbour at the much-thatched village of Kilmore Quay inside the Saltee Islands.

Round the corner beyond the impressive Hook Head, home to Ireland's oldest lighthouse, Wexford faces west across its own shoreline along the beauties of Waterford estuary. Here, there's another of county's fine beaches, at Duncannon, while nearby other sheltered little ports of west Wexford - Arthurstown and Ballyhack - move at their own sweet and gentle pace.

Local Attractions and Information

Ballygarrett	Shrule Deer Farm 055 27277
Ballyhack	Castle (renovated tower house c 1459) 051 389468
Coolgreaney	Gorey, Ram House Gardens (garden "rooms") 0402 37238
Dunbrody	Abbey & Visitor Centre 051 388603
Johnstown	Castle Demesne & Agricultural Museum 053 42888
New Ross	John F Kennedy Arboretum 051 388171
Rosslare	Harbour (terminal building) 053 33622
Tintern	Abbey 051 397124
Wexford	Opera Festival (October), Theatre Royal, 053 22144
Wexford	Tourism Information, 053 23111

Arthurstown

HOTEL/RESTAURANT

Dunbrody Country House

Arthurstown Co Wexford
Tel: 051 389600 Fax: 051 389601
email: info@dunbrodyhouse.com

Irish Bacon Award

Catherine and Kevin Dundon are developing a very special establishment at this spacious and elegant Georgian manor in twenty acres of parkland and gardens, across the estury from Waterford city. Public rooms, including a large entrance hall and gracious drawing room, are well-proportioned and have been tastefully furnished and decorated. The large bedrooms (with fine views) offer all the comforts expected of such a house and includes a recently added new wing which blends admirably with the old house An exceptional breakfast offers a fine buffet - fresh juices, fruit compotes, cheeses - as well as hot dishes from a tempting menu. Conference/banqueting (200/120). Business centre, secretarial services. Equestrian.Garden. Children welcome (under 5s free in parents' room). Pets by arrangement. **Rooms 19** (all en-suite, 3 no-smoking, 4 suites, 2 mini-suites, 8 executive, 1 disabled). B&B £65pps; ss£20. Wheelchair access. Closed 24-26 Dec. Amex, Diners, MasterCard, Visa.

The Harvest Room: The restaurant looks out onto a pleasure garden and beyond, to an organic vegetable and fruit garden. A well-proportioned, elegant room with an open fire in winter, it presents a striking blend of classic and contemporary style - bold recent additions include some beautiful modern rugs, specially commissioned from Ceadogan Rugs at Wellington Bridge. Likewise, chef/proprietor Kevin offers a tempting à la carte that succeeds unusually well in combining classical and international influences with local produce and Irish themes - thus a warm leek and potato cake with pieces of pan-fried crab and topped with crème fraîche, and oven-roasted rack of Wexford lamb with an orange and marmalade glaze. Specialities of the house marked on the menu with a rosette, include temptations such as seared magret de canard foie gras and local salmon baked on an oak plank and scented with smoked hickory chips - and the dish that specially caught the Guide's admiring attention on a recent visit, Roast Loin of Bacon with a Clove & Irish Mist Glaze, served on a Bed of Braised Cabbage & a Potato Cake. Despite the importance of the pig in our culinary history - and indeed the present - too few chefs are currently making the best use of pork and bacon so this dish came as a breath of fresh air. In it, Kevin works with the best local produce to combine familiar traditional themes with contemporary elements - this is an excellent example of New Irish Cuisine and we applaud it. Catherine leads the dining room staff with charm and panache. **Seats 70** (private room, 20). No-smoking area. Toilets wheelchair accessible. D Mon-Sat 6:30-9:15. L, Sun only 1-2.3. Set Sun L £16. House wines £12.50. SC discretionary. Children welcome until 8pm. Closed 25-26 Dec. Amex, Diners, MasterCard, Visa. **Directions:** N11 to Wexford, R733 from Wexford.

Ballyhack   *Neptune Restaurant & Ballyhack Cookery Centre*

Ballyhack Co Wexford

RESTAURANT   Tel: 051 389284 Fax: 051 389356

Near the Passage East car ferry, just under Ballyhack Castle, this welcoming restaurant has been run with style by Pierce and Valerie McAuliffe since 1983. Pierce, a Euro-Toques chef, takes pride in using the best of fresh local ingredients, especially the seafood (for which the restaurant is renowned) in meals that reflect the sunny temperament of this south-eastern corner. Likewise Valerie, an interior designer, has created a cheerful, slightly Mediterranean atmosphere and relaxed ambience in the three rooms which make up the restaurant – a main dining room with open kitchen (used for the cookery demonstrations), a cosy snug (where smoking is allowed) and a non-smoking conservatory with views over the river. Pierce's strongly seasonal à la carte menus and daily short dinner menus reflect his interest in traditional Irish food but have a modern slant and include some French classics too. Specialities include Neptune creamy fish soup (with delicious brown bread) and a hot crab bake with gin, also seafood pancakes, local salmon – and, of course, a Wexford cheeseboard. The cookery school – of which Martin Dwyer, of Dwyers Restaurant in Waterford city is a course director – offers a wide range of courses for both amateur cooks and caterers.(A morning demonstration of traditional Irish dishes with recipes and lunch is £20). **Seats 35** No-smoking area. D Mon-Sat 7-9. À la carte. House wines £12 (BYO permitted: corkage £5). Children over 10 welcome. Closed Xmas and Jan. Amex, Diners, MasterCard, Visa. **Directions:** 7 mile from Waterford via car ferry, 25 miles from Wexford Town.

Ballymurn   *Ballinkeele House*

Ballymurn Co Wexford

HISTORIC HOUSE   Tel: 053 38105 Fax: 053 38468 email: info@ballinkeele.com

Set in 350 acres of game-filled woods and farmland, this fine big house – which was designed by Daniel Robertson and has been the Maher family home since it was built in 1840 – is at the centre of a working farm. It is a grand house, with some wonderful features, including a lofty columned hall with a big open fire in the colder months, beautifully proportioned reception rooms with fine ceilings and furnishings which have changed very little since the house was built. Nevertheless, it is essentially a family house and has a refreshingly hospitable and down to earth atmosphere. Large bedrooms are furnished with antiques and have wonderful countryside views. Margaret is a keen amateur painter and plans to run small art workshops at Ballinkeele.Garden. Children welcome. No pets. **Rooms 5** (all en-suite, all no-smoking).B&B £55pps; ss£10. Closed Mid-Nov -28 Feb. MasterCard, Visa. Residents Set D £15 at 7:30 (book by noon). Private parties up to 14. **Directions:** From Wexford N11 north to Oilgate Village,turn right at signpost.

Campile
Kilmokea Country Manor

Campile Co Wexford

COUNTRY HOUSE   Tel: 051 388109 Fax: 051 388776 email: kilmokea@indigo.ie

This most peaceful and relaxing late Georgian country house is set in formal walled gardens (open to the public between 9-5). The house itself is most tastefully and comfortably furnished, with a drawing room overlooking the Italian Loggia, an honesty library bar, and an elegant dining room. Cream teas, shared with garden visitors, are served in a delightful conservatory. The individually-designed and immaculately maintained bedrooms command lovely views over the gardens and towards the estuary beyond. They have no TVs to disturb the tranquillity (though there's one in the lounge). Owner Emma Hewlett (husband Mark helps out at weekends) does practically everything herself, from preparing and cooking the evening meal on the trusty Aga (a typical dinner might include asparagus hollandaise, honeyed trout, rhubarb compote with home-made orange biscuits and Irish farmhouse cheeses) to offering aromatherapy treatments (for which she holds several qualifications) during the day. Conference/banqueting (20/40). Snooker.Children welcome (under 3s free in parents' room, cots available). Pets in some areas. No smoking establishment. * Two new garden suites and a billiards room (where smoking will be allowed) to be completed by January 2000. **Rooms 4** (all no-smoking, 1 shower only, 1 private, 1 for disabled). B&B £55pps; ss£10. Wheelchair access. Closed 1 Nov-1 Feb. Amex, MasterCard, Visa. **Directions:** Off R733 from New Ross to Ballyhack, follow signs to Kilmokea Gardens.

Carne ˣ
The Lobster Pot

Carne Co Wexford

PUB/RESTAURANT   Tel: 053 31110 Fax: 053 31401

Near Carnsore Point, Ciaran and Anne Hearne's fine, good-looking country pub – in elegant dark green with lots of well maintained plants – is a welcome sight indeed. Inside the long, low building several interconnecting bar areas are furnished in simple, practical style, with sturdy furniture designed for comfortable eating. For fine summer days there are picnic tables outside at the front. One room is a slightly more formal restaurant, but the atmosphere throughout is very relaxed and the emphasis is on putting local seafood to the best possible use, providing good value and efficient service. There's fresh lobster and some more unusual choices, such as Lobster Pot Pot-Pourri (an assortment of seafood served in a white wine sauce) plus half a dozen options "for landlubbers". Meals£-££. Closed 25 Dec & Good Fri.Amex, MasterCard, Visa.

Courtown Harbour
Harbour House

Courtown Harbour Gorey Co Wexford

B&B   Tel/Fax: 055 25117

Donal and Margaret O'Gorman's spick-and-span guesthouse is situated a stone's throw from the harbour and a few minutes from the resort's sandy beaches. Comfortable bedrooms offer TV, tea-making facilities and hairdryer, and there's a well-appointed residents' lounge. Start the day with a traditional breakfast with all the trimmings from Irish soda bread to black pudding. As an alternative, ask about their self-catering in mobile homes. Garden. Playroom; children's playground. Parking. Children under 4 free in parents' room; cots available. No pets. **Rooms 13** (all en-suite, no-smoking; some shower only). B&B £22.50pps; ss£5. Closed Nov-Feb. MasterCard, Visa. **Directions:** 4 miles off the main Rosslare-Dublin N11 route.

Ferrycarrig Bridge
Ferrycarrig Hotel

Ferrycarrig Bridge Wexford Co Wexford

HOTEL/RESTAURANT   Tel: 053 20999 Fax: 053 20982
email: ferrycarrig@griffingroup.ie

The recent addition of 51 bedrooms (including several suites) and an award-winning leisure centre have enhanced the appeal of this modern hotel overlooking the Slaney estuary. Outside, a new terrace patio has been constructed, and the steeply sloping gardens re-landscaped, with steps up to the car park. One of the great advantages of this hotel is that all bedrooms (some with balconies) have splendid views across the water. It's a few minutes' drive from Wexford, and about twenty minutes from Rosslare Harbour, where guests can enjoy a round of golf at the cliff-top St Helen's Bay course. The leisure centre boasts a heated floor, alongside a 20-metre swimming pool, children's splash pool, fully equipped gym and saunas. Conference/banqueting (400/350). ISDN lines. Leisure centre. Garden. Parking. Children welcome (under 4s free in parents' room, cots available).No pets. **Rooms 90** (4 suites, 8 executive). B&B £70pps; ss£15. Lift. Wheelchair access. Open all year. Amex, Diners, MasterCard, Visa.

Tides Restaurant:

The smaller, more formal of the hotel's restaurants offers guests modern French cuisine. **Seats 50** (private room, 50). No-smoking area. Air conditioning. Toilets wheelchair accessible. L 12:30-2:15 daily. D 6:30-9:15 daily. Set Sun L £11.95. A la carte also available. House wines £11.50. sc discretionary. Children welcome before 8pm.*160-seater Boathouse Bistro, serves modern Irish cooking B, L & D daily). *Bar food served 12:30-6 daily. **Directions:** 2 miles outside Wexford Town on N11

Gorey 🏨🏛 *Marlfield House*

Courtown Rd Gorey Co Wexford
Tel: 055 21124 Fax: 055 21572
email: marlf@iol.ie

COUNTRY HOUSE/RESTAURANT

Twenty years on and the Bowe family is still running the country house hotel par excellence. Marlfield House remains at the forefront of Irish hospitality. This is no ordinary hotel, but an example of how to transform a fine 19th-century house into an elegant oasis of unashamed luxury, where guests are cosseted and pampered in surroundings that can only be described as sumptuous. You enter the wooded drive through imposing gates, observing the enclosed wildfowl reserve with its own island and lake; to the rear of the house are further well-maintained gardens and manicured lawns, including a fine kitchen garden that provides much of the produce used in the restaurant. The interior features marble fireplaces, antiques, notable paintings, glittering chandeliers and fine fabrics. The hand of Mary Bowe is very much in evidence, perhaps even more noticeable in the bedrooms (including four-posters and half-testers), six of which are on the ground floor. These are 'State Rooms', larger and even more grand than those upstairs. All offer fine bedding and exquisite furnishings, plus every conceivable amenity, from fresh flowers and fruit to books and magazines. Bathrooms, many in marble, some with separate walk-in shower and spa tub, are equally luxurious and well-appointed, naturally providing bathrobes and top-quality toiletries. Housekeeping is immaculate throughout, service from committed staff thoughtful and unobtrusive. The house is now under the direction of daughter Margaret Bowe, continuing the family tradition.Conference/banqueting (20/40). Tennis. Children under 2 free in parents' room, cots available. Dogs and children are welcome by prior arrangement. **Rooms 14** (6 staterooms). B&B from £83pps; ss from £5. Wheelchair access. Closed mid-Dec end of Jan. Amex, Diners, MasterCard, Visa. **Restaurant:** The graceful dining-room and resplendent conservatory merge into one, allowing views out across the gardens. The conservatory, with its hanging baskets, plants and fresh flowers (not to mention the odd stone statue), is one of the most romantic spots in the whole of Ireland, further enhanced at night by candlelight – a wonderful setting in which to enjoy chef Henry Stone's's accomplished cooking. The fixed-price dinner (£37) offers firstly an amuse-gueule, then four courses with choices. Typical examples: seared scallops nicoise; carrot and coriander soup; roasted guinea fowl with crushed garlic potato, cassoulet of leeks and smoked ham. Vegetarian choices are always offered - homemade pasta with ratatouille,boilie cheese and tomato oil perhaps - and there are updated classic desserts (cappuccino crème brulée) or an Irish cheeseboard.The extensive wine list, long on burgundies and clarets, is informative. **Seats 60** (private room, 20). Non-smoking restaurant. Toilets wheelchair accessible. Air conditioning. Sun L only 12-1:45. D 7-9, Sun to 8. Set L £22. Gourmet D £37. Light à la carte lunches served daily in Library. House wines £17. SC discretionary. **Directions:** 1 mile outside Gorey on Courtown Road.

Kilmore Quay [PUB★] *Kehoe's Pub & Maritime Heritage Centre*

Kilmore Quay Co Wexford
Tel: 053 29830 Fax: 053 29820

PUB

Recent harbour developments, and especially the new marina, have brought an extra surge of activity to this thriving fishing village – and well-informed visitors all head straight for Kehoe's – family-owned for generations (James and Eleanor Kehoe have been running it since 1987). Changes have been made over the years, the most obvious being in 1994 when they decided to do a really good refurbishment job, to enhance the pub's traditional ambience – everything was done correctly, from the roof slates to the old pitchpine flooring (and ceiling in the Parlour). At the same time the interior was used to display a huge range of maritime artefacts, some of them recovered from local wrecks by

James and his diving colleagues. They have created what amounts to a maritime museum; even the beer garden at the back of the pub is constructed from a mast and boom discarded by local trawlers. The other major change has been to the food side of the business, which has crept up on Kehoe's gradually: a few years ago they did little more than soup and sandwiches but now the pub has a growing reputation for the quality and range of its bar meals – seafood, as well as vegetarian dishes and other main courses such as lasagne and stuffed chicken breasts wrapped in bacon. There's a short but very adequate wine list in addition to normal bar drinks. Children welcome. Wheelchair access. Open daily for food 12:30-8. Closed Good Friday, Xmas day. MasterCard, Visa, Laser. **Directions:** From Wexford take N25, then R739 to Kilmore Quay.

Kilmore Quay | *Quay House*

Kilmore Quay Co Wexford
GUESTHOUSE/CAFÉ   Tel: 053 29988 Fax: 053 29808 email: kilmore@esatclear.ie

Siobhan and Pat McDonnell's pristine guesthouse is centrally located in the village (not on the quay as might be expected) and is especially famous for its support of sea angling and diving – they have an annexe especially geared for anglers with drying/storage room, fridges and freezers, live bait and tackle sales. They can also provide packed lunches as well as evening meals. The whole place is ship shape, with attractive, slightly nautical bedrooms ("a place for everything and everything in its place"), practical pine floors (a bit cold underfoot) and neat en-suite facilities (most shower only). The breakfast room/coffee shop has a a maritime theme and a patio overlooking the village's pretty thatched cottages, the sea and beach; food, ranging from breakfast to bar-style meals – home-made soups with brown breads, lasagne etc – is available all day (7.30 am-6 pm). Garden. Parking. Children welcome (under 2s free in parents' room, cots available). Pets by arrangement. **Rooms 10** (all en-suite, 6 shower only). B&B £25pps; ss£5. MasterCard, Visa. **Directions:** N11 towards Rosslare, turn off for Kilmore Quay, left hand side in village.

Kilmore Quay | *The Silver Fox*

Kilmore Quay Co Wexford
RESTAURANT   Tel: 053 29888

Absolute freshness is the key to chef Nicky Cullen's reputation at this middle-market seafood restaurant close to the harbour, where popular dishes and more ambitious seafood creations appear unselfconsciously side by side. Menus at The Silver Fox are wide-ranging and offer some poultry and meat dishes (also vegetarian dishes, by arrangement) as well as the wide choice of seafood for which they have become famous; in the Guide's experience, simplest choices have always been wisest. Harbour developments at Kilmore Quay, including a marina, have been done with an admirable regard for the size and character of the village, but the growing number of visitors means booking is almost essential, at least in summer.Children welcome. **Seats 130** (private room, 35). No-smoking area. Air conditioning.Toilets wheelchair accessible. Open Mon-Sat, L 12:30-6, D 6-9:30. Sun L 12:30-2:30, Sun D 6-9. Set L £4.95, set Sun L £8.95. L&D à la carte available. House wines £9.50. SC discretionary. Closed 24-26 Dec, Jan 10 days. MasterCard, Visa. **Directions:** 20 min. drive from Rosslare ferry, Wexford Town and Ballyhack ferry.

Rosslare | *Churchtown House*

Tagoat Rosslare Co Wexford
COUNTRY HOUSE   Tel/Fax: 053 32555

Patricia and Austin Cody's converted Georgian house, set in some 8 acres of wooded gardens, is a well-run and comfortable country guesthouse, (extremely handy for the Rosslare ferryport about five minutes away). If you're lucky enough to arrive at around teatime, you'll be served delicious home-made cake and tea in the drawing room. A fine Irish breakfast and dinner (notice required) is served in the bright dining room. En-suite bedrooms have pretty co-ordinating fabrics and TV. Garden. Parking. Children welcome (cots available). Pets by arrangement. **Rooms 12** (all en-suite & no-smoking, 6 shower only, 1 mini-suite, 1 for disabled). B&B £35pps; ss£10. Wheelchair access. Closed 30 Nov-1 Mar. Amex, MasterCard, Visa. **Directions:** On R736 half-mile from M25, at Tagoat between pub and church.

Rosslare   *Great Southern Hotel*

Rosslare Co Wexford

HOTEL   Tel: 053 33233 Fax: 053 33543 email: res@rosslare.gsh.ie

A popular family venue, this 1960s hotel is perched on a clifftop overlooking the harbour – very handy for the port and an excellent place to get a fortifying breakfast if you're coming off an overnight ferry. It has good facilities and recent refurbishment has included the exterior, all public areas, the restaurant, maritime bar (with extensive collection of memorabilia covering the history of shipping in the area), function rooms and two-thirds of the bedrooms. Conference/banqueting (200/150). Leisure centre. Tennis. Snooker. Parking. Children welcome (under 2s free in parents' room, cots available). Crèche. No pets. **Rooms 100** (all en-suite, 8 no-smoking, 1 for disabled). B&B £61.50pps; ss£22. Lift. Wheelchair access. Closed Jan to mid-Feb. Amex, Diners, MasterCard, Visa. **Directions:** Overlooking Rosslare Harbour and ferry terminal.

Rosslare   *Kelly's Resort Hotel*

Rosslare Co Wexford
Tel: 053 31148 Fax: 053 32222
email: kellyhot@iol.ie

HOTEL + RESTAURANT

Constant renovating, refurbishing and building work each winter keep raising standards even higher each year at this renowned hotel, up-dating and creating bedrooms, altering public rooms and constructing new areas. The snooker room has grown up and an Italian lunchtime buffet bar has been installed next to the Ivy Room. This complements the contemporary restaurant, La Marine bistro, which has its own separate entrance and a stunning zinc bar imported from France. Note, too, the adjacent wine cellar, visible through a large glass window; several wines are own-label (William's wife is French and her family own vineyards in the Cotes-du-Rhone). Others are imported directly. Quite simply, the hotel has everything, for both individuals and families, many of whom return year after year (the number of children is limited at any one time, so as not to create an imbalance). There is a wide variety of public rooms, ranging from a quiet reading room and the snooker room to a supervised crèche and gallery lounge. Pictures (mostly modern) throughout the hotel form an outstanding art collection. Many of the bedrooms, some with balconies, have sea views and housekeeping throughout is immaculate. Leisure facilities are second to none, including a therapeutic spa and beauty centre, two indoor swimming pools, indoor tennis, and, continuing the French theme, boules. Outside the summer holiday season (end June-early Sept), ask about activity and special interest midweek spring/autumn breaks, weekends and Bank Holidays when rates are reduced. Banqueting (40). Leisure centre, indoor swimming pool. Tennis. Fishing (sea). Snooker. Hairdresser. Playroom. Children's playground. Garden. Parking. No pets. **Rooms 99** (all en-suite, 92 executive, 1 for disabled). B&B from £48pps. Lift. Wheelchair access. Closed early Dec to late Feb. Amex, MasterCard, Visa.

Main Dining Room: In 1998 chef de cuisine Jim Aherne celebrated 25 years at the helm, and he continues to satisfy literally hundreds of guests (hotel and locals) daily. A typical table d'hôte dinner menu – note the use of local ingredients – might include Bannow oysters or St Helen's white crabmeat with couscous and spring greens to start, followed by roast Rosslare spring lamb (an 'uncle' Kelly rears the lamb) or steamed turbot with dill hollandaise. Orange parfait with rhubarb compôte or a selection of Irish cheeses finishes the meal in style, and after coffee you can dance the night away to live music in the Ivy Room. Children welcome before 7pm. **Seats 200** (private room, 40). No-smoking area. Air conditioning.Toilets wheelchair accessible.L daily 1-2:15, Sun to 2. D daily 7:30-9. Set L £15. Set D £25. House wines from £12. SC discretionary.

La Marine: The bistro has proved to be an unqualified success, offering an alternative, more casual option for dining. Chef Eugene Callaghan is one of a new breed of young Irish chefs with the confidence to adapt traditional continental/Mediterranean dishes to Irish produce; thus pasta quills with fresh crab, cream and chives; escalopes of veal Parmigiano with buttered tagliatelle, tomato and parsley, or crusted fillet of salmon served on a bed of champ with a scallion cream sauce. Pear and cinnamon crème brûlée or a chocolate cappuccino cup round off things nicely. Sunday lunch is more traditional and features roast rib of beef. Wines (a selection off the main restaurant list), reflecting the style of food, are fairly priced. Service is swift and friendly.*Bar food daily 12:30-6. **Seats 60** L 12:30-3. D 6:30-9:30. Set L £15, Set D£25; sc discretionary. **Directions:** Take the signs for Wexford/Rosslare.

Wexford   *La Dolce Vita*

Westgate Wexford Co Wexford

RESTAURANT   Tel: 053 23935

Roberto Pons has settled in quickly during his first year as chef-proprietor at this Wexford restaurant, which is already well-established as one of the area's best. A committed Euro-Toques chef, Roberto cooks in traditional Italian style - risotto, osso bucco, rombo in sala verde - and, except for necessary Italian imports, everything is based on the freshest and best of local Irish produce. **Seats 60** No-smoking area. Wheelchair access. D daily 6:30-9:30, à la carte. House wines £9.95. Children welcome. Closed Sun (winter), Mon (summer), 2 wks Jan or Feb. MasterCard, Visa. **Directions:** Around the corner from Dunnes Stores in Redmond Square.

Wexford ✼   Mange 2

100 South Main Street Wexford Co Wexford

RESTAURANT   Tel: 053 44033 email: balyt@indigo.ie

Mange 2 is at the less fashionable end of Wexford's main street and the restaurant itself is pretty basic - farmhouse-style pine tables, plastic flowers and terracotta red painted walls - although it does have views through to the kitchen. A blackboard menu offers a selection of tempting specials. There is something here for everybody, the dishes span all corners of the globe and efficient service means they reach the diner with exemplary speed. Exciting cooking is demonstrated in dishes like perfectly cooked seared scallops on pak choy with ginger & soy dressing and char-grilled monkfish in a citrus & rosemary butter sauce with basmati rice. Carnivores might prefer well-fattened noisettes of lamb with onion marmalade & red berry jus (which, on the Guide's visit, might have benefitted from harder trimming). Mixed side vegetables are attractively served in a parchment cone and there might also be some baby potatoes tossed in butter. An excellent dessert menu should not not disappoint. A great addition to the Wexford dining scene, Mange 2 offers creative cooking which is also good value for money. **Seats 40** Wheelchair access. Air conditioning. D 6-11, Sun 6-10. A la carte. House wines £9.95. SC discretionary. Children welcome. Closed Mondays and 2-18 Jan. MasterCard, Visa. **Directions:** Wexford Town centre.

Wexford   *McMenamin's Townhouse*

3 Auburn Terrace Redmond Rd Wexford Co Wexford

B&B   Tel/Fax: 0503 46442 email: mcmem@indigo.ie

Seamus and Kay McMenamin's redbrick end-of-terrace Victorian house is one of the most highly-regarded places to stay in this area. It makes an excellent first or last night overnight stop for travellers on the Rosslare ferry, a fine base for the Wexford Opera or for a short break in this undervalued corner of Ireland. It's a lovely house throughout, notable for the fine beds the McMenamins provide and a special quality of hospitality unique to these outstanding hosts – the local knowledge passed on to guests to help them make the most of every day out and the terrific breakfasts, which include old-fashioned treats like kippers and lambs' kidneys in sherry sauce, as well as all the other usual breakfast dishes, served with freshly baked breads and home-made preserves. Own parking. Children welcome (under 2s free in parents' room, cots available). No pets. **Rooms 5** (en-suite, shower only, no-smoking). B&B £25pps; ss£5. Closed 20-30 Dec. MasterCard, Visa. **Directions:** Wexford Town centre opp. bus/rail station.

Wexford   *La Riva*

Crescent Quay Wexford Co Wexford

RESTAURANT   Tel: 053 24330

Just off the quays, Frank and Anne Chamberlaine's first floor restaurant has been doing a good job since 1991. It's up a steep flight of stairs – which do not give a very good first impression – however, once inside, a warm welcome offsets any negative impressions. The restaurant itself is delightful in a bright, informal way, with views through to the kitchen. A blackboard menu offers tempting specials, notably seafood - roast monkfish and parmesan, prawns with garlic & chilli sauce, scallops with rosemary & orange.Pasta dishes can be starters or main courses, and there are more serious main courses also, like rack of lamb (with roast shallots and garlic, perhaps). **Seats 42** No-smoking area. Air conditioning. D daily 6-10:30. A la carte menu. House wines £9.95. SC discretionary. Children welcome before 8pm. Closed 2 wks Jan. MasterCard, Visa.

Wexford ❄

Restaurant Mirabeau

6 Anne Street Wexford, Co Wexford

RESTAURANT
Tel: 053 21777

Hans & Pauline Lahme opened here in April 99 and their little restaurant has been an immediate hit; Pauline looks after front of house and Hans is the chef. Daily blackboard specials augment a menu that is quite wide-ranging and always includes some vegetarian options. Seafood and game are particular strengths, seen in starters like venison terrine with hazelnuts & salad and a main course house speciality of mixed fish in a white wine seafood sauce. **Seats 39** No-smoking area. L 12-2. D 6-10. Opera Festival times 4-11 daily. A la carte menu. House wines 310. Children over 10 welcome before 6. Closed Sun & Mon. MasterCard, Visa. **Directions:** Centrally located on the quay.

Wexford

White's Hotel

George Street Wexford Co Wexford

HOTEL
Tel: 053 22311 Fax: 053 45000 email: info@whiteshotel.iol.ie

An extensive refurbishment programme is in progress at this famous town centre hotel. From the outside it looks relatively modern, certainly when approached from the car park, but the reality is that there was a hostelry on this site in the late 18th century, which is more apparent when viewed from George Street. Bedrooms have been modernised, there's a health and fitness club (but no swimming pool) in the basement and a new entrance and lobby are planned shortly. Conference/banqueting (350/350). Secretarial services. Parking. Children welcome (under 3s free in parents' room, cots available). Pets by arrangement. **Rooms 82** (all en-suite, 10 no-smoking, 1 mini-suite). B&B £45pps; ss£15. Lift. Open all year. Amex, Diners, MasterCard, Visa. **Directions:** Follow signs when leaving N25 or N11.

WICKLOW

In this first year of the 21st century, Wicklow is a miracle. Although the booming presence of Dublin is right next door, this sublimely and spectacularly lovely county is very much its own place, a totally away-from-it-all world of moorland and mountain, farmland and garden, forest and lake, seashore and river. It's all right there, just over the nearest hill, yet it all seems so gloriously different.

In times past, Wicklow may have been recorded - by those who kept the official histories - as a mountain stronghold where rebels and hermits alike could keep their distance from the capital. But modern Wicklow has no need to be in a state of rebellion, for it is an invigorating and inspiring place which captivates everyone who lives there, so much so that while many of its citizens inevitably work in Dublin, they're Wicklow people a very long way first and associate Dubs - if at all - an extremely long way down the line.

Their attitude is easily understood, for even with today's traffic, it is still only a very short drive to transform your world from the crowded city streets right into the heart of some of the most heart-stoppingly beautiful scenery in all Ireland. Such scenery generates its own strong loyalties and sense of identity, and Wicklow folk are rightly and proudly a race apart. Drawing strength from their wonderful environment, they have a vigorous local life which keeps metropolitan blandness well at bay. And though being in a place so beautiful is almost sufficient reason for existence in itself, they're busy people too, with sheep farming and forestry and all sorts of light industries, while down in the workaday harbour of Arklow in the south of the county - a port with a long and splendid maritime history - they've been so successful in organising their own seagoing fleet of freighters that there are now more ships registered in Arklow than any other Irish port.

Local Attractions and Information

Ashford	Mount Usher Gardens 0404 40116
Blessington	Russborough (Beit Collection) 045 865239
Bray	Kilruddery House & Gardens 01 2863405
Enniskerry	Powerscourt Gardens & House Exhibition 01 204 6000
Wicklow Gardens Festival (May-July)	Wicklow Co Tourism 0404 66058
Wicklow Mountains	May & Autumn Walking Festivals 0404 66058

Arklow   *Plattenstown House*

COUNTRY HOUSE

Coolgreaney Rd Arklow Co Wicklow
Tel/Fax: 0402 37822

Margaret McDowell describes her period farmhouse well as having "the soft charm typical of the mid 19th century houses built in scenic Wicklow". About halfway between Dublin and Rosslare (each about an hour's drive away) and overlooking parkland, this quiet, peaceful place is set in 50 acres of land amidst its own lovely gardens close to the sea. There are riding stables, forest walks and golf. There's a traditional drawing room overlooking the back garden and a dining room where breakfast is served (and evening meals provided by arrangement). They have very different characters, but all are comfortably furnished. Garden. Children welcome (under 3s free in parents' room). No pets. **Rooms 4** (3 en-suite with shower only, 1 private bathroom, all no-smoking). B&B £26pps, ss£6.Closed Nov-Feb except by arrangement. MasterCard, Visa. **Directions:** Top of Arklow Main Street across roundabout to Coolgreaney Road, 2.5 miles on left.

Ashford *X*   *Il Cacciatore*

RESTAURANT

Ashford Co Wicklow
Tel: 0404 40054

This unpretentious little restaurant is furnished and decorated in trattoria style, with simple wooden furniture, a decorative roman-tiled "roof" and scenic Italian pictures. Expect simple Italian classics – starters like insalata di mare (a salad of crab claws, prawns and squid rings) and spaghetti alla carbonara, followed perhaps by a mixture of grilled fish or veal Milanese. Desserts may not be inspiring, but you can finish with an excellent espresso anyway. **Directions:** On the main road as you drive through Ashford.

Aughrim   *Lawless Hotel*

Aughrim Co Wicklow

HOTEL   Tel: 0402 36146 Fax: 0402 36384 email: lawhotel@iol.ie

Picturesquely situated beside the river in the lovely village of Aughrim, this delightful hotel dates back to 1787. Under the energetic management of the O'Toole family since 1990, the hotel has undergone major refurbishment, and some degree of extension recently. It is to the credit of the proprietors that everything has been done with great respect for the character of the original building. Bedrooms are cosily decorated, in character with a country inn, although on the small side which has limited bathroom design. The "Thirsty Trout" bar and the "Snug" lounge are appealing and a there's a lovely dining room overlooking the river. A recently completed entrance/reception was successfully built to match both design and materials to the original building - which makes it all the more disappointing that the nearby self-catering holiday houses currently under construction by the hotel are so obtrusive, in number and uniformity of size, colour and positioning. A paved area at the back beside the river is used for informal summer food and makes it a romantic spot for wedding photographs. Conference/banqueting (200/250). Secretarial services. Fishing. Garden. Parking. Children welcome. No pets. **Rooms 14** (all en-suite, 10 shower only, 5 no-smoking). B&B £47pps. Wheelchair access (ground floor only). Closed 24-26 Dec. MasterCard, Visa. **Directions:** Follow signs for 8 miles from roundabout at Arklow's Upper Main Street.

Avoca Village ✳   *Avoca Handweavers*

Avoca Village Co Wicklow

CAFÉ   Tel: 0402 35105 Fax: 0402 35446

Avoca handweavers, established in 1723 is Ireland's oldest business. It's a family owned craft design company which now has half a dozen branches throughout Ireland (most of which feature in this Guide) and the business originated here, at Avoca village, where weavers still produce the lovely woven woollen rugs and fabrics which became the hallmark of the company. Today the appeal of Avoca shops is threefold: the high standard of crafts sold, their beautiful locations and restaurants that have built up a reputation for imaginative, wholesome homecooked food. Garden. Parking. Children welcome. Pets in certain areas. **Seats 75** Open all day (10-5) Mon-Sun; No-smoking area. No service charge. Wheelchair access. Closed 25-26 Dec; Amex, Diners, MasterCard, Visa. **Directions:** Leave N11 at Rathnew and follow signs to Avoca Village.

Vale of Avoca ✳   *The Old Coach House*

Vale of Avoca Co Wicklow
Tel: 0402 35408 Fax: 0402 35720

COUNTRY HOUSE + RESTAURANT   email: coach_house@email.com

This lovely old roadside guesthouse and restaurant near Avoca village has recently been taken over by Suzy Caillabet, previously of Les Freres Jacques restaurant in Dublin. The accommodation, although comfortable, was dated and a little rundown at the time of the Guide's visit but refurbishment is planned for the winter of 1999/2000. The restaurant is already looking promising however, with softly draped sheer curtains, antique furniture, oriental rugs and classic white-clothed table settings. Suzy supervises the kitchen personally and menus offer a nice balance between traditional country fare - roast leg of lamb, Irish apple cake with cream - and more cosmopolitan flavours, as in roast tomato & basil soup and Sicilian roasted vegetable lasagne. Garden. Parking. Children welcome (under 3s free in parents' room). Pets by arrangement. **Rooms 6** (6 suites, all shower only, all no-smoking). B&B £25pps; ss£7. MasterCard, Visa. Restaurant. **Seats 45.** No smoking area. Dinner 7-10 Wed-Sun. L Sun only 1-3. Set Sun L £12.50. Set D £16-20 à la carte available. House wine £10.50. Service charge discretionary. Closed Mon-Tues. **Directions:** Between Avoca and Meeting of the Waters (100 yds).

Blessington   *Downshire House Hotel*

Blessington Co Wicklow

HOTEL   Tel: 045 865199 Fax: 045 865331

Situated just 18 miles from Dublin on the N81, in the tree-lined main street of Blessington, this friendly village hotel offers unpretentious comfort which is very winning. Blessington is an attractive village in an area of great natural beauty and archaeological interest – and it's also very close to Ireland's great Palladian mansion, Russborough

House, home of the world-famous Beit art collection. The present owner, Rhoda Byrne, has run the hotel since 1959 and instigated many improvements, including conference facilities for up to 200 and refurbishment of public areas. Simply furnished bedrooms, which include two single rooms, all have en-suite bathrooms with full bath and shower. Conference/banqueting (200/300). Garden. Parking. Children welcome; cots available (£5). **Rooms 25** (all en-suite). B&B £88pps; ss£6. Closed 22 Dec-6 Jan. MasterCard, Visa. **Seats 50** (private room, 20). No-smoking area. L 12:30-3 daily, D 5:30-9:30 daily. SC discretionary. **Directions:** 18 miles from Dublin on N81.

Bray   *The Tree of Idleness*

RESTAURANT

The Seafront Bray Co Wicklow
Tel: 01 286 3498 Fax: 01 282 8183

This much-loved seafront restaurant opened in 1979 when the owners, Akis and Susan Courtellas, arrived from Cyprus bringing with them the name of their previous restaurant (now in Turkish-held north Cyprus). A collection of photographs of old Cyprus in the reception area establishes the traditional Mediterranean atmosphere of the restaurant – and the menu cover bears a drawing of the original Tree of Idleness. Since Akis' death some years ago, Susan has run the restaurant herself with the help of Tom Monaghan, restaurant manager since 1980 and, since last year, a talented new head chef, Robert Fitzharris, who offers modern Greek Cypriot/Mediterranean menus based on the style which has made this restaurant famous. Introduction of young talent has of course brought in new ideas, but this has widened the choice rather than taken away from the character of the restaurant and, as Robert Fitzharris's training included a spell in Athens, he is well qualified to maintain old traditions while also blending in creations of his own. Alongside the classics – tzatziki, humus, taramosalata, Greek salad, dolmades, moussaka (including a vegetarian variation), souvlaki – there are some specialities which have had the world beating a path to the door for 20 years. First, there is the suckling pig: boned and filled with apple and apricot stuffing, it is served crisp-skinned and tender, with a wonderful wine and wild mushroom sauce. Then there is the dessert trolley, which is nothing less than temptation on wheels: it always carries a range of fresh and exotic fruits, baklava, home-made ice creams, several chocolate desserts, Greek yogurt mousse and much else besides. Service is excellent and the wine list includes many rare vintages. No children under 12 after 8 pm. **Seats 50** (private room, 20). No-smoking area. D 7:30-10:30. Set D £21.50, à la carte available. House wines from £11.00. 10% SC. Closed Mondays, Bank Holidays, Christmas & 2 wks end Aug. Amex, MasterCard, Visa. **Directions:** On seafront towards Bray Head.

Dunlavin 🏛   *Rathsallagh House*

COUNTRYHOUSE/RESTAURANT

Dunlavin Co Wicklow
Tel: 045 403112 Fax: 045 403343
email: info@rathsallagh.com

Country House of the Year

This large, rambling country house is just an hour from Dublin, but it could be in a different world. Although it's very professionally operated, the O'Flynn family insists it is not an hotel and – despite the relatively recent addition of an 18-hole golf course with clubhouse in the grounds – the gentle rhythms of life around the country house and gardens ensure that the atmosphere is kept decidedly low-key. Day rooms are elegantly furnished in country house style, with lots of comfortable seating areas and open fires. Accommodation is comfortable to the point of being luxurious, although, as in all old houses, rooms do vary; some are very spacious with lovely country views while other smaller, simpler rooms in the stable yard have a special cottagey charm. The Edwardian breakfast buffet, with its whole ham and silver chafing dishes full of good things like liver, kidneys and juicy field mushrooms, is a sight to gladden the heart of any guest Conference/banqueting (40/120). Fishing, horseriding, hunting, & deer-stalking by arrangement. Clay pigeon shooting.Tennis. Golf (18).Garden. Indoor swimming pool.Not suitable for children under 12. Pets by arrangement. **Rooms 17** (1 suite,1 room for disabled). Wheelchair access. B&B from £55pps; ss£30; Closed 22-28 Dec, January. Amex, Diners, MasterCard, Visa. **Restaurant:** Head chef Niall Hill creates interesting menus based on local produce, much of it from Rathsallagh's own walled garden. A drink in the old kitchen bar is recommended while reading the 4-course menu – country house with world influences – then guests can settle down in the graciously furnished dining room overlooking the gardens and the golf course. Roast local beef is a speciality, as is Wicklow lamb. Leave some room for a treat from the magnificent traditional dessert trolley, or some Irish farmhouse cheese. * Food served all day at Rathsallagh Golf Club (Closed Jan). **Seats 120** (private room, 40). No-smoking area. Toilets wheelchair accessible. D 7-9 daily. Set D £35.40. SC discretionary. Closed Xmas, 3 days. **Directions:** 15 miles south of Naas off Carlow Road, take Kilcullen bypass (M9), turn left 2 miles south Priory Inn, follow signposts.

Enniskerry *Enniscree Lodge*

Enniskerry Co Wicklow
Tel: 01 286 3542 Fax: 01 286 6037
HOTEL/RESTAURANT email: enniscre@iol.ie

Raymond and Josephine Power's comfortable inn is beautifully located, high up on the sunny side of Glencree. Steady renovations and refurbishments have been ongoing since the Powers took over in 1996 but to the relief of its many fans they have not made any radical changes. Attractive features of this former hunting lodge include a cosy bar with open log fire for winter and a south-facing terrace for warm days. More important, perhaps, is the relaxed rural atmosphere. Most of the comfortably furnished, individually decorated bedrooms have lovely views and all of the en-suite bathrooms were refurbished in 1998. Children welcome (under 10s free in parents' room, cots available). **Rooms 10** (4 shower only). B&B £45pps. Closed Jan. Amex, Diners, MasterCard, Visa. **Restaurant:** Sweeping views across Glencree to the Tanduff, Kippure and Sugarloaf peaks provide a dramatic outlook for this well-appointed dining room. Head chef Martin Barry moved up from Tinakilly in July 1999 and, true to his training under Euro-Toques chef John Moloney, bases his cooking on local produce – Wicklow lamb, fresh fish and game in season. **Seats 30** (private room, 10). No-smoking area. Toilets wheelchair accessible. L 1-2 (Sun 12:30-2) & D 7-9 daily. Set L £16.50. Set D £27.50; sc discretionary. House wine £12.50. **Directions:** From Enniskerry Village go up Kilgarron Hill for 4 miles, Lodge is on right.

Enniskerry *Powerscourt Terrace Café*

Powerscourt House Enniskerry Co Wicklow
CAFÉ Tel: 01 2046070 Fax: 01 2046072

Situated in a stunning location overlooking the famous gardens and fountains of Powerscourt House, the Pratt family of Avoca Handweavers opened this self-service restaurant in the summer of 1997, under the management of head chef Leylie Hayes. It is a delightfully relaxed space, with a large outdoor eating area as well as the 160-seater café, and the style and standard of food is similar to the original Avoca restaurant at Kilmacanogue. So expect everything to be freshly made, using as many local ingredients as possible – including organic herbs and vegetables – with lots of healthy food, especially interesting salads and good pastries, and including vegetarian dishes such as oven-roasted vegetable and goat's cheese tart. Parking (some distance from the house). Children welcome. **Seats 160** (indoor), additional 140 outside terrace (private room, 40). No-smoking area. Toilets wheelchair accessible. Open daily 9:30-5(Sun to 5:30). House wine £9.95. Closed 25-26 Dec. Amex, MasterCard, Visa. **Directions:** 2 miles from Enniskerry Village.

Glen O'The Downs *Glenview Hotel*

.Glen O'The Downs Delgany Co Wicklow
HOTEL/RESTAURANT Tel: 01 287 3399 Fax: 01 287 7511 email: glenview@iol.ie

Famous for its views over the Glen O'The Downs, this well-located hotel has all the advantages of a beautiful rural location, yet is just a half hour's drive from Dublin. Major renovations and additions to the hotel have just been completed, resulting in a dramatic upgrade of all facilities. A new conference area has state-of-the-art facilities and there's now an excellent Health and Leisure Club, a new reception area and 74 new bedrooms (including a penthouse suite). All this, together with landscaping and upgrading of the hotel exterior, gives a vastly improved impression of the hotel on arrival.Special breaks (golf, health and fitness, riding) offer good value.Conference/banqueting (220/180). Business centre, secretarial services, executive room, ISDN lines, video conferencing. Leisure centre (indoor swimming pool). Garden. Children welcome before 7pm. Pets by arrangement. **Rooms 74** (2 suites, 19 executive rooms, 35 no-smoking rooms, 1 for disabled). B&B £63pps. Wheelchair access. Lift. Amex, Diners, MasterCard, Visa. **Woodlands Restaurant:** The restaurant has a great natural asset in forest views over the Glen-O'-the Downs although it can otherwise be somewhat short on atmosphere. The presence of head chef Derek Dunne, a well-known successful competitor in the Irish

Culinary Team, puts the food on a more ambitious level than most hotel dining rooms. He presents interesting table d'hote and à la carte menus based on local ingredients - quite a lot of seafood, Wicklow lamb, venison - and mainly classical French in style. Both cooking and service are very professional. **Seats 120** (private room,180). No-smoking area. Toilets wheelchair accessible. Air conditioning. Open daily. L 12:30-2:30, Sun L 12-2:30, D 7- 10, Sun D 7-9:30. Set L £15, set Sun L £17.50. Set D £25. L&D à la carte available. House wines from £15. **Directions:** 4 miles south of Bray on N11.

Glendalough   *Derrybawn House*

Laragh nr Glendalough Co Wicklow
COUNTRY HOUSE   Tel: 0404 45134 Fax: 0404 45109

This appealing house was built in the style of a north Italian villa in the early 19th century, to replace an earlier one burnt down at the time of the 1798 rising. Set well back from the road in its own parkland, the house is approached by a sweeping drive and has an elegant overhanging roof, shuttered windows and pretty wisteria-covered verandah. Very much a family home, reception rooms and the main bedrooms are large, gracious and furnished with antiques, but not too grand. Back bedrooms are smaller but have an appealing country character and all have country views or a pleasant outlook over a courtyard garden. Evening meals are available by arrangement – please book a day ahead. Snooker. Garden. Parking. Not suitable for children under 12, except small babies. Pets permitted in certain areas by arrangement. **Rooms 6** (all private or en-suite, 4 shower only, 4 no-smoking). B&B £30pps; ss£10. Closed Christmas week. No credit cards. **Directions:** 1km south of Laragh on R755.

Glendalough ❋   *Derrymore*

Derrymore Lake Road Glendalough Co Wicklow
B&B   Tel/Fax: 0404 45493 email: patkelleher@eircom.net

Very close to Glendalough, up the hill a little which means you're looking over (not at) the road, Penny Kelleher's friendly B&B seems like an oasis of calm when there are too many visitors around for comfort. Bedrooms are appropriately furnished in a fresh country style with neat en-suite shower rooms and, in fine weather, it is very pleasant to have a private garden to sit in and a quiet base for the outdoor pursuits which can be so enjoyable in the area.. Home-baked bread for breakfast. Own parking. Children over 7 welcome. No pets. **Rooms 4** (all en-suite, all no-smoking). B&B £19pps; ss£6. Closed Nov-Feb. MasterCard, Visa. **Directions:** Follow the road signs to Glendalough Lakes.

Greystones   *The Hungry Monk*

Greystones Co Wicklow
RESTAURANT   Tel: 01 287 5759/7892 Fax: 01 287 7183

Well-known wine buff Pat Keown has run this hospitable first floor restaurant on the main street since 1988. Pat is a great and enthusiastic host; his love of wine is infectious and the place is spick and span – and the monk-related decor is a bit of fun. It all adds up to a great winding-down exercise. A combination of hospitality and interesting good quality food at affordable prices are at the heart of this restaurant's success – sheer generosity of spirit ensures value for money as well as a good meal. Seasonal menus offered include a well-priced Sunday lunch (£13.95) – a particularly popular event running from 12.30 to 8pm – and an evening à la carte menu. Main courses include traditional dishes – rack of Aughrim lamb, roast Cavan duck – as well as more adventurous ones such as chorizo risotto diablo (arborio rice, prawns, red beans and chilli) and a couple of vegetarian dishes. There is also the golfers' special: an incredible 18 oz T-bone steak served with peppercorn sauce and vegetables at a very reasonable £17.95. Blackboard specials include the day's seafood dishes and also any special wine offers. Desserts tend to be classical, there's always a farmhouse cheese plate and the outstanding wine list includes a choice of 50 half bottles. Children welcome. **Seats 40** No-smoking area. Air conditioning. D Wed-Sat 7-11. Open Sun 12:30-8. Set Sun L £13.95. Dinner à la carte. House wine £12.10% service charge. Closed Mon, Tue, Christmas, Bank Holidays. Amex, MasterCard, Visa. **Directions:** Centre of Greystones Village.

Kilmacanogue

Avoca Handweavers

Kilmacanogue Co Wicklow
Tel: 01 286 7466 Fax: 01 286 2367

RESTAURANT/CAFÉ

Happy Heart Eat Out Award

Avoca Handweavers is one of the country's most famous craft shops but it is also well worth allowing time for a meal when you visit.Head chef Johanna Hill has been supervising the production of the famously wholesome home-cooked food at Avoca Handweavers Restaurant since 1995 and people come here from miles around to tuck into fare which is as healthy as it is delicious, meeting the Irish Heart Foundation's definition of a Healthy Choice, i.e. dishes with lots of fruit and vegetables that are high in fibre and low in fat, especially saturated fat. While tarts and quiches are always popular, they also offer lots of healthy dishes bursting with vitamins, including a wide range of salads. Hot food includes traditional dishes such as beef and Guinness casserole and vegetarians are especially well catered for, both in special dishes – nut loaf, vegetable-based soups – and the many that just happen to be meatless. Although traditional home cooking is the overall theme, many dishes, such as Mediterranean vegetable & chevre tart, roasted vegetable & chicken pancake stack and green bean and coconut soup, have a welcome contemporary twist. Johanna Hill and her team - some of whom have moved on to other Avoca Handweavers outlets - have proved that healthy, natural foods are very much in demand - and, to underline the point, Avoca is shortly publishing a cookery book based on their restaurant dishes. Farmhouses cheeses are another strong point, as is the baking – typical breads made daily include traditional brown soda, cheese bread and a popular multigrain loaf. There is also a wide range of excellent delicatessen fare for sale in the shop. **Seats 260.** No-smoking area. Toilets wheelchair accessible. Air Conditioning. Open all day (10-5), Sun 10-5:30. No service charge. Children welcome. Closed 25-26 Dec. Amex, Diners, MasterCard, Visa. **Directions:** On the N11 4 miles south of Bray.

Kiltegan ❋

Barraderry Country House

Kiltegan Co Wicklow
Tel/Fax: 0508 73209

COUNTRY HOUSE

Olive and John Hobson's delightful Georgian house is in a quiet rural area close to the Wicklow mountains and, now that their family has grown up, the whole house has undergone extensive refurbishment and alteration for the comfort of guests. Big bedrooms with country views are beautifully furnished with old family furniture and have well-finished bathrooms and there's a spacious sitting room for guests' use too. Barraderry would make a good base for touring the lovely counties of Wicklow, Kildare, Carlow and Wexford and there's plenty to do nearby, with six golf courses within a half hour drive, several hunts and equestrian centres within easy reach and also Punchestown, Curragh and Naas racecourses. Garden. Children welcome (under 3s free in parents room). Pets allowed in some areas. **Rooms 4** (all en-suite, all no-smoking). B&B £25pps; ss£5. Closed 15 Dec- 15 Jan. No credit cards. **Directions:** 7km from Baltinglass on R747, 1km Kiltegan.

Kiltegan 🏛

Humewood Castle

Kiltegan Co Wicklow
Tel: 0508 73215 Fax: 0508 73382
email: humewood@iol.ie

COUNTRY HOUSE HOTEL

Humewood was the Guide's Romantic Hideaway of the Year for 1999 and it's easy to see why. You arrive on a perfectly ordinary Irish country road, stop at a large (but not especially impressive) gate and press the intercom button, as instructed. Slowly the gate creaks open – and you are transported into a world of make-believe. It's impossible to imagine anywhere more romantic to stay than Humewood Castle. A fairytale 19th-century Gothic Revival castle in private ownership (under the professional management of Hans Velders) set in beautiful parkland in the Wicklow Hills, it has been extensively renovated and stunningly decorated. While the castle is very large by any standards, many of the rooms are of surprisingly human proportions. Thus, for example, while the main dining room provides a fine setting for some two dozen guests, there are more intimate rooms suitable for smaller numbers. Similarly, the luxuriously appointed bedrooms and bathrooms, while indisputably grand, are also very comfortable. Country pursuits are an important part of life at Humewood too, but even if you do nothing more energetic than just relaxing beside the fire, this is a really special place for a break

Conference/banqueting (120/120). Business centre, secretarial services. Garden. Parking. Children welcome. Pets by arrangement. **Rooms 14** (4 en-suite, 1 shower only, all no-smoking). Room rate with breakfast, from £200 high season. L 1-2.30; D 8-10; Set D £42; house wine £17.50; 15% service charge. Open all year. Amex, MasterCard, Visa. **Directions:** On N81 Blessington-Baltinglass, Kiltegan.

Macreddin Village ✳   *The BrookLodge*

Macreddin Village Co Wicklow

HOTEL   Tel: 0402 36444 Fax: 0402 36580 email: brooklodge@macreddin.ie

Imagine, if you can, a completely new village in a Wicklow valley. The Guide has visited the site twice during the construction period and, while there was much work to be done at the time of going to press, the individuals concerned with this unlikely family enterprise make the necessary leap of the imagination possible. The driving force is Evan Doyle, who proved himself at The Strawberry Tree in Killarney, a fine restaurant outstanding for its commitment to using wild, free-range and organic produce long before these became buzz words among a wider public. Wisely, The Strawberry Tree is to be relocated at Macreddin and Freda Wolfe, who made her name at Dublin's Eden Restaurant, will be executive chef. While there will be much more to this new development than accommodation and a restaurant, these will be a promising start. Conference/banqueting (250/175). Business centre, secretarial services, ISDN lines, video conferencing. Snooker. Garden. Parking. Children welcome (under 3s free in parents' room, cots available). Pets by arrangement. **Rooms 4** (all en-suite, 1 suite, 4 no-smoking, 2 disabled, 12 executive). B&B £70pps; ss£25. Lift. Wheelchair access. Open all year. Amex, Diners, MasterCard, Visa. The Strawberry Tree **Seats 85** (private room, 24). No-smoking area. Toilets wheelchair accessible. Air conditioning. D 7-10 daily. Sun L 12:30-5. Set Sun L £14.50. Set D £25. Tasting menu £35. House wines £15. SC discretionary. William Actons Pub Bar food daily from 12:30-10. **Directions:** From N11 take R752 to Rathdrum, then R763 to Aughrim, right to Macreddin (2 km).

Rathdrum   *Avonbrae Guesthouse*

Laragh Road Rathdrum Co Wicklow

GUESTHOUSE   Tel/Fax: 0404 46198

Paddy Geoghegan's hospitable guesthouse makes a comfortable and relaxed base for a visit and is especially popular with lovers of the outdoor life - walking, cycling, riding, pony-trekking, golf and fishing are major attractions to this beautiful area but it's also ideal just for a quiet break. Simply furnished bedrooms vary in size and outlook but all have tea and coffee trays and en-suite facilities (only the smallest room has a bath). There are open fires as well as central heating and a comfortable guest sitting room. For fine weather there's a tennis court in the well-kept garden, and although this sounds grander than it is, there is even a nice little indoor swimming pool. Evening meals £14 at 6.30pm) and packed lunches (from £3.50) are available by arrangement. Snooker. Garden. Parking. Children welcome (free in parent's room under 12 months). Pets permitted. **Rooms 20** (all en-suite, 6 shower only). B&B £24pps; ss£5. Closed Nov-Feb. MasterCard, Visa. **Directions:** A few hundred yards outside Rathdrum on right hand side of Laragh Road.

Rathnew   *Hunter's Hotel*

Newrath Bridge Rathnew Co Wicklow

Tel: 0404 40106 Fax: 0404 40338

HOTEL/RESTAURANT   email: reception@hunters.ie

A rambling old coaching inn set in lovely gardens alongside the River Vartry, this much-loved hotel has a long and fascinating history – it's one of Ireland's oldest coaching inns, with records indicating that it was built around 1720. In the same family now for five generations, the colourful Mrs Maureen Gelletlie is currently at the helm and takes pride in running the place on traditional lines. This means old-fashioned comfort and food based on local and home-grown produce – with the emphasis very much on 'old fashioned' – which is where its character lies. There's a proper little bar, with chintzy loose-covered furniture and an open fire, a traditional dining room with fresh flowers – from the riverside garden where their famous afternoon tea is served in summer – and comfortable country bedrooms (all en-suite with full bath and shower). Conference (40). Garden. Parking. Children welcome. Pets in certain areas. **Rooms 16** (1 disabled). B&B £25pps. Wheelchair access. Open all year. Amex, MasterCard, Visa. **Restaurant:** Gerald

Meade's seasonal lunch and dinner menus change daily. In tune with the spirit of the hotel, the style is traditional country house cooking: simple food with a real home-made feeling about it - no mean achievement in a restaurant and much to be applauded. Expect classics such as chicken liver pâté with melba toast, soups based on fish or garden produce, traditional roasts – rib beef, with Yorkshire pudding or old-fashioned roast stuffed chicken with bacon – and probably several fish dishes, possibly including poached salmon with hollandaise and chive sauce. Desserts are often based on what the garden has to offer, and baking is good, so fresh raspberries and cream or baked apple and rhubarb tart could be wise choices. **Seats 54.** Non-smoking restaurant. Toilets wheelchair accessible. L 1-3 daily. D 7:30-9 daily. Set L £15. Set D £25. No SC. House wine £9.50. Closed 3 days Xmas. **Directions:** Off N11 at Ashford or Rathnew

Rathnew 🏛

Tinakilly House Hotel

Rathnew Co Wicklow
Tel: 0404 69274 Fax: 0404 67806
email: wpower@tinakilly.ie

HOTEL/RESTAURANT

William and Bee Power have run Tinakilly as an hotel since 1983, after completing a senstive restoration programme and the first of many extensions, all carefully designed to harmonise with the orginal building. Since then, caring owner-management and steadily improving amenities have combined to make this country house hotel a favourite destination for both business and leisure. It's a place of great local significance, having been built in the 1870s for Captain Robert Halpin, a local man who became Commander of The Great Eastern, which laid the first telegraph cable linking Europe and America. Now, there's always a welcoming fire burning in the lofty entrance hall, where a fascinating collection of Halpin memorabilia is of special interest and an original chandelier takes pride of place among many fine antiques. Tinakilly is one of the country's top business and corporate venues, but there is also a romantic side to its nature as bedrooms all have views across a bird sanctuary to the sea, and there are also period rooms, some with four-posters. To all this, add friendly, well-trained staff, lovely grounds and a very fine kitchen and the recipe for success is complete. Conference/banqueting (80/90). Secretarial services. Fitness suite. Tennis. Garden. Parking. Children welcome (under 2s free in parents' room, cots available). No pets. **Rooms 53** (all en-suite, some no-smoking, 5 suites, 35 mini-suites, 13 executive). B&B £72pps; ss£45. Lift. Wheelchair access. Open all year. Amex, Diners, MasterCard, Visa. **Brunel Dining Room:** Dining arrangements at Tinakilly have improved since the completion of a panelled split level restaurant in the west wing, which has a relaxed, intimate atmosphere. John Moloney, head chef since 1989, presents a range of menus including a seasonal à la carte and a daily table d'hôte. The kitchen garden produces an abundance of fruit, vegetables and herbs for most of the year and this, plus local meats – notably Wicklow lamb and venison – and seafood, provides the basis for his cooking. An old-fashioned chef in the best sense of the term, John oversees everything from the stockpots through to the preparation of preserves and chocolates. At its best, Tinakilly's very successful house style is sophisticated country house cooking with the main influence – classic French – showing in well-made sauces and elegant presentation. **Seats 80** (private room, 30). No-smoking area. Toilets wheelchair accessible. Air conditioning. L 12:30-2:30 daily, Sun to 2. D 7:30-9:30 daily, Sun to 9. Set D £36. A la carte available. House wine from £12. sc discretionary. **Directions:** N11/M11 to Rathnew, 500 metres from village on R750 to Wicklow.

Roundwood [PUB★]

Roundwood Inn

Roundwood Co Wicklow
Tel: 01 281 8107

PUB/RESTAURANT

Jurgen and Aine Schwalm have owned this 17th century inn in the highest village in the Wicklow Hills since 1985. There's a public bar at one end, with a snug and an open fire, and in the middle of the building the main bar food area, furnished in traditional style with wooden floors and big sturdy tables. The style that the Schwalms and head chef Paul Taube have developed over the years is their own unique blend of Irish and German influences. Excellent bar food includes substantial soups, specialities such as Galway oysters, smoked Wicklow trout, smoked salmon and hearty hot meals such as the house variation on Irish stew. Blackboard specials often include home-made gravad lachs, lobster salad and a speciality dessert, Triple Liqueur Parfait. The food at Roundwood has always had a special character which, together with the place itself and a consistently high standard of hospitality, has earned it an enviable reputation with hillwalkers, Dubliners out for the day and visitors alike. Meals 12.30-9.30 (Sun 12.30-2 & 4-9.30).Closed 25 Dec & Good Fri. Amex, MasterCard, Visa. **Restaurant:** The restaurant is in the same style and only slightly more formal than the main bar, with fires at each end of the room (now converted to gas, alas) and is available by reservation. Restaurant menus overlap somewhat with the bar food, but offer a much wider choice, leaning towards more substantial dishes such as rack of Wicklow lamb, roast wild Wicklow venison, venison ragout and other game in season. German influences are again evident in long-established specialities such as smoked Westphalian ham and wiener schnitzel and a feather-light Baileys Cream gateau which is not to be missed. A mainly European wine list favours France and Germany. **Seats 70** (Private room,32). LTue-Sun, 1-2.15, D Tue-Sat 7.30-9.30. House wine from £12.95; service discretionary; reservations advised. Closed D Sun, all Mon. **Directions:** In the centre of Rounwood village.

Wicklow   *The Bakery Restaurant & Café*

Church Street Wicklow Co Wicklow
RESTAURANT/CAFE   Tel: 0404 66770 Fax: 0404 66717

Sally Stevens' lovely restaurant has great character – the fine stone building has retained some of its old bakery artefacts, including the original ovens in the café downstairs. Lots of candles in the reception area and restaurant set a warm tone which is then complemented by an admirably restrained theme – stone walls and beams provide a dark background for quite austere table settings which work wonderfully well in this room. earning The Bakery the Guide's Table Presentation of the Year award in 1999. Imaginative menus offer eight starters – probably including a house speciality, Sushi Nori - selection of three traditional Japanese seaweed-wrapped rice cakes stuffed with smoked salmon, crab and prawn respectively, served with a soy vinaigrette. Main courses could include a generous rack of Wicklow spring lamb with a light garlic and rosemary jus and good fish dishes such as baked silver hake with a herby pesto crust – strong flavours that balance well with a parmesan cream sauce. Vegetables are highly rated - a seasonal selection is served in a big dish to help yourselves and a separate vegetarian menu is offered. To finish, a Bakery Tasting Plate, perhaps, or plated farmhouse cheeses. Good coffee and friendly service. Children welcome. *Downstairs, the Bistro offers a 2-3 course table d'hote menu,£18-£20 including coffee. **Seats 70** (private room, 36). No-smoking area. Toilets wheelchair accessible. D daily in summer 6-10, (Sun to 9); L Sun only 1-4. Set D £18-21, à la carte available upstairs. Set L £16-18. Early Bird 6-7.30, £18. House wines under £15. SC discretionary. Closed D Sun in winter, Good Friday, 24 Dec-3 Jan. MasterCard, Visa. **Directions:** Off Wicklow main street, opp. main car park.

Wicklow *x*   *The Grand Hotel*

Abbey Street Wicklow Co Wicklow
HOTEL   Tel: 0404 67337 Fax: 0404 69607 email: grandhotel@tinet.ie

At the centre of local activities, this friendly hotel has large public areas including the Glebe Bar, which is very popular for bar meals (especially the lunchtime carvery). The conference/banqueting facilities for up to 300/350 are in constant use, especially for weddings. Pleasant, comfortably furnished bedrooms are all en-suite (two with shower only) and warm, with all the necessary amenities. Acc££ Meals.£ Amex, Diners, MasterCard, Visa.

Wicklow   *The Old Rectory*

Wicklow Co Wicklow
Tel: 0404 67048 Fax: 0404 69181
COUNTRY HOUSE/RESTAURANT   email: mail@oldrectory.ie

Paul and Linda Saunders' pretty early Victorian house is quite small but makes up for its size through great attention to detail. Colourfully decorated bedrooms are all en-suite and have many homely extras including fresh flowers. Breakfast – served with your choice of newspapers – offers many unusual options, and vegetarian and other special dietary requirements will be met by Linda with creativity and enthusiasm. Small conferences (16) Fitness suite; sauna. Garden. Parking. Children welcome. No pets. **Rooms 8** (all en-suite). B&B £54pps; ss£27. No SC. Closed Jan-Feb. Amex, MasterCard,Visa. **Restaurant:** Linda's imaginative food is prepared with an artist's eye, notably for special floral dinners, held in conjunction with the County Wicklow Gardens Festival each summer. Dinner is served by Paul in an attractive new Victorian style conservatory called the Orangery. (No smoking.) Interest in The Old Rectory's food is so great that Linda runs a series of full and half-day cookery courses on topics such as wild food, vegetarian food, and Christmas cookery. **Seats 16.** Non-smoking restaurant. D daily at 8. Gourmet menu £31.50. House wines £10. SC discretionary. **Directions:** N11 to Rathnew then R750 to Wicklow, on left after Statoil station.

NORTHERN IRELAND

BELFAST

Belfast is rediscovering its architectural heritage in 2000, with a growing awareness of the quieter 18th Century architectural styles which preceded the exuberance of the 19th Century's Victorian expansion. In terms of urban significance, the cities of Ireland tend to be relatively recent developments which started as Viking trading settlements that later "had manners put on them" by the Normans. But Belfast is even newer than that. When the Vikings in the 9th century raided what is now known as Belfast Lough, their target was the wealthy monastery at Bangor, and thus their bases were at Ballyholme and Groomsport further east. Then when the Normans held sway in the 13th Century, their main stronghold was at Carrickfergus on the northern shore of the commodious inlet known for several centuries as Carrickfergus Bay.

At the head of that inlet beside the shallow River Lagan, the tiny settlement of beal feirste - the 'mouth of the Farset or the sandspit' - wasn't named on maps at all until the late 15th Century. But Belfast proved to be the perfect greenfield site for rapid development as the industrial revolution got under way. Its rocketing growth began with linen manufacture in the 17th Century, and this was accelerated by the arrival of skilled Huguenot refugees in 1685. There was also scope for ship-building on the shorelines in the valleymouth between the high peaks crowding in on the Antrim side on the northwest, and the Holywood Hills to the southeast, though the first shipyard of any significant size wasn't in being until 1791, when William and Hugh Ritchie opened for business. The Lagan Valley gave convenient access to the rest of Ireland for the increase of trade and commerce to encourage development of the port, while the prosperous farms of Down and Antrim fed a rapidly expanding population.

So, at the head of what was becoming known as Belfast Lough, Belfast took off in a big way, a focus for industrial ingenuity and manufacturing inventiveness, and a magnet for entrepreneurs and innovators from all of the north of Ireland, and the world beyond. Its population in 1600 had been less than 500, yet by 1700 it was 2,000, and by 1800 it was 25,000. The city's growth was prodigious, such that by the end of the 19th Century it could claim with justifiable pride to have the largest shipyard in the world, the largest ropeworks, the largest linen mills, the largest tobacco factory, and the largest heavy engineering works, all served by a greater mileage of quays than anywhere comparable, and all contributing to a situation whereby, in 1900, the population had soared through the 300,000 mark.

Expansion had become so rapid in the latter half of the 19th Century that it tended to obliterate the influence of the gentler intellectual and philosophical legacies inspired by the Huguenots and other earlier developers, a case in point being the gloriously flamboyant and baroque new Rennaissance-style City Hall, which was completed in 1906. It was the perfect expression of that late-Victorian energy and confidence in which Belfast shared with total enthusiasm. But its site had only become available because the City Fathers authorised the demolition of the quietly elegant White Linen Hall, which had been a symbol of Belfast's more thoughtful period of development in the 18th Century.

However, Belfast Corporation was only fulfilling the spirit of the times. And in such a busy city, there was always a strongly human dimension to everyday life. Thus the City Hall may have been on the grand scale, but it was nevertheless right at the heart of the city itself. Equally, while the gantries of the shipyard may have loomed overhead as they still do today, they do so near the houses of the workers in a manner which softens their sheer size. Admittedly this theme of giving great projects a human dimension seems to have been forgotten in the later design and location of the Government Building at Stormont east of the city. But back in the vibrant heart of Belfast, there is continuing entertainment and accessible interest in buildings as various as the Grand Opera House, St Anne's Cathedral, the Crown Liquor Saloon, Sinclair Seamen's Church, the Linenhall Library, and Smithfield Market, not to mention some of the impressive Victorian banking halls, while McHugh's pub on Queen's Square, and Tedford's Restaurant just round the corner on Donegall Quay, provide thoughtful reminders of the earlier restrained style.

In more modern times, aerospace manufacture has displaced many of the old smokestack industries in the forefront of the city's work patterns, and some of the energy of former times has been channelled into impressive urban regeneration along the River Lagan. Here, the flagship building is the Waterfront Hall, a large state-of-the-art concert venue which has won international praise. In the southern part of the city, Queen's University (founded 1845) is a beautifully balanced 1849 Lanyon building at the heart of a pleasant university district which includes the city's noted Lyric Theatre as well as the respected Ulster Museum & Art Gallery, while the University itself is particularly distinguished for its pioneering work in medicine and engineering.

Thus there's a buzz to Belfast which is reflected in its own cultural and warmly sociable life, which includes the innovative energy of its young chefs. Yet in some ways it is still has marked elements of a country town and port strongly rooted in land and sea. The hills of Antrim can be glimpsed from most streets, and the farmland of Down makes its presence felt. They are quickly reached by a somewhat ruthlessly implemented motorway system. So although Belfast may have a clearly defined character of its own, it is also very much part of the varied countryside around it.

Local Attractions and Information

Arts Theatre	Botanic Avenue 02890 316900
Belfast Garden Festival	Balmoral (June)
Belfast Zoo & Castle	Antrim Road 02890 776277
Grand Opera House	Great Victoria St 02890 241919
King's Hall (exhibitions, concerts)	Lisburn Road 02890 665225
Lyric Theatre	Ridgeway Street 02890 381081
Palm House Botanic Gardens	02890 324902
Pat's Bar	Prince's Dock (traditional music) 02890 744525
Tourist Information	02890 246609
Ulster Hall	Bedford Street 02890 323900
Ulster Museum	Stranmillis Road 02890 383000
Waterfront Hall	Laganside 02890 334455

Belfast ✳ — *Aldens*

229 Upper Newtownards Road, Belfast BT4 3JF
RESTAURANT Tel: 02890 650079 Fax: 02890 650032

A discreet public face belies the warmth and elegance of this contemporary restaurant - and it is greatly to proprietor Jonathan Davis's credit that he had the courage and foresight to introduce this shaft of bright light to an area until now bereft of good eating places. Head chef Cath Gradwell brings a raft of cosmopolitan experience to this unlikely spot (Roux restaurants, Kensington Place, 5th Floor at Harvey Nichols to name but three), showing in lively international menus that make the most of local and seasonal ingredients - and a recent dinner confirmed all our hopes. Menus change daily, but specialities that indicate the style include grilled squid with black bean dressing, grilled seabass with lemon aioli, chips & rocket salad.Local produce is used as much as possible and seafood, especially, is a major feature. Classic dishes like steamed mussels with white wine, parsley & garlic sit easily beside fashionable fare and it's good to see an ingredients like venison (probably from the Clandeboye Estate near Bangor) brought out of the casserole category and served as a rare grilled steak with bacon & garlic butter. There's also an interesting, well-priced wine list and excellent service from smartly-uniformed staff. **Seats** 70 No smoking area. Air conditioning. L 12-2.30 Mon-Fri, D 6-10 daily; Set L £12.50, Set D £14.50,; Sun L12-2 £15.95; à la carte also available. House wine from £11; sc discretionary. Toilets wheelchair accessible Children welcome. Closed 2 wks July and Public Hols. Amex, Diners, MasterCard, Visa.

Directions: On main Belfast-Newtownards road at Ballyhackamore

---

Belfast ✗ — *Ashoka*

363 Lisburn Road Belfast BT9 7EP
RESTAURANT Tel: 02890 660362 Fax: 02890 660228

This long-established Indian restaurant came into new ownership in late 1996 and since then it has undergone extensive refurbishment. Loyal customers will be pleased to know that head chef Ishtiaque Mohammed, who has been here since 1983, still rules the kitchen. Often described as a "popular" restaurant, Ashoka can put a different spin on the term, by listing an impressive array of celebrities it has entertained, so you never know who you might meet here. Billy Connolly, perhaps, or Lenny Henry, or Chris Patten.... Restaurant D only. Closed 12-13 Jul. Amex, MasterCard, Visa.

Belfast   *La Belle Epoque*

61 Dublin Road Belfast BT2 7HE

RESTAURANT   Tel: 02890 323244 Fax: 02890 203111

Since 1984 Alain Rousse's authentic French cooking has been giving Belfast diners a flavour
of old Paris. Set menus include "Le Petit Lunch" (Mon-Sat), which is terrific value and a
keenly priced set dinner, which offers a choice of three options within each course and is
augmented by an equally fairly priced à la carte.Children welcome before 9 pm. **Seats 84** L
12-5 Mon-Fri, D 5-11 Mon-Sat, Set L £5.92, Set D £15. A la carte available. House wine
£8. sc discretionary. Toilets wheelchair accessible. Closed 12 &13 Jul & Xmas. Amex, Diners,
MasterCard, Visa. **Directions:** On Dublin Road, 5 minutes walk from city centre.

Belfast ❊   *Benedict's of Belfast*

7-21 Bradbury Place Belfast BT7 IRQ

HOTEL   Tel: 02890 591999 Fax: 02890 591990 email: info@benedictshotel.co.uk

Very conveniently located - a wide range of attractions including the Botanic Gardens,
Queen's University, Queen's Film Theatre and Ulster Museum are within a few minutes
walk - this new hotel combines comfort and contemporary style with moderate
prices.ISDN lines. Parking arrangement with nearby carpark. Not suitable for children
after 9pm. No pets. **Rooms 32** (12 executive rooms, 2 for disabled) Lift.Wheelchair
accessible B&B £35pps, ss £25. Open all year. Amex, Diners, MasterCard, Visa.
Directions: City centre hotel situated in Bradbury Place – just off Shaftsbury Square – in
the heart of Belfast's "Golden Mile".

Belfast   *Café Altos*

Unit 6 Fountain Street Belfast 1

RESTAURANT   Tel: 02890 323087 email: cafealtos@hotmail.com

This buzzy, high-ceilinged daytime place in the city centre, near the City Hall is a sister
restaurant to Dieter Bergmann's Dublin establishment, Il Primo - and also the new
Belfast Il Primo due to open on Shaftsbury Square at the time of going to press. They
share some unusual qualities. Dieter, an importer of French and Italian wines, can be
relied on to offer some special vinous treats: in addition to an exceptional main list, any
wine under £40 a bottle is available by the glass. Il Primo, Dublin, was way ahead of the
current fashion for modern Italian food and prizes authenticity, so a visit to any of the
Bergmann restaurants is sure to be interesting. **Seats 70.** No smoking area; air
conditioning. L only, 12.30-4.30 (except private parties). [Il Primo open evenings only
5-11 daily). A la carte. MasterCard, Visa.

Belfast   *Café Society*

3 Donegall Square East Belfast 1

RESTAURANT   Tel: 02890 439525 Fax: 02890 233749

Handy to the main shopping area, the ground floor bistro is ideal for a quick bite during
the day and there are pavement tables for fine weather. The first floor restaurant
overlooks the City Hall and is popular for dinner and more leisurely lunches; business
lunch is treated seriously (special 2/3 course menu) and there's a separate room suitable
for private dining or small conferences, with projection and secretarial services available
Monday-Thursday. Lively international menus might include smoked haddock & potato
chowder with spiced harrisa, char-grilled sirloin beef with tapenade mash, mustard butter
& wild mushrooms and lovely desserts such as burnt orange crème brûlée. Good details
include home-baked bread, freshly brewed coffee and home-made truffles to finish. L£,
D££. MasterCard, Visa.

Belfast   *Cargoes*

613 Lisburn Road Belfast BT9 7GT

CAFÉ   Tel: 02890 665451

This is a special little place run by partners Radha Patterson and Mary Maw, who take a
lot of trouble sourcing fine produce for the delicatessen side of the business and apply
the same philosophy to the food served in the café. Modern European, Thai and Indian
influences work well together here; simple preparation and good seasonal ingredients
dictate menus - where you might find dishes like smokey bacon & potato soup, Moroccan
chicken with couscous, vegetarian dishes such as goats cheese & tarragon tart or wild

mushroom risotto. There are classic desserts like lemon tart or apple flan, and a range of stylish sandwiches. Children welcome. **Seats 30.** No smoking restaurant. Open 9 am-5 pm Mon-Sat, L 12-3. (Sun 9.30-4.30). A la carte; sc discretionary. Toilets wheelchair accessible. MasterCard, Visa.

Belfast ✵   *Conor Café Bar*

11A Stranmillis Road, Belfast.
CAFÉ   Tel: 02890 663266 Fax: 02890 200233

Just across the road from the Ulster Museum, this unusual high-ceilinged room is bright with natural light from a lantern roof and was originally the Conor William studio. The art theme is carried through to having original work always on show - there's a permanent exhibition of Neill Shawcross's work. Open for breakfast and brunch, through coffee, lunch, afternoon tea and eventually dinner, this is a casual place with a distinctive style - light wood booths along the walls and a long refectory-style table down the centre. Good coffee, home-baked scones, informal food such as warm chicken salad, hot paninis with mozzarella, modern European dishes including lots of pastas, comfort food (like fish & chips with mushy peas) and classic dishes such as moules mariniere and steak & Guinness pie. **Seats 45.** Open all day 9.30-11pm. A la carte. Licensed. Own parking. Closed 25 Dec. MasterCard, Visa. **Directions:** Opposite Ulster museum.

Belfast   *Crescent Townhouse & Metro Brasserie*

13 Lower Crescent Belfast BT7 1NR
HOTEL/RESTAURANT   Tel: 02890 323349 Fax: 02890 320646

This is an elegant building on the corner of Botanic Avenue, just a short stroll from the city centre,. The ground floor is taken up by the Metro Brasserie and Bar/Twelve, a stylish club-like bar with oak panelling and snugs, particularly lively and popular at night (necessitating 'greeters' for the entrance). The reception lounge is on the first floor. Bedrooms are furnished in country house style, with practical furniture, colourful fabrics and good tiled bathrooms. In addition, there are two luxury suites, decorated in a more period style with canopied beds. Breakfast is taken in the contemporary split-level Metro Brasserie, which is also open for lunch and dinner. Several wines by the glass. Street parking free from 6pm-8am, otherwise ticketed. **Rooms 11** (all en-suite) B&B £47.50pps, ss £27.50.Metro Brasserie **Seats 70** L 12-3 Mon-Sat, D 6-9.30 Mon-Thurs (6-10 Fri-Sat). Set D £25; early evening menu £9.95, 6-7 pm only. A la carte; sc discretionary. Closed 24-26 Dec. Amex, Diners, MasterCard, Visa. **Directions:** On corner of Botanic Avenue, in university area

---

Belfast [PUB★]   *Crown Liquor Saloon*

46 Great Victoria Street Belfast BT2 7BA
PUB   Tel: 02890 279901   Fax: 02890 279902

Belfast's most famous pub, The Crown Liquor Saloon, was perhaps the greatest of all the Victorian gin palaces which once flourished in Britain's industrial cities. Remarkably, considering its central location close to the Europa Hotel, it has survived The Troubles virtually unscathed. Although now owned by the National Trust (and run by Bass Taverns) the Crown is far from being a museum piece and attracts a wide clientele of locals and visitors. A visit to one of its famous snugs for a pint and half a dozen oysters served on crushed ice, or a bowl of Irish Stew, is a must. The upstairs section, Flannigans, is built with original timbers from the SS Britannic, sister ship to the Titanic. Bar food served Mon-Sat 12-3. MasterCard, Visa. **Directions:** City centre, opposite Europa Hotel

---

Belfast ⛫   *Culloden Hotel*

Bangor Road Holywood BT18 0EX
Tel: 02890 425223 Fax: 02890 426777
HOTEL   email: res.cull@hastingshotels.com

Hasting Hotels' flagship property, on the main Belfast to Bangor road, is set in 12 acres of beautifully secluded gardens and woodland overlooking Belfast Lough and the County Antrim coastline. The building was originally the official palace for the Bishops of Down, and is a fine example of 19th-century Scottish Baronial architecture – though we do wonder what the bishops would have made of the glass cabinet containing yellow plastic ducks signed by visiting dignitaries. The elegant and luxurious surroundings include fine paintings, antiques, chandeliers, plasterwork ceilings, stained glass windows and an imposing staircase. The spacious bedrooms (most in a side extension, including seven suites and the Presidential Suite with the best views) are lavishly furnished and decorated and offer the usual facilities, plus additional extras such as a bowl of fruit and biscuits. Bathrobes and fine toiletries feature in the splendidly equipped bathrooms. The hotel also has a fine health club, the 'Cultra Inn' (an informal bar and restaurant in the grounds), and an association with The Royal Belfast Golf Club, four minutes away by car (book the complimentary hospitality limousine). Conference/banqueting (400/400) Leisure centre. Hairdresser. Tennis, snooker, walking, pitch & putt, garden. Ample parking. Wheelchair accessible/Lift.Children welcome (cots available). No pets. **Rooms 80** (10 suites, 70 executive rooms, 22 no-smoking) B&B £80pps, ss £47. Open all year. Amex, Diners, MasterCard, Visa. **Directions:** 6 miles from Belfast city centre on A2 towards Bangor

Belfast ★   *Restaurant at Deanes*

38-40 Howard Street Belfast

RESTAURANT/BRASSERIE   Tel: 02890 560000 Fax: 02890 560001

Chef-proprietor Michael Deane offers seriously good cooking in exceedingly grand and elegant surroundings. The main restaurant is on the first floor (downstairs there is a more informal brasserie), and is almost club-like, with various hues of brown and subdued lighting. The dining area is small, the table settings elegant, and there is an open kitchen in which the chefs can be observed at work. Supremely professional staff are well attired and polite, enhancing the atmosphere of fine and elegant dining. The style and presentation of cooking is modern, with prime ingredients given influences from around the world; Michael Deane's special talent for "fusion food" is given full rein in exciting, wide-ranging menus that represent good value for a restaurant of this class. Menus are designed to give reasonable flexibility - there's a very fine dinner menu, which can be two- or three-course, also a separate vegetarian menu and an eight-course tasting selection, the Menu Prestige. Michael Deane is an exceptionally talented chef, very creative, extraordinarily precise and, as is obvious from watching them at work in the open kitchen strong on teamwork. Dishes are luxurious and complex, but the elements within each dish retain their special character and every dish has a special harmony. He is especially interesting when working with several variations of an ingredient to create a single dish - as in an impresssive starter 'Study of Cod' (brandade, terrine & carpaccio) and, especially, a stunning dessert (apple caramel, apple sorbet & jus of Bramley), which has a wonderfully restrained beauty and, despite artistic presentation, is utterly natural. This fine dining at its best and bound to be a memorable experience. The extensive wine list is quite grand and particularly impressive are the temperature-controlled wine cabinets. Deane's was our 1999 Restaurant of the Year. **Seats 40.** Air conditioning. D 7-9.30 daily, Set D £33.50. Menu Prestige £55. Closed Sun & Mon. House wine from £12.95; sc discretionary (10% added to bills of 6+). Closed 24-26 Dec, 1 week July, Jan 1. Amex, MasterCard, Visa

*Brasserie at Deane's, on the ground floor, is open Monday-Saturday, L 12.00-2.45 (no reservations), D 5-10.45. Head chef Raymond McArdle's "Thai-influenced modern British" menu includes vegetarian dishes. There's a great buzz, cooking is stylish and prices reasonable. Closed Sun, Dec 24-26, Jul 12/13, 1 Jan.

Directions: Rear of Belfast City Hall

Belfast   *Dukes Hotel*

65/67 University Street Belfast BT7 1HL

HOTEL   Tel: 02890 236666   Fax: 02890 237177

First opened in 1990, within an imposing Victorian building, the hotel is modern inside with an interesting waterfall descending down one wall, floor by floor, into a rock pool in the foyer. This is flanked on either side by a restaurant/mezzanine bar and the intriguingly-shaped Dukes Bar, a popular rendezvous for locals. Double-glazed bedrooms are spacious with practical furniture and good fabrics, and in addition to the usual facilities there's an ironing board and iron hidden in the wardrobe. Conference/banqueting (150/150) secretarial services. Wheelchair accessible. Street parking (ticketed 8am-6pm). Mini-gym; sauna. Children (Under 12s free in parents' room; cots available). Pets by arrangement. **Rooms 21** (all en-suite) B&B £50pps, ss £35. Amex, Diners, MasterCard, Visa. **Directions:** City centre adjacent to Queens University.

Belfast

Europa Hotel

Great Victoria Street Belfast BT2 7AP
HOTEL   Tel: 02890 327000 Fax: 02890 327800

Belfast's tall, central landmark hotel has undergone many changes since it first opened in the '70s. Now owned by Hastings Hotels, it has been renovated and refurbished to a high standard, with a facade that is particularly striking when illuminated at night. Off the entrance foyer, with its tall columns, is the all-day brasserie (6am-midnight) and the lobby bar, featuring Saturday afternoon jazz and other live musical entertainment. Upstairs on the first floor you'll find the Gallery lounge (afternoon teas served here to the accompaniment of a pianist) and a cocktail bar with circular marble-topped counter. Attractive and practical bedrooms offer the usual up-to-date facilities, but perhaps the hotel's greatest assets are the function suites, ranging from the Grand Ballroom to the twelfth floor Edinburgh Suite with its panoramic views of the city. Nearby parking (special rates apply) can be added to your account. Staff are excellent (porters offer valet parking), and standards of housekeeping and maintenance very good. Children welcome (under 14s free in parents' room; cots available).Conference/banqueting (750/600); video-conferencing; business centre; secretarial services. Wheelchair accessible/Lift Pets by arrangement **Rooms 184** (5 suites, 89 executive rooms, 42 no-smoking, 2 for disabled). Lift. B&B £95pps. Closed 24-26 Dec. Amex, Diners, MasterCard, Visa. **Directions:** City Centre, opposite Crown Liquor Saloon.

Belfastx ❋ 🏛

Hilton Belfast

4 Lanyon Place, Belfast BT1 3LP
HOTEL   Tel: 02890 277000 Fax: 02890 277277

Occupying a prominent position on a rise beside the Waterfront hall, the interior of this landmark hotel turns out to be even more impressive than anticipated. The scale is grand, the style throughout is of contemporary clean-lined elegance - the best of modern materials have been used and the colour palette selected is delicious - and, best of all, it makes the best possible use of its superb waterside site, with the Sonoma Restaurant and several suites commanding exceptional views. Outstanding conference and business facilities include the state-of-the-art Hilton Meeting 2000 service tailored to individual requirements and three executive floors with a Clubroom. All rooms have air-conditioning, satellite TV, in-room movies, no-stop check out in addition to the usual facilities. Recreational facilities are also excellent.The absence of private parking could be a problem, as the multi-storey carpark next door is not owned by the hotel. Conference/banqueting (450/250); secretarial services; business centre; video conferencing; ISDN lines. Leisure centre; indoor swimming pool. Arrangement with nearby carpark.Wheelchair access. Children welcome (under 12s free in parents' room; cots available). No pets. **Rooms 195** (13 suites, 7 mini-suites, 38 executive rooms, 67 no-smoking,10 for disabled). Lift B&B £103.50pps, ss £30. Closed 24-26 Dec. MasterCard, Visa. **Directions:** Belfast city centre, beside Waterfont Hall.

Belfast ☆

Holiday Inn Express

106 University Street Belfast BT7 1HP
HOTEL   Tel/Fax: 02890 311910

At this environmentally-friendly hotel long-term guests are asked if they want their bed linen – duvets here – and towels changed daily, in order to save energy and water resources and reduce detergent pollution. Good-size bedrooms offer plenty of workspace, multi-channel satellite TV (including payable in-house movies and radio) and compact bathrooms (most with shower). A modest continental breakfast is included in the rate. Conference/banqueting 345/260. Business centre. Video-conferencing & secretarial services by arrangment. Secure parking to the rear. Beer garden. No pets. **Rooms 114** (100 shower only, 76 no-smoking, 6 for disabled) B&B £64.95pps. Max 2 guests per room. Open all year. Amex, Diners, MasterCard, Visa. **Directions:** From Shaftesbury Square take Botanic avenue, turn left onto University Street.

Belfast ✗

Jurys Belfast Inn

Fisherwick Place Great Victoria Street Belfast BT2 7AP
HOTEL   Tel: 02890 533500 Fax: 02890 533511 email: bookings@jurys.com

Located in the heart of the city, close to the Grand Opera House and City Hall and just a couple of minutes walk from the major shopping areas of Donegall Place and the Castlecourt Centre, Jurys Belfast Inn opened in 1997, setting new standards for the city's budget accommodation. The high standards and excellent value of all Jurys Inns applies here too: all rooms are en-suite (with bath and shower) and spacious enough to accommodate two adults and two children (or three adults) at a fixed price. Rooms are well-designed and furnished to a high standard, with outstanding amenities for a hotel in the budget class. Acc£. Closed 24-25 Dec. Amex, Diners, MasterCard, Visa.

Belfast — Manor House Restaurant

RESTAURANT

43/47 Donegall Pass Belfast BT7 1DQ
Tel/Fax: 02890 238755

Easily found just off Shaftesbury Square, this well-established Cantonese restaurant has been in the Wong family since 1982, with expansion and renovation in 1989. In common with many other Chinese restaurants the menu is long, but Joyce Wong's menu offers more unusual choices. in addition to the many well-known popular dishes. There is, for example, a wide range of soups and specialities include Cantonese-style crispy chicken and seafood dishes like steamed whole seafish with ginger and scallions. **Seats 80** (private room, 35) L 12-2.30 Mon-Fri, D 5-11 daily, Set L £5.50, Set D £13-17, gourmet D £19, early evening menu £12.95 (5-7 pm only). à la carte available. House wine £9. Air conditioning. sc discretionary. Children welcome. Parking in nearby carpark. Closed 25-26 Dec. MasterCard, Visa. **Directions:** Off Shaftesbury Square

Belfast — The McCausland Hotel

HOTEL/RESTAURANT

34–38 Victoria Street Belfast BT1 3GH
Tel: 02890 220200 Fax: 02890 220220
email: info@mccauslandhotel

Well-located close to the Waterfront Hall, this sister establishment to The Hibernian Hotel in Dublin is in a magnificent landmark building designed by William Hastings in the 1850s in Italianate style, with an ornate four storey facade (with carvings depicting the five continents). It looks particularly impressive when floodlit at night. Classic contemporary design and high quality materials combine to create an exclusive venue for business and leisure guests. Individually appointed bedrooms - decorated in a contemporary country house style, all with some items of antique furniture - include wheelchair-friendly and lady executive rooms (with thoughtful little emergency overnight kits in the bathroom for unplanned visits). Rooms also have fax/modem points and entertainment systems which include TV/CD/radio and VCR. Conference/banqueting (60/75); business centre; secretarial services. Children welcome (under 2s free in parents' room; cots available). No pets. **Rooms 60** (9 mini-suites, 3 for disabled) Lift. B&B £150 room rate. Parking in nearby carpark (Mon-Sat). Closed 24-27 Dec. Amex, Diners, MasterCard, Visa. **Merchants Restaurant:** The executive chef at this appealing restaurant is Eamonn O'Cathain, well-known for various interesting enterprises including Shay Beano restaurant in Dublin and, currently, his parallel career as a broadcaster. Food is lively and colourful in the contemporary style - roast pave of cod with a bloody mary & avocado salsa, chorizo crisps & saffron rice is typical. Children welcome before 8 pm. **Seats 60.** No smoking area; air conditioning. L 12-2.15 Tues-Fri, D 7-9.45 daily. Set L £17.50, Set D £30, à la carte available. House wine £10.50; sc discretionary. Toilets wheelchair accessible. Closed 24-27 Dec. & Bank Hols for L. Also Cafe Marco Polo, an informal cafe-bar at the front of the hotel. **Seats 60** Continental style fare daily, 12 noon-10 pm. **Directions:** On Victoria Street in central Belfast

Belfast ✳ — McHugh's

PUB/RESTAURANT

29-31 Queen's Square, Belfast BT1
Tel: 02890 247830 Fax: 02890 249842

This remarkable pub is in one of Belfast's few remaining eighteenth century buildings. It has recently been extensively and caringly renovated allowing the original bar (which has many interesting maps, photographs and other memorabilia of old Belfast) to retain its character while blending in a new cafe-bar and two restaurants (one in the basement, the other upstairs). Good food includes a lunchtime carvery/salad bar, evening meals and light food - soup, sandwiches etc - through the day. **Seats 80** (private room, 35) Air conditioning. L 12-3 daily, D 5-10.30 daily, all à la carte. Toilets wheelchair accessible. Parking in nearby carpark. Closed Xmas and 12 Jul. Diners, MasterCard, Visa. **Directions:** Behind the Albert Clock in central Belfast

Belfast ✗   *The Morning Star*

17-19 Pottinger's Entry Belfast BT1 4DT
PUB   Tel: 02890 235986 Fax: 02890 438696

Situated in a laneway in the middle of the city, The Morning Star is a listed building and has many interesting features. It's been trading as a public house since about 1840 (although it was mentioned even earlier in the Belfast Newsletter of 1810 as a terminal for the Belfast to Dublin mail coach). The Morning Star always had a good name for food and, when Corinne and Seamus McAlister took over the business in 1989, they wanted to build on that. With due respect for the special character of the pub, the McAlisters have made changes that now allow an impressive range of menus through the day, beginning with breakfast at 9.30, then Morning Star 'Morning Tea' with a full range of teas and coffees, on to lunch and so on. Between them, an astonishing range of food is served, including traditional specialities like Irish stew, champ and sausage, local Strangford mussels, roast Antrim pork and aged Northern Ireland beef (which is a particular source of pride), as well as many universal pub dishes. Daily chef's specials, blackboard specials, there seems no end to the choices offered each day. There's also a restaurant upstairs where more ambitious meals are served, including themed dinners and special wine evenings. On a recent visit the whole building, and especially the downstairs bar, seemed disappointingly scruffy but this can sometimes happen in any pub and the standard of care and maintenance at The Morning Star is usually high. Bar food daily. Amex, MasterCard, Visa.

Belfast   *Nick's Warehouse*

35/39 Hill Street Belfast BT1 2LB
RESTAURANT   Tel: 02890 439690 Fax: 02890 230514

Nick's Warehouse is a clever conversion on two floors, with particularly interesting lighting and efficient aluminium duct air-conditioning. It's a lively spot, notable for attentive, friendly service and excellent food, in both the wine bar and the restaurant. Lively contemporary menus offer a wide range of dishes which are consistently interesting and include some unusual items - rare breed pork, for example (with a Thai coconut curry sauce perhaps). Menus are also considerately marked with symbols indicating dishes containing nuts/oils and also seafood. The cheese selection is interesting too - you can choose between house cheeses (Brie, Caerphilly & Shropshire Blue) or Irish cheeses (Ardrahan, Cashel Blue & St Brendan). Wide choice of teas of coffees and an informative, well-priced wine list that makes good reading - and includes nine house wines under a tenner. Children welcome before 9 pm. **Seats 135** downstairs, 45 upstairs, (private room, 45) Air conditioning. L 12-3 Mon-Fri, D 6-9.30 Tue-Sat, all à la carte. House wines from £8.95. Toilets wheelchair accessible. Closed 25-26 Dec, Easter Mon/Tues, 12-13 July. Amex, Diners, MasterCard, Visa. **Directions:** Behind St.Anne's Cathedral, off High Street.

Belfast   *Posthouse Belfast*

300 Kingsway, Dunmurry, Belfast BT17 9ES
HOTEL   Tel: 02890 612101 Fax: 02890 626546

Situated in 14 acres of grounds on the edge of Belfast city, this hotel will operate until the end of April 2000, when business is transferring to the new city centre hotel on Ormeau Avenue. The new hotel will offer conveniently located luxurious accommodation, with health and leisure facilities. Conference/banqueting (400/350). Business centre; secretarial services. Own parking. Children welcome (under 13s free in parents' room; cots available). Wheelchair accessible. No pets. **Rooms 82** (45 no-smoking).Lift B&B £95 room rate. Amex, Diners, MasterCard, Visa. **Directions:** From M1, take junction 3 for Dunmurry, from Belfast hotel is on left hand side just through village.

Belfast   *Roscoff*

7 Lesley House Shaftesbury Square Belfast BT2 7DB
RESTAURANT   Tel: 02890 331532 Fax: 02890 312093

Paul and Jeanne Rankin's famous restaurant is about to close as we go to press. A major makeover is expected, including a change of name. The whole enterprise will emerge in a totally different style but it will be in the same premises. Amex, Diners, MasterCard, Visa.

Belfast   *Hastings Stormont Hotel*

Upper Newtownards Road Belfast BT4 3LP
Tel: 02890 355500 Fax: 02890 748152
HOTEL   email: conf.stor@hastingshotels.com

Four miles east of the city centre, the hotel is directly opposite the imposing gates leading to Stormont Castle and Parliament Buildings. There's a huge entrance lounge, with stairs up to a more intimate mezzanine area overlooking the castle grounds. The main restaurant and informal modern bistro are pleasantly located. Spacious, practical bedrooms have good worktops and offer the usual facilities; several rooms are designated for female executives. The hotel also has eight self-catering apartments with their own car parking area, featuring a twin bedroom, lounge and kitchen/dinette, available for short stays or long periods. The self-contained Confex Centre, comprising ten trade rooms, complements the function suites in the main building. Own parking. Wheelchair accessible/Lift. No pets. **Rooms 109** (2 suites, 34 executive rooms, 23 no-smoking, 1 for disabled) Lift. B&B £85pps, ss £15. Closed 25 Dec. Amex, Diners, MasterCard, Visa. **Directions:** 4 miles east of Belfast city centre, directly oposite Stormont Parliament Buildings.

Belfast   *Sun Kee Restaurant*

38 Donegall Pass, Belfast BT7 1BS
RESTAURANT   Tel: 02890 312016

Edmund Lau's little place just off Shaftesbury Square has earned widespread recognition as the city's most authentic Chinese restaurant. What you get here is a combination of the classic Chinese dishes which are already familiar - but created in uncompromising Chinse style, without the usual "blanding down" typical of most oriental restaurants. They also offer more unusual dishes, which offer a genuine challenge to the jaded western palate, be prepared to be adventurous It is unlicensed (but you may bring your own). The main difficulty is getting a reservation, as its popularity is matched only by its tiny size. Children welcome. **Seats 30.** Air conditioning. D 5-11 daily, all à la carte. Closed mid-Jul – mid-Aug. No credit cards. **Directions:** Beside Police Station.

Belfast ❋   *Tedfords Restaurant*

5 Donegall Quay, Belfast BT1 3EF
RESTAURANT   Tel: 02890 434000 Fax: 02890 248889

Sailing folk may remember Tedfords as a ships chandlers - you can almost smell the sisal even now, especially as there are reminders a-plenty of this listed building's venerable maritime past.The informal ground floor restaurant, called The Chart Room for reasons which will be obvious when you visit, is pleasantly arranged on two levels with a railing around the upper one, which makes the small area seem more spacious and allows staff to whisk easily around the tables without disturbing diners too much. Although not exclusively a fish restaurant there's an appropriate emphasis on things from the sea: a random list of one day's offerings includes crab, eel, Glenarm salmon, smoke cod, langoustine, brill, halibut, lemon sole. If you want a simple example of how good head chef Paul Dorothy's seafood cooking is, just try the Mediterranean fish soup with croutons and rouille; soups are always a good test and this one was a good as you'll get. However, should you prefer non-fishy fare, you'll find plenty of other temptations like foie gras of duck with toasted brioche, roulade of free range corn fed chicken lightly stuffed and wrappped in a fresh thyme flavoured pancake or entrecote bearnaise (Aberdeen Angus beef) and there's always a vegetarian dish of the day. Informative, fairly priced wine list. *The upstairs Dining Room is totally different - cool and elegant in shades of white, cream and sand. Open for dinner only, Fri & Sat. Reservations essential. **Seats 46** (private room, 14) No smoking area.L 12.30-3 Mon-Fri, D 6-10.30 Mon-Sat, Set L £9.75, Set D £19.25-24.95. à la carte available. House wine £12; sc discretionary. Toilets wheelchair accessible. Children welcome. Parking in multi-storey carpark next door. Closed Sun, Sat L, 25 Dec. MasterCard, Visa. **Directions:** Overlooking river, near Waterfront Hall.

Belfast ❋   *Travelodge*

15 Brunswick Street Belfast BT2 7GE
HOTEL   Tel 02890 333555

Comfortable, inexpensive city centre accommodation, close to City Hall.Payment on arrival. Room Rate £49.95. Amex, Diners, MasterCard, Visa.

Belfast ❋ ✗   *Waterfront Hall*
                                                    2 Lanyon Place BT1
CAFE/RESTAURANT   Tel: 02890 244966

Pleasant, brasserie-style first floor restaurant serving wholesome all-day food, including breakfast and afternoon tea, with more substantial lunch and dinner menus also available. Contemporary cooking. Meals 10am-9pm, daily.

Belfast   *Wellington Park Hotel*
                                                    21 Malone Road Belfast BT9 6RU
HOTEL   Tel: 02890 381111 Fax: 02890 665410

Situated close to the University, just five minutes from the city centre, this hotel is quite a Belfast institution and has been greatly improved by the recent addition of twenty-five new bedrooms and a dedicated business centre with its own secure parking (the main conference facilities remain on the first floor of the redesigned building). Individual guests need not worry about being overrun by conference delegates, since one of the bars is exclusively for their use. The spacious foyer and public areas are comfortably furnished, as are the refurbished bedrooms, featuring the usual facilities, some with modem points and voice-mail. Guests have free use of Queen's University sports centre, a few minutes from the hotel. The Dunadry Hotel & Country Club, a fifteen minute drive from the city, is in the same ownership. Conference (400);secretarial services. Business centre. Own parking. Wheelchair accessible. Children welcome (under 4s free in parents' room; cots available). No pets. **Rooms 75** (3 suites). Lift. B&B £47.50pps, ss £30. Closed 24-26 Dec. Amex, Diners, MasterCard, Visa. **Directions:** From Queen's University, head south up Malone Road – hotel is on right hand side.

ANTRIM

The Antrim Coast may be timeless in its beauty, but 2000 sees its picturesque little ports enjoying restoration and development at places as various as Ballycastle, Glenarm and Carrickfergus. With its boundaries naturally defined by the sea, the River Bann, Lough Neagh and the River Lagan, County Antrim has always had a strong sense of its own clearcut geographical identity. This is further emphasised by the extensive uplands of the Antrim Plateau, wonderful for the sense of space with the moorland rising to heights such as Trostan (551m) and the distinctive Slemish (438m), famed for its association with St Patrick. The plateau eases down to fertile valleys and bustling inland towns such as Ballymena, Antrim and Ballymoney, while the coastal towns ring the changes between the traditional resort of Portrush in the far north, the ferryport of Larne in the east, and historic Carrickfergus with its well-preserved Norman castle overlooking a harbour complex which today places its emphasis on recreation. In the spectacularly beautiful northeast of the county, the most rugged heights of the Plateau are softened by the nine Glens of Antrim, havens of beauty descending gently from the moorland down through small farms to hospitable villages clustered at the shoreline and connected by the renowned Antrim Coast Road. Between these sheltered bays at the foot of the Glens, the sea cliffs of the headlands soar with remarkable rock formations which, on the North Coast, provide the setting for the Carrick-a-Rede rope bridge and the Giant's Causeway. From the charming town of Ballycastle, Northern Ireland's only inhabited offshore island of Rathlin is within easy reach by ferry, a mecca for ornithologists and perfect for days away from the pressures of mainstream life.

Local Attractions and Information

Annaghmore	Ardress (Stapleton decor) 02838 851236
Antrim	Castle Gardens 02894 428000
Bushmills	World's Oldest Distillery
Carrickfergus Castle	02893 351273
Giant's Causeway Centre	028207 31855
Moy, Dungannon	The Argory ("time capsule") 02877 84753
Lisburn	Irish Linen Centre/Lisburn Museum 02891 663377
Portrush	Dunluce Castle 028207 31206

Ballycastle ✗   *House of McDonnell*

71 Castle Street Ballycastle Co Antrim BT64 6AS

PUB   Tel: 028207 62586

The House of McDonnell has been in the caring hands of Tom and Eileen O'Neill since 1979 and in Tom's mother's family for generations before that – they can even tell you not just the year, but the month the pub first opened (April 1766). Tom and Eileen delight in sharing the history of their long, narrow bar with its tiled floor and mahogany bar (which was once a traditional grocery-bar and is now a listed building). The only change in the last hundred years or so, says Tom, has been a toilet block "but outside the premises you understand". Music is important too – they have a good traditional music session every Friday and love to see musicians coming along and joining in. Open Mon-Thurs eves, Fri/Sat & Sun 12pm & 1pm respectively

---

Ballycastle ✳   *Number 10*

90 North Street Ballycastle Co Antrim BT54 6BE

RESTAURANT   Tel: 02820 7 68110

Proprietor-chef John McQuaide's dashing contemporary restaurant on the harbourfront is a great asset to Ballycastle - and very handy to the new marina. You can look forward to modern international cooking with a healthy emphasis on local seafood (as in a starter of fresh crab and potato cakes with tomato sweet & sour sauce with a light leaf salad moistened with walnut oil), but also offering a good choice of red meat and poultry main courses and some imaginative vegetarian options. Tempting desserts, wide-ranging, reasonably priced wine list.**Seats 50** D Tue-Sun 6-10, L12.30-2.30 Sun only, Set Sun L £12, à la carte available, house wine £8.45. no smoking area. sc discretionary . Unsuitable for children. Parking. Closed 15 Jan-12 Feb, (Rest.closed Mon).MasterCard, Visa. **Directions:** On the seafront.

Ballymena ˣ | *Adair Arms Hotel*

Ballymoney Road Ballymena Co Antrim BT43 4BS
HOTEL   Tel: 02825 6 53674

Located in the centre of Ballymena town, this attractive creeper-covered hotel has been owned and managed by the McLarnon family since 1995. Very much the centre of local activities – the bar and lounge make handy meeting places, and there are good conference and banqueting facilities – it's also a popular base for visitors touring the Glens of Antrim and the coastal beauty spots. Bedrooms are not especially big, but they are comfortably furnished and well-maintained, with all the usual amenities. Acc££ Amex, Diners, MasterCard, Visa.

Ballygally ✳ | *Ballygally Castle Hotel*

274 Coast Road Ballygally Co Antrim BT40 2QZ
HOTEL   Tel: 028 2858 3212 Fax: 028 2858 3681 e-mail: res.bgc@hastingshotels.com

This coastal hotel really has got a (very) old castle at the heart of it - and they've even got a ghost. (You can visit her room at the top of the castle).The whole thing is quite unlike any of the other Hastings hotels, although investment is now going into upgrading accommodation and public areas. At the moment rooms vary quite considerably but all are comfortable, some are quite romantic and the hotel has character. The beach is just a stone's throw away, across the road. Conference/banqueting (200/150) Children (Under 12s free in parents' room (£5 extra for breakfast); cots available). Wheelchair accessible. **Rooms 31** (1 suites, 1 mini-suite,all en-suite, 8 executive rooms, 6 shower only) B&B £38pps, ss £14. **Seats 50** (private room, 36) Toilets wheelchair accessible. no sc. Children welcome. Parking. Open all year. Amex, Diners, MasterCard, Visa. **Directions:** Situated on the coast road between Larne and Glenarm.

Ballygally ✳ | *Lynden Heights Restaurant*

971 Drumnagreagh Rd Ballygally Larne Co Antrim BT40 2RR
RESTAURANT   Tel: 02828 583560

On a clear day this restaurant high up above the coast road has the most amazing views - and the dining room is in a conservatory, to make the most of it. There's a cosy bar, where orders are taken by friendly, neatly uniformed waiting staff. A recent Sunday lunch visit confirmed local recommendations: the menu was more interesting than that ultra-traditional meal implies - and both food and service were spot on.Well-balanced evening menus offer a wide choice in a fairly classic style given the occasional contemporary twist; half roast crispy duckling with tangy plum & blackcurrant liqueur is typical. Children welcome Parking. **Seats 60** D 6-9.15 Wed-Sun, Set D £14.95, à la carte available. L12-2 Sun only, Set Sun L £12.95; sc discretionary. Toilets wheelchair accessible. Closed Mon & Tues. Amex, MasterCard, Visa. **Directions:** Situated between Larne and Glenarm- signed off the coast road.

Ballymena 🏛 | *Galgorm Manor Hotel*

136 Fenaghy Road Ballymena Co Antrim BT42 1EA
Tel: 02825 881001 Fax: 02825 880080
HOTEL/RESTAURANT   email: mail@galgorm.com

Set amidst beautiful scenery, with the River Maine running through the grounds, this converted gentleman's residence was completely refurbished before opening under the present management in 1993 and it is now one of Ireland's leading country house hotels. Approaching through well-tended parkland, one passes the separate banqueting and conference facilities to arrive at the front door of the original house, (which is a mere 100 yards from the river). An impressive reception area with antiques and a welcoming log fire sets the tone of the hotel, which is quite grand but also friendly and relaxed. Day rooms include an elegant drawing room and a traditional bar, as well as the more informal Ghillies Bar in characterful converted buildings at the back of the hotel (where light meals are also served). Accommodation includes three suites; two rooms have four-posters. All rooms are very comfortably furnished with good bathrooms, and most have views over the river. The latest phase of development will add 48 new bedrooms, a new conference suite and a leisure centre with swimming pool, jacuzzi and fitness suite.Conference/banqueting (500/450) golf (9/18), fishing, horse-riding,walking & garden. Wheelchair accessible. **Rooms 24** (3 suites, all en-suite, 4 executive rooms,8 for disabled) B&B £60pps, ss £39. Closed 24-26 Dec Amex, Diners, MasterCard, Visa

Restaurant: Galgorm Manor has had a good reputation for its food since opening. Head chef Jean-Yves Annino (who joined the hotel in February 1999) offers table d'hôte menus for lunch and dinner, with an emphasis on local produce. Menus are changed monthly and always include vegetarian dishes. The panelled Board Room has an antique dining table seating 12, for private parties. **Seats 73** (private room, 16) L 12-2.30 daily (Sun 12-2) D 7-9.30 daily (6-8.30 Sun), Set Sun L £14.95 Set D £25.50, house wine £14; sc discretionary. Toilets wheelchair accessible Children welcome Parking **Directions:** From the Galgorm roundabout, take the 3rd exit for Cullybackey (Feneghy road). About 2 miles, on the left.

Bushmills   *Bushmills Inn*

9 Dunluce rd. Bushmills Co Antrim BT57 8QG
Tel: 028 207 32339 Fax: 028 207 32048
HOTEL/RESTAURANT   e-mail: info@bushmills-inn.com

Only a couple of miles from the Giant's Causeway, Bushmills is home to the world's oldest distillery – a tour of the immaculately maintained distillery is highly recommended. The Bushmills Inn is one of Ireland's best-loved hotels. It has grown since its establishment as a 19th-century coaching inn, but its development under the current ownership – including complete restoration before re-opening in 1987 – has been thoughtful. The latest addition, a completely new wing (with 22 bedrooms, a conference centre, new kitchen and staff facilities, car park and an additional entrance) was so skilfully done that it is hard to work out where the old ends and the new begins. Inside, it's the same story: all the features which made the old Inn special have been carried through and blended with new amenities. The tone is set by the turf fire and country seating in the hall and public rooms – bars, the famous circular library, the restaurant, even the Pine Room conference room – carry on the same theme. Bedrooms are individually furnished in a comfortable cottage style and even have "antiqued" bathrooms – but it's all very well done and avoids a theme park feel. Conferences are held in an oak-beamed loft. Small conferences (50). Wheelchair accessible. Garden.Fishing. Children welcome. Pets permitted by arrangement. **Rooms 32** (1 suites, all en-suite, 7 shower only, 1 for disabled) B&B £49pps, ss £29. Open all year. Amex, MasterCard, Visa. Restaurant **Seats 120** (private room, 50) D 7-9.30 daily (Sun 6-9), L12-6 Sun only, Set D from £19, house wine £9.85;.sc discretionary . Toilets wheelchair accessible. **Directions:** On the A2-Antrim coast road, in Bushmills village.

Carnlough   *Londonderry Arms Hotel*

20 Harbour Road Carnlough Co Antrim BT44 0EU
HOTEL   Tel: 02828 885255 Fax: 02828 885263 email: ida@glensofantrim.com

Carnlough, with its charming little harbour and genuinely old-fashioned atmosphere (they still sell things like candyfloss in the little shops) is one of the most delightful places in Northern Ireland – and, to many people, the Londonderry Arms Hotel is Carnlough. Built by the Marchioness of Londonderry in 1848 as a coaching inn, it was inherited by her great grandson, Sir Winston Churchill, in 1921. Since 1948 it has been in the caring hands of the O'Neill family. The original building and interior remain intact, giving the hotel great character. Guests can enjoy good home-made bar meals or afternoon tea. Bedrooms, which are all en-suite and include 14 recently added at the back of the hotel, are comfortable and well-furnished in keeping with the character of the building. Many of the older rooms have sea views. Conferences (120) Parking. Wheelchair accessible. Children under 4 free in parents' room; cots available. Pets permitted by arrangement. **Rooms 35** (all en-suite, 2 for disabled). Lift B&B £40pps, ss £8. Closed 25 Dec. Amex, Diners, MasterCard, Visa. **Restaurant:** Well-known chef Donal Keane has recently joined the hotel, so the style of cooking has moved up serveral notches from the good, unpretentious fare that the hotel has been known for in the past. Local ingredients – wild salmon , crab, lobster and mountain lamb – will still feature, but the style is now contemporary international cooking, with an emphasis on seafood. Typical starters, for example, are tempura of prawn, panfried crab cake with avocado guacomole, crème fraîche & sweet potato crisps - but it's not all seafood, as you could equally begin with confit of duck and follow with a main course of char-grilled beef fillet on Chinese greens with beetroot, pesto & saute potatoes. Children welcome. 7-9 D daily (Sun to 8.30). L Sun only, 12.30-3. No sc. * Barfood served daily. **Directions:** On the A2-Antrim coast road.

Carnlough ✗

The Waterfall

1 High Street Carnlough Co Antrim BT44 0EU

PUB   *No phone*

One row back from the harbour, this friendly pub has a welcoming atmosphere. Although much of the work has been done more recently than it might appear, its red tiled floor and low beamed ceiling are authentic enough, and both the fireplace and the bar itself are made of reclaimed bricks from an old mill across the road. Behind, there's a cosy lounge bar with a stained glass window, decorative plates and another brick fireplace. All very cosy and relaxed. No credit cards.

Carrickfergus ✗

Quality Hotel

75 Belfast Road Carrickfergus Co Antrim BT38 8PH

HOTEL   Tel: 02893 364556 Fax: 02893 351620

The opening of the Quality Hotel in 1997 added a much needed boost to accommodation in this area – and at prices which are far from outrageous. Conveniently located to Belfast airport (10 miles) and the scenic attractions of the Antrim coast, the hotel makes a good base for business and leisure visitors. It has good conference facilities (600), meeting rooms (max 60) and in-room amenities (desk, fax/modem line) for business guests. Bedrooms include three suitable for disabled guests, two suites, two junior suites and 20 non-smoking rooms; all are furnished to a high standard with good en-suite bathrooms (all with bath and shower). The Glennan Suite ("simply the best suite on the island") has jacuzzi bath and separate shower, his & hers washbasins, private dining room, leather furniture and a raised American king size bed overlooking Belfast Lough through balcony doors. Acc££ Open all year. Amex, Diners, MasterCard, Visa.

Crumlin

Aldergrove Airport Hotel

Belfast International Airport Crumlin Co Antrim BT29 4ZY

HOTEL   Tel: 028 9442 2033 Fax: 028 9442 3500

This pleasant modern hotel opened in 1993 and is just 50 metres from the main terminal entrance at Belfast International Airport (and 17 miles from Belfast city centre). Spacious, attractively furnished bedrooms include three designed for disabled guests and a non-smoking floor; all are double-glazed, sound-proofed and have good bathrooms with bath and shower. Fully air-conditioned throughout, the hotel has spacious public areas and good facilities, including a fitness suite with sauna, conference and banqueting facilities, ample parking, a sun terrace and garden. At the time of going to press plans were in hand for an extra 60 bedrooms. To address the needs of longstay business guests, a full leisure centre and games room will also be added, plus a public bar to meet local demand. High security around the airport is seen as a bonus by the hotel, as it helps guests to feel relaxed. Conference/banqueting (250/200) Children's playground & garden. Children (Under 15s free in parents' room; cots available). Wheelchair accessible.No Pets. **Rooms 108** (all en-suite, 50 no-smoking, 3 for disabled) Lift . B&B £37.50pps, no ss. Open all year. Amex, Diners, MasterCard, Visa

---

Dunadry ✗

Dunadry Hotel & Country Club

2 Islandreagh Drive Dunadry Co Antrim BT412HA

HOTEL   Tel: 02894 432474 Fax: 02894 433389

The riverside Dunadry Hotel & Country Club was formerly a mill and it succeeds very well in combining the character of its old buildings with the comfort and efficiency of an international hotel. Set in ten acres of grounds, the hotel has excellent business and leisure facilities, plus banqueting for 180. Stylish, spacious bedrooms include three suites and eleven executive rooms – all have good amenities, including satellite TV, and executive rooms have computer points and fax machines. The most desirable rooms have French windows opening onto the gardens or the inner courtyard and a new informal restaurant makes the most of its situation overlooking the river. Leisure facilities within the grounds include a professional croquet lawn, fun bowling, trout fishing and cycling, as well as a leisure centre which rates as one of the best in Britain and Ireland. Sister establishment to the Wellington Park Hotel in Belfast city (see entry). Acc£££ Closed 25-26 Dec. Amex, Diners, MasterCard, Visa.

Portballintrae

Sweeney's Public House & Wine Bar

6b Seaport Avenue Portballintrae Co Antrim BT57 8SB
RESTAURANT   Tel: 028207 32405 Fax: 028207 31850

This attractive stone building is on the sea side of the road as you drive into Portballintrae and is very handy to both the Royal Portrush Golf Club and the Giant's Causeway. It's a pleasant place, with a welcoming open fire in the bar and a choice of places to drink or have a bite to eat. During the day the conservatory is an attractive option. On chillier days, however, the fireside in the main bar wins over the conservatory and its view. The food, prepared by Pauline Gallagher, is in the modern international café/bar style with no gourmet pretensions. Although likely to suit all age groups during the day, it can get very busy during the evening, especially on live music nights (there is a late licence to 1 am on Friday and Saturday). Wheelchair accessible. Children welcome before 10pm. **Seats 120** (private room, 32) No smoking area; air conditioning. Restaurant open all day (12-9.30pm), à la carte; house wines from £5; sc discretionary. Toilets wheelchair accessible Own parking. No reservations. Open all year. No credit cards. **Directions:** 1 mile from Bushmills, 5 miles from Portrush.Situated on the sea side of the main road, overlooking the bay.

Ballymena ✗

Crosskeys Inn

Portglenone Ballymena Co Antrim BT42
PUB   Tel: 028256 50694

This pretty thatched country pub dates back to 1740. It is one of Ireland's most famous pubs for traditional music, with sessions every Saturday night (and other impromptu sessions, with singing and storytelling, that happen at the drop of a hat). There are occasional blues sessions as well as traditional Irish. It's a characterful cottagey place, with a fire in the old kitchen and several small, low-ceilinged rooms that fill up easily on a busy night. Open all day, all wk No credit cards.

Portrush

Maddybenny Farmhouse

18 Maddybenny Park off Loguestown Road Portrush Co Antrim BT52 2PT
FARMHOUSE/B&B   Tel/Fax: 02870 823394

Farmhouse of the Year

Just two miles from Portrush, Rosemary White's Plantation Period farmhouse was built before 1650. Since extended and now modernised, it makes a very comfortable and exceptionally hospitable place to stay, with a family-run equestrian centre nearby (including stabling for guests' own horses). There is also snooker, a games room and quiet sitting places, as well as an area for outdoor children's games. The accommodation is just as thoughtful. The bedrooms are all en-suite and there are all sorts of useful extras – electric blankets, a comfortable armchair, hospitality tray complete with teacosy, a torch and alarm clock beside the bed, trouser press, hair dryer – and, on the landing, an ironing board, fridge and pay phone for guest use. Across the yard there are also six self-catering cottages, open all year (one wheelchair friendly). Golf, fishing, tennis and pitch & putt nearby. No evening meals, but Rosemary guides guests to the local eating places that will suit them best. Horse-riding,snooker & garden on the premises. **Rooms 3** (all en-suite) B&B £27.50pps, ss £5 Children welcome Parking Closed 16 Dec-6 Jan. MasterCard, Visa. **Directions:** Take the A29 Portrush/Coleraine-signposted to riding centre.

Portrush

Ramore Restaurant

The Harbour Portrush Co Antrim BT56 8BM
RESTAURANT   Tel: 02870 824313 Fax: 02870 823194

George and Jane McAlpin's remarkable restaurant overlooks Portrush harbour and was established well ahead of the other "new wave" restaurants in Northern Ireland, such as Roscoff, Shanks and Deane's. The sheer cosmopolitan buzz of the place – sleek modern style, well-dressed tables and the drama of an open kitchen – is impressive. However - like Roscoff - the McAlpin's have decided it is time for a change of direction. In January 2000 the restaaurant is to close for a total re-vamp - and will emerge as a "new concept in dining". (The following information may change for summer 2000) **Seats 70** D 6.30-10.30 Tues-Sat Toilets wheelchair accessible. Children welcome. Parking Closed 24-26 Dec (Rest. closed Sun & Mon, all Bank hols. except Easter Monday) MasterCard, Visa*

Ramore Wine Bar (underneath the restaurant): Tel: 02870 823444 Fax: 02870 823194 **Seats** 75 L 12.15-2.15 daily, D 5-9.30 daily. A la carte; sc discretionary. Toilets wheelchair accessible. Closed Xmas day & Sun. No credit cards. **Directions:** At the harbour

---

Portrush   *The Royal Court Hotel*

233 Ballybogey Road Whiterocks Portrush Co Antrim BT56 8NF

HOTEL   Tel: 02870 822236 Fax: 02870 823176

Set in a spectacular clifftop location just outside Portrush, and a 10 minute drive from the Giant's Causeway, the Royal Court offers the most desirable hotel accommodation in the area. Public areas are spacious and comfortable – the dining room has the sea view. Bedrooms are all well-furnished with good bathrooms, but vary considerably in size and outlook – the best are on the sea side and have little private balconies. Very handy to a number of golf links including the Royal Portrush and an excellent base for touring this lovely area.Wheelchair accessible. Children under 5 free in parents' room; cots available. No pets. **Rooms 18** (5 suites, all en-suite, 3 executive rooms) B&B £45pps, no ss. Closed 24-26 Dec & Good Fri. Amex, MasterCard, Visa

---

Portrush   *The Harbour Bar*

5-6 Harbour Road Portrush Co Antrim

PUB/RESTAURANT   Tel: 02870 822430 Fax: 02870 823194

The McAlpin's (see Ramore)recently bought the wonderful old pub, the Harbour Bar. They have retained the main ground floor bar area in its traditional form, but now offer food upstairs and plan other changes in the near future. Own parking. **Seats 100** L 12.15-2.30 (Tues-Sat) D 5.30-10 (Tues-Sat) L 12.30-3 Sun only; sc discretionary. Closed 25 Dec & Mondays. No Credit cards.

Templepatrick^x   *Hilton Park Templepatrick*

Castle Upton Estate Templepatrick Co Antrim BT33 0DD

HOTEL   Tel: 02894 435500 Fax: 02894 435511

This brand new purpose-built hotel opened in June 1998 and very soon changed its name from Stakis to Hilton. Facilities are very good, especially for golf - in the hotel as well as on the course, which was opened in autumn 1999. Conference/banqueting (500/400). Video conferencing; secretarial services. Business centre. Leisure centre. Fishing, golf (18), tennis, pitch & putt. Garden.Wheelchair accessible. Children under 5 free in parents' room; cots available. Pets permitted by arrangement.**Rooms 130** (1 suite, all en-suite, 68 executive rooms, 68 no-smoking, 7 for disabled). Lift. B&B £42pps, ss £20; no sc. Open all year. Amex, Diners, MasterCard, Visa. **Directions:** M2 from Belfast; Templepatrick roundabout; 3rd exit.

ARMAGH

With a miniature cathedral city at its heart, Armagh in 2000 finds itself providing fresh interest for those who like to balance urban days with rural respite. Mention Armagh, and most people will think of apples and archbishops. In the more fertile northern part of the county, orchards are traditionally important in the local economy, and the lore of apple growing and their use is part of County Armagh life. As for the pleasant town of Armagh itself - recently restored to its ancient status as a city - it is of course the ecclesiastical capital of all Ireland, and many a mitre is seen about it. But in fact Armagh city's significance long pre-dates Christian times. Emhain Macha - Navan Fort- to the west of the town, was a royal stronghold and centre of civilisation more than 4,000 years ago. Today, its past is explained in a deservedly-praised interpretive centre which is an architectural gem in itself. As with anywhere in Ireland, we are never far from water, and even inland Armagh has its own "coastline" of 25 kilometres along the southern shores of Lough Neagh, Ireland's most extensive lake and Europe's largest eel fishery. Today, Lough Neagh provides sand for the construction industry, eels for gourmets, and recreational boating of all sorts. In times past, it was part of the route which brought coal to Dublin from the mines in Coalisland in Tyrone, the main link to the seaport of Newry being the canal from Portadown which, when opened in 1742, was in the forefront of canal technology. That County Armagh was a leader in canal technology is only one of its many surprises - the discerning traveller will find much of interest, whether it be in the undulating farmland and orchards, the pretty villages, or the handsome uplands rising to Carrigatuke above Newtownhamilton, and on towards the fine peak of Slieve Gullion in the south of the county.

Local Attractions and Information

Armagh	County Museum	02837 523070
Armagh	Planetarium	02837 523689
Armagh	Apple Blossom Time; May trail in apple country (signed)	02837 521800
Armagh	Navan Fort (prehistoric)	02837 525550
Armagh	Palace Stables (18c stables, carriage rides)	02837 5299629
Lough Neagh	Discovery Centre, Oxford Island	02838 322205
Portadown	Moneypenny's Lock (restored lock keeper's house)	02838 322205
Tourist Information		02837 521800

Armagh ✗ | | **Navan Centre**

Killylea Road Armagh Co Armagh
VISITOR CENTRE/CAFÉ | Tel: 02837 525550

In the Navan Centre the coffee shop in the interpretative centre serves wholesome hot food and light snacks. All day Mon-Sun, light meals£

Armagh ✳ | | **Dean's Hill**

College Hill Armagh BT619DF
ACCOMMODATION | Tel/Fax: 028 37 524923

Jill and Edward Armstrong's delightful 18th century family home offers a real taste of the country within a very short walk of the centre of Armagh. Bedrooms are very comfortable, with good bathrooms and beautiful antiques, one with a four-poster - they don't make them like this any more. Reception rooms are equally remarkable - this is a real treasure. Garden.Wheelchair accessible. Children welcome. Pets permitted by arrangement. **Rooms 3** (2 suites, 1 en-suite) B&B £25pps. No Credit cards. **Directions:** From roundabout at Courthouse, take the A3-Portadown proceeding along college Hill on left after Planetarium/playing fields opposite Tower Hill.

Portadown ✳ ✗ | | **Seagoe Hotel**

Upper Church Lane Portadown Co Armagh BT63 5JE
HOTEL | Tel: 028 3833 3076 Fax: 028 3835 0210

Attractively situated in its own grounds on the edge of Portadown, this stunning hotel has been in the same ownership for many years but has recently undergone a complete makeover. The design is innovative and exceptionally easy on the eye and, once inside, the tone of the whole development is set by stylish public areas which are outstanding not only for grace and scale of design, but also the use of extremely high quality materials in construction, furnishing and decor. Easy wheelchair access throughout the building has been thought through in detail (the pay phone in the lobby is wheelchair accessible, for example). Bedrooms have contemporary simplicity teamed with warm, rich fabrics and good work space for business guests; executive rooms also have modem and fax facilities. Business/ conference facilities are equally special - but it's not all work, as there's a separate function entrance (popular for weddings as well as conferences), with its own dramatic lobby/reception area and two superb honeymoon suites. Bar and restaurant areas are designed with equal care, looking onto a delightful courtyard garden in the centre of the building. Own parking. Garden. **Rooms 34** (all en-suite), B&B £45 pps, ss £20. Wheelchair accessible. Lift. Open all year. Credit cards accepted. (Phone to check details). **Directions:** Off the A27 (Old Lurgan Road).

DOWN

While the visitor in 2000 may be left with an abiding impression of County Down as a focal point of the comfortable modern lifestyle, in fact you can expect to find more scenic variety in County Down than most other Irish counties as it rings the changes in its own quiet way from the affluent southern shoreline of Belfast Lough - the "Gold Coast" - through the rolling drumlin country which provides Strangford Lough's many islands, and on then past the uplands around Slieve Croob with the view southward increasingly dominated by by the soft purple slopes of the Mountains of Mourne.

But although the Mournes may soar to Northern Ireland's highest peak of Slieve Donard (850m), and provide within them some excellent hill-walking and challenging climbing, nevertheless when seen across Down's patchwork of prosperous farmland they have a gentleness which is in keeping with the county's well-groomed style. In the same vein, Down is home to some of Ireland's finest gardens, notably Mount Stewart on the eastern shore of Strangford Lough, and Rowallane at Saintfield, while the selection of forest and country parks is also exceptional. Throughout the contemporary landscape, history is much in evidence. St Patrick's grave is in Downpatrick, while the Ulster Folk and Transport Museum near Holywood provides an unrivalled overview of the region's past. The coastline is much-indented, so much so that when measured in detail County Down provides more than half of Northern Ireland's entire shoreline. Within it, the jewel of Strangford Lough is an unmatched attraction for naturalists and boat enthusiasts, while Portaferry has one of Ireland's longest established salt-water aquariums in Explopiris. Throughout the county, there is greater interaction with the sea than anywhere else in Northern Ireland. Bangor in the north of the county has Ireland's largest marina, an award-winning facility, while all three of Northern Ireland's main fishing ports - Portavogie, Ardglass and Kilkeel - are in County Down.

Local Attractions and Information

Ballycopeland	Windmill, Millisle	02891 861413
Castle Espie	Wildfowl and Wetlands Centre	02891 874146
Cultra	Ulster Folk & Transport Museum	02890 428428
Downpatrick Cathedral		02844 614922
Newtownards	Mount Stewart (house, gardens & Temple of the Winds)	028427 88387
Portaferry	Aquarium (Exploris)	028427 28062
Rathfriland	Bronte Interpretive Centre	028406 31152
Saintfield Ballynahinch	Rowallane (National Trust garden)	02897 51031
Strangford	Castle Ward National Trust house, Opera Festival June	02844 881204

Bangor   *Clandeboye Lodge Hotel*

10 Estate Road Clandeboye Bangor Co Down BT19 1UR

HOTEL   Tel: 02892 852500 Fax: 02892 852772

Set in woodland on the edge of the Clandeboye estate, this comfortable modern hotel fits in well with its rural surroundings. The stylish foyer creates a good impression, with a welcoming fire and plentiful seating areas. Off it is the Lodge Restaurant with gothic-style windows and furnishings (where breakfast is also served). Good-sized, bedrooms have neat, well-planned bathrooms (suites have whirlpool baths); standard amenities include phones with voicemail and fax/modem points. Although not seriously dated, decor seemed a little tired on a recent visit and furniture was showing signs of wear. A country-style pub, The Poacher's Arms, is in an original Victorian building beside the hotel. Conference/banqueting (300/300) Golf (18/9), walking & garden available. Children under 4 free in parents' room; cots available). Wheelchair accessible. No Pets. Credit card numbers are taken when booking - and the deduction may be made before your arrival. **Rooms 43** (2 suites, all en-suite,13 no-smoking, 2 for disabled) B&B £35pps, ss £11 Lift Children welcome Parking Closed 24-26 Dec Amex, Diners, MasterCard, Visa. **Directions:** 15 minutes from Belfast, on outskirts of Bangor

Bangor ❋   *Genoa Restaurant*

RESTAURANT

1A Seacliff Road Bangor Co Down BT20 5HD
Tel/Fax: 02891 469253

On the harbour side of the road on Bangor's seafront, this attractive little stone building was once a harbourmaster's lookout office.There's a welcoming first-floor reception bar with contemporary lightwood furniture and a large seaward window and the restaurant itself is in a larger, informally well-appointed room downstairs (Also a patio area for al fresco dining. weather permitting.) Proprietor Rob Mulholland is an excellent host , heading up a charming front of house team, and Gary Beattie's cooking is confident and creative. His sound philosophy is declared on the menu : "Seasonality is respected and herbs, vegetables and salad leaves come from organic suppliers or the Mulholland garden. Fish and shellfish are a speciality and include hand diver scallops and rope mussels from Strangford, lobster from Ballywalter and fish and shrimps from Portavogie, all supplied by individuals". A starter of air-dried Italian ham with black olives and shavings of Parmeggiano Reggiano and a drizzling of white truffle oil indicates the style, with local seafood prominent among the main courses, as in perfectly cooked fillet of hake, set atop a bed of braised bok-choi (Chinese cabbage) and served in a mussel broth, with saffron, baby onion and tomato. A choice of liqueur coffees makes a tempting altenative to dessert. Wheelchair accessible.Children welcome. **Seats 52.** No smoking area. L 12-2.30 (Tues-Sat) D 6.30-9.30 (Tues-Sat) (off-season, phone to check opening times). Gourmet menu £35; also à la carte; house wine £9.50 sc discretionary (10% on tables of 6+) Closed 25 Dec & first 2wks Jan & every Sun and Mon MasterCard, Visa **Directions:** At the Bangor Marina carpark.

Bangor   *Marine Court Hotel*

HOTEL

The Marina Bangor Co Down BT20 5ED
Tel: 02891 451100 Fax: 02891 451200 email: marine.court@dial.pipex.com

Excellent leisure facilities at the Marine Court's Oceanis Health & Fitness Club are this hotel's greatest strength – these include an 18 metre pool, steam room, whirlpool and sunbeds, plus a well-equipped, professionally-staffed gym. As a result the club is extremely popular with locals as well as hotel residents. The hotel overlooks the marina (beyond a public carpark) but the first-floor restaurant is the only public room with a real view and only a few bedrooms are on the front – most have views of dull but tidy service areas. Decor is unispired but furnishings are good quality, with plenty of worktop and tea/coffee tray, hair dryer and trouser press standard in all rooms. Noise from a disco at the back of the hotel can be a problem on some nights. Patrick McCrystal, head chef at the hotel since 1995, oversees three restaurants in the hotel, two informal ones and the first-floor Lord Nelson's Bistro, overlooking the marina. Conference/banqueting (500/300). Leisure centre. Wheelchair accessible. Children (Under 10s free in parents' room; cots available). No Pets. **Rooms 52** (2 suites, all en-suite, 15 executive rooms). Lift. B&B £45pps, ss £35. Secure parking at rear. Closed 25 Dec Amex, Diners, MasterCard, Visa

Bangor ❋   *Royal Hotel*

HOTEL

26/28 Quay Street Bangor Co Down BT20 5ED
Tel: 02891 271866 Fax: 02891 467810

This old hotel near the marina came into new ownership a few years ago but has lost none of its friendliness or old-fashioned charm. There's a warm personal welcome, a clear willingness to help guests in any way possible and the building has some endearing idiosyncracies - particularly an early 20th century lift (the date is on it) with folding grille doors and a mind of its own, which guests get used to after one or two ascents. Rooms vary - the best are the new ones on the front, overlooking the marina. Small conferences (40); Children (Under 5s free in parents' room; cots available). Wheelchair accessible/Lift. No Pets.Children welcome. **Rooms 50** (all en-suite, 7 executive rooms, 8 shower only, 1 for disabled) B&B £47.50pps, ss £15. Nearby parking. Closed 25 Dec Amex, Diners, MasterCard, Visa. **Directions:** A2 from Belfast,at bottom of main street turn right (keeping in left lane). Hotel is 300 yards on right facing marina.

Bangor   *Shanks*

RESTAURANT

The Blackwood Golf Centre 150 Crawfordsburn Road Bangor Co Down BT19 1GB
Tel: 02891 853313 Fax: 02891 852493

The setting is unusual for Robbie and Shirley Millar's restaurant, which was designed by Sir Terence Conran's company. On two floors (the first floor is mostly taken up by the bar and reception area, with some tables in use for extra-busy sittings, and a balcony for al fresco eating), the main restaurant is downstairs, simple, minimalist and bright. There is lots of light wood, some banquette seating, smart table settings, and a windowed kitchen where you can observe chef-patron Robbie Millar and his team of chefs at work. Shirley supervises the front-of-house team. Robbie's contemporary cooking brings together the best local ingredients in dishes often demonstrating Mediterranean and Asian, influences.On arrival, a basket of home-made breads is served with tapenade, followed by an amuse-gueule. Grilled Portavogie prawns with ratatouille puff, fresh basil butter attracts a supplement which, on a recent visit, did not seem justifiable for just four prawns, although rare fillet of beef on grilled onion bread with shitake mushrooms & balsamic vinegar was an outstanding, if perhaps too substantial, dish. Summer main courses might include sliced loin of lamb with tapenade, fennel & parmesan gratin, white beans and rosemary aioli (an attractive sounding combinbation although disappointingly executed) and fillet of hake with sauteed charlotte potatoes, organic spinach & fresh summer truffles, which was much more successful. Desserts also failed to sparkle on this occasion but the cheeseboard looked as good as ever - a great selection, in tip-top condition, although they also attract a supplement. Early bookings may be rushed through the meal or sent up to finish at a table upstairs, which is not acceptable in a restaurant of this calibre.The wine list is very well balanced and, for the quality on offer, inexpensive. Children welcome. Parking. **Seats 60** (private room, 36) L 12.30-2.30 (Tues-Fri) D 7-10 (Tues-Sat). Set L £17.95 Set D £29.50. House wine £12.50; sc discretionary. Toilets wheelchair accessible Closed 25-26 Dec, 1 Jan & 2wks in July Amex, MasterCard, Visa. **Directions:** 2km off A2 Dual Carriageway from Belfast to Bangor

---

Castlewellan ❋ ✗   *Hillyard House*

ACCOMMODATION/RESTAURANT

1-5 Castle Avenue Castlewellan BT31 5BX
Tel: 028 44 770141 Fax: 028 22 723111

Hillyard House is a conference centre on the edge of the Mournes, with simple residential accommodation - an interesting place to break a journey or to stay, for an inexpensive family break perhaps, with an outdoor focus. (There are twin rooms and 4-bedded rooms, all with shower en-suite). Conference room; wheelchair accessible. Lift. Meals are served in a pleasant informal restaurant 11am-9 pm; morning coffee, daily specials based on local produce, scones, high tea. No-smoking restaurant.

Comber   *The Old Schoolhouse Inn*

RESTAURANT/ACCOMMODATION

100 Ballydrain Road Comber Co Down BT23 6EA
Tel: 02897 541182 Fax: 02897 542583

Almost next door to Castle Espie, The Old Schoolhouse is run by Avril (chef) and Terry (the genial host) Brown. It's a magnet for returning regulars, who are treated as long-lost friends and enjoy the straightforward and traditional cooking (with a hint of modernism). The separate bedroom block is self-contained with its own breakfast room and honesty bar/lounge. Each of the twelve comfortable and well-furnished ensuite rooms is named after American presidents of Ulster descent. Conference/banqueting (100) & Video Conferencing available. Children under 5 free in parents' room; cots available. Wheelchair accessible. Garden. **Seats 100.** No smoking area (private room, 60).D 7-10 Mon-Sat, L 12-4, Sun only. Set D £18.95, Set Sun L £11.95 - £13.95; no sc. Toilets wheelchair accessible. Open all year. Amex, MasterCard, Visa. **Rooms** 20 (12 suites,1 for disabled) B&B £37.50pps, ss £7.50. **Directions:** 3 miles south of Comber beside Castle Espie

---

Crawfordsburn   *Old Inn*

HOTEL

15 Main Street Crawfordsburn Co Down BT19 1JH
Tel: 02891 853255 Fax: 02891 852775

The pretty village setting of this famous 16th century inn – the oldest in continuous use in all Ireland – belies its convenient location close to Belfast and its City Airport. Oak beams, antiques and gas lighting emphasise the natural character of the building, an attractive venue for business people and private guests alike. Individually decorated bedrooms vary in size and style, most have antiques, some have four-posters and a few have private sitting rooms. Recent extensions at the back of the hotel have been completed with admirable sympathy for the existing building and include a neat carpark extension and a delightful little garden popular for wedding photographs (perhaps with a nice little ginger cat). The Ulster Folk and Transport Museum and the Royal Belfast Golf Club are nearby. Conference/banqueting (100/90) Ample parking. Garden. Wheelchair accessible. Children welcome. Pets permitted. **Rooms 32** (3 suites, all en-suite, 12 no-smoking, 2 for disabled) B&B £45pps, ss £15 Open all year Amex, Diners, MasterCard, Visa **Directions:** Off A2 Belfast-Bangor road. 6 miles after Holywood, Crawfordsburn is signed left at lights junction; 1 mile to village; hotel on left.

Donaghadee   *Grace Neill's*

33 High Street Donaghadee Co Down BT21 0AH
PUB/RESTAURANT   Tel: 02891 884595 Fax: 02891 882553

Dating back to 1611, Grace Neill's lays a fair claim to be one of the oldest inns in all Ireland; Grace Neill herself was born when the pub was more than two hundred years old and died in 1916 at the age of 98. Extensions and improvements under the present ownership have been done with due sensitivity to the age and character of the original front bar, which has been left simple and unspoilt. The back of the building has been imaginatively developed in contemporary style, creating Bistro Bistro, a bright, high-ceilinged area. Food is along the lines of shredded duck & red onion tortillas with sundried tomato, rack of lamb with chargrilled vegetables and (a great favourite this) homemade pork sausage with mash potato & onion gravy; good desserts follow, all at very reasonable prices. Sunday Brunch is a speciality, with live jazz. Children welcome before 7 pm. **Seats 72.** No smoking area. L 12-2.30 (Tues-Sat) Sun L 12.30-3.30 D 6-9.30 (Tues-Sat); à la carte; sc discretionary.Toilets wheelchair accessible. Own parking Closed Mondays,25-26 Dec,1 Jan & 12,13 July Amex, MasterCard, Visa. **Directions:** Through an arch, off the main High Street

---

Downpatrick ✳   *Denvirs*

14 English Street Downpatrick Co Down BT30 6AB
HOTEL   Tel: 02844 612012

What a gem this ancient place is. It's a wonderful pub with two old bars. There's an interesting informal restaurant, genuinely olde-worlde with an amazing original fireplace and chimney discovered during renovations. There's delightful accommodation in sympathetically updated rooms. And there's a first floor room, with some remarkable original features, suitable for meetings or private parties. Go and see it - there can't be another place in Ireland anything like it. Conferences (70). Wheelchair accessible. Pets permitted. **Rooms 6** (all en-suite) B&B £30pps, ss £5 Bar/Restaurant: Food served from 12-2.30pm daily & 6-8pm Mon-Fri (6-9pm Sat). Children welcome. Parking Closed Xmas day. Amex, Diners, MasterCard, Visa. **Directions:** On same street as Cathedral and court house in Downpatrick.

Dundrum   *The Buck's Head Inn*

77 Main Street Dundrum Co Down BT33 0LU
RESTAURANT   Tel: 02843 7 51868 Fax: 02843 7 51898

Michael and Alison Crothers have developed this attractive, welcoming place from a pub with bar food and a restaurant, to its present position as a restaurant with bar.Alison teams up in the kitchen with head chef Fergus King to source local produce, especially seafood, including oysters from Dundrum Bay and other fish, such as mionkfish, which might be marinated in citrus juices and served with a mussel & cider cream. Note that many dishes on the dinner menu, including Dover sole, red snapper, fillet steak and cheeses attract supplements. Desserts are tempting and a short but imaginative vegetarian menu is also offered. Good service under the direction of the proprietor Michael Crothers. Children welcome. **Seats 70** (private room, 35) No smoking area L 12-2.30, Tea 5-7 & D 7-9 daily (Sun D 5-8.30). Set Sun L £12.50, Set D £20. House wine from £10; sc discretionary. Toilets wheelchair accessible. Own parking. Closed 25 Dec & Mondays 1 Oct-1 Mar. Amex, MasterCard, Visa. **Directions:** On the main Belfast-Newcastle road, approx 3 miles from Newcastle

---

Gilford   *The Yellow Door Restaurant*

2 Bridge Street Gilford Co Down BT63 6EP
RESTAURANT   Tel: 02838 831543 Fax: 02838 831180

Tucked away in a far corner of County Down, alongside the River Bann, The Yellow Door is in a series of rooms, creating a cottage-like atmosphere – offset by an element of contemporary style, especially in the comfortable, elegant reception room/bar area. The restaurant changed hands in 1999 but, as head chef Michael Donaghy has stayed on, there is no obvious change of style. Tables set with Irish linen table mats and napkins, fresh flowers and generous, gleaming wine glasses suggest a serious restaurant, a feeling confirmed by Michael's modern, international menus. Seven or eight choices are offered on each course at dinner, rather less at lunch; the cooking is contemporary. Well-balanced main courses include a strong vegetarian option – maybe a trio of dishes to include a mille feuille of potato & mushroom,Chinese greens and curry roast cauliflower– and there might be a fine example of New Irish Cuisine in char-grilled pork log with pomme fondant, sauted cabbage and grain mustard sauce. Finish with farmhouse cheese or good desserts, perhaps including a refreshing assiette of ice creams and sorbets with seasonal poached fruit. Unsuitable for children. **Seats 45** (private room, 20). No smoking area; air conditioning. L 12.30-2.30, D 6.30-9.30 daily; Set L £14.95, Set Sun L £15.95, Set D £27.50; also à la carte. House wine £10.95; sc discretionary. Parking. Closed Mon, 25-26 Dec & 1wk July. Amex, MasterCard, Visa. **Directions:** Up from mini roundabout.

Groomsport
The Anchorage

49 Main Street Groomsport Co Down BT19 6JR
RESTAURANT
Tel: 02891 465757 Fax: 02891 479863

A discreet brass plaque beside the door of one of the oldest buildings in the village of Groomsport identifies The Anchorage, Jenny McCrea and Michael Scott's restaurant. This unusual establishment is divided into two areas, with a different atmosphere on each side – one has a wooden floor, large mirrors and Scandinavian simplicity – while the other, which is carpeted, has a much more intimate atmosphere. The Anchorage has earned a great reputation in the locality for interesting menus in the modern idiom, good cooking and a relaxed atmosphere. Wheelchair accessible.Children welcome before 8 pm **Seats 50** (private room, 30) D Wed-Sat 5.30-9 (Sat 7-10),L 12.30-2.30 Sun only; à la carte; house wine £10; sc discretionary. Closed Mon,Tue & all Jan. MasterCard, Visa. **Directions:** 2 miles east of Bangor, in Groomsport village.

Groomsport
Islet Hill

21 Bangor Road Groomsport Co Down BT19 6JF
COUNTRY HOUSE
Tel: 02891 464435

Just outside the town of Bangor, Islet Hill is a lovely old farmhouse set in fields overlooking the North Channel. It is a comfortable place to stay but it is the hospitality offered by Denis and Anne Mayne that make it really special. Children are particularly welcome and can play safely in the lovely garden. Both bedrooms are suitable for family use – one has a double bed and a single, the other a kingsize bed and adjoining bunk room; and, in addition to en-suite showers, there's a shared guest bathroom on the landing. Short on rules and regulations and long on welcome, there is no set time for breakfast, guests can use the house at any time and there's a fire in the guests' private sitting room in winter. Garden, walking. Children under 2 free in parents' room; cots available . Pets permitted by arrangement. **Rooms 2** (both shower only & no-smoking) B&B £18.50pps, no ss   Children under 14 B&B £10. Parking. No Credit cards. **Directions:** On B511, 1/4 mile west of Groomsport

---

Hillsborough *x*
Hillside Restaurant & Bar

21 Main Street Hillsborough Co Down BT26 6AE
PUB/RESTAURANT
Tel:02892 682765 Fax: 02892 689888

Peel off the Belfast-Dublin motorway when you see the Hillsborough sign and you'll soon find Diane Shields' Hillside Bar in the steep main street. Established in 1777, it's an attractive pub in fine country style, with a welcoming atmosphere, soothing natural colours and plenty of tables. Real ale is one of the major attractions of the Hillside (they run a Real Ale Festival in late July and have 20-30 real ales on tap) and so is the food. The Refectory (bar food) and restaurant are run independently, with separate kitchens. Colin Elder, head chef in the Refectory kitchen, presents lively international seasonal menus which change with the time of day and provide a wide selection of consistently interesting food throughout – everything from ploughman's with brie, cheddar, apple, chutney and wheaten bread to sweet chilli steak strips served in a pitta pocket. Refectory/bar meals£ **Restaurant:** Dark-walled and low-ceilinged, the restaurant is inviting, with antique mirrors and well-appointed tables. There's a compact dinner menu and an à la carte: world cuisine with a nod to Irish traditions. D££ Tues-Sat Amex, Diners, MasterCard, Visa.

Hillsborough — *The Plough Inn*

3 The Square Main Street Hillsborough Co Down BT26 6AG

PUB/RESTAURANT   Tel: 02892 682985 Fax: 02892 682472

Established in 1752,this former coaching inn enjoys a fine position at the top of the hill. Since 1984 it has been owned by the Patterson family, who have built up a national reputation for hospitality and good food, especially seafood. Somehow they manage to run three separate food operations each day, so pleasing customers looking for a casual daytime meal and more serious evening diners. Derek Patterson, who has been head chef since 1989, creates menus offering a nicely judged combination of traditional food – bacon loin with champ & colcannon, for example – and the world cuisine which is currently so popular, such as Thai-style steamed mussels with lemongrass, chilli, ginger & coconut cream. The evening restaurant is in the old stables at the back of the pub and booking is required; here Derek creates his renowned seafood menus – assorted shellfish soup & crème fraîche, seared king scallops, semi-dried tomato & basil sauce, mediterranean seafood ragout rustic style, with seasalted garlic focaccia. Seafood certainly rules here, but carnivores and vegetarians are not completely ignored – a sprinkling of meat and poultry dishes will always include fine Angus steaks – a fillet with cracked peppercorn crust and Bushmills whiskey cream perhaps – and there's a vegetarian menu available. **Seats** 150 (private room, 40) L 12-2.30 daily D 5-9.30 daily (Sun 5-8) Set Sun L £10. Set D from £15, early evening menu £12-14 5-8pm only. house wine £6-£10. No smoking area. Air conditioning. sc discretionary. Children unsuitable. Parking. Closed Xmas day. Amex, Diners, MasterCard, Visa. **Directions:** Off the main Dublin-Belfast Dual Carriageway.

The Pattersons also own The Pheasant Inn, at Annahilt.

Hillsborough ✗ — *White Gables Hotel*

14 Dromore Road Hillsborough Co Down

HOTEL   Tel: 02892 682755

About ten miles south of Belfast, off the A1 Dublin road, in the historic Georgian village of Hillsborough. The hotel, designed for business travellers, is modern, though already somewhat dated. Uniform and practical bedrooms provide the usual facilities, and there are conference facilities for up to 150. Acc£££ Open all year

Holywood — *Bay Tree Coffee House*

118 High Street Holywood Co Down BT18 9HW

RESTAURANT   Tel: 02890 421419

Since 1988 The Bay Tree has been attracting people from miles around to its delightful craft shop and coffee house on the main street. The craft shop, which sells exclusively Irish wares, is a busy, colourful place specialising in pottery, with over two dozen Irish potters represented. There is also a gallery exhibiting the work of Irish artists and – perhaps best of all – Sue Farmer's delicious food. Baking is a strength, especially the cinnamon scones which are a house speciality. There's quite a strong emphasis on vegetarian dishes – soups, pates, main courses such as red bean & aubergine stew with spiced mash – and organic salads, especially in summer, when you can also eat out on a patio in fine weather. No reservations for lunch but they are required on Friday evenings, when the Bay Tree is open for dinner; it's then that Sue might augment her informal lunch time fare with more serious dishes such as crown of Irish lamb with garlic, redcurrant and rosemary. Wheelchair accessible. **Seats** 34 L 12-2.30 Mon-Sat D 7.30-9.30 Fr only. Non smoking restaurant. sc discretionary. Children welcome. Parking. Closed Sundays, Xmas & 12,13 July. No Credit cards. **Directions:** Opposite the police station .

Holywood ❋ — *Fontana*

61A High Street, Holywood, Co.Down BT18 9AE

RESTAURANT   Tel: 02890 809908 Fax: 02890 422475

A first floor restaurant over a classy kitchen shop ("down the alley & up the satirs"), Fontana is fresh and bright - very bright, in fact, with clear yellow walls which work very well with the polished wood floor and leather seating. Proprietor chef Colleen Bennett is one of the new wave of chefs making a name for themselves in the area at the moment and she offers lovely zesty, loosely structured menus that suit the atmosphere of the room. Starters and main courses overlap to a great extent, with small and large portions of some dishes offered. Caesar salad with garlicky croutons, black olives and char-grilled chicken comes in two sizes, for example and is also on both the lunch and dinner menus (a little more charring and few more olives would have made this an even better dish). Seafood features strongly - in an updated chowder with white wine, coriander & garlic aioli, for example, or - a dish admired on a recent visit - seared cod on new spinach with baby potatoes and sundried tomato butter. Moderate prices come up considerably when side vegetables and salads are charged separately. Outside eating area.Children welcome **Seats 56** L 12-3 Tues-Sat (Sun 11-3), D 6.30-10 Tues-Sat., all à la carte, house wine from £9.95; sc discretionary, 10% added on tables of 6+. Toilets wheelchair accessible. On street parking. Closed Mon, 25-26 Dec & 1 Jan. MasterCard, Visa. **Directions:** Three doors from the Maypole

---

Holywood   *Rayanne Country House*

                                            60 Demesne Road Holywood Co Down BT18 9EX
COUNTRY HOUSE   Tel: 02890 425859 Fax: 02890 423364

Situated almost next to the Holywood Golf Club and Redburn Country Park, and with views across to Belfast Lough, this is a tranquil spot in which to unwind and a fine alternative to 'faceless hotel syndrome'. It's a wonderful and relaxing place, family-run and offering one of the best breakfasts in Ireland, with dishes such as prune soufflé and bacon, Stilton and avocado kedgeree, grilled kippers and baked fresh herring fillets tossed in oatmeal. Dinner is served Wed-Sat incl. and open to non-residents. Garden, Parking. Wheelchair accessible. No Pets. **Rooms 9** (all en-suite, 9 no-smoking) B&B £35pps, ss £22 Own parking Closed 23 Dec-2 Jan MasterCard, Visa. Restaurant **Seats 36.** D only 7-9 Mon-Sat; Set D £25; House wine from £10; sc 10%. Closed Sun. Non-residents welcome. **Directions:** 6 miles from Belfast city on Bangor road.

Holywood   *Sullivans*

                                            Sullivan Place Holywood Co Down BT18 9JF
RESTAURANT   Tel: 02890 421000 Fax: 02890 426664

In the morning or afternoon you can pop in to chef-proprietor Simon Shaw's bright, friendly and informal espresso bar and restaurant for tea or coffee and light snacks. At lunch time some more substantial dishes are offered, from a home-made soup such as lentil & bacon served with crusty bread to a McCartney's sausages & champ, with wholegrain sauce. Vegetarians are well catered for (pasta with sundried tomato and mangetout and vegetarian dishes are highlighted on both lunch and dinner menus.Generous proportions of dishes such as braised lamb shank with Moroccan cous-cous, or salmon & sole with puff pastry are most enjoyable - this is first-class cooking, confirmed by lovely desserts such as crème brûlée or chocolate terrine, or you can finish with a plate of Cashel Blue, served with pears. Excellent coffee, fair prices. **Seats 65.** Air conditioning Open all day (10-10).L 12-2.30 daily, D 5-10 Mon-Sat. Set Sun L £11.50; early evening menu £8.50, 5-7 pm only; also à la carte; house wine £9.95; sc 10% on parties of 6+. Toilets wheelchair accessible. Parking nearby. Closed Sun D, 25-26 Dec. Amex, MasterCard, Visa. **Directions:** Off the main street.

Newcastle   *Burrendale Hotel & Country Club*

                                            51 Castlewellan Road Newcastle Co Down
HOTEL   Tel: 02844 22599   Fax: 02844 22328

Just outside the traditional seaside holiday town of Newcastle, and close to the championship links of the Royal County Down golf course, this area on the edge of the Mourne mountains has an isolated atmosphere yet is just an hour's drive from Belfast. Public areas in the hotel are spacious and include the Cottage Bar with an open log fire, welcome on chilly days. Well-appointed accommodation includes some family rooms. Conference/banqueting (150 /180) Leisure centre (12 metre pool). Beauty salon. Own parking. Children under 4 free in parents' room; cots available. Wheelchair accessible.**Rooms 68** (3 mini-suites, 17 executive rooms, 12 for disabled) Lift B&B £65pps, ss £15. Open all year. Amex, Diners, MasterCard, Visa. **Directions:** On A50 Castlewellan road.

Newcastle   *Hastings Slieve Donard Hotel*

                                            Downs Road Newcastle Co Down BT33 0AH
HOTEL   Tel: 028437 23681 Fax: 028437 24830 email: gmsdh@hastingshotels.com

This famous hotel stands beneath the Mournes in six acres of public grounds, adjacent to the beach and the Royal County Down Golf Links. The Victorian holiday hotel par excellence, the Slieve Donard first opened in 1897 and has been the leading place to stay in Newcastle ever since. Recent years have seen great improvements in both the public rooms and accommodation. Bedrooms are finished to a high standard and all the bathrooms sport one of the famous yellow Hastings ducks. The nearby Tollymore Forest Park provides excellent walking on clearly marked trails, just one of the many outdoor pursuits that attract guests; should the weather be unsuitable, the Elysium health club has enough facilities to keep the over-energetic occupied for weeks - and is soon to be extended. The hotel also offers a wide range of special breaks. Conference/banqueting (825/440). Secretarial services. Business centre. Leisure centre. Tennis, golf (18), fishing, snooker. Own parking. Children under 14 free in parents' room; cots available. No pets. **Rooms 126** (3 suites, 10 mini-suites, 114 executive rooms, 10 no-smoking, 1 for disabled). 2 Lifts. B&B £70pps, ss £20. Open all year. Amex, Diners, MasterCard, Visa. **Directions:** Along sea front from town centre.

Newry ❋ ✗   *Canal Court Hotel*

Merchants Quay Newry Co Down BT35 8HF
HOTEL   Tel: 028 41 751234 Fax: 028 41 751177

This new canalside hotel has brought badly needed facilities to Newry, including business/conference services as well as a health & leisure complex and spacious, comfortable accommodation.

Newtownards   *Edenvale House*

130 Portaferry Road Newtownards Co Down BT22 2AH
COUNTRY HOUSE   Tel: 02891 814881 Fax: 02891 826192

Diane Whyte's charming Georgian house is set peacefully in seven acres of garden and paddock, with views over Strangford Lough to the Mourne mountains and a National Trust wildfowl reserve. The house has been sensitively restored and modernised, providing a high standard of accommodation and hospitality. Guests are warmly welcomed and well fed, with excellent traditional breakfasts and afternoon tea with homemade scones. For evening meals, Diane directs guests to one of the local restaurants. Edenvale is close to the National Trust properties Mount Stewart and Castle Ward. Children under 2 free in parents' room; cots available. Pets permitted. **Rooms 3** (1 mini-suite, all no-smoking). B&B £27.50pps, ss £5. Closed Xmas. MasterCard, Visa **Directions:** 2 miles from Newtownards on A20 going towards Portaferry.

Portaferry   *The Narrows*

8 Shore Road Portaferry Co Down BT22 1JY
Tel: 02891 28148 Fax: 02891 28105
ACCOMMODATION/RESTAURANT   email: the.narrows@dial.pipex.com

On the Portaferry waterfront, an archway in the middle of a primrose yellow facade attracts attention to the inspired eighteenth century courtyard development that is central to Will and James Browns' unusual guesthouse and conference facilities. The ground floor includes a cosy sitting room with an open fire and a spacious restaurant; the style throughout is light and bright, with lots of natural materials and local art. Minimalist bedrooms are all different and have a serene, almost oriental atmosphere; all are en-suite but only three have baths. For guests with special needs, all the shower rooms are wheelchair-friendly, eight are specially designed and there is a lift. There are two interconnecting rooms and two family rooms; children's tea is available at 5 pm. A fine room over the archway, opening onto a private balcony, provides banqueting/conference facilities for 40/70 respectively. Own parking.Children under 2 free in parents' room; cots available. Pets by arrangement. **Rooms 13** (all no-smoking, 9 for disabled). Lift. B&B £39pps, ss £15. Open all year. Amex, Diners, MasterCard, Visa. **Restaurant:** At lunch and dinner every day, head chef Danny Millar presents lively modern menus based on carefully sourced local ingredients – notably seafood, including lobster, but also local meats and organic vegetables and herbs from their own garden. Lunch menus tend to include some homely dishes like black bean & bacon soup and hot smoked cod with champ and mustard butter. A disappointing recent visit suggests that inconsistency may be a problem; however good management should ensure a return to the normally high standards achieved at this exciting establishment. Children welcome. **Seats** 36 L 12-2.30, D 6-9.15 daily; à la carte; sc discretionary. Toilets wheelchair accessible. **Directions:** A20 to Portaferry on shore front.

Portaferry

Portaferry Hotel

The Strand Portaferry Co Down BT22 1EP

HOTEL   Tel: 02891 728231 Fax: 02891 728999 email: info@portaferryhotel.com

This18th-century waterfront terrace presents a neat, traditional exterior overlooking the Lough to the attractive village of Strangford and the National Trust property, Castleward, home to an opera festival each June. Extensions and refurbishment undertaken by John and Marie Herlihy, who have owned the hotel since 1980, have been sensitively done and the inn is now one of the most popular destinations in Northern Ireland – not least for its food. There's an excellent lunchtime bar menu (including 'Children's Choice') available every day except Sunday. Accommodation is comfortable and most of the individually decorated en-suite bedrooms have views of the water. Small conference/private parties (14/85); Own parking. Children (Under 2s free in parents' room; cots available). No pets. **Rooms 14** (4 no-smoking) B&B £45pps, ss £10. Closed 24-25 Dec. Amex, Diners, MasterCard, Visa. **Restaurant:** The restaurant has been recently refurbished but not too noticeably so – its slightly cottagey style provides the perfect background for good unpretentious food. Local produce features prominently in prime Ulster beef, Mourne lamb and game from neighbouring estates – but it is, of course, the seafood from daily landings at the nearby fishing villages of Ardglass and Portavogie that take pride of place. Gerry Manley, head chef since early 1998, presents well-balanced table d'hôte lunch and dinner menus plus a short carte, providing plenty of choice although majoring on local seafood. Not suitable for children under 12 after 8 pm. **Seats 80.** Food served daily: 12.30-2.30, 5.30-7, 7-9 (Sat to 10). Set Sun L £15, Set D £22.50; à la carte L available; house wine from £11.50; sc discretionary.Toilets wheelchair accessible. **Directions:** On Portaferry seafront.

Sketrick Island

Daft Eddy's

Sketrick Island Killinchy Co Down BT23 6QH

PUB   Tel/Fax: 02897 541615

Reached by a short causeway, this well-known pub enjoys a stunning position on a small island, with views to Strangford Lough. It was taken over by the Stronge family in 1996 and virtually rebuilt in 1997. To those with a sentimental attachment to the old pub it may now seem more ordinary; however it is an attractive building and serves its purpose well, with a split-level bar and a restaurant. The maritime decor reflects the pub's large sailing clientele, as well as its location. Head chef Gordon Potts prepares good bar food, which is strongest on fresh fish dishes. Children welcome. **Seats 90.** Air conditioning. Open all day (12-9.30) L 12-3 daily, D 5-9.30, Set Sun L £12 Set D from £12.50, à la carte available, house wine £10; sc discretionary.Toilets wheelchair accessible. Own parking. Open all year. MasterCard, Visa. **Directions:** From Killinchy drive to shore and turn left for o.5 mile – pub is on island over causeway.

FERMANAGH

Fermanagh in 2000 is moving into a central role in Ireland's myriad inland waterways. Ireland is a watery place of many lakes, rivers and canals. So it's quite an achievement to be the most watery county of all, yet this is is but one of Fermanagh's many claims to distinction. It is the only county in Ireland where you can travel the complete distance between its furthest extremities throughout the heart of its territory entirely by boat. For Fermanagh is divided - or linked if you prefer - throughout its length by the handsome waters of the River Erne. Southeast of Enniskillen, Upper Lough Erne is a maze of small waterways. Northwest of the historic and characterful town, the riverway opens out into the broad spread of Lower Lough Erne, a magnificent inland sea set off against the spectacular heights of the Cliffs of Magho. Boating has always been central to life in Fermanagh, so much so that in ancient times the leading local family, the Maguires, reputedly had a fleet of pleasure craft on Lough Erne as long ago as the 12th Century. It's a stunningly beautiful county with much else of interest, including the Marble Arch caves, and the great houses of Castle Cooole and Florence Court, the latter with its own forest park nestling under the rising heights of Cuilcagh (667m). And if you think lakes are for fishing rather than floating over, then in western Fermanagh the village of Garrison gives access to Lough Melvin, an angler's heaven.

Local Attractions and Information

Belleek	(porcelain & Explore Erne Exhibition)	028686 58866
Enniskillen	Castle	02866 325000
Enniskillen	Castle Coole	02866 322690
Enniskillen	Florence Court	02866 348249
Lough Erne Cruises		02866 322882
Marble Arch Caves		02866 348855
Newtownbutler	Crom Estate (National Trust conservation site)	02866 738174
Tourist Information		02866 323110

Enniskillen ✗   *Blakes of the Hollow*

6 Church Street Enniskillen Co Fermanagh BT74 6JE
PUB   Tel: 02866 322143 Fax: 02866 748491

One of the great classic pubs of Ireland, Blakes has been in the same family since 1887 and, up to now, has always been one of the few places that could be relied upon to be unchanged. Not a food place, a pub. Maybe a sandwich, but mainly somewhere to have a pint and put the world to rights. It will be a great relief to Blakes' many fans all over the world that the building is listed both inside and out because major changes at this historic establishment include three new bars, a café/wine bar and a restaurant. Open all year

Enniskillen   *Killyhevlin Hotel*

Dublin Road Enniskillen Co Fermanagh BT74 6RW
HOTEL   Tel: 02866 323481 Fax: 02866 324726 e-mail: info@killymevlin.com

Just south of Enniskillen, on the A4, this pleasant modern hotel on the banks of the Erne has fishing and river cruising as particular local attractions in addition to other outdoor activities such as golf and horseriding. The hotel was completely refurbished in 1997 and is spacious, with conference/banqueting facilities as well as a warm welcome and comfortable accommodation for private guests. A new leisure complex is planned for completion 2000/2001.There are also some holiday chalets in the grounds, with private jetties. Conference/banqueting (600/400) Fishing, cycling & walking available. Ample parking. Children under 12 free in parents' room; cots available for £5. Wheelchair accessible. Pets permitted by arrangement. **Rooms 43** (1 suite, all en-suite, 1 for disabled) B&B £50pps, ss £15; sc incl. Closed 24-25 Dec. Amex, Diners, MasterCard, Visa. **Directions:** On the A4 just south of Enniskillen

Kesh

Lough Erne Hotel

Main Street Kesh Co Fermanagh

HOTEL   Tel: 028686 31275 Fax: 028686 31921 e-mail:loughernehotel@lakelands.net

In a very attractive location on the banks of the Glendurragh River, this friendly town centre hotel has twelve comfortable rooms with en-suite bath/shower rooms, TV and tea/coffee facilities. The hotel is understandably popular for weddings, as the bar and function rooms overlook the river and have access to an attractive paved riverside walkway and garden. Popular for fishing holidays, it would also make a good base for a family break; there is plenty to do in the area, including golf, watersports and horseriding. Conferences (250). Fishing, cycling, walking. Off-season breaks. Garden. Limited wheelchair access. Own parking. Children welcome. Pets permitted in some areas. **Rooms 12** (all en-suite) B&B £70pps, ss £5; sc discretionary. Closed 25 Dec. Amex, Diners, MasterCard, Visa. **Directions:** On north-eastern corner of Lough Erne, where A42 joins the A35.

Kesh ❋ ✗

Lusty Beg Island

Boa Island Kesh Co Fermanagh BT93 8AD

ACCOMMODATION/PUB   Tel: 028 686 32032 Fax: 028 686 32033

If you arrive by road, a little ferry takes you over to the island (leave your car on the mainland unless you will be staying on the island), or of course, you can call in by boat. It's an unusual place and worth a visit, if only to call into the pleasant waterside pub for a drink, a cup of tea or an informal meal. However, you could stay much longer as accommodation is available in lodges, chalets and a motel, all spread relatively inconspicuously around the wooded island. Conferences, corporate entertaining and management training is a speciality and all sorts of activity breaks. Leisure centre with swimming pool, tennis court, fitness suite, sauna. Canoes. Mountain bikes for hire. Nature trail. Price guide: B&B £32.50 pps. ss £12.50. Chalets £490 high season. Open all year. Credit cards accepted.

LONDONDERRY

In the new mood of 2000, the City of Derry has established itself as a formidable pace-setter. When the boundaries of its surrounding county were first defined in modern times, this was actually the County of Coleraine, named for the busy little port 30 miles to the northeast, on the River Bann a few miles inland from the Atlantic coast. It was an area long favoured by settlers, for Mountsandel on the salmon-rich Bann a mile south of Coleraine, is where the 9,000 year old traces of one of the sites of some of the oldest-known houses in Ireland have been found.

Today, Coleraine is the main campus of the University of Ulster, with the vitality of student life spreading to the nearby coastal resorts of Portstewart and Portrush in the area known as the "Golden Triangle", appropriately fringed by the north by the three golden miles of Portstewart Strand. Southwestward from Coleraine the county - which was re-named after the City of Derry became Londonderry in 1613 - offers a fascinating variety of places and scenery, with large areas of fine farmland being punctuated by ranges of hills, while the rising slopes of the Sperrin Mountains dominate the County's southern boundary.

The road from Belfast to Derry sweeps through the Sperrins by way of the stirringly-named Glenshane Pass, and from its heights you begin to get the first glimpses westward of the mountains of Donegal. This is an appropriate hint of the new atmosphere in the City of Derry itself. This lively place could reasonably claim to be the most senior of all Ireland's modern cities, as it can trace its origins back to a monastery of St Colmcille, otherwise Columba, founded in 546AD. Today, the city - with up-dated port facilities on the River Foyle and a cheerfully restored urban heart - is moving into a vibrant future in which it thrives on the energy drawn from its natural position as the focal point of a larger catchment area which takes in much of Donegal to the west in addition to Londonderry to the east.

Local Attractions and Information

Derry City	Tourist Information 02871 267284
Derry	Harbour Museum 02871 377331
Magherafelt	Springhill (17th century furnished house) 02879 7 48210

Aghadowey   *The Brown Trout Golf & Country Inn*

Aghadowey Co Londonderry BT51 4AD
Tel: 02870 868209 Fax: 02870 868878
HOTEL/RESTAURANT   email: bill@browntroutinn.com

Golf is the major attraction at this lively country inn, both on-site and in the locality. Newcomers will soon find friends in the convivial bar, where food is served from noon to 10 pm every day. Spacious en-suite rooms with plenty of space for golfing gear are all on the ground floor, arranged around a garden courtyard. New cottage suites overlooking the golf course (just 100 yards from the main building) are the first of this standard to be completed in Northern Ireland. **Restaurant:** Up a steep staircase (with chair lift for the less able), the restaurant overlooks the garden end of the golf course. Jane O'Hara's good home cooking is based on fresh local ingredients – trout fillet with fresh herbs & lemon butter or sirloin steak with a Bushmills whiskey sauce. High Tea (very popular in this part of the country) is followed by an à la carte dinner menu. Small conference/private parties (40/50); Tennis, horse-riding, golf (9/18), fishing, walking, garden & children's playground available. Children under 4 free in parents' room; cots available). Pets permitted. **Rooms 25** (4 mini-suites, all en-suite) B&B £42.50pps, ss £15 Lift. **Seats 42** (private room, 40) No smoking restaurant. Open all day (7am-10pm) L 12-3 daily, Set Sun L £10; also à la carte; house wine £7.95; sc discretionary Toilets wheelchair accessible. Open all year. Amex, Diners, MasterCard, Visa. **Directions:** On A54 the main road between Kilrea and Coleraine

---

Coleraine   *Greenhill House*

24 Greenhill Road Aghadowey Co Londonderry BT51 4EU
FARMHOUSE   Tel: 02870 868241 Fax: 02870 868365

Framed by trees with lovely country views, the Hegarty family's Georgian farmhouse is at the centre of a large working farm. In true Northern tradition, Elizabeth Hegarty is a great baker and greets guests in the drawing room with an afternoon tea which includes a vast array of home-made teabreads, cakes and biscuits. There are two large family rooms (6 in total) and, although not luxurious, the thoughtfulness that has gone into their furnishing makes them exceptionally comfortable – everything is in just the right place to be convenient. Little touches like fresh flowers, a fruit basket, After Eights, tea & coffee making facilities, hair dryer, bathrobe, good quality clothes hangers and even a torch are way above the standard expected of farmhouse accommodation. Elizabeth provides dinner for residents by arrangement – please book by noon. (No wine). Children welcome, No pets. **Rooms 6** (all en-suite) Closed 1 Nov-end Feb. MasterCard, Visa **Directions:** On B66 off A29, 7 miles south of Coleraine, 3 miles north of Garvagh.

Limavady　　　　　　　　　　　　　　　　　　*The Lime Tree*

60 Catherine st. Limavady Co Londonderry BT49 9DB
RESTAURANT　　　　　　　　　　　　　　　　Tel: 028777 64300

Stanley and Maria Matthews' restaurant is on a main street of this handsome, wide-streeted town in a beautiful and prosperous part of the country. There is a great sense of contentment about The Lime Tree; the room is pleasant but quite modest, Stanley is a fine chef and Maria a welcoming and solicitous hostess. Ingredients are carefully sourced, many of them local; menus are generous, with a classical base that Stanley works on to introduce new ideas, thus duck rillettes listed beside crab and prawn filo parcels with a chilli oil dressing; prime fillet steak with a green peppercorn sauce and breast of chicken with a couscous, almond and raisin filling served with a cumin scented sauce. In addition to set menus, they operate a very good à la carte lunch menu, with a dressier version in the evening. They also do theme nights "to try out different dishes and ideas". Good cooking and good value go hand in hand with warm hospitality at The Lime Tree. Limavady is lucky to have it. Nearby Parking. Children welcome. **Seats 30.** L 12-2 (Wed-Sun) D 6-9 (Wed-Sun) Set L £6.95, Set Sun L £12.95. Early evening menu £12.95, 6-7 pm only; also à la carte; house wine £9; sc discretionary Toilets wheelchair accessible. Closed Mon,Tue (Sat. lunch booking only), 1 wk Feb/Mar, 1 wk July & Nov. Amex, MasterCard, Visa. **Directions:** On the outskirt of the town, main Derry-Limavady road.

Limavady　　　　　　　　　　　　　　　　　　*Streeve Hill*

25 Dowland Road Limavady Co Londonderry BT49 0HP
COUNTRY HOUSE　　　　　Tel: 028777 66563 Fax: 028777 68285

Peter and June Welsh have welcomed guests to their lovely 18th century home since they moved here in 1996. It is a very charming house, with a Palladian facade of rose brick and fine views over parkland towards the Sperrin mountains – but there is also beauty closer to home, in and around the house itself and in the nearby gardens of their former home, Drenagh. The stylish country house accommodation at Streeve Hill is extremely comfortable and the food and hospitality exceptional. Although the maximum number they can accommodate is six, they are happy for guests to bring friends to dine (provided 24 hour notice is given). They also cater for private dinner parties. Breakfast is another high point and, in the event of fine summer weather, it can be even more enjoyable if served on the terrace outside the drawing room Horse-riding, walking, fishing, garden available. Children welcome (under 5s free in parents' room; cots available). No Pets. Residents D £30 (inc. their friends). Please give 24hrs notice. **Rooms 3** (all en-suite & no-smoking,1 shower only). B&B £45pps, ss £5; sc discretionary. Closed Xmas & New Year. Amex, MasterCard, Visa. **Directions:** From Limavady take B021 for Castlerock, follow Estate wall on right. 200 yards past Lodge turn right at end of wall

---

Londonderry 🏛　　　　　　　*Beech Hill Country House Hotel*

32 Ardmore Road Londonderry Co Londonderry BT47 3QP
Tel: 02871 349279 Fax: 02871 345366
COUNTRY HOUSE　　　　　　　　email: beechhill@nisecrets.com

Beech Hill is just a couple of miles south of Londonderry, in a lovely setting of 42 acres of peaceful woodland, waterfalls and gardens. Built in 1729, the house has retained many of its original details and proprietor Patsy O'Kane makes an hospitable and caring hostess. Bedrooms vary in size and outlook – many overlook the gardens – but all are very attractively furnished with antiques. Public rooms include a good-sized bar, a fine restaurant (in what was originally the snooker room, now extended into a new conservatory overlooking the gardens) and an elegant room seating up to 20 for meetings or private parties. Conference/banqueting (100/80) secretarial services. Fitness centre. Tennis, garden, walking available. Children welcome (under 2s free in parents' room;

cots, £10). No Pets. **Rooms 27** (4 suites, 2 mini-suites, 21 executive rooms, 2 no-smoking, 2 for disabled).Lift. B&B £45pps, ss £25 sc discretionary. Closed 25 Dec. Amex, MasterCard, Visa. **Directions:** From main A6 L'Derry-Belfast road,turn off at Faughan bridge,drive 1 mile to Ardmore chapel - entrance is opposite.

Londonderry   *Everglades Hotel*

Prehen Road Londonderry Co Londonderry BT47 2NH
Tel: 02871 346722 Fax: 02871 349200
HOTEL   email: res.egh@hastingshotel.com

Situated on the banks of the River Foyle, close to City of Derry airport and just a mile from the city centre, this modern hotel is well located for business and pleasure. Like all the Hastings Hotels, Everglades Hotel undergoes an ongoing system of refurbishment and upgrading, a policy which pays off in comfortable well-maintained bedrooms and public areas which never feel dated. Accommodation is all of a high standard, with good amenities including airconditioning, a spacious desk area and, on request, female executive.The hotel is well located for golf, with the City of Derry course just a couple of minutes away and six other courses, including Royal Portrush, within driving distance. Conference/banqueting (500/350); secretarial services.Video Conferencing.Wheelchair accessible. Own parking. Children under 4 free in parents' room; cots available.Pets permitted by arrangement. **Rooms 64** (2 suites, 4 mini-suites, 2 no-smoking, 1 executive room, 4 for disabled) Lift. B&B £45pps, ss £15. no sc. Open all year. Amex, MasterCard, Visa. **Directions:** On the outskirts of Derry, main Derry-Omagh road.

Londonderry ✳   *The Trinity Hotel*

22-24 Strand Road Londonerry Co Londonerry BT48 7AB
HOTEL   Tel: 02871 271271 Fax: 02871 271277

Entry to this new hotel is a little strange - you by-pass the ground floor bar and head upstairs, as reception is on the first floor. However, once there it's worth the trip, as it's a very pleasant contemporary hotel, conveniently located, moderately priced and a great asset to the city. Bedrooms aren't especially big, but they are cosy and comfortably furnished - a good base for doing Derry on foot. At the time of our visit, a second (larger) hotel was planned just along the street. Conference/banqueting (160/80) secretarial services. Children welcome (under 2s free in parents' room; cots available). Wheelchair accessible. No Pets. **Rooms 40** (all en-suite,2 suites, 2 for disabled). Lift. B&B £45pps, ss £25. Children welcome Nearby Parking. Amex, Diners, MasterCard, Visa. **Directions:** At end of Strand road opposite pedestrianised area.

Magherafelt   *Trompets*

25 Church Street Magherafelt Co Londonderry BT45 6AP
Tel: 028796 32257 Fax: 028796 34441
RESTAURANT   e-mail: eclectic.trompets@dnet.co.uk

After working abroad Noel McMeel made his name at Beech Hill Country House, Londonderry, before opening this smart little restaurant in the centre of Magherafelt in July 1997. At the time of going to press he is poised to move again, to set up a new restaurant in Belfast. Call the restaurant at the above number for further information.

Upperlands 🏛   *Ardtara House*

8 Gorteade Road Upperlands Nr Maghera Co Londonderry BT46 5SA
COUNTRY HOUSE   Tel: 028796 44490 Fax: 028796 45080

Former home to the Clark linen milling family, Ardtara is now an attractive, elegantly decorated Victorian country house with a genuinely hospitable atmosphere. Well-proportioned rooms have antique furnishings and fresh flowers. All the large, luxuriously furnished bedrooms enjoy views of the garden and surrounding countryside and have king size beds and original fireplaces, while bathrooms combine practicality with period details, some including freestanding baths and fireplaces. Breakfast is a high point, so allow time to enjoy it. Private parties catered. Tennis, woodland walk, golf practice tee. No dogs. Small conferences (50). **Rooms 8** (all en-suite) B&B £70pps, ss £30. MasterCard, Visa. **Restaurant:** In a dining room converted from its previous use as a snooker room – still with full Victorian skylight and original hunting frieze, head chef Paul Twells continues the philosophy of using seasonal and local ingredients and offers a balanced choice on his menus, with game well represented in season. **Seats 50** (private room, 20) No smoking restaurant. D 7-9 daily, L from12.30, Sun only; Set L £14.50, Set D £23.50; sc discretionary. Closed 25-26 Dec Mastercard, Visa **Directions:** A29 to Maghera/Coleraine; follow the sign to Kilrea until reaching Ardtara.

TYRONE

As the USA confidently leads the world into 2000 and the years beyond, it's worth reflecting that some of the key people in that great nation's creation had family roots in Tyrone. This is Northern Ireland's most extensive county, so it is something of a surprise for the traveller to discover that its geography appears to be largely dominated by a range of modestly high mountains of which nearly half seem to be in the neighbouring county of Londonderry.

Yet such is the case with Tyrone and the Sperrins. The village of Sperrin itself towards the head of Glenelly may be in Tyrone, but the highest peak of Sawel (678 m), which looms over it, is actually right on the county boundary. But as well, much of the county is upland territory and moorland, giving the impression that the Sperrins are even more extensive than is really the case.

In such a land, the lower country and the fertile valleys gleam like jewels, and there's often a vivid impression of a living - and indeed prosperity - being wrested from a demanding environment. It's a character-forming sort of place, so it's perhaps understandable that it was the ancestral homeland of a remarkable number of early American Presidents, and this connection is commemorated in the Ulster American Folk Park a few miles north of the county town of Omagh.

Forest parks abound, but as well attractive towns like Castlederg and Dungannon, as well as villages such as those in the uplands and along the charming Clogher Valley, provide entertainment and hospitality for visitors refreshed by the wide open spaces of the moorlands and the mountains.

Local Attractions and Information
CO TYRONE
Omagh   Ulster-American Folk Park Tel: 02882 243292

Clogher ✗   *Corick House*

COUNTRY HOUSE

20 Corick Road Clogher Co Tyrone BT76 OB2
Tel: 028855 48216 Fax: 028855 49531

Corick House is a charming 17th century William and Mary House, a listed building overlooking the river Blackwater in the scenic Clogher Valley area of South Tyrone. The house is built on a grand scale, with large well-proportioned reception rooms and surrounded by fine gardens. After period conversion, extension and refurbishment by Jean Beacon, who took over the house in 1995, it was opened as a licensed country house with ten luxurious bedrooms (all individually decorated, with antiques – giving it a private house atmosphere) and a restaurant which is open to non-residents. All facilities are accessible to wheelchair users and one of the bedrooms is specially adapted for disabled guests. The romantic setting and good banqueting facilities (up to 250) makes it an excellent venue for weddings, but banqueting is kept separate from the rest of the house. The novelist William Carleton grew up in the area and an annual Summer School, which attracts some highly distinguished speakers, is held at Corick House to honour his memory. A number of special breaks are available. Acc££ Open all year Amex, Diners, MasterCard, Visa.

Cookstown   *Tullylagan Country House*

HOTEL/RESTAURANT

40B Tullylagan Road Cookstown Co Tyrone BT80 8UP
Tel: 028867 65100 Fax: 028867 61715

Halfway between Dungannon and Cookstown, this impressive country house hotel is set in 30 acres of grounds, with the Tullylagan river flowing through the estate. The lovely setting enhances a hotel which is particularly notable for friendly and enthusiastic staff. The public areas include a spacious foyer/reception with a fine staircase leading up to a range of well-appointed bedrooms, which vary according to their position in the house (five are shower only), but are all attractively decorated in country house style. The hotel takes pride in its dining room and has recently added an extra dimension, the Tullylagan Wine Bar, situated in a separate building which is used for banqueting (open Friday-Sunday 7-12pm). The hotel is within 10 minutes drive of two golf courses, and equestrian activities and fishing are also available nearby; weekend and other special breaks offer good value. Conference/banqueting (150/125); video conferencing. Fishing, Walking.Garden. Children's playground; children under 2 free in parents' room; cots available. Wheelchair accessible. Pets permitted. **Rooms 15** (1 suite, 1 mini-suite, 2 no-smoking, 2 for disabled).Lift. B&B £35pps, ss£14.95.Closed 24-26 Dec [Restaurant **Seats 36** (private room, 20) Open L 12-2.15 daily, D 7-9.15 daily L12.30-2.30 Sun only, Set L £13.95. Set D £19.95, house wine £10.50 Toilets wheelchair accessible.Closed Sun D.] Amex, MasterCard, Visa. **Directions:** 6 miles from Dungannon,4 miles from Cookstown.

Dungannon 🏛 *Grange Lodge*

7 Grange Road Dungannon Co Tyrone BT71 7EJ
COUNTRY HOUSE   Tel: 02887 784212 Fax: 02887 784313

Norah and Ralph Brown's renowned Georgian retreat offers comfort, true family hospitality and extremely good food. The house is on an elevated site just outside Dungannon, with about 20 acres of grounds; mature woodland and gardens (producing food for the table and flowers for the house) with views over lush countryside. Improvements over the years have been made with great sensitivity and the feeling is of gentle organic growth, culminating in the present warm and welcoming atmosphere. Grange Lodge is furnished unselfconsciously, with antiques and family pieces throughout. Bedrooms (and bathrooms) are exceptionally comfortable and thoughtful in detail. Norah's home cooking is superb and, although they no longer accept bookings from non-residents for dinner, they will cater for groups of 10-30. Grange Lodge is fully licensed and dinner menus change daily (in consultation with guests). Breakfasts are also outstanding, so allow time to indulge. Banqueting (30) Garden. Walking.Not suitable for children under 12. **Rooms 5** (all en-suite) B&B £35pps, ss£14. Closed 20 Dec-1 Feb. MasterCard, Visa. Parking. **Directions:** 1 mile from M1 junction 15. A29 Armagh, left at sign Grange; next right & first gates on right.

Omagh *Hawthorn House*

72 Old Mountfield Road Omagh Co Tyrone BT79 7EN
RESTAURANT/ACCOMMODATION   Tel/Fax: 028 82 25 2005

On the edge of the town, in a lovely part of the country at the foot of the Sperrin Mountains, Hawthorn House was only established in the autumn of 1997 and yet is already recognised as one of the leading guesthouses and restaurants in Ulster. Owner-manager Michael Gaine is putting years of experience in the hotel business to work in this fine venture supported by an excellent team. Bedrooms are large and comfortable, with all the amenities expected of top quality accommodation. Public areas are also furnished to a high standard. Warm hospitality and helpful staff ensure guests' comfort, in both the accommodation and the restaurant. Conference/banqueting (40/65).Garden. Children (Under 10s free in parents' room; cots available).Wheelchair accessible.No Pets. **Rooms 5** (4 en-suite,1 shower only). B&B £25pps, ss £10. Open all year. MasterCard, Visa. **Restaurant:** Head chef Barry Emerson presents tempting modern menus for both lunch and dinner. Sunday lunch offers a nicely judged combination of traditional and more adventurous dishes. **Seats 60** (private room, 20) L 12-3 daily D 7-10 daily Set Sun L £15, Set L £10. à la carte available, house wines from £9.Toilets wheelchair accessible no smoking area; sc discretionary. Children welcome. Parking. **Directions:** From Dublin/Belfast; go through 3 sets of traffic lights,turn right at 4th set (Mountjoy Road) Turn right again at 5th set (health centre) Premises on the left.